CHILD GROWTH AND DEVELOPMENT 97/98

Fourth Edition

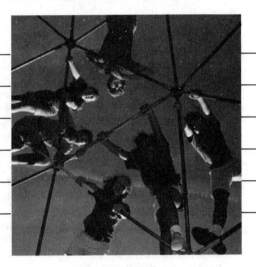

Editor

Ellen N. Junn
California State University, Fullerton

Ellen Junn is a professor of child development, Administrative Fellow in the Office of the Vice President of Academic Affairs, and Director of the Office of Educational Equity at California State University, Fullerton. She received a B.S. in experimental psychology from the University of Michigan and her M.A. and Ph.D. in cognitive and developmental psychology from Princeton University. In addition to her work on educational equity issues, Dr. Junn's research and publications focus on developments in children's conceptions regarding adult social relationships and on college teaching effectiveness.

Editor

Chris J. Boyatzis
Bucknell University

Chris Boyatzis is an assistant professor of psychology at Bucknell University. He received a B.A. in psychology from Boston University and his M.A. and Ph.D. in developmental psychology from Brandeis University. Many of his research interests lie at the intersection of social and cognitive development in early childhood. Dr. Boyatzis has published research on children's nonverbal behavior and social status, media effects on children, symbolic development, and play and art. He has also written on the use of literature and film to teach developmental psychology.

Annual Editions E
A Library of Information from the Public Press
Dushkin/McGraw-Hill
Sluice Dock, Guilford, Connecticut 06437

Visit us on the Internet—http://www.dushkin.com

The Annual Editions Series

ANNUAL EDITIONS is a series of over 65 volumes designed to provide the reader with convenient, low-cost access to a wide range of current, carefully selected articles from some of the most important magazines, newspapers, and journals published today. ANNUAL EDITIONS are updated on an annual basis through a continuous monitoring of over 300 periodical sources. All ANNUAL EDITIONS have a number of features that are designed to make them particularly useful, including topic guides, annotated tables of contents, unit overviews, and indexes. For the teacher using ANNUAL EDITIONS in the classroom, an Instructor's Resource Guide with test questions is available for each volume.

VOLUMES AVAILABLE

Abnormal Psychology
Adolescent Psychology
Africa
Aging
American Foreign Policy
American Government
American History, Pre-Civil War
American History, Post-Civil War
American Public Policy
Anthropology
Archaeology
Biopsychology
Business Ethics
Child Growth and Development
China
Comparative Politics
Computers in Education
Computers in Society
Criminal Justice
Criminology
Developing World
Deviant Behavior
Drugs, Society, and Behavior
Dying, Death, and Bereavement

Early Childhood Education
Economics
Educating Exceptional Children
Education
Educational Psychology
Environment
Geography
Global Issues
Health
Human Development
Human Resources
Human Sexuality
India and South Asia
International Business
Japan and the Pacific Rim
Latin America
Life Management
Macroeconomics
Management
Marketing
Marriage and Family
Mass Media
Microeconomics

Middle East and the
   Islamic World
Multicultural Education
Nutrition
Personal Growth and Behavior
Physical Anthropology
Psychology
Public Administration
Race and Ethnic Relations
Russia, the Eurasian Republics,
   and Central/Eastern Europe
Social Problems
Social Psychology
Sociology
State and Local Government
Urban Society
Western Civilization,
   Pre-Reformation
Western Civilization,
   Post-Reformation
Western Europe
World History, Pre-Modern
World History, Modern
World Politics

Cataloging in Publication Data
Main entry under title: Annual Editions: Child growth and development. 1997/98.
        1. Child psychology—Periodicals. I. Junn, Ellen N., *comp.* II. Boyatzis, Chris J.,
comp. III. Title: Child growth and development.
ISBN 0-697-37221-9   155.4'.05   ISSN 1075-5217

Fourth Edition

Cover image © 1996 PhotoDisc, Inc.

Printed in the United States of America   Printed on Recycled Paper

Editors/Advisory Board

Members of the Advisory Board are instrumental in the final selection of articles for each edition of ANNUAL EDITIONS. Their review of articles for content, level, currentness, and appropriateness provides critical direction to the editor and staff. We think that you will find their careful consideration well reflected in this volume.

EDITORS

Ellen N. Junn
California State University, Fullerton

Chris J. Boyatzis
Bucknell University

ADVISORY BOARD

Mary Belcher
Orange Coast College

Patrick M. Drumm
*Indiana University–
Purdue University*

Gene V. Elliott
Rowan College of New Jersey

JoAnn M. Farver
University of Southern California

Kathy Fite
Southwest Texas State University

Trisha Folds-Bennett
College of Charleston

Charles D. Hoffman
*California State University
San Bernardino*

Richard J. Ida
Solano Community College

Marcia Lasswell
California State Polytechnic University

Nancy G. McCarley
Mississippi State University

Joann Montepare
Tufts University

Derek Price
Wheaton College

Mary Helen Spear
Prince George's Community College

Connie Steele
University of Tennessee

Faye B. Steuer
College of Charleston

Harold R. Strang
University of Virginia

Staff

Ian A. Nielsen, Publisher

EDITORIAL STAFF

Roberta Monaco, Developmental Editor
Addie Raucci, Administrative Editor
Cheryl Greenleaf, Permissions Editor
Deanna Herrschaft, Permissions Assistant
Diane Barker, Proofreader
Lisa Holmes-Doebrick, Program Coordinator
Joseph Offredi, Photo Coordinator

PRODUCTION STAFF

Brenda S. Filley, Production Manager
Charles Vitelli, Designer
Shawn Callahan, Graphics
Lara M. Johnson, Graphics
Laura Levine, Graphics
Mike Campbell, Graphics
Juliana Arbo, Typesetting Supervisor
Jane Jaegersen, Typesetter
Marie Lazauskas, Word Processor
Larry Killian, Copier Coordinator

To the Reader

In publishing ANNUAL EDITIONS we recognize the enormous role played by the magazines, newspapers, and journals of the *public press* in providing current, first-rate educational information in a broad spectrum of interest areas. Many of these articles are appropriate for students, researchers, and professionals seeking accurate, current material to help bridge the gap between principles and theories and the real world. These articles, however, become more useful for study when those of lasting value are carefully *collected, organized, indexed,* and *reproduced* in a *low-cost format,* which provides easy and permanent access when the material is needed. That is the role played by ANNUAL EDITIONS. Under the direction of each volume's *academic editor,* who is an expert in the subject area, and with the guidance of an *Advisory Board,* each year we seek to provide in each ANNUAL EDITION a current, well-balanced, carefully selected collection of the best of the public press for your study and enjoyment. We think that you will find this volume useful, and we hope that you will take a moment to let us know what you think.

We are delighted to welcome you to this fourth volume of *Annual Editions: Child Growth and Development 97/98.* The amazing sequence of events of prenatal development that lead to the birth of a baby is an awe-inspiring process. Perhaps more intriguing is the question of what the future may hold for this newly arrived baby—for instance, will this child become a doctor, a lawyer, an artist, beggar, or thief? Although philosophers and prominent thinkers such as Charles Darwin and Sigmund Freud have long speculated about the importance of infancy on subsequent development, not until the 1960s did the scientific study of infants and young children flourish. Since then, research and theory in infancy and childhood has exploded, resulting in a wealth of new knowledge about child development. Past accounts of infants and young children as passive, homogeneous organisms have been replaced with investigations aimed at studying infants and young children at a "microlevel"—as active individuals with many inborn competencies, who are capable of shaping their own environment—as well as at a "macrolevel," by considering the larger context surrounding the child. In short, children are not "blank slates," and development does not take place in a vacuum; children arrive with many skills and grow up in a complex web of social, historical, political, economic, and cultural spheres.

As was the case for previous editions, we hope to achieve at least four major goals with this volume. First, we hope to present you with the latest research and thinking to help you better appreciate the complex interactions that characterize human development in infancy and childhood. Second, in light of the feedback we received on previous editions, we placed greater emphasis on important contemporary issues and challenges, exploring topics such as understanding development in the context of current societal and cultural influences. Third, attention is given to articles that also discuss effective, practical applications. Finally, we hope that this anthology will serve as a catalyst to help students become more effective future professionals and parents.

To achieve these objectives, we carefully selected articles from a variety of sources, including scholarly research journals and texts as well as semiprofessional journals and popular publications. Every selection was scrutinized for readability, interest level, relevance, and currency. In addition, we listened to the valuable input and advice from members of our advisory board, consisting of faculty from a range of institutions of higher education, including community and liberal arts colleges as well as research and teaching universities. We are most grateful to the advisory board as well as to the excellent editorial staff of Dushkin Publishing Group/Brown & Benchmark Publishers.

Annual Editions: Child Growth and Development 97/98 is organized into five major units. Unit 1 focuses on conception, prenatal development, and childbirth. Unit 2 presents information regarding developments in cognition, language, and learning. Unit 3 focuses on social and emotional development. Unit 4 is devoted to parenting and family issues such as working parents, marital transitions, siblings, and discipline. Finally, unit 5 focuses on larger cultural and societal influences (such as poverty, media) and on special challenges (such as childhood victimization and abuse, children with attention deficits).

Instructors for large lecture courses may wish to adopt this anthology as a supplement to a basic text, whereas instructors for smaller sections might also find the readings effective for promoting student presentations or for stimulating discussions and applications. Whatever format is utilized, it is our hope that the instructor and the students will find the readings interesting, illuminating, and provocative.

As the title indicates, *Annual Editions: Child Growth and Development* is by definition a volume that undergoes continual review and revision. Thus, we welome and encourage your comments and suggestions for future editions of this volume. Simply fill out and return the comment card found at the end of this book. Best wishes, and we look forward to hearing from you!

Ellen N. Junn
Editor

Chris J. Boyatzis
Editor

Contents

UNIT 1

Conception to Birth

Seven articles discuss the development of the child from the prenatal stage to birth.

UNIT 2

Cognition, Language, and Learning

Nine selections consider the growth of a child's cognitive and language abilities and their experiences in the learning process in school.

The concepts in bold italics are developed in the article. For further expansion please refer to the Topic Guide and the Index.

The concepts in bold italics are developed in the article. For further expansion please refer to the Topic Guide and the Index.

UNIT 3

Social and Emotional Development

Five articles follow a child's emotional development into the larger social world.

The concepts in bold italics are developed in the article. For further expansion please refer to the Topic Guide and the Index.

UNIT 4

Parenting and Family Issues

Five articles assess the latest implications of child development with regard to attachment, marital transitions, day care, and discipline.

The concepts in bold italics are developed in the article. For further expansion please refer to the Topic Guide and the Index.

UNIT 5

Cultural and Societal Influences

Ten selections examine how society and culture impact on the development of the child.

The concepts in bold italics are developed in the article. For further expansion please refer to the Topic Guide and the Index.

Topic Guide

This topic guide suggests how the selections in this book relate to topics of traditional concern to students and professionals involved with the study of infant and child development. It is useful for locating articles that relate to each other for reading and research. The guide is arranged alphabetically according to topic. Articles may, of course, treat topics that do not appear in the topic guide. In turn, entries in the topic guide do not necessarily constitute a comprehensive listing of all the contents of each selection.

TOPIC AREA	TREATED IN	TOPIC AREA	TREATED IN
Aggression/Violence	1. Eugenics Revisited 20. Children without Friends 26. Why Spanking Takes the Spunk Out of Kids 29. Why Leave Children with Bad Parents? 31. Violence, Reel to Real 33. Victimization of Children	**Developmental Disabilities and Challenges**	7. Most Intimate Bond 35. Young Children with Attention Deficits 36. Life in a Parallel World
Attachment	8. Amazing Minds of Infants 23. Fathers' Time 24. Life-Span Adjustment of Children to Their Parents' Divorce	**Discipline**	9. Ten Myths about Child Development 18. Moral Power of Good Stories 25. How Children Learn to Resolve Conflicts in Families 26. Why Spanking Takes the Spunk Out of Kids
Birth and Birth Defects/ Reproduction/ Teratogens	2. Making Babies 3. Waiting Game 4. In the Name of the Children 5. Fantastic Voyage of Tanner Roberts 6. Putting a New Spin on the Birth of Human Birth	**Divorce/Stepparents**	24. Life-Span Adjustment of Children to Their Parents' Divorce 29. Why Leave Children with Bad Parents?
Brain and Physical Development	6. Putting a New Spin on the Birth of Human Birth 10. Your Child's Brain 13. Malnutrition, Poverty, and Intellectual Development 17. Early Experience and Emotional Development 35. Young Children with Attention Deficits 36. Life in a Parallel World	**Drug Abuse**	4. In the Name of the Children 29. Why Leave Children with Bad Parents?
		Economic Issues/Poverty	13. Malnutrition, Poverty, and Intellectual Development 29. Why Leave Children with Bad Parents? 30. Child Labor in Pakistan 32. Get 'em While They're Young
Child Abuse	26. Why Spanking Takes the Spunk Out of Kids 29. Why Leave Children with Bad Parents? 33. Victimization of Children	**Emotional Development**	1. Eugenics Revisited 7. Most Intimate Bond 10. Your Child's Brain 17. Early Experience and Emotional Development 18. Moral Power of Good Stories 19. EQ Factor 20. Children without Friends 23. Fathers' Time 24. Life-Span Adjustment of Children to Their Parents' Divorce 25. How Children Learn to Resolve Conflicts in Families 26. Why Spanking Takes the Spunk Out of Kids 34. Resilience in Development 36. Life in a Parallel World
Cognitive Development	8. Amazing Minds of Infants 10. Your Child's Brain 11. Vygotsky's Theory 12. How Do Infants Learn about the Physical World? 13. Malnutrition, Poverty, and Intellectual Development 14. What Should Children Learn? 15. How Kids Learn 16. IQ Puzzle 35. Young Children with Attention Deficits 36. Life in a Parallel World		
Creativity	10. Your Child's Brain 11. Vygotsky's Theory 28. Buried Alive	**Family/Parenting**	9. Ten Myths about Child Development 18. Moral Power of Good Stories 22. Little Big People 23. Fathers' Time 24. Life-Span Adjustment of Children to Their Parents' Divorce 25. How Children Learn to Resolve Conflicts in Families 26. Why Spanking Takes the Spunk Out of Kids 27. School and Family in a Postmodern World 28. Buried Alive 29. Why Leave Children with Bad Parents? 32. Get 'em While They're Young 33. Victimization of Children 34. Resilience in Development
Cross-Cultural Influences	30. Child Labor in Pakistan		

TOPIC AREA	TREATED IN	TOPIC AREA	TREATED IN
High-Risk Infants/Children	4. In the Name of the Children 7. Most Intimate Bond 13. Malnutrition, Poverty, and Intellectual Development 20. Children without Friends 24. Life-Span Adjustment of Children to Their Parents' Divorce 29. Why Leave Children with Bad Parents? 30. Child Labor in Pakistan 33. Victimization of Children 34. Resilience in Development 35. Young Children with Attention Deficits 36. Life in a Parallel World	**Personality Development**	7. Most Intimate Bond 18. Moral Power of Good Stories 19. EQ Factor 20. Children without Friends 22. Little Big People 23. Fathers' Time 24. Life-Span Adjustment of Children to Their Parents' Divorce 28. Buried Alive 32. Get 'em While They're Young 34. Resilience in Development
Hyperactivity/ Attention Deficit Disorder	35. Young Children with Attention Deficits	**Play**	11. Vygotsky's Theory 20. Children without Friends 21. Girls and Boys Together . . . but Mostly Apart 28. Buried Alive
Infant Development	8. Amazing Minds of Infants 10. Your Child's Brain 12. How Do Infants Learn about the Physical World? 17. Early Experience and Emotional Development	**Prenatal Development and Diagnoses**	2. Making Babies 3. Waiting Game 4. In the Name of the Children 5. Fantastic Voyage of Tanner Roberts 6. Putting a New Spin on the Birth of Human Birth 7. Most Intimate Bond
Intelligence	1. Eugenics Revisited 9. Ten Myths about Child Development 10. Your Child's Brain 13. Malnutrition, Poverty, and Intellectual Development 16. IQ Puzzle 19. EQ Factor	**Preschoolers/ Toddlers**	10. Your Child's Brain 20. Children without Friends 21. Girls and Boys Together . . . but Mostly Apart 25. How Children Learn to Resolve Conflicts in Families 26. Why Spanking Takes the Spunk Out of Kids 32. Get 'em While They're Young
Language Development	10. Your Child's Brain 15. How Kids Learn	**Schooling**	11. Vygotsky's Theory 14. Why Should Children Learn? 15. How Kids Learn 21. Girls and Boys Together . . . but Mostly Apart 27. School and Family in the Postmodern World 35. Young Children with Attention Deficits
Learning/Literacy	10. Your Child's Brain 11. Vygotsky's Theory 14. What Should Children Learn? 15. How Kids Learn 18. Moral Power of Good Stories 27. School and Family in the Postmodern World 35. Young Children with Attention Deficits		
Memory	8. Amazing Minds of Infants 12. How Do Infants Learn about the Physical World? 15. How Kids Learn	**Self-Esteem/Self-Control**	19. EQ Factor 20. Children without Friends 25. How Children Learn to Resolve Conflicts in Families 26. Why Spanking Takes the Spunk Out of Kids
Mental Illness	1. Eugenics Revisited 24. Life-Span Adjustment of Children to Their Parents' Divorce 33. Victimization of Children	**Sex Differences/Roles/ Characteristics**	21. Girls and Boys Together . . . but Mostly Apart
Moral Development	18. Moral Power of Good Stories	**Socialization**	18. Moral Power of Good Stories 20. Children without Friends 21. Girls and Boys Together . . . but Mostly Apart 22. Little Big People 23. Fathers' Time 25. How Children Learn to Resolve Conflicts in Families 27. School and Family in the Postmodern World 28. Buried Alive 31. Violence, Reel to Real 32. Get 'em While They're Young
Nature/Nurture Issue	1. Eugenics Revisited 6. Putting a New Spin on the Birth of Human Birth 8. Amazing Minds of Infants 10. Your Child's Brain 13. Malnutrition, Poverty, and Intellectual Development 17. Early Experience and Emotional Development		
Peers/Social Skills	19. EQ Factor 20. Children without Friends 21. Girls and Boys Together . . . but Mostly Apart 25. How Children Learn to Resolve Conflicts in Families	**Television/Media**	22. Little Big People 28. Buried Alive 31. Violence, Reel to Real 32. Get 'em While They're Young

Conception to Birth

- **Prenatal Development (Articles 1–4)**
- **Birth and Babies (Articles 5–7)**

Our understanding of conception and prenatal development is not what it used to be. We are now witness to dramatic changes in reproductive technology. Advances in this new "prenatal science" include fertility treatments for couples who have difficulty conceiving and a host of prenatal diagnostic tests, such as amniocentesis and alpha-fetaprotein testing, which assess the well-being of the fetus as well as detect genetic or chromosomal problems. These technological developments are discussed in the articles "Making Babies" and "Waiting Game."

Perhaps the oldest debate in the study of human development is the "nature versus nurture" question. Scientists have moved beyond thinking of development as due to either genetics *or* environment, now recognizing that nature *and* nurture interact to shape us. Each human is a biological organism, and each is surrounded, from the moment of conception, by environmental forces. John Horgan's essay, "Eugenics Revisited," helps us to consider the nature and nurture of our IQ, mental health, sexual orientation, and other aspects of who we are. This selection is especially valuable because it helps the reader appreciate several crucial facts about the nature/nurture debate. First, although both genes and experience are crucial in shaping us, many scientists have recently emphasized the power of genes. However, the research evidence shows that there are fewer certainties about genetic influence than some scientists might imply. Second, findings from the nature/nurture debate can always be interpreted from more than one perspective to support more than one view. Finally, whether we embrace genes or environment as the primary factor in determining development, there may be ethical, political, legal, and societal consequences of taking a particular stance.

Students of child development should realize that the classic nature/nurture controversy applies as much to prenatal development as to other stages of childhood. While prenatal development is largely the result of the unfolding of an individual's genetic blueprint, the fetus is also in an environment within the mother's womb. Hence, the

fetus is vulnerable to teratogens, hazards from the environment that interfere with normal prenatal development. One potential teratogen is alcohol. Thousands of babies are born every year with fetal alcohol syndrome, a constellation of permanent physical, behavioral, and neurological defects that result from the mother's heavy alcohol use during pregnancy. We are learning more about potential harm to the developing fetus due to increasing rates of maternal use of illegal drugs. As a consequence, pregnant women are being held to more stringent legal standards, culminating in legal battles that pit the rights of pregnant women against the rights of their fetuses. Barry Siegel's report, "In the Name of the Children," presents a case study that puts in sharp relief some of these troubling and controversial issues.

Our notions of childbirth have themselves evolved throughout history. Although in earlier decades many women gave birth to their babies at home or in comfortable, natural settings, the vast majority of births in Western societies now occur in hospitals. Some critics claim that childbirth is seen by the medical community not as a natural life event but as a disease; women are often treated during childbirth as passive, immobilized patients, and they are subjected to many specialized tools and surgical techniques. Also, more than one in five births in the United States is now by cesarean section, making it one of the most common surgical procedures in this country. A personal account of the birth of one baby is given in "The Fantastic Voyage of Tanner Roberts," which details, in a contraction-by-contraction analysis, the emotional and technical aspects of childbirth.

In a related theme, "Putting a New Spin on the Birth of Human Birth" provides readers with an anthropological perspective on the possible evolutionary significance of human birth and its relation to neonate head size and development.

Finally, the last article in this section, "The Most Intimate Bond," chronicles the very rare incidence of conjoined twins and raises hard questions about human nature and individuality. How is it that these twins can share identical genes, inhabit the same body, and yet have two unique personalities that relate to each other in a remarkably warm and special way?

Looking Ahead: Challenge Questions

Where do you stand on the nature/nurture issue? Does it comfort you—or unsettle you—to know that the genes you inherited influence your intelligence, mental health, susceptibility to some diseases, and so on? Given the information in the article "Eugenics Revisited," how would you respond to someone who claimed that a person's IQ, personality, or sexual orientation is "determined" by nature?

In light of the vast array of prenatal diagnostics and medical procedures now used, does technology play too great a role in determining who can have children? Defend your answer.

How would you balance the personal wish for a child and the expense and ethical complications of available reproductive technology? Assuming that new procedures continue to be developed, what options might be available to parents in the future?

Labor and delivery represents a momentous occasion for everyone concerned—mother, father, and newborn. Given that women have been giving birth for centuries, do you think the medical community or the public's view of birthing has changed over the years? What suggestions would you have to make the experience of birthing easier?

Should society pit the rights of a pregnant woman against those of her fetus? Rather than determining how pregnant women should be punished for alcohol and drug abuse, should there be more emphasis on prevention of abuses that can cause birth defects?

Eugenics Revisited

Scientists are linking genes to a host of complex human disorders and traits, but just how valid—and useful—are these findings?

John Horgan

Senior Writer

"How to Tell If Your Child's a Serial Killer!" That was the sound bite with which the television show *Donahue* sought to entice listeners February 25. On the program, a psychiatrist from the Rochester, N.Y., area noted that some men are born with not one Y chromosome but two. Double-Y men, the psychiatrist said, are "at special risk for antisocial, violent behavior." In fact, the psychiatrist had recently studied such a man. Although he had grown up in a "Norman Rockwell" setting, as an adult he had strangled at least 11 women and two children.

"It is not hysterical or overstating it," Phil Donahue told his horrified audience, "to say that we are moving toward the time when, quite literally, just as we can anticipate . . . genetic predispositions toward various physical diseases, we will also be able to pinpoint mental disorders which include aggression, antisocial behavior and the possibility of very serious criminal activity later on."

Eugenics is back in fashion. The message that genetics can explain, predict and even modify human behavior for the betterment of society is promulgated not just on sensationalistic talk shows but by our most prominent scientists. James D. Watson, co-discoverer of the double-helix structure of DNA and former head of the Human Genome Project, the massive effort to map our entire genetic endowment, said recently, "We used to think that our fate was in our stars. Now we know, in large part, that our fate is in our genes."

Daniel E. Koshland, Jr., a biologist at the University of California at Berkeley and editor of *Science,* the most influential peer-reviewed journal in the U.S., has declared in an editorial that the nature/nurture debate is "basically over," since scientists have shown that genes influence many aspects of human behavior. He has also contended that genetic research may help eliminate society's most intractable problems, including drug abuse, homelessness and, yes, violent crime.

Some studies cited to back this claim are remarkably similar to those conducted over a century ago by scientists such as Francis Galton, known as the father of eugenics. Just as the British polymath studied identical twins in order to show that "nature prevails enormously over nurture," so do modern researchers. But the primary reason behind the revival of eugenics is the astonishing successes of biologists in mapping and manipulating the human genome. Over the past decade, investigators have identified genes underlying such crippling diseases as cystic fibrosis, muscular dystrophy and, this past spring, Huntington's disease. Given these advances, researchers say, it is only a matter of time before they can lay bare the genetic foundation of much more complex traits and disorders.

The political base for eugenics has also become considerably broader in recent years. Spokespersons for the mentally ill believe demonstrating the genetic basis of disorders such as schizophrenia and manic depression—and even alcoholism and drug addiction—will lead not only to better diagnoses and treatments but also to more compassion toward sufferers and their families. Some homosexuals believe society will become more tolerant toward them if it can be shown that sexual orientation is an innate, biological condition and not a matter of choice.

But critics contend that no good can come of bad science. Far from moving inexorably closer to its goals, they point out, the field of behavioral genetics is mired in the same problems that have always plagued it. Behavioral traits are extraordinarily difficult to define, and practically every claim of a genetic basis can also be explained as an environmental effect. "This has been a huge enterprise, and for the most part the work has been done shoddily. Even careful people get sucked into misinterpreting data," says Jonathan Beckwith, a geneticist at Harvard University. He adds, "There are social consequences to this."

The skeptics also accuse the media of having created an unrealistically optimistic view of the field. Richard C. Lewontin, a biologist at Harvard and a prominent critic of behavioral genetics, contends that the media generally give much more prominent coverage to dra-

"EERIE" PARALLELS between identical twins raised apart—such as Jerry Levey *(left)* and Mark Newman, who both became firefighters—are said to support genetic models of human behavior. Yet skeptics say the significance of such coincidences has been exaggerated.

matic reports—such as the discovery of an "alcoholism gene"—than to contradictory results or retractions. "Skepticism doesn't make the news," Lewontin says. "It only makes the news when you find a gene." The result is that spurious findings often become accepted by the public and even by so-called experts.

The claim that men with an extra Y chromosome are predisposed toward violence is a case in point. It stems from a survey in the 1960s that found more extra-Y men in prison than in the general population. Some researchers hypothesized that since the Y chromosome confers male attributes, men with an extra Y become hyperaggressive "supermales." Follow-up studies indicated that while extra-Y men tend to be taller than other men and score slightly lower on intelligence tests, they are otherwise normal. The National Academy of Sciences concluded in a report published this year that there is no evidence to support the link between the extra Y chromosome and violent behavior.

MINNESOTA TWINS

No research in behavioral genetics has been more eagerly embraced by the press than the identical-twin studies done at the University of Minnesota. Thomas J. Bouchard, Jr., a psychologist, initiated them in the late 1970s, and since then they have been featured in the *Washington Post, Newsweek,* the *New York Times* and other publications worldwide as well as on television. *Science* has favorably described the Minnesota team's work in several news stories and in 1990 published a major article by the group.

The workers have studied more than 50 pairs of identical twins who were separated shortly after birth and raised in different households. The assumption is that any differences between identical twins, who share all each other's genes, are caused by the environment; similarities are attributed to their shared genes. The group estimates the relative contribution of genes to a given trait in a term called "heritability." A trait that stems entirely

from genes, such as eye color, is defined as 100 percent heritable. Height is 90 percent heritable; that is, 90 percent of the variation in height is accounted for by genetic variation, and the other 10 percent is accounted for by diet and other environmental factors.

The Minnesota group has reported finding a strong genetic contribution to practically all the traits it has examined. Whereas most previous studies have estimated the heritability of intelligence (as defined by performance on intelligence tests) as roughly 50 percent, Bouchard and his colleagues arrived at a figure of 70 percent. They have also found a genetic component underlying such culturally defined traits as religiosity, political orientation (conservative versus liberal), job satisfaction, leisure-time interests and proneness to divorce. In fact, the group concluded in *Science,* "On multiple measures of personality and temperament . . . monozygotic twins reared apart are about as similar as are monozygotic twins reared together." (Identical twins are called monozygotic because they stem from a single fertilized egg, or zygote.)

The researchers have buttressed their statistical findings with anecdotes about "eerie," "bewitching" and "remarkable" parallels between reunited twins. One case involved Oskar, who was raised as a Nazi in Czechoslovakia, and Jack, who was raised as a Jew in Trinidad. Both were reportedly wearing shirts with epaulets when they were reunited by the Minnesota group in 1979. They also both flushed the toilet before as well as after using it and enjoyed deliberately sneezing to startle people in elevators.

Some other celebrated cases involved two British women who wore seven rings and named their firstborn sons Richard Andrew and Andrew

Behavioral Genetics: A Lack-of-Progress Report

CRIME: Family, twin and adoption studies have suggested a heritability of 0 to more than 50 percent for predisposition to crime. (Heritability represents the degree to which a trait stems from genetic factors.) In the 1960s researchers reported an association between an extra Y chromosome and violent crime in males. Follow-up studies found that association to be spurious.

MANIC DEPRESSION: Twin and family studies indicate heritability of 60 to 80 percent for susceptibility to manic depression. In 1987 two groups reported locating different genes linked to manic depression, one in Amish families and the other in Israeli families. Both reports have been retracted.

SCHIZOPHRENIA: Twin studies show heritability of 40 to 90 percent. In 1988 a group reported finding a gene linked to schizophrenia in British and Icelandic families. Other studies documented no linkage, and the initial claim has now been retracted.

ALCOHOLISM: Twin and adoption studies suggest heritability ranging from 0 to 60 percent. In 1990 a group claimed to link a gene—one that produces a receptor for the neurotransmitter dopamine—with alcoholism. A recent review of the evidence concluded it does not support a link.

INTELLIGENCE: Twin and adoption studies show a heritability of performance on intelligence tests of 20 to 80 percent. One group recently unveiled preliminary evidence for genetic markers for high intelligence (an IQ of 130 or higher). The study is unpublished.

HOMOSEXUALITY: In 1991 a researcher cited anatomic differences between the brains of heterosexual and homosexual males. Two recent twin studies have found a heritability of roughly 50 percent for predisposition to male or female homosexuality. These reports have been disputed. Another group claims to have preliminary evidence of genes linked to male homosexuality. The data have not been published.

Richard; two men who both had been named Jim, named their pet dogs Toy, married women named Linda, divorced them and remarried women named Betty; and two men who had become firefighters and drank Budweiser beer.

Other twin researchers say the significance of these coincidences has been greatly exaggerated. Richard J. Rose of Indiana University, who is collaborating on a study of 16,000 pairs of twins in Finland, points out that "if you bring together strangers who were born on the same day in the same country and ask them to find similarities between them, you may find a lot of seemingly astounding coincidences."

Rose's collaborator, Jaakko Kaprio of the University of Helsinki, notes that the Minnesota twin studies may also be biased by their selection method. Whereas he and Rose gather data by combing birth registries and sending questionnaires to those identified as twins, the Minnesota group relies heavily on media coverage to recruit new twins. The twins then come to Minnesota for a week of study—and, often, further publicity. Twins who are

"interested in publicity and willing to support it," Kaprio says, may be atypical. This self-selection effect, he adds, may explain why the Bouchard group's estimates of heritability tend to be higher than those of other studies.

One of the most outspoken critics of the Minnesota twin studies—and indeed all twin studies indicating high heritability of behavioral traits—is Leon J. Kamin, a psychologist at Northeastern University. In the 1970s Kamin helped to expose inconsistencies and possible fraud in studies of separated identical twins conducted by the British psychologist Cyril Burt during the previous two decades. Burt's conclusion that intelligence was mostly inherited had inspired various observers, notably Arthur R. Jensen, a psychologist at the University of California at Berkeley, to argue that socioeconomic stratification in the U.S. is largely a genetic phenomenon.

In his investigations of other twin studies, Kamin has shown that identical twins supposedly raised apart are often raised by members of their family or by unrelated families in the same neighborhood; some twins had extensive contact with each other while

growing up. Kamin suspects the same may be true of some Minnesota twins. He notes, for example, that some news accounts suggested Oskar and Jack (the Nazi and the Jew) and the two British women wearing seven rings were reunited for the first time when they arrived in Minnesota to be studied by Bouchard. Actually, both pairs of twins had met previously. Kamin has repeatedly asked the Minnesota group for detailed case histories of its twins to determine whether it has underestimated contact and similarities in upbringing. "They've never responded," he says.

Kamin proposes that the Minnesota twins have particularly strong motives to downplay previous contacts and to exaggerate their similarities. They might want to please researchers, to attract more attention from the media or even to make money. In fact, some twins acquired agents and were paid for appearances on television. Jack and Oskar recently sold their life story to a film producer in Los Angeles (who says Robert Duvall is interested in the roles).

Even the Minnesota researchers

The Huntington's Disease Saga: A Cautionary Tale

The identification of the gene for Huntington's disease, which was announced in March, was hailed as one of the great success stories of modern genetics. Yet it provides some rather sobering lessons for researchers seeking genes linked to more complex human disorders and traits.

The story begins in the late 1970s, when workers developed novel techniques for identifying polymorphisms, sections of the human genome that come in two or more forms. Investigators realized that by finding polymorphisms linked—always and exclusively—to diseases, they could determine which chromosome the gene resides in. Researchers decided to test the polymorphism technique on Huntington's disease, a devastating neurological disorder that affects roughly one in 10,000 people. Scientists had known for more than a century that Huntington's was caused by a mutant, dominant gene. If one parent has the disease, his or her offspring have a 50 percent chance of inheriting it.

One of the leaders of the Hun-

tington's effort was Nancy Wexler, a neuropsychologist at Columbia University whose mother had died of the disease and who therefore has a 50 percent chance of developing it herself. She and other researchers focused on a poor Venezuelan village whose inhabitants had an unusually high incidence of the disease. In 1983, through what has now become a legendary stroke of good fortune, they found a linkage with one of the first polymorphisms they tested. The linkage indicated that the gene for Huntington's disease was somewhere on chromosome 4.

The finding led quickly to a test for determining whether offspring of carriers—either in utero or already born—have inherited the gene itself. The test requires an analysis of blood samples from several members of a family known to carry the disease. Wexler herself has declined to say whether she has taken the test.

Researchers assumed that they would quickly identify the actual gene in chromosome 4 that causes Huntington's disease. Yet it took 10 years for six

teams of workers from 10 institutions to find the gene. It is a so-called expanding gene, which for unknown reasons gains base pairs (the chemical "rungs" binding two strands of DNA) every time it is transmitted. The greater the expansion of the gene, researchers say, the earlier the onset of the disease. The search was complicated by the fact that workers had no physical clues about the course of the disease to guide them. Indeed, Wexler and others emphasize that they still have no idea how the gene actually causes the disease; treatments or cures may be years or decades away.

The most immediate impact of the new discovery will be the development of a better test for Huntington's, one that requires blood only from the person at risk and not other family members. By measuring the length of the mutant gene, the test might also predict more accurately when carriers will show symptoms.

As difficult as it was to pinpoint the gene for Huntington's, it will be almost infinitely harder to discover genes for behavioral disorders, says Evan S. Balaban, a biologist at Harvard University. Unlike Huntington's disease, he notes, disorders such as schizophrenia and alcoholism cannot be unambiguously diagnosed. Furthermore, they stem not from a single dominant gene but from many genes acting in concert with environmental effects. If researchers do find a statistical association between certain genes and a trait, Balaban says, that knowledge may never be translated into useful therapies or tests. "What does it mean to have a 10 percent increased risk of alcoholism?" he asks.

NANCY WEXLER helped to find the gene responsible for Huntington's disease by studying a population in Venezuela that has been ravaged by the disorder.

caution against overinterpretation of their work. They agree with their critics that high heritability should not be equated with inevitability, since the environment can still drastically affect the expression of a gene. For example, the genetic disease phenylketonuria, which causes profound retardation, has a heritability of 100 percent. Yet eliminating the amino acid phenylalanine from the diet of affected persons prevents retardation from occurring.

Such warnings tend to be minimized in media coverage, however. Writers often make the same inference that Koshland did in an editorial in *Science:* "Better schools, a better environment, better counseling and better rehabilitation will help some individuals but not all." The prime minister of Singapore apparently reached the same conclusion. A decade ago he cited popular accounts of the Minnesota research in defending policies that encouraged middle-class Singaporeans to bear children and discouraged childbearing by the poor.

SMART GENES

Twin studies, of course, do not indicate which specific genes contribute to a trait. Early in the 1980s scientists began developing powerful ways to unearth that information. The techniques stem from the fact that certain stretches of human DNA, called polymorphisms, vary in a predictable way. If a polymorphism is consistently inherited together with a given trait—blue eyes, for example—then geneticists assume it either lies near a gene for that trait or actually is the gene. A polymorphism that merely lies near a gene is known as a marker.

In so-called linkage studies, investigators search for polymorphisms co-inherited with a trait in families unusually prone to the trait. In 1983 researchers used this method to find a marker linked to Huntington's disease, a crippling neurological disorder that usually strikes carriers in middle age and kills them within 10 years. Since then, the same technique has pinpointed genes for cystic fibrosis, muscular dystrophy and other diseases. In association studies, researchers compare the relative frequency of polymorphisms in two unrelated populations, one with the trait and one lacking it.

Workers are already using both methods to search for polymorphisms associated with intelligence, defined as the ability to score well on standardized intelligence tests. In 1991 Shelley D. Smith of the Boys Town National Institute for Communication Disorders in Children, in Omaha, and

David W. Fulker of the University of Colorado identified polymorphisms associated with dyslexia in a linkage study of 19 families exhibiting high incidence of the reading disorder.

Two years ago Robert Plomin, a psychologist at Pennsylvania State University who has long been active in behavioral genetics, received a $600,000 grant from the National Institute of Child Health and Human Development to search for genes linked to high intelligence. Plomin is using the association method, which he says is more suited than the linkage technique to identifying genes whose contribution to a trait is relatively small. Plomin is studying a group of 64 school children 12 to 13 years old who fall into three groups: those who score approximately 130, 100 and 80 on intelligence tests.

Plomin has examined some 25 polymorphisms in each of these three groups, trying to determine whether any occur with greater frequency in the "bright" children. The polymorphisms have been linked to genes thought to have neurological effects. He has uncovered several markers that seem to occur more often in the highest-scoring children. He is now seeking to replicate his results in another group of 60 children; half score above 142 on intelligence tests, and half score less than 74 (yet have no obvious organic deficiencies). Plomin presented his preliminary findings at a meeting, titled "Origins and Development of High Ability," held in London in January.

At the same meeting, however, other workers offered evidence that intelligence tests are actually poor predictors of success in business, the arts or even advanced academic programs. Indeed, even Plomin seems ambivalent about the value of his research. He suggests that someday genetic information on the cognitive abilities of children might help teachers design lessons that are more suited to students' innate strengths and weaknesses.

But he also calls his approach "a fishing expedition," given that a large number of genes may contribute to intelligence. He thinks the heritability of intelligence is not 70 percent, as the

Minnesota twin researchers have claimed, but 50 percent, which is the average finding of other studies, and at best he can only find a gene that accounts for a tiny part of variance in intelligence. "If you wanted to select on the basis of this, it would be of no use whatsoever," he remarks. These cautions did not prevent the *Sunday Telegraph,* a London newspaper, from announcing that Plomin had found "evidence that geniuses are born not made."

Evan S. Balaban, a biologist at Harvard, thinks Plomin's fishing expedition is doomed to fail. He grants that there may well be a significant genetic component to intelligence (while insisting that studies by Bouchard and others have not demonstrated one). But he doubts whether investigators will ever uncover any specific genes related to high intelligence or "genius." "It is very rare to find genes that have a specific effect," he says. "For evolutionary reasons, this just doesn't happen very often."

The history of the search for markers associated with mental illness supports Balaban's view. Over the past few decades, studies of twins, families and adoptees have convinced most investigators that schizophrenia and manic depression are not caused by psychosocial factors—such as the notorious "schizophrenogenic mother" postulated by some Freudian psychiatrists—but by biological and genetic factors. After observing the dramatic success of linkage studies in the early 1980s, researchers immediately began using the technique to isolate polymorphic markers for mental illness. The potential value of such research was enormous, given that schizophrenia and manic depression each affect roughly one percent of the global population.

They seemed to have achieved their first great success in 1987. A group led by Janice A. Egeland of the University of Miami School of Medicine claimed it had linked a genetic marker on chromosome 11 to manic depression in an Amish population. That same year another team, led by Miron Baron of Columbia University, linked a marker on the X chromosome to manic depression in three Israeli families.

The media hailed these announcements as major breakthroughs. Far less attention was paid to the retractions that followed. A more extensive analysis of the Amish in 1989 by a group from the National Institute of Mental Health turned up no link between chromosome 11 and manic depression. This year Baron's team retracted its claim of linkage with the X chromosome after doing a new study of its Israeli families with more sophisticated markers and more extensive diagnoses.

SCHIZOPHRENIC RESULTS

Studies of schizophrenia have followed a remarkably similar course. In 1988 a group headed by Hugh M. D. Gurling of the University College, London, Medical School announced in *Nature* that it had found linkage in Icelandic and British families between genetic markers on chromosome 5 and schizophrenia. In the same issue, however, researchers led by Kenneth K. Kidd of Yale University reported seeing no such linkage in a Swedish family. Although Gurling defended his result as legitimate for several years, additional research has convinced him that it was probably a false positive. "The new families showed no linkage at all," he says.

These disappointments have highlighted the problems involved in using linkage to study mental illness. Neil Risch, a geneticist at Yale, points out that linkage analysis is ideal for studying diseases, such as Huntington's, that have distinct symptoms and are caused by a single dominant gene. Some researchers had hoped that at least certain subtypes of schizophrenia or manic depression might be single-gene disorders. Single-gene mutations are thought to cause variants of breast cancer and of Alzheimer's disease that run in families and are manifested much earlier than usual. But such diseases are rare, Risch says, because natural selection quickly winnows them out of the population, and no evidence exists for distinct subtypes of manic depression or schizophrenia.

Indeed, all the available evidence suggests that schizophrenia and manic depression are caused by at least several genes—each of which may exert only a tiny influence—acting in concert with environmental influences. Finding such genes with linkage analysis may not be impossible, Risch says, but it will be considerably more difficult than identifying genes that have a one-to-one correspondence to a trait. The difficulty is compounded by the fact that the diagnosis of mental illness is often subjective—all the more so when researchers are relying on family records or recollections.

Some experts now question whether genes play a significant role in mental illness. "Personally, I think we have overestimated the genetic component of schizophrenia," says E. Fuller Torrey, a psychiatrist at St. Elizabeth's Hospital in Washington, D.C. He argues that the evidence supporting genetic models can be explained by other biological factors, such as a virus that strikes in utero. The pattern of incidence of schizophrenia in families often resembles that of other viral diseases, such as polio. "Genes may just create a susceptibility to the virus," Torrey explains.

THE DRINK LINK

Even Kidd, the Yale geneticist who has devoted his career to searching for genes linked to mental illness, acknowledges that "in a rigorous, technical, scientific sense, there is very little proof that schizophrenia, manic depression and other psychiatric disorders have a genetic origin. "Virtually all the evidence supports a genetic explanation, but there are always other explanations, even if they are convoluted."

The evidence for a genetic basis for alcoholism is even more tentative than that for manic depression and schizophrenia. Although some studies discern a genetic component, especially in males, others have reached the opposite conclusion. Gurling, the University College investigator, found a decade ago that identical twins were slightly *more* likely to be discordant for alcoholism than fraternal twins. The drinking habits of some identical

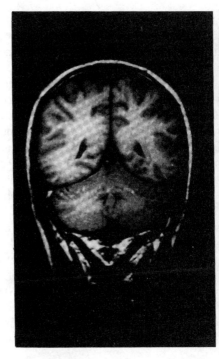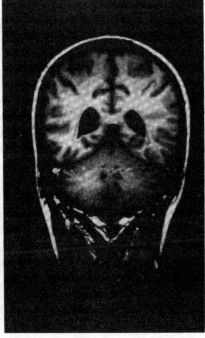

BRAIN OF SCHIZOPHRENIC (*right*) appears different from the brain of his identical twin in these magnetic resonance images. Such findings suggest that factors that are biological but not genetic—such as viruses—may play a significant role in mental illness.

"Better Breeding"

Fairly or not, modern genetics research is still haunted by the history of eugenics. "It offers a lot of cautionary lessons," says Daniel J. Kevles, a historian at the California Institute of Technology, who wrote the 1985 book *In the Name of Eugenics.* The British scientist Francis Galton, cousin to Charles Darwin, first proposed that human society could be improved "through better breeding" in 1865 in an article entitled "Hereditary Talent and Character." He coined the term eugenics, from the Greek for "good birth," in 1883.

Galton's proposal had broad appeal. The American sexual libertarian John Humphrey Noyes bent eugenics into an ingenious argument for polygamy. "While the good man will be limited by his conscience to what the law allows," Noyes said, "the bad man, free from moral check, will distribute his seed beyond the legal limit."

A more serious advocate was the biologist Charles B. Davenport, founder of Cold Spring Harbor Laboratory and of the Eugenics Record Office, which gathered information on thousands of American families for genetic research. After demonstrating the heritability of eye, skin and hair color,

Davenport went on to "prove" the heritability of traits such as "pauperism," criminality and "feeble-mindedness." In one monograph, published in 1919, he asserted that the ability to be a naval officer is an inherited trait, composed of subtraits for thalassophilia, or love of the sea, and hyperkineticism, or wanderlust. Noting the paucity of female naval officers, Davenport concluded that the trait is unique to males.

Beginning in the 1920s the American Eugenics Society, founded by Davenport and others, sponsored "Fitter Families Contests" at state fairs around the U.S. Just as cows and sheep were appraised by judges at the fairs,

so were human entrants (such as the family shown above at the 1925 Texas State Fair). Less amusingly, eugenicists helped to persuade more than 20 U.S. states to authorize sterilization of men and women in prisons and mental hospitals, and they urged the federal government to restrict the immigration of "undesirable" races.

No nation, of course, practiced eugenics as enthusiastically as Nazi Germany, whose program culminated in "euthanasia" ("good death") of the mentally and physically disabled as well as Jews, Gypsies, Catholics and others. As revelations of these atrocities spread after World War II, popular support for eugenics programs waned in the U.S. and elsewhere.

---

twins were strikingly different. "In some cases, one drank a few bottles a day, and the other didn't drink at all," Gurling says.

Nevertheless, in 1990 a group led by Kenneth Blum of the University of Texas Health Science Center at San Antonio announced it had discovered a genetic marker for alcoholism in an association study comparing 35 alcoholics with a control group of 35 non-alcoholics. A page-one story in the *New York Times* portrayed the research as a potential watershed in the diagnosis and treatment of alcoholism without mentioning the considerable skepticism aroused among other researchers.

The Blum group claimed that its marker, called the A1 allele, was associated with a gene, called the D2 gene,

that codes for a receptor for the neurotransmitter dopamine. Skeptics noted that the A1 allele was actually some 10,000 base pairs from the dopamine-receptor gene and was not linked to any detectable variation in its expression.

Since the initial announcement by Blum, three papers, including an additional one by Blum's group, have presented more evidence of an association between the A1 allele and alcoholism. Six groups have found no such evidence (and received virtually no mention in the popular media).

In April, Risch and Joel Gelernter of Yale and David Goldman of the National Institute on Alcohol Abuse and Alcoholism analyzed all these studies on the A1 allele in a paper in the *Journal of the American Medical Asso-*

ciation. They noted that if Blum's two studies are cast aside, the balance of the results shows no association between the D2 receptor and alcoholism, either in the disorder's milder or most severe forms. "We therefore conclude that no physiologically significant association" between the A1 allele and alcoholism has been proved, the group stated. "It's a dead issue," Risch says.

Gelernter and his colleagues point out that association studies are prone to spurious results if not properly controlled. They suggest that the positive findings of Blum and his colleagues may have derived from a failure to control for ethnic variation. The limited surveys done so far have shown that the incidence of the A1 allele varies wildly in different ethnic groups, ranging from 10 percent in certain Jewish groups to about 50 percent in Japanese.

Blum insists that the ethnic data, far from undermining his case, support it, since those groups with the highest prevalence of the A1 allele also exhibit the highest rates of "addictive behavior." He contends that the only reason the Japanese do not display higher rates of alcoholism is that many also carry a gene that prevents them from metabolizing alcohol. "They're pretty compulsive," explains Blum, who recently obtained a patent for a genetic test for alcoholism.

These arguments have been rejected even by Irving I. Gottesman of the University of Virginia, who is a strong defender of genetic models of human behavior. He considers the papers cited by Blum to support his case to be ambiguous and even contradictory. Some see an association only with alcoholism that leads to medical complications or even death; others discern no association with alcoholism but only with "polysubstance abuse," including cigarette smoking. "I think it is by and large garbage," Gottesman says of the alleged A1-alcoholism link.

By far the most controversial area of behavioral genetics is research on crime. Last fall complaints by civil-rights leaders and others led the National Institutes of Health to withdraw its funding from a meeting entitled "Genetic Factors in Crime: Findings, Uses and Implications." The conference brochure had noted the "apparent failure of environmental approaches to crime" and suggested that genetic research might yield methods for identifying and treating potential criminals—and particularly those prone to violence—at an early age.

Critics contend that such investigations inevitably suggest that blacks are predisposed to crime, given that blacks in the U.S. are six times more likely than whites to be arrested for a violent crime. In fact, some prominent scientists, notably Richard J. Herrnstein, a psychologist at Harvard, have made this assertion. Others reject this view but insist biological research on attributes linked to violent crime, such as aggression, may still have some value.

"People who are unwilling to address genetic and biochemical factors are just putting their heads in the sand," says Goldman, the alcoholism expert. "It is not fair to say that just because there have been geneticists who have had a very narrow view of this in the past, we shouldn't explore this now."

In fact, investigations of the biology of violent crime continue, albeit quietly. Workers at City of Hope Hospital in Duarte, Calif., claim to have found an association between the A1 allele—the alleged alcoholism marker—and "criminal aggression." Last year a group led by Markus J. P. Kruesi of the University of Illinois at Chicago presented evidence of an association between low levels of the neurotransmitter serotonin and disruptive-behavior disorders in children. Kruesi concedes there is no way to determine whether the serotonin levels are genetically influenced. In fact, the serotonin levels might be an effect—a reaction to an environmental trauma—rather than a cause. "This might be a scar marker," he says.

One reason such research persists is that studies of families, twins and adoptees have suggested a genetic component to crime. Glenn D. Walters, a psychologist at the Federal Correctional Institution in Schuylkill, Pa., recently reviewed 38 of these studies, conducted from the 1930s to the present, in the journal *Criminology*. His meta-analysis turned up a small genetic effect, "but nothing to get excited about." He observes that "a lot of the research has not been very good" and that the more recent, better-designed studies tended to turn up less evidence. "I don't think we will find any biological markers for crime," he says. "We should put our resources elsewhere."

GAY GENES

The ostensible purpose of investigations of mental illness, alcoholism and even crime is to reduce their incidence. Scientists studying homosexuality have a different goal: simply to test whether homosexuality is innate, as many homosexuals have long professed. That claim was advanced by a report in

Science in 1991 by Simon LeVay of the Salk Institute for Biological Studies in San Diego. LeVay has acknowledged both that he is gay and that he believes evidence of biological differences between homosexuals and heterosexuals will encourage tolerance toward gays.

LeVay, who recently left the Salk Institute to found the Institute of Gay and Lesbian Education, focused on a tiny neural structure in the hypothalamus, a region of the brain known to control sexual response. He measured this structure, called the interstitial nucleus, in autopsies of the brains of 19 homosexual males, 16 heterosexual males and six heterosexual women. LeVay found that the interstitial nucleus was almost twice as large in the heterosexual males as in the homosexual males or in the women. He postulated that the interstitial nucleus "is large in individuals oriented toward women"—whether male or female.

Of course, LeVay's finding only addresses anatomic differences, not necessarily genetic ones. Various other researchers have tried to establish that homosexuality is not just biological in its origin—caused, perhaps, by hormonal influences in utero—but also genetic. Some have sought evidence in experiments with rats and other animals. A group headed by Angela Pattatucci of the National Cancer Institute is studying a strain of male fruit flies—which wags have dubbed either "fruity" or "fruitless"—that court other males.

In December 1991 J. Michael Bailey of Northwestern University and Richard C. Pillard of Boston University announced they had uncovered evidence of a genetic basis for male homosexuality in humans. They studied 161 gay men, each of whom had at least one identical or fraternal twin or adopted brother. The researchers determined that 52 percent of the identical twins were both homosexual, as compared with 22 percent of the fraternal twins and 11 percent of the adopted brothers.

Bailey and Pillard derived similar results in a study of lesbians published this year in the *Archives of General Psychiatry*. They compared 147 gay women with identical or fraternal twins or adopted sisters: 48 percent of the identical twins were both gay, versus 16 per-cent of the fraternal twins (who share only half each other's genes) and 6 per-cent of the adopted sisters. "Both male and female sexual orientation appeared to be influenced by genetic factors," Bailey and Pillard concluded.

This conclusion has disturbed some of Bailey and Pillard's own subjects. "I have major questions about the validity of some of the assumptions they are making," says Nina Sossen, a gay woman living in Madison, Wis., whose identical twin is heterosexual. Her doubts are shared by William Byne, a psychiatrist at Columbia University. He notes that in their study of male homosexuality Bailey and Pillard found more concordance between unrelated, adopted brothers than related (but non-twin) brothers. The high concordance of the male and female identical twins, moreover, may stem from the fact that such twins are often dressed alike and treated alike—indeed, they are often mistaken for each other—by family members as well as by others.

"The increased concordance for homosexuality among the identical twins could be entirely accounted for by the increased similarity of their developmental experiences," Byne says. "In my opinion, the major finding of that study is that 48 percent of identical twins who were reared together were discordant for sexual orientation."

Byne also criticizes LeVay's conclusion that homosexuality must be biological—although not necessarily genetic—because the brains of male homosexuals resemble the brains of women. That assumption, Byne points out, rests on still another assumption, that there are significant anatomic differences between heterosexual male and female brains. But to date, there have been no replicable studies showing such sexual dimorphism.

Byne notes that he has been suspected of having an antigay motive. Two reviewers of an article he recently wrote criticizing homosexuality research accused him of having a "right-wing agenda," he says. He has also been contacted by conservative groups

hoping he will speak out against the admittance of homosexuals to the military. He emphasizes that he supports gay rights and thinks homosexuality, whatever its cause, is not a "choice." He adds that genetic models of behavior are just as likely to foment bigotry as to quell it.

"HIERARCHY OF WORTHLESSNESS"

Despite the skepticism of Byne and others, at least one group, led by Dean Hamer of the National Cancer Institute, is searching not merely for anatomic or biochemical differences in homosexuals but for genetic markers. Hamer has done a linkage study of numerous small families, each of which has at least two gay brothers. He says his study has turned up some tentative findings, and he plans to submit his results soon. Hamer's colleague Pattatucci is planning a similar study of lesbians.

What purpose will be served by pinpointing genes linked to homosexuality? In an information sheet for prospective participants in his study, Hamer expresses the hope that his research may "improve understanding between people with different sexual orientations." He adds, "This study is not aimed at developing methods to alter either heterosexual or homosexual orientation, and the results of the study will not allow sexual orientation to be determined by a blood test or amniocentesis."

Yet even Pillard, who is gay and applauds Hamer's work, admits to some concern over the potential uses of a genetic marker for homosexuality. He notes that some parents might choose to abort embryos carrying such a marker. Male and female homosexuals might then retaliate, he says, by conceiving children and aborting fetuses that lacked such a gene.

Balaban, the Harvard biologist, thinks the possible dangers of such research—assuming it is successful—outweigh any benefits. Indeed, he sees behavioral genetics as a "hierarchy of worthlessness," with twin studies at

the bottom and linkage studies of mental illness at the top. The best researchers can hope for is to find, say, a gene associated with a slightly elevated risk of schizophrenia. Such information is more likely to lead to discrimination by insurance companies and employers than to therapeutic benefits, Balaban warns.

His colleague Lewontin agrees. In the 1970s, he recalls, insurance companies began requiring black customers to take tests for sickle cell anemia, a genetic disease that primarily affects blacks. Those who refused to take the test or who tested positive were denied coverage. "I feel that this research is a substitute for what is really hard—finding out how to change social conditions," Lewontin remarks. "I think it's the wrong direction for research, given that we have a finite amount of resources."

Paul R. Billings, a geneticist at the California Pacific Medical Center, shares some of these concerns. He agrees that twin studies seem to be inherently ambiguous, and he urges researchers seeking markers for homosexuality to consider what a conservative government—led by Patrick Buchanan, for example—might allow to be done with such information. But he believes some aspects of behavioral genetics, particularly searches for genes underlying mental illness, are worth pursuing.

In an article published in the British journal *Social Science and Medicine* last year, Billings and two other scientists offered some constructive criticism for the field. Researchers engaged in association and linkage studies should establish "strict criteria as to what would constitute meaningful data." Both scientists and the press should emphasize the limitations of such studies, "especially when the mechanism of how a gene acts on a behavior is not known." Billings and his colleagues strive to end their article on a positive note. "Despite the shortcomings of other studies," they say, "there is relatively good evidence for a site on the X chromosome which is associated with [manic depression] in some families." This finding was retracted earlier this year.

Making Babies

*The Boom in the Infertility Business Is Raising Hopes,
and Increasing Criticism*

Nancy Wartik

Nancy Wartik, who lives in Brooklyn, N. Y., is a contributing editor for American Health *magazine.*

In his spotless embryology lab at the Center for Reproductive Medicine at Century City Hospital, David Hill is peering into the viewer of a formidable-looking microscope, trying to make a baby. On a monitor next to the scope is the vastly magnified image of a woman's egg–smaller, in reality, than a tiny speck of dust–and of the microscopic suction rod holding it in place. Right now, Hill's attention is on the semen sample next to the egg. With his right hand, he's manipulating controls that send a needle far finer than a hair chasing after what looks to be a batch of teeny, wriggling long-tailed polliwogs.

"The best sperm tend to go off to the edge and go around and around the drop like little race cars," Hill says as he hunts down a pack of them. "It's very fortuitous for embryologists."

When he's zeroed in on the sperm he wants, Hill draws them up into the needle by sucking on a rubber mouthpiece that's connected to a slender hose and clenched between his teeth–an oddly low-tech note in this whole sophisticated operation. After he's drawn some 50 sperm into the needle, he moves it over to the egg and presses down against its translucent outer shell (the *zona pellucida*). Under the pressure of the needle, the egg squashes in on itself alarmingly, like a beach ball poked with a stick. But as soon as Hill punctures the *zona pellucida,* deposits a fraction of the sperm and retracts the needle, the egg springs back into shape. Beneath its cloudy shell, the sperm buzz madly about like trapped insects.

The procedure he's just completed is a subzonal insertion, usually known by its friendly acronym, SUZI. Eggs and sperm that Hill manipulate in this way can't, for one reason or another, achieve fertiliza-

tion on their own. So he's helping them bypass the arduous trek to conception. The sperm-injected eggs (usually a total of seven or eight for each couple) go into an incubator and are maintained at body temperature for 14 to 18 hours. Depending on the number that make the leap to embryo status, about four of the best quality will be loaded into a catheter and inserted into the woman's womb.

"I can't wait to come into the lab, open up the incubator and see whether any of our efforts have resulted in decent embryos," says Hill. "It's just like opening a little Christmas present. I never get tired of it."

In Hill's sterilized lab, surrounded by the tools of his trade, it's easy to lose sight of what's actually happening. For couples who come to Century City, as to a fast-growing number of similar clinics around the country, these procedures represent a last chance to achieve a desire as old as human history: that of giving birth to a child. On behalf of these couples, Hill is waging a daily battle of technology against nature. And despite a swelling arsenal of controversial new techniques and procedures, nature usually wins.

Three years ago, John Taylor [this name and those of the other patients have been changed] got the call from his doctor, just before a weekend business trip to New Orleans. After months of trying unsuccessfully to conceive, John and his wife, Leslie, had sought medical help. Now they were awaiting results of his sperm test. The voice at the other end of the line had bad news. "The doctor told me I had absolutely no sperm," recalls Taylor, 36, a television lighting designer.

"The two of us stood in the kitchen and bawled our eyes out. I was destroyed. I felt emasculated. I come from a large family, and the fact that I'd never be able to have my own children–never, there wasn't a hope in hell–was devastating."

1. CONCEPTION TO BIRTH: Prenatal Development

At the end of his weekend trip, in a bizarre twist of events, Taylor returned to hear that there had been a mix-up at the lab, and he did have a sperm count. But it was low, the doctor warned him; pregnancy would still be problematic. "If the guy had been standing there, I'd have decked him for putting me through all that," he says. "But I was also pleased. At least he'd given us back some hope."

Today, $20,000 poorer and their insurance coverage for infertility exhausted, the Taylors wonder whether there was much point in those hopes being raised. Both partners have undergone surgery to correct reproductive-tract problems; each has tried fertility drugs. They've tried timed insemination, with John's sperm inserted directly into Leslie's uterus when ultrasound scanning showed she was ovulating. Twice they've attempted, and failed at, "test tube" conception at Century City. To cut costs on the pricey medication a woman takes during such attempts, they've journeyed to Tijuana to purchase their drugs at cut-rate prices.

Running the gantlet of these treatments has "put an incredible strain on our marriage," says Taylor. "Frankly, I'm surprised we're still together. In many respects, our lives have been on hold with this thing for three years."

In a few months, the Taylors will return to Century City to try a new procedure developed in Belgium that Hill has recently begun working on. The ultimate refinement of existing sperm-injection methods, it involves shooting a single sperm directly into the heart of an egg and seems to produce higher fertilization rates than multiple-sperm procedures such as SUZI; the Belgian clinic that first used it is now claiming pregnancy rates of more than 30%.

This could be the Taylors' winning ticket in the baby lottery. But Leslie, 38, a small, jeans-clad TV director who sits curled on the sofa in their North Hollywood home, is tiring of the demands of the pregnancy chase. "I only want to try direct injection once," says Leslie. "John wants to try it twice. I'm emotionally and physically beyond it. I've been on hormone injections for three solid months; I feel fat and bloated and like I could cry at the drop of a hat. Why is it that we cannot conceive a child? Why?"

"It can make you feel guilty," says John. "You look back over your life, you say: 'I've always tried to be a decent person. Did I do something wrong? Is God trying to punish me? Was it my lifestyle?'"

He's not willing to give up, however, and his determination is carrying both of them. "All through this, we've had a willingness to fight, not to take the first defeat and say, 'OK, it's over,'" he says. "When you start something like this, you've got to finish. Otherwise you spend the rest of your life wondering 'What if?' I'm still not convinced we're finished."

To Leslie, he adds, "I won't ask for more than two tries. But you go in every time thinking, this is the time it's going to work."

More often than not, however, you'll be wrong.

Inside the administrative offices at the Century City reproductive clinic, which occupies part of a floor in this small private hospital, are homey touches: stuffed animals nesting on file cabinets, a sign that reads "Never give up!" On the outer walls hang photos of children conceived as a result of treatment here and letters from their grateful parents. There is praise for the "incredible staff" at Century City, and the word *miracle* shows up often.

Each year, more than 300 couples come here seeking children. For many, it's a court of last appeal, after months or years of lower-tech efforts such as drugs or surgery have failed. In general, those who choose high-tech conception follow a similar regimen. A woman begins with daily injections of powerful hormone-regulating drugs to stimulate her ovaries to mature more eggs than the single one that normally matures each month. If the therapy succeeds, the crop of eggs—about 10 on average but in some cases more than 30—is "harvested." While a patient is under local or general anesthesia, a doctor inserts a needle either vaginally or through an incision in the stomach to suck the eggs from her ovaries.

In regular in-vitro fertilization (IVF), eggs are then combined in a petri dish with the sperm sample, fresh or frozen, that a man has dutifully provided. In gamete intra-Fallopian transfer (GIFT), developed as a slightly more "natural" alternative to IVF—eggs and sperm don't unite in glassware, but are inserted together into the Fallopian tubes. The resulting embryos are transferred into the uterus, the Fallopian tubes or, sometimes, both. At many IVF centers, extra embryos now can be frozen, meaning a woman doesn't have to go through the stressful process of an egg retrieval at each attempt.

Louise Brown, the first baby conceived through IVF, was born in Britain in 1978. Three years later, the first American high-tech baby was born at a Norfolk, Va., clinic. Since then, the infertility business in the United States has mushroomed into a $2-billion-a-year enterprise, much of its expansion spurred by the development of assisted reproductive technologies, including IVF and the many different methods it has spawned for manipulating eggs and sperm outside the body. It is, at best, an imperfect science—expensive, unregulated and relatively untested, especially in the area of long-term effects.

But the market for reproductive technologies is sizable. According to the National Center for Health Statistics, about 2.3 million married American couples are infertile (meaning they haven't been able to conceive after a year or more of trying). For up to 15% of them, according to the American Fertility Society, high-tech approaches are considered the only hope. With the U.S. government disinclined to allocate research dollars to a politically touchy area such as reproductive technology, this country has lagged behind Australia and parts of Europe—but not too far. There are now about 350 U.S. infertility clinics, including at least two multi-state chains; at least 45 reproductive clinics that perform IVF and other assisted technologies are crowded into California alone. More than 33,000 assisted-reproductive-technology procedures were initiated in 1991, the last year for which figures are available, up 30% from 1990.

Originally used only to treat blocked tubes, assisted reproductive technologies are now applied to a range of female infertility problems, including endometriosis, ovulatory disorders and the catch-all condition of "unexplained infertility." More recently, researchers have zeroed in on male infertility. Women had long been accorded the lion's share of the blame when a marriage was barren, but when reproductive specialists peered closely into their petri dishes, they discovered that the man was wholly or partly responsible for a couple's problem 40% to 60% of the time.

For some men, approaches that range from eschewing hot tubs to undergoing corrective surgery will do the trick. But others have sperm that are so few in number, sluggish, malformed or otherwise defective that doctors could do nothing but point them toward the nearest sperm bank—until recently. In the late 1980s, embryologists found it was possible to aid recalcitrant sperm in fertilization by opening the egg's outer shell to give the sperm easier access. This type of "micromanipulation," known as partial zona dissection, was followed by SUZI. Then, in 1992, came the Belgians' encouraging announcement of intracytoplasmic sperm injection, or ICSI (pronounced ICK-see by those in the field), the no-nonsense technique in which a single sperm is propelled to the egg's center.

"It's actually somewhat surprising the technique works," admits Jacques Cohen, scientific director of assisted reproduction at New York City's Cornell Medical Center and a pioneer in the development of micromanipulation. "We used to think there was a certain sequence of processes that was absolutely necessary before the sperm was able to fertilize the egg. Now we know that's not true; those processes can be completely surpassed."

As these dazzling technologies establish themselves as the wave of the future, troubling issues surround their use. Most conspicuous are the ethical dilemmas that seem to grab headlines weekly. There is much outrage at the idea of 60-year-old women becoming mothers and apprehension that scientists might soon start using eggs from aborted fetuses to produce babies—meaning that a child could have a biological mother who was never born. And last fall, two U.S. scientists "cloned" a human embryo, making an exact genetic copy of the original and raising the specter of an assembly-line baby-manufacturing industry.

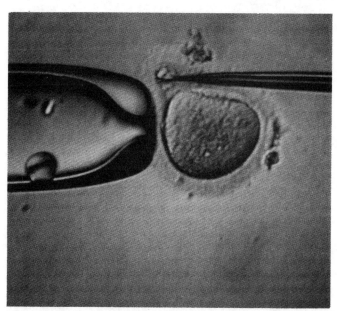

The needle on the right contains a semen sample to be inserted into the egg, center.

But at the moment, these issues don't apply in clinical practice—or apply to only a tiny handful of those who visit programs. (Realistically, not many 60-year-old women crave new motherhood.) For most infertile couples, the considerations are more mundane: In 1991, only 15% of individual attempts at test-tube conception produced what's known in the field as a "take-home baby"—with figures higher or lower depending on the procedure and the patient involved.

'The door never completely closes on the infertile couple,' says David Hill. 'They can end up childless and financially depleted.'

If success rates are low, however, prices are not. A completed attempt (some women drop out early because they don't respond to initial hormone therapy) ranges from $8,000 to $13,000 or more. Lumped into the category of "luxury" treatments such as tummy-tucks or orthodontia, assisted reproductive technologies in many cases are not covered, or only minimally covered, by insurance. And there's no money-back guarantee.

In worst-case scenarios, patients run up huge tabs in repeated futile efforts to have a baby. "The door never, ever completely closes on an infertile couple," acknowledges Hill. "There's always the latest snazzy technique to rekindle hope. They can end up at the end of the line childless and financially depleted."

Contemplating this scenario, a small but vocal number of critics, several of them on Capitol Hill, have raised their voices in a growing chorus of complaint.

Too often, they say, the assisted-reproductive-technology field is battening on emotional desperation. "The technology doesn't work," says Ann Pappert, who's working on a book to be titled "Cruel Promises: Inside the Reproductive Industry," and one of a group of experts who attended a 1990 World Health Organization policy conference on IVF. "A lot of couples go into it thinking: 'All right, I know the reality but I'm going to be the exception.' I've heard that over and over and over again. The whole technology is presented in a manner that encourages them to think that way. A lot of clinics, the way they talk to the patients sort of pumps them up to keep going back. It's a business, and like any business, you have to keep your clients coming.

"How many people would go to an IVF clinic if they read that 85% of couples go home without a baby?" she asks. "It's not that I think clinics should only emphasize the negative, but there isn't a balanced picture presented. If you go to your OB-GYN, does he have a wall of baby pictures? It's a form of emotional manipulation."

Advocates of reproductive technology see things differently. Diane Aronson, executive director of the Somerville, Mass.-based national infertility consumer group RESOLVE, came to the organization years ago with her own problems. "These couples may be in a vulnerable position, but that doesn't mean they're not thinking, rational folks," she says. "Plenty of people decide, 'IVF is not for me.' That's their option. But everyone should have the right to become informed about IVF, to assess the risk and evaluate it for themselves." The question, though, is whether couples have a chance to make a truly informed decision. Does the data exist to help them weigh whether the short- and long-term risks are worth the potential benefit? Many in the field admit that the answer is no.

In 1989, the Canadian government assembled a royal commission to come up with guidelines and funding recommendations for the country's use of reproductive technology. The commissioners reviewed hundreds of studies from international research on the use of reproductive technologies for infertility problems. Last year, they concluded that only one procedure—standard IVF for treatment of blocked tubes—had been proven in studies to give women a better chance of birth—about 10% per attempt—than no treatment at all. It recommended that no other form of the procedure get health-care coverage.

The commission didn't say whether IVF works for other types of infertility, or that procedures such as GIFT or micromanipulation are not effective. But, says Dr. Patricia Baird of the University of British Columbia in Vancouver, the pediatrician and geneticist who headed the inquiry, "we were really rather disturbed by the quality of the studies out there. Many of them have methodological weaknesses or small sample sizes. There's a real hodgepodge of women being treated, so you can't judge what the success rate is for different categories of diagnosis. There may be categories for which it's really not doing any good, and we need to sort that out, because IVF is invasive and expensive, and there are risks involved."

She adds: "It seems to us that everything except IVF for blocked tubes should be offered in the context of research trials, in which women are told these aren't proven treatments. They shouldn't have to pay, and they should have full information and informed consent."

The World Health Organization also has criticized the profit-driven proliferation of reproductive technology in countries around the globe and called for more clinical trials. Ask Dr. Maria Bustillo, current president of the Society for Assisted Reproductive Technology, if the United States should begin offering these in the context of clinical trials, and she laughs.

"I'd love it," says Bustillo, who is the director of reproductive endocrinology at Mt. Sinai Medical Center in New York. "I'd love to be able to go back and do some really basic studies. It would be wonderful if people didn't have to pay these high costs, when we don't yet have the data to give them answers. But we can't even get money for doing basic research on endometriosis. Where would we get the dollars to do this?

"A lot of things in medicine related to women's health get started and adopted without sufficient study; the purse strings have not been controlled by women."

But without the data that clinical trials would provide, reproductive centers are operating in a questionably gray area. For example, programs typically tell couples that their odds of giving birth stay the same for each IVF attempt, up through the fourth try (after which birth rates are known to dip precipitously). That may, in fact, not be so. A 1992 study by a Yale University professor, frustrated at his own and his wife's failure with multiple attempts, suggests that the chance of pregnancy drops even before the fourth try. Of 571 women who started treatment at Yale, 13% got pregnant on the first attempt, 10.7% succeeded on the second go-round, 6.9% on the third and 4.3% on the fourth. Edward H. Kaplan, professor of management sciences and of medicine at Yale, who authored the study, is cautious about applying his results to other clinics, but he believes that "you could end up spending a whole lot of money trying to get pregnant when the chance is really very small."

Roberta Geist, 43 and a real estate agent, *has* spent a whole lot of money—more than $30,000—trying to get pregnant. She's tried GIFT once and IVF once. At the moment, she's lying in a Century City recovery room after her third egg retrieval; she's preparing to try IVF again. Geist's chances of pregnancy, she's been told, are 10% to 14%. "While you have your period, you can still have a child," she says hopefully. "This should work."

Married at 38, Geist discovered after a year of trying

to conceive that her tubes were blocked, her hormonal levels not optimal. "My husband won't let me adopt," Geist says. But she very much wants a baby. "I have that maternal instinct now," she says. "I want to be a mother. I'd love for this to work. If it doesn't, I don't know, I'll deal with it, but...." A nurse standing nearby gives Geist a hug. "This is going to work," she says.

It doesn't. In fact, a month later, after her fourth failed attempt, Geist gave up on the idea of genetic motherhood and was going to try again with a donor egg.

Further complicating the picture for patients confronting the assisted-reproductive technology labyrinth is the dramatic fluctuation in take home baby rates from clinic to clinic. Rates can vary from less than 5% at some programs to a high of more than 30% at others, according to Dr. David Meldrum, director of the Center for Advanced Reproductive Care at South Bay Hospital in Redondo Beach. "These are very complex procedures, with many different variables," Meldrum says. "The research hasn't been done yet that will show you, you must do this particular thing at this particular time to get the best results. Without that knowledge, each program varies in the small details that make the difference between success and lack of it."

He adds: "I've visited programs having great difficulty. They have individuals trying extremely hard to have a good outcome, they're very well trained, they're in agony, and yet it's difficult to put your finger on exactly where the problem is."

Couples can improve their odds by using groups like RESOLVE or the resources of the American Fertility Society to get success rate data on clinics that register with the society (most do). But checking on a particular clinic's rates in that manner still won't reveal how many of those who signed on at the clinic actually took a baby home, because the group presents such rates in terms of how many births a program has had, per egg retrieval, rather than in terms of births per started attempt.

"About 15% of women don't get to egg retrieval, but those failures are discounted as if they never happened," notes Michael Katz, a supervisory investigative specialist with the Division of Service Industry Practices at the Federal Trade Commission. "The [American Fertility Society] position is that the whole process doesn't start until the egg is recovered. Our position is that the process starts when the consumer begins kicking over dollars; those drugs cost quite a bit of money."

In recent years, the FTC, virtually the only agency to watchdog these clinics, has chastised several for representing their success rates in a misleading way, exacting promises from each to practice truth-in-advertising. But that's virtually as much outside regulation as the industry has been subject to. Although a voluntary lab accreditation program was recently initiated by the Society for Assisted Reproductive Technology, nothing currently mandates that IVF labs be licensed or prove their competency in any way.

That could change. In 1992, Congress approved a bill scheduled to go into effect at the end of this year that gives each state the option to require that its IVF programs be licensed according to a national standard. It also demands that such clinics annually report success rates—including numbers of started attempts as well as of egg retrievals—to the government. Still, Rep. Ron Wyden (D-Ore.), who sponsored the initial bill, refers to it as "baby steps," and some complain that because clinic licensing won't be federally administered, the law has no teeth in it.

Such minimal scrutiny, combined with a technology evolving at warp speed, and stiff competition (billboards, radio spots, ads in upscale magazines designed to win business) to attract the minority of infertile couples who can afford assisted reproductive techniques, leaves a margin for abuse.

The new ICSI procedure could be a case in point. In Britain, embryologists who want to use it must prove their competence, then apply for a treatment license. In the United States, any lab that wants to offer the technique can do so. Last fall, the procedure won its 15 minutes of fame here, touted in headlines and on "Donahue" and "Eye to Eye With Connie Chung," as the panacea for male infertility. "In big urban centers, people will call around to clinics asking, 'Do you offer it?'" notes Barry Behr, director of the human embryology and andrology lab at Stanford University. "If you say no, they'll call elsewhere. It's a rat race; you almost have to stay one-up on the program down the road to get business."

As the hype flew, embryologists from around the country took off to Brussels to do a workshop at the clinic where ICSI had been developed. They returned to the United States with certificates to hang on their walls, stating that they'd taken the course. Yet, says micromanipulation pioneer Jacques Cohen of Cornell, "I'm afraid it is going to be used quite wrongly by most programs. It's one of the most difficult technologies I've ever been involved with. A lot of people think you can just take a needle, put a sperm in it and stick it in the egg. But you need the expertise to apply the procedure correctly."

Century City's David Hill, who spent several days studying the procedure at Reproductive Biology Associates in Atlanta, where the first U.S. ICSI baby was born last fall, readily admits that he's still straddling a learning curve. The fertilization rates he's getting aren't better yet than those with SUZI. "It is more challenging than other micromanipulation procedures," says Hill, "but we won't charge extra for it until I've gotten three pregnancies. As I feel more comfortable with it, we may slowly, slowly start using it in lieu of SUZI."

Not all clinics may be that circumspect. Behr also fears that some programs will move straight to prescribing this more high-tech, and pricey, treatment for infertile couples when lower-tech solutions might do instead. That sort of practice, he adds, is relatively common. "It's one of the big controversies in the field today: At what point do you resort to these aggressive, invasive procedures?" he asks. "Some labs claim success using these aggressive treatments, while others can have success without them. In my mind, it's when you don't have to resort to pulling out every stop that you're doing a good job."

Today is a good day at Century City; there have been two positive pregnancy tests. Although the chance of a miscarriage during assisted-reproductive-technology pregnancies is 25% (slightly higher than the percentage in the general population), positive tests are still cause for rejoicing. "I have a whistle I blow when someone gets pregnant," embryologist David Hill says. "I used to take Polaroids of myself doing handstands, but I stopped because of my back."

Hill's concern for the patients he works with is evident. Why aren't they getting pregnant? he says of the Taylors. I wish I knew. If I could bleed a pint of my own blood to get them pregnant, I would do it. In this business, that's not an infrequent feeling."

Now sitting behind his desk, Hill is contemplating another troubling subject. Early last year, a collaborative study by epidemiologists from around the country suggested that the hormones used to stimulate women's ovaries to release extra eggs might raise their risk for ovarian cancer. Let's assume for the sake of argument that there is an inherent risk," says Hill. "Now I happen not to believe it. I think no study yet clearly shows that association. But let's say there was an association. This may still be something patients are willing to undertake, as long as they have a realistic estimate of the ratio of risk to benefit."

The problem is, the information doesn't exist to help patients make that assessment. Moreover, Robert Spirtas, chief of the contraceptive and reproductive evaluation branch at the National Institutes of Health, disagrees that this particular study should be discounted. He admits that the research had methodological flaws because the author had limited data. Still, he says, "the study raises an issue that we had really better look at" and notes that the institute plans to fund its own study on ovarian cancer and fertility drugs, which millions of American women have now taken.

To date, the potential risks of reproductive technologies have gone virtually unexplored. In 1990, the World Health Organization sharply criticized the infertility community for doing more research on "new and expanded uses for the technology" than its effects on women using it, or on their children.

"This is one vast clinical trial, and no one is monitoring it," says author Ann Pappert. "No one has a clue about what the long-term effects of these technologies will be on the babies or on women, and nobody's doing much to try to find out. The whole history of reproductive medicine is filled with these breakthroughs that, 10 or 20 years down the road, fill hospitals with patients having breast implants or IUDs removed, or DES problems [related to the drug given to pregnant women in the '50s that caused cancer in some of their daughters]. The truth is that instead of waking up after the fact, we should stop now and see if we're creating another problem."

With 23,000 high-tech babies born in this country, the American Fertility Society puts the birth defect rate in these children at less than 3%, a figure equivalent to that in the general population. Preliminary data from Australia, however, suggests that the rate of certain defects may be elevated in high-tech babies. Moreover, about one in three assisted reproductive-technology babies is a multiple birth—twins, triplets or, rarely, a higher number—a result of transferring several embryos at once into a woman's reproductive tract. Children of multiple births are significantly likelier to suffer a range of health and developmental problems that can be a consequence, as pediatrician and geneticist Patricia Baird puts it, "of being born too soon and too small."

And the advent of micromanipulation has raised an entirely new series of concerns. For some years, scientists have subscribed to a theory of natural selection to explain why 200 million or more sperm are in the average ejaculate when only one is needed to fertilize the egg. The thinking has been that it's the hardiest sperm that helps create a human being. But when an embryologist assumes godlike stature by arbitrarily selecting that single sperm from a marginal batch, it stands the concept of natural selection on its head. Critics fear that the children of ICSI could be the products of a conception not "meant" to occur.

IVF practitioners disagree. "Natural selection is baloney," scoffs Michael Tucker, scientific director of Reproductive Biology Associates. "The female reproductive tract is not an assault course, OK? It's not simply that Sparky Sperm, the biggest, meanest, toughest one, runs the marathon and gets to the top of the egg first. Other than the simple fact that sperm move toward the egg, the fertility event is close to being random."

Still, Tucker concedes it would have been preferable if direct injection could have been tested in animals before being used in people. Earlier forms of micromanipulation were evaluated on non-human subjects, but ICSI is tricky to perform with animal sperm and eggs. In Belgium, where efforts are under way to track

ICSI babies into young adulthood, rates of genetic defects seem to be no higher than in the general population. And for the most part, geneticists agree that a sperm can be malformed or sluggish without those attributes affecting its chromosomal content. Still, they point out that the generation of male children produced by micromanipulation is likely to endure its own infertility problems.

Patricia Olds-Clark, a Temple University medical school geneticist who is studying a mouse model of infertility, says: "Their sperm are carrying genes that won't allow the sperm of their sons to fertilize in a normal way. And what's true in mice is going to be true in humans."

Moreover, Cornell's Jacques Cohen admits that there may be "problem groups" for whom micromanipulation is riskier. "Patients with unexplained fertilization failure who come to micromanipulation because regular IVF didn't work may have an increased incidence of congenital malformations," he notes. "But those patients are rare, and they are counseled accordingly." At least, they are at Cornell. Whether other clinics tell similar patients of this risk is not clear.

The Society for Assisted Reproductive Technology's Maria Bustillo has heard it all before. She knows that when the negative side of the assisted-reproductive-technology balance sheet is totaled up, it smacks of a conspiracy being perpetrated by avaricious doctors on hapless couples. But she doesn't buy that point of view.

'You can tell a patient till your face is blue that her chances are less than 2%,' says Maria Bustillo. 'Then she goes through with it.'

"We make a mistake if we just blame the providers of this technology," she insists. "A lot of this is patient-driven. You have a couple in front of you, she's 43 with a borderline FSH level (a hormonal measure) and you tell her till your face is blue that her chances of having a baby are less than 2% with IVF. And she goes through with it and gets an embryo or two, then wants to do it all again. Do I withhold that, as a doctor? If I do, they may go and get worse treatment somewhere else."

In fact, infertile couples themselves remain among the most ardent defenders of their right to persevere in the face of slender odds or possible risks. Between 1990 and 1992, Maria DiPaulo, 40, of Queens, N.Y., and her husband, Stan, 41, tried IVF seven times, thanks to insurance that paid all but $4,000 of their $70,000 in medical bills. The two knew their chances would plummet after attempt No. 4. But, says Maria, "I wouldn't have cared if it was just a 1% chance." She was also aware, since she repeatedly mainlined hormones, that "there could be repercussions in the years to come from all the drugs I took. But I guess I think about today; I don't worry about that far down the road. You get so set on doing whatever you can to make this pregnancy happen that risk isn't an obvious factor anymore."

The DiPaulos, who recently adopted a little girl, say that as frustrating as their experience was, it was ultimately a positive one. "I think we never could have adopted if we hadn't gone through all this," Tony says. "It meant a lot to say we did everything we could."

Then there's Terry Matthews [her real name], 33, a New Hampshire travel agent who was born with only one ovary and lost the other to a cyst at age 24. Matthews, who tried to adopt but couldn't find an available birth mother, was told that, using a donor egg, she had a 30% to 35% likelihood of success—a decent gamble. But she says slimmer odds wouldn't have deterred her. "When you make these decisions, they're not based on facts and figures; it's pure emotion," she says. "I don't know how low they would have had to have gone for me to say forget it—10%, 5%? I don't know. This was the only chance I had to have a child." In November, 1992, on a second IVF attempt, she gave birth to a boy, from her sister's donor egg.

Ultimately, not even the sternest critics believe the IVF industry should grind to a halt. "I'm not calling for a moratorium," says author Pappert. "I just think there needs to be a hell of a lot more work done on determining the safety margin and on deciding who really needs it. And there needs to be more supervision."

As for the Taylors, their determination to try ICSI hasn't wavered, but their focus is shifting slightly. As they prepare to return to Century City, they're also beginning the paperwork for adoption proceedings. "You grow up, as a woman, envisioning yourself going through the process of giving birth to a child that is biologically yours and your husband's," says Leslie. "I think that physical void will probably always exist, but from what I understand, when they put a baby in your arms, it's yours."

Adds John: "It's difficult. We're definitely going to give it another shot. But time keeps passing. We want an end to this. And I think this year we'll see that. One way or another. I think by the end of the year, we'll have a child."

WAITING GAME

*Advances in prenatal testing can reduce the time women
spend weighing the numbers against their nerves.*

SUSAN GILBERT

Susan Gilbert is a journalist in New York

PREGNANCY IS A STATE OF WAITING. FOR women who decide to have a prenatal test to diagnose serious health problems in the fetus, the waiting can be most difficult early on, as they count the weeks until the test can be performed and then until they get the results. There have long been just two options. One is amniocentesis, the safest and most widely used prenatal genetic test, which often doesn't yield results until the 17th week of pregnancy. The other is chorionic villus sampling, or C.V.S., a newer test that can cut the waiting time in half, but at a price—a higher miscarriage rate and the possibility of causing birth defects.

Play it safe and wait. Take a risk in exchange for earlier answers. Women find themselves weighing the numbers against their own nerves, all the while wishing there was a truly safe test that could be performed in the first trimester, before too many people know they are pregnant and before they grow too much in love with the idea themselves.

The prospect is no longer unthinkable. Seizing advances in medical technology and a certain quixotic spirit, obstetricians around the country have disproved the long-held assumption that amniocentesis cannot be performed before 16 weeks. Indeed, in the last few years it has become routine to do the test at 14 weeks, and innovations in the laboratory have trimmed the wait for results from two or more weeks to one. A handful of doctors have begun offering a third option: early amniocentesis performed in the 12th or 13th week of pregnancy.

Still more choices are on the horizon. "There's a big push for early right now," says Dr. James E. Haddow, medical director of the Foundation for Blood Research in Scarborough, Me. Dr. Haddow is one of several researchers working to develop a first-trimester blood test to diagnose Down syndrome, a leading cause of mental retardation. Other doctors are experimenting with ultrasound as a means of seeing severe and sometimes life-threatening abnormalities in the fetus within the first 12 weeks.

Early testing holds the promise of treatment or even cures for crippling, disfiguring or fatal conditions. C.V.S. has already made it possible to prevent one genetic disease, a hormonal imbalance called congenital adrenal hyperplasia, which masculinizes females. If the flawed gene that causes it is identified before a fetus's genitals have formed, the mother can be given corticosteroids and the fetus will develop normally. "We're hoping that with early diagnosis, other conditions will one day be treated with gene therapy," says Dr. Sherman Elias, director of reproductive genetics at the University of Tennessee Health Sciences Center in Memphis.

For the most part, however, the push for early diagnosis is less about heroics than about reducing the time a woman, or a couple, spends waiting and worrying. "Couples are anxious," says Dr. Elias. "The earlier we can reassure them, the happier the pregnancy will be."

Virginia L. Corson, a genetic counselor at John Hopkins Hospital in Baltimore, says that most of the expectant parents she sees would probably have an abortion if their test results were positive. But she adds that "some families would be nervous without the knowledge, even if they wouldn't consider abortion. They want to prepare themselves."

A majority of the couples who are asking for earlier prenatal testing are baby boomers, the demographic slice of the population on whom most such tests are performed. These are the people who put of having children until their careers were established, who didn't want to assume the responsibility of parenthood until they were financially secure. What many of them didn't take into account, however, is that the risk of having a baby with Down syndrome jumps from 1 in 952 for a 30-year-old woman to 1 in 385 once she reaches 35, and it doubles every two and a half years thereafter. There are twice as many pregnant women age 35 and older today as there were in 1976, and their numbers, combined with their tendency to question their doctors about their medical options, have made their wishes for better diagnostic tests difficult to ignore.

The first prenatal test, introduced in the mid-1970's, was amniocentesis, a procedure that involves inserting a long needle through the abdomen and into the uterus to aspirate a sample of amniotic fluid. The fluid contains two clues to a fetus's health. One is sloughed-off fetal skin cells, which can be analyzed for hundreds of chromosomal and genetic defects. Although Down syndrome, the most common of these disorders, is the only one that is routinely checked for, amniocentesis can also reveal conditions like Tay-Sachs, cystic fibrosis, sickle-cell disease and thalassemia. The other clue is the level of a protein called alpha-fetoprotein. A large amount of alpha-fetoprotein in the amniotic fluid is a sure sign that the fetus has a deadly or extremely disabling spinal defect, such as open spine, or spina bifida. Such deformities are the most common birth defects, affecting 1 in 1,000 fetuses regardless of the mother's age.

CHORIONIC VILLUS SAMPLING, WHICH IS generally done between the ninth and eleventh week of pregnancy, can find virtually all of the chromosomal and genetic flaws that amniocentesis can. Cells from the placenta are gathered by inserting a catheter through the cervix or a needle through the abdomen. But there are several limitations to C.V.S. It can't diagnose spina bifida, so women must wait until they are 15 weeks pregnant to have a blood test that can screen for the disorder. The accuracy of the blood test, however, is only 85 percent, and ultrasound or amniocentesis is required to confirm a positive result. A woman who chooses C.V.S. might also find herself having an anmiocentesis for another reason: C.V.S. is inconclusive about 1 percent of the time.

Both anmiocentesis and C.V.S. can cause miscarriages, but C.V.S. carries more than double the risk, about 2.4 percent. And over the last few years there have been reports linking the test to fetal deformities, such as missing fingers and toes and malformed limbs and mouths. "If a couple is deciding between the two procedures, they're weighing the early timing of C.V.S. against the slightly higher risks," says Virginia Corson. "The higher-risk patients tend to go with the earlier test, but the 33-year-olds are slightly more comfortable with amnio."

Birnist O'Reilly, who is 43 years old and lives in New Jersey, chose amniocentesis when she was pregnant with her first child five years ago and C.V.S. when she became pregnant again two years ago. Her decision to take the added risk was influenced by her age and the difficulty she'd had conceiving. "It would probably have taken a long time for me to get pregnant again," she says, "and my biological clock was ticking."

The assumption that amniocentesis couldn't be performed before the 16th week of pregnancy was grounded only partly in fact. It's a fact that in the early days of the procedure, laboratories needed a larger sample of amniotic fluid than could be obtained in the first trimester without a risk of interfering with the development of the fetus's lungs or causing the placenta to become detached from the uterus. It's also a fact that in the first trimester the layers of the amniotic sac are most vulnerable to damage because they haven't yet fused together. A needle poked through the abdomen and into the uterus can rupture the layers, jeopardizing the fetus's life. In addition, in the mid-1970's, when amniocentesis was usually done at 13 weeks, doctors sometimes had trouble getting any amniotic fluid on the first try and had to repeat the procedure, which increased the chance of a miscarriage. Putting off the test until the 16th week increased the success rate.

BUT ABOUT A DECADE AGO, SOME DOCtors questioned the need to wait so long, and began tinkering with the procedure to make it safer and more effective during the earlier weeks of pregnancy. When C.V.S. was introduced in 1982, many of the doctors who were doing amniocentesis realized that some of their patients were "going down the street," says Dr. Laird G. Jackson, director of the division of medical genetics at Jefferson Medical College in Philadelphia and a pioneer in the development of chorionic villus sampling. "So they wanted to try early amnios."

In experiments involving women who were less than 16 weeks pregnant, doctors found that they could get accurate results with smaller samples of fluid. They also discovered that they could avoid damaging the amniotic sac if they inserted the needle quickly. More recently, laboratory technology has emerged that can extract genetic information from far fewer fetal cells than before. The size of the fluid samples has thus ceased to be an obstacle to performing anmiocentesis before the 16th week of pregnancy.

Another obstacle fell away as a result of improvements in ultrasound. When ultrasound could show only a still image, amniocentesis was essentially a shot in the dark. Doctors would look inside the uterus to find a pocket of amniotic fluid and mark a spot on the pregnant woman's abdomen with a pen. Then they'd turn off the ultrasound and insert the needle, hoping that they were tapping the right area within the uterus. Sometimes they weren't. The needle might hit the fetus or the placenta, or fail to draw enough amniotic fluid and have to be withdrawn and inserted again. Any of these problems could cause a miscarriage.

By the mid-1980's, ultrasound machines could show a moving image. That meant doctors could use the image as a guide and see exactly where the needle was going.

Several recent studies have concluded that amniocentesis using ultrasound guiding done between 11 and 14 weeks is nearly as safe as anmiocentesis later in a pregnancy. Last year, Dr. Miller reported that his miscarriage rate from week 11 to week 24 was 1.6 percent. That's higher than the rate at 14 to 16 weeks, estimated at 0.5 percent nationwide. But it's lower than the rate following C.V.S.

Still, most doctors feel it's premature to recommend that all women who want early prenatal testing have an amniocentesis before 14 weeks. For one thing, there's no way to know for sure whether early amniocentesis is really safer than C.V.S., because no studies have directly compared the two procedures. In addition, an amnocentesis done before 13 weeks is less accurate in diagnosing spinal defects, because the level of alpha-fetoprotein in the amniotic fluid isn't high enough. Finally, although a few doctors have done thousands of anmiocentesis before 14 weeks, most obstetricians haven't done any. Since the more procedures doctors do, the more skilled they become, the low miscarriage rate reported in studies like Dr. Miller's probably reflects a best-case scenario.

High-risk patients are the best candidates for early amniocentesis.

Even the champions of early amniocentesis believe it's appropriate only for high-risk patients: women in their 40's and those who have a family history of an inherited disease like Down syndrome.

"Other women would be better off having an amniocentesis at 14 weeks," says Dr. Fay O. Redwine, associate professor of obstetrics, gynecology and human genetics at the Medical College of Virginia in Richmond. "They'd get the results by 15 weeks and still be able to have a first-trimester abortion."

The ultimate goal is the development of first-trimester procedures that pose no risk at all to the fetus. One candidate is ultrasound, which can show anatomical details that were invisible a decade ago. At 12 weeks, for example, an ultrasound can reveal treatable conditions like a missing kidney or a blockage of the bladder. Also at 12 weeks, an ultrasound is often sensitive enough to show a cystic hygroma, a cyst on a fetus's neck that is sometimes associated with chromosomal abnormalities like Down syndrome. "How accurate the ultrasound is in identifying these chromosomal abnormalities remains to be seen," says Dr. Redwine.

The most promising prospect is a simple blood test that could be offered in the early weeks of pregnancy, along with numerous other routine blood tests. Dr. Haddow, of the Foundation for Blood Research, is refining the mid-trimester blood test now used to screen for spina bifida and Down syndrome in the hope of making it accurate enough to be done earlier. "If every woman had this test, it could reduce the number of amnios that needed to be done," says Dr. Haddow. No doubt more women in their 20's and 30's would end up having an amniocentesis because the blood test would show their risk of having a baby with birth defects was higher than predicted on the basis of age or family history. But Dr. Haddow believes that significantly fewer older women would have amniocentesis, because the blood test would reveal, to the pleasant surprise of many of them, that their risk was negligible.

Another test, developed by Dr. Elias and several other scientists, searches for the few fetal cells that make their way into a pregnant woman's blood. Preliminary experiments have been encouraging: the blood test has diagnosed three chromosomal abnormalities, including Down syndrome, during the 10th week of pregnancy. A full-blown trial funded by the National Institutes of Health involving 3,000 women could get under way later this year. If the test's effectiveness is confirmed, and if it can also diagnose genetic diseases, it could make obsolete the routine use of amniocentesis or C.V.S. for high-risk patients, eliminating the need for women to weigh the pros and cons of two imperfect tests. That's just what women have been waiting for.

In the Name of the Children

Get Treatment or Go to Jail, One South Carolina Hospital Tells Drug-Abusing Pregnant Women. Now It Faces a Lawsuit and a Civil-Rights Investigation.

Barry Siegel

Times national correspondent Barry Siegel's last piece for this magazine was on a Georgia doctor accused of murdering an infant.

IT ALL BEGAN, NURSE SHIRLEY BROWN AND HER COLLEAGUES at the Medical University of South Carolina now say, with the pregnant woman who appeared at the emergency room one morning in October, 1988.

The woman was suffering from abruptio placentae—an abrupt separation of the placenta before labor. Her fetus was stillborn. They'd been seeing an increasing number of these abruptions at the hospital, a state institution in Charleston serving a largely indigent black population. The usual causes were conditions such as high blood pressure or trauma such as auto accidents. But the more recent cases didn't appear to have such causes. This case didn't appear to have any cause.

Brown and her boss, Dr. Edgar O. Horger III, then head of fetal-maternal medicine at the hospital, turned to the medical literature. In both professional journals and the popular press, they found, pregnant substance abusers were a hot topic. The figures were startling: One out of 10 fetuses in the United States is exposed to cocaine in the womb, affecting 375,000 babies a year. To Brown and Horger, sitting in genteel Charleston, such numbers sounded like a big-city problem. Still, article after article was suggesting cocaine as one cause for abruptions.

So Brown and her colleagues ran an urine drug screen on their patient. The woman tested positive for cocaine.

That was ground zero, they all agreed later. Their eyes now opened, Brown and her colleagues started running drug screens on other pregnant patients. Of the first four, three tested positive. Within one year, they had 119 positives, all but 15 of them women who'd first visited the hospital at the time of delivery.

They still didn't have a solution, though. Try as she might, Brown—a manager for high-risk obstetrical cases—could not get these women to the Charleston County Substance Abuse Commission. Despite counseling and cajoling, not a single woman kept her appointment for drug treatment. Of the 15 who came in before delivery, only one even came back for additional prenatal care. The hospital next saw the others when they returned in pre-term labor and once again tested positive for cocaine.

What to do? How to stop this?

What to do, the hospital staff eventually decided, was to cross a treacherous line. Prosecutors across the country, they knew, increasingly were going after pregnant substance abusers, charging dozens with distribution to minors and child neglect. We will join them, Brown and Horger resolved. If our patients test positive and refuse treatment, we'll hand them over to the law.

At the time, it seemed an ideal, if unprecedented, solution. The goal, after all, was not to put these women in jail; the goal was to coerce them into treatment. But not everyone has applauded. Nor has everyone entirely shared the hospital's preference for treatment over jail. The decision to traffic with police and prosecutors, in fact, has drawn the hospital into an increasingly nasty quagmire, one that is as rich in calculated political posturing as in tortured ethical soul-searching.

Does society have a duty to intervene between a woman and her fetus? If so, when? Who or what public agent is responsible? What are the boundaries of government intrusion?

For having kicked up such questions, hospital and Charleston officials now face a $3-million civil lawsuit, a federal civil-rights investigation, a complaint filed with the National Institutes of Health and a chance of losing the hospital's federal funding, if not its accreditation. Everyone from the American Civil Liberties Union to the U.S. Department of Health and Human Services has rushed here to join what is at once a revealing test of difficult national issues and a scorching clash between law and medicine.

All sorts of agendas, reaching well beyond the perplexing world of medical ethics, are being played out in Charleston. New York lawyers jump off airplanes waving the Constitution and stacks of legal briefs. Southern politicians lean into microphones to orate about "personal responsibility." Feminists, hearing obvious echoes of the abortion debate, talk about control of the body and autonomy in the reproductive process. Such repercussions, coming from forces so far beyond their own world, have visibly shaken Horger, Brown and others on the hospital staff. They have not, however, persuaded them to back down.

1. CONCEPTION TO BIRTH: Prenatal Development

Brown and Horger see the complexities, the imponderables, the obstacles, but they also see spontaneous abortions, pre-term deliveries, stillbirths and underdeveloped newborns with jumpy nervous systems. "It's a real difficult issue here," Shirley Brown says. "I can see both sides, I can see where everyone's coming from. But don't we finally have to make a decision? Don't we finally have to make a choice?"

IT WAS IN AUGUST, 1989, THAT BROWN MADE HER FATEFUL DECISION TO call Charles Condon, at the time the elected solicitor, or prosecutor, for Charleston and Berkeley counties.

By then, MUSC's drug-testing program had evolved considerably from its genesis nine months before. At first, the hospital's criteria for such screening had been informal, if not random; when doctors suspected a patient of substance abuse, for whatever reason, they simply ordered a test. This approach had made some at the hospital uneasy. Might they be ordering tests for other than medical reasons? Might they be ordering tests because the patient was poor or black or sullen or not like them? Virtually all those getting screened and testing positive, after all, were indigent blacks.

Listening to such concerns, it occurred to Brown that MUSC could be accused of discrimination. So in April, 1989, seeking to standardize the process, the hospital adopted a more formal protocol. Drug screens would be ordered for patients with any of six indicators: no prenatal care; abruptio placentae; intrauterine fetal death; pre-term labor, intrauterine growth retardation and previously known drug or alcohol abuse. Using these criteria, MUSC still found that it was mainly screening poor blacks—in part because they composed much of the hospital's patient pool—but hospital staffers no longer felt as uneasy about the selection process. Instead, they worried about the results they were seeing.

Month by month, the number of positive drug screens at the hospital kept rising. By summer, a full quarter of screened patients were testing positive for drugs—up to 24 a month. Not one went for drug treatment. Brown and Horger felt more than frustrated; they felt they were witnessing a crime.

Cocaine, they knew, easily travels through the placenta to the fetus. There is no conclusive evidence about the drug's lasting impact on infants, since follow-up studies are scarce, and anecdotal reports of "neuro-behavioral problems" don't separate cocaine's impact from influences such as poverty and family instability. But its immediate effects were often apparent at MUSC. Withdrawal, irritability, lethargy, stiff muscle tone, problems sleeping and eating, cardiovascular dysfunction, aversion to loud sounds or handling—doctors could usually spot the exposed newborns.

It seemed to Brown and Horger that these were abused children. If so, wasn't the hospital staff legally responsible? Weren't they morally responsible? "We were not trying to rid the streets of cocaine," Horger recalled. "We were trying to stop harm to the fetus."

To Charleston solicitor's interest, however, proved somewhat different. Charles Condon nearly climbed out of his chair when Brown and others from MUSC, sitting in his office, revealed that they'd identified and treated more than 100 pregnant substance abusers in the past 12 months.

"This has been going on?" he demanded. "This has been going on?" In Condon's view, the hospital had been doing nothing less than harboring criminals. He had a little problem with the fact that they'd known about cocaine users for a year. The hospital, he believed, had to report these cases once they had viable fetuses.

Condon's response reflected, in part, his particular bent. A Charleston native from a large Catholic family, Condon is, at 41, running for state attorney general after 12 years as county solicitor, a post he first won at age 27—"the youngest circuit solicitor ever elected in the history of South Carolina," his résumé proudly notes. A Republican, Condon possesses the type of unabashed political streak that leads him to reveal, out of sheer delight, the pragmatic calculations—Who could complain? Who has an interest in this?—that shape his positions. "That's the real world" is among his favorite observations.

But even more than his personal propensity, Condon's response reflected a growing pattern in law enforcement across the country. With medical advances giving fetuses ever more social recognition, a number of prosecutors have been inspired to treat fetuses as children. In the past decade, they've charged more than 160 pregnant substance abusers in 24 states with child neglect and distribution of drugs to minors. That appellate courts have overturned virtually every conviction on such charges, flatly rejecting the notion of applying child protection laws to fetuses, was no discouragement to Condon.

"It's nice you came in," Condon told Brown and the others sitting before him. "But the fact is, you have to come in. There's no patient-doctor privilege on this. If you don't report it, it's a crime."

From there, events moved rather swiftly.

Together with Charleston Police Chief Reuben Greenberg, Condon called an interagency community meeting to "develop a policy as to possible prosecution" of pregnant substance abusers. Within three weeks, this task force had hammered out its plan. That same day, Police Capt. R. H. Roberts explained it in a memo to all central detectives, declaring it "effective immediately."

When a prenatal patient at the hospital tested positive, she would be counseled, usually by Brown, then presented a letter from the solicitor offering to defer prosecution if she successfully completed a drug treatment program. If she refused, failed to complete or tested positive again, MUSC would notify the police, who would issue an arrest warrant. If a patient was already at the stage of delivering a child and she or the baby tested positive, there would be no such warnings or second chances. The Department of Social Services would be notified to take the newborn, and the woman would be arrested immediately after her release from the hospital. The hospital contact in all cases would be Shirley Brown. If the fetus was "viable," the charges would include drug distribution and child neglect. The basis for arrests would not be limited to positive drug-screen results; written or oral statements made by the patient to "third parties" would suffice.

There were, it should be said, more than a few expressions of early concern at the hospital about this "interagency policy," as it came to be called. A medical resident named Birgit Pols expressed discomfort about acting as an arm of the law. She was distressed that MUSC was applying this policy only to a selected population of indigent blacks; if nurses and doctors screened everybody, she knew from studies and private reports, they'd be amazed at how many positives they'd get. Kathleen Straight, then nurse manager of the neonatal intensive-care unit, told a documentary film team that she thought it dangerous to be setting infants against mothers and labeling substance abusers and their babies as bad. The medical director of the neonatal intensive-care unit, Dr. Celeste Patrick, wrote the Medical University president to point out serious flaws in the program, including insufficient drug-treatment facilities in Charleston and "thinly veiled discrimination against . . . poor black women." The hospital's general counsel, Joseph C. Good Jr., worried about legal liability as well as other problems. In one letter, he asked the police to obtain a subpoena for medical records when they came calling with arrest warrants, in order "to protect the Medical University . . . from any allegations of breach of confidentiality." In another letter to a senior assistant state attorney general, he wrote, "This is not a perfect program. . . . I would prefer to have the mothers sign an informed consent for a drug screen. . . . I would also prefer the DSS be notified rather than law enforcement. . . . The other weakness in this program is that the main prosecutions have been against black indigent mothers. . . ."

Such moments of hesitation, however, apparently were overwhelmed by the enthusiasm of those in charge. In fact, according to neonatologist Patrick, the hospital warned doctors that "nonsupport" of the program "may result in revocation of our MUSC-provided malpractice insurance." Months later, perhaps as a result, Horger could not even recall the plan's early critics. "Not only didn't I have a problem with the policy, I was happy with it," he said. "I welcomed it. I thought at the time it was right."

By then, though, the hospital's objections might not have mattered. In joining hands with the world of law enforcement, the medical community plainly had lost considerable control. By the time MUSC's board of directors officially adopted the interagency policy on Nov. 27—some six weeks after Capt. Roberts' memo had declared it "effective immediately"—the arrests had already begun, without use of subpoenas.

Pregnant substance abusers' first awareness of the new policy usually came not from the hospital but from their television sets. There they began seeing a series of public-service announcements featuring the county solicitor. "And not only will you live with guilt, you could be arrested," Condon explained in one spot. "This is a tragedy you can prevent. . . . If you stay with the (treatment] program, you won't be arrested. Wake up from the nightmare. Think about your baby first. . . ."

Since MUSC was the only high-risk obstetrical center within 50 miles for indigents, even those frightened by Gondon's words had little choice but to go there, particularly if they depended on Medicaid. Once at the hospital, they had to sign a general consent for medical treatment that—without ex-

plicitly saying so—allowed, among many other things, a drug screen. Those who tested positive soon found themselves receiving visits from Shirley Brown. Those unpersuaded by Brown soon found themselves being introduced to a police detective.

It is hard to verify all these women's stories, partly because many are homeless or rootless. Those who do come forward do so in the foreign milieu of their attorneys' offices, where it is difficult to get past carefully phrased statements that often, in their personal details, happen to dovetail nicely with the lawyers' general legal arguments. Nonetheless, it seems clear that at least some of those arrested were taken from their hospital room hours or days after delivering and led to jail in handcuffs and shackles. Others sat in jail cells waiting to give birth, then, when in labor, were brought by ambulance, in handcuffs and shackles, to the hospital. One tells of being seized in a chokehold, near full-term, and escorted forcefully into treatment. Most describe impoverished lives supported by food stamps, Aid to Families with Dependent Children and, in some instances, prostitution. Several talk of backgrounds full of missing husbands, mentally ill parents and early shunting to foster homes. Virtually all make a point of calling Brown "nasty" or "cold" or "degrading."

"Shirley Brown and another nurse came to my room and told me my baby tested positive," said Ellen Laverne Knight, recalling the day she delivered her third child at MUSC in November, 1989. "I gotta sign this and do more tests, they said. Next day, they brought my roommate's baby to her, but not mine. Nurse Brown was a bitch. She came and said I had to go into a room to talk to someone. It was the police. They said I have the right to remain silent. I found out I was going to jail. They brought my clothes, they handcuffed me, they put a sheet over my hands, they pushed me out in a wheelchair. I spent the night in city jail without a sanitary napkin. . . ."

Telling this story, Knight was sitting in a lawyer's conference room in downtown Charleston, dressed in a business suit. Drug-free after undergoing two three-month treatment programs, she spoke with composure, but also with obvious bitterness. Yes, she said, she'd done coke two days before her baby's birth. But she took care of her children, made them meals. She never got high in her home. Depression is what drove her to drugs, depression from being unable to find a job, depression from being unable to get her children's father to make court-ordered support payments. "It's hard to explain the reality of the addict," she said. "When you get the urge, it overrides everything. I definitely would have gone to treatment if they'd offered. Instead, they sent me to jail and took my baby."

After watching 10 such arrests in three months, Brown and others at the hospital felt compelled to remind the solicitor that they wanted patients going to treatment, not jail. Automatically sending women to jail after they'd delivered their babies was purely punitive, Brown pointed out. Treatment would help after delivery as much as before. Everyone should get warnings, everyone should be offered treatment.

"Amnesty for all," Condon called it, consenting only reluctantly to give options to those delivering, instead of hauling them directly to jail. For the good of the program, he'd compromise—but it rankled.

"The truth is, we have an abysmal record of prosecution in this," Condon said later. "If we wanted to be punitive, we would have marched them down, given high bonds, packed that jail. If they want to see punitive, we can get punitive. This may be punitive in New York, but here, it's a kid-glove approach. Practically speaking, they've got to break into jail to get there."

Not everyone agreed. Agitated word of Charleston's program soon began to spread. One day in early 1990, the phone rang in Lynn M. Paltrow's office at the ACLU Reproductive Freedom Project in New York. Paltrow, then 31, was already one of the nation's leading litigators responding to "fetal rights" cases, already one of the most visible warriors in the field of reproductive-rights law.

Her caller wondered: Have you heard what's going on in South Carolina?

ALTHOUGH THE CHARLESTON POLICY WAS IN SOME WAYS SINGULAR, ITS underpinnings were, to Paltrow, all too familiar.

The same anti-abortion argument that she'd been fighting for years—the premise that the fetus has rights—was exactly what she now was hearing across the country as justification for punishing pregnant substance abusers. Although she didn't think all the prosecutors in these substance-abuse cases were necessarily anti-abortion, she still feared the ramifications.

After all, she reasoned, if it's a crime to endanger the life, health and welfare of a fetus, then virtually any action by pregnant women could become the basis for criminal prosecution. You could require women to take folic acid, you could prevent them from having babies as teen-agers or after 40, you could mandate what they eat, how they exercise, whether they have sex.

Paltrow already had served as co-counsel in virtually all of the most critical early prosecutions of pregnant substance abusers. She'd successfully fought Jennifer Johnson's prosecution in Florida, Kimberly Hardy's in Michigan, Pamela Rae Stewart's in California. Now, in early 1990, South Carolina seemed to be presenting a still larger battlefield. This was about even more than women's rights or fetal rights. This was about civil rights and racial discrimination. This was about sane public-health policy.

It didn't take Paltrow long to find a host of esteemed professors, doctors and medical groups that agreed. The list eventually included such experts in their fields as Dr. Barry Zuckerman, chairman of the department of pediatrics at the Boston University School of Medicine and Boston City Hospital, and Dr. Jay Katz, professor emeritus of law, medicine and psychiatry at the Yale University Law School. In the mound of essays, declarations and studies on Paltrow's desk, these specialists offered all manner of objection to Charleston's policy.

The policy, they argued, violates the right to privacy in medical information, the right to refuse medical treatment, the right to procreate, the right to equal protection under the 14th Amendment. The policy forces doctors to be cops and gives the judgment of doctors—or nurse Brown—the force of law. The policy treats drug addiction as a crime rather than an illness and allows for no relapses, which are expected at treatment centers. The policy frays the doctor's relationship with patients. The policy violates all notions of informed consent. The policy is tantamount to human research, without the required approvals. The policy, no matter what criteria are used, targets poor blacks by screening only at an indigent center such as MUSC. The policy leads society down a slippery slope—if you're going after women for harming their fetuses, what about drinkers and smokers, whose behavior produces, overall, greater and more lasting harm each year than cocaine users?

Above all, the academics and doctors assembled by Paltrow argued that the policy, while mandating treatment if you want to avoid jail, ignores the fact that appropriate treatment programs for pregnant addicts just don't exist in the Charleston area. By "appropriate," they mean outpatient programs that provide transportation and day-care and long-term residential programs where mothers can live with their children, isolated from the type of potentially violent male addicts they're all too familiar with.

On this point there can be little dispute. Until the recent opening of the Sojourner Center for Women, which serves only one ZIP code in the city, there was no outpatient program in Charleston that offered day-care or direct door-to-door transportation; there is still no residential program specifically for women and their children. The Department of Alcohol and Other Drug Abuse Services (formerly the Charleston County Substance Abuse Commission), where MUSC directs most pregnant substance abusers, counsels all kinds of abusers, often in group therapy sessions. MUSC itself, in applying for grants, has expressed "serious concern" that needed services "are not available" at the hospital or in the Charleston community. Counselors obliged to ask anxious, depressed mothers to leave their children and ride buses an hour or more across town readily confirm such concerns. Women will come, the counselors claim, only if they feel they and their children are safe. Otherwise, threats and coercion will just drive them away.

That, some believe, is precisely what's been happening in Charleston. In a South Carolina medical journal article, at various professional gatherings and even in Condon's résumé, the trio of Brown, Horger and Condon have hailed a "marked" decrease in positive drug screens—from 24 to four or five a month—but specialists such as Zuckerman think this MUSC report "deeply flawed." How do they know the hospital hasn't merely driven most substance abusers away?

It is hard to judge all these arguments. It is true, for example, that Charleston is targeting poor blacks by screening only at MUSC—but it is also true that the 1991 South Carolina Prevalence Study found black women nearly six times more likely to use cocaine than white women, and women without medical insurance 17 to 18 times more likely. While it is true that more appropriate treatment programs are needed, it is also true that no one really knows if such programs would attract all the pregnant substance abusers who now stay away. Whether to talk about a "failure of personal responsibility" or "the disease of addiction" is in some way, finally, a question of philosophy, not fact.

The central argument against coercion echoes that of many prominent medical organizations. The American Medical Assn., the American Academy of Pediatrics, the American Nurses Assn., the American Public Health Assn., the March of Dimes—in recent years they have all ringingly condemned the national trend toward use of coercion and legal threats. "Criminal sanctions or civil liability for harmful behavior by the pregnant woman toward her fetus are inappropriate," resolves the AMA. "The public must be assured of non-punitive access to comprehensive health care which will meet the needs of the substance-abusing pregnant woman," proclaims the AAP. "The threat of criminal prosecution is counterproductive," declares the ANA.

As the debate in Charleston has developed, such statements have meant more and more to Paltrow, for they've helped in her critical effort to keep the matter from being framed as a collision between women's rights and fetal rights. This is the tricky heart of the controversy.

Personally, Paltrow's heart goes out to pregnant substance abusers; having grown up on Long Island watching her parents regularly march for social justice, she is one of those inclined to talk about "the disease of addiction" and "the burdens of poverty." But she knows these substance abusers are enormously unpopular with others. She knows that, as impressive as the intellectual arguments might be in favor of women's reproductive rights, they pale for many in the face of a sickly newborn twitching from a cocaine rush. She knows she'd lose support, even among those committed to women's rights, if people felt forced to choose between pregnant substance abusers and their babies.

The medical community's policy statements provide Paltrow with a way to avoid this perilous choice. "Even if you care only about the baby, even if you don't give a damn about the mother, you should still oppose Charleston's policy," Paltrow finds herself able to argue. "All evidence is, this frightens them away from prenatal health care that's good for the baby. You can't punish the woman without punishing the fetus. You need to come up with policies that help both. Threats don't make sense. Jail doesn't make sense."

That sentiment is, in a sense, the heart of her case. To challenge Charleston's policy in court, however, Paltrow needed not just experts and arguments. She also needed clients who'd actually been prosecuted. So she sent feelers to South Carolina attorneys, and she waited. Not until early last year—by then she'd left the ACLU to co-found the Center for Reproductive Law & Policy in New York—did Paltrow locate the women she wanted.

One was Crystal Ferguson, a tall, thin, outspoken 31-year-old African American who had not taken kindly to her treatment at MUSC. She lived in a trailer with two sons, 10 and 11, and a daughter, 2. She was happy to join a civil suit; she thought someone should pay for what they'd done.

She'd been using drugs when she became pregnant with her little girl, she told Paltrow and Susan Dunn, a local Charleston attorney who'd joined the case. But she hadn't consid-

ered herself an addict. She thought she could stop using, she thought she had it under control. She went to a local health clinic for prenatal care, where she denied drug use, since she'd seen the solicitor talking on TV and was afraid of being arrested. Instead, she tried to overcome her addiction herself, but couldn't. At 32 weeks, she was referred to MUSC, where she tested positive for cocaine. You go to a residential substance-abuse program for two weeks, Shirley Brown informed her, or you get arrested. At first, Ferguson agreed, but when she went home to pack, "I saw the situation my kids were in. There was no one to take care of them. Someone had stolen our food stamps and my unemployment check while I was at the hospital. There was no way I was going to leave my children for two weeks, knowing the environment they were in." She called the hospital and asked if there was a place she could go with her sons. Told there was not, she refused treatment and avoided prenatal care the last two months of pregnancy. She returned to the hospital only to deliver a full-term baby girl—and to once again test positive for cocaine.

The other woman was Theresa Joseph, a 35-year old African American who came to be known in court papers anonymously as Monica Roe. Small and flashy looking, with light skin and a Yankee accent, she was more reluctant to fight than Ferguson; she was more inclined to disappear than stand her ground. Yet she, too, was angry. Supported by AFDC and disability payments, she had a 10-year-old son who lives with her and other children living elsewhere.

She'd used drugs during her pregnancy, she told Paltrow and Dunn, and avoided prenatal care entirely because Condon's TV announcements frightened her. She'd ended up at MUSC anyway because of a severe foot infection. There, Brown, learning of her history of drug use, came to visit. Joseph had heard about Brown, had heard people talk about her as if she were a witch. Brown told her she'd lose her baby and go to jail if she didn't go into treatment. Afraid of being arrested, she left the hospital that night—just put on her clothes and ran out. Later, realizing she needed help, she returned to the hospital to ask Brown for entry into a treatment program, but they gave her an appointment for 3½ weeks later. By then, she'd lost her nerve and didn't keep the appointment. She next came to MUSC in pre-term labor at 7½ months. They didn't let her see her baby after it was born. The baby, Shirley Brown told her, had tested positive for cocaine.

In both cases, MUSC had called the police, who'd arrested, handcuffed and led the women to jail, Ferguson from her home, Joseph from her hospital bed. Ferguson felt like she was dying; Joseph screamed and cried as they led her away. At bond hearings, David Schwacke—Condon's successor as solicitor—had charged them with distribution of drugs to a minor. Ferguson stayed in jail 11 hours, Joseph three weeks.

"I now understand more about addiction," Ferguson said in an affidavit to the court. "I was a sick person. I made a mistake, but MUSC did not make it better. The staff was very insensitive, especially nurse Shirley Brown. . . . I was just another black drug addict to them. . . . They locked me up like I was a mass murderer. Is someone had offered me a program where I could have brought my children, I would have gone. . . ."

Getting Ferguson and Joseph's cases dropped would prove to be the easiest of Paltrow's legal tasks. Few South Carolina judges were buying the attempt to treat fetuses as children; in 1992, a state appellate court had tossed out the child-neglect conviction of a pregnant substance abuser, basically ruling it a nonexistent charge. So when Paltrow and public defender Ted Phillips—supported by the American Public Health Assn. and 17 other medical and civil rights groups—moved in May, 1993, to quash the distribution charges against Joseph and Ferguson, Schwacke surrendered without a fight. By agreeing to dismiss the charges against those two and rescind the bench warrants on five others similarly charged, Schwacke hoped to preserve the Charleston policy's options and avoid an even worse legal precedent.

Paltrow wasn't finished, though. In October, she filed a $3-million class-action complaint seeking compensatory and punitive damages as well as a preliminary injunction "to prevent defendants from continuing to conduct an unconstitutional experiment on African-American women. . . ." In January, she filed a formal complaint to the National Institutes of Health Office for Protection from Research Risks, accusing MUSC—because it published a medical journal article—of "conducting research on human subjects, including our clients," without the review and approval required by the National Research Act. In February, the federal government, perhaps taking the cue, revealed it had opened a civil-rights investigation of the MUSC program. Civil rights investigator Roosevelt H. Freeman started knocking on doors and asking questions in Charleston. By then, four more women had come forward, signed affidavits and joined the lawsuit.

For the moment, Paltrow seemed on a roll. The hospital's medical staff was reeling and ducking. That week, several MUSC doctors declined invitations to testify in the state capital about pregnant substance abusers, while others didn't even return phone calls from the hospital's own public-relations office.

Soon enough, though, a certain resistance to Paltrow's attack became apparent. Soon enough, the abiding aversion in the south Carolina low country to pregnant substance abusers, and to folks from out of state delivering moral instruction, began to emerge. When the federal civil rights investigator asked the county solicitor to document everything he said—every trifling fact, every off-hand statement—more than a few began to grumble.

"That's not the way it's done down here," Schwacke later observed. "Down here, people trust each other."

CHARLESTON IS A UNIQUE PLACE, AT ONCE CIVILIZED AND DISINCLINED to embrace imported notions. On the winding cobblestone and brick roads of this gracious but insular Southern town of 80,000, dozens of grand Colonial and antebellum homes are still occupied by direct descendants of the families that built them in the early 1700s. Cannons on the East Battery still aim across the confluence of the Cooper and Ashley rivers at Ft. Sumter, as they did at the start of the Civil War. This is a town

that was flourishing well before the Revolution under management of a sophisticated aristocracy, leaders who grew wealthy in the rice, indigo and slave trades, leaders who were the first to fire on and secede from the Union.

References here are to "our cocaine problem," not "our interagency policy problem." Charleston's policy is still in place; Shirley Brown still requires women who test positive to choose, sometimes on the spot, between treatment and immediate arrest.

"There's no controversy here," announces Reuben Greenberg, Charleston's purposefully provocative police chief, as he paces about his office, eyes glinting. "Only California types and ACLU types are bothered by this, and no one cares about those types here. They have no power here."

That surely is overstatement, but not by much. The policy's supporters are many, and they are little swayed by Paltrow's pile of briefs, reports and affidavits. They are more impressed by the fact that of some 200 women facing prosecution under the policy, 154 went to treatment and only two of the 46 arrested actually received sentences. They remain impressed even when told that no one really knows that happened to those women once in treatment.

How can you say we're driving patients from prenatal care, they ask, when most substance abusers never even come for prenatal care? How can you say women don't go to drug treatment because existing programs are "inappropriate," when most haven't even tried them once, haven't even seen what they're like? How can you say doctors shouldn't cooperate with the law, when they already must report everything from gunshot wounds and rapes to child abuse? How can you compare cocaine to alcohol, when one is legal and one illegal? How can you say cocaine's impact isn't lasting when its enormous cost drains a world of shrinking medical resources?

It is not hard to see why this last point draws particular attention from the policy's supporters. The average initial hospital visit for a cocaine-exposed baby costs $24,000 at MUSC, compared to $500 for a normal delivery. One drug-exposed baby stayed a year, costing $731,000; then his mother delivered another drug-exposed infant who stayed four months and cost $167,132. What with developmental follow-up, special education and foster care, one federal report calculates the total cost of each drug-exposed baby at $1 million.

When not talking about such cost issues, Charles Condon focuses on the theme of personal responsibility.

"Are we really to blame society?" he asks. "These women want day care and free transportation, but who's taking care of their kids when they're on coke? Who's providing transportation to go get the drugs? Suddenly they're supermoms who won't abandon their kids. That these two women want a South Carolina jury to give them $3 million for what happened to them. . . . It's frightening. If we can't act in situations like this, when can we act?"

Equally adamant is Police Chief Greenberg, who readily addresses the charges of racial discrimination. A black Jew (by way of his Russian immigrant grandfather), a former Berkeley activist, a onetime sailor, rodeo bull rider and college professor, he is a man given far more to irreverence than Southern gentility. He is also a man given regularly to expressing impatience with "all that psychological sociological crap" that blames criminal activity on impoverished social conditions or bad parenting. Once, at a drug forum in Washington, D.C., after listening to Lynn Paltrow explain that cocaine wasn't permanently damaging, he rushed up to her, got right in her face, even though they'd never met. "How can you say that?" he demanded. "Cocaine mothers are killing their babies; how can you say that?"

Sitting in his office another day, he explained: "I see hordes of people, mainly black, walk around in a daze. The drug crisis has a tremendous impact on the black community. I wouldn't care if it were all blacks who got arrested. This policy is helping black kids. The racial aspects don't bothers me. God, this whole political correctness thing. . . ." With that, Greenberg jumped up and fell on his knees. "I pray for when the majority of blacks in jail are there for tax evasion," he said, raising his arms to the ceiling. "Then we will have made it—then we'll be part of the American scene."

In the end, those in Charleston and elsewhere who support the policy just don't buy Paltrow's effort to close off the fetal-rights debate. To them a mother and a fetus's interests are not always the same. To them, what's most important here is not abortion rights or women's rights or civil rights. To them, what's most important here, finally, is the health of the child when born.

"I'm not a lawyer," Shirley Brown said with a shrug. "I have two patients, mother and unborn child. One patient can talk, one can't, and people on drugs don't always make the best decision for themselves. Sometimes you've got to choose between your two patients. We took the stance that you've got to choose for the unborn patient."

Speaking these words, Brown was sitting in the hospital's public-relations office, having arrived 90 minutes late for an interview. She blamed her delay on the need to deal with an agitated addict high on heroin and cocaine. The legal complaints and news media commotion, she said, "create an ominous portrait and make patients very apprehensive. You take people using drugs, who already are afraid, and make them more afraid. This is making my job harder."

The mother of a 19-year-old daughter, Brown is an earnest woman in her early 40s, born and raised in small-town South Carolina, who enjoys piloting a private plane around the state in her off hours "to see the world from a different, more peaceful perspective." Watching her march into the room with self-assured composure, hearing her speak evenly and directly, even the more generous involved in the Charleston controversy have felt inspired to call her "steely."

Now, however, she sounded more wounded than belligerent.

She was raised in a religious home, Brown explained; she was raised in church. Her parents—her dad had a small insurance agency, her mom worked in a bank—loved her, loved her two sisters, Sundays, the whole family would get together with her mom's seven brothers and sisters, the gathering full of children, the cousins like siblings to her. Family mattered, she believed. Children are a precious asset, children are our future, children are our dreams. She didn't understand this fu-

ror, she didn't understand why people thought her a witch, she didn't understand why people didn't want to help children.

"You start to talk with care and compassion," she said of her visits with patients. "But you must make them understand. So you tell them—get treatment, don't get arrested, I don't want you arrested. But if you continue using drugs, you . . . will . . . be . . . arrested. I don't yell. I also don't say"—here Brown momentarily adopts a soft, cooing voice—" 'don't worry about it.' I tell them some have been arrested. That's why they get upset. If you're on drugs, and you're told you will go to jail if you don't stop, and you don't want to stop, then the person telling you is mean."

Brown blinked hard, her face flushed. "How would you feel?" she continued. "How would you feel? I've had patients looking through their pocketbook to get a card from that attorney [Lynn Paltrow] to sue me. 'You can't make me go into treatment,' they say. 'You're violating my rights. I'm going to call this attorney.' How'd you like it if you were threatened with a lawsuit each time you walked into a room?"

After two hours of conversation, her visitor rose to leave, but Brown did not want to stop.

"No patient was publicly seen being arrested at MU," she said. "It was always done low-key and quietly. Plainclothes officer, cloth over the handcuffs, out the back door, unannounced. . . . We're trying to help pregnant women. . . . I don't know anyone who's perfect."

Her visitor now at the door, Brown still couldn't let go.

"How would you like it? I can combat the truth, but this, what they're saying about me. . . . Once said, there's no recovering. . . . Do you see that bad, mean monster nurse Brown? Is that what you see? Does it look like I have horns? Is that what you see?"

"THIS IS NOT YOUR GARDEN VARIETY CASE," A VISIBLY DISGRUNTLED U.S. District Judge C. Weston Houck muttered during his first morning of exposure to the various arguments in the case titled Crystal Ferguson and Monica Roe vs. City of Charleston et al. "This is going to be a complicated constitutional case."

That was on Wednesday, Feb. 16, at a hearing called to consider Paltrow's motion for a preliminary injunction. Charles Condon and Shirley Brown were sitting at the defendants' table, Paltrow and Susan Dunn and two other lawyers at the plaintiffs' table. Within minutes, it was apparent that Paltrow's momentum had hit something of a brick wall in Judge Houck.

Called to speak first, Paltrow, having spent hours the night before preparing, rose clutching a legal pad full of notes. The mission she faced was daunting; to get an injunction, she needed to prove her two particular clients faced imminent, irreparable danger.

"I would like to begin . . . by explaining what we're not asking for today," she said. "We are not asking this court to enjoin MUSC from counseling its pregnant patients—"

That's about as far as she got.

"Tell me what you are asking for," Judge Houck interrupted. MUSC does "a lot of things. And I can't go down to everything. . . ."

Paltrow tried again. "All that we are asking this court to do is to restore [MUSC] to what it is supposed to be—a health-care facility, not a conduit to jail—"

"Look, look, look, look, look, look" the judge interrupted again. "Tell me what you want.... I don't need all that surplusage ... OK?"

Paltrow tried shifting from description to legal argument, but that didn't work either.

"How is that going to the failure for me to grant relief?" Houck asked. "How is that going to cause your clients irreparable harm?"

Paltrow tried summarizing her claims.

"That's what the lawsuit is all about," Houck barked. "That's been done. I can't stop that by a preliminary injunction."

Paltrow tried citing case precedents.

"Just hand me those cases," Houck growled. "But I mean, it doesn't do any good for you to read cases here in court. I can't read them now and hear your arguments as well."

As the day wore on, it grew harder and harder to ignore the good ol' boy routines. The more the judge addressed Bobby Hull, local attorney for the hospital, the more their voices thickened into a distinct Southern drawl. The term "fussin' at" began appearing with some frequency, as in Hull's suggestion that "it's the state they all fussin' at, not the individuals." (By suing MUSC, a state institution, Paltrow is effectively suing South Carolina.) Although the judge called the hospital's lawyer "Mr. Hull," he could not bring himself to address Paltrow by name or even, at times, look directly at her.

"I believe there is some evidence the goal of this program has been achieved to some extent," Judge Houck said, upon finally revealing that he was going to deny Paltrow's motion for an injunction. "I do believe if the program continues, some mothers who are addicted and in prenatal care will not continue treatment. Then I must conclude that the discontinuation of the program is going to cause at least one or more children to be born with addiction to drugs.... That is very serious harm.... The public undoubtedly is interested in its institutions not violating the constitutional rights of citizens.... I also believe that the public interest of this state is focused now, more than probably at any other time, on drugs and [their] effects.... It may be that the public interest is not well founded.... It may be that they should be more concerned about the deprivation of constitutional rights of the plaintiff, but I really don't think that's the case. I think the public is concerned about children who, through no fault of their own ... are conceived by a mother who is addicted to drugs.... To avoid that ... is of great public interest...."

Paltrow's obvious dismay and Condon's satisfied smile as they left the hearing told the whole story. There were many months to go, many more chances coming for Paltrow to persuade and educate; at a second hearing in early June, Paltrow would in fact prevail on several procedural matters. Still, if not readily apparent before, it was now: No matter how much you debate the issues and assemble the experts, this case was not, in the end, only about right or wrong, good or bad, legal or illegal, moral or immoral. This case was also very much about political will—of what the public wants and will support.

Condon, for one, understands this quite well.

Just last summer, after all, Charleston residents—including Mayor Joseph Riley Jr., and Police Chief Greenberg—fought fiercely against locating a residential drug- and alcohol-treatment center near the city, even though it had federal funding and was to include precisely the type of residential facility that specialists believe would attract pregnant substance abusers with children. Expressing concern about the "frequent mental dysfunction" of substance abusers, noting that "even the best treatment programs are only partially effective," Greenberg declared that he "would not like to see this facility located in my neighborhood or the proposed location."

By the time everyone finally agreed last fall to build the facility near the MUSC complex, it was clear that the dispute, although ostensibly over location, was also being driven by a more fundamental fear and animosity. "There was a great resentment against people who don't follow rules ending up in a better position than those who do," is how Condon put it. "Of people pulling the cart being told what to do by those in the cart."

Walking to the courthouse from his law office, Condon began to explain, with all the relish of a pragmatic political scientist, the principles underlying such community resistance.

"First, be cognizant that it takes taxpayer money to pay for these programs," he advised. "That's the real world. So they must meet harsh tests: Are they necessary? Bare bones? You're handing out free food, shelter, access to better medical plans than we have. I'm not at all against these programs, but you can't get resources for them; there's not great support in this country for them. That's the real world, just like there's not enough political will to move after pregnant women who use alcohol or cigarettes. There is, though, a political basis for this interagency program. Leaders can take a position against crack. Our legal system reflects our cultural mores. That's our system. That's the real world...."

Condon stopped in mid-sentence, at the moment he reached the television cameras waiting at the courthouse steps. Instantly, he turned from his companion and hit his cue.

"The left-wing ACLU doesn't represent the American people," he began, leaning into the microphone. "The left-wing ACLU doesn't represent the people of South Carolina. MUSC deserves an award. If the plaintiff prevails, in effect we'd be legalizing the use of crack cocaine during pregnancy...." Staring into the camera, Condon posed the enduring question that so grips Charleston: "Who is speaking for the babies in this courtroom?" he asked. "Who is speaking for the babies?"

Then Condon turned back to his private conversation. "Tell Lynn thanks for suing me," he smiled, as he walked into the courthouse. "Running in South Carolina for attorney general, the best thing you can have happen is to be sued by the ACLU."

The Fantastic Voyage of Tanner Roberts

Pamela Warrick

Times Staff Writer

At 10:04 a.m. on Jan. 30 Tanner Max Roberts ended a remarkable journey.

On that sunny Thursday in a suite at St. Joseph Medical Center in Burbank, Tanner was born. As births go, this one was uneventful. But being born—the original voyage from darkness into light—is by its very nature a most extraordinary experience. It has been variously described as euphoric, traumatic, even catastrophic for the baby.

Many of the mysteries surrounding the process, including questions as basic as how labor begins, remain unsolved. Yet over the last decade, ultrasound and other diagnostic devices have opened a window into the womb. Today, it is scientifically possible to, at the very least, imagine what it is like to be born. Here, according to medical texts, published research and expert interviews, is the story of how it might have been for one baby.

Day 266

On the afternoon of the 266th day of Cindy Roberts' pregnancy, the onetime champion freestyle swimmer lowers her swollen body into a warm bath. Submerged, she feels almost weightless.

All morning, she had been out walking around shopping malls, hoping to hurry the start of labor. She is tired of being pregnant, tired of being big. This pregnancy, she sighs, has gone on long enough.

Inside her belly, another beautiful swimmer floats in his own watery world. On other afternoons, he would stretch and tumble in his amino bubble. Now, there is no room for acrobatics.

Even with arms and knees pulled in tight in classic fetal position, his body fills the entire uterine envelope. The womb has stretched to almost 60 times its normal size, but its occupant's world is shrinking. . . .

Why labor begins when it does is a mystery. The pressure of the fetus on the pelvic floor might have something to do with it. The fetus might trigger it by excreting certain chemicals that signal a level of anxiety about the increasingly cramped surroundings.

The placenta, once spongy with nourishing blood vessels, is growing tough and fibrous in anticipation of its impending functional failure. Just as the fetus's days *in utero* are numbered, the placenta too has a finite life span.

At nearly nine pounds—three pounds more than he weighed just a month ago—Tanner is physiologically ready to be born. Cartilage nicely shapes his ears, hair decorates his head and the soles of his feet are sufficiently creased to give him an identifiable footprint.

His head is big and heavy—25% of his body weight. So it is gravity, as much as biological destiny, that pulls him head down into the pelvic basin.

The Pain Begins

That night in the frozen-food aisle at Lucky, Cindy Roberts stops short. A sharp pain, starting in the small of her back and reaching around her middle like fingers of flame, causes her to gasp.

She grabs her contracted belly; from rib cage to pelvis, she is as hard as a basketball.

For weeks, painless Braxton Hicks spasms (named from the gynecologist who discovered them) have been flexing her uterine muscles. But these practice contractions, which stretch the uterus and pump it up for the rigors of labor, have prepared neither Tanner nor his mother for the ordeal to come.

After 20 minutes in the checkout line and only one more serious contraction, Cindy loads a week's worth of groceries into the trunk of her gray Suzuki and heads home, smiling. It hurts but at least something is happening.

After six hours of mild and irregular spasms, the uterus settles into a predictable rhythm, contracting every 10 to 15 minutes, each contraction lasting 10 to 15 seconds. By now Tanner 'knows'—if only by the flood of anxiety-producing proteins in his system—that something is happening.

Prostaglandins, the hormones that have kept Cindy Roberts' cervix intact and the uterine contents secure, have stopped circulating. Suddenly released from these chemical inhibitors, the uterine muscles begin the natural process of expelling the foreign body the uterus has hosted for the last 9 months and 7 days.

The walls of the uterus begin to randomly contract—and with them, the very walls of Tanner's home. Even without a fully developed nervous system, the fetus at term is capable of experiencing pressure, confinement, restraint. And that might well be what Tanner is feeling.

After six hours of mild and irregular spasms, the uterus settles into a predictable rhythm, contracting every 10 to 15 minutes, each contraction lasting 10 to 15 seconds.

By now, Tanner "knows"—if only by the flood of anxiety-producing proteins in his system—that something is happening.

3 O'Clock Wake-Up Call

At 3 a.m., Cindy and Tom Roberts are wide awake. With son Kevin, 3, asleep in another room, they time Cindy's contractions with a stopwatch. Six to eight minutes apart. Tom rubs Cindy's back during each spasm. The contractions are growing more frequent and more intense. Time to call the hospital.

Cindy goes to the kitchen and downs two glasses of Gatorade and two Carnation Instant Breakfast bars for energy. When the time between contractions has narrowed to five minutes, Tom calls a friend to stay with Kevin.

Until now, the pre-dawn hours have been Tanner's favorite time for "dreaming." Being suspended in body-temperature amino fluid is not unlike being adrift in a sensory deprivation tank.

Before the onset of labor, the fetus also takes advantage of these quiet hours to "breathe." Even though his lungs are still collapsed and full of fluid, Tanner heaves his tiny chest and abdomen up and down, simulating the inhaling and exhaling that will sustain him outside the womb.

Each breathing episode is marked by a flurry of rapid eye movements of the sort measured in REM sleep—the stage when most dreaming is known to occur. (By seven months, a fetus is neurologically equipped to dream.)

But now, with the first real breath just hours ahead, breathing practice is over and dreams are put away. Tanner's activity is reduced to internal functions and basic reflexive responses.

Even Cindy's ingestion of glucose-heavy Gatorade—a predictable fetal stimulant—provoked only slight reaction. And the ride to the hospital does not seem to startle this small passenger.

The Pain Begins II

"How soon can I get an epidural?" Cindy Roberts wants to know.

It is 5 a.m. and her cervix is dilated 2 centimeters. It must open to 10 centimeters (about 4 inches) for the baby's head to push through. Each contraction thins and widens the cervical ring, but only slightly and awfully slowly. Or so it seems to Cindy.

In the meantime, she wants an anesthetic.

Tanner is stressed. Every time the uterus contracts, it flattens the placenta, which does his breathing for him. It also compresses the umbilical cord, which delivers the oxygen and removes carbon dioxide.

At the height of each contraction, Tanner is cut off. He can't get oxygen and he can't get rid of the toxic gases. With every spasm, he grows hypoxic (oxygen deprived): a life-threatening condition in an older child or in an adult, but the fetus is equipped to respond. Peppering the outside of his aorta are reddish-brown nodules—factories for making the hormones that will sustain him through labor and disappear during childhood.

In a distinctly fetal version of the "fight or flight" response, the stress hormone noradrenaline surges through Tanner's system. Instead of rushing blood to the skeletal muscles for "flight" (unnecessary for a fetus with nowhere to go), this specialized protein directs fresh blood to the heart and brain—the two organs most vulnerable to permanent damage from lack of oxygen.

In the Labor Room

When Cindy arrived at St. Joseph Medical Center, her contractions were 4 to 5 minutes apart. Now they have slowed to every 7 minutes. "I hate this," she says. "I hate this."

"When babies see the hospital door, they say 'Forget it!' " jokes nurse Rita Yates, who has seen this happen before.

Cindy is not laughing.

In Labor-Delivery Suite 2, a hotel-like room with furniture that converts from Danish modern to OR traditional, Yates pulls a webbed belt and fetal monitor around Cindy's middle to measure the labor.

She rubs petroleum jelly over the mother's taut abdomen to form a seal around the monitor microphone to enhance transmission. As the monitor begins to pick up the fetal heartbeat, a pen on the nearby console inscribes the rate on a long strip of graph paper.

Above the jagged line that is Tanner's changing heart rate, a second pen charts the variations in uterine muscle tone, drawing a picture of each contraction.

The nurse turns up the volume as the monitor picks up the sound of Tanner's heartbeat. From inside the mother's body, it ker-thumps and whooshes, ker-thumps and whooshes.

"There's that washing machine," says Tom Roberts. "Doesn't he sound great? It's supposed to be a boy. That's what they said."

Tanner's world is not a silent one. The most familiar sounds are a muffled version of his mother's voice and the sounds inside her body—the gurgling, rumbling and slurping noises of her internal organs and vessels as they pump, vibrate, murmur and digest.

Because fluid is a great conductor of sound, Tanner's fully developed hearing registers noise from outside his mother as well. Tanner is especially attuned to—and easily stimulated by—his father's distinctive baritone and the sweet, little-boy voice of brother Kevin.

Now, a new sound booms through his world: The echo of his own heartbeat. As broadcast by the sensitive fetal monitor, it is an imposing sound.

With each contraction of the uterine wall, Tanner's heartbeat jumps from its resting rate of about 140 beats per minute to its "stressed" rate of 160 to 170.

When the cervix is dilated to more than 4 centimeters, or almost half open, Tanner's mother is given her first medication. As Demerol begins to drip into her vein, Cindy relaxes.

Tanner, heart rate dipping to 130, then 120, begins to fall asleep.

'Breathe, Cindy!'

"Breathe through it, Cindy. Breathe! The baby needs you to BREATHE. . . ."

Contractions are coming every 3 to 4 minutes, each one lasting 25 seconds. The Demerol does not stop the pain, Cindy growls. She hugs her husband's old blue bathrobe tight against her chest as nurse Cindy Cox urges her to "relax those muscles. Breathe deep. Relax. You're almost done, almost done. . . . Done.

"Pretty soon," Cox announces, "you'll have him in your arms."

"He'd better be," snaps the exhausted Cindy.

Tanner's nap is over. With each contraction, his heart rate soars to 160, 170, 180 beats per minute.

Blood cells rich in oxygen-loving hemoglobin supply the oxygen-heavy blood Tanner needs to cope. Without these specialized cells, interruptions in the fetal oxygen supply would be damaging indeed.

While each contraction cuts off Tanner's only source of oxygen, the minutes of rest between each contraction resupply the deprived placenta and umbilical cord. The mother's deep breathing during contractions helps rush the fresh blood to the fetal heart and brain.

During a lull between two particularly intense contractions, a new sound is heard: metal instruments being lined up on a sterile-clothed bedside table.

Clank, clank. Tanner's heart rate leaps for a moment and then returns to its normal pace.

The Doctor Arrives

At 8 a.m., the Verdugo Mountains behind the hospital are still pink from the sunrise. Cindy Roberts' obstetrician, Dr. Wayne Furr, arrives and determines her cervix is almost completely dilated. But the "bag of waters" still has not ruptured.

Using a tool made for the purpose, the doctor reaches into the birth canal and tears the diaphanous membranes of the amino sac. About half a liter of clear fluid spills out.

Before he leaves the room, the doctor tells Cindy her labor is progressing well and she can have that epidural anesthetic now. Between contractions, Cindy sighs, "Thank you."

Tanner is startled by the rush of the escaping fluid. And, with the next contraction, he is startled again by the impact of the loss. No longer are the contractions diffused across a watery bed. Now Tanner's head, knees and shoulders are pressed hard against the muscular uterine wall.

Because the spinal anesthetic acts only on the mother's spinal nerves, the 8 cubic centimeters of Marcain have no direct effect on the fetus. But for the next 30 minutes, the drug eases the frequency and intensity of contractions. It also reduced the mother's blood pressure and slows her breathing.

After 30 minutes, contractions resume with as much or greater force. They are coming every 2 minutes now. Each one lasts a full minute. Between spasms, the mother sleeps. But not Tanner.

For him, this is the start of the most stressful part of his journey.

Head First

By 9 a.m., Cindy's cervix is fully dilated and her labor suite has been transformed into a delivery room. The upholstered rocker and blond wood furniture have been covered with sterile blue drapes. A chest in the corner has become a high-tech warming table. And doctor, nurse and father are gloved, capped and gowned for the imminent birth.

As Tanner is pushed farther and farther down the birth canal, his body stretches out, like toothpaste being squeezed from the tube. Each expulsive push by the uterus impels his head against the pelvic girdle.

His feet kick out behind him, jabbing his mother's rib cage. The pressure on his skull is enormous from all sides as it makes its way through the narrow passage. (The skull of an adult could not easily withstand such pressure.)

But the flexible fetal skull is designed for this very event. Instead of a single fused bone, Tanner's head consists for four bony plates. As his skull is compressed, the plates slide over one another to allow the head to pass through.

The stress of contractions is formidable indeed. Skull compression, coupled with Tanner's increasing lack of oxygen, causes stress hormones to explode through his system. In an adult, this level of stress would mean that a stroke or a heart attack is occurring. But once more the fetal constitution is prepared.

As in earlier episodes of stress, blood rushes to the heart and head. But this time the stress is so strong, it causes more of Tanner's system to shut down. Like sea mammals during lengthy underwater stays, Tanner's body instinctively reacts to save itself. The heartbeat slows to a frightening 100, 90, 80 beats per minute and then leaps again to 180.

His body is compressed by his mother's contractions and her pushes. And as he nears his entrance to the world, the compressions help press the fluid from his lungs in preparation for the first breath.

Tanner's body, now wedged between his mother's sacral bone in back and pubic bone in front, suddenly turns slightly to fit through.

The Final Countdown

"1 - 2 - 3 - 4 - 5 - 6 - 7 - 8 - 9 - 10! 1 - 2 - 3 - 4 - 5 - 6 - 7 - 8 - 9 - 10! 1-2-3-4-5-6-7-8-9-10-11-12!"

Tom Roberts, who as Thomas Kane makes his living as the voice for such companies as Lincoln Mercury and Exxon, booms out the numbers as Cindy bears down, down, down to push out the baby.

"Here we go. Go, go, go, go, go, go, go!" cheers nurse Yates.

"Oh!" pants Cindy as the top of the baby's head emerges.

Tanner is squeezed tight in the birth canal as his head "crowns." The doctor gently touches the top of his wet, curly haired head. Over the next few seconds, Tanner's head, face down, emerges. As his chin clears the mother's body, his head spontaneously turns left.

His face is puffy and scrunched. Although squinting fiercely against the sudden light, Tanner's dark blue eyes are open. His lips are fluttering and he is making tiny bubbles with the clear mucus around his mouth.

Before any more of the body emerges, the doctor cradles Tanner's head and suctions his nose and mouth. Tanner takes his first breath—actually a large gasp, followed by whimpering, and then a lusty cry.

The tiny air sacs in his lungs suddenly inflate and he is ready for the next gasp. After a few minutes, the big gasp will settle into routine inhalations and exhalations.

Tanner's left shoulder is delivered, immediately (although gently) followed by the right shoulder. The rest of Tanner slides out easily.

His trunk and head are luminescent pink; his limbs are still gray-blue from lack of oxygen. His fingers and toes are gray. Tanner's body is wet, but only slightly bloody as the doctor lifts him onto his mother's abdomen.

It's a Boy

"Hello, baby, Hello, baby," whispers Cindy to the dazed but alert infant balanced on her belly.

"He's beautiful, just beautiful," reports nurse Yates.

"Very healthy. A real solid guy," adds the doctor.

"Isn't he just great!" announces the father.

Tanner seems to be able to focus slightly on objects about 8 inches from his face—the distance to his mother's face as she cradles him in her arms. Wrapped in a white flannel blanket, Tanner, drawn by his mother's voice, seems to gaze into her eyes. Unquestionably, he knows her.

The umbilical cord, still connecting baby and mother, slows and then stops pulsing. The obstetrician clamps the cord at both ends and hands the father a pair of surgical shears. Tom severs Tanner's final connection to the interior world.

Now Tanner's blood flows not to his mother for nourishment, but to his own lungs, intestines and other organs. The fetal path of blood through the heart is abandoned and blood is rerouted to Tanner's newly inflated lungs.

The baby is laid on a table next to the mother's bed to be dried and warmed. He cries loudly as eye-drops are put in. Meanwhile, the placenta is delivered from the mother.

Tanner can see very little, mostly shadows, mostly black and white. He seems to be able to focus slightly on objects about 8 inches from his face—the distance to his mother's face as she cradles him in her arms.

Wrapped in a white flannel blanket, Tanner, drawn by his mother's voice, seems to gaze into her eyes. Unquestionably, he knows her.

The room is quiet now, but everything about his new environment is intense to Tanner. The baby is overwhelmed from the avalanche of stimuli—first sounds, first sights, first touches. His mother lightly strokes his cheek. "Everything's going to be fine," she tells him. "Just fine."

□

Today, Tanner is 4½ weeks old and weighs 11 pounds. His eyes are still blue, but his hair is growing blond like his mother's.

His pediatrician, Dr. Gary Smithson of Glendale, reports that despite a brief bout of non-threatening jaundice, Tanner has been healthy since the day he was born. "He did have some of the longest fingernails I've seen on a baby," says Smithson, who gave Tanner his first manicure two hours after birth.

He sleeps up to three hours at a time and is a good eater. He still responds vigorously to the sound of his father's and his big brother's voices. On his third day home from the hospital, his mother awakened from a nap to find Tanner's chubby hands clutching her cheeks.

"Our eyes met for an instant," says Cindy, "and it was like he was looking right into my heart. . . ."

Putting a New Spin on the Birth of Human Birth

Humans do any number of things better than other animals, but giving birth is not one of them. Among the apes, our closest relatives, females bring infants into the world through a roomy birth canal with little fuss. In contrast, human babies often spend hours corkscrewing their way down a narrow birth canal, finally emerging head down, away from the mother—the only primates to do so. That makes human birth a risky business. Because babies don't bend backward, mothers can't pull them out without risk of serious injury, nor can they clear their newborns' airways if they are in trouble. Says University of Delaware anthropologist Karen Rosenberg wryly, "it's not the type of system you would invent if you were designing it today."

The process wasn't invented today, of course; it evolved over millions of years. But exactly when and how it did so has for decades perplexed anthropologists, who lacked the fossil evidence that could answer those questions. Over the past 8 years, however, they have been able to reconstruct a few bones associated with the birth canal from human ancestors dating as far back as 3 million years. At a symposium at last month's meeting of the American Association of Physical Anthropologists in Denver, researchers used those bones to begin tracing the evolution of human birth.

Those reconstructed bones, however, haven't given birth to a single scenario. In fact, they've produced a pair of decidedly nonidentical twins: Some researchers at the symposium presented new evidence that modern birth developed only very recently in our evolutionary history, while others countered with an intriguing speculation that it developed very early on.

Resolving this "when" question is important, says Wenda Trevathan, an anthropologist at New Mexico State University in Las Cruces, because of the insights it can produce about the social abilities of the creatures who evolved into human beings. "Human birth is so painful and risky," explains Trevathan, whose analysis puts her into the early camp, "that mothers need help from others to deliver a baby successfully." As a result, its development created a powerful selective force for empathy, communication, and cooperation—skills important to being human. And when those traits emerged is another date that anthropologists would love to pin down.

One thing researchers do know is why modern birth gives women such a difficult turn. The human pelvis, which surrounds the birth canal, crimps that canal partway down. At the top, the canal is widest from side to side. The longest dimension of a baby's head is from the nose to the back of the skull, and so the baby enters the canal facing sideways. But lower down, the canal changes its shape so that the longest dimension is from front to back. As a result, the infant must rotate 90 degrees. And there's one more twist: The baby's head is broadest at the back, but the lower canal is a bit broader at the front. So the infant enters the world facing down.

Apes, which have small heads and relatively larger pelves, don't have to go through these gyrations. In 1960, anthropologist Sherwood Washburn of the University of California, Berkeley, speculated that humans took this turn for the worse because the lineage was caught in an "obstetrical dilemma." The pelvis narrowed in response to two-legged walking, since this helps center our legs under our bodies. But as babies' heads and brains started getting bigger, the fit became really tight. The theory seemed sound, but the first hard evidence of when and how the pelvic girdle changed didn't come until 1986.

That was the year Owen Lovejoy of Kent State University in Ohio and Robert Tague, now at Louisiana State University, reconstructed the pelves of two australopithecines (the oldest known nonape human forerunners), including one belonging to "Lucy," the famous 3-million-year-old fossil female. They found that the australopithecine pelvis had changed from an apelike pattern. The back, which supports most of the upper body, had moved closer to the hip joints, giving the pelvis the shape of an oval stretched from hip to hip. The change helped "to adjust posture in a biped," says Tague.

But it also had implications for how australopithecine babies were born. Unlike newborn apes, which can ride into the world facing up all the way, australopithecine babies had to face sideways, Tague and Lovejoy argued. Only then could the head pass through the birth canal.

In Denver, Chris Ruff of the Johns Hopkins University School of Medicine argued that's probably the way hominid babies came into the world until just a few hundred thousand years ago. He based this conclusion on an analysis of two different parts of the skeleton of early *Homo*, human ancestors who appeared at least 2 million years ago, and some of their successors. First, Ruff measured the curve of the iliac brim, a bony feature that forms part of the start of the birth canal, and extrapolated from it the overall shape of the birth canal opening in early *Homo*. He concluded that the canal of this ancestor was oval, much like its shape in australopithecines.

The second feature Ruff examined was related to the width at the lower end of the canal: the shape of the thigh bones just below where some muscles attach them to the side of the pelvis. Bones change shape in response to the force of muscle tugs. And Ruff noted that in nine early *Homo* specimens, ranging in age from 1.9 to 0.7 million years old, the thigh bone shapes indicated these muscles were pulling very hard. "They would only do that if the hip joints were wider apart" than in modern humans, Ruff says. The muscles pull to counterbalance the weight of the air-borne hip and leg during a step; the farther away that hip is, the harder they have to pull. The wide pelvis implied by these muscle actions also implies a wide birth canal "broadened to fit the head sideways all the way down," Ruff says. In other words, no rotation.

In fact, he continues, there's no evidence that the lower pelvis changed much from the australopithecine pattern until the last few hundred thousand years, with early modern humans and the Neanderthals. By that time, average brain size had shot up from about 800 milliliters in early *Homo* to more than 1200 milliliters (modern human brains are about 1400 milliliters, though there is a huge range of variation). "The head had become a critical component" in birth, says Ruff. To let it through, the lower end of the bony birth canal had to enlarge. It couldn't get any wider from side to side than it already was, because that would splay the legs out, Ruff says, and so it elongated from front to back.

And that change meant that human infants had to spin as they traversed the canal, first facing sideways, then turning so that they emerge face down.

Aware of the fragmentary nature of the fossils that Ruff used, other researchers were reserved in their reactions, although many found the argument plausible. "This is a very creative approach, because there are so few [whole pelves]," says Tague. "And Ruff is always very thorough in his work." One who does disagree is Lovejoy, who, though he did not hear Ruff's talk, says that in general "there's too much slop in the relationship between the [top of the thigh bone] and the birth canal to draw a reliable conclusion."

Another demurral comes from Trevathan, though for different reasons: She thinks rotation may have arisen very early—even in the australopithecines. She pointed out that if australopithecine babies did face sideways as they came through the canal, the next part of their anatomy coming through would cause problems: the shoulders, which would stretch across the narrowest diameter of the oval. "The shoulders are rigid, and they'd get caught," she says. The best way out, Trevathan suggests, was a rotational birth. The anthropologist, who was trained as a midwife, points out that even in modern humans the shoulders are a problem, particularly in larger babies.

As with Ruff's work, this notion was greeted with caution, but not rejection. Anthropologist Alan Mann of the University of Pennsylvania noted that "Obstetricians have been telling me for years about the great difficulty in fitting the shoulders through," yet anthropologists seem to have left them out of the evolutionary picture. Rosenberg, who likes the idea, says, however, that "I worry a bit that we may be exaggerating the importance of the shoulders. I'm not saying it's wrong, but Wenda only suggested it was a real problem with big babies," and australopithecine babies could have been rather small. And Ruff simply suggests that the babies could have turned their necks, lining

their heads up with their shoulders and avoiding the problem altogether.

The time when this rotation entered the picture might seem like a detail, but anthropologists feel that it's a crucial one, because that's when mothers began to need outside help. "Chimps hide at the time of birth; humans do exactly the opposite and seek assistance," Rosenberg says. The pain and difficulty of labor put a premium on companionship, Trevathan contends; studies by Marshall Klaus at Children's Hospital in Oakland, California, have shown that the presence of a support person during labor reduces the rate of Caesarean sections and other birth complications. Since aid at birth increases the chance of reproductive success, traits that support this aid become products of natural selection. Emotional empathy, communication, and responsiveness all fall into this category. "Of course, birth isn't the only pressure for social relationships, but it's got to be an important one," Rosenberg says.

Mann adds that "if a female needs assistance, it means complex interaction between mother and assistant. If this was occurring in australopithecines, it would suggest they are more complicated than the field appears to view them at the moment—something more than simple apes." He has argued that australopithecine babies went through a prolonged period of dependence, and this too would put a premium on social cooperation. "Of course," Rosenberg notes, "if Wenda's idea isn't true, then it means that rotation and cooperation probably didn't arrive until much later."

How, then, can this timing issue be resolved? "I hate to say this, because anthropologists always say it," Rosenberg says, "but we need more fossils. We have two female australopithecines, and I'd like some female early *Homo* pelves as well." There are none at present, preventing scientists from getting a more direct look at the birth canal and all it entails. Researchers are waiting for that chance—expectantly.

–Joshua Fischman

THE MOST INTIMATE
BOND

*Conjoined for life, the Hensel twins are a medical mystery
and a lesson in cooperation for us all*

CLAUDIA WALLIS

IT'S PLAY PERIOD IN CONNIE STAHLKE's kindergarten room. Abigail and Brittany Hensel are at the Play-Doh table, when a visitor asks, How much is 10 plus 10? Britty starts counting on her fingers. Abby helpfully lays down her hand on the table. They count fingers and toes with all the accuracy their six-year-old minds can muster. "Nineteen," they conclude. Then the clearly ancient guest asks, "Guess how old I am." Britty can't resist the chance to tease: "900,000!" she shrieks. The sisters dissolve into giggles. They reach up and slap a celebratory high five.

The Hensel twins love to share a joke. A puckish sense of humor is one of their best tools for contending with all the other sharing they must do day in and day out—a sharing of a more profound and intimate nature than most of us can imagine. The two hands that meet in a high five, offer fingers for counting and clasp their adored parents in an embrace belong to a single body. Abby controls the right limbs, Britty the left. Although they have separate necks and heads, separate hearts, stomachs and spinal cords, they share a bloodstream and all organs

below the waist. In medical terms, they are known as "conjoined twins." In human terms, though, they are two very different people, with separate opinions, tastes and dreams.

For six years the Hensel twins have lived a quiet existence in a tiny Midwestern town where everyone knows them. (The family does not want the town to be identified.) They go shopping with their parents and younger brother and sister, attend school and even play in Little League T-ball games. But until recently when their parents opened their doors and hearts to a Life magazine reporter and photographer, the twins have been shielded from media attention. Their touching story, which appears on the cover of Life's April issue, has made them instant celebrities.

But the girls are more than curiosities. Their smiling faces and apparent good health seem a rebuke to the current medical trend of trying to separate, via surgery, ever more complexly conjoined twins—a trend that often means sacrificing one child so the other can live "normally." And their tale of lives un-

punctuated by solitude has much to teach all of us about the real meaning of individuality and the limitless power of human cooperation.

Conjoined twins are a rare event in the world's delivery rooms. They occur about once in every 50,000 births, but 40% are stillborn, and, curiously, 70% are female. Conjoined twins are always identical: the product of a single egg that for some unknown reason failed to divide fully into separate twins during the first three weeks of gestation. In the U.S. there are perhaps 40 live cases each year; ordinary identical twins are 400 times as common.

The popular term Siamese twins originated with a celebrated pair named Eng and Chang, born in Siam (Thailand today) and exhibited across the U.S. from 1829 to 1840. Eng and Chang, who lived to the ripe old age of 63—still a record for conjoined twins—were connected at the chest by a flexible band of cartilage. (Modern surgeons could have separated them easily.) Connections at the chest and abdomen are the most frequent configuration for conjoined twins, though medical texts list more than a dozen possible permutations. Dicephalic twins like the Hensels, who have two heads but share one two-legged body, are among the rarest. Only three or four cases are on record.

"I just want people to know that they're two separate kids with their own personalities. If they had to be put together, I think they were put together perfectly."

—PATTY HENSEL

Patty and Mike Hensel had no idea what they were in for when Patty's first pregnancy came to term six years ago. A spunky, attractive emergency-room nurse, Patty, now 37, had no signs that there was anything unusual about her pregnancy. Ultrasound tests indicated a single, normal fetus. (Doctors later guessed that the girls' heads must have been aligned during the sonogram.) Mike, who works as a landscaper and carpenter, thought he had heard two heartbeats at one point, but that impression was soon dismissed.

Because the fetus appeared to be in a buttocks-first, or breech position, Patty was scheduled for a Caesarean section. She was woozy with anesthesia, and Mike was not in the room, when doctors attempted the delivery. They pulled out the buttocks, then the legs and finally, to their astonishment, two heads. "We all stood in silence for about 30 seconds," recalls Dr. Joy Westerdahl, the family's physician, who assisted at the birth. "It was extremely silent."

Mike recalls the painful way he was given the news. "They had a pretty crude way of telling me. They said, 'They've got one body and two heads.' " Patty, still under sedation, heard the word Siamese and couldn't quite grasp it. "I had cats?" she asked.

The girls were whisked off to a children's hospital in a nearby city. "We thought they were going to die," recalls Patty, who remained bedridden in the community hospital where she works, suffering from dangerously high blood pressure. Her sister, Sandy Fiecke, acted as her surrogate for several days at the children's hospital. She held the tiny girls for hours, offered them bottles and wore Patty's or Mike's sweatshirts so the girls would come to know their parents' scents. The task of informing friends and family fell to Mike. "It's pretty hard to explain to your folks how the kids were put together."

But once it was clear that the twins were healthy and the family could fall into a normal routine of bathing, feeding and cuddling, "we knew it would be fine," recalls Patty. And so it has been. Aside from an operation at four months to remove a third arm that projected awkwardly between their heads, the girls have not needed surgery. They have been hospitalized briefly three times: twice for pneumonia in Britty's lung and once for a kidney infection.

Westerdahl says it is impossible to guess about their long-term prognosis but for now they are "healthy and stable." Brittany is more prone to colds and coughs than Abigail. Since their circulation is linked, notes Patty, "we know that if Abby takes the medicine, Britty's ear infection will go away." The twins need only one set of vaccinations, says Westerdahl: "They like that they don't have to get two shots!"

Though they share many organs, including a single large liver, a bladder, intestines and a reproductive tract, their nervous systems are distinct. Tickle Abby on her side anywhere from head to toe, and Britty can't feel it—except along a narrow region on their back where they seem to share sensation. The girls experience separate hungers and separate urges to urinate and sleep.

The fact that they learned to walk at 15 months seems a miracle of determination, encouragement and teamwork. "We praised them so much," remembers Nancy Oltrogge, the twins' day-care provider, who presided over the process. No one ever instructed the girls about who should move which foot when. "They knew what to do," marvels Oltrogge. "We just had to make sure we watched them because they were a little bit top-heavy and could tip over." Occasionally, though, the twins would disagree on which way

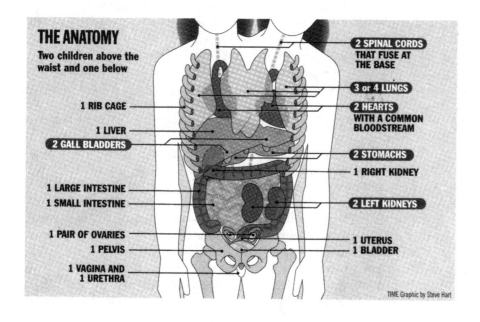

THE ANATOMY
Two children above the waist and one below

- 1 RIB CAGE
- 1 LIVER
- 2 GALL BLADDERS
- 1 LARGE INTESTINE
- 1 SMALL INTESTINE
- 1 PAIR OF OVARIES
- 1 PELVIS
- 1 VAGINA AND 1 URETHRA

- 2 SPINAL CORDS THAT FUSE AT THE BASE
- 3 or 4 LUNGS
- 2 HEARTS WITH A COMMON BLOODSTREAM
- 2 STOMACHS
- 1 RIGHT KIDNEY
- 2 LEFT KIDNEYS
- 1 UTERUS
- 1 BLADDER

TIME Graphic by Steve Hart

to go. "All of a sudden," says Oltrogge, "they're going in circles." The twins have graduated to swimming and riding a bike.

No one can say how two separate brains can synchronize such complex motions. It is possible that the girls have developed an unconscious awareness of the placement of each other's limbs. "How do they coordinate upper-body motion like clapping hands?" asks Westerdahl. "I don't know if we can ever answer that."

The idea of separating the twins was dismissed by both parents right from the start, when doctors said there was little chance that both could survive the procedure. "How could you pick between the two?" asks Mike. Even if separation were possible, Patty, as a nurse, could picture all too vividly a pathway of pain, multiple surgeries and lives spent mostly in wheelchairs. "If they were separated, they would pretty much cut them right down the middle. You can see that," she says.

This view is supported by Dr. Benjamin Carson, chief of pediatric neurosurgery at Johns Hopkins Children's Center in Baltimore, Maryland, who has helped separate other twins. "If we were to separate them, we would basically take a couple of individuals who are mobile and change them into invalids." He doubts that both could survive.

Perhaps the closest case in which separation was attempted is that of Eilish and Katie Holton of Ireland. Born in a configuration similar to the Hensels' but with four arms rather than three, the Holton twins were separated in 1992 at age 3 in a 15-hour operation involving 25 doctors at London's Great Ormond Street Children's Hospital. Katie died of heart problems four days later. Eilish survives and hobbles around quite nimbly with an artificial leg. Eilish and her parents visited the Hensels in December 1994. For each family, the visit, recorded for ABC's 20/20, was a stunning encounter with the road not traveled.

Patty and Mike worry about what will happen when the girls enter adolescence. "It's going to be tough on them," Mike suspects. Should there come a point where the girls insist on being separated, says Carson, the possibility could be explored, though conjoined twins have never been successfully divided after early childhood. "They would have to say, 'We can't stand this anymore.'" Aside from the physical difficulty, such a separation, he says, would present a "major emotional trauma."

Right now the girls seem content with their lot. "I'm not going to be separated," Britty insists. (Having met just one Holton twin, she has some sense of the risks.) Each girl seems to have established a remarkably solid sense of self. "They do their own work," says Stahlke, their teacher. "When we take tests, they could copy each other so easily, but they don't. If Abby makes a mistake, Batty has that one right. It just amazes me."

Abby wants to be a dentist. Britty dreams of piloting planes. "It's gonna be kind of hard in the cockpit when one's flying and the other one's working on someone's teeth," jokes Mike. They are already asking if they might someday find husbands. And why not? says Mike. Other conjoined twins have married. "They're good-looking girls. They're witty. They've got everything going for them, except," he pauses, "they're together." —*Reported by Jen M. R. Doman with the Hensels*

Cognition, Language, and Learning

• Early Cognitive and Language Development (Articles 8–13)
• Learning in School (Articles 14–16)

We have come a long way from the days when the characterization of cognition of infants and young children included phrases like "tabula rasa" and "booming, buzzing, confusion." Infants and young children are no longer viewed by researchers as blank slates, passively waiting to be filled up with knowledge. Today, experts in child development are calling for a reformulation of assumptions about children's cognitive abilities, as well as calling for reforms in the ways we teach children in our schools.

Hence, the articles in the first subsection highlight some of the new knowledge on the cognitive abilities of infants and preschoolers. Recent research indicates that babies have wonderfully active minds. The essays "The

Amazing Minds of Infants," "Your Child's Brain," and "How Do Infants Learn about the Physical World?" describe how scientists are discovering, by employing ingenious experimental techniques, that infants possess many heretofore unrealized skills.

For many people, mentioning the word "infant" conjures up images of the round, cherubic faces of babies that grace most baby food labels. Unfortunately, not all infants are lucky enough to receive adequate nutrition. The importance of a supportive physical environment in promoting cognitive development is highlighted by the information found in "Malnutrition, Poverty, and Intellectual Development."

The ideas of Lev Vygotsky, a Russian psychologist who wrote decades ago, are having increasing impact on child development and education. "Vygotsky's Theory: The Importance of Make-Believe Play" is a rich presentation of his ideas about the value of play in cognitive growth and the role of parents and peers in promoting play and intellectual development.

As Erik Erikson noted, from about age 6 to 12 years, children enter the period of "industry versus inferiority" and become preoccupied with learning the tools of their culture. In our culture, these tools are the "three R's"—learning to read, write, and do arithmetic in school. Thus, the second subsection of this unit addresses developments in school-age children.

Researchers now recognize that children's learning in school, as well as educational philosophies and practices, are affected by cultural and societal norms. The author of "What Should Children Learn?" takes on the controversial issue of educational reform in the United States. What do we expect children in our country to know as a result of schooling, and how do we know if students have attained these skills? This article will offer much food for thought for those who believe the United States should change its educational values and practices.

Without question, the writings of Jean Piaget have dominated and reshaped researchers' views about the active nature of children's thinking abilities. This notion of the inherently active and cognitively competent child has clear and important implications for maximizing learning among children. Hence, the author of the article "How

Kids Learn" joins Piaget in stressing the importance of creative, imaginative play and active hands-on experiences as effective vehicles for promoting cognitive growth and learning in preschoolers and school-age children.

"The IQ Puzzle" presents interesting data on how national IQ scores have changed in recent years and offers some intriguing proposals for why we may be seeing subtle shifts in scores as a result of environmental influences.

Looking Ahead: Challenge Questions

Given that infants are more cognitively competent than once thought, what do you think about accelerated, formalized efforts to speed up infants' cognitive skills? What advantages or disadvantages do you envision for infants who are exposed to teaching and drilling at early ages? Do you think that there are "critical periods" in the very early years of development that will forever determine later cognitive growth? Imagine that you are a parent; would you rush to expose your infant to classical music or mathematics? Why or why not?

Why might pretend play or imaginative art activities be useful in promoting children's cognitive development and intelligence? How could you educate classroom teachers to utilize more creative forms of artwork or imaginative play as a regular part of their classroom instructional practices?

How would you rate American schools in terms of their ability to help children learn? What things would you change about our educational system? Why? Do you think that all American children should be required to pass national standards or tests? Why is educational reform so difficult in this country? In your view, how have teachers contributed to or hindered educational reform?

Do you know your own IQ? What do you think IQ tests measure? Is IQ a fixed mental capacity that does not change once an individual reaches adulthood? In what ways do you think environmental experiences may affect IQ? Is IQ a useful construct when assessing an individual? Why or why not? Why do you think IQ tests receive so much attention and weight by both researchers and the general public?

The Amazing Minds of Infants

Looking here, looking there, babies are like little scientists, constantly exploring the world around them, with innate abilities we're just beginning to understand.

Text by **Lisa Grunwald**
Reporting by **Jeff Goldberg**

Additional reporting: **Stacey Bernstein, Anne Hollister**

A light comes on. Shapes and colors appear. Some of the colors and shapes start moving. Some of the colors and shapes make noise. Some of the noises are voices. One is a mother's. Sometimes she sings. Sometimes she says things. Sometimes she leaves. What can an infant make of the world? In the blur of perception and chaos of feeling, what does a baby know?

Most parents, observing infancy, are like travelers searching for famous sites: first tooth, first step, first word, first illness, first shoes, first full night of sleep. Most subtle, and most profound of all, is the first time the clouds of infancy part to reveal the little light of a human intelligence.

For many parents, that revelation may be the moment when they see their baby's first smile. For others, it may be the moment when they watch their child show an actual

---

At three months, babies can learn—and remember for weeks—visual sequences and simple mechanical tasks.

---

preference—for a lullaby, perhaps, or a stuffed animal. But new evidence is emerging to show that even before those moments, babies already have wonderfully active minds.

Of course, they're not exactly chatty in their first year of life, so what—and how—babies truly think may always remain a mystery. But using a variety of ingenious techniques that interpret how infants watch and move, students of child development are discovering a host of unsuspected skills. From a rudimentary understanding of math to a

sense of the past and the future, from precocious language ability to an innate understanding of physical laws, children one year and younger know a lot more than they're saying.

MEMORY

Does an infant remember anything? Penelope Leach, that slightly scolding doyenne of the child development field, warns in *Babyhood* that a six- to eight-month-old "cannot hold in his mind a picture of his mother, nor of where she is." And traditionally psychologists have assumed that infants cannot store memories until, like adults, they have the language skills needed to form and retrieve them. But new research suggests that babies as young as three months may be taking quite accurate mental notes.

In his lab at the University of Denver, psychologist Marshall

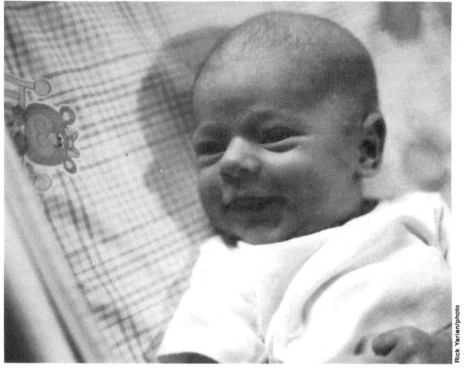

Babies show an unexpected ability to remember surprisingly intricate details.

Haith has spent much of the past four years putting infants into large black boxes where they lie and look up at TV screens. The program they see is a Haith invention: a sequence of colorful objects appearing on different sides of the monitor. Using an infrared camera linked to a computer, Haith follows the babies' eye movements and has found that after only five tries the babies can anticipate where the next object will appear. With a little more practice, they can foresee a four-step sequence. And up to two weeks later, most can still predict it. Says Haith: "The babies are not just looking. They're analyzing, creating little hypotheses."

Similar findings by Carolyn Rovee-Collier, a psychologist at Rutgers University, suggest that infants can remember surprisingly intricate details. In a typical experiment, she places a baby in a crib beneath an elaborate mobile, ties one of the baby's ankles to it with a satin ribbon, then observes as the baby kicks and—often gleefully—makes it move. When, weeks later, the baby's feet are left untied and the mobile is returned to the crib, the baby will try to kick again, presumably recalling the palmy days of kicking the last time. But if the mobile's elements are changed even slightly, the baby will remain unmoved—and unmoving. "When we change things," explains Rovee-Collier, "it wipes out the memory. But as soon as we bring back what had become familiar and expected, the memory comes right back. What we've learned from this is that even at two and a half months, an infant's memory is very developed, very specific and incredibly detailed."

Rachel Clifton, a psychologist at the University of Massachusetts, says that an infant's experience at six months can be remembered a full two years later. Clifton stumbled upon her findings while researching motor and hearing skills. Three years ago she placed 16 six-month-olds in a pitch-dark room with objects that made different sounds. Using infrared cameras like Haith's, she observed how and when the infants reached for the objects. Later, realizing she had created a unique situation that couldn't have been duplicated in real life, she wondered if the babies would remember their experience. Two years after the original experiment, collaborating with psychologist Nancy Myers, she brought the same 16 children back to the lab, along with a control group of 16 other two-and-a-half-year-olds. Amazingly, the experimental group showed the behavior they had at six months, reaching for objects and showing no fear. Fewer control-group toddlers reached for the objects, and many of them cried.

Says Myers: "For so long, we didn't think that infants could rep-

At five months, babies have the raw ability to add.

resent in their memories the events that were going on around them, but put them back in a similar situation, as we did, and you can make the memory accessible."

MATH

A t least a few parental eyebrows—and undoubtedly some expectations—were raised by this recent headline in *The New York Times:* "Study Finds Babies at 5 Months Grasp Simple Mathematics." The story, which reported on the findings of Karen Wynn, a psychologist at the University of Arizona, explained that infants as young as five months had been found to exhibit "a rudimentary ability to add and subtract."

Wynn, who published her research in the renowned scientific journal *Nature,* had based her experiments on a widely observed phenomenon: Infants look longer at things that are unexpected to them, thereby revealing what they do expect, or know. Wynn enacted addition and subtraction equations for babies using Mickey Mouse dolls. In a typical example, she had the babies watch as she placed a doll on a puppet stage, hid it behind a screen, then placed a second doll behind the screen (to represent one plus one). When she removed the screen to reveal three, not two, Mickey Mouse dolls, the infants stared longer at such incorrect outcomes than they had at correct ones. Wynn believes that babies' numerical understanding is "an innate mechanism, somehow built into the biological structure."

Her findings have been met with enthusiasm in the field—not least from Mark Strauss at the University of Pittsburgh, who a decade ago found that somewhat older babies could distinguish at a glance the difference between one, two, three and four balls—nearly as many objects as adults can decipher without counting. Says Strauss: "Five-month-olds are clearly thinking about quantities and applying numerical concepts to their world."

Wynn's conclusions have also inspired skepticism among some researchers who believe her results may reflect infants' ability to perceive things but not necessarily an ability to know what they're perceiving. Wynn herself warns parents not to leap to any conclusions, and certainly not to start tossing algebra texts into their children's cribs. Still, she insists: "A lot more is happening in infants'

At six months, babies recognize their native tongue.

---

minds than we've tended to give them credit for."

LANGUAGE

In an old stand-up routine, Robin Williams used to describe his son's dawning ability as a mimic of words—particularly those of the deeply embarrassing four-letter variety. Most parents decide they can no longer speak with complete freedom when their children start talking. Yet current research on language might prompt some to start censoring themselves even earlier.

At Seattle's University of Washington, psychologist Patricia Kuhl has shown that long before infants actually begin to learn words, they can sort through a jumble of spoken sounds in search of the ones that have meaning. From birth to four months, according to Kuhl, babies are "universal linguists" capable of distinguishing each of the 150 sounds that make up all human speech. But by just six months, they have begun the metamorphosis into specialists who recognize the speech sounds of their native tongue.

In Kuhl's experiment babies listened as a tape-recorded voice repeated vowel and consonant combinations. Each time the sounds changed—from "ah" to "oooh," for example—a toy bear in a box was lit up and danced. The babies quickly learned to look at the bear when they heard sounds that were new to them. Studying Swedish and American six-month-olds, Kuhl found they ignored subtle variations

in pronunciation of their own language's sounds—for instance, the different ways two people might pronounce "ee"—but they heard similar variations in a foreign language as separate sounds. The implication? Six-month-olds can already discern the sounds they will later need for speech. Says Kuhl: "There's nothing external in these six-month-olds that would provide you with a clue that something like this is going on."

By eight to nine months, comprehension is more visible, with babies looking at a ball when their mothers say "ball," for example. According to psychologist Donna Thal at the University of California, San Diego, it is still impossible to gauge just how many words babies understand at this point, but her recent studies of slightly older children indicate that comprehension may exceed expression by a factor as high as a hundred to one. Thal's studies show that although some babies are slow in starting to talk, comprehension appears to be equal between the late talkers and early ones.

PHYSICS

No, no one is claiming that an eight-month-old can compute the trajectory of a moon around a planet. But at Cornell University, psychologist Elizabeth Spelke is finding that babies as young as four months have a rudimentary knowledge of the way the world works—or should work.

Spelke sets her young subjects up before a puppet stage, where she shows them a series of unexpected actions: a ball seems to roll through a solid barrier, another seems to leap between two platforms, a third seems to hang in

EMOTIONS: THE SHY AND THE LIVELY

A growing number of researchers believe early temperament may indicate later troubles.

One thing that infants are *not* good at is hiding what they feel. Fear, glee, rage, affection: Long before babies start talking, emotions tumble out of them in gestures, tears and belly laughs. But measuring infant temperament—finding a way to quantify its traits—has always been harder than measuring skills.

Around the country, researchers are now combining questionnaires filled in by parents, home visits by trained observers, and newly devised lab tests to explore the mystery of temperamenat. Concentrating on babies older than eight months (the age at which the full range of infant emotions has emerged), investigators have designed more than 50 experimental situations to provoke emotions from fear to sadness, from interest to pleasure. Most children's reactions fall within an average range on such tests. But there are babies on either extreme, and psychologist Nathan Fox at the University of Maryland has begun to explore their responses. Putting his babies in electroencephalogram (EEG) helmets, he has found that particularly inhibited babies show a distinctive brain-wave pattern, which others believe may predict later emotional problems, including depression. Although some scientists agree that early behavior can predict later temperament, other researchers argue that enduring character traits are the exception, not the rule. For psychiatrist Stanley Greenspan of Bethesda, Md., the ability of infants to change is an article of faith. Specializing in babies as young as three months, Greenspan says he can treat what he calls the garden-variety problems of sleep disorders, tan-

Long before babies begin talking, emotions are graphically expressed in their gestures and facial expressions.

trums and anger in a few sessions. (Don't imagine tiny couches for infant patients; although the babies are closely observed, it's the parents who often get treatment.) For more severe problems, such as suspected learning disorders, he recommends more intensive early intervention—often involving a team of therapists—and has found that this can make a huge difference: "Babies who were very scared, shy and inhibited can completely change and become very assertive, outgoing and confident over a number of months."

The University of Washington's Mary Rothbart has compared infants in Japan, the Netherlands and the U.S. and notes that northern European mothers are most prone to ignore their babies' fussiness with a stiff-upper-lip approach. When tested at one year by having their mothers leave a room, the Dutch babies are the most distressed and ignore their mothers upon their return. Psychologists call this response an "insecure attachment relationship," and some regard it as an early warning of later anxiety disorders. Says Rothbart: "In the process of soothing a baby, you're helping to teach it to shift its attention away from negative sensations. Adults with anxiety disorders may never have learned to do this." Tellingly, when Dutch mothers were instructed to soothe and play with their fussy babies, the follow-up sessions showed positive results. "With intervention," concludes Rothbart, "you can turn things around."

TAKING INFANTS SERIOUSLY

The ultimate question becomes, should education begin at three months?

One question that might leap to the minds of parents newly informed of their infants' skills is a simple one: So what? What does it mean if children really have these unexpected abilities?

Pointing to the findings on memory that she has published with partner Rachel Clifton, Nancy Myers suggests that if memories of the babies' experience allowed them to be unafraid in the pitch-black room, then exposing children to a wide variety of events and places may make them more accepting of similar situations later on. "I don't want to say that mothers should make an extreme effort to stimulate their babies," Myers says, "but taking a baby to different places, allowing him to see and smell different things, is an important means of establishing familiarity. It will allow the baby to feel freer in the future."

But what about other kinds of skills: Should infants' innate abilities with language or math be consciously nurtured and pushed along?

In Philadelphia, instructors at the Institutes for the Achievement of Human Potential have been coaching parents since 1963 to teach their babies to read from birth. Touting "genetic potential," their program recommends that parents write out on cards everything from "nose" to "kiss" to "Mommy." The new findings about infants' skills have hardly gone unnoticed at the Institutes, where director Janet Doman says: "For the past thirty years, we've been saying that children can learn at very early ages. It's nice to know that science is finally validating what we've known all along."

Yet many of the scientists performing the experiments question the value of such intensive efforts. Says Rutgers's Carolyn Rovee-Collier: "Most of us agree that an infant could be taught to recognize letters and numbers. But the problem is that parents who do these kinds of programs start investing a lot in their infants and become very bound up in their success. It puts great strain on the infants and the parents."

University of Denver psychologist Marshall Haith agrees: "Babies are born prepared to take on the world. We've got to get away from the feeling that we've got this wonderful brain sitting there and we've got to keep pumping information into it. Nature wouldn't have done anything so stupid."

To most researchers, the moral of the story seems to be: Respect your baby, but don't go nuts. "Don't waste your child's fun months," says Karen Wynn, who says her findings about math "should be viewed as no more than a new insight for parents who have young children." Says the University of Pittsburgh's Mark Strauss: "Ideally, we can tell parents a lot more about subtle things they can watch happening in their infants, and that will make watching and getting involved more fun."

---

midair. Like Karen Wynn with her math experiments, Spelke measures the babies' looking time and has recorded longer intervals for unexpected actions than for expected ones. Again like Wynn, Spelke believes that babies must have some "core" knowledge—in this case, about the way physical objects behave. Says Spelke: "At an age when infants are not able to talk about objects, move around objects, reach for and manipulate objects, or even see objects with high resolution, they appear to recognize where a moving object is

when it has left their view and make inferences about where it should be when it comes into sight again."

The notion of an infant's possessing any innate mechanism—other than reflexes like sucking that fade with time—would have shocked the shoes off the pioneers of child development research, who believed, as some still do, that what we know can be learned only through experience. But the belief in biologically programmed core knowledge lies at the heart of the current research—not only with

math and physics but with other cognitive skills as well. Indeed, Carnegie Mellon's Mark Johnson believes that the ability of infants to recognize the human face is not learned, as previously thought, but is present at birth. Studying infants, some only 10 minutes old, Johnson has observed a marked preference for pictures of faces to pictures of blank ovals or faces with scrambled features. He believes that we are born with a "template" of the human face that aids our survival by helping us recognize our meal ticket.

10 Myths About Child Development

Modern research helps us sort out fact from fiction when it comes to theories about raising our children.

Mastering motor skills early is *not* a sign of superior intelligence.

Julius Segal

Julius Segal, Ph.D., a contributing editor of *Parents* Magazine, is a psychologist, author, and lecturer whose latest book is *Winning Life's Toughest Battles* (Ballantine).

"The 'evil eye' can bring harm to children admired by strangers."
"The fatter the child, the healthier."

"Spare the rod, and spoil the child." When I was a youngster, those were among the erroneous beliefs voiced by adults on my block. If you are like most parents, you, too, probably have theories about what makes kids tick—what determines the shape of a child's personality and behavior. Some of these notions have been passed along to you by your parents, others picked up from friends, still others culled from convincing TV talk-show guests.

In previous generations little scientific information was available by which parents could assess the validity of such theories. Today, however, child-development researchers have accumulated a rich store of knowledge to help us understand how and why children unfold as they do.

Based on today's scientific evidence, it appears that many of the ideas parents have about child development are rooted in myth rather than reality. Over the past few years I have kept a record of such unfounded notions as they were expressed to me by mothers and fathers during lectures and workshops around the country. Here are ten of them, all dealing with the child's early years.

1 You can tell in infancy how bright a child is likely to be later on.

Many parents continue to believe, as mine did, that the pace and quality of a baby's early achievements—reaching, sitting, crawling, babbling—are sure indications of that child's later capacities.

To examine this notion, researchers have conducted studies in which the same children were tested over long periods—in some cases from the first weeks of life to adulthood. As babies, the children were given so-called infant IQ tests, tapping such sensory and motor skills as the ability to recognize their mother, turn the pages of a book, or imitate words. Their scores were correlated with the results of later IQ tests, which tap mainly problem-solving, reasoning, and verbal skills.

The correlations have turned out to be negligible. Except, of course, in cases of extreme retardation, scores on even the most reputable tests of infant intelligence bear virtually no relationship to the scores that children achieve on standard IQ tests later on. Clearly the child's proficiency in mastering early sensory and motor tasks tells us little, if anything, about later intellectual ability.

Thus, for example, early agility in building blocks or skill in imitating an adult stirring with a spoon (two items in the widely used Bayley Scale of Infant Development) provides scant indication of the child's "smarts" later on, when schooling begins in earnest, and virtually no indication of how the child will function intellectually in the later years of childhood. Most researchers agree that regardless of the hype surrounding recently developed tests, the world of the infant and the world of the nine-year-old, say, are just too different to allow us to make either the triumphant ("a bud-

ding Einstein") or dismal ("a slow learner") projections many parents make about their little ones.

2 The more stimulation a baby gets, the better.

There is no doubt that babies are more receptive to stimulation from the outside world than either psychologists or parents had ever imagined in the past. Thus it is for good reason that mothers and fathers have been encouraged to begin right from the start to exercise the baby's senses—for example, placing bright, intriguing objects around the room and over the crib, playing music, reading, talking. The notion that a stimulating environment can have a positive effect on the intellectual capacities of babies—perhaps by actually influencing the brain's rate of growth—is no myth.

But it *is* a myth to assume that the larger the amount of early stimulation you provide, the more beneficial it will be. The truth is that babies can be *over*stimulated—which is what many parents, intent on beginning to groom their progeny for college in the cradle, end up doing. Indeed, bombarding newborns with heavier doses of new sensations than they are physiologically prepared for can sometimes inhibit progress. Psychologists Paul H. Mussen, Ph.D., John J. Conger, Ph.D., and Jerome Kagan, Ph.D., cite an example in their textbook, *Essentials of Child Development and Personality* (Harper & Row): "It is possible that the three-week-old baby, biologically too immature to reach for the brightly-colored mobile, may become more upset by the presence of the mobile than if nothing were present."

Observant parents have probably noticed that too much stimulation can be very disconcerting for the baby who is still not up to dealing with the pressure of all that input. Some simply become agitated or cry. Others try to push away the irritating stimulus—the intrusive rattle, toy, talking face, or finger. Still others withdraw, turning inward to avoid the relentless assault on their senses, and some simply tune out altogether and wisely drop off to sleep. Given such clues, parents are wise to curb the "enrichment activity." What the baby seems to be saying is "Enough already! My nervous system isn't quite ready for all that stuff."

3 If a baby cries every time Mother leaves her, it is an early sign of emotional insecurity.

If this were so, virtually every child would have to be regarded as emotionally insecure. Experiments throughout the world have shown that at a certain point in their early development, all babies become agitated, cry, and show an increased heart rate typical of a state of anxiety when separated from their mother or other steady caretaker. Starting at about eight months for some children—but usually peaking at about twelve to fifteen months for most—the experience is almost sure to bring distress and tears, and then the impact begins to weaken. The pattern applies equally in every region in which children have been studied, including American cities, isolated villages in the Guatemalan highlands, towns in Israel, and remote areas of the Kalahari Desert, in Africa.

Babies reared at home by their mother and those who spend much of their early life at a day-care center are equally likely to show separation anxiety. There are individual differences among kids, of course, in how soon the experience begins and how long it lasts, but overall it appears to be a universal phenomenon of early childhood—regardless of other aspects of the child's personality or of the nature of child-rearing practices.

4 You'll spoil the baby if you respond to his demands too quickly.

University of Virginia psychologist Mary D. Salter Ainsworth, Ph.D., and her associates carefully analyzed mother-infant interactions as they actually took place in the home. Some mothers responded to their babies as soon as they fussed or cried. Others did not, out of the belief that in doing so they would be overindulging the child and thus hampering normal development.

The results of this and related studies show that in the first year or so of life, children—still dependent and needy—are not "spoiled" by parents who are responsive and attentive. Babies tend to become more compliant—and more independent as well—when their signals of distress are responded to without delay. It is babies whose calls for help are answered slowly or ignored altogether who tend to make a habit of crying and whining and who are more hesitant about beginning to explore the world on their own.

5 "Bonding" between parent and infant must take place immediately after the baby's birth.

The idea of a now-or-never time for skin-close contact between mother or father and newborn arose from research with animals. Scientists have shown that there is indeed a period shortly after birth when infant sheep, chickens, geese, swans, and other animals are genetically programmed to latch on to the first moving object they see—their mother—and to follow it around. The process is called imprinting because the image of Mother becomes so indelibly imprinted in the "mind" of the infant animal that it cannot be erased. Moreover, when this imprinting process is disrupted, the system of signals that guides the mother-infant relationship becomes disorganized—and so does the newborn's behavior.

It is a gigantic leap, however, from chicks to children. A similarly critical period has never been reliably demonstrated for human infants, who form attachments to their caretakers much more gradually. Instead of being a static, one-time event, bonding is a process, a dynamic and continuous one. Thus a reciprocal, loving attachment is still realizable even when early contact is delayed—as it is for many mothers and their prematurely born infants, or when illness of either the newborn or mother intervenes. Moreover, secure bonds can and often do develop between children and their adoptive parents, coming together months or even years after the children's birth.

The bottom line is clear: There is no brief, miraculous period of early parent-child interaction that will define the child's future. Opportunities to build the kind of emotional intimacy that helps children thrive are available well beyond the opening hours and days of parenthood.

6 Special talents surface early or not at all.

Many kids who are born with

unique aptitudes do not find the opportunities to discover them—let alone express them—until their childhood has passed. Robert Albert, Ph.D., at Pitzer College, in Claremont, California, has studied the developmental patterns of exceptionally gifted youngsters. He concludes that it is only in early adolescence that many kids recognize their skills and begin to build their identity around them. "During the early years," says Albert, "sometimes as a result of crystallizing experiences in the high school science lab or the theater workshop, a talented scientist or performer emerges, and a dazzling career takes shape."

We know today that it is simply not possible to view a child's inherent nature and life experiences as independent forces. In order to become a football star, for example, a child would have to inherit a combination of such traits as agility, speed, and endurance. But without exposure to the sport and opportunity to practice, even the best-endowed child would not become truly outstanding at this activity.

Consider the case of jazz musician Louis Armstrong, a true genius who helped propel a new musical art form. He was actually a neglected and abandoned child. It was only years later, while Armstrong was living in the New Orleans Colored Waifs Home for boys, that someone taught him to play an instrument and his profound talent was ignited.

There are instances, of course, in which enormous endowment and exposure come together early. Mozart was clearly born with a remarkable genius for musical creation—and his magnificent products began to emerge at age five as a result of his father's steady instruction and because a harpsichord quickly became the center of his life. But no deadline exists for such a happy merger between innate talent and the opportunity to express it.

7 An only child is likely to have problems relating to other people.

Influenced by this widespread myth, many parents of single children expect them to become maladjusted loners with a self-centered approach to life. However, as University of Wisconsin psychologist Diane E. Papalia, Ph.D., and Sally

Wendkos Olds document in their textbook, *Human Development* (McGraw-Hill), research does not bear out this negative view—a fact that should be of special interest to that 10 percent of American couples opting to have only one child.

Instead, Papalia and Olds point out that only children are inclined in their early years to be bright, successful, self-confident, resourceful, and popular with their peers. Moreover, they are "just as likely to grow up to be successful in jobs, marriages, and parenthood experiences."

Studies do show that only children tend to be somewhat less eager for social intimacy. For example, they become involved with fewer organizations, have fewer friends, and generally lead a less intense social life than kids who grow up with siblings. On the other hand, they are likely to become the leaders of the organizations they do join, and they generate close friendships. Most important, their lives are marked by no less contentment than those of youngsters raised with siblings.

8 Children who suffer early neglect and deprivation will not realize their normal potential.

Many couples, seeking to adopt a child who has already endured traumatic beginnings, are unduly troubled by this belief. While there is little doubt that prolonged early stress and privation can hamper development, the ill effects are more often reversible than either parents or professionals have assumed. Under the proper conditions for growth, initial handicapping circumstances can be overcome. Indeed, Lewis P. Lipsitt, Ph.D., professor of psychology and medical science and director of the Brown University Child Study Center, in Providence, observes that such circumstances may spark the quest to succeed. "In some cases," says Lipsitt, "early adversity may serve as a launching pad for self-realization and achievement."

University of London child psychiatrist Michael Rutter, M.D., points out that even severely deprived children, not rescued from their appalling situations until the age of six or seven, are capable of achieving normal intellectual functions. One study, for example, showed an increase of about 30 IQ points among orphaned kids who'd been moved from a poor institution to a better one at age six. "It is quite clear," writes Rutter in *Maternal Deprivation Revisited* (Penguin Books), "that major environmental improvements in middle-class childhood can lead to substantial increases in IQ."

The same pattern applies when early impairments are due to physical rather than psychological causes. A group of Hawaiian children who suffered birth trauma—including potentially dangerous periods of anoxia, or lack of oxygen—were studied over a span of eighteen years. Their initial impairments were linked to later problems in development only when combined with persistently poor environmental circumstances such as chronic poverty, family instability, or illness of the mother. Those children who were raised in an intact family and with nurturing, stimulating parents showed few, if any, negative effects of the complications endured at birth—unless, of course, they had suffered severe damage to the central nervous system.

The data strike an optimistic note. Although a highly unfavorable environment can produce damage, young kids often prove to be resilient and malleable—capable of changing when circumstances change. Under the proper conditions, early deficits can be erased and the potential for a productive life fulfilled.

9 Spare the rod, and spoil the child.

Probably no child-rearing fiction has been as convincingly disproved as this one—yet it is still devoutly believed by countless parents, who inflict physical pain in the name of discipline as a cornerstone of their child-rearing techniques.

The myth that corporal punishment pays dividends undoubtedly carries higher stakes for our kids than any other discussed in this article. Research has convincingly demonstrated that using the "rod" creates children who are not more obedient but who are instead simply more angry and aggressive than other kids. Parents who routinely slap or strike their children are actually handing them a model of violence to imitate—and many do indeed grow to be abusive, some even murderously so.

Physical punishment may initially appear effective. For example, a three-year-old "strapped" for scratching up Mom's new coffee table is not likely to go near that table for a while, but ultimately the child-victim learns mainly how important it is not to get caught—and to even the score. In the long run, corporal punishment is surely not a proficient technique for inducing children to adhere to parental standards. As they grow, children will tend to follow the guidance of those who inspire affection and admiration, not fear or contempt.

10 Parental conflicts don't affect children who don't yet talk.

Most parents are aware that it is disturbing to children of school age when Mother and Father carry on arguments in their presence. We know from youngsters' responses to parental quarrels how sensitive they are to the tensions that sometimes descend like a cloud on the household—and to hearing expressions of suspicion, anger, or contempt. For good reason, therefore, we try to avoid exposing our quarrels to the kids in the household.

But it has been assumed by most parents that the same care need not necessarily be taken in the case of infants and toddlers, who, to quote one neighbor, "are too young to know and understand." That assumption, it now turns out, does not hold up. In studies conducted both in the natural environment of the home and in research laboratories, it is clear that even very young children can be acutely sensitive to arguments and other displays of interpersonal static in their environment.

At the National Institute of Mental Health, in Bethesda, Maryland, psychologists Carolyn Zahn-Waxler, Ph.D., and Mark Cummings, Ph.D., have found that in homes where conflict is high, children as young as eighteen months to two years become sufficiently upset to actually make efforts to break up their parents' battles. Moreover, they have shown that when two-year-olds at play become aware of arguments around them—even between strangers—they get rattled and begin acting more aggressively toward their peers. The evidence is compelling: Even before they can tell us about it, many children are remarkably well "tuned in" to the quality of the interpersonal relationships in their environment.

A baby's brain is a work in progress, trillions of neurons waiting to be wired into a mind. The experiences of childhood, pioneering research shows, help form the brain's circuits—for music and math, language and emotion.

Your Child's Brain

Sharon Begley

YOU HOLD YOUR NEWBORN SO his sky-blue eyes are just inches from the brightly patterned wallpaper. *ZZZt:* a neuron from his retina makes an electrical connection with one in his brain's visual cortex. You gently touch his palm with a clothespin; he grasps it, drops it, and you return it to him with soft words and a smile. *Crackle:* neurons from his hand strengthen their connection to those in his sensory-motor cortex. He cries in the night; you feed him, holding his gaze because nature has seen to it that the distance from a parent's crooked elbow to his eyes exactly matches the distance at which a baby focuses. *Zap:* neurons in the brain's amygdala send pulses of electricity through the circuits that control emotion. You hold him on your lap and talk . . . and neurons from his ears start hard-wiring connections to the auditory cortex.

And you thought you were just playing with your kid.

When a baby comes into the world her brain is a jumble of neurons, all waiting to be woven into the intricate tapestry of the mind. Some of the neurons have already been hard-wired, by the genes in the fertilized egg, into circuits that command breathing or control heartbeat, regulate body temperature or produce reflexes. But trillions upon trillions

more are like the Pentium chips in a computer before the factory preloads the software. They are pure and of almost infinite potential, unprogrammed circuits that might one day compose rap songs and do calculus, erupt in fury and melt in ecstasy. If the neurons are used, they become integrated into the circuitry of the brain by connecting to other neurons; if they are not used, they may die. It is the experiences of childhood, determining which neurons are used, that wire the circuits of the brain as surely as a programmer at a keyboard reconfigures the circuits in a computer. Which keys are typed—which experiences a child has—determines whether the child grows up to be intelligent or dull, fearful or self-assured, articulate or tongue-tied. Early experiences are so powerful, says pediatric neurobiologist Harry Chungani of Wayne State University, that "they can completely change the way a person turns out."

By adulthood the brain is crisscrossed with more than 100 billion neurons, each reaching out to thousands of others so that, all told, the brain has more than 100 trillion connections. It is those connections—more than the number of galaxies in the known universe—that give the brain its unrivaled powers. The traditional view was that the wiring diagram is predetermined, like one for a new house,

by the genes in the fertilized egg. Unfortunately, even though half the genes—50,000—are involved in the central nervous system in some way, there are not enough of them to specify the brain's incomparably complex wiring. That leaves another possibility: genes might determine only the brain's main circuits, with something else shaping the trillions of finer connections. That something else is the environment, the myriad messages that the brain receives from the outside world. According to the emerging paradigm, "there are two broad stages of brain wiring," says developmental neurobiologist Carla Shatz of the University of California, Berkeley: "an early period, when experience is not required, and a later one, when it is."

Yet, once wired, there are limits to the brain's ability to create itself. Time limits. Called "critical periods," they are windows of opportunity that nature flings open, starting before birth, and them slams shut, one by one, with every additional candle on the child's birthday cake. In the experiments that gave birth to this paradigm in the 1970s, Torsten Wiesel and David Hubel found that sewing shut one eye of a newborn kitten rewired its brain: so few neurons connected from the shut eye to the visual cortex that the animal was blind even after its eye was reopened.

The Logical Brain

SKILL: Math and logic

LEARNING WINDOW: Birth to 4 years

WHAT WE KNOW: Circuits for math reside in the brain's cortex, near those for music. Toddlers taught simple concepts, like one and many, do better in math. Music lessons may help develop spatial skills.

WHAT WE CAN DO ABOUT IT: Play counting games with a toddler. Have him set the table to learn one-to-one relationships—one plate, one fork per person. And, to hedge your bets, turn on a Mozart CD.

Such rewiring did not occur in adult cats whose eyes were shut. Conclusion: there is a short, early period when circuits connect the retina to the visual cortex. When brain regions mature dictates how long they stay malleable. Sensory areas mature in early childhood; the emotional limbic system is wired by puberty; the frontal lobes—seat of understanding—develop at least through the age of 16.

The implications of this new understanding are at once promising and disturbing. They suggest that, with the right input at the right time, almost anything is possible. But they imply, too, that if you miss the window you're playing with a handicap. They offer an explanation of why the gains a toddler makes in Head Start are so often evanescent: this intensive instruction begins too late to fundamentally rewire the brain. And they make clear the mistake of postponing instruction in a second language (see box, "Why Do Schools Flunk Biology?"). As Chugani asks, "What idiot decreed that foreign-language instruction not begin until high school?"

Neurobiologists are still at the dawn of understanding exactly which kinds of experiences, or sensory input, wire the brain in which ways. They know a great deal about the circuit for vision. It has a neuron-growth spurt at the age of 2 to 4 months, which corresponds to when babies start to really notice the world, and peaks at 8 months, when each neuron is connected to an astonishing 15,000 other neurons. A baby whose eyes are clouded by cataracts from birth will, despite cataract-removal surgery at the age of 2, be forever blind. For other systems, researchers know what happens, but not—at the level of neurons and molecules—how. They nevertheless remain confident that cognitive abilities work much like sensory ones, for the brain is parsimonious in how it conducts its affairs: a mechanism that works fine for wiring vision is not likely to be abandoned when it comes to circuits for music. "Connections are not forming willy-nilly," says Dale Purves of Duke University, "but are promoted by activity."

Language: Before there are words, in the world of a newborn, there are sounds. In English they are phonemes such as sharp ba's and da's, drawn-out ee's and ll's and sibilant sss's. In Japanese they are different—barked hi's, merged rr/ll's. When a child hears a phoneme over and over, neurons from his ear stimulate the formation of dedicated connections in his brain's auditory cortex. This "perceptual map," explains Patricia Kuhl of the University of Washington, reflects the apparent distance—and thus the similarity—between sounds. So in English-speakers, neurons in the auditory cortex that respond to "ra" lie far from those that respond to "la." But for Japanese, where the sounds are nearly identical, neurons that respond to "ra" are practically intertwined, like L.A. freeway spaghetti, with those for "la." As a result, a Japanese-speaker will have trouble distinguishing the two sounds.

Researchers find evidence of these tendencies across many languages. By 6 months of age, Kuhl reports, infants in English-speaking homes already have different auditory maps (as shown by electrical measurements that identify which neurons respond to different sounds) from those in Swedish-speaking homes. Children are functionally deaf to sounds absent from their native tongue. The map is completed by the first birthday. "By 12 months," says Kuhl, "infants have lost the ability to discriminate sounds that are not significant in their language. And their babbling has acquired the sound of their language."

Kuhl's findings help explain why learning a second language after, rather than with, the first is so difficult. "The perceptual map of the first language constrains the learning of a second," she says. In other words, the circuits are already wired for Spanish, and the remaining undedicated neurons have lost their ability to form basic new connections for, say, Greek. A child taught a second language after the age of 10 or so is unlikely ever to speak it like a native. Kuhl's work also suggests why related languages such as Spanish and French are easier to learn than unrelated ones: more of the existing circuits can do double duty.

With this basic circuitry established, a baby is primed to turn sounds into words. The more words a child hears, the faster she learns language, according to psychiatrist Janellen Huttenlocher of the University of Chicago. Infants whose mothers spoke to them a lot knew 131 more words at 20 months than did babies of more taciturn, or less involved, mothers; at 24 months, the gap had widened to 295 words. (Presumably the findings would also apply to a father if he were the primary caregiver.) It didn't matter which words the mother used—monosyllables seemed to work. The sound of words, it seems, builds up neural circuitry that can then absorb more words, much as creating a computer file allows the user to fill it with prose. "There is a huge vocabulary to be acquired," says Huttenlocher, "and it can only be acquired through repeated exposure to words."

Music: Last October researchers at the University of Konstanz in Germany reported that exposure to music rewires neural

The Language Brain

SKILL: Language

LEARNING WINDOW: Birth to 10 years

WHAT WE KNOW: Circuits in the auditory cortex, representing the sounds that form words, are wired by the age of 1. The more words a child hears by 2, the larger her vocabulary will grow. Hearing problems can impair the ability to match sounds to letters.

WHAT WE CAN DO ABOUT IT: Talk to your child—a lot. If you want her to master a second language, introduce it by the age of 10. Protect hearing by treating ear infections promptly.

circuits. In the brains of nine string players examined with magnetic resonance imaging, the amount of somatosensory cortex dedicated to the thumb and fifth finger of the left hand—the fingering digits—was significantly larger than in nonplayers. How long the players practiced each day did not affect the cortical map. But the age at which they had been introduced to their muse did: the younger the child when she took up an instrument, the more cortex she devoted to playing it.

Like other circuits formed early in life, the ones for music endure. Wayne State's Chugani played the guitar as a child, then gave it up. A few years ago he started taking piano lessons with his young daughter. She learned easily, but he couldn't get his fingers to follow his wishes. Yet when Chugani recently picked up a guitar, he found to his delight that "the songs are still there," much like the muscle memory for riding a bicycle.

Math and logic: At UC Irvine, Gordon Shaw suspected that all higher-order thinking is characterized by similar patterns of neuron firing. "If you're working with little kids," says Shaw, "you're not going to teach them higher mathematics or chess. But they are interested in and can process music." So Shaw and Frances Rauscher gave 19 preschoolers piano or singing lessons. After eight months, the researchers found, the children "dramatically improved in spatial reasoning," compared with children given no music lessons, as shown in their ability to work mazes, draw geometric figures and copy patterns of two-color blocks. The mechanism behind the "Mozart effect" remains murky, but Shaw suspects that when children exercise cortical neurons by listening to classical music, they are also strengthening circuits used for mathematics. Music, says the UC team, "excites the inherent brain patterns and enhances their use in complex reasoning tasks."

Emotions: The trunk lines for the circuits controlling emotion are laid down before birth. Then parents take over. Perhaps the strongest influence is what psychiatrist Daniel Stern calls attunement—whether caregivers "play back a child's inner feelings." If a baby's squeal of delight at a puppy is met with a smile and hug, if her excitement at seeing a plane overhead is mirrored, circuits for these emotions are reinforced. Apparently, the brain uses the same pathways to generate an emotion as to respond to one. So if an emotion is reciprocated, the electrical and chemical signals that produced it are reinforced. But if emotions are repeatedly met with indifference or a clashing response—Baby is proud of building a skyscraper out of Mom's best pots, and Mom is terminally annoyed—those circuits become confused and fail to strengthen. The key here is "repeatedly": one dismissive harrumph will not scar a child for life. It's the pattern that counts, and it can be very powerful: in one of Stern's studies, a baby whose mother never matched her level of excitement became extremely passive, unable to feel excitement or joy.

Experience can also wire the brain's "calm down" circuit, as Daniel Goleman describes in his best-selling "Emotional Intelligence." One father gently soothes his crying infant, another drops him into his crib; one mother hugs the toddler who just skinned her knee, another screams "It's your own stupid fault!" The first responses are attuned to the child's distress; the others are wildly out of emotional sync. Between 10 and 18 months, a cluster of cells in the rational prefrontal cortex is busy hooking up to the emotion regions. The circuit seems to grow into a control switch, able to calm agitation by infusing reason into emotion. Perhaps parental soothing trains this circuit, strengthening the neural connections that form it, so that the child learns how to calm herself down. This all happens so early that the effects of nurture can be misperceived as innate nature.

Stress and constant threats also rewire emotion circuits. These circuits are centered on the amygdala, a little almond-shaped structure deep in the brain whose job is to scan incoming sights and sounds for emotional content. According to a wiring diagram worked out by Joseph LeDoux of New York University, impulses from eye and ear reach the amygdala before they get to the rational, thoughtful neocortex. If a sight, sound or experience has proved painful before—Dad's drunken arrival home was followed by a beating—then the amygdala floods the circuits with neurochemicals before the higher brain knows what's happening. The more often this pathway is used, the easier it is to trigger: the mere memory of Dad may induce fear. Since the circuits can stay excited for days, the brain remains on high alert. In this state, says neuroscientist Bruce Perry of Baylor College of Medicine, more circuits attend to nonverbal cues—facial expressions, angry noises—that warn of impending danger. As a result, the cortex falls behind in development and has trouble assimilating complex information such as language.

Movement: Fetal movements begin at 7 weeks and peak between the 15th and 17th weeks. That is when regions of the brain controlling movement start to wire up. The critical period lasts a while: it takes up to two years for cells in the cerebellum, which controls posture and movement, to form functional circuits. "A lot of organization takes place using information gleaned from when the child moves about in the world," says William Greenough of the University of Illinois. "If you restrict activity you inhibit the formation of synaptic connections in the cerebellum." The child's initially spastic movements send a signal to the brain's motor cortex; the more the arm, for instance, moves, the stronger the circuit, and the better the brain will become at moving the arm intentionally and fluidly. The window lasts only a few years: a child immobilized in a body cast until the age of 4 will learn to walk eventually, but never smoothly.

The Musical Brain

SKILL: Music

LEARNING WINDOW: 3 to 10 years

WHAT WE KNOW: String players have a larger area of their sensory cortex dedicated to the fingering digits on their left hand. Few concert-level performers begin playing later than the age of 10. It is much harder to learn an instrument as an adult.

WHAT WE CAN DO ABOUT IT: Sing songs with children. Play structured, melodic music. If a child shows any musical aptitude or interest, get an instrument into her hand early.

THERE ARE MANY MORE CIRCUITS to discover, and many more environmental influences to pin down. Still, neuro labs are filled with an unmistakable air of optimism these days. It stems from a growing understanding of how, at the level of nerve cells and molecules, the brain's circuits form. In the beginning, the brain-to-be consists of only a few advance scouts breaking trail: within a week of conception they march out of the embryo's "neural tube," a cylinder of cells extending from head to tail. Multiplying as they go (the brain adds an astonishing 250,000 neurons per minute during gestation), the neurons clump into the brain stem which commands heartbeat and breathing, build the little cerebellum at the back of the head which controls posture and movement, and form the grooved and rumpled cortex wherein thought and perception originate. The neural cells are so small, and the distance so great, that a neuron striking out for what will be the prefrontal cortex migrates a distance equivalent to a human's walking from New York to California, says developmental neurobiologist Mary Beth Hatten of Rockefeller University.

Only when they reach their destinations do these cells become true neurons. They grow a fiber called an axon that carries electrical signals. The axon might reach only to a neuron next door, or it might wend its way clear across to the other side of the brain. It is the axonal connections that form the brain's circuits. Genes determine the main highways along which axons travel to make their connection. But to reach particular target cells, axons follow chemical cues strewn along their path. Some of these chemicals attract: this way to the motor cortex! Some repel: no, *that* way to the olfactory cortex. By the fifth month of gestation most axons have reached their general destination. But like the prettiest girl in the bar, target cells attract way more suitors—axons—than they can accommodate.

How does the wiring get sorted out? The baby neurons fire electrical pulses once a minute, in a fit of what Berkeley's Shatz calls auto-dialing. If cells fire together, the target cells "ring" together. The target cells then release a flood of chemicals, called trophic factors, that strengthen the incipient connections. Active neurons respond better to trophic factors than inactive ones, Barbara Barres of Stanford University reported in October. So neurons that are quiet when others throb lose their grip on the target cell. "Cells that fire together wire together," says Shatz.

The same basic process continues after birth. Now, it is not an auto-dialer that sends signals, but stimuli from the senses. In experiments with rats, Illinois's Greenough found that animals raised with playmates and toys and other stimuli grow 25 percent more synapses than rats deprived of such stimuli.

Rats are not children, but all evidence suggests that the same rules of brain development hold. For decades Head Start has fallen short of the high hopes invested in it: the children's IQ gains fade after about three years. Craig Ramey of the University of Alabama suspected the culprit was timing: Head Start enrolls 2-, 3- and 4- year-olds. So in 1972 he launched the Abecedarian Project. Children from 20 poor families were assigned to one of four groups: intensive early education in a day-care center from about 4 months to age 8, from 4 months to 5 years, from 5 to 8

SCHOOLS

Why Do Schools Flunk Biology?

BY LYNNELL HANCOCK

BIOLOGY IS A STAPLE AT MOST American high schools. Yet when it comes to the biology of the students themselves—how their brains develop and retain knowledge—school officials would rather not pay attention to the lessons. Can first graders handle French? What time should school start? Should music be cut? Biologists have some important evidence to offer. But not only are they ignored, their findings are often turned upside down.

Force of habit rules the hallways and classrooms. Neither brain science nor education research has been able to free the majority of America's schools from their 19th-century roots. If more administrators were tuned into brain research, scientists argue, not only would schedules change, but subjects such as foreign language and geometry would be offered to much younger children. Music and gym would be daily requirements. Lectures, work sheets and rote memorization would be replaced by hands-on materials, drama and project work. And teachers would pay greater attention to children's emotional connections to subjects. "We do more education research than anyone else in the world," says Frank Vellutino, a professor of educational psychology at State University of New York at Albany, "and we ignore more as well."

Plato once said that music "is a more potent instrument than any other for education." Now scientists know why. Music, they believe, trains the brain for higher forms of thinking. Researchers at the University of California, Irvine, studied the power of music by observing two groups of preschoolers. One group took piano lessons and sang daily in chorus. The other did not. After eight months the musical 3-year-olds were expert puzzlemasters, scoring 80 percent higher than their playmates did in spatial intelligence—the ability to visualize the world accurately.

This skill later translates into complex math and engineering skills. "Early music training can enhance a child's ability to reason," says Irvine physicist Gordon Shaw. Yet music education is often the first "frill" to be cut when school budgets shrink. Schools on average have only one music teacher for every 500 children, according to the National Commission on Music Education.

Then there's gym—another expendable hour by most school standards. Only 36 percent of schoolchildren today are required to partic-

The Windows of Opportunity

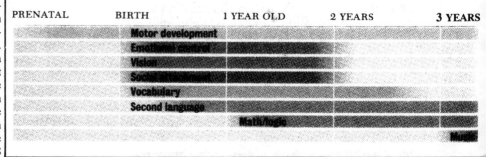

PRENATAL	BIRTH	1 YEAR OLD	2 YEARS	3 YEARS
	Motor development			
	Emotional control			
	Vision			
	Social attachment			
	Vocabulary			
	Second language			
		Math/logic		
				Music

ipate in daily physical education. Yet researchers now know that exercise is good not only for the heart. It also juices up the brain, feeding it nutrients in the form of glucose and increasing nerve connections—all of which make it easier for kids of all ages to learn. Neuroscientist William Greenough confirmed this by watching rats at his University of Illinois at Urbana-Champaign lab. One group did nothing. A second exercised on an automatic treadmill. A third was set loose in a Barnum & Bailey obstacle course requiring the rats to perform acrobatic feats. These "supersmart" rats grew "an enormous amount of gray matter" compared with their sedentary partners, says Greenough.

Of course, children don't ordinarily run such gantlets; still, Greenough believes, the results are significant. Numerous studies, he says, show that children who exercise regularly do better in school.

The implication for schools goes beyond simple exercise. Children also need to be more physically active in the classroom, not sitting quietly in their seats memorizing subtraction tables. Knowledge is retained longer if children connect not only aurally but emotionally and physically to the material, says University of Oregon education professor Robert Sylwester in "A Celebration of Neurons."

Good teachers know that lecturing on the American Revolution is far less effective than acting out a battle. Angles and dimensions are better understood if children chuck their work sheets and build a complex model to scale. The smell of the glue enters memory through one sensory system, the touch of the wood blocks another, the sight of the finished model still another. The brain then creates a multidimensional mental model of the experience—one easier to retrieve. "Explaining a smell," says Sylwester, "is not as good as actually smelling it."

Scientists argue that children are capable of far more at younger ages than schools generally realize. People obviously continue learning their whole lives, but the optimum "windows of opportunity for learning" last until about the age of 10 or 12, says Harry Chugani of Wayne State University's Children's Hospital of Michigan. Chugani determined this by measuring the brain's consumption of its chief energy source, glucose. (The more glucose it uses, the more active the brain.) Children's brains, he observes, gobble up glucose at twice the adult rate from the age of 4 to puberty. So young brains are as primed as they'll ever be to process new information. Complex subjects such as trigonometry or foreign language shouldn't wait for puberty to be introduced. In fact, Chugani says, it's far easier for an elementary-school child to hear and process a second language—and even speak it without an accent. Yet most U.S. districts wait until junior high to introduce Spanish or French— after the "windows" are closed.

Reform could begin at the beginning. Many sleep researchers now believe that most teens' biological clocks are set later than those of their fellow humans. But high school starts at 7:30 a.m., usually to accommodate bus schedules. The result can be wasted class time for whole groups of kids. Making matters worse, many kids have trouble readjusting their natural sleep rhythm. Dr. Richard Allen of Johns Hopkins University found that teens went to sleep at the same time whether they had to be at school by 7:30 a.m. or 9:30 a.m. The later-to-rise teens not only get more sleep, he says; they also get better grades. The obvious solution would be to start school later when kids hit puberty. But at school, there's what's obvious, and then there's tradition.

Why is this body of research rarely used in most American classrooms? Not many administrators or school-board members know it exists, says Linda Darling-Hammond, professor of education at Columbia University's Teachers College. In most states, neither teachers nor administrators are required to know much about how children learn in order to be certified. What's worse, she says, decisions to cut music or gym are often made by noneducators, whose concerns are more often monetary than educational. "Our school system was invented in the late 1800s, and little has changed," she says. "Can you imagine if the medical profession ran this way?"

With Pat Wingert *and* Mary Hager *in Washington*

Circuits in different regions of the brain mature at different times. As a result, different circuits are most sensitive to life's experiences at different ages. Give your children the stimulation they need when they need it, and anything's possible. Stumble, and all bets are off.

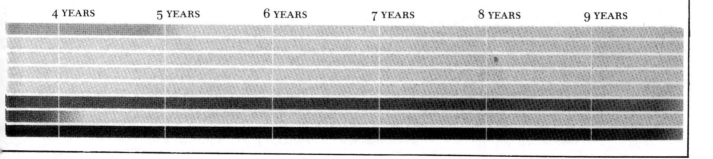

| 4 YEARS | 5 YEARS | 6 YEARS | 7 YEARS | 8 YEARS | 9 YEARS |

years, or none at all. What does it mean to "educate" a 4-month-old? Nothing fancy: blocks, beads, talking to him, playing games such as peek-a-boo. As outlined in the book "Learningames,"* each of the 200-odd activities was designed to enhance cognitive, language, social or motor development. In a recent paper, Ramey and Frances Campbell of the University of North Carolina report that children enrolled in Abecedarian as preschoolers still scored higher in math and reading at the age of 15 than untreated children. The children still retained an average IQ edge of 4.6 points. The earlier the children were enrolled, the more enduring the gain. And intervention after age 5 conferred no IQ or academic benefit.

All of which raises a troubling question. If the windows of the mind close, for the most part, before we're out of elementary school, is all hope lost for children whose parents did not have them count beads to stimulate their math circuits, or babble to them to build their language loops? At one level, no: the brain retains the ability to learn throughout life, as witness anyone who was befuddled by Greek in college only to master it during retirement. But on a deeper level the news is sobering. Chil-dren whose neural circuits are not stimulated before kindergarten are never going to be what they could have been. "You want to say that it is never too late," says Joseph Sparling, who designed the Abecedarian curriculum. "But there seems to be something very special about the early years."

And yet . . . there is new evidence that certain kinds of intervention can reach even the older brain and, like a microscopic screwdriver, rewire broken circuits. In January, scientists led by Paula Tallal of Rutgers University and Michael Merzenich of UC San Francisco described a study of children who have "language-based learning disabilities"—reading problems. LLD affects 7 million children in the United States. Tallal has long argued that LLD arises from a child's inability to distinguish short, staccato sounds—such as "d" and "b." Normally, it takes neurons in the auditory cortex something like .015 second to respond to a signal from the ear, calm down and get ready to respond to the next sound; in LLD children, it takes five to 10 times as long. (Merzenich speculates that the defect might be the result of chronic middle-ear infections in infancy: the brain never "hears" sounds clearly and so fails to draw a sharp auditory map.) Short sounds such as "b" and "d" go by too fast—.04 second—to process. Unable to associate sounds with letters, the children develop reading problems.

The scientists drilled the 5- to 10-year-olds three hours a day with computer-produced sound that draws out short consonants, like an LP played too slow. The result: LLD children who were one to three years behind in language ability improved by a full two years after only four weeks. The improvement has lasted. The training, Merzenich suspect, redrew the wiring diagram in the children's auditory cortex to process fast sounds. Their reading problems vanished like the sounds of the letters that, before, they never heard.

Such neural rehab may be the ultimate payoff of the discovery that the experiences of life are etched in the bumps and squiggles of the brain. For now, it is enough to know that we are born with a world of potential—potential that will be realized only if it is tapped. And that is challenge enough.

With MARY HAGER

*Joseph Sparling and Isabelle Lewis (226 pages. Walker. $8.95).

Vygotsky's Theory:
The Importance of Make-Believe Play

Laura E. Berk

Laura E. Berk is professor of psychology at Illinois State University. Her research interests include Vygotsky's theory on children's private, or self-directed, speech and applications of Vygotsky's ideas to education. She has been NAEYC's Research in Review editor for the past three years.

In most theories of cognition and cognitive development, the social and the cognitive make contact only minimally. Rather than being truly joined and interactive, they are viewed as separate domains of functioning. At best, the social world is a surrounding context for cognitive activity, not an integral part of it. Early childhood educators have a long tradition of regarding what the young child knows as personally rather than socially constructed—a tradition that follows from the massive contributions of Piaget's cognitive-developmental theory to our field.

The ideas of the Russian developmental psychologist Lev Vygotsky, who early in this century forged an innovative theory granting great importance to social and cultural experience in development, have gained increasing visibility over the past decade. In Vygotsky's ([1933] 1978) sociocultural theory, the "mind extends beyond the skin" and is inseparably joined with other minds (Wertsch 1991, p. 90). Social experience shapes the ways of thinking and interpreting the world available to individuals. And language plays a crucial role in a socially formed mind because it is our primary avenue of communication and mental contact with others, it serves as the major means by which social experience is represented psychologically, and it is an indispensable tool for thought (Vygotsky [1934] 1987). A basic premise of Vygotsky's theory is that all uniquely human, higher forms of mental activity are jointly constructed and transferred to children through dialogues with other people.

Vygotsky's ideas are stimulating a host of new ways to educate young children that emphasize opportunities for discussion and joint problem solving. A central Vygotskian concept that has played a formative role in these efforts is the *zone of proximal development,* which refers to a range of tasks that the child cannot yet handle alone but can accomplish with the help of adults and more skilled peers. As children engage in cooperative dialogues with more mature partners, they internalize the language of these interactions and use it to organize their independent efforts in the same way (Berk 1992). According to sociocultural theory, supportive guidance from adults that creates a *scaffold* for children's learning is essential for their cognitive development. Such communication sensitively adjusts to children's momentary progress, offering the necessary assistance for mastery while prompting children to take over more responsibility for the task as their skill increases (Wood & Middleton 1975; Wood 1989). Furthermore, *cooperative learning*—in which small groups of peers at varying levels of competence share responsibility and resolve differences of opinion as they work toward a common goal—also fosters cognitive maturity (Forman 1987; Tudge 1992).

The vast literature on children's play reveals that its contributions to child development can be looked at from diverse vantage points.

These Vygotskian ideas about teaching and learning have largely been implemented in academically relevant early childhood contexts, such as literacy, mathematics, and science (Moll 1990; Forman, Minick, & Stone 1993); but a close look at Vygotsky's writings reveals that they recur as major themes in his view of play. Although Vygotsky's works contain only a brief 12-page statement about play, his discussion is provocative, innovative, and ahead of his time. In accord with his emphasis on social experience and language as vital forces in cognitive development, Vygotsky ([1933] 1978) emphasized representational play—the make-believe that blossoms during the preschool years and evolves into the games with rules that dominate middle childhood. Vygotsky

Nancy P. Alexander

Social and cultural experience are very important in development. Children learn a lot through the social activity we call play, where communication—the sharing of information and ideas—abounds. This is especially true if children are of different backgrounds and ages. Of course children learn a lot through discussions and conversations with adults, too.

broadly influential zone of proximal development within which *children advance themselves* to ever-higher levels of psychological functioning. Consequently, Vygotsky's theory has much to say to teachers about the importance of promoting make-believe in preschool and child care programs.

Development and significance of make-believe play

Vygotsky began his consideration of the importance of play by suggesting that if we can identify its defining features, we can gain insight into its functions in development. To isolate the distinctiveness of play, Vygotsky explored characteristics regarded by other theorists as central to playful activity and found them wanting. For example, the common assumption that play is pleasurable activity is not specific to play. Many other experiences, such as eating a favorite treat, being granted the undivided attention of a parent, or listening to an exciting story, are at least as gratifying and sometimes more so than is play. Furthermore, certain playful experiences—games that can be won or lost—are not pure fun for the child when they result in disappointing outcomes.

A second way of understanding play is to highlight its symbolic features, as Piaget ([1945] 1951) did in his characterization of make-believe as a means through which children practice representational schemes. Yet symbolism is another feature that is not exclusive to play. Both Piaget and Vygotsky noted that it also characterizes language, artistic, and literacy activities during the preschool years.

Vygotsky concluded that play has two critical features that, when combined, describe its uniqueness and shed light on its role in development. First, all representational play *creates an imaginary situation* that permits the child to grapple with unrealizable desires. Vygotsky pointed out that fantasy play first appears at a time when children must learn to postpone gratification of impulses and accept the fact that certain desires will remain unsatisfied. During the second year, caregivers begin to insist that toddlers delay gratification (e.g., wait for a turn) and acquire socially approved behaviors involving safety, respect for property, self-care (e.g., washing hands), and everyday routines (e.g., putting toys away) (Gralinski & Kopp 1993).

The creation of an imaginary situation in play, however, has often been assumed to be a way in which children attain immediate fulfillment of desires not satisfied in real life. Vygotsky pointed out that this commonly held belief is not correct. A second feature of all representational play is that it *contains rules for behavior* that children must follow to successfully act out the play scene. Games that appear in the late preschool period and flourish during the school years are clearly

accorded fantasy play a prominent place in his theory, granting it the status of a "leading factor in development" (p. 101), as the following frequently quoted remarks reveal:

Play creates a zone of proximal development in the child. In play, the child always behaves beyond his average age, above his daily behavior; in play it is as though he were a head taller than himself. As in the focus of a magnifying glass, play contains all developmental tendencies in a condensed form and is itself a major source of development. (p. 102)

As we discuss Vygotsky's theory and the research stimulated by it, we will see that he situated play squarely within a sociocultural context. Adults and peers scaffold young children's play, nurturing the transition to make-believe and its elaboration throughout the preschool years. Representational play serves as a unique, rule based. Even the simplest imaginative situations created by very young children proceed in accord with social rules, although the rules are not laid down in advance. For example, a child pretending to go to sleep follows the rules of bedtime behavior. Another child, imagining himself to be a father and a doll to be a child, conforms to the rules of parental behavior. Yet a third child playing astronaut observes the rules of shuttle launch and space walk. Vygotsky ([1933] 1978) concluded, "Whenever there is an imaginary situation, there are rules" (p. 95). A child cannot behave in an imaginary situation without rules.

These attributes of play—an imaginary situation governed by rules—provide the key to its role in development. According to Vygotsky, play supports the emergence of two complementary capacities: (a) the ability to separate thought from actions and objects, and (b) the capacity to renounce impulsive action in favor of deliberate, self-regulatory activity.

Separating thought from actions and objects

In creating an imaginary situation, children learn to act not just in response to external stimuli but also in accord with internal ideas. Infants and very young children, Vygotsky ([1933] 1978) explained, are reactive beings; momentary perceptions trigger their behavior. A baby who sees an attractive toy grabs for it without delay. A toddler runs after a ball that has rolled into the street without considering consequences. "[I]n play, things lose their determining force. *The child sees one thing but acts differently in relation to what he sees. Thus, a condition is reached in which the child begins to act independently of what he sees*" (p. 97).

Just how does imaginative play help children separate thought from the surrounding world and rely on ideas to guide behavior? According to Vygotsky, the object substitutions that characterize make-believe are crucial in this process. When children use a stick to represent a horse or a folded blanket to represent a sleeping baby, their relation to reality is dramatically changed. The stick becomes a pivot for separating the meaning "horse" from a real horse; similarly, the blanket becomes a pivot

for distinguishing the meaning "baby" from a real baby. This adjustment in thinking occurs because children change the substitute object's real meaning when they behave toward it in a pretend fashion.

Vygotsky emphasized that young children have difficulty severing thinking—or the meaning of words—from objects; they do so only gradually. Indeed, such research reveals that object substitutions become more flexible as children get older. In early pretense, toddlers use only realistic objects—for example, a toy telephone to talk into or a cup to drink from. Around age 2, children use less realistic toys, such as a block for a telephone receiver. Sometime during the third year, children can imagine objects and events without any direct support from the real world, as when they say to a play partner, "I'm calling Susie on the phone!" while pretending to dial with their hands or without acting out the event at all. By this time, a play symbol no longer has to resemble the object or behavior for which it stands (Bretherton et al. 1984; Corrigan 1987).

According to Vygotsky ([1930] 1990), in helping children separate meaning from objects, the pretending of early childhood serves as vital preparation for the much later development of abstract thought, in which symbols are manipulated and propositions evaluated with-

© Nancy P. Alexander

Vygotsky concluded that play has two critical features that, when combined, describe its uniqueness and shed light on its role in development. First, all representational play creates an imaginary situation that permits the child to grapple with unrealizable desires. Games that appear in the late preschool period and flourish during the school years are clearly rule based. Even the simplest imaginative situations created by very young children proceed in accord with social rules, although the rules are not laid down in advance. A second feature of all representational play is that it contains rules for behavior that children must follow to successfully act out the play scene.

Psychoanalytic theorists have highlighted the emotionally integrative function of pretense, pointing out that anxiety-provoking events—such as a visit to the doctor's office or discipline by a parent—are likely to be revisited in the young child's play but with roles reversed so that the child is in command and compensates for unpleasant experiences in real life.

---

out referring to the real world. And in detaching meaning from behavior, make-believe also helps teach children to choose deliberately from among alternative courses of action. This capacity to think in a planful, self-regulatory fashion is also strengthened by the rule-based nature of play, as we will see in the following section.

Renouncing impulsive action

Vygotsky pointed out that the imaginative play of children contains an interesting paradox. In play, children do what they most feel like doing, and to an outside observer, the play of preschoolers appears free and spontaneous. Nevertheless, play constantly demands that children act against their immediate impulses because they must subject themselves to the rules of the make-believe context or the game they have chosen to play. According to Vygotsky ([1933] 1978), free play is not really "free"; instead, it requires self-restraint—willingly following social rules. As a result, in play the young child displays many capacities that "will become her basic level of real action and morality" in the future (p. 100). By enacting rules in make-believe, children come to better understand social norms and expectations and strive to behave in ways that uphold them. For example, a child occupying the role of parent in a household scene starts to become dimly aware of parental responsibilities in real situations and gains insight into the rule-governed nature of the parent–child relationship (Haight & Miller 1993).

When we look at the development of play from early to middle childhood, the most obvious way in which it changes is that it increasingly emphasizes rules. The greater stress on the rule-oriented aspect of play over time means that children gradually become more conscious of the goals of their play activities. Vygotsky ([1933] 1978) summarized, "The development from games with an overt imaginary situation and covert rules to games with overt rules and a covert imaginary situation outlines the evolution of children's play" (p. 96). From this perspective, the fantasy play of the preschool years is essential for further development of play in middle childhood—specifically, for movement toward game play, which provides additional instruction in setting goals, regulating one's behavior in pursuit of those goals, and subordinating action to rules rather than to impulse—in short, for becoming a cooperative and productive member of society. Play, in Vygotsky's theory, is the preeminent educational activity of early childhood.

Impact of imaginative play on development

Was Vygotsky correct in stating that make-believe serves as a zone of proximal development, supporting the emergence and refinement of a wide variety of competencies? A careful examination of his theory reveals that the benefits of play are complex and indirect; they may take years to be realized (Nicolopoulou 1991). Still, considerable support exists for Vygotsky's view that play contributes to the development of a diverse array of capacities in the young child.

Sociodramatic play, the coordinated and reciprocal make-believe with peers that emerges around age 2½ and increases rapidly until age 4 to 5, has been studied thoroughly. Compared to social nonpretend activities (such as drawing or putting together puzzles), during social pretend activities, preschoolers' interactions last longer, show more involvement, draw larger numbers of children into the activity, and are more cooperative (Connolly, Doyle, & Reznick 1988). When we consider these findings from the standpoint of Vygotsky's emphasis on the social origins of cognition, it is not surprising that preschoolers who spend more time at sociodramatic play are advanced in general intellectual development and show an enhanced ability to understand the feelings of others. They are also seen as more socially competent by their teachers (Burns & Brainerd 1979; Connolly & Doyle 1984).

Piaget underscored the opportunities that make-believe affords for exercising symbolic schemes.

A growing body of research reveals that make-believe play strengthens a variety of specific mental abilities. For example, it promotes memory. In a study in which 4- and 5-year-olds were asked either to remember a set of toys or to play with them, the play condition produced far better recall. Rather than just naming or touching the objects (strategies applied in the "remember" condition), children who played with the toys engaged in many spontaneous organizations and uses of the materials that enabled them to memorize effortlessly (Newman 1990). In this way, play may provide a vital foundation for more sophisticated memory strategies mastered during middle childhood that depend on establishing meaningful relationships among to-be-remembered information. Other research confirms that opportunities to engage in fantasy play promote children's storytelling and story memory (Saltz, Dixon, & Johnson 1977; Pellegrini & Galda 1982).

Language is also greatly enriched by play experiences. As children engage in play talk, they often correct one another's errors, either directly or by demonstrating acceptable ways to speak. For example, in enacting a telephone conversation, one kindergartner said, "Hello, come to my house please." Her play partner quickly countered with appropriate telephone greeting behavior: "No, first you've get to say 'what are you doing?'" (Ervin-Tripp 1991, p. 90). Vocabulary expands during make-believe as children introduce new words they have heard during recent experiences. One 4-year-old playing nurse remarked to an agemate, "I'm going to give you a temperature" (p. 90). Although her first use of the term was not correct, active experimentation increases the chances that she will notice more about the context in which "temperature" is applied and move toward correct usage. Furthermore, the linguistic skills required to express different points of view, resolve disputes, and persuade peers to collaborate in play are numerous. Play offers an arena in which all facets of conversational dialogue can be extended.

Make-believe also fosters young children's ability to reason about impossible or absurd situations—a finding highly consistent with Vygotsky's emphasis that fantasy play assists children in separating meanings from the objects for which they stand. A repeated finding in the cognitive development literature is that through much of early and middle childhood, thinking is tied to the here and now—to concrete reality; but under certain conditions, young children attain a "theoretical" mode of reasoning.

Consider the following syllogism: All cats bark. Rex is a cat. Does Rex bark? Researchers had a group of 4- to 6-year-olds act out problems like this with toys. A second group of children were told that the events were taking place on a pretend planet rather than on Earth. A contro! group merely listened and answered the question. Children in the two "play" conditions gave more theoretical than factual responses and were also able to justify their answers with theoretical ideas—for example, "In the story, cats bark, so we can pretend they bark" (Dias & Harris 1988, 1990). Entering the pretend mode seems to enable children to reason with contrary facts as if they were true—findings that provide striking verification of Vygotsky's ([1933] 1978) assumption that in play, the child is well "beyond his average age, above his daily behavior" (p. 102).

Finally, young children who especially enjoy pretending or who are given encouragement to engage in fantasy play score higher on tests of imagination and creativity. When children use play objects in novel ways, the objects seem to stimulate the discovery of new relationships and enhance children's ability to think flexibly and inventively (Dansky 1980; Pepler & Ross 1981).

In sum, fantasy play contributes to social maturity and the construction of diverse aspects of cognition. For people who have questioned whether play activities, so indigenous and absorbing to children, must be curbed in favor of more "productive" activities or whether play constitutes a powerful zone of proximal development, the findings just reviewed clearly grant play a legitimate and fruitful place in children's lives.

Scaffolding children's make-believe play

The Piagetian view, dominant for the past three decades, claims that make-believe emerges spontaneously when children become capable of representational thought. Piaget and his followers assumed that children lack the cognitive competencies to share play symbols with others—both adults and peers—until well into the preschool period (e.g., Fein 1981). Not until recently have researchers seriously addressed the social context of children's play experiences. Their findings challenge the notion that fantasy play is an unprompted phenomenon arising solely from tendencies within the child. Instead, new evidence suggests that make-believe, like other higher mental functions, is the product of social collaboration.

Adult–child play

Twenty-four-month-old Elizabeth is being carried upstairs for a diaper change by her mother.

Elizabeth: My going Sherman Dairy. (Sherman Dairy is the family's favorite dessert restaurant.)

Mother: You're going to Sherman Dairy?

Elizabeth: Yeah.

Mother: Is Andrew the cook? (Andrew is a 4-year-old friend who is playing with Elizabeth's sister.)

Elizabeth: Yep. (Pause) *My* cook.

Mother: (Putting Elizabeth on the changing table and beginning to change her) You're the cook? You can cook with your dishes, right? Do you have some pots and pans?

Elizabeth: Yep. (Adapted from Haight & Miller 1993, p. 46)

In the play sequence above, 2-year-old Elizabeth initiates a make-believe scenario in which a trip upstairs for a diaper change is transformed into a journey to buy

---

All theorists recognize that pretense permits children to become familiar with social role possibilities in their culture, providing important insights into the link between self and wider society.

ice cream. Her mother encourages her to expand the imaginative theme and act it out with toys. The play episode is elaborated and sustained as her mother asks questions that help Elizabeth clarify her intentions and think of new ideas.

Vygotskian-based research on play emphasizes that make-believe is, from its beginnings, a social activity (El'konin 1966; Garvey 1990). In Western industrialized societies, play first appears between caregivers and children; children initially learn pretense and games under the supportive guidance of experts. From these interactions, children acquire the communicative conventions, social skills, and representational capacities that permit them to carry out make-believe on their own.

In the most extensive study of caregiver scaffolding of make-believe, Haight and Miller (1993) followed the development of pretend play at home of nine middle-class children between 1 and 4 years of age. Social make-believe was common across the entire age span, consuming from 68 to 75% of children's total pretend time. Furthermore, mothers were the children's principal play partners until 3 years of age. By age 4, children played approximately the same amount with their mothers as they did with other children (siblings and peers). Children's pretending with mothers, however, was not caused by a lack of child playmates at the youngest ages. Several investigations reveal that 1- and 2-year-olds who have fairly continuous access to other children prefer to play with their mothers (Dunn & Dale 1984; Miller & Garvey 1984). These findings confirm the Vygotskian view that play with caregivers gradually gives way to play with peers as children's competence increases.

Further evidence that caregivers teach toddlers to pretend stems from Haight and Miller's observation that at 12 months, make-believe was fairly one sided; almost all play episodes were initiated by mothers. From age 2 on, when pretending was better established, mothers and children displayed mutual interest in getting make-believe started; half of pretend episodes were initiated by each. At all ages, mothers typically followed the child's lead and elaborated on the child's contribution. Thus, although pretense was first introduced to 12-month-olds by their mothers, it quickly became a joint activity in which both partners participated actively in an imaginative dialogue and in which the adult gradually released responsibility to the child for creating and guiding the fantasy theme.

Children's object substitutions during make-believe are also largely traceable to episodes in which their mothers showed them how to engage in object renaming or suggested a pretend action to the child (Smolucha 1992). By the time their children are 2 years old, mothers talk more about nonexistent fantasy objects, a change that may prompt children to widen the range of object substitutions in their play (Kavanaugh, Whittington, & Cerbone 1983). Furthermore, many parents and early childhood teachers surround children with toys designed to stimulate pretend themes. By offering an array of objects specialized for make-believe, caregivers communicate to children that pretense is a valued activity and maximize opportunities to collaborate with them in integrating props into fantasy scenes.

Consequences of supportive caregiver–child play

In their longitudinal study, Haight and Miller (1993)

carefully examined the play themes of mother–child pretense and found that it appeared to serve a variety of functions, including communicating feelings, expressing and working through conflicts, enlivening daily routines, and teaching lessons. These diverse social uses of caregiver–child play suggest that adult support and expansion of preschoolers' make-believe should facilitate all the developmental outcomes of play already discussed, although as yet, no systematic research on the topic exists.

Accumulating evidence does show that children's make-believe play with their mothers is more sustained and complex than is their solitary make-believe play. One- to 3-year-olds engage in more than twice as much make-believe while playing with mothers than while playing alone. In addition, caregiver support leads early make-believe to include more elaborate themes (Dunn & Wooding 1977; O'Connell & Bretherton 1984; Zukow 1986; Slade 1987; Fiese 1990; Tamis-LeMonda & Bornstein 1991; Haight & Miller 1993; O'Reilly & Bornstein 1993). In line with Vygotsky's zone of proximal development, very young children, for whom make-believe is just emerging, act more competently when playing with a mature partner than they otherwise would. In Haight and Miller's study, suggestive evidence emerged that mother–child play promotes effective child–child play. Children whose mothers ranked high in pretending when their children were 1 year old ranked high in peer play at 4 years. And children of the most enthusiastic and imaginative parents were among the most highly skilled preschool pretenders.

Critical features of adult–child play

Although mother–child play has been granted considerable research attention, a search of the literature revealed no studies of teachers' participation in young children's play. Yet evidence on the effect of adult–child play suggests that it is vital for teachers in preschool and child care programs to engage in joint play with children.

Teachers' effective playful involvement with children requires early childhood environments that are developmentally appropriate. Especially important are generous adult–child ratios, a stable staff that relates to children sensitively and responsively, and settings that are richly equipped to offer varied opportunities for make-believe. These factors are critical because they ensure that teachers have the necessary time, rapport, and play props to encourage children's imaginative contributions and to scaffold them toward social pretend play with peers.

At the same time, adults walk a fine line in making effective contributions to children's pretense. The power of adult–child play to foster development is undermined by communication that is too overpowering or one sided. Fiese (1990) found that maternal questioning, instructing, and intrusiveness (initiating a new activity unrelated to the child's current pattern of play) led to immature, simple exploratory play in young children. In contrast, turn taking and joint involvement in a shared activity resulted in high levels of pretense. Furthermore, adult intervention that recognizes children's current level of cognitive competence and builds on it is most

Vygotsky's special emphasis on the imaginative and rule-based nature of play adds an additional perspective to the viewpoints just mentioned—one that highlights the critical role of make-believe in developing reflective thoughts, as well as self-regulatory and socially cooperative behavior.

successful in involving children. Lucariello (1987) reported that when 24- to 29-month-olds were familiar with a play theme suggested by their mother, both partners displayed advanced levels of imaginative activity and constructed the scenario together. When the theme was unfamiliar, the mother took nearly total responsibility for pretense.

Promoting social pretend play with peers

At preschool, Jason joins a group of children in the block area for a space shuttle launch. "That can be our control tower," he suggests to Vance, pointing to a corner by a bookshelf.

"Wait, I gotta get it all ready," states Lynette, who is still arranging the astronauts (two dolls and a teddy bear) inside a circle of large blocks, which represent the rocket.

"Countdown!" Jason announces, speaking into a small wooden block, his pretend walkie-talkie.

"Five, six, two, four, one, blastoff!" responds Vance, commander of the control tower.

Lynette makes one of the dolls push a pretend button and reports, "Brrm, brrm, they're going up!" (Berk 1993, p. 311)

When pretending with peers, children make use of the many competencies they acquire through their play with adults. Yet pretend play with peers must also be responsive and cooperative to result in satisfying play experiences and to serve as a zone of proximal development in which children advance their skills and understanding. According to Göncü (1993), social play with peers requires *intersubjectivity*—a process whereby individuals involved in the same activity who begin with different perspectives arrive at a shared understanding. In the play episode just described, the children achieve a high level of intersubjectivity as they coordinate several roles in an elaborate plot and respond in a smooth, complementary fashion to each other's contributions.

The importance of intersubjectivity for peer social play is suggested by the work of several major theorists.

A basic premise of Vygotsky's theory is that all uniquely human, higher forms of mental activity are jointly constructed and transferred to children through dialogues with other people.

Piaget ([1945] 1951) notes that for children to play together, they must collectively construct play symbols. Likewise, Vygotsky ([1933] 1978) claimed that in pretense with peers, children jointly develop rules that guide social activity. And Parten (1932) labeled the most advanced form of peer social participation *cooperative play,* in which children orient toward a common goal by negotiating plans, roles, and divisions of labor.

Recent evidence indicates that intersubjectivity among peer partners increases substantially during the preschool years, as the amount of time children devote to sociodramatic play rises. Between 3 and 4-½ years, children engage in more extensions and affirmations of their partners' messages and fewer disagreements, assertions of their own opinions, and irrelevant statements during play (Göncü 1993). Interestingly, preschoolers have much more difficulty establishing a cooperative, shared framework in "closed-end" problem solving, in which they must orient toward a single correct solution to a task (Tudge & Rogoff 1987). Here again is an example of how children's competence during play is advanced compared to other contexts. By middle childhood, the social skills mastered during sociodramatic activities generalize to nonplay activities.

When we look at the features of harmonious child–child play, the relevance of warm, responsive adult communication for encouraging such play becomes even clearer. Even after sociodramatic play is well underway and adults have reduced their play involvement, teachers need to guide children toward effective relations with agemates. Observational evidence indicates that teachers rarely mediate peer interaction except when

For teachers who have always made sure that play is a central feature of the early childhood curriculum, Vygotsky's theory offers yet another justification for play's prominent place in programs for young children.

intense disagreements arise that threaten classroom order or children's safety. When teachers do step in, they almost always use directive strategies, in which they tell children what to do or say (e.g., "Ask Daniel if you can have the fire truck next") or solve the problem for them (e.g., "Jessica was playing with that toy first, so you can have a turn after her") (File 1993, p. 352).

A Vygotskian-based approach to facilitating peer interaction requires that teachers tailor their intervention to children's current capacities and use techniques that help children regulate their own behavior. To implement intervention in this way, teachers must acquire detailed knowledge of individual children's social skills—the type of information teachers typically gather only for the cognitive domain. When intervening, they need to use a range of teaching strategies because (like cognitive development) the support that is appropriate for scaffolding social development varies from child to child and changes with age. At times the adult might model a skill or give the child examples of strategies (e.g., "You could tell Paul, 'I want a turn'"). At other times, she might ask the child to engage in problem solving ("What could you do if you want a turn?") (File 1993, p. 356). In each instance, the teacher selects a level of support that best matches the child's abilities and momentary needs and then pulls back as the child acquires new social skills.

Vygotsky's ideas are stimulating a host of new ways to educate young children that emphasize opportunities for discussion and joint problem solving.

Children can be socialized into sociodramatic play by a variety of expert partners. In a recent comparison of the make-believe play of American and Mexican siblings, Farver (1993) found that American 3-½- to 7-year-olds tended to rely on intrusive tactics; they more often instructed, directed, and rejected their younger siblings' contributions. In contrast, Mexican children used more behaviors that gently facilitated—invitations to join, comments on the younger child's actions, suggestions, and positive affect. In this respect, Mexican older siblings were similar to American mothers in their scaffolding of play, a skill that appeared to be fostered by the Mexican culture's assignment of caregiving responsibilities to older brothers and sisters.

These findings suggest that multi-age groupings in early childhood programs offer additional opportunities to promote make-believe and that older siblings from ethnic-minority families may be particularly adept at such scaffolding—indeed, they may be as capable as adults! Because of their limited experience with the caregiving role and their more conflictual relationships with siblings, children from ethnic-majority families may need more assistance in learning how to play effectively with younger peers. In classrooms with a multicultural mix of children, children of ethnic minorities who are skilled at scaffolding can serve as models and scaffolders for agemates, showing them how to engage young children in pretense.

Conclusion

The vast literature on children's play reveals that its contributions to child development can be looked at from diverse vantage points. Psychoanalytic theorists have highlighted the emotionally integrative function of pretense, pointing out that anxiety-provoking events—

such as a visit to the doctor's office or discipline by a parent—are likely to be revisited in the young child's play but with roles reversed so that the child is in command and compensates for unpleasant experiences in real life. Piaget underscored the opportunities that make-believe affords for exercising symbolic schemes. And all theorists recognize that pretense permits children to become familiar with social role possibilities in their culture, providing important insights into the link between self and wider society.

Vygotsky's special emphasis on the imaginative and rule-based nature of play adds an additional perspective to the viewpoints just mentioned—one that highlights the critical role of make-believe in developing reflective thought as well as self-regulatory and socially cooperative behavior. For teachers who have always made sure that play is a central feature of the early childhood curriculum, Vygotsky's theory offers yet another justification for play's prominent place in programs for young children. For other teachers whose concern with academic progress has led them to neglect play, Vygotsky's theory provides a convincing argument for change—a powerful account of why pretense is the ultimate activity for nurturing early childhood capacities that are crucial for academic as well as later-life success.

References

Berk, L.E. 1992. Children's private speech: An overview of theory and the status of research. In *Private speech: From social interaction to self-regulation*, eds. R.M. Diaz, & L.E. Berk. 17–53. Hillsdale, NJ: Erlbaum.

Berk, L.E. 1993. *Infants, children, and adolescents*. Boston: Allyn & Bacon.

Have You Read These Articles?

Blau, R., A. Zavitkovsky, & D. Zavitkovsky. 1989. Play is . . . . *Young Children* 45 (1): 30–31.

Chenfeld, M.B. 1991. "Wanna play?" *Young Children* 46 (6): 4–6.

Elkind, D. 1988. From our president. Play. *Young Children* 43 (5): 2.

Myhre, S.M. 1993. Enhancing your dramatic-play area through the use of prop boxes. *Young Children* 48 (5): 6–11.

Nourot, P.M., & J.L. Van Hoorn. 1991. Research in review. Symbolic play in preschool and primary settings. *Young Children* 46 (6): 40–50.

Trawick-Smith, J. 1988. "Let's say you're the baby, OK?" Play leadership and following behavior of young children. *Young Children* 43 (5): 51–59.

You may obtain copies of these **or any other** *Young Children* articles.

• For articles **from the past 5 years,** contact the Institute for Scientific Information, 3501 Market St., Philadelphia, PA 19104; phone 215-386-0100; fax 215-386-6362.

• For articles **more than 5 years old,** send $5, your address, and the title of the article to NAEYC's Editorial Department.

Bretherton, I., B. O'Connell, C. Shore, & E. Bates. 1984. The effect of contextual variation on symbolic play: Development from 20 to 28 months. In *Symbolic play and the development of social understanding,* ed. I. Bretherton. 271–98. New York: Academic.

Burns, S.M., & C.J. Brainerd. 1979. Effects of constructive and dramatic play on perspective taking in very young children. *Developmental Psychology* 15: 512–21.

Connolly, J.A., & A.B. Doyle. 1984. Relations of social fantasy play to social competence in preschoolers. *Developmental Psychology* 20: 797–806.

Connolly, J.A., A.B. Doyle, & E. Reznick. 1988. Social pretend play and social interaction in preschoolers. *Journal of Applied Developmental Psychology* 9: 301–13.

Corrigan, R. 1987. A developmental sequence of actor-object pretend play in young children. *Merrill-Palmer Quarterly* 33: 87–106.

Dansky, J.L. 1980. Make-believe: A mediator of the relationship between play and associative fluency. *Child Development* 51: 576–79.

Dias, M.G., & P.L. Harris. 1988. The effect of make-believe play on deductive reasoning. *British Journal of Developmental Psychology* 6: 207–21.

Dias, M.G., & P.L. Harris. 1990. The influence of the imagination of reasoning by young children. *British Journal of Developmental Psychology* 8: 305–18.

Dunn, J., & N. Dale. 1984. I a daddy: 2-year-olds' collaboration in joint pretend with sibling and with mother. In *Symbolic play,* ed. I. Bretherton. 131–58. New York: Academic Press.

Dunn, J., & C. Wooding. 1977. Play in the home and its implications for learning. In *Biology of play,* eds. B. Tizard, & D. Harvey. 45–58. London: Heinemann.

El'konin, D. 1966. Symbolics and its functions in the play of children. *Soviet Education* 8: 35–41.

Ervin-Tripp, S. 1991. Play in language development. In *Play and the social context of development in early care and education,* eds. B. Scales, M. Almy, A. Nicolopoulou, & S. Ervin-Tripp. 84–97. New York: Teachers College Press.

Farver, J.M. 1993. Cultural differences in scaffolding pretend play: A comparison of American and Mexican mother–child and sibling–child pairs. In *Parent–child play,* ed. K. MacDonald. 349–66. Albany, NY: State University of New York Press.

Fein, G. 1981. Pretend play: An integrative review. *Child Development* 52: 1095–118.

Fiese, B. 1990. Playful relationships: A contextual analysis of mother–toddler interaction and symbolic play. *Child Development* 61: 1648–56.

File, N. 1993. The teacher as guide of children's competence with peers. *Child & Youth Care Forum* 22: 351–60.

Forman, E.A. 1987. Learning through peer interaction: A Vygotskian perspective. *Genetic Epistemologist* 15: 6–15.

Forman, E.A., N. Minick, & C.A. Stone. 1993. *Contexts for learning.* New York: Oxford University Press.

Garvey, C. 1990. *Play.* Cambridge, MA: Harvard University Press.

Göncü, A. 1993. Development of intersubjectivity in the dyadic play of preschoolers. *Early Childhood Research Quarterly* 8: 99–116.

Gralinski, J.H., & C.B. Kopp. 1993. Everyday rules for behavior: Mothers' requests to young children. *Developmental Psychology* 29: 573–84.

Haight, W.L., & P.J. Miller. 1993. *Pretending at home: Early development in a sociocultural context.* Albany, NY: State University of New York Press.

Kavanaugh, R.D., S. Whittington, & M.J. Cerbone. 1983. Mothers' use of fantasy in speech to young children. *Journal of Child Language* 10: 45–55.

Lucariello, J. 1987. Spinning fantasy: Themes, structure, and the knowledge base. *Child Development* 58: 434–42.

Miller, P., & C. Garvey. 1984. Mother–baby role play: Its origins in social support. In *Symbolic play,* ed. I. Bretherton. 101–30. New York: Academic.

Moll, L.C. 1990. *Vygotsky and education.* New York: Cambridge University Press.

Newman, L.S. 1990. Intentional versus unintentional memory in young children: Remembering versus playing. *Journal of Experimental Child Psychology* 50: 243–58.

Nicolopoulou, A. 1991. Play, cognitive development, and the social world. In *Play and the social context of development in early care and education,* eds. B. Scales, M. Almy, A. Nicolopoulou, & S. Ervin-Tripp. 129–42. New York: Teachers College Press.

O'Connell, B., & I. Bretherton. 1984. Toddler's play alone and with mother: The role of maternal guidance. In *Symbolic play,* ed. I. Bretherton. 337–68. New York: Academic.

O'Reilly, A.W., & M.H. Bornstein. 1993. Caregiver–child interaction in play. In *New directions for child development,* eds. M.H. Bornstein, & A.W. O'Reilly. 55–66. San Francisco: Jossey-Bass.

Parten, M. 1932. Social participation among preschool children. *Journal of Abnormal and Social Psychology* 27: 243–69.

Pellegrini, A.D., & L. Galda. 1982. The effects of thematic-fantasy play training on the development of children's story comprehension. *American Educational Research Journal* 19: 443–52.

Pepler, D.J., & H.S. Ross. 1981. The effect of play on convergent and divergent problem solving. *Child Development* 52: 1202–10.

Piaget, J. [1945] 1951. *Play, dreams, and imitation in childhood.* New York: Norton.

Saltz, E., D. Dixon, & J. Johnson. 1977. Training disadvantaged preschoolers on various fantasy activities: Effects on cognitive functioning and impulse control. *Child Development* 46: 367–80.

Slade, A. 1987. A longitudinal study of maternal involvement and symbolic play during the toddler period. *Child Development* 58: 367–75.

Smolucha, F. 1992. Social origins of private speech in pretend play. In *Private speech: From social interaction to self-regulation,* eds. R.M. Diaz, & L.E. Berk. 123–41. Hillsdale, NJ: Erlbaum.

Tamis-LeMonda, C.S., & M.H. Bornstein. 1991. Individual variation, correspondence, stability, and change in mother and toddler play. *Infant Behavior and Development* 14: 143–62.

Tudge, J.R.H. 1992. Processes and consequences of peer collaboration: A Vygotskian analysis. *Child Development* 63: 1364–79.

Tudge, J.R.H., & B. Rogoff. 1987. Peer influences on cognitive development: Piagetian and Vygotskian perspectives. In *Interaction in human development,* eds. M.H. Bornstein, & J.S. Bruner. 17–40. Hillsdale, NJ: Erlbaum.

Vygotsky, L.S. [1933] 1978. The role of play in development. In *Mind in society,* eds. M. Cole, V. John-Steiner, S. Scribner, & E. Souberman. 92–104. Cambridge, MA: Harvard University Press.

Vygotsky, L.S. [1934] 1987. Thinking and speech. In *The collected works of L.S. Vygotsky: Vol. 1. Problems of general psychology,* eds. R. Rieber & A.S. Carton, trans. N. Minick. 37–285. New York: Plenum.

Vygotsky, L.S. [1930] 1990. Imagination and creativity in childhood. *Soviet Psychology* 28: 84–96.

Wertsch, J.W. 1991. A sociocultural approach to socially shared cognition. In *Perspectives on socially shared cognition,* eds. L.B. Resnick, J. M. Levine, & S.D. Teasley. 85–100. Washington, D.C: American Psychological Association.

Wood, D.J. 1989. Social interaction as tutoring. In *Interaction in human development,* eds. M.H. Bornstein, & J.S. Bruner. 59–80. Hillsdale, NJ: Erlbaum.

Wood, D.J., & D. Middleton. 1975. A study of assisted problem solving. *British Journal of Psychology* 66: 181–91.

Zukow, P.G. 1986. The relationship between interaction with the caregiver and the emergence of play activities during the one-word period. *British Journal of Developmental Psychology* 4: 223–34.

How Do Infants Learn About the Physical World?

Renée Baillargeon

Renée Baillargeon is a Professor of Psychology at the University of Illinois at Urbana-Champaign. Address correspondence to Renée Baillargeon, Department of Psychology, University of Illinois, 603 East Daniel, Champaign, IL 61820.

Until recently, young infants were assumed to lack even the most fundamental of adults' beliefs about objects. This conclusion was based largely on analyses of young infants' performance in object manipulation tasks. For example, young infants were said to be unaware that an object continues to exist when masked by another object because they consistently failed tasks that required them to search for an object hidden beneath or behind another object.[1]

In time, however, researchers came to realize that young infants might fail tasks such as search tasks not because of limited physical knowledge, but because of difficulties associated with the planning and execution of action sequences. This concern led investigators to seek alternative methods for exploring young infants' physical knowledge, methods that did not depend on the manipulation of objects.

Infants' well-documented tendency to look longer at novel than at familiar events[2] suggested one alternative method for investigating young infants' beliefs about objects.

In a typical experiment, infants are presented with two test events: a possible and an impossible event. The possible event is consistent with the expectation or belief examined in the experiment; the impossible event, in contrast, violates this expectation. The rationale is that if infants possess the belief being tested, they will perceive the impossible event as more novel or surprising than the possible event, and will therefore look reliably longer at the impossible than at the possible event.

Using this violation-of-expectation method, investigators have demonstrated that even very young infants possess many of the same fundamental beliefs about objects as adults do.[3,4] For example, infants aged 2.5 to 3.5 months are aware that objects continue to exist when masked by other objects, that objects cannot remain stable without support, that objects move along spatially continuous paths, and that objects cannot move through the space occupied by other objects.

The repeated demonstration of sophisticated physical knowledge in early infancy has led investigators in recent years to focus their efforts in a new direction. In addition to exploring what infants know about the physical world, researchers have become interested in the question of how infants attain their physical knowledge.

My colleagues and I have begun to build a model of the development of young infants' physical reasoning.[5–7] The model is based on the assumption that infants are born not with substantive beliefs about objects (e.g., intuitive notions of impenetrability, continuity, or force), as researchers such as Spelke[8] and Leslie[9] have proposed, but with highly constrained mechanisms that guide the development of infants' reasoning about objects. The model is derived from findings concerning infants' intuitions about different physical phenomena (e.g., support, collision, and unveiling phenomena). Comparison of these findings points to two developmental patterns that recur across ages and phenomena. We assume that these patterns reflect, at least indirectly, the nature and properties of infants' learning mechanisms. In this review, I describe the patterns and summarize some of the evidence supporting them.

FIRST PATTERN: IDENTIFICATION OF INITIAL CONCEPT AND VARIABLES

The first developmental pattern is that, when learning about a new physical phenomenon, infants first form a preliminary, all-or-none concept that captures the essence of the phenomenon but few of its details. With further experience, this *initial concept* is progressively elaborated. Infants slowly identify discrete and continuous *variables* that are relevant to the initial concept, study the

From *Current Directions in Psychological Science*, October 1994, pp. 133-140. © 1994 by the American Psychological Society. Reprinted by permission of Cambridge University Press.

effects of those variables, and incorporate this accrued knowledge into their reasoning, resulting in increasingly accurate predictions over time.

To illustrate the distinction between initial concepts and variables, I summarize experiments on the development of young infants' reasoning about support phenomena (conducted with Amy Needham, Julie DeVos, and Helen Raschke), collision phenomena (conducted with Laura Kotovsky), and unveiling phenomena (conducted with Julie DeVos).[3,5–7]

Support Phenomena

Our experiments on young infants' ability to reason about support phenomena have focused on simple problems involving a box and a platform. Our results indicate that by 3 months of age, if not before, infants expect the box to fall if it loses all contact with the platform and to remain stable otherwise. At this stage, any contact between the box and the platform is deemed sufficient to ensure the box's stability. At least two developments take place between 3 and 6.5 months of age. First, infants become aware that the locus of contact between the box and the platform must be taken into account when judging the box's stability. Infants initially assume that the box will remain stable if placed either on the top or against the side of the platform. By 4.5 to 5.5 months of age, however, infants come to distinguish between the two types of contact and recognize that only the former ensures support. The second development is that infants begin to appreciate that the amount of contact between the box and the platform affects the box's stability. Initially, infants believe that the box will be stable even if only a small portion (e.g., the left 15%) of its bottom surface rests on the platform (see Fig. 1). By 6.5 months of age, however, infants expect the box to fall unless a significant portion of its bottom surface lies on the platform.

These results suggest the following developmental sequence. When learning about the support relation between two objects, infants first form an initial concept centered on a distinction between contact and no contact. With further experience, this initial concept is progressively revised. Infants identify first a discrete (locus of contact) and later a continuous (amount of contact) variable and incorporate these variables into their initial concept, resulting in more successful predictions over time.

Collision Phenomena

Our experiments on infants' reasoning about collision events have focused on simple problems involving a moving object (a cylinder that rolls down a ramp) and a stationary object (a large, wheeled toy bug resting on a track at the bottom of the ramp). Adults typically expect the bug to roll down the track when hit by the cylinder. When asked how far the bug will be displaced, adults are generally reluctant to hazard a guess (they are aware that the length

Fig. 1. Paradigm for studying infants' understanding of support phenomena. In both events, a gloved hand pushes a box from left to right along the top of a platform. In the possible event (top), the box is pushed until its leading edge reaches the end of the platform. In the impossible event (bottom), the box is pushed until only the left 15% of its bottom surface rests on the platform.

of the bug's trajectory depends on a host of factors about which they have no information). After observing that the bug rolls to the middle of the track when hit by a medium-size cylinder, however, adults readily predict that the bug will roll farther with a larger cylinder and less far with a smaller cylinder made of identical material.

Our experiments indicate that by 2.5 months of age, infants already possess clear expectations that the bug should remain stationary when not hit (e.g., when a barrier prevents the cylinder from contacting the bug) and should be displaced when hit. However, it is not until 5.5 to 6.5 months of age that infants are able to judge, after seeing that the medium cylinder causes the bug to roll to the middle of the track, that the bug should roll farther with the larger but not the smaller cylinder (see Fig. 2). Younger infants are not surprised to see the bug roll to the end of the track when hit by either the larger or the smaller cylinder, even though all three of the cylinders are simultaneously present in the apparatus, so that their sizes can be readily compared, and even though the infants have no difficulty remembering (as shown in other experiments) that the bug rolled to the middle of the track with the medium cylinder. These results suggest that prior to 5.5 to 6.5 months of age, infants are unaware that the size of the cylinder can be used to reason about the length of the bug's trajectory.

One interpretation of these findings is that when learning about collision events between a moving and a stationary object, infants first form an initial concept centered on a distinction between impact and no impact. With further experience, infants begin to identify variables that influence this initial concept. By 5.5 to 6.5 months of age, infants realize that the size of the moving object can be used to predict how far the stationary object will be displaced. After seeing how far a stationary object travels with a moving object of a given size, infants readily use this information to calibrate their predictions about how far the stationary object will travel with moving objects of different sizes.

Unveiling Phenomena

Our experiments on unveiling phenomena have involved problems in which a cloth cover is removed to reveal an object. Our results indicate that by 9.5 months of age, infants realize that the presence (or absence) of a protuberance in the cover signals the presence (or absence) of an object beneath the cover. Infants are surprised to see a toy retrieved from under a cover that lies flat on a surface, but not from under a cover that displays a marked protuberance.

At this stage, however, infants are not yet aware that the size of the protuberance in the cover can be used to infer the size of the object beneath the cover. When shown a cover with a small protuberance, they are not surprised to see either a small or a large toy retrieved from under the cover. Furthermore, providing infants with a reminder of the protuberance's size has no effect on their performance. In one experiment, for example, infants saw two identical covers placed side by side; both covers displayed a small protuberance (see Fig. 3). After a few seconds, a screen hid the left cover; the right cover remained visible to the right of the screen. Next, a hand reached behind the screen's right edge twice in succession, reappearing first with the cover and then with a small (possible event) or a large (impossible event) toy dog. Each dog was held next to the visible cover, so that their sizes could be readily compared. At 9.5 months of age, infants judged that either dog could have been hidden under the cover behind the screen. At 12.5 months of age, however, infants showed reliable surprise at the large dog's retrieval.

Together, these results suggest the following developmental sequence.

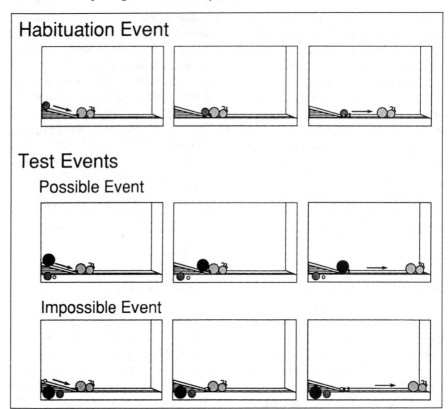

Fig. 2. Paradigm for studying infants' understanding of collision phenomena. First, infants are habituated to (i.e., repeatedly shown) an event in which a blue, medium-size cylinder rolls down a ramp and hits a bug resting on one end of a track; the bug then rolls to the middle of the track. In the test events, two new cylinders are introduced, and the bug now rolls to the end of the track. The cylinder used in the possible event is a yellow cylinder larger than the habituation cylinder; the cylinder used in the impossible event is an orange cylinder smaller than the habituation cylinder.

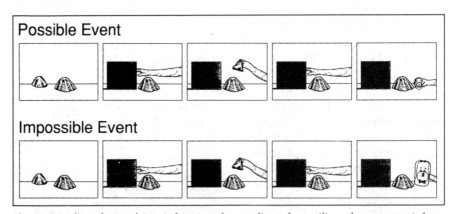

Fig. 3. Paradigm for studying infants' understanding of unveiling phenomena. Infants first see two identical covers placed side by side; both covers display a small protuberance. Next, a screen hides the left cover, and a gloved hand reaches behind the screen twice in succession, reappearing first with the cover and then with a small (top) or a large (bottom) toy dog. Each dog is held next to the visible cover, so that their sizes can be readily compared.

When learning about unveiling phenomena, infants first form an initial concept centered on a distinction between protuberance and no protuberance. Later on, infants identify a continuous variable that affects this concept: They begin to appreciate that the size of the protuberance in the cover can be used to infer the size of the object under the cover.

Comments

How can the developmental sequences described in this section be explained? As I mentioned earlier, we assume that these sequences reflect not the gradual unfolding of innate beliefs, but the application of highly constrained, innate learning mechanisms to available data. In this approach, the problem of explaining the age at which specific initial concepts and variables are understood is that of determining (a) what data—observations or manipulations—are necessary for learning and (b) when these data become available to infants.

For example, one might propose that 3-month-old infants have already learned that objects fall when released in midair because this expectation is consistent with countless observations (e.g., watching their caretakers drop peas in pots, toys in baskets, clothes in hampers) and manipulations (e.g., noticing that their pacifiers fall when they open their mouths) available virtually from birth. Furthermore, one might speculate that it is not until 6.5 months that infants begin to appreciate how much contact is needed between objects and their supports because it is not until this age that infants have available pertinent data from which to abstract such a variable. Researchers have reported that the ability to sit without support emerges at about 6 months of age; infants then become able to sit in front of tables (e.g., on a parent's lap or in a high chair) with their upper limbs and hands relieved from the encumbrance of postural maintenance and thus free to manipulate objects.[10] For the first time, infants may have the opportunity to deposit objects on tables and to note that objects tend to fall unless significant portions of their bottom surfaces are supported. In the natural course of events, infants would be unlikely to learn about such a variable from observation alone because caretakers rarely deposit objects on the edges of surfaces. There is no a priori reason, however, to assume that infants could not learn such a variable if given appropriate observations (e.g., seeing that a box falls when released on the edge of a platform). We are currently conducting a "teaching" experiment to investigate this possibility; our preliminary results are extremely encouraging and suggest that very few observations may be necessary to set infants on the path to learning.

SECOND PATTERN: USE OF QUALITATIVE AND QUANTITATIVE STRATEGIES

In the previous section, I proposed that when learning about a novel physical phenomenon, infants first develop an all-or-none initial concept and later identify discrete and continuous variables that affect this concept. The second developmental pattern suggested by current evidence concerns the strategies infants use when reasoning about continuous variables. Following the terminology used in computational models of everyday physical reasoning,[11] a strategy is said to be *quantitative* if it requires infants to encode and use information about absolute quantities (e.g., object A is "this" large or has traveled "this" far from object B, where "this" stands for some absolute measure of A's size or distance from B). In contrast, a strategy is said to be *qualitative* if it requires infants to encode and use information about relative quantities (e.g., object A is larger than or has traveled farther than object B). After identifying a continuous variable, infants appear to succeed in reasoning about the variable qualitatively before they succeed in doing so quantitatively.

To illustrate the distinction between infants' use of qualitative and quantitative strategies, I report experiments on the development of infants' ability to reason about collision phenomena (conducted with Laura Kotovsky), unveiling phenomena (conducted with Julie DeVos), and barrier phenomena.[3,5-7]

Collision Phenomena

As I explained earlier, 5.5- to 6.5-month-old infants are surprised, after observing that a medium-size cylinder causes a bug to roll to the middle of a track, to see the bug roll farther when hit by a smaller but not a larger cylinder. Such a finding suggests that by 5.5 to 6.5 months of age, infants are aware that the size of the cylinder affects the length of the bug's trajectory.

In these initial experiments, the small, medium, and large cylinders were placed side by side at the start of each event, allowing infants to compare their sizes directly. In subsequent experiments, only one cylinder was present in the apparatus in each test event. Under these conditions, 6.5-month-old infants were no longer surprised when the small cylinder caused the bug to roll to the end of the track; only older, 7.5-month-old infants showed surprise at this event.

Our interpretation of these results is that at 5.5 to 6.5 months of age, infants are able to reason about the cylinder's size only qualitatively: They can predict the effect of modifications in the cylinder's size only when they are able to encode such modifications in relative terms (e.g., "this cylinder is smaller than the one used in the last trial"). When infants are forced to encode and compare the absolute sizes of the cylinders, because the cylinders are never shown side by side, they fail the task. By 7.5 months of age, however, infants have already overcome this initial limitation and succeed in the task even when they must rely on their representation of the absolute size of each cylinder to do so.[12]

Unveiling Phenomena

In the previous section, I reported that 9.5-month-old infants are not surprised to see either a small or a large toy dog retrieved from under a cover with a small protuberance, even when a second, identical cover is present. Unlike these younger infants, however, 12.5-month-old infants *are* surprised when the large dog is brought into view. This last finding suggests that by 12.5 months of age, infants are aware that the size of the protuberance in a cloth cover can be used to infer the size of the object under the cover.

In our initial experiment, 12.5-month-old infants were tested with the second cover present to the right of the screen (see Fig. 3). Subsequent experiments were conducted without the second cover (see Fig. 4, top panel) or with the second cover placed to the left, rather than to the right, of the screen (see Fig. 4, bottom panel); in the latter condition,

infants could no longer compare in a single glance the size of the dog to that of the cover. Our results indicated that 12.5-month-old infants fail both of these conditions: They no longer show surprise when the large dog is retrieved from behind the screen. By 13.5 months of age, however, infants are surprised by the large dog's retrieval even when no second cover is present.

These results suggest that at 12.5 months of age, infants are able to reason about the size of the protuberance in the cover only qualitatively: They can determine which dog could have been hidden under the cover only if they are able to compare, in a single glance, the size of the dog with that of a second, identical cover (e.g., "the dog is bigger than the cover"). When infants are forced to represent the absolute

size of the protuberance in the cover, they fail the task. By 13.5 months of age, however, infants have already progressed beyond this initial limitation; they no longer have difficulty representing the absolute size of the protuberance and comparing it with that of each dog.

Barrier Phenomena

Our experiments on barrier phenomena have focused on problems involving a moving object (a rotating screen) and a stationary barrier (a large box). In the test events, infants first see the screen lying flat against the apparatus floor; the box stands clearly visible behind the screen. Next, the screen rotates about its distant edge, progressively occluding the box. At 4.5 months of age, infants expect the screen to stop when it reaches the occluded box; they are surprised if the screen rotates unhindered through a full 180° arc. However, infants are initially poor at predicting at what point the screen should encounter the box and stop. When shown a possible event in which the screen stops against the box (112° arc) and an impossible event in which the screen stops after rotating through the top 80% of the space occupied by the box (157° arc), 6.5-month-old infants give evidence of detecting this 80% violation, but 4.5-month-old infants do not: They judge both the 112° and the 157° stopping points to be consistent with the box's height and location (see Fig. 5).

In subsequent experiments, we examined whether 4.5-month-old infants would succeed in detecting the 80% violation if provided with a second, identical box. In one condition, this second box was placed to the right of and in the same frontoparallel plane as the box behind the screen (see Fig. 6, left panel). In the possible event, the screen stopped when aligned with the top of the second box; in the impossible event, the screen rotated past the top of the second box. In another condition,

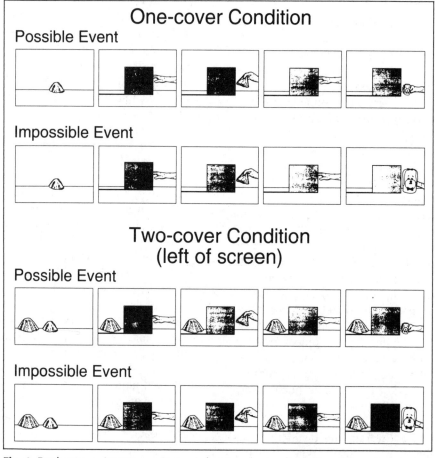

Fig. 4. Further experiments examining infants' understanding of unveiling phenomena. These test events are identical to those depicted in Figure 3 except that only one cover is used (top) or the second, identical cover is placed to the left of the screen (bottom). In the latter condition, infants can no longer compare in a single glance the height of the dog to that of the second cover.

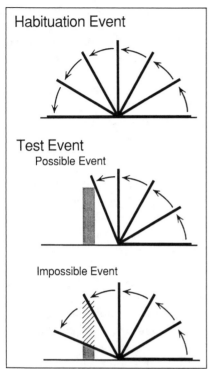

Habituation Event

Test Event
Possible Event

Impossible Event

Fig. 5. Paradigm for studying infants' understanding of barrier phenomena. Infants are first habituated to a screen that rotates through a 180° arc, in the manner of a drawbridge. Next, a large box is placed behind the screen. In the possible event, the screen stops when it encounters the box (112° arc); in the impossible event, the screen stops after rotating through the top 80% of the space occupied by the box (157° arc).

the second box was placed to the right of but slightly in front of the box behind the screen (see Fig. 6, right panel). In this condition, the screen rotated past the top of the second box in each test event. The infants succeeded in detecting the 80% violation in the first but not the second condition.

These results suggest that at 4.5 months of age, infants are able to reason about the box's height and location only qualitatively: They can predict the screen's stopping point only when they are able to rely on a simple alignment strategy (e.g., "the screen is aligned with the top of the visible box"). By 6.5 months of age, however, infants have already progressed beyond this point; they can use their representations of the occluded box's height and distance

from the screen to estimate, within broad limits, at what point the screen will stop.

Comments

How should the developmental sequences described in this section be explained? We think it unlikely that these sequences reflect the maturation of infants' general quantitative reasoning or information processing because the same pattern recurs at different ages for different phenomena. What phenomenon-specific changes could account for the findings reported here? At least two hypotheses can be advanced. On the one hand, it could be that when first reasoning about a continuous variable, infants either do not spontaneously encode information about this variable or do not encode this information swiftly enough or precisely enough for it to be of use in the tasks examined here (e.g., infants do not encode the size of the protuberance in the cover and hence are unable to judge which dog could have been hidden beneath it). On the other hand, infants could encode the necessary quantitative information but have difficulty accessing or processing this information in the context of deriving new and unfamiliar predictions (e.g., infants encode the protuberance's size and realize that they must compare it with that of the dog, but are thwarted in performing this comparison by the added requirement of having to retrieve part of the information from memory). Future research will no doubt help determine which, if either, of these hypotheses is correct.

CONCLUDING REMARKS

I have argued that in learning to reason about a novel physical phenomenon, infants first form an all-or-none concept and then add to this initial concept discrete and continuous variables that are discovered to affect the phenomenon. Further-

more, I have proposed that after identifying continuous variables, infants succeed in reasoning first qualitatively and only later quantitatively about the variables.

This sketchy description may suggest a rather static view of development in which accomplishments, once attained, are retained in their initial forms. Nothing could be further from the truth, however. Our data suggest that the variables infants identify evolve over time, as do the qualitative and quantitative strategies infants devise. When judging whether a box resting on a platform is stable, for example, infants initially focus exclusively on the amount of contact between the box's bottom surface and the platform, and as a consequence treat symmetrical and asymmetrical boxes alike. By the end of the 1st year, however, infants appear to have revised their definition of this variable to take into account the shape (or weight distribution) of the box.[5] Similarly, evidence obtained with the rotating-screen paradigm suggests that infants' quantitative reasoning continues to improve over time (e.g., 6.5-month-old infants can detect 80% but not 50% violations, whereas 8.5-month-old infants can detect both), as does their qualitative reasoning (e.g., 6.5-month-old infants will make use of a second box to detect a violation even if this second box differs markedly in color from the box behind the screen, whereas 4.5-month-old infants will not).[3]

The model of the development of infants' physical reasoning proposed here suggests many questions for future research. In particular, what are the innate constraints that guide this development? Are infants born with core principles (e.g., intuitive notions of impenetrability and continuity) that direct their interpretations of physical events? Or are infants, as I suggested earlier, equipped primarily with learning mechanisms that are capable, when applied to coherent sets of observations, of producing appropriate generalizations? What

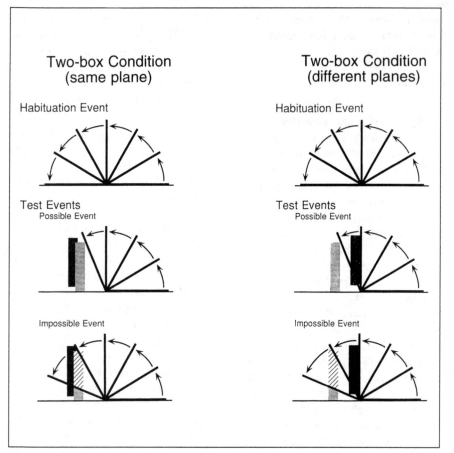

Fig. 6. Further experiments examining infants' understanding of barrier phenomena. These events are identical to those depicted in Figure 5 except that a second, identical box stands to the right of and in the same fronto-parallel plane as the box behind the screen (left) or to the right and in front of the box behind the screen (right).

evidence would help distinguish between these two views?

Some insight into this question may be gained by considering two predictions that proponents of the innate-principles view might offer. The first prediction is that when reasoning about a physical event involving a core principle, infants should succeed at about the same age at detecting all equally salient violations of the principle. Thus, researchers who deem impenetrability a likely core principle might expect infants who realize that a small object cannot pass through a gapless surface to understand also that a large object cannot pass through a small gap; provided that the two situations violate the impenetrability principle to a similar degree, they would be expected to yield identical interpretations. The second prediction is that infants should succeed at

about the same age at reasoning about different physical events that implicate the same underlying core principle. Thus, it might be proposed that infants who are successful at reasoning about objects' passage through gaps should be just as adept at reasoning about objects' entry into containers, because both phenomena would trigger the application of the impenetrability principle.

The model presented here departs systematically from the two predictions just described. First, the model predicts explicitly that when reasoning about physical events, infants succeed in detecting certain types of violations before others. Thus, in contrast to the innate-principles view, the model would expect infants to recognize that a small object cannot pass through a gapless surface before they recognize that a

large object cannot pass through a smaller gap. This developmental sequence would be cast in terms of the formation of an initial concept centered on a distinction between gap and no gap, followed by the identification of size as a continuous variable relevant to the phenomenon.

Second, the present model also diverges from the prediction that different physical events that implicate the same core principle should be understood at about the same age. The results summarized in the preceding sections and elsewhere[6]— such as the finding that unveiling tasks yield the same developmental patterns as rotating-screen tasks, but at much later ages—suggest that infants respond to physical events not in terms of abstract underlying principles, but in terms of concrete categories corresponding to specific ways in which objects behave or interact. Thus, according to our model, it would not be at all surprising to find that infants succeed in reasoning about gaps several weeks or months before they do containers; the order of acquisition of the two categories would be expected to depend on the content of infants' daily experiences. The model does not rule out the possibility that infants eventually come to realize that superficially distinct events—such as those involving gaps and containers, or rotating screens and cloth covers—can be deeply related; unlike the innate-principles view, however, the model considers such a realization a product, rather than a point of departure, of learning.

One advantage of the view that infants process physical events in terms of concrete categories focusing on specific types of interactions between objects is that this view makes it possible to explain incorrect interpretations that appear to stem from miscategorizations of events. Pilot data collected in our laboratory suggest that young infants expect a moving object to stop when it encounters a tall, thin box but not a short, wide box, even when the latter is considerably larger in volume than the former. We suspect that infants are led by the dominant vertical axis of the tall box to perceive it as a wall-like, immovable object, and hence categorize the event as an instance of a barrier phenomenon; in contrast, infants tend to view the wide box as a movable object, and hence categorize the event as an instance of a collision phenomenon, resulting in incorrect predictions.

The foregoing discussion highlighted several types of developmental sequences that would be anticipated in an innate-mechanisms view but not (without considerable elaboration) in an innate-principles view. To gain further insight into the nature and origins of these developmental sequences, we have adopted a dual research strategy. First, we are examining the development of infants' understanding of additional physical phenomena (e.g., gap, containment, and occlusion phenomena) to determine how easily these developments can be captured in terms of the patterns described in the model and to compare more closely the acquisition time lines of phenomena that are superficially distinct but deeply related. Second, as was alluded to earlier, we are attempting to teach infants initial concepts and variables to uncover what kinds of observations, and how many observations, are required for learning. We hope that the pursuit of these two strategies will eventually allow us to specify the nature of the learning mechanisms that infants bring to the task of learning about the physical world.

Acknowledgments—This research was supported by grants from the Guggenheim Foundation, the University of Illinois Center for Advanced Study, and the National Institute of Child Health and Human Development (HD-21104). I would like to thank Jerry DeJong, for his support and insight, and Susan Carey, Noam Chomsky, Judy DeLoache, Cindy Fischer, John Flavell, Laura Kotovsky, Brian Ross, and Bob Wyer, for many helpful comments and suggestions.

Notes

1. J. Piaget, The Construction of Reality in the Child (Basic Books, New York, 1954).

2. E.S. Spelke, Preferential looking methods as tools for the study of cognition in infancy, in Measurement of Audition and Vision in the First Year of Postnatal Life, G. Gottlieb and N. Krasnegor, Eds. (Ablex, Norwood, NJ, 1985).

3. R. Baillargeon, The object concept revisited: New directions in the investigation of infants' physical knowledge, in Visual Perception and Cognition in Infancy, C.E. Granrud, Ed. (Erlbaum, Hillsdale, NJ, 1993).

4. E.S. Spelke, K. Breinlinger, J. Macomber, and K. Jacobson, Origins of knowledge, Psychological Review, 99, 605–632 (1992).

5. R. Baillargeon, L. Kotovsky, and A. Needham, The acquisition of physical knowledge in infancy, in Causal Understandings in Cognition and Culture, G. Lewis, D. Premack, and D. Sperber, Eds. (Oxford University Press, Oxford, in press).

6. R. Baillargeon, A model of physical reasoning in infancy, in Advances in Infancy Research, Vol. 9, C. Rovee-Collier and L. Lipsitt, Eds. (Ablex, Norwood, NJ, in press).

7. R. Baillargeon, Physical reasoning in infants, in The Cognitive Neurosciences, M.S. Gazzaniga, Ed. (MIT Press, Cambridge, MA, in press).

8. E.S. Spelke, Physical knowledge in infancy: Reflections on Piaget's theory, in The Epigenesis of Mind: Essays on Biology and Cognition, S. Carey and R. Gelman, Eds. (Erlbaum, Hillsdale, NJ, 1991).

9. A.M. Leslie, ToMM, ToBy, and Agency: Core architecture and domain specificity, in Causal Understandings in Cognition and Culture, G. Lewis, D. Premack, and D. Sperber, Eds. (Oxford University Press, Oxford, in press).

10. P. Rochat and A. Bullinger, Posture and functional action in infancy, in Francophone Perspectives on Structure and Process in Mental Development, A. Vyt, H. Bloch, and M. Bornstein, Eds. (Erlbaum, Hillsdale, NJ, in press).

11. K.D. Forbus, Qualitative process theory, Artificial Intelligence, 24, 85–168 (1984).

12. This example focused exclusively on the size of the cylinder, but what of the distance traveled by the bug in each event? It seems likely that infants encode this information not in quantitative terms (e.g., "the bug traveled x as opposed to y distance"), but rather in qualitative terms, using as their point of reference the track itself (e.g., "the bug rolled to the middle of the track"), their own spatial position (e.g., "the bug stopped in front of me"), or the brightly decorated back wall of the apparatus (e.g., "the bug stopped in front of such-and-such section of the back wall").

Malnutrition, Poverty and Intellectual Development

Research into childhood nutrition reveals that a poor diet influences mental development in more ways than expected. Other aspects of poverty exacerbate the effects.

J. Larry Brown and Ernesto Pollitt

J. LARRY BROWN and ERNESTO POLLITT have collaborated for several years on the policy implications of childhood nutrition. Brown, director of the Center on Hunger, Poverty and Nutrition Policy at Tufts University, is also professor of nutrition and health policy at the School of Nutrition Science and Policy and at the School of Medicine. Pollitt is professor of human development in the department of pediatrics at the School of Medicine at the University of California, Davis, and is also a member of the Program of International Nutrition.

The prevalence of malnutrition in children is staggering. Globally, nearly 195 million children younger than five years are undernourished. Malnutrition is most obvious in the developing countries, where the condition often takes severe forms; images of emaciated bodies in famine-struck or war-torn regions are tragically familiar. Yet milder forms are more common, especially in developed nations. Indeed, in 1992 an estimated 12 million American children consumed diets that were significantly below the recommended allowances of nutrients established by the National Academy of Sciences.

Undernutrition triggers an array of health problems in children, many of which can become chronic. It can lead to extreme weight loss, stunted growth, weakened resistance to infection and, in the worst cases, early death. The effects can be particularly devastating in the first few years of life, when the body is growing rapidly and the need for calories and nutrients is greatest.

Inadequate nutrition can also disrupt cognition—although in different ways than were previously assumed. At one time, underfeeding in childhood was thought to hinder mental development solely by producing permanent, structural damage to the brain. More recent work, however, indicates that malnutrition can impair the intellect by other means as well. Furthermore, even in cases where the brain's hardware is damaged, some of the injury may be reversible. These new findings have important implications for policies aimed at bolstering achievement among underprivileged children.

Scientists first investigated the link between malnutrition and mental performance early in this century, but the subject did not attract serious attention until decades later. In the 1960s increasing evidence of undernutrition in industrial nations, including the U.S., along with continuing concern about severe malnutrition in developing countries, prompted researchers to examine the lasting effects of food deprivation. A number of studies in Latin America, Africa and the U.S. reported that on intelligence tests children with a history of malnutrition attained lower scores than children of similar social and economic status who were properly nourished. These surveys had various experimental limitations that made them inconclusive, but later research has firmly established that undernutrition in early life can limit long-term intellectual development.

Worry over Brain Damage

For many years, scientists considered the connection between nutrition and intellectual development to be straightforward. They assumed that poor nutrition was primarily a worry from conception to age two, when the brain grows to roughly 80 percent of its adult size. In this critical period, any degree of malnutrition was thought to halt the normal development of the brain and thereby to inflict severe, lasting damage.

Gradually, though, investigators recognized that the main-effect model, as we have termed this view, was too simplistic. For instance, the emphasis on

Effects of Poverty and Malnutrition: The Guatemalan Project

In a project carried out by the Institute of Nutrition of Central America and Panama, children and young adults in Guatemala who had received nutritional supplements in infancy were studied to assess the influence of early diet and poverty on later intellectual development. Subjects, including the boys at the right, were given a battery of cognitive tests. Individuals who regularly consumed a highly nutritious supplement called Atole before the age of two performed at about the same level on most tests, such as tests of vocabulary skills, regardless of economic status (*bottom left*). But the performance of those given a less nutritious supplement called Fresco varied with poverty level. Evidently, good nutrition early in life can help counteract the destructive effects of poverty on intellectual development. Among individuals who had more than two years of formal education, those who consumed Atole scored significantly higher than those who received Fresco (*bottom right*)—an indication that poor nutrition in infancy can subsequently undermine the benefits of schooling. —*E.P.*

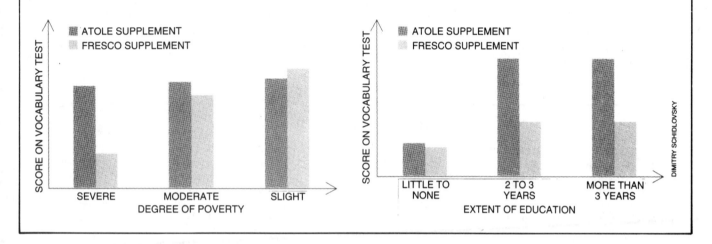

the first two years of life proved somewhat misguided. Brain growth in that period is not always terminated irreversibly in undernourished children. Rather it may be put on hold temporarily; if diet improves by age three or so, growth of the brain may continue at close to a normal pace. Conversely, injury to the brain can occur even when a child suffers malnutrition after the first two years of life—a sign that providing adequate nutrition throughout childhood is important to cognitive development. Focusing exclusively on the first two years of life is thus inadequate.

Furthermore, although severe underfeeding in infancy can certainly lead to irreparable cognitive deficits, as the main-effect model predicts, the model cannot fully account for intellectual impairment stemming from more moderate malnutrition. This flaw became apparent in the 1960s, when researchers showed that mildly undernourished children from middle- or upper-income families (whose nutrient deficits stemmed from medical conditions) did not suffer the same intellectual troubles as did mildly underfed children in impoverished communities. If poor nutrition impaired cognition only by structurally altering the brain, the two groups should have performed alike. Something

else had to be at work as well. In other words, factors such as income, education and other aspects of the environment could apparently protect children against the harmful effects of a poor diet or could exacerbate the insult of malnutrition.

No Energy to Learn

In the 1970s research by David A. Levitsky and Richard H. Barnes of Cornell University helped to clarify how malnutrition might hinder cognitive development in ways other than injuring the brain. Levitsky and Barnes studied rodents to examine the effects of malnutrition. Levitsky concluded that the malnourished animals performed less well on tests of mental ability, such as maze running, not because they suffered brain damage but mostly because, lacking energy, they essentially withdrew from contact with their peers and the objects in their environment. In addition, mothers coddled the less mobile infants, further hindering their growth and independence.

By extrapolation, the findings implied that cognitive disability in undernourished children might stem in part from reduced interaction with other people and with their surroundings. This fun-

damental shift in understanding produced increased optimism about the prospects for remediation; if decreased social interaction was partly at fault for cognitive impairment, then social and intellectual remediation could presumably help make up for deficits in the youngsters' experiences.

Although the new ideas were compelling, scientists did not have much human evidence to buttress the changing views. A recent study by one of us (Pollitt) and several collaborators adds strong support to the notion that malnutrition affects intellectual development in part by compromising many different aspects of a child's development. The research also provides added insight into how poor diet and economic adversities during childhood combine to impede intellectual functioning later in life. Pollitt's collaborators included Reynaldo Martorell of Emory University, Kathleen S. Gorman of the University of Vermont, Patrice L. Engle of California Polytechnic State University and Juan A. Rivera of the Institute of Nutrition of Central America and Panama.

The project was an extensive follow-up of Guatemalan children who were studied by other scientists many years earlier. In 1969 the Institute of Nutrition of Central America and Panama, with the help of various U.S. government agencies and private foundations, began a massive effort to examine the value of nutritional supplements in preventing the health problems of malnutrition. For eight years, residents of four villages in Guatemala received one of two nutritional supplements. When this phase of the study was being planned, researchers felt that protein was the most important nutrient missing from diets in developing countries. Therefore, project workers looked specifically at how children would respond to added protein in their diets. The mothers and children in two of the villages received a high-protein supplement called Atole (the Guatemalan name for a hot maize gruel). Inhabitants of the other two villages—who constituted the control group—received Fresco, a sweet, fruit-flavored drink, which contained no protein. Both supplements provided vitamins and minerals as well as calories; Fresco provided a third the calories of Atole.

When the study began, all pregnant women, and all children under the age of seven in the villages, were invited to participate. During the course of the study, children under seven who moved into the villages and women who became pregnant were also asked to join the project. More than 2,000 children and mothers participated between 1969 and 1977. Regular medical exams of the children revealed that both supplements improved the health of the participants, but Atole performed more impressively. For instance, in all four villages, the rate of infant mortality decreased. But in the villages that received Atole, infant mortality decreased 69 percent, whereas in villages receiving Fresco, the rate went down by just 24 percent. Also, only Atole improved growth rates in children under three.

Gains in Guatemala

In the follow-up study, carried out in 1988 and 1989, Pollitt and his colleagues visited the villages to assess how these early nutritional supplements affected intellectual development over

Avoiding Malnutrition

Opinions on what constitutes malnutrition—and recommendations for avoiding the problem—have been refined over time. Early studies considered lack of protein to be the most troubling deficiency in the diets of underfed children, especially in developing countries. Ingested protein is broken down into amino acids, which are then recycled to build the specific proteins needed by the individual at any given time. Proteins form many structural elements of the body and carry out most cellular processes. By the 1970s, though, investigators had begun to worry about calories, too. When faced with a lack of calories, the body breaks down amino acids for energy instead of using them to make new proteins.

In more recent years, nutrition research has emphasized that shortages of vitamins and minerals—particularly vitamin A, iodine and iron—contribute to significant health problems. Vitamin A is important for good vision, bone growth, tooth development and resistance to infection. Iodine, which tends to be scarce in developing countries, is needed for proper operation of the central nervous system. Iron is a constituent of hemoglobin, which transports oxygen to tissues. Iron also helps the body fight infections; levels of the mineral are low in diets of many poor children in the U.S. Hence, most investigators now believe malnutrition is best avoided by a diet that supplies enough protein, calories, vitamins and minerals to ensure normal growth. Some standard guidelines for optimal nutrition in children are listed below. —J.L.B.

DIETARY requirements for children can be met by eating several servings a day from each of five food categories.

RODICA PRATO

FOOD CATEGORY	SERVINGS PER DAY	SERVING SIZE*		
		AGE 1 TO 3 YEARS	4 TO 6 YEARS	7 TO 10 YEARS
WHOLE-GRAIN OR ENRICHED BREADS, CEREALS, RICE, PASTA	6 OR MORE	1/2 SLICE BREAD OR 1/4 CUP RICE OR NOODLES	1 SLICE BREAD OR 1/2 CUP RICE OR NOODLES	1 TO 2 SLICES BREAD OR 1/2 TO 1 CUP RICE OR NOODLES
VEGETABLES	3 OR MORE	2 TO 4 TBSP OR 1/2 CUP JUICE	1/4 TO 1/2 CUP OR 1/2 CUP JUICE	1/2 TO 3/4 CUP OR 1/2 CUP JUICE
FRUITS	2 OR MORE	2 TO 4 TBSP OR 1/2 CUP JUICE	1/4 TO 1/2 CUP OR 1/2 CUP JUICE	1/2 TO 3/4 CUP OR 1/2 CUP JUICE
LEAN MEATS, FISH, POULTRY, EGGS, NUTS, BEANS	2 OR MORE	1 TO 2 OZ	1 TO 2 OZ	2 TO 3 OZ
MILK AND CHEESE	3 TO 4	1/2 TO 3/4 CUP MILK OR 1/2 TO 3/4 OZ CHEESE	3/4 CUP MILK OR 3/4 OZ CHEESE	3/4 TO 1 CUP MILK OR 3/4 TO 1 OZ CHEESE

*Data from "Growth and Nutrient Requirements of Children." P. M. Queen and R. R. Henry in Pediatric Nutrition, edited by R. J. Grand et al. Butterworth, 1987

LISA BURNETT

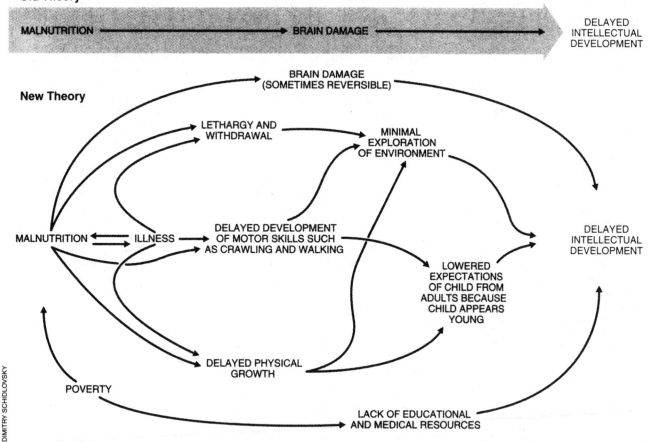

Old Theory

New Theory

MALNUTRITION HINDERS COGNITIVE ABILITIES through several interacting routes, according to recent research. Early models of malnutrition considered cognitive deficiencies to result only from damage to the brain (*top*). Now scientists also believe (*bottom*) that malnutrition alters intellectual development by interfering with overall health as well as the child's energy level, rate of motor development and rate of growth. In addition, low economic status can exacerbate all these factors, placing impoverished children at particular risk for cognitive impairment later in life.

the long term. More than 70 percent of the original participants—by then, ranging in age from 11 to 27 years old—agreed to take part in the follow-up. In particular, the team's analysis concentrated on the group of roughly 600 people who were exposed to Atole or Fresco both prenatally and for at least two years after birth. These adolescents and young adults took literacy, vocabulary and reading comprehension tests, a general knowledge exam, an arithmetic test and a standard nonverbal intelligence test. The researchers then determined how education and economic status (measured by house quality, father's occupation and mother's education) correlated with test scores.

The subjects who received Atole in early life performed significantly better on most tests of cognition than those who received Fresco. The strongest effects of Atole were observed among those at the low end of the social and economic ladder: these children performed as well as the more privileged

children in their villages [*see box, Effects of Poverty and Malnutrition: The Guatemalan Project*]. Atole thus served as a kind of social equalizer, helping children from low-income families achieve at the same level as their slightly more economically advantaged peers within the village. But the children of this study all lived in extreme poverty and did not perform at the same level as, say, a child from a middle-class household in a more prosperous area of Guatemala. Hence, adequate nutrition by itself could not fully compensate for the negative effects of poverty on intellectual growth.

In addition, Atole appeared to have increased the advantage of education. With every additional year of schooling, the differences in achievement between the adolescents who received Atole and those who consumed Fresco increased. This result indicates that poor nutrition can essentially negate some typical benefits of education. In separate

but related studies, Pollitt and his collaborators, working in Peru, and Sally Grantham-McGregor of the University of the West Indies, working in Jamaica, have demonstrated that learning capabilities are affected by how recently one has eaten. So breakfast every day before school is indeed important, particularly among children at risk for undernutrition.

The better long-term effects in the Atole group can largely be explained by the differences in the children's motor skills, physical growth, and social and emotional development. The youngsters who received Fresco in their early life suffered more physical disadvantages— a slower rate of growth and a slower rate of recovery from infection, for example—compared with those who received Atole. Because development was hindered, these children also learned to crawl and walk slightly later on average than the infants who received Atole. Pollitt and his colleagues speculate that for the infants who took Fresco, this limitation delayed the acquisition of the cognitive skills that children develop when they explore their social and physical environment.

Furthermore, because these undernourished toddlers remained small for their age, adults might have tended to treat them as if they were younger than their actual age. Such a response would very likely slow cognitive development, if the toddlers were not challenged—to talk, for instance—in the same way that other children their age were. Children who consumed Atole, in contrast, avoided malnutrition, grew up faster and were presumably exposed to more challenges in their social environment. Of course, the results do not rule out the possibility that the Fresco recipients may have suffered some degree of brain damage that impeded their later functioning. The findings, however, imply that additional factors, such as the child's social environment, played a major role as well.

The results in Guatemala are also consistent with the prevailing understanding of the interactions between poor nutrition, poverty and education. Nutritional supplements combat the effects of poverty, but only somewhat. A well-nourished child may be better able to explore the environment, but an impoverished community may offer little to investigate. And although schools can provide much of the stimulation children need, early malnutrition can undermine the overall value of education. Most important, this study demonstrates that poor nutrition in early childhood can continue to hinder intellectual performance into adulthood.

Because the early planners of the Guatemalan study chose to examine protein, these results emphasize protein's importance to intellectual growth. The supplements also included calories, vitamins and minerals; consequently, their role should be taken into account, but the arrangement of this particular study makes isolating the effects difficult.

Other work links essential vitamins and minerals to mental ability. For example, in one study in West Java, Pollitt and his colleagues showed a close association between iron-deficiency anemia (the most common consequence of malnutrition) and poor mental and motor skills in children. The researchers gave iron supplements to babies between 12 and 18 months old who were suffering from iron-deficiency anemia. The mineral significantly improved the infants' scores on mental and motor skills tests. Sadly, children with iron-deficiency anemia are more susceptible to lead poisoning, which produces its own set of neurological disorders that interfere with proper cognition. Consequently, poor children face a double jeopardy: they are more likely to be anemic and more likely to live where lead poisoning is widespread.

Correcting and Preventing Impairment

Studies such as the one in Guatemala have prompted many scholars, including one of us (Brown), to suggest that when the social and economic aspects of a child's environment cannot be easily changed, providing adequate nutrition during infancy and later will at least lessen the cognitive deficits engendered by poverty. Nutritional supplements cannot by themselves reverse the long-term adverse effects of earlier undernutrition, however. The ideal would be to provide additional support, such as tutoring, opportunities to develop new social skills and guidance from an involved parent or another concerned adult. Recent studies have shown that enriched education programs for children in economically impoverished communities can often ameliorate some of the problems associated with previous malnutrition.

To have the best chance at being useful, such intervention should be comprehensive and sustained. Most undernourished children face persistent challenges that can exacerbate the effects of underfeeding. They frequently live in areas with substandard schools and with little or no medical care. Their parents are often unemployed or work for very low wages. And the children may suffer from illnesses that sap energy needed for the tasks of learning.

On balance, it seems clear that prevention of malnutrition among young children remains the best policy—not only on moral grounds but on economic ones as well. The U.S., for example, invests billions of dollars in education, yet much of this money goes to waste when children appear at the school door intellectually crippled from undernutrition. The immediate expense of nutrition programs and broader interventions should be considered a critical investment in the future. Malnutrition alters educational preparedness and, later, workforce productivity, making it an unacceptable risk for its victims as well as for a nation's strength and competitiveness. Steps taken today to combat malnutrition and its intellectual effects can go a long way toward improving the quality of life—and productivity—of large segments of a population and thus of society as a whole.

Further Reading

NUTRITION AND BEHAVIOR. Edited by Janina R. Galler. Plenum Press, 1984.

THE EFFECTS OF IMPROVED NUTRITION IN EARLY CHILDHOOD: THE INSTITUTE OF CENTRAL AMERICA AND PANAMA (IN-CAP) FOLLOW-UP STUDY. Edited by Reynaldo Martorell and Nevin S. Scrimshaw. Supplement to *Journal of Nutrition*, Vol. 125, No. 4S; April 1995.

THE RELATIONSHIP BETWEEN UNDER-NUTRITION AND BEHAVIORAL DEVELOPMENT IN CHILDREN. Edited by Ernesto Pollitt. *Supplement to Journal of Nutrition*, Vol. 125, No. 8S; August 1995.

WHAT SHOULD CHILDREN LEARN?

PAUL GAGNON

Paul Gagnon is a senior research associate at the School of Education at Boston University, and a former director of the Fund for the Improvement and Reform of Schools and Teaching of the U.S. Department of Education. He is the author of two books on the teaching of history in high schools.

Can the wishes of two Presidents, Republican and Democratic, of most governors, of several Congresses, and of up to 80 percent of the American public and teachers simply be ignored? So it seems. Over the past five years all of them have called for national academic standards, to make schools stronger and more equal. But their will has been frustrated by the century-old habits of American educators unable to conceive of excellence and equity co-existing in the schools most children have to attend. This makes a depressing story, but some of it needs telling if those children are to see a happy ending. For to succeed where national efforts failed, state and local school leaders, teachers, parents, and citizens need to understand what they are up against, what has to be done differently, and how much is at stake.

They can begin by recognizing, and tolerating no longer, the vast inertia of an educational establishment entrenched in many university faculties of education; in well-heeled interest associations, with their bureaucracies, journals, and conventions; in hundreds of research centers and consulting firms; in federal, state, and local bureaucracies; in textbook-publishing houses and the aggressive new industries of educational technology and assessment. On the whole this establishment is well-meaning, and it is not monolithic, all of one mind. But its mainstream, trained and engrossed in the means rather than the academic content of education, instinctively resists any reform that starts with content and then lets it shape everything else—most certainly the means.

Starting school reform by first deciding what every child should learn strikes most people as only common sense. But to many American educators, it spells revolutionary change. The standards strategy for school reform would give subject-matter teachers and scholars, and the educated public, unprecedented power to spur genuine change—change far deeper than questions of school choice, methods, or management. Means and management are not the problem. The overused business analogy breaks down: business first decides the content of its product; means follow. But educators, unwilling to focus on subject matter, have never decided what content everyone should know; the curriculum stays frozen, incoherent and unequal. For more than a decade American citizens have wanted high, common standards—the only new idea for their schools in a century. But to get them, they will have to work around the establishment, and overturn the status quo.

The first step toward change was taken in 1983, when the National Commission on Excellence in Education delivered a ringing wake-up call: "If an unfriendly foreign power had attempted to impose on America the mediocre educational performance that exists today, we might well have viewed it as an act of war." The commission's report, *A Nation at Risk*, told us that other countries' schools were doing better in both quality and equality of learning—and ours were losing ground on each count. In the commission's words, "a rising tide of mediocrity" belied our democratic promise that "all, regardless of race or class or economic status, are entitled to a fair chance and to the tools for developing their individual powers of mind and spirit to the utmost."

A Nation at Risk gave rise to the standards strategy for school improvement, talk or the avoidance of which has preoccupied American educators ever since. It said that all high school students, regardless of background or vocational prospects, needed a common core curriculum of four years of English, three years each of mathematics, science, and social studies, and a semester of computer science. The college-bound should add two years of foreign language. In the early 1980s only 13.4 percent of our high school graduates had taken the first four of those "new basics." Adding the computer semester dropped the percentage all the way to 2.7, and adding foreign language made it 1.9. "Mediocrity" was a mild word for what was going on. But the public paid attention: many states and districts raised their core academic requirements, over the objections of experts who declared that dropout rates would soar, for minorities most of all.

By 1990, the National Center for Education Statistics found, 39.8 percent of high school graduates had taken the recommended years of English, mathematics, science, and social studies; 22.7 percent added the computer semester; 17.3 percent added both computers and the foreign language. Instead of rising, the dropout rate for African-Americans declined, and for Hispanics remained roughly stable. The percentage of African-American students taking the required years of academic subjects rose from 10.1 to 41.1; for Hispanics it rose from 6.3 to 32.7. "Top-down" recommendations, with state and local implementation, had made a difference, and they continue, albeit at a slower rate, to do so.

The glass, however, is still at best half full. And by comparison with the democratization of public schools in other countries, it is well under half empty. Our 25 percent dropout rate means that the roughly 40 percent of high school graduates in 1990 who got the recommended classes made up only 30 percent of all young people of that age. In 1991, in two school systems at opposite ends of the earth, about two thirds of the corresponding Japanese and French age groups completed markedly more-demanding academic programs, which included foreign languages. In both countries about half the students were in programs combining technical and liberal education. Even disregarding foreign languages, relatively few of our young people graduate from academic programs that are as rigorous as those abroad. For fully equivalent programs, a generous estimate of American completion would be 15 percent—about a quarter of the French and Japanese completion rate.

We used to say—and too many educators still say—that we cannot compare our schools with those of other countries, because they educate only an elite and we try to educate everybody. Untrue for thirty years, this is now the opposite of the truth. They educate the many, and we the few. To our shame, a disadvantaged child has a better chance for an equal and rigorous education, and whatever advancement it may bring, in Paris or Copenhagen than in one of our big cities.

Comparing curricula makes us look bad enough, but what is behind the course titles on student transcripts? Are American courses as substantial as those abroad? To make them so, President George Bush and the nation's governors launched a movement to set national standards for course content at meetings in Charlottesville, Virginia, in 1989. Goal Three of their statement insisted that course content be academically "challenging," comparable to that in the best schools here and overseas, and—for equity—that all students be offered such content and be expected to master it. Polls showed overwhelming public support, even for a national curriculum.

> Had we looked overseas after midcentury, we could have learned from both our allies and our enemies in the Second World War. But we did not and still do not. Those most reluctant to look abroad are the promoters of giddy educational fixes that no foreign country would take seriously, from subjecting schools to the "free market" all the way to killing off academic disciplines in favor of "issue-based inquiry."

Shortly after, Congress set up a National Council on Education Standards and Testing, to "advise on the desirability and feasibility of national standards and tests." In its report of January, 1992, the council recommended both. National content standards, it said ought to "define what students should know and be able to do" in English, geography, history, mathematics, and science, "with other subjects to follow." A core of common content was needed to "promote educational equity, to preserve democracy and enhance the civic culture, and to improve economic competitiveness." It should set high expectations, not minimal competencies; it should provide focus and direction, not a national curriculum.

The ball was handed off to the U.S. Department of Education, which in turn funded privately based consortia of scholars and teachers to decide what was most worth learning in each major subject. The stage was set to open equal opportunities for learning, to temper the curricular chaos of 15,000 school districts, so that children would no longer be entirely at the mercy of where or to whom they were born. Some of us in the Department of Education were sure it could be done. We were wrong. The department itself never decided how the standards strategy ought to work, or how to explain it to others. Last year four of the national projects it had commissioned—in the arts, civics, geography, and history—issued their documents. (Science and foreign-language projects are still under way. A math project had been separately completed in 1991.) After spending more than $900,000, the English project had been defunded for nonperformance, its professional associations unable to do for our language and literature what other nations have done for theirs. (One sub-committee solemnly voted that the phrase "standard English" be replaced by "privileged dialect.") Only the civics document earned countrywide respect. The others met with disbelief and complaint over their length and extravagant demands. The American-history standards set off an ideological conflict that is still boiling, an issue for presidential candidates at campaign stops. (For an examination of the disappointing standards for world history, see "Botched Standards.")

A year after the standards projects reported, the national version of standards-based reform is dead of multiple wounds, some self-inflicted, others from our culture wars, still others from congressional antipathy to any federal initiative, and most from American educators who have long resisted establishing a common core of academic learning. Recovery now depends on the states' choosing their own standards. But where a well-funded nationwide effort collapsed, how can states step in and do it right? Are we as a people ready to apply the standards of our very best schools, public and private, to all the others, and reform a system that is generally mediocre and shamefully unequal? A century of avoidance says no.

THE TEN
AND THE NINE

THE idea that democratic education requires a rigorously academic core for every student is not new. The report of the illustrious Committee of Ten, published in 1894, forcefully articulated it, calling for an established academic curriculum for all high school students, *whether or not they were going to college.* Italics are needed, for the committee was falsely accused in its time of caring only for the college-bound, and thus of being elitist and anti-democratic. This line is still taken by educators who have not read the report.

The story of the Ten's defeat and the triumph of progressive education's dumbed-down version of John Dewey's ideas, which reads eerily like the failure of the national-standards movement today, is best told in Richard Hofstadter's *Anti-Intellectualism in American Life,* which won the Pulitzer Prize in 1964. Chaired by Charles William Eliot, the president of Harvard, the Committee of Ten was made up of six university scholars (several had taught in secondary schools), three high school principals, including the head of the Girls' High School in Boston, and William T. Harris, the U.S. Commissioner of Education. The common core they advocated required four years of foreign language and English language and literature, three to four years of math and science, and two to four years of history. Young Americans taking on the profession of citizen, they said, needed a demanding curriculum, not the "feeble and scrappy" courses offered in too many high schools. This was doubly important for "school children who have no expectation of going to college," so that they might have at maturity "a salutary influence" upon the affairs of the country.

The report could have been written today. It anticipated the progressive pedagogical agenda and our latest "innovations" as well. It decried the "dry and lifeless system of instruction by text-book." Facts alone were repellent; schooling was for "the invaluable mental power which we call the judgment." It deplored mere coverage. To reach a common core of essentials, less was more: "select the paramount." The committee argued for active inquiry in original sources, studies in depth, individual and group projects, seminars, debates and re-enactments, field trips, museum work, mock legislatures and conventions. All possible teaching aids should be used: engravings, photographs, maps, globes, and the "magic lantern." To make time, school hours needed to be longer and more flexible.

For the new curriculum the Ten urged that history, civil government, and geography be taught as one. They wanted history and English "intimately connected," with constant cross-referencing to other countries and eras, to literature and art. They wanted more time for foreign languages, starting in the elementary grades. The continuing education of teachers needed more rigor—courses during the school year, taught by university scholars, for teachers who needed "the spirit or the apparatus to carry their classes outside . . . [the] narrow limits" of textbooks. Educators today reinvent these century-old ideas and declare them "exciting," as though nobody before—least of all academicians—could have thought such things.

The Ten's marriage of common substance and varied methods—exactly the object of today's standards strategy—was broken by the advent of a new corps of nonacademic educators who argued that common requirements would force a multitude of students to drop out. In 1911 a Committee of Nine on the Articulation of High School and College turned the Ten on their heads. The Nine, primarily public school administrators, insisted that school "holding power" depended on meeting interests that "each boy and girl has at the time." To focus on academics was to enslave the high school to the college, and lead students away from "pursuits for which they are adapted" toward those "for which they are not adapted and in which they are not needed." Schools should focus on industrial arts, agriculture, and "household science."

The influence of what Hofstadter called an "anti-intellectualist movement" also stood out in *Cardinal Principles of Secondary Education,* issued in 1918 by the National Education Association's Commission on the Reorganization of Secondary Education, and nationally distributed by the U.S. Office of Education. Again made up of administrators, the commission included no academic subjects in its list of seven things high schools ought to teach: health, command of fundamental processes (the three Rs), "worthy" home membership, "worthy" use of leisure, vocation, citizenship, and ethical character. This report, too, could have been written today, by the promoters of content-free brands of "outcomes-based education," which they celebrate as new and "transformational."

MASS TRIAGE

FROM the 1920s on, vast numbers of children were locked into curricular tracks and "ability groups" on the basis of surface differences—race, ethnicity, language, social class, sex, "deportment," and intelligence as categorized by inane notions of testing—that had nothing to do with their potential. At the low point of this mass triage, leaders of the "Life Adjustment" movement of the 1940s consigned up to 80 percent of all American children and adolescents to the nonacademic heap. Hofstadter called it the most anti-democratic moment in the history of schooling. In the next decade James Bryant Conant's influential book *The American High School Today* (1959) still sought no common academic core and considered no more than 20 percent of students as "academically talented." The rest, Conant said, should "follow vocational goals and . . . develop general interests." And in *The Education of American Teachers* (1963), Conant added that at the university level "a prescription of general education is impossible unless one knows, at least approximately, the vocational aspirations of the group in question."

Thus spoke mainstream American educators, habitually failing to recall the three distinct purposes of schooling—for work, for public affairs, for private culture—and ever unable to imagine what free people could be as citizens or private personalities outside their daily work. From the report of the Nine to the present, educators (including those at many universities) have put socializing the masses and job training ahead of intellect. At different times socializing takes on various looks from group to group, left to right. But its common root is distrust of ordinary people's minds and spirit. Unable to think and seek the good, ordinary people must be socially engineered to amuse themselves and to behave. We boast of escaping the old world's class system, but cherish our own brand of social privilege. Academic standards, educators have said for a century, are not for everyone—as though most people do not deserve or need a liberal education, as though we want them not as equals but only to work and to buy, Beta-minuses out of Aldous Huxley's *Brave New World.* To feel better, we tell one another the story that schools can be "different but equal," a swindle still outliving its twin, "separate but equal."

In contrast, the cataclysms of depression and war brought educators in Europe to other views by the 1950s: it was time to democratize their schools, by leveling upward. As European secondary schools were opened to all, the political parties of the left resolved that the children of workers and the poor should gain whatever personal and

> Starting school reform by first deciding what every child should learn strikes most people as only common sense. But to many American educators, it spells revolutionary change. This strategy would give subject-matter teachers, and the educated public, unprecedented power to spur genuine change—change far deeper than questions of school choice, methods, or management.

political power they could from the same academic curriculum formerly reserved to the few.

A generation earlier America had leveled downward, accepting a dual, unequal school system sold to trusting citizens with warm words of solicitude by expert-specialists. In fact those specialists were perpetuating elitism by denouncing liberal education as elitist. Europeans were not so trusting as we, either of experts or of one another. Out of revolution and class conflict they had raised wariness to a high art, looking behind words for consequences. In Europe the schools had been battlegrounds for ideas about human nature, religion, history, national honor, and democracy itself. European democrats who had suffered Nazi occupation were not about to accept the notion that schools could be different but equal.

Had we looked overseas after midcentury, we could have learned from both our allies and our enemies in the Second World War. But we did not and still do not. Those most reluctant to look abroad are the promoters of giddy educational fixes that no foreign country would take seriously, from subjecting schools to the "free market" all the way to killing off academic disciplines in favor of "issue-based inquiry." Albert Shanker, the president of the American Federation of Teachers, puts it squarely, as usual: Americans tolerate a "marked inequality of opportunity in comparison with Germany, France, or Japan." Why do students work harder in those countries, with the same TV and pop culture to distract them? Because their educators have decided what all students should know by the end of high school, Shanker says, and they have "worked back from these goals to figure out what children should learn by the time they are ages fourteen and nine." Standards are universal and known by everyone, so "fewer students are lost—and fewer teachers are lost."

CONTENT-BASED REFORM

GRANTED, the U.S. Department of Education's own ambivalence did not help the standards strategy's reception. What could easily have been explained as a necessarily slow four-step process—in which most important decisions would be left to states, local districts, schools, and teachers—remained in confusion. And when expensive standards projects refused to discipline themselves and lugged forth great tomes that looked like national curricula, the department gave up trying. It let go the idea of a national core of essential learning and decided to say that setting standards was now up to the states.

Having fifty sets of standards need not mean disaster. But the Committee of Ten was right: something close to national agreement on a vital common core is indispensable to educational equity, to dislodge and replace the empty, undemanding programs that leave so many children untaught and disadvantaged. Without some such agreement, the much-heralded devolution of reform leadership to the states could make things worse.

The four steps essential to content-based school reform are no mystery. But conventional educators will object to them, for they focus on subject matter and must be carried out by subject-matter teachers and scholars, not by curriculum specialists unlearned in academic disciplines. In step one, teachers and scholars work together under public review to write the content standards—brief, scrupulously selected lists of what is most worth knowing in each academic subject. These have but one function: to lay before students, parents, teachers, and the university teachers of teachers the essential core of learning that all students in a modern democracy have the right not to be allowed to avoid. "Core" means what it says: teaching it should take no more than two thirds of the time given to each subject, the rest being left to local school and teacher choice.

This step is the most critical but most often misunderstood. What is a subject-matter essential, or "standard," and what is not? It is specific, not abstract, but it does not descend to detail. In history a typical standard asks students to understand the causes of the First World War, with an eye to the technological, economic, social, and political forces at work, together with the roles of individuals, of accident, and of ordinary confusion. It does not ask students to "master the concept of conflict in world history." Nor does it ask them to memorize the names of the twenty central characters in the tragedy of the summer of 1914.

As they select each standard, scholars and teachers must consider whether they can explain its importance when students ask "So what?" The First World War is an easy example. What it did to Americans was to shape their lives and deaths for the rest of the twentieth century—from the Depression and the Second World War to the end of the Cold War, from our hubris of 1945 to our present fantasy that we have spent ourselves too poor even to keep our parks clean or our libraries open. If a standard cannot be explained to the young, or to an educated public, it is either too general or too detailed. In a hurry, some states have issued "common cores of learning" that are lists of healthy attitudes and abstract "learning outcomes." Others have copied detail directly out of the overstuffed national standards documents. Neither is a help to teachers or curriculum makers.

Step two was never "national" business: writing a state curriculum framework, saying in which grades the essentials should be taught. Its function is to end the plague of gaps and repetitions that only American educators seem resigned to accept as normal. Articulating subject matter across the elementary and secondary years also requires a collaboration of equals—teachers, scholars, and learning specialists—each of whom has things to say that the others need to hear. The word "framework," too, means what it says; it leaves the third step—course design and pedagogy—to the school and the teacher. They must have the authority to make the choices most important to them and to their students: the topics and questions by which to teach the essentials, the day-to-day content of instruction, the materials and methods best suited to their students and to their own strengths.

Step four, writing performance standards and tests of achievement, can sensibly follow only when the others have been taken. But some states are hurrying to award expensive contracts to outside testing firms before anyone has thought about, much less decided, what is worth testing. To leave this to experts and let the rush to "accountability"—which now has a potent assessment lobby behind it—drive standards and course content will kill all chances for school improvement. Not everything precious can be measured, and not everything measurable is worth teaching; pap is pap, a drop or a gallon. So once more it is teachers and scholars who must decide what to assess.

Content-based reform will not always be easy even for teachers and scholars. All who teach, from the grades to graduate school, will have to be differently educated than they now are and teach differently than they now teach. For example, the history learned at any level depends on the prior education of both student and teacher. And the decision about what history to teach must anticipate what is to be learned at higher levels. But this is not how American schools and universities work. Teachers and academicians habitually shape each course as an island entire to itself, as though what they teach, or do not teach, matters to nobody but themselves—as if others had no right to notice, and none to intervene. That must change.

Schoolteachers and university scholars will have to accept

each other as equals, because aligning subject matter demands seamless, collaborative work from pre-school through Ph.D. They rarely do so now. Nor do elementary and high school teachers confer, or teachers in the same building. Apart from ego, insecurity, and worries over turf, collaboration takes time, which schools and universities rarely provide, and personal commitment, which they rarely reward. Moreover, to choose essentials and to design frameworks and assessments, educators will have to debate priorities. What *is* truly most worth knowing? What must be left out? Academicians avoid such questions at all cost; witness their chaotic college curricula. University faculties will have to alter their major programs, giving up pet courses for others that better prepare the next generation of teachers and help those already teaching. They will have to battle colleagues into coherent general-education requirements for underclassmen. To do all this, academicians will need to be broadly educated, and be differently rewarded by administrative and trustee policies.

States whose educators accept this degree of change will accomplish standards-based reform. Where change is rejected, they will fail. The hard fact is that anchoring school reform in academic learning—and putting teachers and scholars in charge—is foreign in all senses. It would redirect the mainstream of American education as the twentieth-century parade of much-hyped fashions never has. Life Adjustment, "greening," the open classroom, "back to basics," career education, "futures learning," global consciousness, "doing-a-value," critical and creative thinking, and "outcomes-based" education (are there other kinds?)—not one of these has ruffled the establishment or gotten beneath the surface to substantial subject matter, and so not one has improved the schools of most American children. Indeed, by leaving weary teachers awash in the debris from successive tides of obsession and indifference, they have made things worse.

OBSTACLES AND PROSPECTS

OF the obstacles reformers confront, the toughest may be our mad utilitarianism. Consider the three aims of schooling—preparing the worker, the citizen, and the cultivated individual. We put the worker ahead of the other two, as if they had no effect on the nation's economy or the quality of work done. Turning to citizenship, we bypass the substance of history, politics, letters, and ideas and peddle ready-made attitudes. Thus American educators have never had to think consistently about the moral, aesthetic, or intellectual content of public schooling for the masses—the gifts that academic subjects open for everyone.

Since academics have been for the few, it follows that our teacher corps is academically undereducated, ill prepared to offer challenging content to all its charges. Teachers are not to blame. Since so little is expected from most students, the university teachers of teachers—whether in content or pedagogy—see no reason to ask much of *them*. The time it will take to re-prepare teachers is itself an obstacle. There are no shortcuts to content-based reform, which makes it vulnerable to hawkers of new fashions from an education industry whose planned obsolescence leaves *haute couture* in the dust.

States will discover that the changes required by academic school reform will call down showers of objection. "Standards alone will not solve our problems"—as if anyone thought they could. "Standards will oppress minorities and the poor"—as if the absence of standards does not leave educators free to offer unequal schooling and tax cutters free to slash school spending. "Standards will stifle innovation"—as though clear and equal standards were not the best friends of innovators. Parents have seen far too many passing fads that skew or empty the curriculum. Settled aims will make it easier to experiment with school structure, school size, and all the ways that schools have to be different from one another to meet different circumstances.

States will find friends in teachers and citizens who, not overspecialized, have no ideology to press, and who understand that the three purposes of education—for work, for citizenship, and for private life—are by their nature distinct, many-sided, requiring different, sometimes opposite, modes of teaching aimed at different, sometimes opposite, results. Schooling for work is a "conservative" function, demanding disciplined mastery of tasks from the world of work as it is, not as we wish it to be, and objective testing of student competence. Schooling for citizenship, in contrast, is a "radical" activity, egalitarian and skeptical in style, mixing the hard study of history and ideas with free-swinging exchange on public issues. The school nurtures both teamwork and thorny individualism, at once the readiness to serve and the readiness to resist, for nobody knows ahead of time which the good citizen may have to do. To educate the private person, the school must detach itself much of the time from the clamor of popular culture. It must be conservative in requiring students to confront the range of arts, letters, and right behavior conceived in the past, toward the liberal end that their choices be informed and thereby free.

People well know that to work at these three purposes, schools must serve both society and the individual, must be close to daily life at some moments and wholly insulated at others. They know that different things are learned best in different ways, from drill to brainstorming, and that schools have to be *both* disciplined and easygoing, hierarchical and egalitarian, at different times for different subjects at different levels—mixing pleasure and pain, each often following upon the other.

In sum, they can understand why Theodore Sizer is not indulging in paradox when he says that only "a loose system that has rigor" can correct what he describes in *Horace's School* (1992) as "the inattention of American culture to serious learning." We need, he says, "generous localism" applied with high and common academic expectations. For a century we have resisted this, treating the majority of our children as though they were learning-disabled. We say that knowledge is power, but we have kept knowledge from millions of children, adolescents, and even college students. Our chance to make this long-delayed turn to democratic education is now in the hands of the states and local schools.

Botched Standards

Which is more important for young people to study—Magna Carta or the Mongol empire? The latest answer may surprise you

THE world-history document issued by the National Center for History in the Schools, at UCLA, and funded by the U.S. Department of Education and the National Endowment for the Humanities, is worth a close look, as a cautionary tale for reformers who may assume that scholars see the role of standards more clearly than others do. Given its 314 pages, and the limited time schools allot to world history, it is not helpful even for picking and choosing, because it has no continuing questions to help readers focus on essentials, as better textbooks do. To avoid the battles among specialists that selection would have set off, its authors, careful to offend no vocal constituency, acted on the dubious principle that all societies and all eras back to prehistory deserve equal space in the education of young Americans. By so doing they buried essentials under mounds of undifferentiated matter, much of it academic exotica and antiquarianism.

The document's failure is surprising, because its opening pages are eloquent on why citizens must study history. No reason, it argues, is "more important to a democratic society than this: *Knowledge of history is the precondition of political intelligence.*" It adds, "Without history, a society shares no common memory of where it has been, what its core values are, or what decisions of the past account for present circumstances." Also in italics is Etienne Gilson's remark *"History is the only laboratory we have in which to test the consequences of thought."* But between the promise and the

execution we find a chasm. The volume is weakest on thought and the consequences of ideas, on core values and common memories, not only the West's but any civilization's. It is thin on political turning points and institutions, and thereby on the drama of human choice and its effects. For all its length and pretentious demands, it scants the artistic, literary, and philosophical legacies of world cultures, and it shortchanges the past 250 years, which saw so many of the decisions that "account for present circumstances."

Its treatment of world history has thirty-nine main standards, 108 subheads, and 526 sub-subheads, all of them called standards. None of the main standards or subheads is devoted to ideas, whether philosophical, religious, ethical, or moral, social, economic, or political. One must descend to the 526 sub-subheads, or to fragments of them. Neither the Judaic nor the Christian principles that are the sources of Western values, morals, and views of justice and of ideas of the individual's dignity and responsibility—even for unreligious or anti-religious thinkers—are given more than one half of a sub-subhead, less than a thousandth of the document's substance. The ideas of Islam and of Protestant reformers fare no better. However, the topic "mastery of horse-riding on the steppes" gets twice that space, the Scythians and the Xiongnu fill two full sub-subheads, and the Olmecs get a main standard all to themselves.

On the secular side, there is nothing of medieval thought about just rules of law, war, economic life, or social responsibility. Later we find nothing of Renaissance or Reformation theory concerning society, economics, or politics. Enlightenment thought and its impact on Church and State are relegated to a single sub-subhead. French revolutionary ideas "on social equality, democracy, human rights, constitutionalism, and nationalism" get one sub-subhead out of ninety-four for the years 1750–1914. For the twentieth century a single sub-subhead asks students to explain the "leading ideas of liberalism, social reformism, conservatism, and socialism as competing ideologies in 20th century Europe." Leninist and Fascist-Nazi ideologies are each assigned half of a sub-subhead, so that only two sub-subheads must do for the political ideas and ideology of the entire twentieth-century world.

In squeezing European civilization, the document is also meager on the political history that makes sophisticated citizens. There is nothing on the failure of Athenian democracy to overcome the forces of pride and demagoguery. The vast questions about Rome's decline that so preoccupied the American Founders are compressed into part of a subhead, less than half the space given the Gupta empire in India. As to politics in the years 1000–1500, a single sub-subhead is devoted to "analyzing how European monarchies expanded their power at the expense of feudal lords and assessing the growth and limitations of representative institutions in these monarchies." So, buried and unnamed in half of that sub-subhead are Magna Carta and the Model Parliament, along with the prime political lesson that true constitutions require a balance of power in society. In the same era entire standards take up the Mongol empire and sub-Saharan Africa.

The seventeenth-century English Revolution gets a single sub-subhead (out of eighty-four for the era 1450–1770)—no more than "evaluating the interplay of indigenous Indian, Persian, and European influences in Mughal artistic, architectural, literary, and scientific achievements." The authors find nothing special about English constitutional history that American citizens should know, in keeping with today's fashion of decrying "Whig history," as though the world-wide struggle for political freedom, and all of its sacrifice, setbacks, and advances, were only a myth to hoodwink the innocent young. All but absent, too, is the history of labor. In the section covering the twentieth century there is no mention of trade unions, their battles and importance to democracy and social justice, and why totalitarians make them their first victims. Even the vast twentieth-century struggle of liberal democracies to overcome Nazism and Soviet communism fades into pale generalities.

Some of the weaknesses in the world-history document are but the reverse side of American virtues: hopefulness and generosity; our eagerness to embrace diversity, to be self-critical, to shun "ethnocentrism." In what other country do people cringe at that word and are students required to study other cultures but not their own? The standards also reflect our impatience with politics, our reluctance to admit that only politics can turn aspirations into reality, and our impatience with the gloomier views of human nature that accept the presence of evil in the world, and the tragedy and imperfection of the human condition.

The fact remains, however, that in deference to current styles in the history profession, the authors played down the Western sources of their own American consciences, and failed to do the work of selecting what would best serve the education of American students, or of society at large. Fortunately, their introduction makes clear why state and local teacher-scholar teams must do better. Nothing less is at stake than our political competence as a people.

Taking the solidity of democratic institutions for granted, educators have worried too little about the hard things they require citizens to understand. Now, in the mid-1990s, we have reasons to pay more attention. For one thing, it takes a perverse effort of will to deny that the effects of technology and economics, demography and nature, make our problems and the world's more complicated than ever. Or to deny that nostrums peddled by the loudest voices in politics and talk TV and radio are more simplistic than ever. Or that blaming "government" for every ill and anxiety—while not yet so virulent as under the Weimar Republic—betrays a flaming ignorance of history and human nature.

WHAT HISTORY TEACHES

WITH respect to world history, what should Americans know and teach? What is the main story? It is not the parade of military, technological, and economic "interactions," or the endless comparisons among often incomparable centers of great power, that global studies dwell upon—although these must, of course, be taken into account. The big story is not the push to modernize but the struggle to civilize, to curb the bestial side of human nature. What students can grasp very well is that this is a common struggle, in which all peoples and races are equal—equal in our natures, equal in the historical guilt of forebears who pursued war, slavery, and oppression. Black Africans, Anglo-Americans, Europeans, Native Americans, North African and Middle Eastern peoples, Mongols, Chinese, and Japanese—all have pursued these things when they have had the power to, afflicting one another and weaker neighbors.

For our time, the first lesson to be learned from world history, the most compelling story, is the age-old struggle of people within each culture to limit aggression and greed, to nourish the better side of human nature, to apply morality and law, to keep the peace and render justice. Students can see the glory and agony of this struggle, and how often it has been lost. Because human evil exists, good intent has never been enough. It has taken brains, courage, self-sacrifice, patience, love, and—always with tragic consequences—war itself to contain the beast. Against the twin temptations of wishfulness and cynicism, history says that evil and tragedy are real, that civilization has a high price but that it, too, is real, and has been won from time to time. In history we find the ideas, the conditions, and the famous and ordinary men and women making it possible.

All peoples have taken part in the struggle to civilize. An honest look at the past reveals a common human mixture of altruism, malevolence, and indifference, and reasons for all of us to feel both pride and shame. Starting from any other point of view is historically false, and blind to human nature. Historians—and standard setters—have a special obligation to be candid. But many popular textbooks are unfailingly pious about other cultures and ultra-critical of our own, preaching a new-style ignorance in reaction against, but just as pernicious as, our older textbook pieties about ourselves and disdain for others. Both are pernicious because both sap the will to civilize. People who are taught to feel specially guilty, or specially victimized, or naturally superior, will not reach out to others as equals; they will not pay the costs in toil, tears, and taxes always imposed by that struggle.

This is not a "conservative" or "liberal" issue but one of trusting children, adolescents, and adults to work with historical truth, however inconvenient or impolite it may seem. History reinforces the rough notion of equality that we learn on the playground and in the street: there are like proportions of admirable and avoidable people in every imaginable human grouping—by age, class, race, sex, religion, or cultural taste. Individuals are not equal in talent or virtue, and certainly not equally deserving of respect. To teach otherwise is to invite ridicule and resentment. Instead what must repeatedly be taught, because it is not quickly learned—but is quickly forgotten in hard times—is that in civilized society it is every person's *rights* that are equally deserving of respect: rights to free expression, equal protection under law, fair judgment, rigorous education, honest work and pay, an equal chance to pursue the good.

This hard truth we accept, and remember, only with the help of historical insight, which is indispensable in forging a democratic conscience—that inner feeling that we ought to do the right thing even if only out of prudence. For we see again and again that societies failing to accord a good measure of liberty, equality, and justice have hastened their own decay, particularly over the past two centuries, since the American and French revolutions told the world that these three were the proper aims of human life and politics, and that it was right and possible to bring them to reality—by force if necessary.

Student-citizens need to be acutely sensitive to the central political drama of world history since the 1770s—what Sigmund Neumann called the "triple revolution" aimed at national unity and independence, at political democracy and civil rights, and at economic and social justice. This, too, is not a liberal or conservative matter. Whether we approve or deplore these ends, or the means to them, does not lessen their force or our need to deal with them, at home and abroad. Modern history tells us that whenever any one of them is frustrated for long, masses of people will sink to envy, self-pity, fury, and a search for scapegoats, führers, and quick, violent solutions.

Good history is not always fun to learn, any more than is chemistry or mathematics, and we should not pretend that it is. The job of citizen is no easier to prepare for than that of doctor or bridge builder. Nor is good history always popular. It denies us the comforts of optimism or pessimism. It gives the lie to nostalgia, whether for left-wing or right-wing or feel-good politics. Its lessons offer no cure for today's problems, only warnings we are silly to ignore. As they select the essentials of U.S. and world history, state and local standard setters and curriculum makers can look for the particulars that teach such lessons best—memorable events, ideas, and people whose stories need telling, but always in the context of longer narrative history.

For example, an American-history standard should require the ability not only to recall points in the Constitution and Bill of Rights but also to understand the ideas and events behind them, back to Greek and Roman thought and institutions, to Judeo-Christian views of human nature and respon-

sibility, to Magna Carta and the English Revolution, to Hobbes, Locke, and Montesquieu, Burke, Paine, the Federalists and the anti-Federalists. These essentials are not grasped by playacting a few quarrels from hot Philadelphia afternoons of 1787—though playacting can make a good start if the script is based on original sources.

Moreover, the lesson of the Constitution is not nearly complete without learning the harrowing consequences of a cheap answer to labor shortages that American planters were sure they had found in the early 1600s—slaves from Africa. A tortured Constitution, belying the Declaration's promise, was only one, early payment. The Civil War followed, and even 620,000 dead did not purchase the free and equal Union for which Lincoln prayed in his Second Inaugural. New chains of bondage were forged, and another century of repression and humiliation followed, before the civil-rights movement of the 1960s restarted a process of liberation whose grinding slowness continues to divide and embitter us.

Likewise, a world-history standard on the Second World War teaches little unless that war is seen as a consequence of the outbreak of the First World War and of the murderous incompetence with which it was fought, of the Bolshevik Revolution, of world depression, of the furies and civic ineptitude that destroyed the Weimar Republic, of Hitler's rise on the shoulders of private armies, and of the liberal democracies' wishful rejection of the costs of collective security, from the Paris Conference of 1919 through the Spanish Civil War to the Nazi occupation of Prague in 1939. Nor can it teach nearly enough without examining the Holocaust, the ultimate horror, itself a consequence of all these things and more since the Middle Ages.

The fiftieth anniversary of the end of the Second World War brought back the war's satanic nature, from Rotterdam to Dresden, Nanking and Bataan to Hiroshima. The debates over guilt revealed widespread avoidance of history's warnings. Some seemed to doubt that evil exists and has to be dealt with, even by making war. Others seemed to deny that any war, launched for whatever cause, will carry frightful human consequences, will be as hellish as weapons permit. And 1945 was not the end. The Cold War followed from the effects of both world wars. Draining lives and resources, fouling our politics, skewing economic life, it divided us against one another, from the Red scares of the 1940s and 1950s through the bloody Korean and Vietnam wars. Its legacy clouds our view of a changing world and its needs, not least our own need to distinguish between force that is necessary and force that is not. All these afflictions are consequences of human choices back to 1914 and earlier, many of them in pursuit of cheap, quick answers in defiance of history's lessons and the imperatives of civilized life.

How Kids Learn

BARBARA KANTROWITZ & PAT WINGERT

Ages 5 through 8 are wonder years. That's when children begin learning to study, to reason, to cooperate. We can put them in desks and drill them all day. Or we can keep them moving, touching, exploring. The experts favor a hands-on approach, but changing the way schools teach isn't easy. The stakes are high and parents can help.

With Howard Manly in Atlanta and bureau reports

It's time for number games in Janet Gill's kindergarten class at the Greenbrook School in South Brunswick, N.J. With hardly any prodding from their teacher, 23 five- and six-year-olds pull out geometric puzzles, playing cards and counting equipment from the shelves lining the room. At one round table, a group of youngsters fits together brightly colored wooden shapes. One little girl forms a hexagon out of triangles. The others, obviously impressed, gather round to count up how many parts are needed to make the whole.

After about half an hour, the children get ready for story time. They pack up their counting equipment and settle in a circle around Gill. She holds up a giant book about a zany character called Mrs. Wishy-washy who insists on giving farm animals a bath. The children recite the whimsical lines along with Gill, obviously enjoying one of their favorite tales. (The hallway is lined with drawings depicting the children's own interpretation of the book; they've taken a few literary liberties, like substituting unicorns and dinosaurs for cows and pigs.) After the first reading, Gill asks for volunteers to act out the various parts in the book. Lots of hands shoot up. Gill picks out four children and

they play their parts enthusiastically. There isn't a bored face in the room.

This isn't reading, writing and arithmetic the way most people remember it. Like a growing number of public- and private-school educators, the principals and teachers in South Brunswick believe that children between the ages of 5 and 8 have to be taught differently from older children. They recognize that young children learn best through active, hands-on teaching methods like games and dramatic play. They know that children in this age group develop at varying rates and schools have to allow for these differences. They also believe that youngsters' social growth is as essential as their academic achievement. Says Joan Warren, a teacher consultant in South Brunswick: "Our programs are designed to fit the child instead of making the child fit the school."

Educators call this kind of teaching "developmentally appropriate practice"—a curriculum based on what scientists know about how young children learn. These ideas have been slowly emerging through research conducted over the last century, particularly in the past 30 years. Some of the tenets have appeared

The Lives and Times of Children

Each youngster proceeds at his own pace, but the learning curve of a child is fairly predictable. Their drive to learn is awesome, and careful adults can nourish it. The biggest mistake is pushing a child too hard, too soon.

● Infants and Toddlers

They're born to learn. The first important lesson is trust, and they learn that from their relationships with their parents or other caring adults. Later, babies will begin to explore the world around them and experiment with independence. As they mature, infants slowly develop gross motor (sitting, crawling, walking) and fine motor (picking up tiny objects) skills. Generally, they remain egocentric and are unable to share or wait their turn. New skills are perfected through repetition, such as the babbling that leads to speaking.

■ 18 months to 3 years

Usually toilet training becomes the prime learning activity. Children tend to concentrate on language development and large-muscle control through activities like climbing on jungle gyms. Attention spans lengthen enough to listen to uncomplicated stories and carry on conversations. Vocabulary expands to about 200 words. They enjoy playing with one other child, or a small group, for short periods, and learn that others have feelings too. They continue to look to parents for encouragement and protection, while beginning to accept limits on their behavior.

▲ 3-year-olds

Generally, they're interested in doing things for themselves and trying to keep up with older children. Their ability to quietly listen to stories and music remains limited. They begin telling stories and jokes. Physical growth slows, but large-muscle development continues as children run, jump and ride tricycles. They begin to deal with cause and effect; it's time to plant seeds and watch them grow.

● 4-year-olds

They develop better small motor skills, such as cutting with scissors, painting, working with puzzles and building things. They can master colors, sizes and shapes. They should be read to and should be encouraged to watch others write; let them scribble on paper but try to keep them away from walls.

■ 5-year-olds

They begin to understand counting as a one-to-one correlation. Improved memories make it easier for them to recognize meaningful words, and with sharper fine motor skills, some children will be able to write their own names.

▲ Both 4s and 5s

Both groups learn best by interacting with people and concrete objects and by trying to solve real problems. They can learn from stories and books, but only in ways that relate to their own experience. Socially, these children are increasingly interested in activities outside their immediate family. They can play in groups for longer periods, learning lessons in cooperation and negotiation. Physically, large-muscle development continues, and skills such as balancing emerge.

● 6-year-olds

Interest in their peers continues to increase, and they become acutely aware of comparisons between themselves and others. It's a taste of adolescence: does the group accept them? Speech is usually well developed, and children are able to joke and tease. They have a strong sense of true and false and are eager for clear rules and definitions. However, they have a difficult time differentiating between minor and major infractions. Generally, children this age are more mature mentally than physically and unable to sit still for long periods. They learn better by firsthand experiences. Learning by doing also encourages children's "disposition" to use the knowledge and skills they're acquiring.

■ 7- to 8-year-olds

During this period, children begin developing the ability to think about and solve problems in their heads, but some will continue to rely on fingers and toes to help them find the right answer. Not until they're 11 are most kids capable of thinking purely symbolically; they still use real objects to give the symbols— such as numbers—meaning. At this stage they listen better and engage in give and take. Generally, physical growth continues to slow, while athletic abilities improve—children are able to hit a softball, skip rope or balance on a beam. Sitting for long periods is still more tiring than running and jumping.

under other names—progressivism in the 1920s, open education in the 1970s. But they've never been the norm. Now, educators say that may be about to change. "The entire early-childhood profession has amassed itself in unison behind these principles," says Yale education professor Sharon Lynn Kagan. In the last few years, many of the major education organizations in the country—including the National Association for the Education of Young Children and the National Association of State Boards of Education—have endorsed remarkably similar plans for revamping kindergarten through third grade.

Bolstered by opinions from the experts, individual states are beginning to take action. Both California and New York have appointed task forces to recommend changes for the earliest grades. And scores of individual school districts like South Brunswick, figuring that young minds are a terrible thing to waste, are pushing ahead on their own.

The evidence gathered from research in child development is so compelling that even groups like the Council for Basic Education, for years a major supporter of the traditional format, have revised their thinking. "The idea of putting small children in front of workbooks and asking them to sit at their desks all day is a nightmare vision," says Patte Barth, associate editor of Basic Education, the council's newsletter.

At this point, there's no way of knowing how soon change will come or how widespread it will be. However, there's a growing recognition of the importance of the early grades. For the past few years, most of the public's attention has focused on older children, especially teenagers. "That's a Band-Aid kind of approach," says Anne Dillman, a member of the New Jersey State Board of Education. "When the product doesn't come out right, you try and fix it at the end. But we really have to start at the beginning." Demographics have contributed to the sense of urgency. The baby boomlet has replaced the baby-bust generation of the 1970s. More kids in elementary school means more parents asking if there's a better way to teach. And researchers say there is a better way. "We've made remarkable breakthroughs in understanding the development of children, the development of learning and the climate that enhances that," says Ernest Boyer of The Carnegie Foundation for the Advancement of Teaching. But, he adds, too often, "what we know in theory and what we're doing in the classroom are very different."

The early grades pose special challenges because that's when children's attitudes toward school and learning are shaped, says Tufts University psychologist David Elkind. As youngsters move from home or preschool into the larger, more competitive world of elementary school, they begin to make judgments about their own abilities. If they feel inadequate, they may give up. Intellectually, they're also in transition, moving from the intensely physical exploration habits of infancy and toddlerhood to more abstract reasoning. Children are born wanting to learn. A baby can spend hours studying his hands; a toddler is fascinated by watching sand pour through a sieve. What looks like play to an adult is actually the work of childhood, developing an understanding of the world. Studies show that the most effective way to teach young kids is to capitalize on their natural inclination to learn through play.

But in the 1980s, many schools have tried to do just the opposite, pressure instead of challenge. The "back to basics" movement meant that teaching methods intended for high school students were imposed on first graders. The lesson of the day was more: more homework, more tests, more discipline. Children should be behind their desks, not roaming around the room. Teachers should be at the head of the classrooms, drilling knowledge into their charges. Much of this was a reaction against the trend toward open education in the '70s. Based on the British system, it allowed children to develop at their own pace within a highly structured classroom. But too many teachers and principals who tried open education thought that it meant simply tearing down classroom walls and letting children do whatever they wanted. The results were often disastrous. "Because it was done wrong, there was a backlash against it," says Sue Bredekamp of the National Association for the Education of Young Children.

At the same time, parents, too, were demanding more from their elementary schools. By the mid-1980s, the majority of 3- and 4-year-olds were attending some form of pre-school. And their parents expected these classroom veterans to be reading by the second semester of kindergarten. But the truth is that many 5-year-olds aren't ready for reading—or most of the other academic tasks that come easily to older children—no matter how many years of school they've completed. "We're confusing the numbers of years children have been in school with brain development," says Martha Denckla, a professor of neurology and pediatrics at Johns Hopkins University. "Just because a child goes to day care at age 3 doesn't mean the human brain mutates into an older brain. A 5-year-old's brain is still a 5-year-old's brain."

As part of the return to basics, parents and districts demanded hard evidence that their children were learning. And some communities took extreme measures. In 1985 Georgia became the first state to require 6-year-olds to pass a standardized test before entering first grade. More than two dozen other states proposed similar legislation. In the beginning Georgia's move was hailed as a "pioneering" effort to get kids off to a good start. Instead, concedes state school superintendent Werner Rogers, "We got off on the wrong foot." Five-year-olds who used to spend their days finger-painting or singing were hunched over ditto sheets, preparing for the big exam. "We would have to spend a month just teaching kids how to take the test," says Beth Hunnings, a kindergarten teacher in suburban Atlanta. This year Georgia altered the tests in favor of a more flexible evaluation; other states have changed their minds as well.

The intense, early pressure has taken an early toll. Kindergartners are struggling with homework. First graders are taking spelling tests before they even understand how to read. Second graders feel like failures. "During this critical period," says David Elkind in his book "Miseducation," "the child's bud-

In Japan, First Grade Isn't a Boot Camp

Japanese students have the highest math and science test scores in the world. More than 90 percent graduate from high school. Illiteracy is virtually nonexistent in Japan. Most Americans attribute this success to a rigid system that sets youngsters on a lock-step march from cradle to college. In fact, the early years of Japanese schooling are anything but a boot camp; the atmosphere is warm and nurturing. From kindergarten through third grade, the goal is not only academic but also social—teaching kids to be part of a group so they can be good citizens as well as good students. "Getting along with others is not just a means for keeping the peace in the classroom but something which is a valued end in itself," says American researcher Merry White, author of "The Japanese Educational Challenge."

Lessons in living and working together grow naturally out of the Japanese culture. Starting in kindergarten, youngsters learn to work in teams, with brighter students often helping slower ones. All children are told they can succeed if they persist and work hard. Japanese teachers are expected to be extremely patient with young children. They go over lessons step by step and repeat instructions as often as necessary. "The key is not to scold [children] for small mistakes," says Yukio Ueda, princi-pal of Mita Elementary School in Tokyo. Instead, he says, teachers concentrate on praising and encouraging their young charges.

As a result, the classrooms are relaxed and cheerful, even when they're filled with rows of desks. On one recent afternoon a class of second graders at Ueda's school was working on an art project. Their as-signment was to build a roof with poles made of rolled-up newspapers. The chil-dren worked in small groups, occasionally asking their teacher for help. The room was filled with the sound of eager youngsters chatting about how to get the job done. In another second-grade class, the subject was math. Maniko Inoue, the teacher, suggested a number game to practice multiplication. After a few minutes of playing it, one boy stood up and proposed changing the rules just a bit to make it more fun. Inoue lis-tened carefully and then asked if the other students agreed. They cheered, "Yes, yes," and the game continued according to the new rules.

Academics are far from neglected in the early grades. The Education Ministry sets curriculum standards and goals for each school year. For example, third graders by the end of the year are supposed to be able to read and write 508 characters (out of some 2,000 considered essential to basic literacy). Teachers have time for play and lessons: Japanese children attend school for 240 days, compared with about 180 in the United States.

Mothers' role: Not all the teaching goes on in the classroom. Parents, especially mothers, play a key role in education. Although most kindergartens do not teach writing or numbers in any systematic way, more than 80 percent of Japanese children learn to read or write to some extent before they enter school. "It is as if mothers had their own built-in curriculum," says Shig-efumi Nagano, a director of the National Institute for Educational Research. "The first game they teach is to count numbers up to 10."

For all their success in the early grades, the Japanese are worried they're not doing well enough. After a recent national curri-culum review, officials were alarmed by what Education Minister Takeo Nishioka described as excessive "bullying and mis-conduct" among children—the result, ac-cording to some Japanese, of too much emphasis on material values. So three years from now, first and second graders will no longer be studying social studies and sci-ence. Instead, children will spend more time learning how to be good citizens. That's "back to basics"—Japanese style.

Barbara Kantrowitz *with* Hideko Takayama *in Tokyo*

---

ding sense of competence is frequently under attack, not only from inappropriate instructional practices . . . but also from the hundred and one feelings of hurt, frustration and rejection that mark a child's entrance into the world of schooling, competition and peer-group involvement." Adults under similar stress can rationalize setbacks or put them in perspective based on previous experiences; young children have none of these defenses. Schools that demand too much too soon are setting kids off on the road to failure.

It doesn't have to be this way. Most experts on child development and early-childhood education believe that young children learn much more readily if the teaching methods meet their special needs:

Differences in thinking: The most important ingre-dient of the nontraditional approach is hands-on learn-ing. Research begun by Swiss psychologist Jean Piaget indicates that somewhere between the ages of 6 and 9, children begin to think abstractly instead of concretely. Younger children learn much more by touching and seeing and smelling and tasting than by just listening. In other words, 6-year-olds can easily understand ad-dition and subtraction if they have actual objects to count instead of a series of numbers written on a blackboard. Lectures don't help. Kids learn to reason and communicate by engaging in conversation. Yet most teachers still talk at, not with, their pupils.

Physical activity: When they get to be 10 or 11, children can sit still for sustained periods. But until they are physically ready for long periods of inactivity, they need to be active in the classroom. "A young child has to make a conscious effort to sit still," says De-nckla. "A large chunk of children can't do it for very long. It's a very energy-consuming activity for them." Small children actually get more tired if they have to sit still and listen to a teacher talk than if they're allowed to move around in the classroom. The frontal lobe, the part of the brain that applies the brakes to children's natural energy and curiosity, is still immature in 6- to 9-year-olds, Denckla says. As the lobe develops, so does what Denckla describes as "boredom tolerance." Simply put, learning by doing is much less boring to young children.

Language development: In this age group, experts say language development should not be broken down into isolated skills—reading, writing and speaking. Children first learn to reason and to express themselves by talking. They can dictate stories to a teacher before they actually read or write. Later, their first attempts at composition do not need to be letter perfect; the important thing is that they learn to communicate ideas. But in many classrooms, grammar and spelling have become more important than content. While mastering the technical aspects of writing is essential as a child gets older, educators warn against emphasizing form over content in the early grades. Books should also be interesting to kids—not just words strung together solely for the purpose of pedagogy. Psychologist Katherine Nelson of the City University of New York says that her extensive laboratory and observational work indicates that kids can learn language—speaking, writing or reading—only if it is presented in a way that makes sense to them. But many teachers still use texts that are so boring they'd put anybody to sleep.

Socialization: A youngster's social development has a profound effect on his academic progress. Kids who have trouble getting along with their classmates can end up behind academically as well and have a higher incidence of dropping out. In the early grades especially, experts say youngsters should be encouraged to work in groups rather than individually so that teachers can spot children who may be having problems making friends. "When children work on a project," says University of Illinois education professor Lillian Katz, "they learn to work together, to disagree, to speculate, to take turns and de-escalate tensions. These skills can't be learned through lecture. We all know people who have wonderful technical skills but don't have any social skills. Relationships should be the first 'R'."

Feelings of competence and self-esteem: At this age, children are also learning to judge themselves in relation to others. For most children, school marks the first time that their goals are not set by an internal clock but by the outside world. Just as the 1-year-old struggles to walk, 6-year-olds are struggling to meet adult expectations. Young kids don't know how to distinguish between effort and ability, says Tynette Hills, coordinator of early-childhood education for the state of New Jersey. If they try hard to do something and fail, they may conclude that they will never be able to accomplish a particular task. The effects of obvious methods of comparison, such as posting grades, can be serious. Says Hills: "A child who has had his confidence really damaged needs a rescue operation."

Rates of growth: Between the ages of 5 and 9, there's a wide range of development for children of normal intelligence. "What's appropriate for one child may not be appropriate for another," says Dr. Perry Dyke, a member of the California State Board of Education. "We've got to have the teachers and the staff reach children at whatever level they may be at . . . That takes very sophisticated teaching." A child's pace is almost impossible to predict beforehand. Some kids learn to read on their own by kindergarten; others are still struggling to decode words two or three years later. But by the beginning of the fourth grade, children with very different histories often read on the same level. Sometimes, there's a sudden "spurt" of learning, much like a growth spurt, and a child who has been behind all year will catch up in just a few weeks. Ernest Boyer and others think that multigrade classrooms, where two or three grades are mixed, are a good solution to this problem—and a way to avoid the "tracking" that can hurt a child's self-esteem. In an ungraded classroom, for example, an older child who is having problems in a particular area can practice by tutoring younger kids.

Putting these principles into practice has never been easy. Forty years ago Milwaukee abolished report cards and started sending home ungraded evaluations for kindergarten through third grade. "If anything was developmentally appropriate, those ungraded classes were," says Millie Hoffman, a curriculum specialist with the Milwaukee schools. When the back-to-basics movement geared up nationally in the early 1980s, the city bowed to pressure. Parents started demanding letter grades on report cards. A traditional, direct-teaching approach was introduced into the school system after some students began getting low scores on standardized tests. The school board ordered basal readers with controlled vocabularies and contrived stories. Milwaukee kindergarten teachers were so up-

A Primer for Parents

When visiting a school, trust your eyes. What you see is what your child is going to get.

● Teachers should talk to small groups of children or individual youngsters; they shouldn't just lecture.

■ Children should be working on projects, active experiments and play; they shouldn't be at their desks all day filling in workbooks.

▲ Children should be dictating and writing their own stories or reading real books.

● The classroom layout should have reading and art areas and space for children to work in groups.

■ Children should create freehand artwork, not just color or paste together adult drawings.

▲ Most importantly, watch the children's faces. Are they intellectually engaged, eager and happy? If they look bored or scared, they probably are.

set by these changes that they convinced the board that their students didn't need most of the standardized tests and the workbooks that go along with the readers.

Some schools have been able to keep the progressive format. Olive School in Arlington Heights, Ill., has had a nontraditional curriculum for 22 years. "We've been able to do it because parents are involved, the teachers really care and the children do well," says principal Mary Stitt. "We feel confident that we know what's best for kids." Teachers say they spend a lot of time educating parents about the teaching methods. "Parents always think school should be the way it was for them," says first-grade teacher Cathy Sauer. "As if everything else can change and progress but education is supposed to stay the same. I find that parents want their children to like school, to get along with other children and to be good thinkers. When they see that happening, they become convinced."

Parental involvement is especially important when schools switch from a traditional to a new format. Four years ago, Anne Norford, principal of the Brownsville Elementary School in Albemarle County, Va., began to convert her school. Parents volunteer regularly and that helps. But the transition has not been completely smooth. Several teachers refused to switch over to the more active format. Most of them have since left the school, Norford says. There's no question that some teachers have trouble implementing the developmentally appropriate approach. "Our teachers are not all trained for it," says Yale's Kagan. "It takes a lot of savvy and skill." A successful child-centered classroom seems to function effortlessly as youngsters move from activity to activity. But there's a lot of planning behind it—and that's the responsibility of the individual teacher. "One of the biggest problems," says Norford, "is trying to come up with a program that every teacher can do—not just the cadre of single people who are willing to work 90 hours a week." Teachers also have to participate actively in classroom activities and give up the automatic mantle of authority that comes from standing at the blackboard.

Teachers do better when they're involved in the planning and decision making. When the South Brunswick, N.J., schools decided in the early 1980s to change to a new format, the district spent several years studying a variety of curricula. Teachers participated in that research. A laboratory school was set up in the summer so that teachers could test materials. "We had the support of the teachers because teachers were part of the process," says teacher consultant Joan Warren.

One residue of the back-to-basics movement is the demand for accountability. Children who are taught in nontraditional classrooms can score slightly lower on commonly used standardized tests. That's because most current tests are geared to the old ways. Children are usually quizzed on specific skills, such as vocabulary or addition, not on the concepts behind those skills. "The standardized tests usually call for one-word answers," says Carolyn Topping, principal of Mesa Elementary School in Boulder, Colo. "There may be three words in a row, two of which are misspelled and the child is asked to circle the correctly spelled word. But the tests never ask, 'Does the child know how to write a paragraph?' "

Even if the tests were revised to reflect different kinds of knowledge, there are serious questions about the reliability of tests on young children. The results can vary widely, depending on many factors—a child's mood, his ability to manipulate a pencil (a difficult skill for many kids), his reaction to the person administering the test. "I'm appalled at all the testing we're doing of small children," says Vanderbilt University professor Chester Finn, a former assistant secretary of education under the Reagan administration. He favors regular informal reviews and teacher evaluations to make sure a student understands an idea before moving on to the next level of difficulty.

Tests are the simplest method of judging the effectiveness of a classroom—if not always the most accurate. But there are other ways to tell if children are learning. If youngsters are excited by what they are doing, they're probably laughing and talking to one another and to their teacher. That communication is part of the learning process. "People think that school has to be either free play or all worksheets," says Illinois professor Katz. "The truth is that neither is enough. There has to be a balance between spontaneous play and teacher-directed work." And, she adds, "you have to have the other component. Your class has to have intellectual life."

Katz, author of "Engaging Children's Minds," describes two different elementary-school classes she visited recently. In one, children spent the entire morning making identical pictures of traffic lights. There was no attempt to relate the pictures to anything else the class was doing. In the other class, youngsters were investigating a school bus. They wrote to the district and asked if they could have a bus parked in their lot for a few days. They studied it, figured out what all the parts were for and talked about traffic rules. Then, in the classroom, they built their own bus out of cardboard. They had fun, but they also practiced writing, problem solving, even a little arithmetic. Says Katz: "When the class had their parents' night, the teacher was ready with reports on how each child was doing. But all the parents wanted to see was the bus because their children had been coming home and talking about it for weeks." That's the kind of education kids deserve. Anything less should get an "F."

The IQ Puzzle

Scores on intelligence tests around the world have risen sharply. Does the baffling increase mean that today's children are near-geniuses? Or do IQ tests reveal less about intelligence than we think?

SHARON BEGLEY

IN THE MYTHICAL TOWN OF LAKE WOBEGON, AS HUMORIST GARRISON Keillor tells it, all the women are strong, all the men good looking . . . and all the children are above average. On the last point, Keillor didn't know how right he was. In a phenomenon overlooked even by scholars who study the nature and roots of intelligence, IQ scores throughout the developed world have soared dramatically since the tests were introduced in the early years of this century—27 points in Britain since 1942 and 24 points in the United States since 1918, for instance, with comparable gains throughout Western Europe, Canada, Japan, Israel, urban Brazil, China, Australia and New Zealand (graph). The rise is so sharp that it implies that the average school-child today is as bright as the near-geniuses of yesteryear. And not only in Lake Wobegon. "We now have data for 20 nations," James R. Flynn, a political philosopher at the University of Otago in New Zealand who stumbled upon the phenomenon, told an IQ conference earlier this month. "And there is not a single exception to massive IQ gains."

But while it is easy to tabulate the IQ gains now known as the Flynn effect, explaining them is harder. Scientists agree that the gains are not a statistical artifact. The tests whose results Flynn analyzed have remained basically unchanged over the generations. And in some cases they have been given to the same populations—every military-age man in the Netherlands, for instance—not self-selected and therefore variable populations, as is the case with the SATs. "The increase in scores is real, it has been empirically demonstrated and it is widely accepted," says psychologist Wendy Williams of Yale University. But beyond that, agreement breaks down in a debate that recalls the controversy over IQ and race rekindled in 1994 by the book "The Bell Curve." For the implications are just as profound. If IQ measures innate intelligence, then there is a serious IQ generation gap: either a large fraction of today's children are gifted, with IQs of 130 or more, or "almost half of white Americans during World War I had IQs so low [below 76] that they lacked the intellectual capacity to understand the basic rules of baseball," says Flynn. But if, instead, the IQ gains are too large to represent true intelligence gains, as Flynn contends, "they throw a wrench into the theory that intelligence is measured by IQ."

To some veterans of the "Bell Curve" debate, the sharp rise in IQ bolsters the argument that intelligence must be determined more by nurture than by nature. Nature, in the form of the prevalence of "smart" genes in a population, does not change at anything like the speed with which IQ has risen, goes the argument. "The gene pool cannot change so much, so fast," says John Boli of Emory University. But the Flynn effect might in fact be "consistent with either a high or a low heritability of intelligence," argues psychologist Stephen Ceci of Cornell University. He draws an analogy to height. Stature is strongly heritable: short parents tend to have shorter children than tall parents do. Yet height, like IQ, has been rising for decades, not because tallness genes are suddenly more common but because of better nutrition. Similarly, intelligence may have a genetic basis yet still be subject to environmental influences. These influences would shape the form that intelligence takes in a particular society. They would also allow more children to attain their maximum intellectual potential—or keep them from doing so.

Are We Getting Smarter?

In every country analyzed, measured IQs have risen sharply. The score for the most recent test in each country is assigned a value of 100; scores for earlier years are adjusted accordingly.

IQ INDEX*

Belgium · Norway · U.S. · Netherlands · Israel · Britain

1940 1950 1960 1970 1980 1990

*SOURCES: FLYNN; GOLDENBERG; RAVEN, RAVEN AND COURT

On a recent April weekend in Atlanta, psychologist Ulrich Neisser of Emory assembled 16 researchers to discuss these intriguing issues. Could rising living standards explain the IQ gain? Of the 20-odd-point rise, socioeconomic factors account for perhaps 5 points, Flynn calculates. Better schools? The greatest IQ gains have come on nonverbal intelligence tests—those that are heavy on mazes and puzzles. Yet these are the very tests that are designed to be free of such cultural influences as education. On tests of "acquired intelligence" (vocabulary or arithmetic or facts such as where turpentine comes from), which are expected to mirror acquired knowledge such as that from schooling, the gains are much smaller.

Might better nutrition and a more stimulating environment of museums and zoos, Legos and Transformers account for the IQ rise? Both can raise IQ scores, but only because they raise true intelligence by, say, giving the Legomaniac a better grasp of spatial relationships. And there is no evidence that real-world intelligence—an ability to learn faster or make creative leaps or do any of the other things that "intelligence" connotes—is rising at anything like the rate of IQ scores. (If it were, remember, the average American of 1918 couldn't have understood baseball.) Flynn calls this "the broken link" between IQ and intelligence.

At the Emory conference, Yale's Williams, an expert on the development of children's intelligence, pointed out that much of the IQ gain may simply reflect the greater familiarity that today's kids have with the sorts of questions posed on the tests. Taking her data from wherever she can find it, Williams has been collecting kids' cereal boxes and fast food bags. Both are covered with mazes and puzzles remarkably similar to what IQ tests ask. "In the 1930s a kid may never have seen a maze before finding one on his IQ test," says Williams. "It seems clear that the tests are not measuring innate, immutable intelligence, but a type of practiced learning and familiarity with the test questions."

But part of the IQ gain may reflect something far more meaningful, Williams suggested. Several studies indicate that a more permissive parenting style gives children a grater facility with language. "If the child is leading the parent, rather than always being directed, language skills develop faster," says Williams. "And language is closely linked to overall cognitive capacity. So while test-taking practice and a culture awash in mazes and puzzles would raise IQ scores without increasing intelligence in any meaningful way, parenting style may produce a true increase in intelligence and also in IQ."

Of all the explanations offered for the Flynn effect, Flynn himself is most taken with the idea that every generation comes of age in a world starkly different from their parents'. "Technological development has been going on in all the Flynn-effect countries," points out psychologist Patricia Greenfield of UCLA. And in some places formal schooling was greatly expanded during the same period. Whatever schools teach, they rely on the basic structure of test questions and answers. "The test question is the most basic convention on an intelligence test," says Greenfield. Children who have not had formal schooling would be unfamiliar with this format and therefore might do worse on standard IQ tests for reasons having nothing to do with their innate intelligence. More recently, Greenfield argues, wave upon wave of other cultural forces has lapped onto children's mental shores. Radio and TV drove up basic vocabulary. Videogames like Tetris enhanced such abilities as assembling a puzzle, a common IQ-test question. Action-packed videogames typically demand navigation through a two-dimensional representation of a 3-D space; mental paper folding, a prominent feature of the Stanford-Binet IQ test, demands the same skill. The spread of these image-intense technologies, says Greenfield, could explain the "spurt [in IQ scores] in the U.S. between 1972 and 1989."

Even Charles Murray, coauthor of "The Bell Curve," concedes that the Flynn effect provides "indirect support" for the idea that differences in blacks' and whites' IQs could reflect environmental factors. "It cautions against taking these differences as etched in stone," he says.

Somewhere out there, potent environmental forces are creating IQ differences. Some may rise both genuine intelligence and IQ; some may raise only IQ. Some may operate within generations as well as between generations, inflating the IQ scores of one child and deflating another's. Yet despite these unknowns, we still use IQ scores to sort out children into stimulating classrooms or dull ones, into prestigious schools or mediocre ones. The debate over the Flynn effect makes it clear that we're still not quite sure what we're measuring.

Social and Emotional Development

- The Child's Feelings: Emotional Development (Articles 17 and 18)
- Entry into the Social World: Peers, Play, and Popularity (Articles 19–21)

One of the truisms about our species is that we are social animals. From birth, each person's life is a constellation of relationships, from family at home to friends in the neighborhood and school. This unit addresses how children's social and emotional development is influenced by important relationships with parents, peers, and teachers.

When John Donne in 1623 wrote, "No man is an island . . . every man is . . . a part of the main," he implied that all humans are connected to each other and that these connections make us who we are. Early in this century, sociologist C. H. Cooley highlighted the importance of relationships with the phrase "looking-glass self" to describe how people tend to see themselves as a function of how others perceive them. Personality theorist Alfred Adler, also writing in the early twentieth century, claimed that personal strength derived from the quality of one's connectedness to others: The stronger the relationships, the stronger the person. The notion that a person's self-concept arises from relations with others also has roots in developmental psychology. As Jean Piaget once wrote, "There is no such thing as isolated individuals; there are only relations." The articles in this unit respect these traditions by emphasizing the theme that a child's development occurs within the context of relationships.

Not only does self-concept arise through relations with parents, but a child's sense of morality does as well. In "The Moral Power of Good Stories," William Kilpatrick discusses how the stories and fables that parents and teachers read with children may promote youngsters' character development and understanding of right and wrong.

Another major influence in the landscape of childhood is friendship. When do childhood friendships begin? Friends become increasingly important during the elementary school years. If forming strong, secure attachments with family members is an important task of early childhood, then one of the major psychological achievements of middle childhood is a move toward the peer group. Across the elementary school years, children spend ever-increasing time with peers in the neighborhood and at school. Janis Bullock, in "Children without Friends," examines children's relationships with peers and describes different kinds of children—popular, rejected, neglected.

This article helps us understand that friends are clearly a developmental and psychological advantage. Similarly, the essay "The EQ Factor" describes new research suggesting that a child's emotional intelligence may be a strong predictor of self-concept and social relationships and may be enhanced by appropriate environmental support.

An interesting characteristic of peer relations in middle childhood is that boys and girls rarely play together. Most of the time, boys play with boys and girls play with girls. "Girls and Boys Together . . . but Mostly Apart" discusses the central role of gender in social and emotional development.

Looking Ahead: Challenge Questions

What are some of the ways that friends can be beneficial or harmful to a child's self-concept and self-esteem? Why is it important for children to become members of a peer group? Can you think of popular books or movies that illustrate the values of friendship and peers?

Do you think you have a high EQ? What sort of emotional characteristics do you think may go into having a high EQ? Do you think personality is something that is innately given or can one's personality be changed in significant ways? If you had a child with a very introverted personality, would it be advisable to try and help this child learn to become more extroverted? Why or why not?

When you were a child, did you experience gender segregation—boys playing with boys, girls with girls? How might this have influenced your social and emotional development? Could gender segregation reinforce differences or create difficulties between boys and girls, and men and women? What could a teacher or parent do to influence gender segregation?

Why might stories and fables be effective tools for teaching children morals and values? Do you recall favorite books or stories from childhood, and how they affected your character development? Do you think the stories available to children today teach children important moral values? If you were a parent today, what sorts of stories or fables would you want to tell your children?

EARLY EXPERIENCE AND EMOTIONAL DEVELOPMENT:
The Emergence of Wariness of Heights

Joseph J. Campos,[1] Bennett I. Bertenthal,[2] and Rosanne Kermoian[1]

[1]University of California at Berkeley, [2]University of Virginia

Abstract—*Because of its biological adaptive value, wariness of heights is widely believed to be innate or under maturational control. In this report, we present evidence contrary to this hypothesis, and show the importance of locomotor experience for emotional development. Four studies bearing on this conclusion have shown that (1) when age is held constant, locomotor experience accounts for wariness of heights; (2) "artificial" experience locomoting in a walker generates evidence of wariness of heights; (3) an orthopedically handicapped infant tested longitudinally did not show wariness of heights so long as he had no locomotor experience; and (4) regardless of the age when infants begin to crawl, it is the duration of locomotor experience and not age that predicts avoidance of heights. These findings suggest that when infants begin to crawl, experiences generated by locomotion make possible the development of wariness of heights.*

Between 6 and 10 months of age, major changes occur in fearfulness in the human infant. During this period, some fears are shown for the first time, and many others show a step-function increase in prevalence (Bridges, 1932; Scarr & Salapatek, 1970; Sroufe, 1979). These changes in fearfulness occur so abruptly, involve so many different elicitors, and have such biologically adaptive value that many investigators propose maturational explanations for this developmental shift (Emde, Gaensbauer, & Harmon, 1976; Kagan, Kearsley, & Zelazo, 1978). For such theorists, the development of neurophysiological structures (e.g., the frontal lobes) precedes and accounts for changes in affect.

In contrast to predominantly maturational explanations of developmental changes, Gottlieb (1983, 1991) proposed a model in which different types of experiences play an important role in developmental shifts. He emphasized that new developmental acquisitions, such as crawling, generate experiences that, in turn, create the conditions for further developmental changes. Gottlieb called such "bootstrapping" processes probabilistic epigenesis. In contrast to most current models of developmental transition, Gottlieb's approach stresses the possibility that, under some circumstances, psychological function may precede and account for development of neurophysiological structures.

There is evidence in the animal literature that a probabilistic epigenetic process plays a role in the development of wariness of heights. Held and Hein (1963), for instance, showed that dark-reared kittens given experience with active self-produced locomotion in an illuminated environment showed avoidance of heights, whereas dark-reared littermates given passive experience moving in the same environment manifested no such avoidance. In these studies, despite equivalent maturational states in the two groups of kittens, the experiences made possible by correlated visuomotor responses during active locomotion proved necessary to elicit wariness of heights.

So long as they are prelocomotor, human infants, despite their visual competence and absence of visual deprivation, may be functionally equivalent to Held and Hein's passively moved kittens. Crawling may generate or refine skills sufficient for the onset of wariness of heights. These skills may include improved calibration of distances, heightened sensitivity to visually specified self-motion, more consistent coordination of visual and vestibular stimulation, and increased awareness of emotional signals from significant others (Bertenthal & Campos, 1990; Campos, Hiatt, Ramsay, Henderson, & Svejda, 1978).

There is anecdotal evidence supporting a link between locomotor experience and development of wariness of heights in human infants. Parents commonly report that there is a phase following the acquisition of locomotion when infants show no avoidance of heights, and will go over the edge of a bed or other precipice if the caretaker is not vigilant. Parents also report that this phase of apparent fearlessness is followed by one in which wariness of heights becomes quite intense (Campos et al., 1978).

In sum, both the kitten research and the anecdotal human evidence suggest that wariness of heights is not simply a maturational phenomenon, to be expected even in the absence of experience. From the perspective of probabilistic epigenesis, locomotor experience may operate as an organizer of emotional development, serving either to induce wariness of heights (i.e., to produce a potent emotional state that would never emerge without such experience) or to facilitate its emergence (i.e., to bring it about earlier than it otherwise would appear). The research reported here represents an attempt to determine whether

This research was supported by grants from the National Institutes of Health (HD-16195, HD-00695, and HD-25066) and from the John D. and Catherine T. MacArthur Foundation.

Address requests for reprints to Joseph J. Campos, Institute of Human Development, 1203 Tolman Hall, University of California at Berkeley, Berkeley, CA 94720.

locomotor experience is indeed an organizer of the emergence of wariness of heights.

Pinpointing the role of locomotion in the emergence of wariness of heights in human infants requires solution of a number of methodological problems. One is the selection of an ecologically valid paradigm for testing wariness of heights. Another is the determination of an outcome measure that can be used with both prelocomotor and locomotor infants. A third is a means of determining whether locomotion is playing a role as a correlate, an antecedent, an inducer, or a facilitator of the onset of wariness of heights.

The ecologically valid paradigm we selected for testing was the visual cliff (Walk, 1966; Walk & Gibson, 1961)—a large, safety-glass-covered table with a solid textured surface placed immediately underneath the glass on one side (the "shallow" side) and a similar surface placed some 43 in. underneath the glass on the floor below on the other side (the "deep" side).

To equate task demands for prelocomotor and locomotor infants, we measured the infants' wariness reactions while they were slowly lowered toward either the deep or the shallow side of the cliff. This descent procedure not only allowed us to assess differences in wariness reactions as a function of locomotor experience in both prelocomotor and locomotor infants but also permitted us to assess an index of depth perception, that is, a visual placing response (the extension of the arms and hands in anticipation of contact with the shallow, but not the deep, surface of the cliff [Walters, 1981]).

To assess fearfulness with an index appropriate to both pre- and postlocomoting infants, we measured heart rate (HR) responses during the 3-s period of descent onto the surface of the cliff. Prior work had shown consistently that heart rate decelerates in infants who are in a state of nonfearful attentiveness, but accelerates when infants are showing either a defensive response (Graham & Clifton, 1966) or a precry state (Campos, Emde, Gaensbauer, & Henderson, 1975).

To relate self-produced locomotion to fearfulness, we used a number of converging research operations. One was an *age-held-constant design,* contrasting the performance of infants who were locomoting with those of the same age who

were not yet locomoting; the second was an analog of an experiential *enrichment* manipulation, in which infants who were otherwise incapable of crawling or creeping were tested after they had a number of hours of experience moving about voluntarily in walker devices; the third was an analog of an experiential *deprivation* manipulation, in which an infant who was orthopedically handicapped, but otherwise normal, was tested longitudinally past the usual age of onset of crawling and again after the delayed acquisition of crawling; and the fourth was a *cross-sequential lag design* aimed at teasing apart the effects of age of onset of locomotion and of duration of locomotor experience on the infant's avoidance of crossing the deep or the shallow side of the cliff to the mother.

EXPERIMENT 1: HR RESPONSES OF PRELOCOMOTOR AND LOCOMOTOR INFANTS

In the first study, a total of 92 infants, half locomoting for an average of 5 weeks, were tested at 7.3 months of age. Telemetered HR, facial expressions (taped from a camera under the deep side of the cliff), and the visual placing response were recorded. Each infant was lowered to each side of the cliff by a female experimenter, with the mother in another room.

As predicted from the work of Held and Hein (1963), locomotor infants showed evidence of wariness of heights, and prelocomotor infants did not. Only on deep trials did the HR of locomotor infants accelerate significantly from baselevels (by 5 beats/min), and differ significantly from the HR responses of prelocomotor infants. The HR responses of prelocomotor infants did not differ from baselevels on either the deep or shallow sides. Surprisingly, facial expressions did not differentiate testing conditions, perhaps because the descent minimized the opportunity to target these expressions to social figures.

In addition, every infant tested, regardless of locomotor status, showed visual placing responses on the shallow side, and no infant showed placing responses on the deep side of the cliff. Thus, all infants showed evidence for depth perception on the deep side, but only locomotor infants showed evidence of fear-related cardiac acceleration in response to heights.

EXPERIMENT 2: ACCELERATION OF LOCOMOTOR EXPERIENCE

Although correlated, the development of locomotion and the emergence of wariness of heights may be jointly determined by a third factor that brings about both changes. Disambiguation of this possibility required a means of providing "artificial" locomotor experience to infants who were not yet able to crawl. This manipulation was achieved by providing wheeled walkers to infants and testing them after their mothers had reported at least 32 hr of voluntary forward movement in the device.

Infants who received walkers were divided into two groups: prelocomotor walkers ($N = $ 9M, 9F, Mean Age = 224 days, Walker Experience = 47 hr of voluntary forward movement) and locomotor walkers ($N = $ 9M, 7F, Mean Age = 222 days, Walker Experience = 32 hr). The performance of infants in these two groups was compared with the performance of age-matched subjects, also divided into two groups: prelocomotor controls ($N = $ 9M, 9F, Mean Age = 222 days) and locomotor controls ($N = $ 9M, 7F, Mean Age = 222 days). The average duration of crawling experience was only 5 days in the locomotor walker and the locomotor control groups. All infants were tested using the same procedure as in the prior study. No shallow trials were administered in order to minimize subject loss due to the additional testing time required for such trials.

As revealed in Figure 1, the three groups of infants with any type of locomotor experience showed evidence of cardiac acceleration, whereas the prelocomotor control infants did not. It is noteworthy that all 16 infants in the locomotor walker group (who had a "double dosage" of locomotor experience consisting of walker training and some crawling) showed HR accelerations upon descent to the cliff. Planned comparisons revealed significant differences between (1) all walker infants and all controls, (2) all spontaneously locomoting infants and prelocomotor controls, and (3) prelocomotor walkers and prelocomotor controls. These findings show that the provision of "artificial" locomotor experience may facilitate or induce wariness of heights, even for infants who otherwise have little or no crawling experience. Locomotor experience thus appears to be an antecedent of the emergence of wariness.

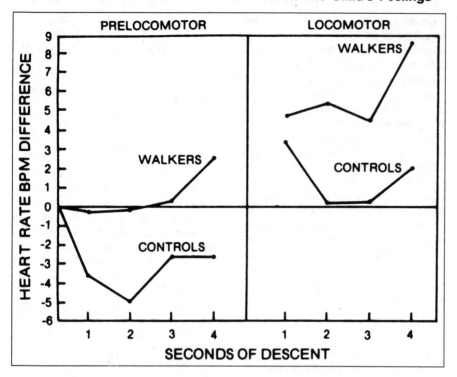

Fig. 1. Heart rate response while the infant is lowered toward the deep side of the visual cliff as a function of locomotor experience. The left panel contrasts the performance of prelocomotor infants with and without "artificial" walker experience. The right panel contrasts the performance of crawling infants with and without "artificial" walker experience. Heart rate is expressed as difference from baseline in beats/min.

sessed separately the effects of age of onset of crawling (early, normative, or late) and of duration of locomotor experience (11 or 41 days), as well as their interaction, using a longitudinal design.

The results of this study demonstrated a clear effect of locomotor experience independent of the age when self-produced locomotion first appeared. This effect of experience was evident with both nominal data (the proportion of infants who avoided descending onto the deep side of the cliff on the first test trial) and interval data (the latency to descend from the center board of the visual cliff onto the deep side on deep trials minus the latency to descend onto the shallow side on shallow trials). At whatever age the infant had begun to crawl, only 30% to 50% of infants avoided the deep side after 11 days of locomotor experience. However, after 41 days of locomotor experience, avoidance increased to 60% to 80% of infants. The latency data revealed a significant interaction of side of cliff with locomotor experience, but not a main effect of age, nor of the interaction of age with experience. The results of this study further suggest that locomotor experience paces the onset of wariness of heights.

EXPERIMENT 3: DEPRIVATION OF LOCOMOTOR EXPERIENCE

Although Experiment 2 showed that training in locomotion accelerates the onset of wariness of heights, it is possible that this response would eventually develop even in the absence of locomotor experience. To determine whether the delayed acquisition of crawling precedes the delayed emergence of wariness of heights, we longitudinally tested an infant with a peripheral handicap to locomotion. This infant was neurologically normal and had a Bayley Developmental Quotient of 126, but was born with two congenitally dislocated hips. After an early operation, he was placed in a full body cast. The infant was tested on the visual cliff monthly between 6 and 10 months of age using the procedures described above. While the infant was in the cast, he showed no evidence of crawling. At 8.5 months of age (i.e., 1.5 months after the normative age of onset of locomotion), the cast was removed, and the infant began crawling soon afterward.

This infant showed no evidence of dif-

ferential cardiac responsiveness on the deep versus shallow side of the cliff until 10 months of age, at which time his HR accelerated markedly on the deep side, and decelerated on the shallow. Although we cannot generalize from a single case study, these data provide further support for the role of self-produced locomotion as a facilitator or inducer of wariness of heights.

EXPERIMENT 4: AGE OF ONSET OF LOCOMOTION VERSUS LOCOMOTOR EXPERIENCE

In the studies described so far, HR was used as an imperfect index of wariness. However, we felt that a study using behavioral avoidance was needed to confirm the link between locomotor experience and wariness of heights. We thus used the locomotor crossing test on the visual cliff, in which the infant is placed on the center of the cliff, and the mother is instructed to encourage the infant to cross to her over either the deep or the shallow side. In this study, we also as-

PROCESSES UNDERLYING THE DEVELOPMENT OF WARINESS OF HEIGHTS

The pattern of findings obtained in these four studies, taken together with the animal studies by Held and Hein (1963), demonstrates a consistent relation between locomotor experience and wariness of heights. We propose the following interpretations for our findings.

We believe that crawling initially is a goal in itself, with affect solely linked to the success or failure of implementing the act of moving. Locomotion is initially not context dependent, and infants show no wariness of heights because the goal of moving is not coordinated with other goals, including the avoidance of threats. However, as a result of locomotor experience, infants acquire a sense of both the efficacy and the limitations of their own actions. Locomotion stops being an end in itself, and begins to be goal corrected and coordinated with the environmental surround. As a result, infants begin to show wariness of heights once locomotion becomes context dependent (cf. Bertenthal & Campos, 1990).

The context-dependency of the infants' actions may come about from falling and near-falling experiences that locomotion generates. Near-falls are particularly important because they are frequent, they elicit powerful emotional signals from the parent, and they set the stage for long-term retention of negative affect in such contexts.

There is still another means by which the infant can acquire a sense of wariness of depth with locomotion. While the infant moves about voluntarily, visual information specifying self-movement becomes more highly correlated with vestibular information specifying the same amount of self-movement (Bertenthal & Campos, 1990). Once expectancies related to the correlation of visual and vestibular information are formed, being lowered toward the deep side of the cliff creates a violation of the expected correlation. This violation results from the absence of visible texture near the infant when lowered toward the deep side of the cliff, relative to the shallow side. As a consequence, angular acceleration is not detected by the visual system, whereas it is detected by the vestibular system. This violation of expectation results in distress proportional to the magnitude of the violation. A test of this interpretation requires assessment of the establishment of visual-vestibular coordination as a function of locomotor experience and confirmation that wariness occurs in contexts that violate visual-vestibular coordination.

LOCOMOTOR EXPERIENCE AND OTHER EMOTIONAL CHANGES

The consequences of the development of self-produced locomotion for emotional development extend far beyond the domain of wariness of heights. Indeed, the onset of locomotion generates an entirely different emotional climate in the family. For instance, as psychoanalytic theories predict (e.g., Mahler, Pine, & Bergman, 1975), the onset of locomotion brings about a burgeoning of both positive and negative affect—positive affect because of the child's new levels of self-efficacy; negative affect because of the increases in frustration resulting from thwarting of the child's goals and because of the affective resonance that comes from increased parental expressions of prohibition (Campos, Kermoian, & Zumbahlen, in press). Locomotion is also crucial for the development of attachment (Ainsworth, Blehar, Waters, & Wall, 1978; Bowlby, 1973), because it makes physical proximity to the caregiver possible. With the formation of specific attachments, locomotion increases in significance as the child becomes better able to move independently toward novel and potentially frightening environments. Infants are also more sensitive to the location of the parent, more likely to show distress upon separation, and more likely to look to the parent in ambiguous situations.

Locomotion also brings about emotional changes in the parents. These changes include the increased pride (and sometimes sorrow) that the parents experience in their child's new mobility and independence and the new levels of anger parents direct at the baby when the baby begins to encounter forbidden objects. It seems clear from the findings obtained in this line of research that new levels of functioning in one behavioral domain can generate experiences that profoundly affect other developmental domains, including affective, social, cognitive, and sensorimotor ones (Kermoian & Campos, 1988). We thus propose that theoretical orientations like probabilistic epigenesis provide a novel, heuristic, and timely perspective for the study of emotional development.

REFERENCES

Ainsworth, M.D.S., Blehar, M., Waters, E., & Wall, S. (1978). *Patterns of attachment.* Hillsdale, NJ: Erlbaum.

Bertenthal, B., & Campos, J.J. (1990). A systems approach to the organizing effects of self-produced locomotion during infancy. In C. Rovee-Collier & L.P. Lipsitt (Eds.), *Advances in infancy research* (Vol. 6, pp. 1–60). Norwood, NJ: Ablex.

Bowlby, J. (1973). *Attachment and loss: Vol. 2. Separation.* New York: Basic Books.

Bridges, K.M. (1932). Emotional development in early infancy. *Child Development, 3,* 324–341.

Campos, J.J., Emde, R.N., Gaensbauer, T.J., & Henderson, C. (1975). Cardiac and behavioral interrelationships in the reactions of infants to strangers. *Developmental Psychology, 11,* 589–601.

Campos, J.J., Hiatt, S., Ramsay, D., Henderson, C., & Svejda, M. (1978). The emergence of fear of heights. In M. Lewis & L. Rosenblum (Eds.), *The development of affect* (pp. 149–182). New York: Plenum Press.

Campos, J.J., Kermoian, R., & Zumbahlen, R.M. (in press). In N. Eisenberg (Ed.), *New directions for child development.* San Francisco: Jossey-Bass.

Emde, R.N., Gaensbauer, T.J., & Harmon, R.J. (1976). Emotional expression in infancy: A biobehavioral study. *Psychological Issues* (Vol. 10, No. 37). New York: International Universities Press.

Gottlieb, G. (1983). The psychobiological approach to developmental issues. In P. Mussen (Ed.), *Handbook of child psychology: Vol. II. Infancy and developmental psychobiology* (4th ed.) (pp. 1–26). New York: Wiley.

Gottlieb, G. (1991). Experiential canalization of behavioral development: Theory. *Developmental Psychology 27,* 4–13.

Graham, F.K., & Clifton, R.K. (1966). Heartrate change as a component of the orienting response. *Psychological Bulletin, 65,* 305–320.

Held, R., & Hein, A. (1963). Movement-produced stimulation in the development of visually-guided behavior. *Journal of Comparative and Physiological Psychology, 56,* 872–876.

Kagan, J., Kearsley, R., & Zelazo, P.R. (1978). *Infancy: Its place in human development.* Cambridge, MA: Harvard University Press.

Kermoian, R., & Campos, J.J. (1988). Locomotor experience: A facilitator of spatial cognitive development. *Child Development, 59,* 908–917.

Mahler, M., Pine, F., & Bergman, A. (1975). *The psychological birth of the human infant.* New York: Basic Books.

Scarr, S., & Salapatek, P. (1970). Patterns of fear development during infancy. *Merrill-Palmer Quarterly, 16,* 53–90.

Sroufe, L.A. (1979). Socioemotional development. In J. Osofsky (Ed.), *Handbook of infant development* (pp. 462–516). New York: Wiley.

Walk, R. (1966). The development of depth perception in animals and human infants. *Monographs of the Society for Research in Child Development, 31*(Whole No. 5).

Walk, R., & Gibson, E. (1961). A comparative and analytical study of visual depth perception. *Psychological Monographs, 75*(15, Whole No. 5).

Walters, C. (1981). Development of the visual placing response in the human infant. *Journal of Experimental Child Psychology, 32,* 313–329.

THE MORAL POWER OF GOOD STORIES

WILLIAM KILPATRICK

William Kilpatrick is a professor of education at Boston College.

ONE OF the simplest but most important things we can do to encourage character development in youngsters is to acquaint them with stories and histories that can give them a common reference point and supply them with a stock of good examples.

Stories help to make sense of our lives. They also create a desire to be good. Plato, who thought long and hard about the subject of moral education, believed that children should be brought up in such a way that they would fall in love with virtue. And he thought that stories and histories were the key to sparking this desire. No amount of discussion or dialogue could compensate if that spark was missing.

Yet today very little attention is paid to this aspect of a child's development. Contemporary educators have for too long assumed that the desire to be good will just be there. But we have learned in recent years that this is not the case. The desire has to be instilled by caring parents and thoughtful teachers. As Plato understood, one of the best ways to do it is with stories. They allow us to identify with models of courage and virtue in a way that "problem solving" or classroom discussion does not.

Stories have always been an important way of transmitting values and wisdom. They become all the more important in a society that, like ours, has experienced so much disruption in the family and in the community. The lessons contained in good stories are lessons the child might not otherwise get in a world of harried adults and fractured social institutions.

One of the early calls for returning stories to the curriculum was made by William Bennett in a speech before the Manhattan Institute:

> Do we want our children to know what honesty means? Then we might teach them about Abe Lincoln walking three miles to return six cents and, conversely, about Aesop's shepherd boy who cried wolf.
>
> Do we want our children to know what courage means? Then we might teach them about Joan of Arc, Horatius at the Bridge, Harriet Tubman and the Underground Railroad.
>
> Do we want them to know about kindness and compassion, and their opposites? Then they should read *A Christmas Carol* and *The Diary of Anne Frank* and, later on, *King Lear.*

It's a long list and one that no doubt would have horrified Rousseau. Among the reasons Bennett puts forward in arguing for the primacy of stories are that "unlike courses in moral reasoning," they provide a "stock of examples illustrating what we believe to be right and wrong," and that they "help anchor our children in their culture, its history and traditions. They give children a mooring." "This is necessary," he continues, "because morality, of course, is inextricably bound both to the individual conscience and the memory of society . . . We should teach these accounts of character to our children so that we may welcome them to a common world . . ."

Bennett's concern over character was not simply a conservative phenomenon. Liberals too were having second thoughts about a moral education that relied on moral reasoning. In a 1988 speech that could easily have been mistaken for one of Bennett's, Derek Bok, the president of Harvard University stated:

> Socrates sometimes talked as if knowledge alone would suffice to ensure virtuous behavior. He did not stress the value of early habituation, positive

From *American Educator,* Summer 1993, pp. 24-35. Adapted from *Why Johnny Can't Tell Right from Wrong: Moral Illiteracy and the Case for Character Education* by William Kilpatrick. © 1992 by William Kilpatrick. Reprinted by permission of Simon & Schuster, Inc.

example and obedience to rules in giving students the desire and self-discipline to live up to their beliefs and to respect the basic norms of behavior essential to civilized communities.

Bok went on to call for "a broader effort to teach by habit, example and exhortation," and unlike Bennett, he was speaking not of the elementary or high school but of the university level.

Nevertheless, one still finds a resistance among many educators toward the kind of stories Bennett recommends—stories that teach by example. I don't mean this in a conspiratorial sense. I find this reaction in student teachers who have never heard of Bennett. Moreover, as far as I know, no committee of educators ever came together to promulgate an anti-story agenda. It has been more a matter of climate, and of what the climate would allow. In my conversations with teachers and would-be teachers, one of the most common themes I hear is their conviction that they simply don't have the right to tell students anything about right and wrong. Many have a similar attitude toward literature with a moral; they would also feel uneasy about letting a story do the telling for them. The most pejorative word in their vocabulary is "preach." But the loss of stories doesn't strike them as a serious loss. They seem to be convinced that whatever is of value in the old stories will be found out anyway. Some are Rousseauians and believe it will be found out through instinct; others subscribe to some version or other of critical thinking and believe it will be found out through reason.

The latter attitude is a legacy of the Enlightenment, but it is far more widespread now than it ever was in the eighteenth century. The argument then and now is as follows: Stories and myth may have been necessary to get the attention of ignorant farmers and fishermen, but intelligent people don't need to have their ethical principles wrapped in a pretty box; they are perfectly capable of grasping the essential point without being charmed by myths, and because they can reach their own conclusions, they are less susceptible to the harmful superstitions and narrow prejudices that may be embedded in stories. This attitude may be characterized as one of wanting to establish the moral of the story without the story. It does not intend to do away with morality but to make it more secure by disentangling it from a web of fictions. For example, during the Enlightenment the Bible came to be looked upon as an attempt to convey a set of advanced ethical ideas to primitive people who could understand them only if they were couched in story form. A man of the Enlightenment, however, could dispense with the stories and myths, mysteries and miracles, could dispense, for that matter, with a belief in God, and still retain the essence—the Christian ethic.

The decision-making approach to moral education—which relies on students to discover values for themselves—is in this tradition. It presents dilemmas that are stories of a sort, but they are stories with the juice squeezed out of them. Once you've thought your way through to a position on the issue, you can forget about the characters. The important thing is to understand the principles involved. Moreover, a real story with well-defined characters might play on a child's emotions and thus intrude on his or her thinking process.

But is it really possible to streamline morality in this way? Can we extract the ethical kernel and discard the rest? Or does something vital get lost in the process? As the noted short story writer Flannery O'Connor put it, "A story is a way to say something that can't be said any other way . . . You tell a story because a statement would be inadequate." In brief, can we have the moral of the story without the story? And if we can, how long can we hold it in our hands before it begins to dissolve?

The danger of such abstraction is that we quickly tend to forget the human element in morality. The utilitarian system of ethics that was a product of the English Enlightenment provides a good illustration of what can happen. It was a sort of debit-credit system of morality in which the rightness or wrongness of acts depended on their usefulness in maintaining a smoothly running social machine. Utilitarianism oiled the cogs of the Industrial Revolution by providing reasonable justifications for child labor, dangerous working conditions, long hours and low wages. For the sake of an abstraction—"the greatest happiness for the greatest number"—utilitarianism was willing to ignore the real human suffering created by the factory system.

Some of the most powerful attacks on that system can be found in the novels of Charles Dickens. Dickens brought home to his readers the human face of child labor and debtors' prison. And he did it in a way that was hard to ignore or shake off. Such graphic "reminders" may come to us through reading or they may come to us through personal experience, but without them, even the most intelligent and best-educated person will begin to lose sight of the fact that moral issues are human issues.

I USE the words "lose sight of" advisedly. There is an important sense in which morality has a visual base—or, if you want, a visible base. In other words, there is a connection between virtue and vision. One has to see correctly before one can act correctly. This connection was taken quite seriously in the ancient world. Plato's most famous parable—the parable of the cave—explains moral confusion in terms of simple misdirected vision: the men in the cave are looking in the wrong direction. Likewise, the Bible prophets regarded moral blindness not only as a sin but as the root of a multitude of sins.

The reason why seeing is so important to the moral life is that many of the moral facts of life are apprehended through observation. Much of the moral law consists of axioms or premises about human beings and human conduct. And one does not arrive at premises by reasoning. You either see them or you don't. The Declaration of Independence's assertion that some truths are "self-evident" is one example of this visual approach to right and wrong. The word "evident" means "present and plainly visible." Many of Abraham Lincoln's arguments were of the same order. When Southern slave owners claimed the same right as Northerners to bring their "property" into the new territories, Lincoln replied: "That is to say, inasmuch as you do not object to my taking my hog to Nebraska, therefore I must not object to your taking your slave. Now, I admit this is perfectly logical, if there is no difference between hogs and Negroes."

Lincoln's argument against slavery is not logical but definitional. It is a matter of plain sight that Negroes are persons. But even the most obvious moral facts can be denied or explained away once the imagination becomes captive to a distorted vision. The point is illustrated by a recent Woody Allen film, *Crimes and Misdemeanors.* The central character, Judah Rosenthal, who is both an ophthalmologist and a philanthropist, is faced with a dilemma: What should he do about his mistress? She has become possessive and neurotic and has started to do what mistresses are never supposed to do: she has begun to make phone calls to his office and to his home, thus threatening to completely ruin his life—a life that in many ways has been one of service. Judah seeks advice from two people: his brother Jack, who has ties to the underworld, and a rabbi, who tries to call Judah back to the vision of his childhood faith. The rabbi (who is nearly blind) advises Judah to end the relationship, even if it means exposure, and to ask his wife for forgiveness. Jack, on the other hand, having ascertained the woman's potential for doing damage and her unwillingness to listen to reason, advises Judah to "go on to the next [logical] step," and he offers to have her "taken care of." The interesting thing is that Jack's reasoning powers are just as good as the rabbi's; and based on his vision of the world, they make perfect sense. You simply don't take the chance that a vindictive person will destroy your marriage and your career. And indeed, Jack finally wins the argument. In an imagined conversation, Judah tells the rabbi, "You live in the Kingdom of Heaven, Jack lives in the real world." The woman is "taken care of."

Jack's reasoning may be taken as an example of deranged rationality or—if you change your angle of vision—as the only smart thing to do. Certain moral principles make sense within the context of certain visions of life, but from within the context of other visions, they don't make much sense at all. From within the vision provided by the rabbi's faith, all lives are sacred; from Jack's viewpoint, some lives don't count.

Many of the moral principles we subscribe to seem reasonable to us only because they are embedded within a vision or worldview we hold to be true—even though we might not think very often about it. In the same way, a moral transformation is often accompanied by a transformation of vision. Many ordinary people describe their moral improvement as the result of seeing things in a different light or seeing them for the first time. "I was blind but now I see" is more than a line from an old hymn; it is the way a great many people explain their moral growth.

If we can agree that morality is intimately bound up with vision, then we can see why stories are so important for our moral development and why neglecting them is a serious mistake. This is because stories are one of the chief ways by which visions are conveyed (a vision, in turn, may be defined as a story about the way things are or the way the world works). Just as vision and morality are intimately connected, so are story and morality. Some contemporary philosophers of ethics—most notably, Alasdair MacIntyre—now maintain that the connection between narrative and morality is an essential one, not

merely a useful one. The Ph.D. needs the story "part" just as much as the peasant. In other words, story and moral may be less separable than we have come to think. The question is not whether the moral principle needs to be sweetened with the sugar of the story but whether moral principles make any sense outside the human context of stories.

In recent years a number of prominent psychologists and educators have turned their attention to stories. In *The Uses of Enchantment* (1975), child psychiatrist Bruno Bettelheim argued that fairy tales are a vital source of psychological and moral strength; their formative power, he said, had been seriously underestimated. Robert Coles of Harvard University followed in the 1980s with three books *(The Moral Life of Children, The Spiritual Life of Children,* and *The Call of Stories),* which detailed the indispensable role of stories in the life of both children and adults. Another Harvard scholar, Jerome Bruner, whose earlier *The Process of Education* had helped stimulate interest in critical thinking, had, by the mid-eighties, begun to worry that "propositional thinking" had been emphasized at the expense of "narrative thinking"—literally, a way of thinking in stories. In *Actual Minds, Possible Worlds,* Bruner suggests that it is this narrative thought, much more than logical thought, that gives meaning to life.

A number of other psychologists had arrived at similar conclusions. Theodore Sarbin, Donald Spence, Paul Vitz, and others have emphasized the extent to which individuals interpret their own lives as stories or narratives. "Indeed," writes Vitz, "it is almost impossible not to think this way." According to these psychologists, it is such narrative plots more than anything else that guide our moral choices. Coles, in *The Moral Life of Children,* observes how the children he came to know through his work not only understood their own lives in a narrative way but were profoundly influenced in their decisions by the stories, often of a religious kind, they had learned.

By the mid-eighties a similar story had begun to unfold in the field of education. Under the leadership of Professor Kevin Ryan, Boston University's Center for the Advancement of Character and Ethics produced a number of position papers calling for a reemphasis on literature as a moral teacher and guide. Meanwhile, in *Teaching as Storytelling* and other books, Kieran Egan of Canada's Simon Fraser University was proposing that the foundations of all education are poetic and imaginative. Even logico-mathematical and rational forms of thinking grow out of imagination, and depend on it. Egan argues that storytelling should be the basic educational method because it corresponds with fundamental structures of the human mind. Like Paul Vitz, he suggests that it is nearly impossible not to think in story terms. "Most of the world's cultures and its great religions," he points out, "have at their sacred core a story, and we indeed have difficulty keeping our rational history from being constantly shaped into stories."

In short, scholars in several fields were belatedly discovering what Flannery O'Connor, with her writer's intuition, had noticed years before: "A story is a way to say something that can't be said any other way . . ."

THIS RECENT interest in stories should not, however, be interpreted as simply another Romantic reaction to rationalism. None of the people I have mentioned could be classified as Romanticists. Several of them (including Flannery O'Connor) freely acknowledge their indebtedness to Aristotle and Aquinas—to what might be called the "realist" tradition in philosophy. Although literature can be used as an escape, the best literature, as Jacques Barzun said, carries us back to reality. It involves us in the detail and particularity of other lives. And unlike the superficial encounters of the workaday world, a book shows us what other lives are like from the inside. Moral principles also take on a reality in stories that they lack in purely logical form. Stories restrain our tendency to indulge in abstract speculation about ethics. They make it a little harder for us to reduce people to factors in an equation.

I can illustrate the overall point by mentioning a recurrent phenomenon in my classes. I have noticed that when my students are presented with a Values Clarification strategy and then with a dramatic account of the same situation, they respond one way to the dilemma and another to the story. In the Values Clarification dilemma called "The Lifeboat Exercise," the class is asked to imagine that a ship has sunk and a lifeboat has been put out from it. The lifeboat is overcrowded and in danger of being swamped unless the load is lightened. The students are given a brief description of the passengers—a young couple and their child, an elderly brother and sister, a doctor, a bookkeeper, an athlete, an entertainer, and so on—and from this list they must decide whom to throw overboard. Consistent with current thinking, there are no right and wrong answers in this exercise. The idea is to generate discussion. And it works quite well. Students are typically excited by the lifeboat dilemma.

This scenario, of course, is similar to the situation that faced the crew and passengers of the *Titanic* when it struck an iceberg in the North Atlantic in 1912. But when the event is presented as a story rather than as a dilemma, the response evoked is not the same. For example, when students who have done the exercise are given the opportunity to view the film *A Night to Remember,* they react in a strikingly different way. I've watched classes struggle with the lifeboat dilemma, but the struggle is mainly an intellectual one—like doing a crossword puzzle. The characters in the exercise, after all, are only hypothetical. They are counters to be moved around at will. We can't really identify them, nor can we be inspired or repelled by them. They exist only for the sake of the exercise.

When they watch the film, however, these normally blasé college students behave differently. Many of them cry. They cry as quietly as possible, of course: even on the college level it is extremely important to maintain one's cool. But this is a fairly consistent reaction. I've observed it in several different classes over several years. They don't even have to see the whole film. About twenty minutes of excerpts will do the trick.

What does the story do that the exercise doesn't? Very simply, it moves them deeply and profoundly. This is what art is supposed to do.

NOT ALL STORIES INSPIRE US TO BE BETTER THAN WE ARE

GOOD LITERATURE doesn't introduce a child to "kids like me" but to others who are better than himself—who are just like he might become if he fulfills his potential for goodness. "When we read," writes novelist John Gardner, "we ingest metaphors of goodness, wordlessly learning to behave more like Levin than like Anna (in *Anna Karenina*), more like the transformed Emma (in Jane Austen's novel) than like the Emma we first meet in the book." We can easily add more examples: learning to behave more like the transformed boy in *Captains Courageous* than the boy we first meet, more like Portia than Shylock, more like the younger brother in *King of the Golden River* than the older brothers (he gives water to a thirsty man; they refuse). When fiction works for us, observes critic Wayne Booth, we have been—at least for the duration—that kind of person.

But not all stories inspire us to be better than we are. By the decade of the seventies, a new type of story was coming into vogue. Psychologist David Elkind refers to it as the "therapeutic" story:

> Previously in much of children's literature, the goals were often to help or to please others—parents, friends, pets—who were needy or endangered. A boy took risks to save a dog, or a girl worked hard to get a desired gift for a sick friend. In children's fiction today, however, the goals are often therapeutic and rehabilitative. Heroes and heroines are healing themselves rather than helping others.

Healing themselves—or increasingly, it appears, simply accepting themselves. The best examples of this literature of self-acceptance are the stories of Judy Blume. Blume, far and away the most successful author of books for young adults, writes: "When I was young I could never find any books about kids like me, and that's what I wanted to read about." The "kids like me" she writes about are self-obsessed, sexually absorbed, shallow, sullen, emotionally numb, contemptuous of adults, and relentlessly materialistic. Youngsters of this sort have, of course, appeared before in fiction: the character of Nellie from *Little House on the Prairie* comes to mind. The novel thing about the Blume books is that her non-judgmental prose contains no suggestion that such children should mend their ways. The main characters in stories such as *Blubber* and *Then Again Maybe I Won't* are nasty and meanspirited—but "so what?" as they might say. "That's the way kids are, and it's okay" seems to mark the limit of the Blume philosophy. There is in her stories no encouragement to look outside the self, and thus, as Michelle Landsberg, a Canadian writer, observes of Blume, no "enlargements of the self." Rather, her books consistently endorse narcissistic self-centeredness. Children didn't exactly stop reading books in the seventies and eighties, but more and more of what they were reading resembled nothing so much as junior versions of Rousseau's *Confessions*.

If you have seen the film, you may recall some of the vivid sketches of the passengers on the dying ship as the situation becomes clear to them: Edith Evans, giving up a place on the last boat to Mrs. Brown, saying, "You go first; you have children waiting at home." Harvey Collyer pleading with his wife, "Go, Lottie! For God's sake, be brave and go! I'll get a seat in another boat." Mrs. Isidor Straus declining a place in the boats: "I've always stayed with my husband, so why should I leave him now?"

The story is full of scenes like this: Arthur Ryerson stripping off his life vest and giving it to his wife's maid; men struggling below-decks to keep the pumps going in the face of almost certain death; the ship's band playing ragtime and then hymns till the very end; the women in boat 6 insisting that it return to pick up survivors; the men clinging to the hull of an overturned boat, reciting the Lord's Prayer; the *Carpathia*, weaving in and out of ice floes, racing at breakneck speed to the rescue. But there are other images as well: the indolence and stupidity of the *California's* crew, who, only ten miles away, might have made all the difference, but did nothing; the man disguised in a women's shawl; the panicked mob of men rushing a lifeboat; passengers in half-empty lifeboats refusing to go back to save the drowning.

The film doesn't leave the viewer much room for ethical maneuvering. It is quite clear who has acted well and who has not. And anyone who has seen it will come away hoping that if ever put to a similar test, he or she will be brave and not cowardly, will think of others rather than of self.

Not only does the film move us, it moves us in certain directions. It is definitive, not open-ended. We are not being asked to ponder a complex ethical dilemma; rather, we are being taught what is proper. There are codes of conduct: women and children first; duty to others before self. If there is a dilemma in the film, it does not concern the code itself. The only dilemma is the perennial one that engages each soul: conscience versus cowardice, faith versus despair.

This is not to say that the film was produced as a moral fable. It is, after all, a true story and a gripping one, the type of thing that almost demands cinematic expression—hardly a case of didacticism. In fact, if we were to level a charge of didacticism, it would have to be against "The Lifeboat Exercise." It is quite obviously an artificially contrived teaching exercise. But this is didacticism with a difference. "The Lifeboat Exercise" belongs to the age of relativism, and consequently, it has nothing to teach. No code of conduct is being passed down; no models of good and bad behavior are shown. Whether it is actually a good thing or bad thing to throw someone overboard is up to the youngster to decide for himself. The exercise is designed to initiate the group into the world of "each man his own moral compass."

Of course, we are comparing two somewhat different things: a story, on the one hand, and a discussion exercise, on the other. The point is that the logic of relativism necessitates the second approach. The story of the *Titanic* was surely known to the developers of "The Lifeboat Exercise." Why didn't they use it? The most probable answer is the one we have alluded to: The story doesn't allow for the type of dialogue desired. It marshals its audi-

ence swiftly and powerfully to the side of certain values. We feel admiration for the radio operators who stay at their post. We feel pity and contempt for the handful of male passengers who sneak into lifeboats. There are not an infinite number of ways in which to respond to these scenes, as there might be to a piece of abstract art. Drama is not the right medium for creating a value-neutral climate. It exerts too much moral force.

Drama also forces us to see things afresh. We don't always notice the humanity of the person sitting next to us on the bus. It is often the case that human beings and human problems must be presented dramatically for us to see them truly. Robert Coles relates an interesting anecdote in this regard about Ruby Bridges, the child who first integrated the New Orleans schools. Ruby had seen *A Raisin in the Sun,* and expressed to Coles the wish that white people would see it: "If all the [white] people on the street [who were heckling her mercilessly] saw the movie, they might stop coming out to bother us." When Coles asked her why she thought that, she answered, "Because the people in the movies would work on them, and maybe they'd listen." Ruby knew that whites who saw her every day didn't really see her. Maybe the movie would make them see.

ADMITTEDLY, I have been mixing media rather freely here, and this raises a question. Films obviously have to do with seeing, but how about books? The paradoxical answer is that the storyteller's craft is not only a matter of telling but also of showing. This is why writing is so often compared to painting, and why beginning writers are urged to visualize what they want to say. So, even when a writer has a moral theme, his work—if he is a good writer—is more like the work of an artist than a moralist. For example, C.S. Lewis's immensely popular children's books have strong moral and religious themes, but they were not conceived out of a moral intent. "All my seven Narnian books," Lewis wrote in 1960, "and my three science fiction books, began with seeing pictures in my head. At first they were not a story, just pictures. *The Lion [The Lion, the Witch and the Wardrobe]* all began with a picture of a faun carrying an umbrella and parcels in a snowy wood."

Stories are essentially moving pictures. That is why they are so readily adaptable to the screen. And a well-made film, in turn, needs surprisingly little dialogue to make its point. When, in *A Night to Remember,* the shawl is torn away from the man's head, we do not have to be told anything. We *see* that his behavior is shameful; it is written on his face.

On the simplest level the moral force of a story or film is the force of example. It shows us examples of men and women acting well or trying to act well, or acting badly. The story points to these people and says in effect, "Act like this; don't act like that." Except that, of course, nothing of the kind is actually stated. It is a matter of showing. There is, for instance, a scene in *Anna Karenina* in which Levin sits by the side of his dying brother and simply holds his hand for an hour, and then another hour. Tolstoy doesn't come out and say that this is what he ought to do, but the scene is presented in such a way that the reader knows that it is the right thing to do. It is, to use a phrase of Bruno Bettelheim's, "tangibly right."

"Do I have to draw you a picture?" That much-used put-down implies that normally intelligent people can do without graphic illustration. But when it comes to moral matters, it may be that we do need the picture more than we think. The story suits our nature because we think more readily in pictures than in propositions. And when a proposition or principle has the power to move us to action, it is often because it is backed up by a picture or image. Consider, for example, the enormous importance historians assign to a single book—*Uncle Tom's Cabin*—in galvanizing public sentiment against slavery. After the novel appeared, it was acted out on the stage in hundreds of cities. For the first time, vast numbers of Americans had a visible and dramatic image of the evils of slavery. Lincoln, on being introduced to author Harriet Beecher Stowe, greeted her with the words "So this is the little lady who started the big war." In more recent times the nation's conscience has been quickened by photo images of civil rights workers marching arm in arm, kneeling in prayer, and under police attack. It is nice to think that moral progress is the result of better reasoning, but it is naive to ignore that role of the imagination in our moral life.

The more abstract our ethic, the less power it has to move us. Yet the progression of recent decades has been in the direction of increasing verbalization and abstraction, toward a reason dissociated from ordinary feelings and cut off from images that convey humanness to us. "At the core of every moral code," observed Walter Lippmann, "there is a picture of human nature." But the picture coming out of our schools increasingly resembles a blank canvas. The deep human sympathies—the kind we acquire from good literature—are missing.

Perhaps the best novelistic portrait of disconnected rationalism is that of Raskolnikov in *Crime and Punishment.* Raskolnikov has mastered the art of asking the question "Why not?" What is wrong with killing a repulsive old woman? he asks himself. What is wrong with taking her money and using it for a worthy cause—namely,

to pay for his own education? With that education, Raskolnikov eventually plans to bring his intellectual gifts to the service of mankind. It is good utilitarian logic.

In commenting on *Crime and Punishment,* William Barrett observes that in the days and weeks after the killing, "a single image breaks into this [Raskolnikov's] thinking." It is the image of his victim, and this image saves Raskolnikov's soul. Not an idea but an image. For Dostoevsky the value of each soul was a mystery that could never be calculated but only shown.

The same theme recurs in *The Brothers Karamazov.* At the very end of the book, Alyosha speaks to the youngsters who love him: "My dear children . . . You must know that there is nothing higher and stronger and more wholesome and useful for life in after years than some good memory, especially a memory connected with childhood, with home. People talk to you a great deal about your education, but some fine, sacred memory, preserved from childhood, is perhaps the best education. If a man carries many such memories with him into life, he is safe to the end of his days, and if we have only one good memory left in our hearts, even that may sometime be the means of saving us."

There is no point in trying to improve on this. Let us only observe that what Dostoevsky says of good memories is true also of good stories. Some of our "sacred" memories may find their source in stories.

We carry around in our heads many more of these images and memories than we realize. The picture of Narcissus by the pool is probably there for most of us; and the Prodigal Son and his forgiving father likely inhabit some corner of our imagination. Atticus Finch, Ebenezer Scrooge, Laura Ingalls Wilder, Anne Frank, David and Goliath, Abraham Lincoln, Peter and the servant girl: for most of us these names will call up an image, and the image will summon up a story. The story in turn may give us the power or resolve to struggle through a difficult situation or to overcome our own moral sluggishness. Or it may simply give us the power to see things clearly. Above all, the story allows us to make that human connection we are always in danger of forgetting.

A SELECTION OF GREAT BOOKS FOR CHILDREN AND TEENS*

One of the difficulties in compiling a list of good books is that there are so many good ones to choose from. What follows is only a short representative list.

The books on the list have been chosen because they are the kinds of books that help youngsters to grow

---

* *From the author's annotated list of over 100 recommended books, space allows us to print only ten from each of the three age-group categories.*

in courage, charity, justice, and other virtues. But they would not be included if they were not also good stories. These are not didactic or preachy books. On the contrary, they are exciting and compelling. They are the kind of stories that throw off sparks.

Since good books do their own work in their own way, it is not necessary or wise for adults to explain the "moral" in each story. Shared reading may prompt youngsters to ask questions about moral issues, but

adults should be careful not to treat books like doses of moral medicine.

The three reading levels are only a rough guide. Children do not seem to have much respect for such age gradings, and tend to tramp back and fourth across them. Some middle readers (roughly eight to twelve years old) can read and enjoy Tolkien. Some children in the same age group may just be getting started on *Little House in the Big Woods*. And the youngster who can read novels may still delight in hearing fairy tales read to younger siblings. Likewise, beginning readers or nonreaders will often enjoy listening to read-alouds selected from a middle reading level.

A word of explanation is in order about the term "older readers." I have used it instead of the more common classification "young adult." Many of the young adult books aimed at teenagers tend to reflect back to them their own limited adolescent world, thus leaving the young reader with the impression that there is nothing more profound in life than the teenage view of things as seen through the lens of popular culture. If teenagers really are to be treated as young adults, then they deserve acquaintance with books that offer a broader and deeper vision of life.

PICTURE BOOKS, STORY BOOKS, BEGINNING READERS

Aesop's Fables. Illus. by Fritz Kredel. Grosset, 1947, 1983. 234 pp.

"The Fox and the Crow," "The Hare and the Tortoise," "The Wolf in Sheep's Clothing," "The Boy Who Cried Wolf": these little stories-with-a-moral go back at least 2,300 years, but their shrewd observations about human foibles are still timely. We still need to be reminded that we can't trust flatterers, that we can't please everyone, and that we shouldn't pretend to be what we're not. Listeners and readers of all ages will take pleasure in these pithy and entertaining lessons in living.

Beauty and the Beast. Retold and illus. by Jan Brett. Clarion, 1989, 1991. 31 pp.

Beauty and the Beast is just the right antidote to our modern obsession with looks, surface charm, and casual sex. It speaks volumes about the meaning of true love and true beauty, and about the importance of restraining our animal nature until love has had time to grow. Children will appreciate the mystery and romance of this story; adults will appreciate its depth and wisdom. Jan Brett's illustrations are elegant and enchanting, but older readers should be directed to Madame Leprince de Beaumont's longer version—especially for Beauty's observation that "handsome looks [may] hide a false and wicked heart."

Dogger. Shirley Hughes. Illus. by the author. Bodley Head, 1977. 32 pp. (First American edition published in 1978 by Prentice-Hall under the title *David and Dog.*)

This is a story about one of those small everyday sacrifices family members make for one another. David takes his worn, stuffed dog, "Dogger," everywhere; but one day on a walk with his mother, David manages to lose Dogger. The whole family joins in the search, but to no avail. The next day at the school fair, Dogger is found in the possession of a little girl who has just purchased him from a toy stall. In order to get Dogger back from the reluctant girl, Bella, David's older sister trades a large and beautiful stuffed bear she has just won.

The Door in the Wall. Marguerite De Angeli. Illus. by the author. Doubleday, 1949. 111 pp. Dell, 1990. 120 pp.

A heartwarming and inspiring tale of a young boy left crippled by illness, and of his victory over his seemingly hopeless situation. With the help of the monks who heal his broken spirit as well as his body, Robin learns that when the way to the future is blocked, there is always a "door in the wall" for those willing to look for it. Set in late-medieval England, this beautifully written tale brings alive the texture and richness of life in castles, monasteries, and market towns.

The Emperor and the Kite. Jane Yolen. Illus. by Ed Young. World, 1967. 31 pp. Philomel, 1988. 28 pp.

Set in ancient China, this simple yet powerful story tells of courage and loyalty. Djeou Seow's brothers are like "four rising suns" and her sisters like "midnight moons" in the eyes of her father, the emperor. But Djeou Seow is the youngest, and so insignificant the emperor often forgets he has a fourth daughter. When the emperor is kidnapped, his children flee and do nothing. All except Djeou Seow. She keeps him alive by using her kite to bring him food. And eventually, with the help of her kite, she effects his escape. Like King Lear, the emperor learns that a daughter's loyalty is shown by deeds, not words. The elegant illustrations are a perfect marriage to the text.

How Many Days to America? A Thanksgiving Story. Eve Bunting. Illus. by Beth Peck. Clarion, 1982, 1988. 32 pp.

"Because we do not think the way they think, my son." In these words, a father explains to his son why they must leave everything behind and flee their country. Together with other families, they make a perilous journey in a small boat in search of America. After encountering storms, pirates, sickness, and near starvation, they finally arrive in America. Unbeknownst to the refugees, it is Thanksgiving Day, and they find a welcoming dinner waiting for them. This powerful, nonpolitical story of modern-day pilgrims conveys courage, hope, and determination.

Keep the Lights Burning, Abbie. Peter and Connie Roop. Illus. by Peter E. Hanson. Carolrhoda, 1985. 40 pp. Houghton Mifflin, 1989. 40 pp.

Abbie's mother is sick, so her father, the lighthouse keeper, must take their small boat to get medicine and other supplies. "Keep the lights burning, Abbie!" is the last thing he says to his eldest daughter, who has never done so by herself. When her father's return is delayed for weeks by a mighty storm, Abbie takes charge of her sisters and keeps the light burning despite many obstacles. The lights give not only safety to ships but comfort to her father. "I was afraid for you," he says on his return. "Every night I watched for the lights. Every night I saw them. Then I knew you were all right." This true story, based in part on Abbie Burgess's own account, is accompanied by marvelous watercolor illustrations.

Little House in the Big Woods. Laura Ingalls Wilder. Illus. by Garth Williams. Harper, 1932. 237 pp. Cornerstone, 1989. 300 pp.

In a small log cabin in the deep woods of Wisconsin, little Laura Ingalls lived with her ma and pa and her sisters, far from other folk. In a style simple yet elegant, the story of Laura's life is told through the course of a year: harvesting and putting by for the winter, hunting and fishing for food, long winter evenings, warm shelter and family times. The description of the hard work involved in maintaining the home, the sense of a family all working together in harmony for a mutual goal, the shared play when work is done: all affirm traditional family roles and values. The most admirable quality of this book and its sequels—except for the last, *The First Four Years*—is its atmosphere of gentle affection among the family. (The last book does not share the harmonious flavor of the earlier volumes; published posthumously from a manuscript found among the author's papers, the story of the first four years of Laura's marriage, when every sort of disaster occurs, has a passive and resentful tone.) Note: boys enjoy the *Little House* series as much as girls do.

The Little Match Girl. Hans Christian Andersen. Illus. by Rachel Isadora. Grosset, 1944. 24 pp. Putnam, 1990. 32 pp.

If you want your children to feel compassion for the plight of the poor, you could belabor them with facts about poverty rates and homelessness, or—better—you could read *The Little Match Girl* to them. The spurt of the matches against the cold brick casts more light on the tragedy of poverty than any number of statistics or news reports. Moreover, the compassion the story evokes is based not on a sense of duty but on a sense of identity. We are brought too far inside the girl's rich imaginative life for it to be otherwise. Rachel Isadora's illustrations nicely capture the mystical quality of Andersen's vision.

A Tale of Three Wishes. Isaac Bashevis Singer. Illus. by Irene Lieblich. Farrar, Straus, 1975, 1976. 27 pp.

Nobel Prize-winner Isaac Bashevis Singer's tales for children are full of wisdom and wonderment, and this one is no exception. Three Jewish children who seek a miraculous shortcut to wisdom, learning, and love discover, by way of a mysterious encounter, that wishes must be earned by effort. When we next meet them, as grown-ups, we find that they have learned the lesson well, and that a much slower but still miraculous transformation has, indeed, taken place in each.

Middle Readers

The Chronicles of Narnia. C. S. Lewis. Illus. by Pauline Baynes. Macmillan, 1950-56, 1988.

Four children enter a wardrobe in an empty room and come out into a strange kingdom of never-ending winter populated by fauns, giants, dwarfs, talking animals, a singularly evil witch, and an extraordinary lion. Thus begins *The Lion, the Witch and the Wardrobe,* the first in the seven-book series that has commanded the loyalty of millions of children worldwide. It is difficult to pinpoint the source of Lewis's success, since he does so many things so well: he has created a thoroughly convincing secondary world, his plots are marvelously constructed, his characters (both human and nonhuman) are closely observed, and his stories are deeply moving. In addition, the *Chronicles* are packed with suspense, surprises, and adventure. As engrossing as the action is, the interior struggles of the several characters are just as compelling. The children battle recurring temptations to cowardice, meanness, pride, and even treachery. Although they don't win all the battles, they do grow in goodness and nobility. Reading the *Chronicles* is, among other things, an education in virtue. It is also satisfying reading for adults. Readers who first chance upon the series at age twenty or thirty are as likely to become loyal subjects of Narnia as are nine- or ten-year-olds. Adult readers may also be interested to know some of the history behind the creation of the series. Together with other friends, Lewis and J. R. R. Tolkien met regularly at an Oxford pub to read aloud from works in progress, and to give and receive criticism. One result was the *Chronicles;* the other was Tolkien's *The Hobbit,* and its sequel, *The Lord of the Rings.* The other titles in the Narnia *Chronicles* are *Prince Caspian, The Voyage of the "Dawn Treader," The Silver Chair, The Horse and His Boy, The Magician's Nephew,* and *The Last Battle.*

The 18th Emergency. Betsy Byars. Illus. by Robert Grossman. Viking, 1973, 1988. 126 pp.

When Benjie, a slight sixth-grade boy whom everyone calls "Mouse," insults Marv Hammerman, the class tough guy, Benjie's first reaction is to flee. Benjie continues to run from his problem (and Marv's vengeance) until he finally realizes that, painful as

it will be, the only honorable thing to do is face the consequences of his actions and confront Marv—even if it means getting beat up. In doing so, Benjie matures emotionally, demonstrated figuratively when his friend stops using his hated nickname. In this book, Byars has made the notion of honor comprehensible to young readers, while maintaining her lively, outrageously funny style.

A Girl Called Al. Constance C. Greene. Illus. by Byron Barton. Viking, 1969. 127 pp. Viking Penguin, 1991.

In this pert, sassy, and honest story of friendship across generations, our narrator (who never gives her name) makes friends with a new girl in her apartment building, a girl who calls herself "Al" rather than "Alexandra," who is too fat, and who literally refuses to let her hair down. Together the two girls befriend old Mr. Richards, the colorful-tattoo-bearing maintenance man who tends their building. This unlikely friendship between the girls and the kind, gentle, delightfully eccentric old fellow becomes especially important to Al, who masks her distress over her absentee father's neglect by gaining weight. The children's sorrow at Mr. Richards's death is touching, and yet entirely in keeping with the lively, clear-sighted, and unsentimental insights of the narrator. This story presents a blueprint of hope for children who might otherwise believe that the lack of an involved, loving father in their lives is an insurmountable handicap; it is also a perceptive tale of loneliness alleviated by loving friendship between old and young.

The Hundred Dresses. Eleanor Estes. Illus. by Louis Slobodkin. Harcourt, 1944, 1974. 80 pp.

Even though she knows it is wrong, Maddie goes along with her friends' daily teasing of Wanda, the daughter of Polish immigrants. The outcast girl's unexpected move to another city leaves Maddie resolved to stand up for others in the future, but it also leaves her smitten with the realization that it is too late to make amends to Wanda herself. As Michelle Landsberg points out, this complex, subtle story stands in refreshing contrast to Judy Blume's amoral treatment of the same theme in *Blubber.*

Island of the Blue Dolphins. Scott O'Dell. Houghton Mifflin, 1960, 1990. 181 pp.

A poignant and powerful story of a twelve-year-old Indian girl who is accidentally abandoned on a remote island. After sacrificing her safe passage to the mainland in an unsuccessful attempt to save her brother's life, Karana spends the next eighteen years in solitude. Relying on skill and inner strength, she manages not only to survive but to grow in serenity and charity (exemplified by her rescue of a wild dog that had previously attacked her). This *Robinson Crusoe-*like story is a tribute to human resilience. O'Dell is a skillful writer whose popularity with young readers is well deserved.

The Rabbi's Girls. Johanna Hurwitz. Illus. by Pamela Johnson. Morrow, 1982. 158 pp. Puffin, 1989. 158 pp.

Carrie Levin is proud to be one of "the rabbi's girls." Her father is rabbi to the small Jewish community in Lorain, Ohio; he is also father to six daughters. In an understated though intensely moving account, Carrie tells of her father's strength, love, and devotion, and of their life as observant Jews, during the year 1923. When the youngest daughter, a tiny baby, develops pneumonia, a terrible tornado devastates the town, and her father's health fails, Carrie learns that life is both bitter and good, that without the bitter, one would be unable to appreciate the good. Her father's death, shortly after the tornado, brings Carrie the realization of all he has given her, especially the knowledge that "the year is a circle, and that life goes on." The love and devotion of this father survives even death.

Roll of Thunder, Hear My Cry. Mildred Taylor. Dial, 1976. 276 pp. Puffin, 1991. 276 pp.

This powerful story of a black family's resistance to injustice and poverty is set during the Depression years in Mississippi, and is observed through the eyes of Cassie, a spirited nine-year-old. Cassie and her family have a strong sense of right and wrong, plus an abundant supply of courage and determination. They need every bit of it. The novel, drawn from stories the author heard as a child, attests to the importance of storytelling as a vehicle for transmitting family virtues.

The Sign of the Beaver. Elizabeth Speare. Houghton Mifflin, 1983. 135 pp. ABC-Clio, 1988. 146 pp.

This story, set in 1768, tells of a young boy's experience of self-discovery when he is left alone on the Maine frontier while his father travels back to Massachusetts to fetch his mother and sister. Young Matt has been left behind to tend the family's new homestead, and though he makes a diligent effort, he is not learned in forest ways, and minor carelessness and impulsiveness on his part result in major disaster. Matt's life is saved only by the intervention of Indians who live nearby. Gradually the boy is forced to acknowledge that the Indians are not brute savages but highly skilled, complex, worthy people from whom he has much to learn. Eventually Matt is able to earn the respect of his Indian friends, though in a totally unexpected way. Here is a well-written frontier survival story which provides much food for thought. A Newbery Honor winner.

Snow Treasure. Marie McSwigan. Dutton, 1942. 197 pp. Scholastic, 1986. 104 pp.

In 1940 the Nazis invaded Norway. This story, which has a basis in fact, tells how Norwegian schoolchildren smuggled $9 million of gold bullion past German sentries and onto a hidden ship bound for America. How did they do it? By sledding right under the noses of the unwitting Nazi guards. A suspenseful plot and a series of close calls make this a real page turner.

Tuck Everlasting. Natalie Babbitt. Farrar, Straus, 1975, 1991. 139 pp.

This profound tale of adventure leads Winnie Foster, an overprotected ten-year-old, into the forest where she encounters the Tuck family, who have received eternal life by drinking from a certain spring. A moral dilemma develops for the young girl as she is forced to choose between mortality and everlasting life. Just as Winnie is caught up in the rapture of the possibility of eternal life, she is sobered by the words of Pa Tuck, who knows the burden it carries: "Us Tucks are stuck. We ain't part of the wheel no more. Dropped off, Winnie. Left behind." A thought-provoking explanation of the meaning of life—and death—this book, like the Tucks, seems destined to last for a good long time.

OLDER READERS

Abraham Lincoln: From Log Cabin to White House. Sterling North. Random House, 1956, 1987. 184 pp.

This excellent introductory biography of our sixteenth president, by a well-known children's author, focuses on Lincoln's career prior to his presidency, and especially on his younger days on the frontier. North writes clearly and concisely, and does full justice to both the nobility and the complexity of Lincoln's character. He does not sentimentalize his subject, and his history is reliable. A memorable story of a man who was truly "self-made," and who overcame both poverty and ignorance.

April Morning. Howard Fast. Bantam, 1961, 1987. 202 pp.

Set in Lexington, Massachusetts, during the American Revolution, Fast's novel tells of a boy's rapid transformation from self-absorption to responsible manhood. While the nation wins its independence, Adam Cooper wins the approval and trust of his elders. Fast paints a detailed and dramatic portrait of the Revolution, and of the men and women who made it happen.

Cheaper by the Dozen. Frank Gilbreth, Jr., and Ernestine Gilbreth Carey. Crowell, 1948. 237 pp. Bantam 1988. 180 pp.

In one of the funniest books ever written, two of the Gilbreth children recall the adventures and high jinks of growing up in a family of twelve boisterous children, governed by a truly memorable father and an equally engaging mother. The family's best-developed trait is their sense of humor (who can forget the car horn incident?—and that's only the beginning). Underlying the fun and high spirits, however, is the father's dedication to the training and education of his children, in order that they may grow into competent, responsible, and fun-loving adults. This book is a happy memorial to an unforgettable father.

Their mother, Lilian Gilbreth, is the

focus of the sequel *Belles on Their Toes* (Crowell, 1950. 237 pp.), also a lively and hilarious story, which tells of the family's struggles, joys, and sorrows after the death of the father.

The Chosen. Chaim Potok. Simon & Schuster, 1967. 284 pp. Knopf, 1992. 284 pp.

The Chosen is a book of a special kind: one of the few modern novels to concern itself with the life of the mind and the joy of intellectual discovery as well as the spiritual aspect of human nature. In form the novel is very simple. It tells of two Jewish boys growing up in Brooklyn, their friendship, their relationships with their fathers, and the choices they face for the future. One boy, Reuven Malter, is Americanized, the son of a prominent Zionist professor. His friend, Danny Saunders, a brilliant young scholar, is the son of the leader of a strict Hasidic sect. As these unlikely friends grow up, they slowly learn to appreciate each other's worlds. *The Chosen* is more than a standard coming-of-age story; it is a story of spiritual and intellectual maturation, of the deepening of two young souls. A specifically Jewish story, its theme and implications are universal.

The Endless Steppe: A Girl in Exile. Esther Hautzig. Scholastic, 1968, 1970. 240 pp.

In June 1941, ten-year-old Esther's sheltered life in Vilna, Poland, was abruptly shattered when Russian soldiers arrested and deported her, her family, and other Polish Jews to work at forced labor in Siberia. The carefree life of Poland, the terror of arrest by the Russians, the grim journey by cattle car to unknown destinations far from home, and the struggle to keep body and soul together in an unfamiliar, hostile land are all vividly depicted in this true-life account. After the war's end, the family learned of the irony of their five years in exile: by removing the Polish Jews from the reach of the Germans, the Russians had unintentionally saved their lives. Those of Esther's large extended family who were not deported had been murdered by the Nazis. Esther's courage, resilience, and strength in the face of these hardships is an inspiring example, made all the more telling by the author's

honest depiction of her own immaturities and moments of self-pity. The reader soon finds himself giving thanks for things taken for granted—peace, freedom, family.

The Hero and the Crown. Robin McKinley. Greenwillow, 1984. 246 pp. ABC-Clio, 1988. *The Blue Sword.* Robin McKinley. Greenwillow, 1982. 272 pp. Ace, 1987. 248 pp.

Fantasy lovers of all ages will appreciate these tales of romantic adventure. Both novels have richly detailed and masterfully crafted plots in which the struggle for adolescent identity is woven together with the battle between good and evil. In *The Hero and the Crown,* the unlikely heroine is Aerin, a Damarian princess. Totally lacking in courtly graces, she is nevertheless strong and independent, and proves her worth by freeing Damar from fire-breathing dragons and an evil wizard. This gracefully written fantasy offers a refreshing twist as the heroine performs the daring deeds. The action of *The Blue Sword* takes place 500 years later and concerns the exploits of another heroine, Harry Crew. Kidnapped by the magic-working Corlath, king of the Old Damarians, Harry soon discovers that she, too, possesses mysterious powers. Like the legendary Aerin who preceded her, Harry finds herself battling the evil forces that threaten the Damarians. McKinley has given us two utterly engrossing stories about heroines who display uncommon courage, ingenuity, and wit.

Narrative of the Life of Frederick Douglass. Frederick Douglass. Boston Anti-Slavery Office, 1845. 126 pp. Belknap, Harvard University Press, 1960. 163 pp.

The early life of one of the great heroes of the antislavery movement in America, as written by himself. Born a slave in Maryland before the Civil War, Douglass educated himself, escaped from bondage after several attempts, and went on to become the most powerful black politician in America. A moving record of one man's triumph over prejudice, ignorance, and oppression.

Old Yeller. Fred Gipson. Harper, 1956, 1990. 184 pp.

The story of a young boy on the Texas frontier and the big yellow dog who becomes his friend and helper. Written in a clear, unsentimental style, it offers a detailed picture of the constant dangers and difficulties of frontier life and the courage and unity with which frontier families confronted those hazards. Reminds us that boys and girls on the frontier had awesome responsibilities thrust on them at a very early age—responsibilities that they met.

Robinson Crusoe. Daniel Defoe. Originally published in 1719. Knopf, 1991. 256 pp.

This book, one of the first novels in the English language, is a classic of adventure. Crusoe, Defoe's first-person narrator, runs away to sea as a young man, and experiences every kind of peril and misfortune, including slavery. He is at length cast away upon a deserted island, where he slowly learns to survive by his wits. Defoe's narrative is full of the accurate minor details that make a story convincing—so convincing, indeed, that when the book first appeared, many took it to be fact. The reader comes to admire the inventiveness, pluck, and hard work of Crusoe, as Crusoe learns to trust in the goodness of a power greater than himself.

Warrior Scarlet. Rosemary Sutcliff. Oxford University Press, 1958, 1979. 207pp.

Among the tribes of Bronze Age Britain, to be different was often the same as being outcast. The boy Drem knows this well. Drem struggles fiercely to overcome the handicap of his withered right arm, and to pass his tribe's test of manhood in order to wear the warrior's red robe, the "warrior scarlet." Because Drem tries so desperately to succeed, his failure is all the more unbearable. The heart of the story is found in Drem's positive response to this failure: sick at heart, he nonetheless faces the loss of all his hopes without becoming resigned or bitter. The deep sorrow he experiences works an inward change in Drem, giving him more compassion toward others who also suffer because they are different. The swift, stirring plot culminates in a satisfying conclusion.

The EQ Factor

New brain research suggests that emotions, not IQ, may be the true measure of human intelligence

NANCY GIBBS

IT TURNS OUT THAT A SCIENTIST can see the future by watching four-year-olds interact with a marshmallow. The researcher invites the children, one by one, into a plain room and begins the gentle torment. You can have this marshmallow right now, he says. But if you wait while I run an errand, you can have two marshmallows when I get back. And then he leaves.

Some children grab for the treat the minute he's out the door. Some last a few minutes before they give in. But others are determined to wait. They cover their eyes; they put their heads down; they sing to themselves; they try to play games or even fall asleep. When the researcher returns, he gives these children their hard-earned marshmallows. And then, science waits for them to grow up.

By the time the children reach high school, something remarkable has happened. A survey of the children's parents and teachers found that those who as four-year-olds had the fortitude to hold out for the second marshmallow generally grew up to be better adjusted, more popular, adventurous, confident and dependable teenagers. The children who gave in to temptation early on were more likely to be lonely, easily frustrated and stubborn. They buckled under stress and shied away from challenges. And when some of the students in the two groups took the Scholastic Aptitude Test, the kids who had held out longer scored an average of 210 points higher.

When we think of brilliance we see Einstein, deep-eyed, woolly haired, a thinking machine with skin and mismatched socks. High achievers, we imagine, were wired for greatness from birth.

But then you have to wonder why, over time, natural talent seems to ignite in some people and dim in others. This is where the marshmallows come in. It seems that the ability to delay gratification is a master skill, a triumph of the reasoning brain over the impulsive one. It is a sign, in short, of emotional intelligence. And it doesn't show up on an IQ test.

For most of this century, scientists have worshipped the hardware of the brain and the software of the mind; the messy powers of the heart were left to the poets. But cognitive theory could simply not explain the questions we wonder about most: why some people just seem to have a gift for living well; why the smartest kid in the class will probably not end up the richest; why we like some people virtually on sight and distrust others; why some people remain buoyant in the face of troubles that would sink a less resilient soul. What qual-

Children who aren't accepted by classmates are up to eight times more likely to drop out

ities of the mind or spirit, in short, determine who succeeds?

The phrase "emotional intelligence" was coined by Yale psychologist Peter Salovey and the University of New Hampshire's John Mayer five years ago to describe qualities like understanding one's own feelings, empathy for the feelings of others and "the regulation of emotion in a way that enhances living." Their notion is about to bound into the national conversation, handily shortened to EQ, thanks to a new book, *Emotional Intelligence* (Bantam; $23.95) by Daniel Goleman. Goleman, a Harvard psychology Ph.D. and a New York *Times* science writer with a gift for making even the chewiest scientific theories digestible to lay readers, has brought together a decade's worth of behavioral research into how the mind processes feelings. His goal, he announces on the cover, is to redefine what it means to be smart. His thesis: when it comes to predicting people's success, brainpower as measured by IQ and standardized achievement tests may actually matter less than the qualities of mind once thought of as "character" before the word began to sound quaint.

At first glance, there would seem to be little that's new here to any close reader of fortune cookies. There may be no less original idea than the notion that our hearts hold dominion over our heads. "I was so angry," we say, "I couldn't think straight." Neither is it surprising that "people skills" are useful, which amounts to saying, it's good to be nice. "It's so true it's trivial," says Dr. Paul McHugh, director of psychiatry at Johns Hopkins University School of Medicine. But if it were that simple, the book would not be quite so interesting or its implications so controversial.

This is no abstract investigation. Goleman is looking for antidotes to restore "civility to our streets and caring to our communal life." He sees practical applications everywhere for how companies should decide whom to hire, how couples can increase the odds that their marriages will last, how parents should raise their children and how schools should teach them. When street gangs substitute for families and schoolyard insults end in stabbings, when more than half

of marriages end in divorce, when the majority of the children murdered in this country are killed by parents and stepparents, many of whom say they were trying to discipline the child for behavior like blocking the TV or crying too much, it suggests a demand for remedial emotional education. While children are still young, Goleman argues, there is a "neurological window of opportunity" since the brain's prefrontal circuitry, which regulates how we act on what we feel, probably does not mature until mid-adolescence.

And it is here the arguments will break out. Goleman's highly popularized conclusions, says McHugh, "will chill any veteran scholar of psychotherapy and any neuroscientist who worries about how his research may come to be applied." While many researchers in this relatively new field are glad to see emotional issues finally taken seriously, they fear that a notion as handy as EQ invites misuse. Goleman admits the danger of suggesting that you can assign a numerical yardstick to a person's character as well as his intellect; Goleman never even uses the phrase EQ in his book. But he (begrudgingly) approved an "unscientific" EQ test in *USA Today* with choices like "I am aware of even subtle feelings as I have them," and "I can sense the pulse of a group or relationship and state unspoken feelings."

"You don't want to take an average of your emotional skill," argues Harvard psychology professor Jerome Kagan, a pioneer in child-development research. "That's what's wrong with the concept of intelligence for mental skills too. Some people handle anger well but can't handle fear. Some people can't take joy. So each emotion has to be viewed differently."

EQ is not the opposite of IQ. Some people are blessed with a lot of both, some with little of either. What researchers have been trying to understand is how they complement each other; how one's ability to handle stress, for instance, affects the ability to concentrate and put intelligence to use. Among the ingredients for success, researchers now generally agree that IQ counts for about 20%; the rest depends on everything from class to luck to the neural pathways that have developed in

the brain over millions of years of human evolution.

It is actually the neuroscientists and evolutionists who do the best job of explaining the reasons behind the most unreasonable behavior. In the past decade or so, scientists have learned enough about the brain to make judgments about where emotion comes from and why we need it. Primitive emotional responses held the keys to survival: fear drives the blood into the large muscles, making it easier to run; surprise triggers the eyebrows to rise, allowing the eyes to widen their view and gather more information about an unexpected event. Disgust wrinkles up the face and closes the nostrils to keep out foul smells.

Emotional life grows out of an area of the brain called the limbic system, specifically the amygdala, whence come delight and disgust and fear and anger. Millions of years ago, the neocortex was added on, enabling humans to plan, learn and remember. Lust grows from the limbic system; love, from the neocortex. Animals like reptiles that have no neocortex cannot experience anything like maternal love; this is why baby snakes have to hide to avoid being eaten by their parents. Humans, with their capacity for love, will protect their offspring, allowing the brains of the young time to develop. The more connections between limbic system and the neocortex, the more emotional responses are possible.

It was scientists like Joseph LeDoux of New York University who uncovered these cerebral pathways. LeDoux's parents owned a meat market. As a boy in Louisiana, he first learned about his future specialty by cutting up cows' brains for sweetbreads. "I found them the most interesting part of the cow's anatomy," he recalls. "They were visually pleasing—lots of folds, convolutions and patterns. The cerebellum was more interesting to look at than steak." The butchers' son became a neuroscientist, and it was he who discovered the short circuit in the brain that lets emotions drive action before the intellect gets a chance to intervene.

A hiker on a mountain path, for example, sees a long, curved shape in the grass out of the corner of his eye. He leaps out of the way before he realizes it is only a stick that looks like a snake. Then he calms down; his cortex gets the message a few milliseconds after his amygdala and "regulates" its primitive response.

Without these emotional reflexes, rarely conscious but often terribly powerful, we would scarcely be able to function. "Most decisions we make have a vast number of possible outcomes, and any attempt to analyze all of them would never end," says University of Iowa neurologist Antonio Damasio, author of *Descartes' Error: Emotion, Reason and the Human Brain*. "I'd ask you to lunch tomorrow, and when the appointed time arrived, you'd still be

Metamood is a difficult skill because emotions so often appear in disguise. A person in mourning may know he is sad, but he may not recognize that he is also angry at the person for dying—because this seems somehow inappropriate. A parent who yells at the child who ran into the street is expressing anger at disobedience, but the degree of anger may owe more to the fear the parent feels at what could have happened.

In Goleman's analysis, self-awareness is perhaps the most crucial ability because it allows us to exercise some self-control. The idea is not to repress feeling (the reaction

to resignation instead of perseverance. Over-worrying about failing increases the likelihood of failure; a salesman so concerned about his falling sales that he can't bring himself to pick up the phone guarantees that his sales will fall even further.

But why are some people better able to "snap out of it" and get on with the task at hand? Again, given sufficient self-awareness, people develop coping mechanisms. Sadness and discouragement, for instance, are "low arousal" states, and the dispirited salesman who goes out for a run is triggering a high arousal state that is incompatible with staying blue. Relaxation works better for

Anxiety is a rehearsal for danger. A little anxiety helps focus the mind; too much can paralyze it

thinking about whether you should come." What tips the balance, Damasio contends, is our unconscious assigning of emotional values to some of those choices. Whether we experience a somatic response—a gut feeling of dread or a giddy sense of elation— emotions are helping to limit the field in any choice we have to make. If the prospect of lunch with a neurologist is unnerving or distasteful, Damasio suggests, the invitee will conveniently remember a previous engagement.

When Damasio worked with patients in whom the connection between emotional brain and neocortex had been severed because of damage to the brain, he discovered how central that hidden pathway is to how we live our lives. People who had lost that linkage were just as smart and quick to reason, but their lives often fell apart nonetheless. They could not make decisions because they didn't know how they felt about their choices. They couldn't react to warnings or anger in other people. If they made a mistake, like a bad investment, they felt no regret or shame and so were bound to repeat it.

If there is a cornerstone to emotional intelligence on which most other emotional skills depend, it is a sense of self-awareness, of being smart about what we feel. A person whose day starts badly at home may be grouchy all day at work without quite knowing why. Once an emotional response comes into awareness—or, physiologically, is processed through the neocortex—the chances of handling it appropriately improve. Scientists refer to "metamood," the ability to pull back and recognize that "what I'm feeling is anger," or sorrow, or shame.

that has made psychoanalysts rich) but rather to do what Aristotle considered the hard work of the will. "Anyone can become angry—that is easy," he wrote in the *Nicomachean Ethics*. "But to be angry with the right person, to the right degree, at the right time, for the right purpose, and in the right way—that is not easy."

Some impulses seem to be easier to control than others. Anger, not surprisingly, is one of the hardest, perhaps because of its evolutionary value in priming people to action. Researchers believe anger usually arises out of a sense of being trespassed against—the belief that one is being robbed of what is rightfully his. The body's first response is a surge of energy, the release of a cascade of neurotransmitters called catecholamines. If a person is already aroused or under stress, the threshold for release is lower, which helps explain why people's tempers shorten during a hard day.

Scientists are not only discovering where anger comes from; they are also exposing myths about how best to handle it. Popular wisdom argues for "letting it all hang out" and having a good cathartic rant. But Goleman cites studies showing that dwelling on anger actually increases its power; the body needs a chance to process the adrenaline through exercise, relaxation techniques, a well-timed intervention or even the old admonition to count to 10.

Anxiety serves a similar useful purpose, so long as it doesn't spin out of control. Worrying is a rehearsal for danger; the act of fretting focuses the mind on a problem so it can search efficiently for solutions. The danger comes when worrying blocks thinking, becoming an end in itself or a path

high-energy moods like anger or anxiety. Either way, the idea is to shift to a state of arousal that breaks the destructive cycle of the dominant mood.

The idea of being able to predict which salesmen are most likely to prosper was not an abstraction for Metropolitan Life, which in the mid-'80s was hiring 5,000 salespeople a year and training them at a cost of more than $30,000 each. Half quit the first year, and four out of five within four years. The reason: selling life insurance involves having the door slammed in your face over and over again. Was it possible to identify which people would be better at handling frustration and take each refusal as a challenge rather than a setback?

The head of the company approached psychologist Martin Seligman at the University of Pennsylvania and invited him to test some of his theories about the importance of optimism in people's success. When optimists fail, he has found, they attribute the failure to something they can change, not some innate weakness that they are helpless to overcome. And that confidence in their power to effect change is self-reinforcing. Seligman tracked 15,000 new workers who had taken two tests. One was the company's regular screening exam, the other Seligman's test measuring their levels of optimism. Among the new hires was a group who flunked the screening test but scored as "superoptimists" on Seligman's exam. And sure enough, they did the best of all; they outsold the pessimists in the regular group by 21% in the first year and 57% in the second. For years after that, passing Selig-

In the corporate world, say personnel executives, IQ gets you hired, but EQ gets you promoted

man's test was one way to get hired as a MetLife salesperson.

Perhaps the most visible emotional skills, the ones we recognize most readily, are the "people skills" like empathy, graciousness, the ability to read a social situation. Researchers believe that about 90% of emotional communication is nonverbal. Harvard psychologist Robert Rosenthal developed the PONS test (Profile of Non-

verbal Sensitivity) to measure people's ability to read emotional cues. He shows subjects a film of a young woman expressing feelings—anger, love, jealousy, gratitude, seduction—edited so that one or another nonverbal cue is blanked out. In some instances the face is visible but not the body, or the woman's eyes are hidden, so that viewers have to judge the feeling by subtle cues. Once again, people with higher PONS scores tend to be more successful in

their work and relationships; children who score well are more popular and successful in school, even then their IQs are quite average.

Like other emotional skills, empathy is an innate quality that can be shaped by experience. Infants as young as three months old exhibit empathy when they get upset at the sound of another baby crying. Even very young children learn by imitation; by watch-

One Way to Test Your EQ

UNLIKE IQ, WHICH IS GAUGED BY THE FAMOUS STANFORD-Binet tests, EQ does not lend itself to any single numerical measure. Nor should it, say experts. Emotional intelligence is by definition a complex, multifaceted quality representing such intangibles as self-awareness, empathy, persistence and social deftness.

Some aspects of emotional intelligence, however, can be quantified. Optimism, for example, is a handy measure of a person's self-worth. According to Martin Seligman, a University of Pennsylvania psychologist, how people respond to setbacks—optimistically or pessimistically—is a fairly accurate indicator of how well they will succeed in school, in sports and in certain kinds of work. To test his theory, Seligman devised a questionnaire to screen insurance salesmen at MetLife.

In Seligman's test, job applicants were asked to imagine a hypothetical event and then choose the response (A or B) that most closely resembled their own. Some samples from his questionnaire:

You forget your spouse's (boyfriend's/girlfriend's) birthday.
A. I'm not good at remembering birthdays.
B. I was preoccupied with other things.

You owe the library $10 for an overdue book.
A. When I am really involved in what I am reading, I often forget when it's due.
B. I was so involved in writing the report, I forgot to return the book.

You lose your temper with a friend.
A. He or she is always nagging me.
B. He or she was in a hostile mood.

You are penalized for returning your income-tax forms late.
A. I always put off doing my taxes.
B. I was lazy about getting my taxes done this year.

You've been feeling run-down.
A. I never get a chance to relax.
B. I was exceptionally busy this week.

A friend says something that hurts your feelings.
A. She always blurts things out without thinking of others.
B. My friend was in a bad mood and took it out on me.

You fall down a great deal while skiing.
A. Skiing is difficult.
B. The trails were icy.

You gain weight over the holidays, and you can't lose it.
A. Diets don't work in the long run.
B. The diet I tried didn't work.

Seligman found that those insurance salesmen who answered with more B's than A's were better able to overcome bad sales days, recovered more easily from rejection and were less likely to quit. People with an optimistic view of life tend to treat obstacles and setbacks as temporary (and therefore surmountable). Pessimists take them personally; what others see as fleeting, localized impediments, they view as pervasive and permanent.

The most dramatic proof of his theory, says Seligman, came at the 1988 Olympic Games in Seoul, South Korea, after U.S. swimmer Matt Biondi turned in two disappointing performances in his first two races. Before the Games, Biondi had been favored to win seven golds—as Mark Spitz had done 16 years earlier. After those first two races, most commentators thought Biondi would be unable to recover from his setback. Not Seligman. He had given some members of the U.S swim team a version of his optimism test before the races; it showed that Biondi possessed an extraordinarily upbeat attitude. Rather than losing heart after turning in a bad time, as others might, Biondi tended to respond by swimming even faster. Sure enough, Biondi bounced right back, winning five gold medals in the next five races.

—By Alice Park

Why do some people remain buoyant in the face of troubles that would sink others?

ing how others act when they see someone in distress, these children acquire a repertoire of sensitive responses. If, on the other hand, the feelings they begin to express are not recognized and reinforced by the adults around them, they not only cease to express those feelings but they also become less able to recognize them in themselves or others.

Empathy too can be seen as a survival skill. Bert Cohler, a University of Chicago psychologist, and Fran Stott, dean of the Erikson Institute for Advanced Study in Child Development in Chicago, have found that children from psychically damaged families frequently become hypervigilant, developing an intense attunement to their parents' moods. One child they studied, Nicholas, had a horrible habit of approaching other kids in his nursery-school class as if he were going to kiss them, then would bite them instead. The scientists went back to study videos of Nicholas at 20 months interacting with his psychotic mother and found that she had responded to his every expression of anger or independence with compulsive kisses. The researchers dubbed them "kisses of death," and their true significance was obvious to Nicholas, who arched his back in horror at her approaching lips—and passed his own rage on to his classmates years later.

Empathy also acts as a buffer to cruelty, and it is a quality conspicuously lacking in child molesters and psychopaths. Goleman cites some chilling research into brutality by Robert Hare, a psychologist at the University of British Columbia. Hare found that psychopaths, when hooked up to electrodes and told they are going to receive a shock, show none of the visceral responses that fear of pain typically triggers: rapid heartbeat, sweating and so on. How could the threat of punishment deter such people from committing crimes?

It is easy to draw the obvious lesson from these test results. How much happier would we be, how much more successful as individuals and civil as a society, if we were more alert to the importance of emotional intelligence and more adept at teaching it? From kindergartens to business schools to corporations across the

country, people are taking seriously the idea that a little more time spent on the "touchy-feely" skills so often derided may in fact pay rich dividends.

In the corporate world, according to personnel executives, IQ gets you hired, but EQ gets you promoted. Goleman likes to tell of a manager at AT&T's Bell Labs, a think tank for brilliant engineers in New Jersey, who was asked to rank his top performers. They weren't the ones with the highest IQs; they were the ones whose E-mail got answered. Those workers who were good collaborators and networkers and popular with colleagues were more likely to get the cooperation they needed to reach their goals than the socially awkward, lone-wolf geniuses.

When David Campbell and others at the Center for Creative Leadership studied "derailed executives," the rising stars who flamed out, the researchers found that these executives failed most often because of "an interpersonal flaw" rather than a technical inability. Interviews with top executives in the U.S. and Europe turned up nine so-called fatal flaws, many of them classic emotional failings, such as "poor working relations," being "authoritarian" or "too ambitious" and having "conflict with upper management."

At the center's executive-leadership seminars across the country, managers come to get emotionally retooled. "This isn't sensitivity training or Sunday-supplement stuff," says Campbell. "One thing they know when they get through is what other people think of them." And the executives have an incentive to listen. Says Karen Boylston, director of the center's team-leadership group: "Customers are telling businesses, 'I don't care if every member of your staff graduated with honors from Harvard, Stanford and Wharton. I will take my business and go where I am understood and treated with respect.'"

Nowhere is the discussion of emotional intelligence more pressing than in schools, where both the stakes and the opportunities seem greatest. Instead of con-

stant crisis intervention, or declarations of war on drug abuse or teen pregnancy or violence, it is time, Goleman argues, for preventive medicine. "Five years ago, teachers didn't want to think about this," says principal Roberta Kirshbaum of P.S. 75 in New York City. "But when kids are getting killed in high school, we have to deal with it." Five years ago, Kirshbaum's school adopted an emotional literacy program, designed to help children learn to manage anger, frustration, loneliness. Since then, fights at lunchtime have decreased from two or three a day to almost none.

Educators can point to all sorts of data to support this new direction. Students who are depressed or angry literally cannot learn. Children who have trouble being accepted by their classmates are 2 to 8 times as likely to drop out. An inability to distinguish distressing feelings or handle frustration has been linked to eating disorders in girls.

Many school administrators are completely rethinking the weight they have been giving to traditional lessons and standardized tests. Peter Relic, president of the National Association of Independent Schools, would like to junk the SAT completely. "Yes, it may cost a heck of a lot more money to assess someone's EQ rather than using a machine-scored test to measure IQ," he says. "But if we don't, then we're saying that a

Deficient emotional skills may be the reason more than half of all marriages end in divorce

test score is more important to us than who a child is as a human being. That means an immense loss in terms of human potential because we've defined success too narrowly."

This warm embrace by educators has left some scientists in a bind. On one hand, says Yale psychologist Salovey, "I love the idea that we want to teach people a richer understanding of their emotional life, to help them achieve their goals." But, he adds, "what I would oppose is training conformity to social expectations." The danger is that any campaign to hone emotional skills in children will end up teaching that there is a "right" emotional response for any given situation—laugh at parades, cry at funerals, sit still at church. "You can teach self-control," says Dr. Alvin Poussaint, professor of psychiatry at Harvard Medical School. "You can teach that it's better to talk out your anger and not use violence. But is it good emotional intelligence not to challenge authority?"

SOME PSYCHOLOGISTS GO further and challenge the very idea that emotional skills can or should be taught in any kind of formal, classroom way. Goleman's premise that children can be trained to analyze their feelings strikes Johns Hopkins' McHugh as an effort to reinvent the encounter group: "I consider that an abominable idea, an idea we have seen with adults. That failed, and now he wants to try it with children? Good grief!" He cites the description in Goleman's book of an experimental program at the Nueva Learning Center in San Francisco. In one scene, two fifth-grade boys start to argue over the rules of an exercise, and the teacher breaks in to ask them to talk about

Square Pegs in the Oval Office?

IF A HIGH DEGREE OF EMOTIONAL INTELLIGENCE IS A PREREQUISITE FOR OUTstanding achievement, there ought to be no better place to find it than in the White House. It turns out, however, that not every man who reached the pinnacle of American leadership was a gleaming example of self-awareness, empathy, impulse control and all the other qualities that mark an elevated EQ.

Oliver Wendell Holmes, who knew intelligence when he saw it, judged Franklin Roosevelt "a second-class intellect, but a first-class temperament." Born and educated as an aristocrat, F.D.R. had polio and needed a wheelchair for most of his adult life. Yet, far from becoming a self-pitying wretch, he developed an unbridled optimism that served him and the country well during the Depression and World War II—this despite, or because of, what Princeton professor Fred Greenstein calls Roosevelt's "tendency toward deviousness and duplicity."

Even a first-class temperament, however, is not a sure predictor of a successful presidency. According to Duke University political scientist James David Barber, the most perfect blend of intellect and warmth of personality in a Chief Executive was the brilliant Thomas Jefferson, who "knew the importance of communication and empathy. He never lost the common touch." Richard Ellis, a professor of politics at Oregon's Willamette University who is skeptical of the whole EQ theory, cites two 19th century Presidents who did not fit the mold. "Martin Van Buren was well adjusted, balanced, empathetic and persuasive, but he was not very successful," says Ellis. "Andrew Jackson was less well adjusted, less balanced, less empathetic and was terrible at controlling his own impulses, but he transformed the presidency."

Lyndon Johnson as Senate majority leader was a brilliant practitioner of the art of political persuasion, yet failed utterly to transfer that gift to the White House. In fact, says Princeton's Greenstein, L. B. J. and Richard Nixon would be labeled "worst cases" on any EQ scale of Presidents. Each was touched with political genius, yet each met with disaster. "To some extent," says Greenstein, "this is a function of the extreme aspects of their psyches; they are the political versions of Van Gogh, who does unbelievable paintings and then cuts off his ear."

History professor William Leuchtenburg of the University of North Carolina at Chapel Hill suggests that the 20th century Presidents with perhaps the highest IQs—Wilson, Hoover and Carter—also had the most trouble connecting with their constituents. Woodrow Wilson, he says, "was very high strung [and] arrogant; he was not willing to strike any middle ground. Herbert Hoover was so locked into certain ideas that you could never convince him otherwise. Jimmy Carter is probably the most puzzling of the three. He didn't have a deficiency of temperament; in fact, he was too temperate. There was an excessive rationalization about Carter's approach."

That was never a problem for John Kennedy and Ronald Reagan. Nobody ever accused them of intellectual genius, yet both radiated qualities of leadership with an infectious confidence and openheartedness that endeared them to the nation. Whether President Clinton will be so endeared remains a puzzle. That he is a Rhodes scholar makes him certifiably brainy, but his emotional intelligence is shaky. He obviously has the knack for establishing rapport with people, but he often appears so eager to please that he looks weak. "As for controlling his impulses," says Willamette's Ellis, "Clinton is terrible." —*By Jesse Birnbaum.*
Reported by James Carney/Washington and Lisa H. Towle/Raleigh

Some EQ is innate. Infants as young as three months show empathy

what they're feeling. "I appreciate the way you're being assertive in talking with Tucker," she says to one student. "You're not attacking." This strikes McHugh as pure folly. "The author is presuming that someone has the key to the right emotions to be taught to children. We don't even know the right emotions to be taught to adults. Do you really think a child of eight or nine really understands the difference between aggressiveness and assertiveness?"

The problem may be that there is an ingredient missing. Emotional skills, like intellectual ones, are morally neutral. Just as a genius could use his intellect either to cure cancer or engineer a deadly virus, someone with great empathic insight could use it to inspire colleagues or exploit them. Without a moral compass to guide people in how to employ their gifts, emotional intelligence can be used for good or evil. Columbia University psychologist Walter Mischel, who invented the marshmallow test and others like it, observes that the knack for delaying gratification that makes a child one marsh-

mallow richer can help him become a better citizen or—just as easily—an even more brilliant criminal.

Given the passionate arguments that are raging over the state of moral instruction in this country, it is no wonder Goleman chose to focus more on neutral emotional skills than on the values that should govern their use. That's another book—and another debate.

—*Reported by Sharon E. Epperson and Lawrence Mondi/New York, James L. Graff/Chicago and Lisa H. Towle/Raleigh*

Children Without Friends

Who Are They and How Can Teachers Help?

This article highlights an area that should be of great concern to educators—children without friends. The author notes the serious implications of growing up friendless: "The uniqueness of peer relationships contributes to a child's normal development." Now, proven techniques of identification allow teachers and other professionals to help such children.—R.J.S.

Janis R. Bullock

Janis R. Bullock is Assistant Professor, Human Development and Counseling, Montana State University, Bozeman.

Children who have difficulty forming friendships and gaining acceptance among peers have received a tremendous amount of interest over the past decade. Research indicates that approximately 6 to 11 percent of elementary school-age children have no friends or receive no friendship nominations from peers (Hymel & Asher, 1977). This figure varies depending upon the assessment procedure used and it may be even higher in some subgroups. For example, children who have learning disabilities (Gresham, 1988) or are mildly retarded (Taylor, Asher & Williams, 1987) may experience even more difficulties forming so-

cial relationships. Nonetheless, many average and above-average children are without friends. Consequently, research and intervention focusing on children with peer relationship problems are becoming more extensive.

Researchers continue to seek information that may contribute to the understanding and awareness of these children. Many children who experience poor peer relations are at risk and need support. Research on the consequences of peer rejection can provide teachers with the foundation and rationale for effective intervention. Teachers working closely with children who lack friends understand the frustration such students experience during attempts to interact with peers.

The uniqueness of peer relationships contributes to a child's normal development. Unlike adult-child relationships, child-child relations are more egalitarian and involve more reciprocal interactions. These interactions help

children achieve competency in many areas. Therefore, children who lack friends do not enjoy many important benefits of interaction. Peer relations should be viewed as necessary for a child's healthy development.

Identifying Children Without Friends

In order to determine a child's status within the peer group, researchers often use two variations of sociometric measurement techniques. These measurements rely on children's perceptions of others and can identify those children who are rejected or neglected by their peer group. A widely used sociometric technique is the peer nomination method (Hymel & Rubin, 1985). In this technique, children are asked to pick from a list the names of three children with whom they like to play and three children with whom they do not like to play. In general, this procedure provides a useful means of assessing children's impact on their peers. Rejected children receive few positive nominations and many negative nominations, while neglected children receive few positive *or* negative nominations.

The rating scale measure (Singleton & Asher, 1977), a slightly different approach, is used to assess social acceptance or preference within the peer group. Children are asked to rate each classmate on a 1-5 Likert-type scale, in response to questions about how much they like to play or work with that class-

From *Childhood Education*, Winter 1992, pp. 92-96. Reprinted by permission of Janis R. Bullock and the Association for Childhood Education International, 11501 Georgia Avenue, Suite 315, Wheaton, MD. © 1992 by the Association.

mate. Rejected children receive very low overall ratings, whereas ratings of neglected children do not differ from those of average children. Although neglected children are generally liked, they very often lack friends.

Sociometric Status and Behaviors in Children

Once researchers were able to identify rejected and neglected children, they became interested in determining the behaviors associated with each status. Information is typically gathered on child behavior in three ways: peer reports, teacher reports and direct observation. The behaviors of the children are then correlated with sociometric status.

Peers can provide an important perspective on the behavior norms within a peer group, providing insight on areas often unavailable or unknown to adults. A common technique requires children to characterize the behavior of peers (e.g., aggressive, helpful, cooperative, shy). A variety of behaviors attributed to children by their peers are related to their sociometric status (Carlson, Lahey & Neeper, 1984; Coie, Dodge & Coppotelli, 1982; Wasik, 1987). Across age groups, peers accept children who are considered helpful, friendly, cooperative, cheerful and prosocial. Peer rejection is generally associated with aggression, disruption and fighting. Shy, quiet children lacking social involvement are often neglected.

Because of their considerable contact with children, teachers can provide a valuable perspective on children's behavior. French and Waas (1988) obtained teacher ratings on popular, rejected and neglected 2nd- and 5th-grade children. Rejected children were characterized as aggressive, hostile and task avoidant, while neglected children were described as having more school behavior problems

than popular children. Coie and Dodge (1988) asked teachers to rank 1st- and 2nd-grade boys of different sociometric statuses on a variety of peer aggression items. Well-accepted and neglected children were described as the least aggressive, whereas rejected children were described as the most aggressive. Rejected children also scored low in conformity to rules and interpersonal sensitivity. In general, teacher assessments coincided with children's perceptions.

Direct observational methods also contribute to research on the assessment of peer group behavior. Trained observers unacquainted with children can provide unbiased information on discrete behaviors of children. Various studies on school-age children (Dodge, Coie & Brakke, 1982; Gottman, Gonso & Rasmussen, 1975; Ladd, 1983) show a high degree of consistency in outcomes. Both popular and average-status children engage in more cooperative play and social conversation than do rejected children. Rejected children show many more inappropriate behaviors than any of the other status groups. Often alone, they wander around the room and are off-task during the work period. They are also more aggressive, argumentative and likely to engage in disruptive peer interactions.

Less observational information is available on neglected children. In general, they spend more time alone and make fewer social contacts. When they do attempt to make a social contact, they are often ignored. They are characterized as being neither aggressive nor disruptive and have difficulty integrating with peers. They engage in more solitary activities than other children (Dodge, Coie & Brakke, 1982). In general, research suggests that children who are rejected and neglected display certain behaviors that may contribute to their failure to interact with peers.

Children's Status and Dropping Out of School

Children who continually experience rejection are considered to be at risk for dropping out of school. Approximately 20 percent of children who enter school do not graduate for various reasons (Weiner, 1980). A small percentage leave reluctantly, generally due to family emergencies or crises. Others do so because of frustrations related to poor social adjustment. Yet, the majority of these students are considered at least average in intelligence with the ability to graduate.

Several studies provide support for the hypothesis that peer assessments of low acceptance can predict future dropouts. Gronlund and Holmlund (1958) reported that 54 percent of low-accepted boys dropped out of school, compared to 19 percent of high-accepted boys. Among girls, the dropout figure was 35 percent for low acceptance, compared to 4 percent for high acceptance. Barclay (1966) reported that low-accepted boys and girls were two to three times more likely to drop out of school.

These early studies did not distinguish between rejected and neglected children, a more recent concern. Kupersmidt's (1983) study does address the subclassification issue. In a 6-year longitudinal study of 5th-graders, she reports the dropout rate included 30 percent of the rejected, 10 percent of the neglected, 21 percent of the average and 4 percent of the popular sample. Although differences were only marginally significant, the rejected group did show a greater dropout rate. Kupersmidt suggests that perhaps only the rejected children are at risk.

In sum, evidence suggests that many adolescents who drop out of school experience poor peer adjustments in their earlier years of school. They are more likely to drop out of school than their more accepted peers. The effects appear to be stronger for boys than girls, yet patterns are consistent regardless of gender. Evidence suggests that peer rejection may be such an adverse experience that adolescents decide to leave school (Kupersmidt, Coie & Dodge, 1990). The relationship between neglected children and dropout rates is not so clear and needs further examination.

Considerations for Teachers

Children who are rejected by their peers often report feelings of loneliness and lower levels of self-esteem. A sensitive and supportive teacher will be aware of these feelings and will attempt to assess each child's situation. Teachers can begin by careful observation of the child. While observing the child who appears to be having difficulty interacting with peers, the teacher can ask:

- Do the children in the class seem to avoid, ignore and reject the child?
- Does the child lack certain social skills necessary for successful interaction with others?
- Does the child have difficulty interpreting other peoples' cues or requests?
- Does the child have difficulty communicating with others about his/her needs and desires?
- Does the child act aggressively while interacting with others?
- Is the child disruptive in the class?

Although there are no plans that work with every child, teachers can choose from several approaches found to be successful. Teachers will need to choose strategies that best fit the child's needs, are adaptable to the classroom and support their philosophy.

Some children are disliked by peers because they lack the skills necessary to get along with others.

Researchers (Oden & Asher, 1977) have developed techniques for coaching children in social skills. Coaching involves identifying the child's problem and providing some form of direct instruction regarding strategies for use when interacting with peers.

Children can be coached on specific concepts that will contribute to more positive interactions. Concepts that were used by Oden and Asher (1977) included participation (e.g., how to get started and the importance of paying attention), cooperation (e.g., the importance of

> *Evidence suggests that peer rejection may be such an adverse experience that adolescents decide to leave school.*

taking turns and sharing materials), communication (e.g., the importance of talking with others and listening) and being friendly and nice (e.g., the importance of smiling, helping and encouraging others). Coaches can assist children by:

- telling them why each concept is important to peer interaction
- asking for examples to assess children's understanding of the concept
- reinforcing the examples or providing suggestions when children have trouble finding their own examples
- discussing both positive and negative behavioral examples that are important to interactions

- trying out some of the ideas in a play situation
- assessing the situation afterward.

Some children may benefit from practice with younger age-mates. Coaching children has contributed to long-term changes in their behavior and sociometric status.

Children who have difficulty reading other children's cues may benefit by watching others who interact successfully. Low-status children can watch a variety of successful interactions on videotape or acted out by adults, other children or puppets. Studies (Gresham & Nagle, 1980; Jakibchuk & Smeraglio, 1976) indicate that low-status children exhibit an increase in positive interaction after viewing models, and the effects are maintained over time. Factors contributing to these positive outcomes seem to be:

- similarity of the model to the target child
- explicitly identifying the model's behavior to the target child
- using simple step-by-step narration to describe the purposes of the behavior (Asher, Renshaw & Hymel, 1982).

Children who act aggressively toward others are often the least liked in the classroom. Self-control training, also referred to as cognitive behavior modification, focuses on the maintenance of positive behaviors through internal cognitive control (Meichenbaum, 1985). In some cases, teaching aggressive children to self-regulate their behavior has proven more effective in reducing inappropriate behaviors than external reinforcers from teachers (Bolstad & Johnson, 1972).

Researchers (Camp, Blom, Herbert & Van Doornick, 1977) have taught children to reinforce

123

themselves directly by following a thinking-out-loud strategy that was found to reduce disruptive behaviors and increase prosocial behaviors. When using the thinking-out-loud strategy, children are trained to say to themselves, first out loud and then silently, "What is my problem? What is my plan? Am I using my plan? How did I do?" This process helps children interrupt their impulsive behavior, keeps them on task and reminds them of the necessary steps to take when carrying out their task. This training often includes social problem-solving skills, whereby children are encouraged to suggest and evaluate solutions to problems (Spivak, Platt & Shure, 1976).

Disruptiveness is another behavior often related to peer rejection. Disruptive children are often off-task and engage in inappropriate classroom behavior. The percentage of rejected children described as disruptive by peers ranges from 36 percent to 38 percent (Coie & Koeppl, 1990). Two techniques for reducing disruptive behavior in the classroom are use of reinforcement and token incentives.

Positive reinforcement, often used in connection with modeling, has produced some immediate positive outcomes (Asher, Renshaw & Hymel, 1982). The behavior of a child or group of children can be subjected to direct reinforcement. Teachers can make a point of praising socially cooperative interactions, while ignoring any undesirable interactions deemed tolerable. Specific praise of a child immediately after a desirable behavior provides the strongest results. Other studies (e.g., Gresham, 1979) used reinforcement procedures to reduce the frequency of negative social behaviors, and these effects were found to maintain over time.

The use of tokens as a reward for desirable behavior, in conjunction with positive reinforcement, tends to reduce disruptiveness and increase on-task behavior (Kazdin, 1977). In a token economy, teachers identify those behaviors deemed desirable and undesirable. When students act in a desirable manner, they are rewarded with a token of the teacher's choice. Tokens can range from a point system, plastic disks or plastic cards that can be exchanged for toys, food or other privileges. Several variations of token economies exist in schools and institutions. Descriptions of procedures, rules and additional considerations of this system can be found in Kazdin (1977).

Although token economies have shown success, they are not without their critics. This procedure focuses on the symptoms rather than the causes, and the effects of the program do not always generalize to other settings—such as home or play settings (Kazdin, 1977). In some cases, the system may not work at all. For example, Coie and Koeppl (1990) point out that children who lack basic skills or are unable to perform classroom tasks may need specific coaching in academic skills.

Communicating with parents will be especially important for teachers working with children who have difficulty interacting with peers. The increasing number of single-parent families or families with both parents working outside the home means that teachers will need to utilize a variety of approaches to maintain contact.

Options may include telephone calls, notes, letters and parent conferences. In order for children to benefit, parents need to have an understanding of their child's development and progress. Teachers can discuss their observations of the child and share what they are doing in the classroom that might also be reinforced at home. In addition, teachers can ask for parental input and suggestions. Teachers can also share information with parents on child guidance or parent discussion groups that might be available in the community.

In some cases, teachers may find that some children will need more assistance than is possible within the classroom. Not all children will respond to the techniques suggested. At some point, teachers must acknowledge the need for additional help. Teachers will need to work with the family and suggest other resources.

A professional teacher will understand the importance of compiling resources and referrals that can be useful for families. This information might include services such as the school psychologist; community mental health clinics; child, family and marriage counselors; and developmental screening clinics.

> *Not having friends contributes to loneliness, low self-esteem and inability to develop social skills.*

Summary

A significant percentage of children are rejected or neglected during childhood. A lack of friends can put children at risk for later problems. More immediately, not having friends contributes to loneliness, low self-esteem and inability to develop social skills. Rejection or neglect by peers is a traumatic experience for some children. Research indicates that identification and intervention may help modify the negative experiences that some children encounter.

References

Asher, S., Renshaw, R., & Hymel, S. (1982). Peer relations and the development of social skills. In S. G. Moore & C. R. Cooper (Eds.), *The young child: Reviews of research*, Vol. 3, pp. 137-158. Washington, DC: NAEYC.

Barclay, J. (1966). Sociometric choices and teacher ratings as predictors of school dropout. *Journal of Social Psychology, 4,* 40-45.

Bolstad, O., & Johnson, S. (1972). Self-regulation in the modification of disruptive classroom behavior. *Journal of Applied Behavioral Analysis, 5,* 443-454.

Camp, B., Blom, G., Herbert, F., & Van Doornick, W. (1977). Think aloud: A program for developed self-control in young aggressive boys. *Journal of Abnormal Child Psychology, 5,* 157-169.

Carlson, C., Lahey, B., & Neeper, R. (1984). Peer assessment of the social behavior of accepted, rejected, and neglected children. *Journal of Abnormal Child Psychology, 12,* 189-198.

Coie, J., & Dodge, K. (1988). Multiple sources of data on social behavior and social status in the school: A cross-age comparison. *Child Development, 59,* 815-829.

Coie, J., Dodge, K, & Coppotelli, H. (1982). Continuities and changes in children's social status: A five-year longitudinal study. *Developmental Psychology, 18,* 557-570.

Coie, J., & Koeppl, G. (1990). Adapting intervention to the problems of aggressive and disruptive rejected children. In S. R. Asher & J. D. Coie (Eds.), *Peer rejection in childhood*, pp. 309-337. New York: Cambridge University Press.

Dodge, K., Coie, J., & Brakke, N. (1982). Behavior patterns of socially rejected and neglected preadolescents: The roles of social approach and aggression. *Journal of Abnormal Child Psychology, 10,* 389-410.

French, D., & Waas, G. (1985). Behavior problems of peer-neglected and peer-rejected elementary-age children: Parent and teacher perspectives. *Child Development, 56,* 246-252.

Gottman, J., Gonso, J., & Rasmussen, B. (1975). Social interaction, social competence, and friendship in children. *Child Development, 46,* 709-718.

Gresham, F. (1979). Comparison of response cost and time out in a special education setting. *Journal of Special Education, 13,* 199-208.

Gresham, F. (1988). Social competence and motivational characteristics of learning disabled students. In M. C. Luang, M. C. Reynolds & H. J. Walberg (Eds.), *Handbook of special education: Research and practice*, Vol. 2, pp. 283-302. Oxford: Pergamon.

Gresham, F., & Nagle, R. (1980). Social skills training with children: Responsiveness to modeling and coaching as a function of peer orientation. *Journal of Consulting and Clinical Psychology, 48,* 718-729.

Gronlund, N., & Holmlund, W. (1958). The value of elementary school sociometric status scores for predicting pupils' adjustment in high school. *Educational Administration and Supervision, 44,* 225-260.

Hymel, S., & Asher, S. (1977, March). *Assessment and training of isolated children's social skills.* Paper presented at the biennial meeting of the Society for Research in Child Development, New Orleans. (Eric Document Reproduction Service No. ED 136 930).

Hymel, S., & Rubin, K. (1985). Children with peer relationships and social skills problems: Conceptual, methodological, and developmental issues. In G. J. Whitehurst (Ed.), *Annals of child development*, Vol. 2, pp. 251-297. Greenwich, CT: JAI Press.

Jakibchuk, Z., & Smeraglio, V. (1976). The influence of symbolic modeling on the social behavior of preschool children with low levels of social responsiveness. *Child Development, 47,* 838-841.

Kazdin, A. (1977). *The token economy: A review and evaluation.* New York: Plenum.

Kupersmidt, J. (1983, April). Predicting delinquency and academic problems from childhood peer status. In J. D. Coie (Chair), *Strategies for identifying children at social risk: Longitudinal correlates and consequences.* Symposium conducted at the biennial meeting of the Society for Research in Child Development, Detroit, MI.

Kupersmidt, J., Coie, J., & Dodge, K. (1990). The role of poor peer relationships in the development of disorder. In S. R. Asher & J. D. Coie (Eds.), *Peer rejection in childhood*, pp. 253-273. New York: Cambridge University Press.

Ladd, G. (1983). Social networks of popular, average, and rejected children in school settings. *Merrill-Palmer Quarterly, 29,* 283-308.

Meichenbaum, D. H. (1985). *Stress innoculation training.* New York: Pergamon Press.

Oden, S., & Asher, S. (1977). Coaching children in social skills for friendship making. *Child Development, 48,* 495-506.

Singleton, L., & Asher, S. (1977). Peer preferences and social interaction among third-grade children in an integrated school district. *Journal of Educational Psychology, 69,* 330-336.

Spivak, G., Platt, J., & Shure, M. (1976). *The problem-solving approach to adjustment.* San Francisco: Jossey-Bass.

Taylor, A., Asher, S., & Williams, G. (1987). The social adaptation of mainstreamed, mildly retarded children. *Child Development, 58,* 1321-1334.

Wasik, B. (1987). Sociometric measures and peer descriptions of kindergarten children: A study of reliability and validity. *Journal of Clinical Child Psychology, 16,* 218-224.

Weiner, I. P. (1980). Psychopathology in adolescence. In J. Adelson (Ed.), *Handbook of adolescent psychology*, pp. 447-471. New York: Wiley.

Girls and Boys Together… But Mostly Apart: Gender Arrangements in Elementary Schools

Barrie Thorne

Michigan State University

Throughout the years of elementary school, children's friendships and casual encounters are strongly separated by sex. Sex segregation among children, which starts in preschool and is well established by middle childhood, has been amply documented in studies of children's groups and friendships (e.g., Eder & Hallinan, 1978; Schofield, 1981) and is immediately visible in elementary school settings. When children choose seats in classrooms or the cafeteria, or get into line, they frequently arrange themselves in same-sex clusters. At lunchtime, they talk matter-of-factly about "girls' tables" and "boys' tables." Playgrounds have gendered turfs, with some areas and activities, such as large playing fields and basketball courts, controlled mainly by boys, and others—smaller enclaves like jungle-gym areas and concrete spaces for hopscotch or jumprope—more often controlled by girls. Sex segregation is so common in elementary schools that it is meaningful to speak of separate girls' and boys' worlds.

Studies of gender and children's social relations have mostly followed this "two worlds" model, separately describing and comparing the subcultures of girls and of boys (e.g., Lever, 1976; Maltz & Borker, 1983). In brief summary: Boys tend to interact in larger, more age-heterogeneous groups (Lever, 1976; Waldrop & Halverson, 1975; Eder & Hallinan, 1978). They engage in more rough and tumble play and physical fighting (Maccoby & Jacklin, 1974). Organized sports are both a central activity and a major metaphor in boys' subcultures; they use the language of "teams" even when not engaged in sports, and they often construct interaction in the form of contests. The shifting hierarchies of boys' groups (Savin-Williams, 1976) are evident in their more frequent use of direct commands, insults, and challenges (Goodwin, 1980).

Fewer studies have been done of girls' groups (Foot, Chapman, & Smith, 1980; McRobbie & Garber, 1975), and—perhaps because categories for description and analysis have come more from male than female experience—researchers have had difficulty seeing and analyzing girls' social relations. Recent work has begun to correct this skew. In middle childhood, girls' worlds are less public than those of boys; girls more often interact in private places and in smaller groups or friendship pairs (Eder & Hallinan, 1978; Waldrop & Halverson, 1975). Their play is more cooperative and turn-taking (Lever, 1976). Girls have more intense and exclusive friendships, which take shape around keeping and telling secrets, shifting alliances, and indirect ways of expressing disagreement (Goodwin, 1980; Lever, 1976; Maltz & Borker, 1983). Instead of direct commands, girls more often use directives which merge speaker and hearer, e.g., "let's" or "we gotta" (Goodwin, 1980).

Although much can be learned by comparing the social organization and subcultures of boys' and of girls' groups, the separate worlds approach has eclipsed full, contextual understanding of gender and social relations among children. The separate worlds model essentially involves a search for group sex differences, and shares the limitations of individual sex difference research. Differences tend to be exaggerated and similarities ignored, with little theoretical attention to the integration of similarity and difference (Unger, 1979). Statistical findings of difference are often portrayed as dichotomous, neglecting the considerable individual variation that exists; for example, not all boys fight, and some have intense and exclusive friendships. The sex difference approach tends to abstract gender from its social context, to assume that males and females are qualitatively and permanently different (with differences perhaps unfolding through separate developmental lines). These assumptions mask the possibility that gender arrangements and patterns of similarity and difference may vary by situation, race, social class, region, or subculture.

Sex segregation is far from total, and is a more complex and dynamic process than the portrayal of separate worlds reveals. Erving Goffman (1977) has observed that sex segregation has a "with-then-apart" structure; the sexes segregate periodically, with separate spaces, rituals, groups, but they also come together and are, in crucial ways, part of the same world. This is certainly true in the social environment of elementary schools. Although girls and boys do interact as boundaried collectivities—an image suggested by the separate worlds approach—there are other occasions when they work or play in relaxed and integrated ways. Gender is less central to the organization and meaning of some situations than others. In short, sex segregation is not static, but is a variable and complicated process.

To gain an understanding of gender which can encompass both the "with" and the "apart" of sex segregation, analysis should start not with the individual, nor with a search for sex differences, but with social relationships. Gender should be conceptualized as a system of relationships rather than as an immutable and dichotomous given. Taking this approach, I have organized my research on gender and children's social relations around questions like the following: How and when does gender enter into group formation? In a given situation, how is gender made more or less salient or infused with particular meanings? By what rituals, processes, and forms of social organization and conflict do "with-then-apart" rhythms get enacted? How are these processes affected by the organization of institutions (e.g., different types of schools, neighborhoods, or summer camps), varied settings (e.g., the constraints and possibilities governing interaction on playgrounds vs. classrooms), and particular encounters?

METHODS AND SOURCES OF DATA

This study is based on two periods of participant observation. In 1976–1977 I observed for 8 months in a largely working-class elementary school in California, a school with 8% Black and 12% Chicano students. In 1980 I did fieldwork for 3 months in a Michigan elementary school of similar size (around 400 students), social class, and racial composition. I observed in several classrooms—a kindergarten, a second grade, and a combined fourth-fifth grade—and in school hallways, cafeterias, and playgrounds. I set out to follow the round of the school day as children experience it, recording their interactions with one another, and with adults, in varied settings.

Participant observation involves gaining access to everyday, "naturalistic" settings and taking systematic notes over an extended period of time. Rather than starting with preset categories for recording, or with fixed hypotheses for testing, participant-observers record detail in ways which maximize opportunities for discovery. Through continuous interaction between observation and analysis, "grounded theory" is developed (Glaser & Strauss, 1967).

The distinctive logic and discipline of this mode of inquiry emerges from: (1) theoretical sampling—being relatively systematic in the choice of where and whom to observe in order to maximize knowledge relevant to categories and analysis which are being developed; and (2) comparing all relevant data on a given point in order to modify emerging propositions to take account of discrepant cases (Katz, 1983). Participant observation is a flexible, open-ended and inductive method, designed to understand behavior within, rather than stripped from, social context. It provides richly detailed information which is anchored in everyday meanings and experience.

DAILY PROCESSES OF SEX SEGREGATION

Sex segregation should be understood not as a given, but as the result of deliberate activity. The outcome is dramatically visible when there are separate girls' and boys' tables in school lunchrooms, or sex-separated groups on playgrounds. But in the same lunchroom one can also find tables where girls and boys eat and talk together, and in some playground activities the sexes mix. By what processes do girls and boys separate into gender-defined and relatively boundaried collectivities? And in what contexts, and through what processes, do boys and girls interact in less gender-divided ways?

In the school settings I observed, much segregation happened with no mention of gender. Gender was implicit in the contours of friendship, shared interest, and perceived risk which came into play when children chose companions—in their prior planning, invitations, seeking-of-access, saving-of-places, denials of entry, and allowing or protesting of "cuts" by those who violated the rules for lining up. Sometimes children formed mixed-sex groups for play, eating, talking, working on a classroom project, or moving through space. When adults or children explicitly invoked gender—and this was nearly always in ways which separated girls and boys—boundaries were heightened and mixed-sex interaction became an explicit arena of risk.

In the schools I studied, the physical space and curricula were not formally divided by sex, as they have been in the history of elementary schooling (a history evident in separate entrances to old school buildings, where the words "Boys" and "Girls" are permanently etched in concrete). Nevertheless, gender was a visible marker in the adult-organized school day. In both schools, when the public address system sounded, the principal inevitably opened with: "Boys and girls . . . ," and in addressing clusters of children, teachers and aides regularly used gender terms ("Heads down, girls"; "The girls are ready and the boys aren't"). These forms of address made gender visible and salient, conveying an assumption that the sexes are separate social groups.

Teachers and aides sometimes drew upon gender as a basis for sorting children and organizing activities. Gender is an embodied and visual social category which roughly divides the population in half, and the separation of girls and boys permeates the history and lore of schools and playgrounds. In both schools—although through awareness of Title IX, many teachers had changed this practice—one could see separate girls' and boys' lines moving, like caterpillars, through the school halls. In the 4th-5th grade classroom the teacher frequently pitted girls against boys for spelling and math contests. On the playground in the Michigan school, aides regarded the space close to the building as girls' territory, and the playing fields "out there" as boys' territory. They sometimes shooed children of the other sex away from those spaces, especially boys who ventured near the girls' area and seemed to have teasing in mind.

In organizing their activities, both within and apart from the surveillance of adults, children also explicitly invoked gender. During my fieldwork in the Michigan school, I kept daily records of who sat where in the lunchroom. The amount of sex segregation varied: It was least at the first grade tables and almost total among sixth graders. There was also variation from classroom to classroom within a given age, and from day to day. Actions like the following heightened the gender divide:

In the lunchroom, when the two second grade tables were filling, a high-status boy walked by the inside table, which had a scattering of both boys and girls, and said loudly, "Oooo, too many girls," as he headed for a seat at the far table. The boys at the inside table picked up their trays and moved, and no other boys sat at the inside table, which the pronouncement had effectively made taboo.

In the end, that day (which was not the case every day), girls and boys ate at separate tables.

Eating and walking are not sex-typed activities, yet in forming groups in lunchrooms and hallways children often separated by sex. Sex segregation assumed added dimensions on the playground, where spaces, equipment, and activities were infused with gender meanings. My inventories of activities and groupings on the playground showed similar patterns in both schools: Boys controlled the large fixed spaces designated for team sports (baseball diamonds, grassy fields used for football or soccer); girls more often played closer to the building, doing tricks on the monkey bars (which, for 6th graders, became an area for sitting and talking) and using cement areas for jumprope, hopscotch, and group games like four-square. (Lever, 1976, provides a good analysis of sex-divided play.) Girls and boys most often played together in kickball, and in group (rather than team) games like four-square, dodgeball, and handball. When children used gender to exclude others from play, they often drew upon beliefs connecting boys to some activities and girls to others:

A first grade boy avidly watched an all-female game of jump rope. When the girls began to shift positions, he recognized a means of access to the play and he offered, "I'll swing it." A girl responded, "No way, you don't know how to do it, to swing it. You gotta be a girl." He left without protest.

Although children sometimes ignored pronouncements about what each sex could or could not do, I never heard them directly challenge such claims.

When children had explicitly defined an activity or a group as gendered, those who crossed the boundary—especially boys who moved into female-marked space—risked being teased. ("Look! Mike's in the girls' line!"; " 'That's a girl over there,' a girl said loudly, pointing to a boy sitting at an otherwise all-female table in the lunchroom.") Children, and occasionally adults, used teasing—especially the tease of "liking" someone of the other sex, or of "being" that sex by virtue of being in their midst—to police gender boundaries. Much of the teasing drew upon heterosexual romantic definitions, making cross-sex interaction risky, and increasing social distance between boys and girls.

RELATIONSHIPS BETWEEN THE SEXES

Because I have emphasized the "apart" and ignored the occasions of "with," this analysis of sex segregation falsely implies that there is little contact between girls and boys in daily school life. In fact, relationships between girls and boys—which should be studied as fully as, and in connection with, same-sex relationships—are of several kinds:

1. "Borderwork," or forms of cross-sex interaction which are based upon and reaffirm boundaries and asymmetries between girls' and boys' groups;
2. Interactions which are infused with heterosexual meanings;
3. Occasions where individuals cross gender boundaries to participate in the world of the other sex; and
4. Situations where gender is muted in salience, with girls and boys interacting in more relaxed ways.

Borderwork

In elementary school settings boys' and girls' groups are sometimes spatially set apart. Same-sex groups sometimes claim fixed territories such as the basketball court, the bars, or specific lunchroom tables. However, in the crowded, multi-focused, and adult-controlled environment of the school, groups form and disperse at a rapid rate and can never stay totally apart. Contact between girls and boys sometimes lessens sex segregation, but gender-defined groups also come together in ways which emphasize their boundaries.

"Borderwork" refers to interaction across, yet based upon and even strengthening gender boundaries. I have drawn this notion from Fredrik Barth's (1969) analysis of social relations which are maintained across ethnic boundaries with-out diminishing dichotomized ethnic status.[1] His focus is on more macro, ecological arrangements; mine is on face-to-face behavior. But the insight is similar: Groups may interact in ways which strengthen their borders, and the maintenance of ethnic (or gender) groups can best be understood by examining the boundary that defines the group, "not the cultural stuff that it encloses" (Barth, 1969, p. 15). In elementary schools there are several types of borderwork: contests or games where gender-defined teams compete; cross-sex rituals of chasing and pollution; and group invasions. These interactions are asymmetrical, challenging the separate-but-parallel model of "two worlds."

Contests
Boys and girls are sometimes pitted against each other in classroom competitions and playground games. The 4th-5th grade classroom had a boys' side and a girls' side, an arrangement that re-emerged each time the teacher asked children to choose their own desks. Although there was some within-sex shuffling, the result was always a spatial moiety system—boys on the left, girls on the right—with the exception of one girl (the "tomboy" whom I'll describe later), who twice chose a desk with the boys and once with the girls. Drawing upon and reinforcing the children's self-segregation, the teacher often pitted the boys against the girls in spelling and math competitions, events marked by cross-sex antagonism and within-sex solidarity:

> The teacher introduced a math game; she would write addition and subtraction problems on the board, and a member of each team would race to be the first to write the correct answer. She wrote two score-keeping columns on the board: 'Beastly Boys' . . . 'Gossipy Girls.' The boys yelled out, as several girls laughed, 'Noisy girls! Gruesome girls!' The girls sat in a row on top of their desks; sometimes they moved collectively, pushing their hips or whispering 'pass it on.' The boys stood along the wall, some reclining against desks. When members of either group came back victorious from the front of the room, they would do the 'giving five' hand-slapping ritual with their team members.

On the playground a team of girls occasionally played against a team of boys, usually in kickball or team two-square. Sometimes these games proceeded matter-of-factly, but if gender became the explicit basis of team solidarity, the interaction changed, becoming more antagonistic and unstable:

> Two fifth-grade girls played against two fifth-grade boys in a team game of two-square. The game proceeded at an even pace until an argument ensued about whether the ball was out or on the line. Karen, who had hit the ball, became annoyed, flashed her middle finger at the other team, and called to a passing girl to join their side. The boys then called out to other boys, and cheered as several arrived to play. 'We got five and you got three!' Jack yelled. The game continued, with the girls yelling, 'Bratty boys! Sissy boys!' and the boys making noises—'weee haw' 'ha-ha-ha'-as they played.

Chasing
Cross-sex chasing dramatically affirms boundaries between girls and boys. The basic elements of chase and elude, capture and rescue (Sutton-Smith, 1971) are found in various kinds of tag with formal rules, and in informal episodes of chasing which punctuate life on playgrounds. These episodes begin with a provocation (taunts like "You can't get me!" or "Slobber monster!"; bodily pokes or the grabbing of possessions). A provocation may be ignored, or responded to by chasing. Chaser and chased may then alternate roles. In an ethnographic study of chase sequences on a school playground, Christine Finnan (1982) observes that chases vary in number of chasers to chased (e.g., one chasing one, or five chasing two); form of provocation (a taunt or a poke); outcome (an episode may end when the chased outdistances the chaser, or with a brief touch, being wrestled to the ground, or the recapturing of a hat or a ball); and in use of space (there may or may not be safety zones).

Like Finnan (1982), and Sluckin (1981), who studied a playground in England, I found that chasing has a gendered structure. Boys frequently chase one another, an activity which often ends in wrestling and mock fights. When girls chase girls, they are usually less physically aggressive; they less often, for example, wrestle one another to the ground.

Cross-sex chasing is set apart by special names—"girls chase the boys"; "boys chase the girls"; "the chase"; "chasers"; "chase and kiss"; "kiss chase"; "kissers and chasers"; "kiss or kill"—and by children's animated talk about the activity. The names vary by region and school, but contain both gender and sexual meanings (this form of play is mentioned, but only briefly analzyed, in Finnan, 1981; Sluckin, 1981; Parrott, 1972; and Borman, 1979).

In "boys chase the girls" and "girls chase the boys" (the names most frequently used in both the California and Michigan schools) boys and girls become, by definition, separate teams. Gender terms override individual identities, especially for the other team ("Help, a girl's chasin' me!"; "C'mon Sarah, let's get that boy"; "Tony, help save me from the girls"). Individuals may call for help from, or offer help to, others of their sex. They may also grab someone of their sex and turn them over to the opposing team: "Ryan grabbed Billy from behind, wrestling him to the ground 'Hey girls, get 'im,' Ryan called."

Boys more often mix episodes of cross-sex with same-sex chasing. Girls more often have safety zones, places like the girls' restroom or an area by the school wall, where they retreat to rest and talk (sometimes in animated postmortems) before new episodes of cross-sex chasing begin.

Early in the fall in the Michigan school, where chasing was especially prevalent, I watched a second grade boy teach a kindergarten girl how to chase. He slowly ran backwards, beckoning her to pursue him, as he called, "Help, a girl's after me." In the early grades chasing mixes with fantasy play, e.g., a first-grade boy who played "sea monster," his arms outflung and his voice growling, as he chased a group of girls. By third grade, stylized gestures—exaggerated stalking motions, screams (which only girls do), and karate kicks—accompany scenes of chasing.

Names like "chase and kiss" mark the sexual meanings of cross-sex chasing, a theme I return to later. The threat of kissing—most often girls threatening to kiss boys—is a ritualized form of provocation. Cross-sex chasing among sixth graders involves elaborate patterns of touch and touch avoidance, which adults see as sexual. The principal told the sixth graders in the Michigan school that they were not to play "pom-pom," a complicated chasing game, because it entailed "inappropriate touch."

Rituals of Pollution

Cross-sex chasing is sometimes entwined with rituals of pollution, as in "cooties," where specific individuals or groups are treated as contaminating or carrying "germs." Children have rituals for transfering cooties (usually touching someone else and shouting "You've got cooties!"), for immunization (e.g., writing "CV" for "cootie vaccination" on their arms), and for eliminating cooties (e.g., saying "no gives" or using "cootie catchers" made of folded paper) (described in Knapp & Knapp, 1976). While girls may give cooties to girls, boys do not generally give cooties to one another (Samuelson, 1980).

In cross-sex play, either girls or boys may be defined as having cooties, which they transfer through chasing and touching. Girls give cooties to boys more often than vice versa. In Michigan, one version of cooties is called "girl stain"; the fourth-graders whom Karkau, 1973, describes, used the phrase "girl touch." "Cootie queens," or "cootie girls" (there are no "kings" or "boys") are female pariahs, the ultimate school untouchables, seen as contaminating not only by virtue of gender, but also through some added stigma such as being overweight or poor.[2] That girls are seen as more polluting than boys is a significant asymmetry, which echoes cross-cultural patterns, although in other cul-

tures female pollution is generally connected to menstruation, and not applied to prepubertal girls.

Invasions

Playground invasions are another asymmetric form of borderwork. On a few occasions I saw girls invade and disrupt an all-male game, most memorably a group of tall sixth-grade girls who ran onto the playing field and grabbed a football which was in play. The boys were surprised and frustrated, and, unusual for boys this old, finally tattled to the aide. But in the majority of cases, boys disrupt girls' activities rather than vice versa. Boys grab the ball from girls playing four-square, stick feet into a jumprope and stop an ongoing game, and dash through the area of the bars, where girls are taking turns performing, sending the rings flying. Sometimes boys ask to join a girls' game and then, after a short period of seemingly earnest play, disrupt the game:

> Two second-grade boys begged to "twirl" the jumprope for a group of second-grade girls who had been jumping for some time. The girls agreed, and the boys began to twirl. Soon, without announcement, the boys changed from "seashells, cockle bells'" to "hot peppers" (spinning the rope very fast), and tangled the jumper in the rope. The boys ran away laughing.

Boys disrupt girls' play so often that girls have developed almost ritualized responses: They guard their ongoing play, chase boys away, and tattle to the aides. In a playground cycle which enhances sex segregation, aides who try to spot potential trouble before it occurs sometimes shoo boys away from areas where girls are playing. Aides do not anticipate trouble from girls who seek to join groups of boys, with the exception of girls intent on provoking a chase sequence. And indeed, if they seek access to a boys' game, girls usually play with boys in earnest rather than breaking up the game.

A close look at the organization of borderwork—or boundaried interactions between the sexes—shows that the worlds of boys and girls may be separate, but they are not parallel, nor are they equal. The worlds of girls and boys articulate in several asymmetric ways:

1. On the playground, boys control as much as ten times more space than girls, when one adds up the area of large playing fields and compares it with the much smaller areas where girls predominate. Girls, who play closer to the building, are more often watched over and protected by the adult aides.

2. Boys invade all-female games and scenes of play much more than girls invade boys. This, and boys' greater control of space, correspond with other findings about the organization of gender, and inequality, in our society: compared with men and boys, women and girls take up less space, and their space, and talk, are more often violated and interrupted (Greif, 1982; Henley, 1977; West & Zimmerman, 1983).

3. Although individual boys are occasionally treated as contaminating (e.g., a third grade boy who both boys and girls said was "stinky" and "smelled like pee"), girls are more often defined as polluting. This pattern ties to themes that I discuss later: It is more taboo for a boy to play with (as opposed to invade) girls, and girls are more sexually defined than boys.

A look at the boundaries between the separated worlds of girls and boys illuminates within-sex hierarchies of status and control. For example, in the sex-divided seating in the 4th-5th grade classroom, several boys recurringly sat near "female space": their desks were at the gender divide in the classroom, and they were more likely than other boys to sit at a predominantly female table in the lunchroom. These boys—two nonbilingual Chicanos and an overweight "loner" boy who was afraid of sports—were at the bottom of the male hierarchy. Gender is sometimes used as a metaphor for male hierarchies; the inferior status of boys at the bottom is conveyed by calling them "girls":

> Seven boys and one girl were playing basketball. Two younger boys came over and asked to play. While the girl silently stood, fully accepted in the company of players, one of the older boys disparagingly said to the younger boys, 'You girls can't play.'[3]

In contrast, the girls who more often travel in the boys' world, sitting with groups of boys in the lunchroom or playing basketball, soccer, and baseball with them, are not stigmatized. Some have fairly high status with other girls. The worlds of girls and boys are assymetrically arranged, and spatial patterns map out interacting forms of inequality.

Heterosexual Meanings

The organization and meanings of gender (the social categories "woman/man," "girl/boy") and of sexuality vary cross-culturally (Ortner & Whitehead, 1981)—and, in our society, across the life course. Harriet Whitehead (1981) observed that in our (Western) gender system, and that of many traditional North American Indian cultures, one's choice of a sexual object, occupation, and one's dress and demeanor are closely associated with gender. However, the "center of gravity" differs in the two gender systems. For Indians, occupational pursuits provide the primary imagery of gender; dress and demeanor are secondary, and sexuality is least important. In our system, at least for adults, the order is reversed: heterosexuality is central to our definitions of "man" and "woman" ("masculinity"/"femininity"), and the relationships that obtain between them, whereas occupation and dress/demeanor are secondary.

Whereas erotic orientation and gender are closely linked in our definitions of adults, we define children as relatively asexual. Activities and dress/demeanor are more important than sexuality in the cultural

meanings of "girl" and "boy." Children are less heterosexually defined than adults, and we have nonsexual imagery for relations between girls and boys. However, both children and adults sometimes use heterosexual language—"crushes," "like," "goin' with," "girlfriends," and "boyfriends"—to define cross-sex relationships. This language increases through the years of elementary school; the shift to adolescence consolidates a gender system organized around the institution of heterosexuality.

In everyday life in the schools, heterosexual and romantic meanings infuse some ritualized forms of interaction between groups of boys and girls (e.g., "chase and kiss") and help maintain sex segregation. "Jimmy likes Beth" or "Beth likes Jimmy" is a major form of teasing, which a child risks in choosing to sit by or walk with someone of the other sex. The structure of teasing, and children's sparse vocabulary for relationships between girls and boys, are evident in the following conversation which I had with a group of third-grade girls in the lunchroom:

> Susan asked me what I was doing, and I said I was observing the things children do and play. Nicole volunteered, 'I like running, boys chase all the girls. See Tim over there? Judy chases him all around the school. She likes him.' Judy, sitting across the table, quickly responded, 'I hate him. I like him for a friend.' 'Tim loves Judy,' Nicole said in a loud, sing-song voice.

In the younger grades, the culture and lore of girls contains more heterosexual romantic themes than that of boys. In Michigan, the first-grade girls often jumped rope to a rhyme which began: "Down in the valley where the green grass grows, there sat Cindy (name of jumper), as sweet as a rose. She sat, she sat, she sat so sweet. Along came Jason, and kissed her on the cheek . . . first comes love, then comes marriage, then along comes Cindy with a baby carriage. . . . Before a girl took her turn at jumping, the chanters asked her "Who do you want to be your boyfriend?" The jumper always preferred a name, which was accepted matter-of-factly. In chasing, a girl's kiss carried greater threat than a boy's kiss; "girl touch," when defined as contaminating, had sexual connotations. In short, starting at an early age, girls are more sexually defined than boys.

Through the years of elementary school, and increasing with age, the idiom of heterosexuality helps maintain the gender divide. Cross-sex interactions, especially when children initiate them, are fraught with the risk of being teased about "liking" someone of the other sex. I learned of several close cross-sex friendships, formed and maintained in neighborhoods and church, which went underground during the school day.

By the fifth grade a few children began to affirm, rather than avoid, the charge of having a girlfriend or a boyfriend; they introduced the heterosexual courtship rituals of adolescence:

In the lunchroom in the Michigan school, as the tables were forming, a high-status fifth-grade boy called out from his seat at the table: 'I want Trish to sit by me.' Trish came over, and almost like a king and queen, they sat at the gender divide—a row of girls down the table on her side, a row of boys on his.

In this situation, which inverted earlier forms, it was not a loss, but a gain in status to publically choose a companion of the other sex. By affirming his choice, the boy became unteasable (note the familiar asymmetry of heterosexual courtship rituals: the male initiated). This incident signals a temporal shift in arrangements of sex and gender.

Traveling in the World of the Other Sex

Contests, invasions, chasing, and heterosexually-defined encounters are based upon and reaffirm boundaries between girls and boys. In another type of cross-sex interaction, individuals (or sometimes pairs) cross gender boundaries, seeking acceptance in a group of the other sex. Nearly all the cases I saw of this were tomboys—girls who played organized sports and frequently sat with boys in the cafeteria or classroom. If these girls were skilled at activities central in the boys' world, especially games like soccer, baseball, and basketball, they were pretty much accepted as participants.

Being a tomboy is a matter of degree. Some girls seek access to boys' groups but are excluded; other girls limit their "crossing" to specific sports. Only a few—such as the tomboy I mentioned earlier, who chose a seat with the boys in the sex-divided fourth-fifth grade—participate fully in the boys' world. That particular girl was skilled at the various organized sports which boys played in different seasons of the year. She was also adept at physical fighting and at using the forms of arguing, insult, teasing, naming, and sports-talk of the boys' subculture. She was the only Black child in her classroom, in a school with only 8% Black students; overall that token status, along with unusual athletic and verbal skills, may have contributed to her ability to move back and forth across the gender divide. Her unique position in the children's world was widely recognized in the school. Several times, the teacher said to me, "She thinks she's a boy."

I observed only one boy in the upper grades (a fourth grader) who regularly played with all-female groups, as opposed to "playing at" girls' games and seeking to disrupt them. He frequently played jumprope and took turns with girls doing tricks on the bars, using the small gestures—for example, a helpful push on the heel of a girl who needed momentum to turn her body around the bar—which mark skillful and earnest participation. Although I never saw him play in other than an earnest spirit, the girls often chased him away from their games, and both girls and boys teased him. The fact that girls seek, and have more access to boys'

worlds than vice versa, and the fact that girls who travel with the other sex are less stigmatized for it, are obvious asymmetries, tied to the asymmetries previously discussed.

Relaxed Cross-Sex Interactions

Relationships between boys and girls are not always marked by strong boundaries, heterosexual definitions, or by interacting on the terms and turfs of the other sex. On some occasions girls and boys interact in relatively comfortable ways. Gender is not strongly salient nor explicitly invoked, and girls and boys are not organized into boundaried collectivities. These "with" occasions have been neglected by those studying gender and children's relationships, who have emphasized either the model of separate worlds (with little attention to their articulation) or heterosexual forms of contact.

Occasions where boys and girls interact without strain, where gender wanes, rather than waxes in importance, frequently have one or more of the following characteristics:

1. The situations are organized around an absorbing task, such as a group art project or creating a radio show, which encourages cooperation and lessens attention to gender. This pattern accords with other studies finding that cooperative activities reduce group antagonism (e.g., Sherif & Sherif, 1953, who studied divisions between boys in a summer camp; and Aronson et al., 1978, who used cooperative activities to lessen racial divisions in a classroom).

2. Gender is less prominent when children are not responsible for the formation of the group. Mixed-sex play is less frequent in games like football, which require the choosing of teams, and more frequent in games like handball or dodgeball which individuals can join simply by getting into a line or a circle. When adults organize mixed-sex encounters—which they frequently do in the classroom and in physical education periods on the playground—they legitimize cross-sex contact. This removes the risk of being teased for choosing to be with the other sex.

3. There is more extensive and relaxed cross-sex interaction when principles of grouping other than gender are explicitly invoked—for example, counting off to form teams for spelling or kickball, dividing lines by hot lunch or cold lunch, or organizing a work group on the basis of interests or reading ability.

4. Girls and boys may interact more readily in less public and crowded settings. Neighborhood play, depending on demography, is more often sex and age integrated than play at school, partly because with fewer numbers, one may have to resort to an array of social categories to find play partners or to constitute a game. And in less crowded environments there are fewer potential witnesses to "make something of it" if girls and boys play together.

Relaxed interactions between girls and boys often depend on adults to set up and legitimize the contact.[4] Perhaps because of this contingency—and the other, distancing patterns which permeate relations between girls and boys—the easeful moments of interaction rarely build to close friendship. Schofield (1981) makes a similar observation about gender and racial barriers to friendship in a junior high school.

IMPLICATIONS FOR DEVELOPMENT

I have located social relations within an essentially spatial framework, emphasizing the organization of children's play, work, and other activities within specific settings, and in one type of institution, the school. In contrast, frameworks of child development rely upon temporal metaphors, using images of growth and transformation over time. Taken alone, both spatial and temporal frameworks have shortcomings; fitted together, they may be mutually correcting.

Those interested in gender and development have relied upon conceptualizations of "sex role socialization" and "sex differences." Sexuality and gender, I have argued, are more situated and fluid than these individualist and intrinsic models imply. Sex and gender are differently organized and defined across situations, even within the same institution. This situational variation (e.g., in the extent to which an encounter heightens or lessens gender boundaries, or is infused with sexual meanings) shapes and constrains individual behavior. Features which a developmental perspective might attribute to individuals, and understand as relatively internal attributes unfolding over time, may, in fact, be highly dependent on context. For example, children's avoidance of cross-sex friendship may be attributed to individual gender development in middle-childhood. But attention to varied situations may show that this avoidance is contingent on group size, activity, adult behavior, collective meanings, and the risk of being teased.

A focus on social organization and situation draws attention to children's experiences in the present. This helps correct a model like "sex role socialization" which casts the present under the shadow of the future, or presumed "endpoints" (Speier, 1976). A situated analysis of arrangements of sex and gender among those of different ages may point to crucial disjunctions in the life course. In the fourth and fifth grades, culturally defined heterosexual rituals ("goin' with") begin to suppress the presence and visibility of other types of interaction between girls and boys, such as nonsexualized and comfortable interaction, and traveling in the world of the other sex. As "boyfriend/girlfriend" definitions spread, the fifth-grade tomboy I described had to work to sustain "buddy" relationships with boys. Adult women who were tomboys often speak of early adolescence as a painful time when they were pushed away from participation in boys' activities. Other adult women speak of the loss of intense, even erotic ties with other girls when they entered puberty and the rituals of dating, that is, when they became absorbed into the institution of heterosexuality (Rich, 1980). When Lever (1976) describes best-friend relationships among fifth-grade girls as preparation for dating, she imposes heterosexual ideologies onto a present which should be understood on its own terms.

As heterosexual encounters assume more importance, they may alter relations in same-sex groups. For example, Schofield (1981) reports that for sixth- and seventh-grade children in a middle school, the popularity of girls with other girls was affected by their popularity with boys, while boys' status with other boys did not depend on their relations with girls. This is an asymmetry familiar from the adult world; men's relationships with one another are defined through varied activities (occupations, sports), while relationships among women—and their public status—are more influenced by their connections to individual men.

A full understanding of gender and social relations should encompass cross-sex as well as within-sex interactions. "Borderwork" helps maintain separate, gender-linked subcultures, which, as those interested in development have begun to suggest, may result in different milieux for learning. Daniel Maltz and Ruth Borker (1983) for example, argue that because of different interactions within girls' and boys' groups, the sexes learn different rules for creating and interpreting friendly conversation, rules which carry into adulthood and help account for miscommunication between men and women. Carol Gilligan (1982) fits research on the different worlds of girls and boys into a theory of sex differences in moral development. Girls develop a style of reasoning, she argues, which is more personal and relational; boys develop a style which is more positional, based on separateness. Eleanor Maccoby (1982), also following the insight that because of sex segregation, girls and boys grow up in different environments, suggests implications for gender differentiated prosocial and antisocial behavior.

This separate worlds approach, as I have illustrated, also has limitations. The occasions when the sexes are together should also be studied, and understood as contexts for experience and learning. For example, assymetries in cross-sex relationships convey a series of messages: that boys are more entitled to space and to the nonreciprocal right of interrupting or invading the activities of the other sex; that girls are more in need of adult protection, and are lower in status, more defined by sexuality, and may even be polluting. Different types of cross-sex interaction—relaxed, boundaried, sexualized, or taking place on the terms of the other sex—provide different contexts for development.

133

By mapping the array of relationships between and within the sexes, one adds complexity to the overly static and dichotomous imagery of separate worlds. Individual experiences vary, with implications for development. Some children prefer same-sex groupings; some are more likely to cross the gender boundary and participate in the world of the other sex; some children (e.g., girls and boys who frequently play "chase and kiss") invoke heterosexual meanings, while others avoid them.

Finally, after charting the terrain of relationships, one can trace their development over time. For example, age variation in the content and form of borderwork, or of cross- and same-sex touch, may be related to differing cognitive, social, emotional, or physical capacities, as well as to age-associated cultural forms. I earlier mentioned temporal shifts in the organization of cross-sex chasing, from mixing with fantasy play in the early grades to more elaborately ritualized and sexualized forms by the sixth grade. There also appear to be temporal changes in same and cross-sex touch. In kindergarten, girls and boys touch one another more freely than in fourth grade, when children avoid relaxed cross-sex touch and instead use pokes, pushes, and other forms of mock violence, even when the touch clearly couches affection. This touch taboo is obviously related to the risk of seeming to *like* someone of the other sex. In fourth grade, same-sex touch begins to signal sexual meanings among boys, as well as between boys and girls. Younger boys touch one another freely in cuddling (arm around shoulder) as well as mock violence ways. By fourth grade, when homophobic taunts like "fag" become more common among boys, cuddling touch begins to disappear for boys, but less so for girls.

Overall, I am calling for more complexity in our conceptualizations of gender and of children's social relationships. Our challenge is to retain the temporal sweep, looking at individual and group lives as they unfold over time, while also attending to social structure and context, and to the full variety of experiences in the present.

ACKNOWLEDGMENT

I would like to thank Jane Atkinson, Nancy Chodorow, Arlene Daniels, Peter Lyman, Zick Rubin, Malcolm Spector, Avril Thorne, and Margery Wolf for comments on an earlier version of this paper. Conversations with Zella Luria enriched this work.

NOTES

1. I am grateful to Frederick Erickson for suggesting the relevance of Barth's analysis.

2. Sue Samuelson (1980) reports that in a racially mixed playground in Fresno, California, Mexican-American, but not Anglo children gave cooties. Racial, as well as sexual inequality, may be expressed through these forms.

3. This incident was recorded by Margaret Blume, who, for an undergraduate research project in 1982, observed in the California school where I earlier did fieldwork. Her observations and insights enhanced my own, and I would like to thank her for letting me cite this excerpt.

4. Note that in daily school life, depending on the individual and the situation, teachers and aides sometimes lessened, and at other times heightened, sex segregation.

REFERENCES

Aronson, E. et al. (1978). *The jigsaw classroom.* Beverly Hills, CA: Sage.

Barth, F. (Ed.). (1969). *Ethnic groups and boundaries.* Boston: Little, Brown.

Borman, K. M. (1979). Children's interactions in playgrounds. *Theory into Practice, 18,* 251–257.

Eder, D., & Hallinan, M. T. (1978). Sex differences in children's friendships. *American Sociological Review, 43,* 237–250.

Finnan, C. R. (1982). The ethnography of children's spontaneous play. In G. Spindler (Ed.), *Doing the ethnography of schooling* (pp. 358–380). New York: Holt, Rinehart & Winston.

Foot, H. C., Chapman, A. J., & Smith, J. R. (1980). Introduction. *Friendship and social relations in children* (pp. 1–14). New York: Wiley.

Gilligan, C. (1982). *In a different voice: Psychological theory and women's development.* Cambridge, MA: Harvard University Press.

Glaser, B. G., & Strauss, A. L. (1967). *The discovery of grounded theory.* Chicago: Aldine.

Goffman, E. (1977). The arrangement between the sexes. *Theory and Society, 4,* 301–336.

Goodwin, M. H. (1980). Directive-response speech sequences in girls' and boys' task activities. In S. McConnell-Ginet, R. Borker, & N. Furman (Eds.), *Women and language in literature and society* (pp. 157–173). New York: Praeger.

Greif, E. B. (1980). Sex differences in parent-child conversations. *Women's Studies International Quarterly, 3,* 253–258.

Henley. N. (1977). *Body politics: Power, sex, and nonverbal communication.* Englewood Cliffs, NJ: Prentice-Hall.

Karkau, K. (1973). *Sexism in the fourth grade.* Pittsburgh: KNOW, Inc. (pamphlet)

Katz, J. (1983). A theory of qualitative methodology: The social system of analytic fieldwork. In R. M. Emerson (Ed.), *Contemporary field research* (pp. 127–148). Boston: Little, Brown.

Knapp, M., & Knapp. H. (1976). *One potato, two potato: The secret education of American children.* New York: W. W. Norton.

Lever, J. (1976). Sex differences in the games children play. *Social Problems, 23,* 478–487.

Maccoby, E. (1982). *Social groupings in childhood: Their relationship to prosocial and antisocial behavior in boys and girls.* Paper presented at conference on The Development of Prosocial and Antisocial Behavior. Voss, Norway.

Maccoby, E., & Jacklin, C. (1974). *The psychology of sex differences.* CA: Stanford University Press.

Maltz, D. N., & Borker, R. A. (1983). A cultural approach to male-female miscommunication. In J. J. Gumperz (Ed.), *Language and social identity* (pp. 195–216). New York: Cambridge University Press.

McRobbie, A., & Garber, J. (1975). Girls and subcultures. In S. Hall and T. Jefferson (Eds.), *Resistance through rituals* (pp. 209–223). London: Hutchinson.

Ortner, S. B., & Whitehead, H. (1981). *Sexual meanings.* New York: Cambridge University Press.

Parrott, S. (1972). Games children play: Ethnography of a second-grade recess. In J. P. Spradley & D. W. McCurdy (Eds.), *The cultural experience* (pp. 206–219). Chicago: Science Research Associates.

Rich, A. (1980). Compulsory heterosexuality and lesbian existence. *Signs, 5,* 631–660.

Samuelson, S. (1980). The cooties complex. *Western Folklore, 39,* 198–210.

Savin-Williams, R. C. (1976). An ethologicai study of dominance formation and maintenance in a group of human adolescents. *Child Development, 47,* 972–979.

Schofield, J. W. (1981). Complementary and conflicting identities: Images and interaction in an interracial school. In S. R. Asher & J. M. Gottman (Eds.), *The development of children's friendships* (pp. 53–90). New York: Cambridge University Press.

Sherif, M., & Sherif, C. (1953). *Groups in harmony and tension.* New York: Harper.

Sluckin, A. (1981). *Growing up in the playground.* London: Routledge & Kegan Paul.

Speier, M. (1976). The adult ideological viewpoint in studies of childhood. In A. Skolnick (Ed.), *Rethinking childhood* (pp. 168–186). Boston: Little, Brown.

Sutton-Smith, B. (1971). A syntax for play and games. In R. E. Herron and B. Sutton-Smith (Eds.), *Child's Play* (pp. 298–307). New York: Wiley.

Unger, R. K. (1979). Toward a redefinition of sex and gender. *American Psychologist, 34,* 1085–1094.

Waldrop, M. F., & Halverson, C. F. (1975). Intensive and extensive peer behavior: Longitudinal and cross-sectional analysis. *Child Development, 46,* 19–26.

West, C., & Zimmerman, D. H. (1983). Small insults: A study of interruptions in cross-sex conversations between unacquainted persons. In B. Thorne, C. Kramarae, & N. Henley (Eds.), *Language, gender and society.* Rowley, MA: Newbury House.

Whitehead, H. (1981). The bow and the burden strap: A new look at institutionalized homosexuality in Native America. In S. B. Ortner & H. Whitehead (Eds.), *Sexual meanings* (pp. 80–115). New York: Cambridge University Press.

Parenting and Family Issues

Few people today realize that the potential freedom to *choose* parenthood—deciding whether to become a parent, deciding when to have children, or deciding how many children to have—is a development due to the advent of reliable methods of contraception and other recent sociocultural changes. Moreover, unlike any other significant job we may aspire to, few, if any, of us will receive any formal training or information about the lifelong responsibility of parenting. For most of us, our behavior is generally based on our own conscious and subconscious recollections of how we were parented, as well as on our observations of the parenting practices of others around us. In fact, our society often behaves as if the mere act of producing a baby automatically confers upon the parents an innate parenting ability, and that a family's parenting practices should remain private and not be subjected to scrutiny or criticism by outsiders.

Given this climate, it is not surprising that misconceptions about many parenting practices continue to persist today. Only within the last 30 years or so have researchers turned their lenses on the scientific study of the family. Social, historical, cultural, and economic forces also have changed dramatically the face of the American family today. For example, Lucinda Frank's article, "Little Big People," discusses some of these potentially negative changes for the American family and alludes to societal changes that may also be troubling for American children.

Another related shift in parenting involves the fact that significant numbers of children in our country will experience the divorce and/or remarriage of their parents at some point during their lifetime. "Life-Span Adjustment of Children to their Parents' Divorce" reviews the data on this topic and concludes that children's responses to marital transitions vary as a function of many other factors, including, for example, a child's temperament and gender and the availability of supports to their parents. These investigators also argue that rather than viewing single-parent or remarried families as inherently atypical or pathological, researchers today are shifting to examining more closely the specific factors that influence positive as well as negative outcomes for children experiencing changes in their family structure.

Another relatively recent sociocultural change has been the growing trend for fathers to be more active participants in all aspects of family life today. As more women have entered the workforce and sex role expectations have become more flexible, fathers have become more involved in the day-to-day activities of parenting and childrearing. In the past, researchers all but ignored the role of fathers when studying parenting and the family. "Fathers' Time" presents some of the recent research on fathering and the many benefits that fathers, children, and families reap when fathers become actively involved in parenting.

All parents must sooner or later face the question of how to discipline their children. When a young child fails to obey, should the parent reach for the paddle? In "Why Spanking Takes the Spunk Out of Kids," Nick Gallo presents evidence that short-term controls such as spanking are not only ineffective in the long run but may also cause lasting psychological and sometimes physical harm. Although spanking is a very common form of discipline (for example, 90 percent of parents of 3- and 4-year-olds report having spanked their children), this article provides parents with more effective and less problematic forms of discipline.

Looking Ahead: Challenge Questions

Where did you get your ideas, values, and beliefs about how a parent behaves? If you were unsure about how to respond to a particular parenting situation, who would you consult in order to make your decision? How do you think your own experience of parenting by your parents has affected your attitudes or possible parenting practices for your current or future children?

How have the growing numbers of mothers entering the workforce affected the roles of men and women in family life today? Describe the different expectations that our society places upon working mothers versus working fathers. How involved was your own father as a parent and caregiver? Why do you think father involvement has such powerful effects on children and the family? Do you think fathers parent differently from mothers? Why or why not?

As compared to past years, much of the stigma associated with being the child of divorce has been greatly reduced in our country. What factors might account for this shift in attitude? Though most children initially experience their parents' divorce and/or remarriage as stressful,

can you think of any positive outcomes for children who experience these family transitions? If you have a friend with several children who is contemplating divorce, what specific advice could you offer your friend regarding his or her children?

Were you ever spanked by a parent or teacher? If so, how did the experience make you feel? Now imagine being hit by your boss or spouse for disobeying or making a mistake. Why is this situation between adults unacceptable, while most find it acceptable for a parent to strike a child? How do you see yourself altering your current or future disciplinary style with children? How might you teach your children to deal with conflict? If you decide not to use spanking, how would you discipline your child?

Little Big People

A generation of affluent parents have raised the precocious, worldly children they wanted to be—and are now confronted with the results of their experiment.

Lucinda Franks

Lucinda Franks, a Pulitzer Prize-winning journalist, is the author of the novel "Wild Apples."

One day last May, my son's third-grade classroom was left in the care of a substitute teacher. For reasons still undetermined, a small riot broke out, with children fighting, shrieking and shoving chairs. Nine-year-olds going berserk in springtime is not unprecedented, but consider what happened next: The new principal lectured them with a sternness they were unaccustomed to. Then she made them write letters of apology and then they fell apart all over again. Those who claimed they had not participated in the brawl came down at dismissal time tearful and incensed at the burden of collective guilt imposed upon them. "Isn't it illegal for her to punish those of us who did nothing?" one boy asked his mother. "Should we sue her?" asked another. When told they should show more respect for authority, one girl said, "Why should we respect her when she showed no respect for us?"

In the office of a child therapist recently, a 10-year-old girl leaned back and gazed at her mother with half-lidded contempt. The child was there because her divorced parents couldn't do anything with her. Her father was bitter because he had brought her along to buy his girlfriend an engagement gift and she had sulked the whole time. Her mother complained that she refused to make friends with the mother's boyfriend. "How do you expect me to have a relationship with him," the girl said with the ennui of a 40-year-old, "when he's always in your bedroom?"

The therapist shook her head when she recounted the visit: "Sometimes I think I'm too old-fashioned to practice in today's world. Half the time the children act like adults and the adults behave like children."

For decades now, children have been growing up faster and faster, each new generation emerging more precocious than the last. But today's crop of under-12's, particularly in middle- and upper-middle-income families and particularly in urban America, seems to have reinvented—or even bypassed—childhood as we knew it. They are proud, independent and strong-willed; they are worldly-wise and morally serious. They are a generation that has been raised to challenge and doubt authority, to take little at face value—in short, to enter the world of maturity long before they are mature.

This was no accident. The parents of many of these children—those of us who began our families later in life—came of age in the Vietnam War years. Our ideas of child rearing were like our ideas about everything else: radically different from our parents, who thought a child was just a child, even when the child got old enough to march against wars and otherwise protest-the way the elder generation ran the world. Those of us who were veterans of the 60's and 70's swore that we would treat our children with respect. We vowed that we would fold our own offspring into our daily lives, treating them like "little people," empowering them with the rights, the importance and the truth telling we had been denied. We wanted to create the children we always yearned to be. And now, many years later, we are confronted with the results. Did it turn out the way we meant it to? Will our independent children thank us for making them the center of the universe, or have we robbed them of a childhood they can never regain?

The explosion in communications—with television and movies thrusting sophisticated material on grade-schoolers—as well as increasing competition for college placement has intensified childhood burnout. The kids of yesterday, who wandered into meadows of fantasy, whose tears were reserved for skinned knees and broken toys, has given way to the kid who is strapped to the competitive fast track before he is out of diapers. The urban, affluent child is crammed with gymnastics and tennis and French lessons and then is crowded with even more activities by working parents who try to make the most of the time they have with their children. The child who could once be seen playing cops and robbers in the park is no longer even in the park but at home simulating the same thing on his Nintendo screen. He is a computer whiz, a little philosopher, a tiny lawyer, bursting with opinions on the President, on the best museums, the best vacation spots and the college he thinks he will attend.

For childish comfort, he is taken into the capricious arms of television: the great cuddly dinosaur Barney leads him in singing "we're a happy family" and then the child switches the channel to see that the man who taught him tennis is a pedophile who has put a bullet through his brain. Language more appropriate to teenagers can be heard in elementary-school halls. One mother of a 7-year-old confided that a boy had told her daughter, "You're so yucky you must have sex with Nazis."

Economic hardship has long stolen childhood from the poor. The severity and the causes of their problems, which have only intensified, are far different from those of affluent children. Yet for the first time, these more privileged children are thrust unshielded into the middle of family crisis that would paralyze an adult: a parent is dying of AIDS or the child is a mediator in violent dramas of drug addiction or divorce.

Even in stable families, small children with two working parents learn to shift for themselves, cooking and caring for siblings and picking up the attitudes of their elders. Our generation—reared in an era in which sex was not discussed, conflict was suppressed and emotional distance was maintained—opened the gates for our children. But each day, the bleak river of honesty that runs through their lives grows dangerously higher.

"I was determined that there was going to be no more scary secrets, no more J. Edgar Hoover, when I got to be a parent; everything was going to be up front," says Marcia Roesch, a school admissions coordinator. "I talked and talked, but I wasn't listening and I wasn't keeping a sense of balance and appropriateness with my children. I hear parents all the time asking their kids 'Is that O.K.?' as though they need their kids to approve every decision."

Says Candace Stern, a New Jersey mother of an 8-year-old: "I used to express my insecurities and everything else to my daughter. One day, we were watching a takeoff of Little Red Riding Hood on Sesame Street and I thought it was hilarious. Then I looked at Caitlin and she was terrified. It was then that I realized that I didn't really know what was in her mind and that what she heard, what she held onto, was much different than what I, an adult, retained."

Contrary to our assumptions, we have found that children are much more than little people. They are the possessors of rather eccentric states of mind that some experts fear are being altered by the early use of computers and other technology.

"There is a period of childhood, until about age 9, when children should exist in a dreamlike state," says Kay J. Hoffman, an educator at a progressive school in Rockland County in New York. "Instead, they are being hardened too early, jarred into an awake adult consciousness that is preventing the natural development of their imaginations. The trend to intellectualize early education is a dangerous one. I see more children with high anxiety levels and learning problems caused by the enormous pressure that is being put on them to think and speak like adults before they are ready."

Highly verbal children will use words, without really understanding them, as coin of the adult realm. "They use them for protection, to push away their own experience as children," says one doctor who asked not to be identified to protect his patients. "One 4-year-old that I tested kept running out of the room saying he had to go get his 'concentration.' He couldn't just be a child and say, 'I don't want to do this test!' He had to parrot an adult concept that he hardly understood because he was afraid to disappoint me."

I think sometimes we cannot know how profound that fear runs in our children, especially since we have burdened them with such a sense of their own importance. At times, their officiousness seems to be bluff; they simply cannot afford to be wrong. In making them feel so trusted and believed, we have not only bridged the generation gap, we might have overlapped it. As we hover over their development as though we were tending orchids in a greenhouse, are we not also guilty of a kind of neglect? In integrating them into our daily lives, have we taken away their freedom to do childish things? Parents or nannies of old stayed at home and babbled and played games; we take them to department stores, to work, to lunch, to movies and plays. Parents push for intimacy so much that one child was overheard telling her mother, "If you say I can have my feelings one more time, I'm going to throw up."

Says Miriam Siffert, a grandmother in Manhattan: "We sent our children to the most progressive schools, but they knew their place. They knew their time. We didn't take them to dinner parties or on trips to Europe. But I see my grandchildren taking over the house, taking over adult conversation."

Peggy Rosenblatt, a mother of two, concurs: "There is so much familiarity and so little distance. We tell them where we are going, what we are doing. We ask their opinion as though they were our best buddies, and then we are surprised when we tell a 10-year-old to do something he doesn't want to do and he says, 'You can't make me.'"

So uncomfortable are we with being in authority that we have made a crusade of elevating our children at the expense of ourselves. Consider the way we portray ourselves in children's movies; no Mary Poppins or Clark Kent these days; instead, enter Hook, so realistically evil that he breaks the bounds of old-time fantasy, or an all-too-believable Mom and Dad who keep leaving their son home alone.

"Sometimes it seems like there is no bottom line anymore," says Sara Adler, a grade-school teacher for 20 years. "I have some kids who yell 'child abuse' if you discipline them. They know tag lines, but they don't know the lines they cannot and should not cross. The parents think, 'What are the teachers doing!' And the teachers wonder what is going on inside the homes."

We have abrogated the moral authority our parents wore as easily as gloves. In Westchester County in New York, for instance, where kids in their early teens come into the city to party until the early hours of the morning, some parents are afraid to give their children curfews for fear they will move out and live with a friend.

Even children themselves think that things sometimes go too far. "Trust me, I know some kids who are guilty of parent abuse," Jonathan Stein, 10, says. "They feel like they own their parents and that they could just take all their parents' money out of their bank account and run away if they wanted."

Michelle Denburg, a high-school senior, adds: "Some of my teachers were afraid to be authority figures. They couldn't control their class and partly it was the fault of the parents because they would say negative stuff about a teacher and then expect their kids to respect those teachers."

In spite of the confusion these children experience, few would disagree that they are, in many ways, a splendid generation. My son, Joshua, 9, and his friends are amazing in their generosity, sensitivity, ability to stretch across an intellectual canyon and meet adults on their own terms. They have highly developed senses of justice and fairness, rejecting stereotypes and embracing oddities in their peers, whether a hair style or a disability. They are disdainful of smoking and drug use, can sniff out hypocrisy and have social consciences that are poignant. They are so worried about the few trees on their block that last year they formed an earth club to keep them free of litter. At times, the child in our children pokes endearingly through the veneer of sophistication. "Mom, please don't buy Ivory soap anymore" as his most recent environmental request. "Why?" I asked. "Be-

cause they shoot elephants to get the ivory, don't they?" he replied.

Paul Shechtman, a New York lawyer, reports that when he argued with his daughter, 6, about going to school with a rip in the knee of her jeans, she asked him for one good reason why she shouldn't wear them. "Because my father never would have let me," he said, exasperated. "Just because your father made a mistake," she replied, "why should you?"

"At that moment," Shechtman said, "I knew that I had succeeded as a parent. Now, of course, I do have to live with my success."

Helene Stein, mother of three children 14 and under, including Jonathan, says she gets "a kind of wicked pleasure when I compare my children's childhood with my own." She and her sister had to be bathed, with hair brushed and bathrobes on, before they came to the table. "My parents were the ones who spoke," she says. "We listened. With my kids, I drop everything if they seem to want to talk."

Since the end of the Victorian era, when children emerged as entities that would be heard as well as occasionally seen, childhood has been considered increasingly precious. Members of my generation, however, gave new definition to the cult of child worship. When I was pregnant, one friend teased me for turning my apartment upside down and buying a king-size bed (big enough for three): "You'd think you were preparing for the arrival of Caesar." After Josh was born, I filled notebooks recording his every wiggle. And my husband insisted on carrying him in a sling on his hip virtually everywhere, including to cocktail parties, where, to everyone's horror, he let him sip beer. Not being able to recall one of my pictures ever gracing my mother's refrigerator door, I later hung his drawings of little people manning complicated machines up and down the hallway. One day, when 4, he smiled indulgently and said, "Mom, you'd think our house was the Metropolitan Museum of Joshua!"

Some parents applaud both the acceleration and involvement of today's children in the real world. A librarian expressed disbelief when a third-grader asked for books on the Holocaust. "We read those books together," his mother, Carol Saper, explains, "and we talk about them. I think it has made my son a more sensitive, caring person."

Nearly all parents, however, feel their best efforts are continually subverted by television. Much of the time, exhausted, overextended parents are caught unawares. "I'm a working mother and I move mountains to organize everything just right—we even manage to eat dinner together, but there's always some crack for the kids to fall through," says Susan Mascitelli, a hospital administrator who has a son, 9, and a daughter, 3. "The kids leave the table early and my husband

and I finally have 10 minutes of peace and then suddenly I hear the kids howling with laughter at "Married with Children," about a couple that hates each other and a child who acts like a hooker. The fact that they even understand this disgusting program stuns me."

Last year, one school on the Upper West Side of Manhattan held parent meetings to discuss a fourth grade whose girls were so sexually precocious that they were hotly pursuing certain boys and refusing to speak to others. "The last straw was when one child invited kids to his home for a dating party when his parents were out," says Ann Beaton, who has children aged 10, 7 and 1. "The kids' parents just delivered them with no questions asked. The girls wore halter tops and tiny bicycle shorts. It's hard to know whether they just wanted to look like Julia Roberts in "Pretty Woman" or whether they knew what they were up to."

Some parents complain that the culture has sexualized children long before they desired it. One third-grader, asked to list questions she had during a sex education course, replied, "Why do we have to know about stuff like this?"

Dr Richard A. Gardner, a child psychiatrist and author who has recently been outspoken in his defense of adults he thinks have been falsely accused of sex abuse, believes that although these crimes do exist, the country is undergoing a wave of sex abuse hysteria: "When I was a child, I had a book about having a fun day with Uncle Ralph. Now, Uncle Ralph is depicted as the kind of guy who, as soon as Mom goes into the kitchen, has his hand in your pants." Gardner says that data show the proliferation of early childhood sex abuse prevention programs are creating confusion and anxiety in youngsters and he predicts those programs will also result in sexual inhibition, mistrust and even long-term sexual dysfunction.

Schools and parents alike have begun taking steps to address these problems. Stephen M. Clement, the headmaster of a boys school in Manhattan, for instance, imposes strict order on the older boys who set standards of behavior for the younger ones: "One of our boys walked in bleeding—he had been mugged for his baseball cap. A school must try to provide a safe haven and some better models."

At Kay Hoffman's school in Rockland, teachers make unilateral decisions for young children so that they will have a good inventory of adult choices on which to base their own decisions later on. "We try to slow children down," Hoffman says. "We don't barrage them all at once. Learning evolves out of their own experience." The school also advises parents to ban television and not to talk about current events. "As soon as I did that, my child began to relax and act like a little girl again," says Candace Stern, whose daughter attends the school. "Her uncle was in Desert Storm and we didn't even tell her he had gone to Jidda until after it was all over. When we finally told her that he had been in a war, she asked, 'What side was he on?'"

Some worry about the repercussions of this generation's having lost its fleeting chance to be a child. "A person who does not have the opportunity to move through the stages of childhood at his own pace ends up with something missing," Jill Comins, a family therapist, says. "As an adult, he will search endlessly for it. He will experience powerful and regressive tugs backward."

Others, however, predict success. "I've been watching these kids grow up, grade by grade," says Gardner P. Dunnan, headmaster of a co-educational school on the Upper East Side. "They have had so much openness, so many opportunities, such a great arena to learn and grow, by the time they are adults they will be wonderful individuals and citizens."

Perhaps our children are simply rebelling against their parents much earlier than we did. And perhaps that means that they won't have to do it later. Perhaps our children will grow up to be the kind of people who wouldn't dream of inventing the motto "Never Trust Anybody Over 30."

"I feel they are in transition," says Sara Lebar, who lives in Greenwich Village. "We changed the rules and we have to expect them to react. I think that the next stage will be that our kids will be our friends, in a way we never were to our parents. Allison may not give me the respect I gave my mother, but I never aspired to be like my parents. And already Allison wants to be an environmentalist just like me.

For those of us who love our wonderful strong-willed children just the way they are—or almost just the way they are—there is a move afoot to readjust certain things ever so slightly. One day not long ago, having asked my own son several times to straighten out his room—which could not be penetrated because of a string that crisscrossed from wall to wall in some obscure scientific experiment—and having received no reply to this apparently trivial request, my voice became significantly louder. He finally looked up. "I'm not comfortable with cleaning out my room right now," he said.

"Get comfortable," I replied.

"Why?" he gazed at me.

"Because," I said, startled, as out of my mouth tumbled words that could have been taken out of a balloon in a comic strip of the 60's, "you are a child and I am the mother. You do not have the right to tell me what to do. On the other hand, I have the right to tell you what to do as long as you live under my roof."

First he gave me a withering look. Then he thought about it for a minute. And then he said "O.K." and headed for his room.

Fathers' Time

Their style is vastly different, but dads can no longer be looked on as second bananas in the parenting biz. New studies show fathers are crucial for the emotional and intellectual growth of their kids, influencing how they ultimately turn out. Writer/father PAUL ROBERTS reports on the importance of being a papa. Actor/father BILL MOSELEY's dispatches reveal what it's like on the front lines.

Paul Roberts

PAUL ROBERTS is a Seattle-based freelance writer. Actor BILL MOSELEY interviewed Timothy Leary for *PT* in 1995.

This was supposed to be the Golden Era of Paternity. After decades of domestic aloofness, men came charging into parenthood with an almost religious enthusiasm. We attended Lamaze classes and crowded into birthing rooms. We mastered diapering, spent more time at home with the kids, and wallowed in the flood of "papa" literature unleashed by Bill Cosby's 1986 best-seller Fatherhood.

Yet for all our fervor, the paternal revolution has had a slightly hollow ring. It's not simply the relentless accounts of fatherhood's dark side—the abuse, the neglect, the abandonment—that make us so self-conscious. Rather, it's the fact that for all our earnest sensitivity, we can't escape questions of our psychological necessity: What is it, precisely, that fathers do? What critical difference do we make in the lives of our children?

Think about it. The modern mother, no matter how many nontraditional duties she assumes, is still seen as the family's primary nurturer and emotional guardian. It's in her genes. It's in her soul. But mainstream Western society accords no corresponding position to the modern father. Aside from chromosomes and feeling somewhat responsible for household income, there's no similarly celebrated deep link between father and child, no widely recognized "paternal instinct." Margaret Mead's quip that fathers are "a biological necessity but

Diary of a Dad

I love this time. Jane Moseley puts her hunter mare through its paces. Time slows to a trot, works up to a canter, drops to a lazy walk.

She announces she won't wear her riding hat. I insist she must. She refuses, would rather not ride. I can't believe she'd give up The Most Important Thing in her Life over this. Fine, don't ride. This triggers an outpouring of vitriol. I pay attention, but don't take it personally. Thirty minutes later she's holding my hand as we walk down Melrose.

a social accident" may be a little harsh. But it does capture the second-banana status that many fathers have when it comes to taking their measure as parents.

Happily, a new wave of research is likely to substantially boost that standing. Over the last decade, researchers like Jay Belsky, Ph.D., at Pennsylvania State University, and Ross Parke, Ph.D., of the University of California/Riverside Center for Family Studies, have been mapping out the psychology of the father-child bond, detailing how it functions and how it differs—sometimes substantially—from the bond between mother and child. What emerges from their work is the beginning of a truly modern concept of paternity, one in which old assumptions are overturned or, at the very least, cast in a radically different light. Far from Mead's "social accident," fatherhood turns out to be a complex and unique phenomenon with huge consequences for the emotional and intellectual growth of children.

Key to this new idea of fatherhood is a premise so mundane that most of us take it for granted: fathers parent differently than mothers do. They play with their children more. Their interactions tend to be more physical and less intimate, with more of a reliance on humor and excitement. While such distinctions may hardly seem revelatory, they can mean a world of difference to kids. A father's more playful interactive style, for example, turns out to be critical in teaching a child emotional self-control. Likewise, father-child interactions appear to be central to the development of a child's ability to maintain strong, fulfilling social relationships later in life.

But it's not simply a matter of paternal behavior differing from maternal methods. The fabric of the father-child bond is also different. Studies show that fathers with low self-esteem have a greater negative impact in their children than do mothers who don't like themselves. In addition, the father-child bond seems to be more fragile—and therefore more easily severed—during periods of strife between parents.

Amid this welter of findings two things are clear. First, given our rapidly evolving conceptions of "father" and "family," fatherhood in the 1990s is probably tougher, psychologically, than at any other time in recent history. Plainly put, there are precious few positive role models to guide today's papas. Yet at the same time, the absence of any guidance holds hidden promise. Given the new information on fatherhood, the potential for a rich and deeply rewarding paternal experience is significantly greater today than even a generation ago. "The possibilities for fathering have never been better," Belsky says. "Culturally speaking, there is so much more that fathers are 'allowed' to do."

Our Forefathers

The surge of interest in fatherhood has a distinctly modern feel, as if after thousands of years of unquestioned maternal preeminence, men are just now discovering and asserting their parental prerogatives. But in fact, this unquestioned maternal dominance is itself a relatively recent development. Up until the mid-1700s, when most fathers worked in or near the home and took a much greater hand in child rearing, Western culture regarded them and not mothers as the more competent parent—and ultimately held them more responsible for how their children turned out. Not only were books and manuals on parenting written chiefly for men, according to R. L. Griswold, author of *Fatherhood in America*, men were routinely awarded custody of their kids in cases of divorce.

With the Industrial Revolution, however, more fathers began working outside their homes and thus were effectively removed from domestic life. As Vicky Phares, Ph.D., assistant professor of psychology at the University of South Florida, wrote in *Fathers and Developmental Psychopathology*, industrialization ushered in the "feminization of the domestic sphere and the marginalization of fathers' involvement with their children." By the mid-1800s, Phares notes, "child-rearing manuals were geared toward mothers, and this trend

After Jane and I had a snack, she wanted to box. So we waltzed around for 20 minutes, floating like a butterfly (me), stinging like a bee (Jane). I've taught her the rudiments of pugilism: how to make a fist (don't wrap your fingers around your thumb); how she should always stand sideways to her opponent, watching the hands not the eyes, etc. After a few fun-filled injury-free rounds, I came to my senses and ended our play.

Jane is an only child, so I figure it's my job to play with her as a brother or provide her with a sibling—playing with her is easier!

continued for the most part until the mid-1970s."

The implication here—that parental roles have largely been defined by economics—is still a subject of cultural debate. Less arguable, however, is the fact that by the turn of the twentieth century, both science and society saw the psychology of parenting largely as the psychology of motherhood. Not only were mothers somehow more "naturally" inclined to parent, they were also genetically better prepared for the task. Indeed, in 1916, Phares notes, one prominent investigator went so far as to "prove" the existence of the maternal instinct—and the lack of paternal equivalent—largely based on the notion that "few fathers were naturally skilled at taking care of infants."

Granted, bogus scientific claims were plentiful in those times. But even Freud, who believed fathers figured heavily in children's development of conscience and sexual identity, dismissed the idea that they had any impact until well past a child's third year. And even then, many psychologists argued, these paternal contributions consisted primarily of providing income, discipline, and a masculine role model, along with periodic injections of what might be called "real world" experience—that is, things that took place outside the home. "The classical psychological view held that a father's 'job' was to expand his children's horizon beyond the bosom of the family and the mother-child relationship," Belsky observes. "Mothers preserved and protected children from discomfort. But fathers imposed a realistic, the world-is-tough perspective."

By the 1920s, the classic "mother-centric" view was showing its cracks. Not only did subsequent empirical studies find little hard evidence of any unique maternal instinct but, as Phares points out, the phenomenon of "mother-blaming"—that is, blaming mothers for all the emotional and behavioral problems of their children—prodded some researchers (and, no doubt, a good many mothers) to ask whether fathers might share some of the responsibility.

By the 1950s, science began to recognize that there was some paternal impact on early childhood—even if it was only in the negative context of divorce or the extended absence of a father. Psychologist Michael Lamb, Ph.D., research director at the National Institute for Child Health and Human Development in Bethesda, Maryland, explains: "The assumption was that by comparing the behavior and personalities of children raised with and without fathers, one could—essentially by a process of subtraction—estimate what sort of influence fathers typically had."

W_{HAT} D_{ADS} D_O

It wasn't until the feminist movement of the 1970s that researchers thought to ask whether dads could be as nurturing as moms. To everyone's astonishment, the answer was yes.

Actually, that was half the answer. Subsequent inquiries showed that while fathers could be as nurturing as mothers, they tended to leave such duties to moms. Hardly news to millions of overworked women, this finding was crucial. For the first time, researchers began systematically studying how and why male and female parenting strategies diverged, and more to the point, what those differences meant for children.

Although the total fatherhood experience runs from conception on, research has focused most keenly on the first few years of the parent-child relationship. It's here that children are most open to parental influence; they function primarily as receivers, consuming not only huge quantities of nourishment and comfort but stimuli as well. For decades, investigators have understood that infants not only enjoy taking in such rudimentary knowledge but absolutely require it for intellectual, physical, and especially emotional growth.

Without such constant interaction, argues W. Andrew Collins, Ph.D., of the University of Minnesota's Institute for Child Development, infants might never fully develop a sense of comfort and security. As important, they might not develop a sense of being connected to—and thus having some degree of control over—the world around them. "The key ingredient is a 'contingent responsiveness,'" says Collins, "where infants learn their actions will elicit certain reliable responses from others."

It's also during this crucial period that one of the most fundamental differences between male and female parenting styles takes place. Work by several psychiatrists, including San Diego's Martin Greenberg, M.D., and Kyle Pruett, M.D., a professor of psychiatry at the Yale Child Study Center, suggests that while new mothers are inclined to relate to their infants in a more soothing, loving, and serious way, new fathers "hold their children differently and have a different kind of patience and frustration cycle than mothers," Pruett observes.

I crave adult company, but I don't have a baby-sitter for tonight. So I'm trying to lug Jane all the way to Santa Monica to see Wing Chun, *a kung-fu movie she says she doesn't want to see. Oh, no you don't, kid, it's my time now, and we're going to Santa Monica. Of course, Jane winds up loving the movie. Later that night we watch a video of* Captains Courageous. *I am reminded of all the songs that the two of us have made up over the past several years: "Feed Lot," "Ain't No Bridge," "Don't Drink the Water," "When the Vulture Swoops," etc. (Lyrics upon request).*

Why it is fathers behave this way isn't entirely clear. (And when fathers are primary caregivers, they are likely to display many of the so-called maternal traits.) Some studies suggest these gender differences are part of a larger male preference for stimulating, novel activities that arises from neurobiological differences in the way stimuli and pleasure are linked in male and female brains, and likely a result of genetics. Individuals high in the sensation-seeking trait are far more likely to engage in new and exciting pastimes. Though not all guys qualify as sensation seekers, the trait is far more common in men—particularly young ones—than it is in women, and might help explain why any young fathers start off having a parenting style that's stimulating for them as well as their child.

T_{HE} D_{ADDY} D_{YNAMIC}

Whatever its origins, this more playful, jocular approach carries major consequences for developing children. Where the "average" mother cushions her baby against irritating stimulation, the "average" father heaps it on, consistently producing a broader range of arousal. The resulting ups and downs force children to "stretch," emotionally and physically.

This emotion-stretching dynamic becomes more pronounced as father-child relationships enter into their second and third years. When playing, fathers tend to be more physical with their toddlers—wrestling, playing tag, and so on—while mothers emphasize verbal exchanges and interacting with objects, like toys. In nearly all instances, says Lamb, fathers are much more likely "to get children worked up, negatively or positively, with fear as well as delight, forcing them to learn to regulate their feelings."

In a sense, then, fathers push children to cope with the world outside the mother-child bond, as classical theory argued. But more than this, fathering behavior also seems to make children develop a more complex set of interactive skills, what Parke calls "emotional communication" skills.

First, children learn how to "read" their father's emotions via his facial expressions, tone of voice, and other nonverbal cues, and respond accordingly. Is Daddy really going to chase me down and gobble me up, or is he joking? Did I really hurt Daddy by poking him in the eye? Is Daddy in the mood to play, or is he tired?

Second, children learn how to clearly communicate their own emotions to others. One common example is the child who by crying lets her daddy know that he's playing too roughly or is scaring her. Kids also learn to indicate when interactions aren't stimulating enough; they'll show they've lost interest by not responding or wandering off.

Finally, children learn how to "listen" to their own emotional state. For instance, a child soon learns that if he becomes too "worked up" and begins to cry, he may in effect drive his play partner away.

The consequences of such emotional mastery are far-reaching. By successfully coping with stimulating, emotionally stretching interactions, children learn that they can indeed ef-

Made Jane cry—down on her for not helping me put away the groceries, make dinner. She wanted to play Super Mario Bros. (So did I.) She called me an idiot. I yelled at her about not pulling her oar—sounded just like my dad—and sent her to her room. I kept her in there for a few minutes, felt bad, knocked on the door, and sat on her bed and apologized for losing my temper. "You hurt my feelings," she sniffed.

Creating a New Patriarchy

Even the most dedicated dads quickly discover that the road to modern fatherhood is strewn with obstacles. Positive role models are in short supply and personal experiences are usually no help. Jerrold Lee Shapiro, Ph.D., professor of psychology at Santa Clara University, says understanding your relationship with your own father is the first step. If not, you're bound to automatically and unconciously replicate things from your childhood.

Here are several strategies both parents can use to strengthen the father-child bond.

◆ Start early. While involvement doesn't always equal intimacy, fathers who immerse themselves in all aspects of parenting from birth on are more likely to be closer to their children. Take part in as many prenatal activities as possible and schedule at least a week away from work after the baby is born to practice parenting skills and overcome anxieties about handling the baby.

◆ Create "fathering space": Schedule times and activities in which you take care of your newborn entirely on your own. The traditional practice of deferring to mothers as "experts" gives new fathers few chances to hone their parenting skills, bolster their confidence, and build solid bonds with baby.

Sue Dickinson, M.S.W., a marriage and family therapist in Cle Elum, Washington, suggests persuading mom to go out of the house so you can have the experience of being the parent. Martin Greenberg, M.D., recommends bundling your baby in a chest pack and going for walks. The feeling of a baby's body—together with his or her warmth and smell—is captivating.

◆ Articulate feelings. Although fatherhood is routinely described as "the most wonderful experience" a man can have, new fathers may feel anxious, fearful, and frustrated. They may also be jealous of the time their wives spend with the baby and of their wives' "natural" parenting skills. These feelings may only make it harder for you to wholeheartedly participate in parenting and create distance between you and your child. New fathers need to identify such feelings and discuss them with their wives.

◆ Mind the details. Tune in to your children and avoid relying on mom to "read" what your baby wants.

◆ Respect diversity. Accept your partner's parenting style without criticizing. Mothers often regard fathers' more boisterous style as too harsh or insensitive. But such criticism can derail a dad's desire for involvement. "Just because he's doing something you wouldn't do doesn't make it wrong," says Jay Belsky, Ph.D. Mothers have to temper their need to protect and remember dads offer things moms don't.

◆ Be realistic. Fathers who want to adopt a more hands-on approach than they themselves experienced are often frustrated when kids don't immediately respond. But children accustomed to having mom as the primary caregiver simply cannot adapt to "sudden" paternal involvement overnight. Above all, parenting requires patience.

fect change both on internal matters (their feelings) and in the outside world (their father's actions). In that regard, links have been found between the quality of father-child interactions and a child's later development of certain life skills, including an ability to manage frustration, a willingness to explore new things and activities, and persistence in problem solving.

As important as learning to regulate the emotional intensity of their interactions is children's ability to master the larger interactive process, the give and take that makes up social communication. "Kids who learn how to decode and encode emotions early on will be better off later when it comes to any social encounter," Parke says.

Such benefits have been intensely studied in the area of sibling relationships. Work by Belsky and Brenda Volling, Ph.D., an assistant professor of psychology at the University of Michigan, suggests that the emotion-management "lessons" learned by children from their fathers during play are applied later in interactions with siblings—and ultimately with people outside the family—and lead to more cooperation and less fighting. The press release announcing Belsky and Volling's research quipped, "If Adam had been a better father, things might have turned out differently for Cain and Abel."

Such findings come with plenty of caveats. A mother's more comforting manner is just as crucial to her children, helping them foster, among other things, a critical sense of security and self-confidence. Indeed, a mere preference for stimulating activities does not a good father make; obviously, the quality of father-child interactions is important. Successful fathers both monitor and modulate their play, maintaining a level of stimulation that keeps children engaged without making them feel like they've been pushed too far. This requires complete engagement—something many of today's busy fathers find difficult to manage. "What often happens is fathers don't pay attention to the cues their kids are sending," Belsky says. "A kid is crying 'uncle' and his father doesn't hear it."

Of course, fathers aren't the only parent who can teach these coping skills. Mothers physically play with their kids and, depending on the dynamics and history of the family, may also be the ones providing more of a "paternal" influence—teaching coping skills through play. Yet this "stretching" role typically falls to fathers because men gravitate toward less intimate, more physical interactions. And, as Reed

Larson, Ph.D., a psychologist at the University of Illinois-Champagne, observes, "when dads stop having fun interacting with their kids, they're more likely than mothers to exit."

Whether these differences are genetic, cultural, or, more likely, a combination of the two, is still hotly debated. But the fact remains that in terms of time spent with children, fathers typically spend more of it playing with their kids than mothers do—a difference that from very early on, children pick up on. Studies show that during stressful situations, one-year-old and 18-month-old babies more often turn to their primary caretaker—in most families, mom—for help. By contrast, when researchers measured so-called affiliative behaviors like smelling and vocalizing, during their first two years, babies showed a preference for their fathers. Just as dramatic, almost as soon as a child can crawl or walk, he or she will typically seek out dad for play and mom for comfort and other needs.

DOWNSIDE OF THE DADDY TRACK

On the face of it, fathers would seem to enjoy considerable advantages over mothers during their children's first years. Not only do they do less of the dirty work, but it's almost as if they've been anointed to handle the fun art of parenting. Yet as time goes on this situation changes dramatically. While a mother's more intimate, need-related approach to parenting generally continues to cement her bond with her children, a father's more playful and stimulating style steadily loses its appeal. By the age of eight or nine, a child may already be angry at his father's teasing, or bored or annoyed by his I'm-gonna-gitcha style.

This discrepancy often becomes quite pronounced as children reach adolescence. Research suggests that preteens and teens of both sexes continue to rely on their mothers for intimacy and needs, and increasingly view her as the favored parent for topics requiring sensitivity and trust. By contrast, Parke says, the joking, playful style that serves fathers so well during children's first years may begin to alienate teens, giving them the impression that their father doesn't take their thoughts and needs seriously.

Adding to this tension is the father's traditional role as the dispenser of discipline and firmness. It's hypothesized that fathers' less intimate interactive style may make it easier—although not more pleasant—for them to play the "heavy." In any case, adolescents come to see

Anna's sleeping over. Earlier in the evening, Jane was on the floor of her bedroom looking up my shorts, laughing, saying she saw my penis. Later, I spy Jane and Anna holding up our cat Jackson. Must be a penis hunt, little-girl style. It's already in full swing and they're seven and eight!

In addition to being cook, chauffeur, maid, and spiritual protector, I am also Sex Authority! Two years ago, I explained, in a general way, the birds and the bees to Jane, correcting the misinformation she'd been given by her good friend Olivia.

their fathers as the harsher, more distant parent. This feeling may increase teenagers' tendency to interact more often and intimately with their mothers, which in turn only heightens the sense of estrangement and tension between fathers and their kids.

As to whether fathers' possibly not being at home as much as mothers makes it easier or more difficult for them to be the disciplinarian, Parke says there are too many other factors involved to make such a determination. He does note, however, that many mothers faced with unruly kids still employ the threat, "Wait 'til your father gets home."

Clearly, the distance between fathers and adolescent children is not solely as result of fathers' playfulness earlier on. A central function of adolescence is a child's gradual movement toward emotional and physical autonomy from both parents. But studies suggest this movement is most directly and forcefully spurred by fathers' less intimate ways.

Does a father's parenting style during adolescence produce more closeness between father and child? The answer is probably no, says Parke. But if the question is, does a father's style serve a launching, independence-gaining function, the answer is probably yes. "Mothers' continued nurturance maintains a child's connectedness to the family, while fathers encourage differentiation," Parke says. In fact, according to a recent survey of adolescents by Israeli researchers Shmuel Shulman, Ph.D., and Moshe Klein, Ph.D., most perceived their fathers as being the primary source of support for their teenage autonomy.

Such notions will undoubtedly strike some as disturbingly regressive, as if researchers have simply found new, complex ways to justify outdated stereotypes of paternal behavior. For as any sensitive observer knows, the totality of fatherhood goes well beyond a tendency toward stimulating interactions and away from intimacy. Nonetheless, this does appear to be a central component of fathering behavior and may help explain why some seemingly antiquated modes of fathering persist. Despite evolution in gender roles, Belsky says, fathers are still more likely to provide less sensitivity, require kids to adjust to 'tough' realities, and perhaps be less understanding and empathetic.

Yet if the father-child bond truly serves as a mechanism for preparing children for the external world, the bond itself seems remarkably sensitive, even vulnerable, to that world. External variables, such as a father's relationships beyond his family—and in particular his experience in the workplace—appear to be linked to both the kinds of fathering behavior he exhibits and the success he achieves with it. Some of these links are obvious. Few would be surprised to learn that fathers with high-stress jobs are apt to be more distant from their kids or use harsher, physical discipline when dealing with youthful infractions.

Other links between a man's external world and the way he fathers are more subtle. According to Parke, there are significant and intriguing fathering differences between men whose jobs involve a great degree of independence and those who are heavily managed. Fathers with workplace autonomy tend to expect and encourage more independence in their children. Moreover, they generally place grater emphasis on a child's intent when assessing misbehavior, and aren't inclined toward physical discipline. By contrast, men in highly supervised jobs with little autonomy are more likely to value and expect conformity from their kids. They're also more likely to consider the consequences of their children's misbehavior when meting out punishment, and discipline them physically.

This so-called spillover effect is hardly mysterious. We would expect parents whose jobs reward them for creativity, independence, and intent to value those qualities, and to emphasize them in their interactions with their children. Not that men have a monopoly on job spillover. A mother whose job is stressful probably isn't able to parent at one hundred percent either.

DADS WHO DISCONNECT

Other factors may also have a greater impact on the father-child bond than on the bond between mother and child. "If things aren't going well in a marriage," says Lamb, "it's more likely to have a negative impact on a father's relationship with his child. " This is surely due in part to a child's history of intimacy with his or her mother. But Lamb also speculates that fathers simply find it easier to "disconnect" from their kids during times of conflict.

Speculations like these raise the specter of some genetic explanation. If fathers are inclined to relate to their children in a less intimate way, they may naturally be less capable of building and maintaining strong parent-child bonds. Yet while Lamb and Parke acknowledge some degree of innate, gender-related parenting differences, they place far more emphasis on cultural or learned factors.

Jane's legs hurt tonight; she calls them growing pains. I got mad, then simmered down (when my fear subsided), gave her Tylenol after she brushed her teeth. Read her a chapter from Great Expectations.

When Jane's sick, her mother takes such good care of her with medicines, doctors. I was raised Christian Scientist, taught that sickness and injury are illusions that should be healed with prayer and proper thinking. I'm just getting over my anger, my fear of disease, doctors, medicine.

4. PARENTING AND FAMILY ISSUES

Lately, I've felt a little more thin-skinned with Jane. I think it dates back to around the time of her Christmas break. Jane's not as cuddly, pliable, obedient as she was before. Rather, she's more headstrong, defiant, sometimes openly mocking of me, my authority.

I guess she's becoming independent, setting her own boundaries. Yipes! Thankfully, Lucinda explained this. I figured Jane was going through a bad patch, or maybe her friends or mother were encouraging her to resist my fine parenting! Instead, it's my parenting that's helped foster her confidence.

Bill Moseley

Of these, the most important may be the parenting models today's men and women have from their own childhoods—models that very likely ran along traditional lines, and most significantly indicated mothering was mandatory and fathering far more discretionary. A mother may be angry and depressed. Lamb says, "but parenting has to be done and the buck stops with her, whereas dads have traditionally been given leeway."

It's changing, of course. New legal sanctions, such as those against deadbeat dads, coupled with a rising sense—not just among conservatives—of fathers' familial obligations, are making it tougher for men to simply walk away physically or emotionally. Today men getting divorced are likely to fight for primary or joint custody of their kids. We may even reach a point where one parent isn't deemed mandatory and the other "allowed" to drop back.

Bringing the Revolution Home

Researchers say the more compelling changes in fathering are, or ought to be, taking place not just on a social level but on a personal one. One of the simplest steps is refiguring the division of parental duties: mom takes on some of the play master role, while dad does more of the need-based parenting—everything from changing diapers to ferrying the kids to dance lessons. By doing more of the "mandatory" parenting, Parke says, fathers will encourage their kids to see them not simply as a playmate, but as a comfort provider too.

No one's advocating a complete role reversal, or suggesting a complete shift is possible. Parke says men have difficulty "giving up their robust interactive styles, even when they are the parent staying at home." Instead, families should take advantage of the difference between men's and women's parenting approaches. Since fathers' boisterous antics seem to help prepare children for life outside the family, mothers shouldn't cancel this out by intervening or being overly protective.

At the same time, a more androgynous approach has its advantages. Children will be less inclined to mark one parent for fun and the other for comfort. For fathers this might mean more opportunities to deal with emotional ups and downs and develop the empathy and emotional depth.

Of course, fathers will experience difficulties making this shift. Yet the potential rewards are huge. Not only will we give our children more progressive examples of parenting—examples that will be crucial when they raise their own children—but we'll greatly enhance our own parenting experiences.

Fatherhood may be more confusing and open-ended than ever before, but the possibilities—for those willing to take the risks—are endless. "In the theater of modern family life," says Belsky, "there are just many more parts that fathers can play."

Life-Span Adjustment of Children to Their Parents' Divorce

Paul R. Amato

Abstract

Children who experience parental divorce, compared with children in continuously intact two-parent families, exhibit more conduct problems, more symptoms of psychological maladjustment, lower academic achievement, more social difficulties, and poorer self-concepts. Similarly, adults who experienced parental divorce as children, compared with adults raised in continuously intact two-parent families, score lower on a variety of indicators of psychological, interpersonal, and socioeconomic well-being.

However, the overall group differences between offspring from divorced and intact families are small, with considerable diversity existing in children's reactions to divorce. Children's adjustment to divorce depends on several factors, including the amount and quality of contact with noncustodial parents, the custodial parents' psychological adjustment and parenting skills, the level of interparental conflict that precedes and follows divorce, the degree of economic hardship to which children are exposed, and the number of stressful life events that accompany and follow divorce. These factors can be used as guides to assess the probable impact of various legal and therapeutic interventions to improve the well-being of children of divorce.

Paul R. Amato, Ph.D., is associate professor of sociology in the Department of Sociology, University of Nebraska at Lincoln.

Children have always faced the threat of family disruption. In the past, death was more likely to disrupt families than was divorce. Around the turn of the century in the United States, about 25% of children experienced the death of a parent before age 15, compared with 7% or 8% who experienced parental divorce.[1] As a result of the increase in longevity, the proportion of dependent children who lost a parent through death decreased during this century; currently, only about 5% of children are so affected. But the divorce rate increased over this same period, and at current rates, between two-fifths and two-thirds of all recent first marriages will end in divorce or separation.[2] The high rate of marital dissolution means that about 40% of children will experience a parental divorce prior to the age of 16.[3] Although a substantial risk of family disruption has always been present, today it is much more likely to be caused by divorce than by death.

Americans traditionally have believed that a two-parent family is necessary for the successful socialization and development of children. Consequently, it was assumed that parental death leads to many problems for children, such as delinquency, depression, and even suicide in later life—assumptions that apeared to be confirmed by early research.[4]

More recent studies indicate that, although parental death disadvantages children, the long-term consequences are not

---

A consensus is beginning to emerge among social scientists about the consequences of divorce for children.

---

as severe as people once believed.[5] Nevertheless, many social scientists assumed that children who "lost" a parent through divorce experienced serious problems similar to those experienced by children who lost a parent through death. Furthermore, whereas the death of a parent is usually unintended and unavoidable, marital dissolution is freely chosen by at least one parent. Consequently, the question of the impact of divorce on children took on moral overtones. These concerns, combined with the dramatic increase in the rate of divorce during the last few decades, resulted in a proliferation of studies on the effects of divorce on children.

This research literature does not always lead to firm conclusions. Many gaps exist in our knowledge, and weaknesses in study methodology mean that many findings are tentative at best. Nevertheless, a consensus is beginning to emerge among social scientists about the consequences of divorce for children. And, in spite of its limitations, this knowledge can help to inform policies designed to improve the well-being of children involved in parental marital dissolution.

How Do Researchers Study Children and Divorce?

To understand how divorce affects children, social scientists predominately rely on two research designs: cross-sectional and longitudinal.[6] In a cross-sectional study,[7] researchers compare children from divorced and continuously intact two-parent families at a single point in time.[8] In a longitudinal study, researchers follow children over an extended period of time following marital dissolution.[8]

Longitudinal studies usually include a comparison group of children from two-parent families as well. Although both types of research designs have methodological advantages and disadvantages, they provide useful information about adjustment.[6,8,9] Cross-sectional studies provide a "snapshot" that shows how children of divorce differ from other children, whereas longitudinal studies allow us to understand how children adjust to divorce over time.

In addition to studies of children, social scientists have studied the long-term consequences of divorce by comparing adults who experienced divorce as children with those who grew up in continuously intact families. Researchers also have carried out a small number of longitudinal studies in which children of divorce are followed into early adulthood.[10]

Three types of samples appear in the literature.[11] *Clinical samples* consist of children or adults who are in therapy or counseling. Clinical samples are useful in documenting the kinds of problems presented by offspring who adjust poorly to divorce, but these results cannot be generalized to the broad majority of people who never receive professional attention. Researchers obtain *convenience samples* of children or adults through community organizations (such as single-parent support groups) or other local sources. Convenience samples are relatively easy and inexpensive to obtain, but people in these groups may be atypical in unknown ways. Researchers select *random samples* of children or adults in a scientific manner such that the sample represents a clearly defined population within known limits.[12] These samples may be obtained from schools, court records, or households. Random samples allow us to make valid generalizations about the majority of children who experience divorce.[13] Unfortunately, these types of samples are also the most difficult and expensive to obtain.

Researchers match (or statistically equate) children or adults in the two samples (divorced and intact) on key variables known to be associated with both divorce and adjustment.[14] For example, parents of low socioeconomic status are more likely than other parents to divorce *and* to have children who exhibit behavioral and academic problems. Consequently, it is necessary to make sure that the socioeconomic backgrounds of parents in the two groups are comparable.

Researchers then select outcome measures that reflect children's and adults' functioning, or well-being. Common outcome measures for children include academic achievement, conduct, psychological adjustment, self-concept, social adjustment, and the quality of relations with parents. Common outcome measures for adults include psychological adjustment, conduct, use of mental health services, self-concept, social well-being, marital quality, separation or divorce, single parenthood, socioeconomic attainment, and physical health.

Social scientists gather information about children by interviewing one or both parents, questioning the child's teachers, administering tests to the child, or directly observing the child's behavior. Information is usually obtained from adults by interviewing them. Researchers then compare outcomes for those in the divorced and the continuously intact family groups. Statistical criteria are used to judge if differences in outcome measures are large enough to rule out the possibility of their being attributable to chance alone. Observed differences that are too large to be attributable to chance are assumed to be caused by divorce, or at least, by some factor(s) associated with divorce.

Unfortunately, because these studies are correlational, it is difficult to know for certain if divorce is responsible for observed differences between groups. It is always possible that groups might differ in ways that researchers cannot anticipate, measure, and control. For example, an unspecified parental personality characteristic might increase the risk of both divorce and child maladjustment. Firm conclusions about causation require experimentation; because we cannot randomly assign children to divorced and nondivorced families, our beliefs about the causal impact of divorce remain tentative.

How Do Children of Divorce Differ from Other Children?

Those who delve into the published literature on this topic may experience some frustration, as the results vary a good deal from study to study. Many studies show that children of divorce have more problems than do children in continuously intact two-parent families.[15] But other studies show no difference,[16] and a few show that children in divorced families are better off in certain respects than children in two-parent families.[17] This inconsistency results from the fact that studies vary in their sampling strategies, choice of what outcomes to measure, methods of obtaining information, and techniques for analyzing data.

A technique known as *meta-analysis* was recently developed to deal with this very situation.[18] In a meta-analysis, the results of individual studies are expressed in terms of an "effect size" which summarizes the differences between children in divorced and intact groups on each outcome. Because these effect sizes are expressed in a common unit of measure, it is possible to combine them across all studies to determine whether significant effects exist for each topic being reviewed. It is also possible to examine how design features of studies, such as the nature of the sample, might affect the conclusions.[19]

Children in divorced families, on average, experience more problems and have a lower level of well-being than do children in continuously intact two-parent families.

In 1991, Amato and Keith pooled the results for 92 studies that involved more than 13,000 children ranging from preschool to college age.[20] This meta-analysis confirmed that children in divorced families, on average, experience more problems and have a lower level of well-being than do children in continuously intact two-parent families.[21] These problems include lower academic achievement, more behavioral problems, poorer psychological adjustment, more negative self-concepts, more social difficulties, and more problematic relationships with both mothers and fathers.[22]

To determine if there are also differences in adjustment when children of divorce grow into adulthood, Amato and Keith carried out a second meta-analysis of 37 studies in which they examined adult children of divorce.[23] These results, based

Figure 1

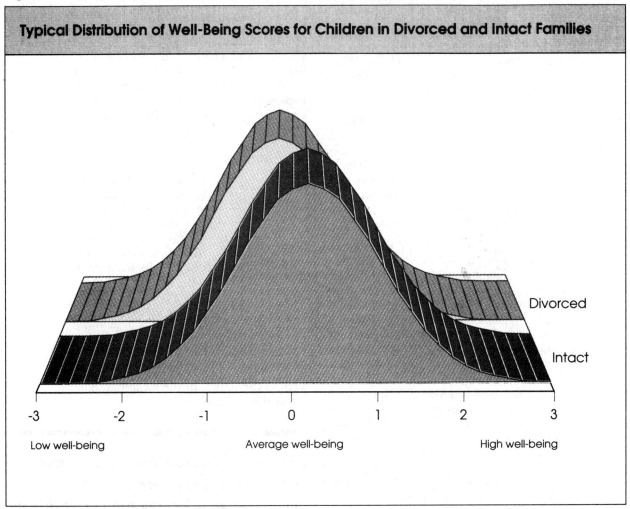

Typical Distribution of Well-Being Scores for Children in Divorced and Intact Families

Divorced

Intact

-3   -2   -1   0   1   2   3

Low well-being   Average well-being   High well-being

on pooled data from 80,000 adults, suggest that parental divorce has a detrimental impact on the life course.[24] Compared with those raised in intact two-parent families, adults who experienced a parental divorce had lower psychological well-being, more behavioral problems, less education, lower job status, a lower standard of living, lower marital satisfaction, a heightened risk of divorce, a heightened risk of being a single parent, and poorer physical health.[25]

The view that children adapt readily to divorce and show no lingering negative consequences is clearly inconsistent with the cumulative research in this area. However, several qualifications temper the seriousness of this conclusion. First, the average differences between children from divorced and continuously intact families are small rather than large. This fact suggests that divorce is not as severe a stressor for children as are other things that can go wrong during childhood. For

example, a recent meta-analysis of studies dealing with childhood sexual abuse revealed average effect sizes three to four times larger than those based on studies of children of divorce.[26] Second, although children of divorce differ, on average, from children in continuously intact two-parent families, there is a great deal of overlap between the two groups.

To illustrate these points, the results of a hypothetical but typical study are shown in Figure 1. This figure shows the distribution of well-being scores (on a representative measure of well-being) for children in divorced and nondivorced families. The height of the curve represents the frequency with which children score at various levels of well-being. Lower scores on the left side of the figure indicate poorer outcomes, whereas higher scores on the right side of the figure indicate better outcomes.

The average for each group of chidren is represented by the highest point in each curve. Note that the average score of children in the divorced group is lower than the average score of children in the nondivorced group, indicating a lower level of well-being. At the same time, a large proportion of children in the divorced group score *higher* than the average score of children in the nondivorced group. Similarly, a large proportion of children in the nondivorced group score *lower* than the average score of children in the divorced group. This overlap reflects the diversity of outcomes for children in both groups. Although the figure is described in terms of children, the same conclusions apply to studies dealing with adults from divorced and intact families of origin.

This diversity helps us to understand why the *average* effects of divorce are relatively weak. Divorce may represent a severe stressor for some children, resulting in substantial impairment and decline in well-being. But for other children, divorce may be relatively inconsequential. And some children may show improvements following divorce. In other words, to inquire about the effects of divorce, as if all children were affected similarly, is to ask the wrong question. A better question would be, "Under what conditions is divorce harmful or beneficial to children?" This point is returned to below.

Variations by Gender of Child

Some researchers are interested in measuring differences in adjustment between children of divorce and children in intact families based on such variables as gender, ethnicity, age, and cohort membership in attempts to identify groups that may respond differently to divorce. Summarized below are the major findings with regard to the relationship between these variables and adjustment.

Several early influential studies found that boys in divorced families had more adjustment problems than did girls.[15] Because these studies have been widely cited, many have come to accept this finding as incontrovertible. Given that boys usually live with their mothers following family disruption, the loss of contact with the same-sex parent could account for such a difference. In addition, boys, compared with girls, may be exposed to more conflict, receive less support from parents and others (because they are believed to be tougher), and be picked on more by custodial mothers (because they resemble their

fathers). Other observers have suggested that boys may be more psychologically vulnerable than girls to a range of stressors, including divorce.[27] However, a number of other studies have failed to find a gender difference in children's reactions to divorce,[17,28] and some studies have found that girls have more problems than do boys.[29]

Amato and Keith tried to clarify this issue in their meta-analytic studies by pooling the results from all studies that reported data for males and females separately.[20,23] For children, the literature reveals one major gender difference: the estimated negative effects of divorce on social adjustment are stronger for boys than for girls. Social adjustment includes measures of popularity, loneliness, and cooperativeness. In other areas, however, such as academic achievement, conduct, or psychological adjustment, no differences between boys and girls are apparent. Why a difference in social adjustment, in particular, should occur is unclear. Girls may be more socially skilled than boys, and this may make them less susceptible to any disruptive effects of divorce. Alternatively, the increased aggressiveness of boys from divorced families may make their social relationships especially problematic, at least in the short term.[30] Nevertheless, the meta-analysis suggests that boys do not always suffer more detrimental consequences of divorce than do girls.

The meta-analysis for adults also revealed minimal sex differences, with one exception: although both men and

---

Although children of divorce differ, on average, from children in continuously intact two-parent families, there is a great deal of overlap between the two groups.

---

women from divorced families obtain less education than do those from continuously intact two-parent families, this difference is larger for women than for men. The reason for the greater vulnerability of women is somewhat unclear. One possibility is that noncustodial fathers are less likely to finance the higher education of daughters than sons.[31]

Variations by Ethnicity of Child

There is a scant amount of research on how divorce affects nonwhite children of divorce. For example, because relatively little research has focused on this population, Amato and Keith were unable to reach any conclusions about ethnic differences in children's reactions to divorce.[20] The lack of information on how divorce affects nonwhite children is a serious omission in this research literature.

With regard to African-American children, some research has suggested that academic deficits associated with living with a single mother are not as pronounced for black children as for white children.[32]

In relation to adults, Amato and Keith show that African Americans are affected less by parental divorce than are whites. For example, the gap in socioeconomic attainment between adults from divorced and nondivorced families of origin is greater among whites than among African Americans. This difference may have to do with the fact that divorce is more common, and perhaps more accepted, among African Americans than among whites.

> *The lack of information on how divorce affects nonwhite children is a serious omission in this research literature.*

Also, because extended kin relations tend to be particularly strong among African Americans, single African-American mothers may receive more support from their extended families than do single white mothers.[33] Alternatively, given the large number of structural barriers that inhibit the attainment of African Americans, growing up in a divorced single-parent family may result in relatively little additional disadvantage.

We need additional research on divorce in different racial and ethnic groups, including African Americans, Asian Americans, Hispanics, and Native Americans. In addition to the adjustment of children of divorce, we need information on relationships between children and custodial and noncustodial parents, the role of extended kin in providing support, and, in general, how culture moderates the impact of marital dissolution on children.

Variations by Age of Child

Some of the best descriptions of how divorce affects children of different ages come from the work of Wallerstein and Kelly, who conducted detailed interviews with children and parents.[34] Although their sample appears to have overrepresented parents who had a difficult time adjusting to divorce, many of their conclusions about age differences have been supported by later studies. Observation of children during the first year after parental separation showed that preschool age children lack the cognitive sophistication to understand the meaning of divorce. Consequently, they react to the departure of one parent with a great deal of confusion. Because they do not understand what is happening, many become fearful. For example, a child may wonder, "Now that one parent is gone, what is to stop the other parent from leaving also?" Young children also tend to be egocentric, that is, they see themselves at the center of the world. This leads some children to blame themselves for their parents' divorce. For example, they may think, "Daddy left because I was bad." Regression to earlier stages of behavior is also common among very young children.

Children of primary school age have greater cognitive maturity and can more accurately grasp the meaning of divorce. However, their understanding of what divorce entails may lead them to grieve for the loss of the family as it was, and feelings of sadness and depression are common. Some children see the divorce as a personal rejection. However, because egocentrism decreases with age, many are able to place the blame elsewhere—usually on a parent. Consequently, older children in this age group may feel a great deal of anger toward one, or sometimes both, parents.

Adolescents are more peer-oriented and less dependent on the family than are younger children. For this reason, they may be impacted less directly by the divorce. However, adolescents may still feel a considerable degree of anger toward one or both parents. In addition, adolescents are concerned about their own intimate relationships. The divorce of their parents may lead adolescents to question their own ability to maintain a long-term relationship with a partner.

The work of Wallerstein and Kelly suggests that children at every age are affected by divorce, although the nature of their reactions differs. But are these reactions more disturbing for one group than for another? Wallerstein and Kelly found that preschool children were the most distressed in the period following parental separation. However, 10 years later, the children of preschool age appeared to have adjusted better than children who were older at the time of family disruption.[35]

Many other studies have examined age at the time of divorce to see if it is associated with children's problems. However, these studies have yielded mixed and often inconsistent results, and the meta-analyses of children[20] and adults[23] were unable to cast much light on these issues.[36] A common problem in many data sets is that age at divorce and time since divorce are confounded. In other words, for a group of children of the same age, the younger they were at the time of divorce, the more time that has elapsed. But if we examine children whose parents all divorced at about the same time, then the more time that has passed, the older children are at the time of the study. Similarly, if we hold constant the age of the child at the time of divorce, then length of time and current age are perfectly correlated. In other words, it is impossible to separate the effects of age at divorce, length of time since divorce, and current age. Given this problem, it is not surprising that research findings are unclear. Nevertheless, it is safe to say that divorce has the potential to impact negatively on children of all ages.

Year of Study

One additional noteworthy finding that emerged from the meta-analyses by Amato and Keith[20,23] concerns the year in which the study was conducted. These researchers found that older studies tended to yield larger differences between children from divorced and intact families than studies carried out more recently. This tendency was observed in studies of children (in relation to measures of academic achievement and conduct) and in studies of adults (in relation to measures of psychological adjustment, separation and divorce, material quality of life, and occupational quality).[23,37] The difference persisted when the fact that more recent studies are more methodologically sophisticated than earlier studies was taken into account.

This finding suggests that more recent cohorts of children are showing less severe effects of divorce than earlier cohorts. Two explanations are worth considering. First, as divorce has become more common, attitudes toward divorce have become more accepting, so children probably feel less stigmatized. Similarly, the increasing number of divorces makes it easier for children to obtain support from others in similar circumstances. Second, because the legal and social barriers to marital dissolution were stronger in the past, couples who obtained a divorce several decades ago probably had more serious problems and experienced more conflict prior to separation than do some divorcing couples today. Furthermore, divorces were probably more acrimonious before the introduction of no-fault divorce. Thus, children of divorce in the past may have been exposed to more dysfunctional family environments and higher levels of conflict than were more recent cohorts of children.

Why Does Divorce Lower Children's Well-Being?

Available research clearly shows an association between parental divorce and children's well-being. However, the causal mechanisms responsible for this association are just beginning to be understood. Most explanations refer to the absence of the noncustodial parent, the adjustment of the custodial parent, interparental conflict, economic hardship, and life stress. Variations in these factors may explain why divorce affects some children more adversely than others.

Parental Absence

According to this view, divorce affects children negatively to the extent that it results in a loss of time, assistance, and affection provided by the noncustodial parent. Mothers and fathers are both considered potentially important resources for children. Both can serve as sources of practical assistance, emotional support, protection, guidance, and supervision. Divorce usually brings about the departure of one parent—typically the father—from the child's household. Over time,

---

A home marked by high levels of discord represents a problematic environment for children's socialization and development.

---

the quantity and quality of contact between children and noncustodial parents often decreases, and this is believed to result in lower levels of adjustment for these children as compared with children from intact families.[38]

The parental absence explanation is supported by several lines of research. For example, some studies show that children who experience the death of a parent exhibit problems similar to those of children who "lose" a parent through divorce.[39] These findings are consistent with the notion that the absence of a parent *for any reason* is problematic for children. Also consistent with a parental absence perspective are studies showing that children who have another adult (such as a grandparent or other relative) to fill some of the functions of the absent parent have fewer problems than do children who have no substitute for the absent parent.[40] In addition, although the results of studies in the area of access to the noncustodial parent and adjustment are mixed,[41] in general,

studies show that a close relationship with both parents is associated with positive adjustment after divorce. One circumstance in which high levels of access may not produce positive adjustment in children is in high-conflict divorces. When conflict between parents is marked, frequent contact with the noncustodial parent may do more harm than good.[42]

Custodial Parental Adjustment and Parenting Skills

According to this view, divorce affects children negatively to the extent that it interferes with the custodial parents' psychological health and ability to parent effectively. Following divorce, custodial parents often exhibit symptoms of depression and anxiety. Lowered emotional well-being, in turn, is likely to impair single parents' child-rearing behaviors. Hetherington and colleagues found that, during the first year following separation, custodial parents were less affectionate toward their children, made fewer maturity demands, supervised them less, were more punitive, and were less consistent in dispensing discipline.[43]

Research provides clear support for this perspective. Almost all studies show that children are better adjusted when the custodial parent is in good mental health[44] and displays good child-rearing skills.[45] In particular, children are better off when custodial parents are affectionate, provide adequate supervision, exercise a moderate degree of control, provide explanations for rules, avoid harsh discipline, and are consistent in dispensing punishment. Also consistent with a parental adjustment perspective are studies showing that, when custodial parents have a good deal of social support, their children have fewer difficulties.[46]

Interparental Conflict

A third explanation for the effects of divorce on children focuses on the role of conflict between parents. A home marked by high levels of discord represents a problematic environment for children's socialization and development. Witnessing overt conflict is a direct stressor for children. Furthermore, parents who argue heatedly or resort to physical violence indirectly teach children that fighting is an appropriate method for resolving differences. As such, children in high-conflict families may not have opportunities to learn alternative ways to manage disagreements, such as negotiating and reaching compromises. Failure to acquire these social skills may interfere with children's ability to form and maintain friendships. Not surprisingly, numerous studies show that children living in high-conflict two-parent families are at increased risk for a variety of problems.[47] It seems likely, therefore, that many of the problems observed among children of divorce are actually caused by the conflict between parents that precedes and accompanies marital dissolution.

Studies show that children in high-conflict intact families are no better off—and often are worse off—than children in divorced single-parent families.[48] Indeed, children in single-parent families may show improvements in well-being following divorce if it represents an escape from an aversive and dysfunctional family environment. Furthermore, a study by Cherlin and colleagues shows that many, but not all, of the difficulties exhibited by children of divorce, such as behavioral problems and low academic test scores, are present *prior* to parental separation, especially for boys.[49] This finding is consistent with the notion that the lowered well-being of children is partly attributable to the conflict that precedes divorce. In addition, conflict may increase around the time of the separation, and parents often continue to fight long after the divorce is final. Indeed, many studies show that children's adjustment is related to the level of conflict between parents following divorce.[50,51] It should be noted here that postdivorce adjustment may also be influenced by residual effects of conflict that occurred during the marriage.

Economic Hardship

Divorce typically results in a severe decline in standard of living for most custodial mothers and their children.[52] Economic hardship increases the risk of psychological and behavioral problems among children[53] and may negatively affect their nutrition and health.[54] Economic hardship also makes it difficult for custodial mothers to provide books, educational toys, home computers, and other resources that can facilitate children's academic attainment. Furthermore, economically pressed parents often move to neighborhoods where schools are poorly financed, crime rates are high, and services are inadequate.[55] Living under these circumstances may facilitate the entry of adolescents into delinquent subcultures. According to this view, divorce affects children negatively to the extent that it results in economic hardship.

Studies show that children's outcomes—especially measures of academic achievement—are related to the level of household income following divorce. For example, Guidubaldi and colleagues found that children in divorced families scored significantly lower than children in intact two-parent families on 27 out of 34 outcomes; taking income differences into account statistically reduced the number of significant differences to only 13.[56]

Studies show that children in high-conflict intact families are no better off—and often are worse off—than children in divorced single-parent families.

Similarly, McLanahan found that income accounted for about half of the association between living in a single-parent family and high school completion for white students.[57] However, most studies show that, even when families are equated in terms of income, children of divorce continue to experience an increased risk of problems. This suggests that economic disadvantage, although important, is not the sole explanation for divorce effects.

Life Stress

Each of the factors noted above—loss of contact with the noncustodial parent, impaired child rearing by the custodial parent, conflict between parents, and a decline in standard of living—represents a stressor for children. In addition, divorce often sets into motion other events that may be stressful, such as moving, changing schools, and parental remarriage. And of course, parental remarriage brings about the possibility of additional divorces. Multiple instances of divorce expose children to repeated episodes of conflict, diminished parenting, and financial hardship.[58] For some children of divorce, stress accumulates throughout childhood.

Research generally supports a stress interpretation of children's adjustment following divorce. Divorces that are accompanied by a large number of other changes appear to have an especially negative impact on children.[59] Furthermore, parental remarriage sometimes exacerbates problems for children of divorce,[17,60] as does a second divorce.[61]

A General Perspective on How Divorce Affects Children

All five explanations for the effects of divorce on children appear to have merit, and a complete accounting for the effect of divorce on children must make reference to each. Because of variability in these five factors, the consequences of divorce differ considerably from one child to the next.

Consider a divorce in which a child loses contact with the father, the custodial mother is preoccupied and inattentive, the parents fight over child support and other issues, the household descends abruptly into poverty, and the separation is accompanied by a series of other uncontrollable changes. Under these circumstances, one would expect the divorce to have a substantial negative impact on the child. In contrast, consider a divorce in which the child continues to see the noncustodial father regularly, the custodial mother continues to be supportive and exercises appropriate discipline, the parents are able to cooperate without conflict, the child's standard of living changes little, and the transition is accompanied by no other major disruptions in the child's life. Under these circumstances, one would predict few negative consequences of divorce. Finally, consider a high-conflict marriage that ends in di-

---

To understand how divorce affects children, it is necessary to assess how divorce changes the total configuration of resources and stressors in children's lives.

---

vorce. As the level of conflict subsides, the previously distant father grows closer to his child, and the previously distracted and stressed mother becomes warmer and more attentive. Assuming no major economic problems or additional disruptive changes, this divorce would probably have a positive impact on the child.

Overall, to understand how divorce affects children, it is necessary to assess how

divorce changes the total configuration of resources and stressors in children's lives.[62] The five factors described above should also be considered when evaluating policy alternatives aimed at improving the well-being of children of divorce.

What Interventions Might Benefit Children of Divorce?

Concern for the well-being of children of divorce leads to a consideration of how various policies and interventions might reduce the risk of problems for them. The most commonly discussed interventions include lowering the incidence of divorce, joint custody, child support reform, enhancing the self-sufficiency of single mothers, and therapeutic programs for children and parents. Interventions suggested in this article are considered in the light of available research evidence.

Lowering the Incidence of Divorce

In the United States during the twentieth century, divorce became increasingly available as the result of a series of judicial decisions that widened the grounds for divorce. In 1970, no-fault divorce was introduced in California; presently it is available in all 50 states.[63] Under most forms of no-fault divorce, a divorce can be obtained without a restrictive waiting period if one partner wants it even if the other partner has done nothing to violate the marriage contract and wishes to keep the marriage together. This fact raises an interesting question: If the law were changed to make marital dissolution more difficult to obtain, and if doing so lowered the divorce rate, would we see a corresponding improvement in the well-being of children?

Several considerations suggest that this outcome is unlikely. First, although legal divorces occurred less often in the past, informal separations and desertions were not uncommon, especially among minorities and those of low socioeconomic status.[64] From a child's perspective, separation is no better than divorce. If the legal system were changed to make divorce more difficult, it would most likely increase the proportion of children living in separated but nondivorced families. It would also increase the proportion of people who spend their childhoods in high-conflict two-parent families. As noted above, high-conflict two-parent families present just as many problems for children as do divorced single-parent families, perhaps more so. Given that the legal system cannot stop married couples from living apart or fighting, changing the legal system to decrease the frequency of divorce is unlikely to improve the well-being of children.

Is it possible to lower the frequency of divorce by increasing marital happiness and stability? The government could enact certain changes toward this end, for example, by changing the tax code to benefit married parents. It is possible that such a policy would enhance the quality and stability of some marriages; however, providing these benefits to married-couple families would increase the relative disadvantage of single parents and their children, an undesirable outcome. Alternatively, the government could take steps to promote marriage preparation, enrichment, and counseling. Increasing the availability of such services would probably help to keep some marriages from ending in divorce. However, as Furstenberg and Cherlin suggest, the rise in divorce is the result of fundamental changes in American society, including shifts in personal values and the growing economic independence of women, factors that cannot be affected easily by government policies.[65] As such, *any* actions taken by government to strengthen marriage are likely to have only minor effects on the divorce rate.

Increasing the Incidence of Joint Physical Custody

The history of custody determination in the United States has changed over time primarily in response to societal influences. In the eighteenth century, fathers usually were awarded custody of their children as they were considered the dominant family figure and were most likely to have the financial means to care for them. In the nineteenth century, the preference for custody moved toward women. The reason for this shift was probably occasioned, in part, by the industrial revolution and the movement of men from the home to the workplace to earn a living. Women, in this circumstance, were needed to care for the children while men were at work and became the primary caretakers of children. At this time, child developmental theorists also focused on the importance of the mother-child relationship, and the as-

sumption was that the children were usually better off under the custody of their mother. Recently, society has moved toward a dual-earner family, and child developmentalists have emphasized the importance of both parents to the child. These changes are currently reflected in the law which emphasizes the importance of maintaining relationships with both parents.[66] The result has been an increased interest in joint custody, which is now available as an option in most states.[59] *Joint physical custody* provides legal rights and responsibilities to both parents and is intended to grant children substantial portions of time with each parent. *Joint legal custody*, which is more common, provides legal rights and responsibilities to both parents, but the child lives with one parent.[66]

Joint physical custody is associated with greater father contact, involvement, and payment of child support.

Joint legal custody may be beneficial to the extent that it keeps both parents involved in their children's lives. However, studies show few differences between joint legal and mother-custody families in the extent to which fathers pay child support, visit their children, and are involved in making decisions about their children, once parental income, education, and other predivorce parental characteristics are taken into account.[66,67] Although joint legal custody may have symbolic value in emphasizing the importance of both parents, it appears to make little difference in practice.

In contrast, joint physical custody is associated with greater father contact, involvement, and payment of child support.[68] Fathers also appear to be more satisfied with joint physical custody than with mother custody. For example, Shrier and colleagues found in 1991 that joint-custody fathers were significantly more satisfied than sole-maternal-custody fathers in two areas, including their legal rights and responsibilities as a parent and their current alimony and child support financial arrangements.[66,69] Joint physical custody may be beneficial if it gives children frequent access to both parents. On the other hand, residential instability may be stressful for some children. Although few studies are available, some show that children in joint physical custody are better adjusted than are children with other custody arrangements,[70] and other studies show no difference.[71]

However, these results may present a picture that is too optimistic. Courts are most likely to grant joint physical custody to couples who request it. A large-scale study by Maccoby and Mnookin in California showed that couples with joint physical custody, compared with those who receive sole custody, are better educated and have higher incomes; further-

---

It does not appear that either mother or father custody is inherently better for children, regardless of the sex of the child.

---

more, couples who request joint custody may be relatively less hostile, and fathers may be particularly committed to their children prior to divorce.[66,72] These findings suggest that some of the apparent positive "effect" of joint custody is a natural result of the type of people who request it in the first place.

It is unlikely that joint physical custody would work well if it were imposed on parents against their will. Under these conditions, joint custody may lead to more contact between fathers and their children but may also maintain and exacerbate conflict between parents.[73] Maccoby and Mnookin found that, although conflict over custody is relatively rare, joint custody is sometimes used to resolve custody disputes. In their study, joint custody was awarded in about one-third of cases in which mothers and fathers had each initially sought sole custody; furthermore, the more legal conflict between parents, the more likely joint custody was to be awarded. Three and one-half years after separation, these couples were experiencing considerably more conflict and less cooperative parenting than couples in which both had wanted joint custody initially. This finding demonstrates that an award of joint custody does not improve the relationship between hostile parents.

As noted above, studies show that children's contact with noncustodial parents is harmful if postdivorce conflict between parents is high. To the extent that joint physical custody maintains contact between children and parents in an atmosphere of conflict, it may do as much (or more) harm than good.[74] Joint custody, therefore, would appear to be the best arrangement for children when parents are cooperative and request such an arrangement. But in cases where parents are unable to cooperate, or when one parent is violent or abusive, a more traditional custody arrangement would be preferable.

Does research suggest that children are better adjusted in mother- or father-custody households? From an economic perspective, one might expect children to be better off with fathers, given that men typically earn more money than do women. On the other hand, children may be cared for more competently by mothers than fathers, given that mothers usually have more child care experience. Studies that have compared the adjustment of children in mother- and father-custody households have yielded mixed results, with some favoring mother custody, some favoring father custody, and others favoring the placement of the child with the same-sex parent.[36]

A recent and thorough study by Downey and Powell,[75] based on a large national sample of children, found little evidence to support the notion that children are better off with the same-sex parent. On a few outcomes, children were better off in father-custody households. However, with household income controlled, children tended to be slightly better off with mothers. This finding suggests that the higher income of single-father households confers certain advantages on children, but if mothers earned as much as fathers, children would be better off with mothers. The overall finding of the study, however, is that the sex of the custodial parent has little to do with children's adjustment. In general then, it does not appear that either mother or father custody is inherently better for children, regardless of the sex of the child.

Child Support Reform

It is widely recognized that noncustodial fathers often fail to pay child support. In a 1987 study by the U.S. Bureau of the Census, about one-third of formerly married women with custody had no child support award. And among those with an award, one-fourth reported receiving no payments in the previous year.[76] In the past, it has been difficult for custodial mothers to seek compliance with awards because of the complications and expense involved. New provisions in the 1988 Family Support Act allow for states to recover child support payments through the taxation system.[77] Starting in 1994, all new payments will be subject to automatic withholding from parents' paychecks.

Child support payments represent only a fraction of most single mothers' income, usually no more than one-fifth.[78] As such, stricter enforcement of child support payments cannot be expected to have a dramatic impact on children's standard of living. Nevertheless, it is usually highly needed income. As noted above, economic hardship has negative consequences for children's health, academic achievement, and psychological adjustment. Consequently, any policy that reduces the economic hardship experienced by children of divorce would be helpful. Furthermore, the extra income derived from child support may decrease custodial mothers' stress and improve parental functioning, with beneficial consequences for children. Consistent with this view, two studies show that regular payment of child support by noncustodial fathers decreases children's behavior problems and increases academic test scores.[79] Furthermore, in these studies, the apparently beneficial effect of child support occurred in spite of the fact that contact between fathers and children was not related to children's well-being.

Research indicates that the majority of fathers are capable of paying the full amount of child support awarded; in fact, most are capable of paying more.[66] Based on these considerations, it would appear to be desirable to increase the economic support provided by noncustodial fathers to their children. This would include increasing the proportion of children with awards, increasing the level of awards, and enforcing child support awards more strictly. A guaranteed minimum child support benefit, in which the government sets a minimum benefit level and assures full payment when fathers are unable to comply, would also improve the standard of living of many children.[80]

Requiring fathers to increase their economic commitment to children may

also lead them to increase visitation, if for no other reason than to make sure that their money is being spent wisely. A number of studies have shown that fathers who pay child support tend to visit their children more often and make more decisions about them than do fathers who fail to pay.[81] If increasing the level of compliance increases father visitation, it may increase conflict between some parents. On the other hand, some children may benefit from greater father involvement. Overall, the benefits of increasing fathers' economic contribution to children would seem to outweigh any risks.

Economic Self-Sufficiency for Single Mothers

As noted above, stricter enforcement of child support awards will help to raise the standard of living of single mothers and their children. However, even if fathers comply fully with child support awards, the economic situation of many single mothers will remain precarious. To a large extent, the economic vulnerability of single mothers reflects the larger inequality between men and women in American society. Not only do women earn less than men, but many married women sacrifice future earning potential to care for children by dropping out of the paid labor force, cut-

Economic hardship has negative consequences for children's health, academic achievement, and psychological adjustment.

ting back on the number of hours worked, taking jobs with more flexible hours, or taking jobs closer to home. Thus, divorcees are disadvantaged both by the lower wages paid to women and by their work histories. In the long run, single mothers and their children will achieve economic parity with single fathers only when women and men are equal in terms of earnings and time spent caring for children.

In the short term, however, certain steps can be taken to allow single mothers receiving public assistance to be economically self-sufficient. These steps would include the provision of job training and subsidized child care.[82] Although these programs operate at government expense, they are cost-effective to the extent that women and children become independent of further public assistance. Furthermore, many single mothers are "penalized" for working because they lose government benefits, such as health care and child care. Welfare reform that removes work disincentives by allowing women to earn a reasonable level of income without losing health care and child care benefits would be desirable. In fact, changes in these directions are being implemented as part of the Family Support Act of 1988.[83] Given that the employment of single mothers does not appear to be harmful to children and can provide a higher standard of living for children than does welfare, and given that economic self-sufficiency would probably improve the psychological well-being of single mothers, it seems likely that these changes will benefit children.

Therapeutic Interventions for Children

According to Cherlin, there are still no firm estimates on the proportion of children who experience harmful psychological effects from parental divorce.[2] Research suggests that, in many cases, children adjust well to divorce without the need for therapeutic intervention. However, our current understanding is that a minority of children do experience adjustment problems and are in need of therapeutic intervention. The

Our current understanding is that a minority of children do experience adjustment problems and are in need of therapeutic intervention.

type of therapeutic intervention suited for children varies according to the type and severity of the adjustment problems and the length of time they are expressed by the child. The major types of therapeutic interventions include child-oriented interventions and family-oriented interventions.[84]

Child-oriented interventions attempt to help children by alleviating the problems commonly experienced by them after divorce. Some intervention programs include private individual therapy. However, many single parents are unable to afford private therapy for their children and may enroll them in programs in which counselors work with groups of children.

Typically, in these sessions, children meet on a regular basis to share their experiences, learn about problem-solving strategies, and offer mutual support. Children may also view films, draw, or participate in role-playing exercises. Small groups are desirable for children of divorce for several reasons. Not only can they reach large numbers of children, but the group itself is therapeutic: children may find it easier to talk with other children than with adults about their experiences and feelings. Most group programs are located in schools; such programs have been introduced in thousands of school districts across the United States.

Evaluations of these programs have been attempted, and in spite of some methodological limitations, most are favorable: children from divorced families who participate, compared with those who do not, exhibit fewer maladaptive attitudes and beliefs about divorce, better classroom behavior, less anxiety and depression, and improved self-concept.[85] Although much of the evidence is positive, it is not entirely clear which components of these programs are most effective. For example, improvement may be brought about by a better understanding of divorce, newly acquired communication skills, or the support of other students. Although more evaluation research is needed, the evidence is positive enough to warrant further development and introduction of therapeutic programs for children.

In addition to child-focused interventions, there are *family-focused interventions* including both educational and therapeutic programs. These programs are aimed at divorcing parents, with the intention of either improving parenting skills or reducing the level of conflict over children.[86] In principle, therapeutic interventions that improve parental child-rearing skills or decrease the level of conflict between parents should benefit children, although this effect has not yet been demonstrated.

What Directions Should Future Research Take?

All things being equal, existing research suggests that a well-functioning nuclear family with two caring parents may be a better environment for children's growth and development than a divorced single-parent family. Children of divorce, as a group, are at greater risk than children from intact families, as a group, for many psychological, academic, and social problems. And adults raised in divorced single-parent families, as a group, do not achieve the same level of psychological and material well-being as those raised in continuously intact two-parent families. However, we need to keep in mind that many children are better off living in single-parent households than in a two-parent families marked by conflict. Furthermore, we need to recognize that most single parents work hard to provide their children with a loving and structured family life. Many single-parent families function well, and most children raised in these settings develop into well-adjusted adults. Blaming single parents as a group for the problems experienced by children of divorce is a pointless exercise.

At this time, our knowledge about children and divorce needs to be expanded in certain directions. The long-term effect of divorce on children is the basic question that needs to be addressed. The answers to this question will inform social policy and the court system, shape models of intervention, and influence parental decision making. This type of information should be obtained from longitudinal and longitudinal-sequential designs. Needed are studies that begin prior to divorce, as well as studies that follow children of divorce through adolescence and into adulthood.[87]

Also needed are data on how a variety of factors—relations with parents, parental adjustment, economic well-being, conflict,

---

It is important to focus on establishing policies that will help narrow the gap in well-being between children of divorce and children from intact families.

---

and exposure to stressors—combine to affect children's response to divorce. This research should make it possible to determine which children lose the most through divorce, which children are relatively unaffected, and which children benefit.

Information on how divorce affects children in different racial and ethnic groups is another area of research that would be informative from the standpoint of both clinical and economic intervention.[33] And more evaluation of various interventions, both legal (joint custody, mediation, child support reform) and therapeutic, are also needed.

It is important to focus on establishing policies that will help narrow the gap in well-being between children of divorce and children from intact families. High divorce rates and single-parent families are facts of life in American society. If it is impossible to prevent children from experiencing parental divorce, steps must be taken to ease the transition.

---

1. Furstenberg, Jr., F.F., and Cherlin, A.J. *Divided families: What happens to children when parents part.* Cambridge, MA: Harvard University Press, 1991, pp. 1–15; Uhlenberg, P. Death and the family. *Journal of Family History* (1980) 5:313–20.

2. Cherlin, A. *Marriage, divorce, remarriage.* Rev. ed. Cambridge, MA: Harvard University Press, 1992.

3. Bumpass, L. Children and marital disruption: A replication and update. *Demography* (1984) 21: 71–82

4. For examples, see the articles in *The child in his family: The impact of disease and death.* E.J. Anthony, ed. New York: Wiley, 1973.

5. Crook, T., and Eliot, J. Parental death during childhood and adult depression: A critical review of the literature. *Psychological Bulletin* (1980) 87:252–59.

6. The cross-sectional and longitudinal designs are used widely in adjustment research and other developmental research because they are suited for studies in which there are one or more nonmanipulable independent variables. In this instance, the researcher must select subjects who already possess different levels of a particular characteristic. Examples of nonmanipulable independent variables include age, sex, marital status of parents, and socioeconomic status. The use of nonmanipulable independent variables in a study usually precludes the use of true experimental designs which involve the random assignment of subjects to groups. Subjects are randomly assigned to eliminate the influence of extraneous

variables. If the influence of extraneous variables has been accomplished in a study and there are significant differences found between groups on a dependent variable, then the researcher may state with confidence that the independent variable caused the results to differ between groups. In studies without random assignment of subjects, including those using cross-sectional and longitudinal designs, statements about cause and effect relationships cannot be made. Researchers are unable to determine which variable caused which or if some other extraneous variable(s) could be responsible for an observed relationship between the variables. It should be noted that this difficulty is inherent in the literature on adjustment to divorce. Although cause and effect relationships may not be known, what is known is that there is a correlation between parental marital status and children's adjustment, and the knowledge that this correlation exists helps to assist the process of policymaking in this area. For a further discussion of the differences between experimental and nonexperimental designs, see Miller, S.A. *Developmental research methods.* Englewood Cliffs, NJ: Prentice-Hall, 1987; Cozby, P.C., Worden, P.E., and Kee, D.W. *Research methods in human development.* Mountain View, CA: Mayfield, 1989.

7. The optimal comparison group would be families that would potentially divorce, but stay together for the sake of the children. However, this population of families would be very difficult to sample. Another available comparison group would be continuously intact two-parent families. However, this comparison group is not consistently used by researchers. Many classifications in cross-sectional research are based on the current marital status of parents. The intact group is heterogeneous as to marital history, and the divorced group is not similar as to the time of divorce or the age of the children when it took place. Some of the most prominent longitudinal studies have no comparison group of intact families. See, for example, Wallerstein, J.S., and Corbin, S.B. Father-child relationships after divorce: Child support and educational opportunity. *Family Law Quarterly* (1986) 20:109–28; Maccoby, E.E., and Mnookin, R.H. *Dividing the child: Social and legal dilemmas of custody.* Cambridge, MA: Harvard University Press, 1992.

8. For example, a researcher using a cross-sectional design might study four different groups of children, grouped by age (for example, 3, 6, 9, and 12) and parental marital status (married or divorced) to see if children from divorced families exhibit significantly more aggression than children from intact families. If the researcher finds that aggressive behavior is, indeed, significantly more likely in children from divorced families, the researcher cannot determine the direction of the relationship, that is, whether the divorce increased aggression in these children or

high levels of aggression in the children caused the divorce. In addition, the researcher is unable to determine if some extraneous variable caused both high aggression and divorce, for example, low socioeconomic status.

For the developmental researcher, there are advantages and disadvantages to using this type of research design. The cross-sectional design is relatively inexpensive and timely, which makes it a popular choice for many researchers. However, a number of difficulties may threaten the validity and reliability of the results. These difficulties include the following: there is no direct measure of age changes; the issue of individual stability over time cannot be addressed; there is a possibility of selection bias; there may be difficulty establishing measurement equivalence; and there is an inevitable confounding of age and time of birth. Some of these problems are avoidable with adequate planning and control; however, the problem of the confounding of age and time of birth (cohort) is intrinsic in the cross-sectional design, and it is impossible to avoid.

Another design that is available to researchers but is seldom used is called the cross-section sequential design. A cross-sectional-sequential study tests separate cross-sectional samples at two or more times of measurement. In comparison to a standard cross-sectional design, this sequential design has the advantage of at least partly unconfounding age and year of birth (because there are at least two different cohorts for each age tested), and it also provides a comparison of the same age group at different times of testing (called a time-lag comparison). It would be advantageous to use this research design in the future for some types of adjustment research.

9. There are major advantages and disadvantages to this type of design. The advantages include the following: a researcher can observe actual changes occurring in subjects over time; irrelevant sources of variability are not of concern; there are no cohort effects because the same cohort is being studied over time and there is no selection bias. Disadvantages that may influence reliability and validity include the following: an expensive and time-consuming design; subject attrition; selective dropout; possible obsolescence of tests and instruments; a potentially biased sample; measurement of only a single cohort; effects of repeated testing; reactivity; difficulty of establishing equivalent measures; and the inevitable confounding of the age of subjects and the historical time of testing. As with the cross-sectional design, some of these problems are avoidable. However, it is impossible to avoid the confounding of age with time of measurement in the longitudinal approach. This confounding follows from the fact that the age comparisons are all within subject. Therefore, if we want to test subjects of different ages, we must test at different times. For an in-depth discussion of longitudinal designs,

see Menard, S. *Longitudinal research.* Series: Quantitative Applications in the Social Sciences, No. 07–076. Newbury Park, CA: Sage, 1991.

A design that is available to developmental researchers and is more complicated but should assist in disentangling the contributions of age, generation, and time of measurement is called the longitudinal-sequential design. In this design, the samples are selected from different cohorts (that is, years of birth), and they are tested repeatedly across the same time span. This design offers at least three advantages over a standard longitudinal design. The longitudinal comparisons are not limited to a single generation or cohort because samples are drawn from different birth years. In addition, there is a cross-sectional component to the design because different age groups are tested at each time of measurement. Finally, the same age group is represented at different times of measurement. More information is provided than in a standard longitudinal design, and there is greater opportunity to disentangle causative factors. See Baltes, P.B., Reese, H.W., and Nesselroade, J.R. *Life-span developmental psychology: Introduction to research methods.* Monterey, CA: Brooks/Cole, 1977.

10. Wallerstein, J.S. Children of divorce: Preliminary report of a ten-year follow-up of young children. *American Journal of Orthopsychiatry* (1984) 54:444–58; Wallerstein, J.S. Children of divorce: Preliminary report of a ten-year follow-up of older children and adolescents. *Journal of the American Academy of Child Psychiatry* (1985) 24:545–53; Wallerstein, J.S. Women after divorce: Preliminary report from a ten-year follow-up. *American Journal of Orthopsychiatry* (1986) 56:65–77; Wallerstein, J.S. Children of divorce: Report of a ten-year follow-up of early latency-age children. *American Journal of Orthopsychiatry* (1987) 57:199–211; Wallerstein, J.S., and Blakeslee, S. *Second chances: Men, women, and children a decade after divorce.* New York: Ticknor and Fields, 1989; Wallerstein, J.S., and Corbin, S.B. Daughters of divorce: Report from a ten-year follow-up. *American Journal of Orthopsychiatry* (October 1989) 59:593–604; Wallerstein, J.S., and Kelly, J.B. *Surviving the breakup: How children and parents cope with divorce.* New York: Basic Books, 1980.

11. For a discussion of sampling, see Kerlinger, F.N. *Foundations of behavioral research.* New York: Holt, Rinehart and Winston, 1973.

12. It should be noted that there are no perfect random samples on this subject. The national studies select ever-divorced families, who are limited by geography, the choice of schools included (rarely private schools, which is a problem in places where a large segment of children, often those with the best advantages, are not enrolled in public schools), or use the court sampling frame, which offers insufficient address data to draw a comprehensive sample.

13. This type of random selection of samples should not be confused with random assignment of subjects to groups.

14. For a discussion of matching, see note no. 6, Miller.

15. See, for example, Guidubaldi, J., Cleminshaw, H.K., Perry, J.D., and McLoughlin, C.S. The impact of parental divorce on children: Report of the nationwide NASP study. *School Psychology Review* (1983) 12:300–23; Hetherington, E.M., Cox, M., and Cox, R. Effects of divorce on parents and children. In *Nontraditional families.* M.E. Lamb, ed. Hillsdale, NJ: Lawrence Erlbaum Associates, 1982, pp. 223–88; see note no. 10, Wallerstein and Kelly.

16. See, for example, Baydar, N. Effects of parental separation and reentry into union on the emotional well-being of children. *Journal of Marriage and the Family* (1988) 50:967–81; Enos, D.M., and Handal, P.J. Relation of parental marital status and perceived family conflict to adjustment in white adolescents. *Journal of Consulting and Clinical Psychology* (1986) 54:820–24; Mechanic, D., and Hansell, S. Divorce, family conflict, and adolescents' well-being. *Journal of Health and Social Behavior* (1989) 30:105–16.

17. Amato, P.R., and Ochiltree, G. Child and adolescent competence in intact, one-parent, and stepfamilies. *Journal of Divorce* (1987) 10:75–96.

18. See Glass, G.V., McGaw, B., and Smith, M.L. An evaluation of meta-analysis. In *Meta-analysis in social research.* Newbury Park, CA: Sage, 1981.

19. The term *meta-analysis* refers to the quantitative combinations of data from independent studies. The procedure is valuable when the result is a descriptive summary of the weight of the available evidence. Summaries are necessary primarily because there are conflicting results in the literature and, at some point, it is valuable to know where the weight of the evidence falls. The primary goals of meta-analysis include determining whether significant effects exist for the topic being reviewed, estimating the magnitude of effects, and relating the existence and magnitude of effects of variations in design and procedure across studies. Proponents of meta-analysis argue that meta-analysis can achieve a greater precision and generalizability of findings than single studies. They then have the potential to provide more definitive evidence for policymaking than can be realized by other means. However, there are logical and methodological difficulties with the technique that need to be understood when interpreting the results of any meta-analysis. First, there is the problem of the selection of studies, that is, how to determine which studies should be included in the meta-analysis. Oakes contends that any rule establishment in this area presents impossible difficulties. A second problem is that, if a researcher includes only published studies in the meta-analysis, there is the danger of overestimating differ-

ences between groups. This danger arises because journal articles are not a representative sample of work addressed in any particular research area. Significant research findings are more likely to be published than nonsignificant research findings. To control for this problem, the researcher must trace unpublished research and incorporate it into the analysis. A third problem is that the use of meta-analysis may overinflate differences between groups because a high proportion of reported statistically significant results are spurious. Finally, because of the diversity of the types of samples that are included in the meta-analysis, it is difficult—if not impossible—to know what population the results are applicable to. For more in-depth discussions of the technique, its advantages, and its disadvantages, see note no. 18, Glass, McGaw, and Smith; Oakes, M. The logic and role of meta-analysis in clinical research. *Statistical Methods in Medical Research* (1993) 2:146–60; note no. 6, Miller; Thompson, S.G., and Pocock, S.J. Can meta-analyses be trusted? *The Lancet* (November 2, 1991) 338:1127–30; Wolf, FM. *Meta-analysis: Quantitative methods for research synthesis.* Series: Quantitative Applications in Social Sciences, No. 07–059. Beverly Hills, CA: Sage, 1986.

20. Amato, P.R., and Keith, B. Parental divorce and the well-being of children: A meta analysis. *Psychological Bulletin* (1991) 100:26–46. Studies were included if they met the following criteria: (1) were published in an academic journal or book, (2) included a sample of children of divorce as well as a sample of children from continuously intact two-parent families, (3) involved quantitative measures of any of the outcomes listed below in note no. 21, and (4) provided sufficient information to calculate an effect size.

21. In the meta-analysis for children, measures of well-being were coded into the following eight categories: academic achievement (standardized achievement tests, grades, teachers' ratings, or intelligence); conduct (misbehavior, aggression, or delinquency); psychological adjustment (depression, anxiety, or happiness); self-concept (self-esteem, perceived competence, or internal locus of control); social adjustment (popularity, loneliness, or cooperativeness); mother-child and father-child relations (affection, help, or quality of interaction), and other.

22. Mean effect sizes ranged from .06 for the "other" category (not significant) to −.23 for conduct (p .001), with an overall effect size of −.17 across all outcomes. Effect sizes reflect the difference between groups in standard deviation units. A negative effect size indicates that children of divorce exhibit lower well-being than do children in intact two-parent families. With the exception of the "other" category, all mean effect sizes were statistically significant (p .001).

23. Amato, P.R., and Keith, B. Parental divorce

and adult well-being: A meta-analysis. *Journal of Marriage and the Family* (1991) 53:43–58.

24. In the meta-analysis for adults, outcomes were coded into the following 15 categories: psychological well-being (emotional adjustment, depression, anxiety, life-satisfaction); behavior/conduct (criminal behavior, drug use, alcoholism, suicide, teenage pregnancy, teenage marriage); use of mental health services; self-concept (self-esteem, self-efficacy, sense of power, internal locus of control); social well-being (number of friends, social participation, social support, contact with parents and extended family); marital quality (marital satisfaction, marital disagreements, marital instability); separation or divorce; one-parent family status; quality of relations with one's children; quality of general family relations (overall ratings of family life); educational attainment (high school graduation; years of education); occupational quality (occupational prestige, job autonomy, job satisfaction); material quality of life (income, assets held, housing quality, welfare dependency, perceived economic strain); physical health (chronic problems, disability), and other.

25. Mean effect sizes ranged from −.02 for relations with children (not significant) to −.36 for becoming a single parent (p .001), with an effect size of −.20 across all outcomes. All mean effect sizes were significant (at least p .01) except for relations with children and self-concept.

26. Kendall-Tackett, K.A., Williams, L.M., and Finkelhor, D. Impact of sexual abuse on children: A review and synthesis of recent empirical studies. *Psychological Bulletin* (1993) 113:164–80. Effect sizes in this meta-analysis ranged from .39 to .66, indicating poorer adjustment for sexually abused children than for nonabused children.

27. Rutter, M. Sex differences in children's responses to family stress. In *The child in his family.* Vol. 1. E.J. Anthony and C. Koupernik, eds. New York: Wiley, 1970.

28. See, for example, Booth, A., Brinkerhoff, D.B., and White, L.K. The impact of parental divorce on courtship. *Journal of Marriage and the Family* (1984) 46:85–94; Smith, T.E. Parental separation and adolescents' academic self-concepts: An effort to solve the puzzle of separation effects. *Journal of Marriage and the Family* (1990) 52:107–18.

29. Slater, E., Steward, K.J., and Linn, M.W. The effects of family disruption on adolescent males and females. *Adolescence* (1983) 18:931–42.

30. See Peterson, J.L., and Zill, N. Marital disruption, parent-child relationships, and behavior problems in children. *Journal of Marriage and the Family* (1986) 48:295–307; Hetherington, E.M., and Chase-Lansdale, P.L. The impact of divorce on life-span development: Short and long term effects. In *Life-span development and behavior.* P.B. Baltes, D.L. Featherman, and R.M.

Lerner, eds. Hillsdale, NJ: Lawrence Erlbaum Associates, 1990.

31. See note no. 7, Wallerstein and Corbin.

32. Hetherington, E.M., Camara, K.A., and Featherman, D.L. Achievement and intellectual functioning of children in one-parent households. In *Achievement and achievement motives*. J.T. Spence, ed. San Francisco: W.H. Freeman, 1983.

33. Del Carmen, R., and Virgo, G.N. Marital disruption and nonresidential parenting: A multicultural perspective. In *Nonresidential parenting: New vistas in family living*. C. Depner and J. Bray, eds. Newbury Park, CA: Sage, 1993, pp. 13–36.

34. See note no. 10, Wallerstein and Kelly.

35. See note no. 10, Wallerstein and Blakeslee.

36. For a summary of these studies, see Amato, P.R. Children's adjustment to divorce: Theories, hypotheses, and empirical support. *Journal of Marriage and the Family* (1993) 55:23–38.

37. See note no. 20, Amato and Keith.

38. Furstenberg, Jr., F.F. and Nord, C.W. Parenting apart: Patterns of child-rearing after marital disruption. *Journal of Marriage and the Family* (1985) 47:893–904; Seltzer, J.A. Relationships between fathers and children who live apart: The father's role after separation. *Journal of Marriage and the Family* (1991) 53:79–101.

39. This trend was confirmed in the meta-analysis by Amato and Keith; see note no. 23. For examples of studies, see Amato, P.R. Parental absence during childhood and depression in later life. *Sociological Quarterly* (1991) 32:543–56; Gregory, I. Introspective data following childhood loss of a parent: Delinquency and high school dropout. *Archives of General Psychiatry* (1965) 13:99–109; Saucier, J., and Ambert, A. Parental marital status and adolescents' optimism about their future. *Journal of Youth and Adolescence* (1982) 11:345–53. Our meta-analysis also showed that, although children who experience parental death are worse off than those in intact two-parent families, they have higher levels of well-being than do children of divorce.

40. Cochran, M., Larner, M., Riley, D., et al. *Extending families: The social networks of parents and their children*. Cambridge, MA: Cambridge University Press, 1990; Dornbusch, S., Carlsmith, J.M., Bushwall, S.J., et al. Single parents, extended households, and the control of adolescents. *Child Development* (1985) 56:326–41.

41. Kelly, J.B. Current research on children's postdivorce adjustment: No simple answers. *Family and Conciliation Courts Review* (1993) 31:29–49.

42. Amato, P.R., and Rezac, S.J. Contact with nonresident parents, interparental conflict, and children's behavior. Paper presented at the Annual Meeting of the Midwest Sociological Society. Chicago, IL, 1993; Healy, J., Jr., Malley, J., and Stewart, A. Children and their fathers after parental separation. *American Journal of Orthopsychiatry* (1990) 60:531–43; see note no. 15, Hetherington, Cox, and Cox.

43. See note no. 15, Hetherington, Cox, and Cox. See also Simons, R.L., Beaman, J., Conger, R.D., and Chao, W. Stress, support, and antisocial behavior traits as determinants of emotional well-being and parenting practices among single mothers. *Journal of Marriage and the Family* (1993) 55:385–98.

44. Kline, M., Tschann, J.M., Johnston, J.R., and Wallerstein, J.S. Children's adjustment in joint and sole physical custody families. *Developmental Psychology* (1989) 25:430–38. Guidubaldi, J., and Perry, J.D. Divorce and mental health sequelae for children: A two year follow-up of a nationwide sample. *Journal of the American Academy of Child Psychiatry* (1985) 24:531–37; and Kalter, N., Kloner, A., Schreiser, S., and Olka, K. Predictors of children's postdivorce adjustment. *American Journal of Orthopsychiatry* (1989) 59:605–18.

45. Guidubaldi, J., Cleminshaw, H.K., Perry, J.D., et al. The role of selected family environment factors in children's post-divorce adjustment. *Family Relations* (1986) 35:141–51; see note no. 15, Hetherington, Cox, and Cox. See note no. 10, Wallerstein and Kelly; note no. 44, Kalter, Kloner, Schreiser, and Olka; note no. 30, Peterson and Zill.

46. Of course, it is also likely that well-behaved children allow parents to behave in a positive and competent manner, whereas ill-behaved children stimulate problematic parental behaviors. Undoubtedly, children influence parents just as parents influence children. However, this does not invalidate the notion that divorce-induced stress can interfere with a person's ability to function effectively as a parent and that a parent's failure to function effectively might have negative consequences for children.

47. Emery, R. Interparental conflict and the children of discord and divorce. *Psychological Bulletin* (1982) 92:310–30; Grych, J.H., and Fincham, F.D. Marital conflict and children's adjustment: A cognitive-contextual framework. *Psychological Bulletin* (1990) 108:267–90.

48. See note no. 28, Booth, Brinkerhoff, and White. See note no. 16, Enos and Handal; and Mechanic and Hansell; Long, N., Forehand, R., Fauber, R., and Brody, G.H. Self-perceived and independently observed competence of young adolescents as a function of parental marital conflict and recent divorce. *Journal of Abnormal Child Psychology* (1987) 15:15–27; see note no. 30, Peterson and Zill.

49. Cherlin, A.J., Furstenberg, Jr., F.F., Chase-Lansdale, P.L., et al. Longitudinal studies of effects of divorce on children in Great Britain and the United States. *Science* (1991) 252:1386–89. Similar findings were reported by Block, J.H., Block, J., and Gjerde, R.R. The personality of children prior to divorce. *Child Development* (1986) 57:827–40.

50. Johnston, J.R., Kline, M., and Tschann,

J.M. Ongoing postdivorce conflict: Effects on children of joint custody and frequent access. *American Journal of Orthopsychiatry* (1989) 59:576–92; Kurdek, L.A., and Berg, B. Correlates of children's adjustment to their parents' divorces. In *Children and divorce*. L.A. Kurdek, ed. San Francisco: Jossey-Bass, 1983; Shaw, D.S., and Emery, R.E. Parental conflict and other correlates of the adjustment of school-age children whose parents have separated. *Journal of Abnormal Child Psychology* (1987) 15:269–81.

51. It is also probable that children's problems, to a certain extent, exacerbate conflict between parents.

52. Duncan, G.J., and Hoffman, S.D. Economic consequences of marital instability. In *Horizontal equity, uncertainty, and economic well-being*. M. David and T. Smeeding, eds. Chicago: University of Chicago Press, 1985; Weitzman, L.J. *The divorce revolution: The unexpected social and economic consequences for women and children in America*. New York: Free Press, 1985.

53. McLeod, J.D., and Shanahan, M.J. Poverty, parenting, and children's mental health. *American Sociological Review* (1993) 58:351–66.

54. Williams, D.R. Socioeconomic differentials in health: A review and redirection. *Social Psychology Quarterly* (1990) 52:81–99.

55. McLanahan, S., and Booth, K. Mother-only families: Problems, prospects, and politics. *Journal of Marriage and the Family* (1989) 51:557–80.

56. See note no. 15, Guidubaldi, Cleminshaw, Perry, and McLoughlin.

57. McLanahan, S. Family structure and the reproduction of poverty. *American Journal of Sociology* (1985) 90:873–901.

58. For a review of the effects of serial marriages (involving three or more marriages) and divorces on child adjustment, see Brody, G.H., Neubaum, E., and Forehand, R. Serial marriage: A heuristic analysis of an emerging family form. *Psychological Bulletin* (1988) 103:211–22.

59. Hodges, W.F, Tierney, C.W., and Buchsbaum, H.K. The cumulative effect of stress on preschool children of divorced and intact families. *Journal of Marriage and the Family* (1984) 46:611–19; Stolberg, A.L., and Anker,J.M. Cognitive and behavioral changes in children resulting from parental divorce and consequent environmental changes. *Journal of Divorce* (1983) 7:23–37.

60. See note no. 16, Baydar. Hetherington and her colleagues found that the remarriage of the custodial mother was associated with increased problems for girls but decreased problems for boys. Hetherington, E.M., Cox, M., and Cox, R. Long-term effects of divorce and remarriage on the adjustment of children. *Journal of the American Academy of Child Psychiatry* (1985) 24:518–30.

61. Amato, P.R., and Booth, A. The consequences of parental divorce and marital unhappi-

ness for adult well-being. *Social Forces* (1991) 69:895–914.

62. For similar perspectives, see Hetherington, E.M. Coping with family transitions: Winners, losers, and survivors. *Child Development* (1989) 60:1–14; Kurdek, L.A. An integrative perspective on children's divorce adjustment. *American Psychologist* 36:856–66.

63. Glendon, M.A. *The transformation of family law: State, law, and family in the United States and Western Europe*. Chicago: University of Chicago Press, 1989. See note no. 52, Weitzman.

64. See note no. 63, Glendon; Sweet, J.A., and Bumpass, L.L. *American families and households*. New York: Russell Sage Foundation, 1990.

65. See note no. 1, Furstenberg and Cherlin.

66. See note no. 7, Maccoby and Mnookin.

67. Seltzer, J. Legal custody arrangements and children's economic welfare. *American Journal of Sociology* (1991) 96:895–929.

68. Arditti, J. A. Differences between fathers with joint custody and noncustodial fathers. *American Journal of Orthopsychiatry* (1992) 62:186–95; Bowman, M., and Ahrons, C.R. Impact of legal custody status on fathers' parenting postdivorce. *Journal of Marriage and the Family* (1985) 47:481–88; Dudley, J.R. Exploring ways to get divorced fathers to comply willingly with child support agreements. *Journal of Divorce* (1991) 14:121–33; Leupnitz, D. A comparison of maternal, paternal, and joint custody: Understanding the varieties of post-divorce family life. *Journal of Divorce* (1986) 9:1–12.

69. See note no. 68, Arditti; Little, M.A. The impact of the custody plan on the family: A five year follow-up. *Family and Conciliation Courts Review* (1992) 30:243–51; Shrier, D.K., Simring, S.K., Shapiro, E.T., and Greif, J. B. Level of satisfaction of fathers and mothers with joint or sole custody arrangements. *Journal of Divorce and Remarriage* (1991) 16:163–69.

70. Buchanan, C.M., Maccoby, E.E., and Dornbusch, S.M. Adolescents and their families after divorce: Three residential arrangements compared. *Journal of Research on Adolescents* (1992) 2:261–91; Glover, R.J., and Steele, C. Comparing the effects on the child of post-divorce parenting arrangements. *Journal of Divorce* (1989) 12:185–201; Wolchik, S.A., Braver, S.L., and Sandler, I.N. Maternal versus joint custody: Children's postseparation experiences and adjustment. *Journal of Clinical Child Psychology* (1985) 14:5–10.

71. Kline, M., Tschann, J.M.,Johnston, J.R., and Wallerstein, J.S. Children's adjustment in joint and sole physical custody families. *Developmental Psychology* (1988) 25:430–38; Leupnitz, D. *Child custody*. Lexington, MA: D.C. Heath, 1982; Pearson, J., and Thoennes, N. Custody after divorce: Demographic and attitudinal patterns. *American Journal of Orthopsychiatry* (1990) 60:233–49.

72. See note no. 68, Arditti; note no. 71, Pear-

son and Thoennes; Steinman, S. The experience of children in a joint custody arrangement: A report of a study. *American Journal of Orthopsychiatry* (1981) 24:554–62.

73. Nelson, R. Parental hostility, conflict, and communication in joint and sole custody families. *Journal of Divorce* (1989) 13:145–57.

74. Buchanan, C.M., Maccoby, E.E., and Dornbusch, S.M. Caught between parents: Adolescents' experience in divorced homes. *Child Development* (1991) 62:1008–29; Johnston, J.R., Kline, M., and Tschann, J.M. Ongoing postdivorce conflict: Effects on children of joint custody and frequent access. *American Journal of Orthopsychiatry* (1989) 59:576–92.

75. Downey, D., and Powell, B. Do children in single-parent households fare better living with same-sex parents? *Journal of Marriage and the Family* (1993) 55:55–71.

76. U.S. Bureau of the Census. *Child support and alimony: 1987.* Current Population Reports, Series P–23, No. 167. Washington, DC: U.S. Government Printing Office, 1990.

77. Public Law No. 100–485, reprinted in 1988 *U.S. Code Cong. & Admin. News,* 102 Stat. 2343.

78. See note no. 52, Duncan and Hoffman.

79. Furstenberg, Jr., F.F, Morgan, S.R, and Allison, R.D. Paternal participation and children's well-being after marital dissolution. *American Sociological Review* (1987) 52:695–701; King, V. Nonresidential father involvement and child well-being: Can dads make a difference? Paper presented at the annual meeting of the Population Association of America. Cincinnati, OH, 1993.

80. For a discussion of child support reform, see Garfinkel, I. *Assuring child support: An extension of Social Security.* New York: Russell Sage Foundation, 1992; Garfinkel, I., and McLanahan, *S.S. Single mothers and their children: A new American dilemma.* Washington, DC: Urban Institute Press, 1986.

81. Seltzer, J.A., and Bianchi, S.M. Children's contact with absent parents. *Journal of Marriage and the Family* (1988) 50:663–77; Seltzer, J., Schaeffer, N.C., and Charng, H. Family ties after divorce: The relationship between visiting and paying child support. *Journal of Marriage and the Family* (1989) 51:1013–32.

82. Britto, K. The Family Support Act of 1988 Welfare Reform (Public Law 100–485). Vol. 2, No. 3. National Conference of State Legislatures. Denver, CO, 1989.

83. Aldous, J. Family policy in the 1980s: Controversy and consensus. *Journal of Marriage and the Family* (1990) 52:1136–51.

84. Grych, J., and Fincham, F.D. Interventions for children of divorce: Toward greater integration of research and action. *Psychological Bulletin* (1992) 111:434–54.

85. Anderson, R.F, Kinney, J., and Gerler, E.R. The effects of divorce groups on children's classroom behavior and attitudes toward divorce. *Elementary School Guidance and Counseling* (1984) 19:70–76; Crosbie-Burnett, M., and Newcomer, L.L. Group counseling children of divorce: The effects of a multimodel intervention. *Journal of Divorce* (1989) 13:69–78. Pedro-Carroll, J., and Cowan, E. L. The children of divorce intervention program: An investigation of the efficacy of a school based intervention program. *Journal of Consulting and Clinical Psychology (1985)* 53:603–11; Stolberg, A.J., and Garrison, K.M. Evaluating a primary prevention program for children of divorce. *American Journal of Community Psychology* (1985) 13:111–24.

86. Bloom, B.L., Hodges, W.F, and Caldwell, R.A. A preventive program for the newly separated: Initial evaluation. *American Journal of Community Psychology* (1982) 10:251–64; Bloom, B.L., Hodges, W.F, Kern, M.B., and McFaddin, S.C. A preventive intervention program for the newly separated: Final evaluations. *American Journal of Orthopsychiatry* (1985) 55:9–26; Zibbell, R.A. A short-term, small-group education and counseling program for separated and divorced parents in conflict. *Journal of Divorce and Remarriage* (1992) 18:189–203.

87. Wallerstein, J.S. The long-term effects of divorce on children: A review. *Journal of the American Academy of Child Adolescent Psychiatry* (1991) 30:349–60.

How Children Learn
to Resolve Conflicts in Families

Susan Crockenberg, Ph.D.

University of Vermont

A parent says to her two-year-old child, "Eat your dinner," and the child says, "No". Events such as this one are ubiquitous in the lives of parents and young children, and serve as windows to family relationships. In studying them, however, researchers, myself included, have taken a characteristically linear approach, focusing on who will prevail, and more specifically, on whether and how quickly the child will comply. As researchers interested in how children become socialized, we have asked, "What control strategies are most effective in eliciting compliance from the child", "What parental behaviors give rise to a defiant response from the child"? These are important questions to parents and researchers alike. Parents have an immediate and legitimate interest in knowing how best to encourage their children to modulate their own interests and goals in ways that allow other family members to pursue their interests and meet their goals. Whether children bear the primary responsibility for achieving this family goal, as the targeting of their behavior implies, is open to debate.

When a parent issues a directive, or makes some claim on the child's time or behavior, there are several possible outcomes. The child may comply, that is, she may simply do what the parent wants. In most families, this is the most frequent child response. It is also common, especially during the second and third years of life, for children to say, "No," or to otherwise indicate that the proposed plan of action is not to their liking. When this latter response occurs, the parent and child have a conflict. Their goals are incompatible; one person wants one thing, the other wants something else. As is the case in any conflict, resolution requires that one or both of them give up or modify their goals. Viewing parent-child interactions of the sort described above as conflicts and their outcomes as conflict resolutions shifts our perspective of these events in significant ways. Most notably, it introduces the possibility that both parent and child may modify their goals in an effort to achieve a resolution.

Parent-child interaction as conflict resolution

In a 1957 treatise on the question of "yes and no," Spitz recognized the significance of negation, describing it as "the most spectacular intellectual and semantic achievement during early childhood" (p.99). He identified the acquisition of "No" as an indicator of a new level of autonomy that accompanies the child's increasing awareness of the "other" and the "self" during the second half of the second year of life. Spitz noted, moreover, that with the child's assertion, the process of negotiation begins. In response to the child's assertion, the parent may alter her approach, perhaps explaining to the child why he or she should comply, or attempting to persuade him or her to do so. She may attempt to engage the child in the task by making it attractive, or she may put it off temporarily. The child may respond by complying, possibly to a much modified directive, or by rejecting the parent's overtures with another "no," in which case the parent may persist in the first response or try another. There is empirical evidence that this pattern of reciprocal interactions characterizes many parent-child exchanges.

One of the most startling observations we made in the course of our study of 95 mothers and their two-year-old children (Crockenberg & Litman, 1990) was the frequency with which negotiation occurred in the context of a parent's expressed desire that the child pick up the toys scattered around our laboratory

---

When mothers combined control (a simple directive) with guidance (explanation, persuasion, or enticement), children who had initially refused a maternal control attempt were more likely to comply than when mothers used any single strategy.

---

playroom and put them in a basket. When children refused, or indicated their reluctance to pick up the toys by continuing to play with them, mothers sometimes repeated their directives, and at other times escalated their demands by increasing the loudness or abruptness of their verbal delivery, or by moving the child bodily first to a toy and then to the basket. Often, however, mothers modified the way they attempted to enlist the child's cooperation so that both mothers and children could obtain their goals. One way they did this was to explain why the pick-up was necessary ("We need to clean up for the next little boy or girl.")

From *Zero to Three*, April 1992, pp. 11-13. © 1992 by the National Center for Clinical Infant Programs. Reprinted by permission.

or appeal to the mutuality of the relationship ("Could you do it for mommy?") Another approach was to integrate play with toy pick-up. A mother might encourage the child, or participate in "driving" the cars and trucks into the basket, in tossing the block into their container, in placing puzzle pieces into the puzzle, in putting the dolly to bed in the basket and the animals to sleep in the farm. Similar exchanges occurred at home. When a child refused a mother's directive to, "Eat your dinner", a mother might respond with a modified proposal that the child, "Have a bite of hot dog." What each of these strategies has in common is that they combine a statement of the parent's goal with some recognition that the child has a different goal and needs to be invited or enticed to respond to the parent's wishes.

Two points are noteworthy about the strategies just described. The first is that they were effective in achieving the mother's goal of having the child put the toys in the basket—our definition of compliance. When mothers combined control, that is a simple directive, with guidance, that is an explanation, persuasion, or enticement, children who had initially refused a maternal control attempt were more likely to comply than when mothers used any other strategy. Neither control nor guidance alone was as predictably related to child compliance under these circumstances as was their combination. This was so, we think, because control alone emphasizes only the mother's wishes, and guidance alone conveys to the child that an invitation has been issued which can be accepted or rejected at will. When they occur together, they convey that both the adult's wishes and the child's wishes are important. The second point is that in explaining, persuading, and accommodating to their children, they conveyed information to them about the way conflicts with others can be resolved.

How conflicts affects children's development

The process of conflict resolution serves as an arena in which children learn to balance the achievement of their goals with the desires of others to achieve theirs. Relationships in which children are involved with important others over a significant period of time are

---

Since children learn relationship skills in families, there should be a long-term developmental payoff for children when parents adopt negotiation as an approach to resolving conflicts between themselves and their children.

---

the most likely contexts for this learning to occur because conflicts inevitably arise, and patterns of interaction around these conflicts will be repeated many times. The achievement is both behavioral and attitudinal. Behaviorally children learn that if another person does not share your goals, you can negotiate—listen to what they want, suggest modifications of what you want that approaches what they want, or simply incorporate what you think they want with what you want. Much of the negotiation that goes on between young children is of this latter type. Like the mothers whose behavior they imitate, the children determine what others want by observing their behavior, and adapting their response accordingly. Thus, a child who wants to play blocks observes that the peer who ignores his overtures is flying an airplane noisily around the room, and she entices him to join her activity by building an airport. Children who exhibit this skill are more effective in entering new groups, and are selected as playmates more frequently than their peers. Attitudinally, children learn from negotiated conflicts that equity in relationships is desirable.

That conflict may have desirable developmental outcomes is not an entirely novel idea, although until recently conflict has been widely viewed as a totally negative event (Hocker & Wilmot, 1985). In a 1989 chapter, Shantz and Hobart proposed some ways conflict might function in the development of social relationships and in the development of self. Following Sullivan (1953) and Piaget (1932), they argued that when conflicts between peers include discussion, argument, negotiation, and compromise, they produce more satisfying and enduring relationships because they are based on mutual consent, rather than on submission to authority. I am extending their argument to parent-child relationships. The likelihood of children negotiating with peers is enhanced when their family relationships offer a model of conflict resolution characterized by direct expression of one's own desires, attentiveness to the expressed desires of others, and verbal and nonverbal compromises that allow each member of the dyad or group to achieve their goals to some extent. Family relationships give rise to child peer relationships of a certain character, and children's ongoing experience of both types of relationship shape their relationships with their adult partners and ultimately with their own children. From this perspective, the potential influence of conflict experiences on the child's behavioral development and life course is substantial. The nature of that influence depends, of course, on the way conflict is expressed and resolved in families.

Although conflict need not be synonymous with aggression and hostility, there is considerable anecdotal and empirical evidence that within as well as outside families individuals often attempt to ensure that their position will prevail over others, or that their goals will be achieved, through the use of coercive and even violent tactics. The high incidence of spouse battering and child abuse in this country, and the related estimate that approximately 3.3 million children witness their parents' marital violence annually (Carlson, 1984) illustrate this reality. Verbal coercion is also pervasive, both between marital partners (Gottman, 1979) and between parent and child (Crockenberg & Covey, 1991). Thus, what children learn from their experience of family conflicts depends on the specific behaviors to which they are exposed in their own family relationships.

Implications for family intervention and research

If family conflicts serve as arenas in which children learn relationship skills, there should be a long-term developmental payoff for children when parents adopt negotiation as an approach to resolving conflicts between themselves and their children. It follows that one way professionals who work with families may further the development of children is to help parents develop negotiation skills they may not have learned in their own previous relationships. How this would be done depends on the context in which the work is taking place. Thomas Gordon's books, *Parent Effectiveness Training* and *Teacher Effectiveness Training*, are excellent sources of information about the skills necessary for adult-children negotiation, and parent-education classes, in which adults role-play conflicts they are currently engaged in with a child, are useful vehicles for helping ordinary parents and other adults develop negotiation skills. The fewer the skills an adult has, and the more firmly established are alternate strategies (e.g. power-assertive or violent approaches to conflict), the more intensive the intervention will need to be in order to effect change.

The ultimate goal of the intervention, of course, is to help children learn strategies they will use in their own relationships with peers and partners. When children have grown up in families characterized by high levels of power assertion or avoidance of conflict, they may have failed to develop appropriate negotiating skills, and interventions will need to focus on directly teaching them skills for resolving conflicts with others. One context in which such interventions may be especially useful is with children who accompany their mothers to battered women's shelters. These children have likely observed interparental violence in the context of conflict, and may have been the recipients of conflict-linked violence as well. Children need not have witnessed or experienced violent family conflicts, however, for them to benefit from opportunities to learn skills for negotiating conflict with peers. Adults who supervise children in any setting can facilitate this learning by negotiating their own adult-child conflicts and by helping children to resolve conflicts with each other. So often in child care settings teachers simply resolve the children's problem themselves ("Give her the scissors") rather than taking the time to have each child state a need and work out a resolution that is acceptable to both.

The proposed interventions are reasonable inferences from the propositions about the learning of conflict-related skills outlined earlier. However, the empirical evidence on which they rest is thin indeed. While it is reasonably certain that children are affected adversely by witnessing violence between their parents (Emery, 1989), it is unclear whether the "effects" are attributable solely to witnessing because observation and direct experiences of aggression frequently occur together in families. Thus, the impact on children we attribute to observing violent conflict may be a joint influence of observation and the direct experience of abuse. Nor do we know whether a parent-child relationship, or any adult-child relationship characterized by respect and negotiation, can mitigate the impact on child behavior of observing violence and coercion between parents. Totally absent from the research literature, moreover, is any consideration of the way observed or experienced conflict in families characterized by negotiation and compromise influence the way children resolve conflicts with peers. It is these questions that require attention if our work with children and families is to be based on sound scientific principles.

References

Carlson, B.E. (1984). Children's observations of interparental violence. In A.R. Roberts (Ed.), *Battered women and their families* (pp. 147-167). New York: Springer Publishing.

Crockenberg, S., & Covey, S.L. (1991). Marital conflict and externalizing behavior in children. In D. Cicchetti (Ed.), *Rochester Symposium on Developmental Psychpathology, Vol. 3.*Hillsdale, NJ: Lawrence Erlbaum Associates.

Crockenberg, S., & Litman, C. (1990). Autonomy as competence in two-year-olds: Maternal correlates of child compliance, defiance, and self-assertion. *Developmental Psychology, 26,* 961-971.

Emery, R.E. (1989). Family violence. *American Psychologist, 44(2),* 321-328.

Gordon, T. (1974). *Teacher effectiveness training.* Reading, MA: Addison-Wesley.

Gordon, T. (1975). *Parent effectiveness training.* Bergenfield, NJ: Dutton.

Gottman, J.M. (1979) *Marital interaction: Experimental investigations.* New York: Academic Press.

Hocker, J.L. & Wilmot, W.W. (1985). *Interpersonal conflict (2nd ed.).* Dubuque, IA: Wm. C. Brown.

Piaget, J. (1932). *The moral judgement of the child.* London: Routledge & Kegan Paul.

Shantz, C., & Hobart, C. (1989). Social conflict and development. In T. Beradt & G. Ladd (Eds.), *Peer relationships in child development* (pp. 71-94). New York: Wiley.

Spitz, R.A. (1957). *No and yes: On the genesis of human communication.* Madison, CT: International Universities Press.

Sullivan, H.S. (1953). *The interpersonal theory of psychiatry.* New York: Norton.

Why *Spanking* Takes the Spunk Out of Kids

Nick Gallo

Nick Gallo is a writer in Seattle.

There was an old woman, who lived in a shoe.

She had so many children she didn't know what to do.

She gave them some broth without any bread,

Then whipped them all soundly and sent them to bed.

W hy did she do that?" my 3-year-old son, Alex, asks, as I turn the page to another nursery rhyme.

"Why?" I repeat. "Well, I guess she. . . ." I pause, fumbling around for a good answer. "She must have, ummm, something must have happened—"

"She's mean," he announces, eyeing me evenly.

"Oh, I don't know, maybe she. . . ." I stop again. "Maybe," I admit, "she *is* mean."

I sit back in the chair and grimace as I remember that last time I "lost it" with my son. Upset for being scolded at a restaurant, he sailed his grilled cheese sandwich at my head. Then, before I had a chance to stop the action, he flung his booster seat across the room. As he howled and howled, I grabbed him and fled. Retreating quickly to the parking lot, I jammed him in his car seat about as gently as Patrick Ewing slamdunks a basketball. I didn't smack him—and I

HOW TO KEEP YOUR COOL WHEN YOUR KID BREAKS THE RULES

Count to 10. It works. Close your eyes. Take a deep breath. Unclench your fists. Go in another room and close the door, if necessary. Resist your first impulse.

Recognize cues. An angry reaction often involves an escalating cycle of frustration, exasperation, and then finally random hitting. Think about what your child does to push your buttons. Try to interrupt the cycle before you are caught up.

Express your hurt. Parents often aren't just mad, but disappointed and hurt when their children displease them. Explaining to your child why a behavior upsets you may help defuse the situation. Experts advise parents to use "I-messages" to relay feelings, yet to avoid recrimination and blame. For example, instead of screaming at a child about a messy room, try something like, "I'm unhappy when the house is messy."

---

haven't yet—but it was obvious I'd shaken him hard enough to hurt him. As we drove home, he was enraged, hysterical, and finally exhausted. I was all of that—and frightened.

Spanking children, of course, is an age-old tradition. It goes back at least 6,000 years according to prescriptions found on clay tablets from southern Babylonia—which recommended a whack on the behind for disobedient youths.

Still, I suspect spanking scares most parents, stirring a dark fear that we may injure our children—psychologically, physically. According to a recent national survey, only 7 percent of parents think spanking is the most effective form of discipline, though that doesn't mean they haven't resorted to it at times.

"Spanking often is a parent's admission of failure," says Lawrence Hartmann, M.D., child psychiatrist at Harvard Medical School, in Cambridge, Massachusetts. "It means you can't stop bad behavior by any other means."

Yet, discipline is essential. Children need structure, a basic framework that provides for rules and limits and order. The child who doesn't learn the world operates by such regulations is more likely to grow up frustrated, insecure, and incapable of self-discipline, at risk for problems with school, drugs, and the law.

As a result of the over-permissive attitudes toward child-rearing popular several years ago, the pendulum may be swinging back. Many parents today have said they want to return to the good old days, with its emphasis on traditional values, basic skills, and strict discipline. But most child experts caution against embracing a return to spanking.

"There is no research that demonstrates spanking is highly effective at changing long-term behavior," says Martin Drell, M.D., chief of child psychiatry at LSU School of Medicine, in New Orleans, Louisiana.

Perhaps there are instances where a swat on the butt has its uses. It shows a child who's boss. It may clear the air sometimes and allow a parent and child to start over. It may even be a beneficial way to improve a child's behavior, provided it doesn't inflict physical harm and is part of a consistent, reliable, and predictable system.

Often, however, it's not so measured or logical. It's the back of the hand when the kid whines once too often. Or it's a slap to the head for playing near the street. Or, as Ralph Welsh, Ph.D., clinical psychologist in private practice, found in his research, it can cross the line into child abuse, involving excessive use of force. In the words of my 3-year-old, it's mean.

Because so many factors are usually intertwined with spanking, its effects are difficult to determine. Certainly, a case can be made against it. Some studies show physical punishment can increase a child's hostility and cause him or her to act, *more,* not less, aggressively. Spanking sends a message to children that "might makes right," that the way to settle disputes is to use physical force and inflict pain, rather than strive for cooperation. Ultimately, it is self-defeating because a child learns that the way to avoid punishment is simply to be increasingly devious.

"At best, corporal punishment is ineffective; at worst, it can cause long-term coping problems," says Temple University psychology professor Irwin Hyman, Ed.D., director of the National Center for Study of Corporal Punishment and Alternatives in Schools in Philadelphia.

Lost in the research and statistical analyses is perhaps a sadder consequence. As my son and I lapsed into a lull following our clash, I saw a

wariness in his eyes that hadn't been there before. I was left with a basic, visceral feeling that hitting isn't something a loving father does to his young son. Trust seems too fragile a thing to risk smothering it with fear.

A BETTER WAY TO DISCIPLINE

Bennett Leventhal, M.D., director of child and adolescent psychiatry at the University of Chicago, reminds us that "punishment" and "discipline" are not synonymous. Punishment, whether it's spanking or what you might call verbal spanking—yelling and name-calling—is pure reaction. Discipline, says Dr. Leventhal, is something you teach. Designed to help children gain self-control and motivation, it often produces conflicts, especially when children are exploring feelings of power and autonomy, but ultimately it should teach a child to respect the rights of others, to act responsibly, and to enjoy freedom within limits. In fact, discipline is derived from the word "disciple," meaning a follower or a learner.

"That's the whole purpose of discipline—to develop *self-discipline,*" says Dr. Hartmann. "The policeman is not always around."

Time-outs can be very effective, but they often are misused. They shouldn't be a form of punishment, but rather a chance for the child to calm down.

Okay, but how does this help an angry parent, say an Italian father with a short fuse who has just caught a grilled cheese sandwich in the face?

Develop alternatives to spanking, answers Dr. Drell, acknowledging that parents need an entire repertoire of options if they wish to avoid resorting to spanking. "If parents

have only one arrow, that's what they'll use," he says. "If they have five arrows in their quiver, then they may not have to use the one marked: 'spanking.' There's a saying: If all you have is a hammer, everything in the world is a nail."

But before you even get to the moment when you need to choose an alternative, there are important steps to take. Try to focus on *prevention,* says Dr. Hyman.

Gary Peterson, M.D., a child psychiatrist and associate professor of psychiatry at the University of North Carolina in Chapel Hill, points out that the real reason most children refrain from bad behavior is fear of disapproval, not spanking. "Generations ago, we didn't have all these behavior-shaping methods," he says. "We need to use them." Here are some of the best.

Set limits. Often it's the little things, such as conduct at the breakfast table, that precipitate discipline problems. If you don't provide specific guidelines on routine, everyday matters, your child will have a harder time knowing what is expected of them, warns Dr. Drell. Clear, firm limits give kids the blueprint for a pattern of behavior.

One note: Sometimes, it's parents, not kids, who don't want to play by the rules. If you're stressed-out and can't tolerate activity that you normally accept, warn your child beforehand.

Establish order. Children are great individualists. Some thrive on structured situations more than others, but, in general, regular schedules for such affairs as eating, sleeping, and brushing teeth reduce opportunities for fights and conflicts, notes Dr. Peterson. "Be consistent," he says. "That's the key."

Adapt your environment to your child. Child-proofing your home as much as possible reduces the number of no-no's you have to say.

Plan ahead. Anticipating difficult times and activities can avoid many problems and frustrations, believes Elizabeth Crary, M.S., author of *Without Spanking or Spoiling* (Parenting

Press, Seattle). If your child gets antsy when you stand in line, make sure to bring along some diversions. If your child gets grouchy because of hunger or tiredness at a certain time of the day, think about rearranging schedules. Be sure, she notes, to allow enough time for transitions, such as bed time, meal times, and departures.

Crary also recommends *foreshadowing*—preparing a child for experiences and events that are new or uncomfortable. Don't wait until you're at the zoo to tell your child what's expected. Explain ahead of time what will take place, what behavior is permitted.

Have the right expectations. Many parents aren't sure what normal behavior is, says Crary. Parents who punish an energetic 2-year-old for not sitting quietly in church may be setting an impossible standard. Be aware, she says, that children learn at different rates, so don't judge your child by another child's progress.

Try distraction. For young toddlers, diversion prevents power struggles. While youngsters at this age can be tremendously willful, their memory and attention span is limited. Steer the 1-year-old headed for a light socket toward fun and games elsewhere.

Offer choices. Problem: It's 7 a.m. and your child won't wear her red shirt. You can insist that she does, accompanying your command with words like, "You have to learn to listen to me." Or you can allow her to choose between the red shirt and a blue one. Presenting alternatives often gets you off the hook. Just as importantly, say child development experts, choices boost children's self-esteem, giving them confidence to make decisions. But don't confuse questions with commands and offer

choices when you don't mean to. You probably aren't really soliciting an opinion when you ask, "Isn't it time to brush you teeth?"

Praise your child. Sometimes, children misbehave because it's the only way they can get attention, notes Cliff Siegel, M.D., director of child psychiatry at Denver Children's Hospital. Verbal praise and attention feed a child's self-esteem, enhancing mastery and control over the world. The likely result: a more confident kid who is less frustrated and less likely to misbehave.

Reward good behavior. The carrot often works better than the stick, remarks Dr. Siegel. Kids respond to positive reinforcement, he says, recalling a mother who spanked her rambunctious 20-month-old with few results. "She never noticed when the boy did anything good," he says. "He'd bring her a toy and she wouldn't acknowledge it. After she changed that, the entire nature of their relationship changed. She didn't have to spank him after that. All she did was say, "Stop that,' and the boy listened."

Sooner or later your child will test you. And that's when it's important to have your options available. One of the most popular methods of discipline today is the use of "timeouts." It involves briefly isolating a child who has misbehaved from the scene of a conflict. The child, removed to an area such as a bedroom, is told to wait five or ten minutes before returning to the scene. Timeouts can be very effective, but they often are misused, says Crary. Properly used, they are a calming device, not punishment; therefore, they're best reserved for children who can understand the concepts of quiet

and waiting—age $2^1/_2$ to $3^1/_2$ and up— and who can substitute acceptable behavior when calmed down.

As children get older, a disciplinary system can include grounding them or restricting television-watching. Dr. Hyman, who counsels parents in Philadelphia, believes your system will have a better change of working if you allow your child to help establish rules—and the consequences for breaking those rules. Include restitution, not just punishment, in your system so that a child who breaks a window after being told not to play ball in the house can work to "pay" for the damage.

Try at all times to avoid humiliating or demeaning your child. Last year in California, a mother was fined for punishing her 7-year-old son by forcing him to sit on a public bench and wear a pig's snout and a sign saying he was a liar and a thief. While the case was extreme, many parents scream, yell, and inflict psychological abuse that can be as harmful as or more so than spanking to a child's self-image.

Parents are fallible, of course, and given to mistakes. Forgive yourself when you lose your patience and temper and vow to do better. An old-fashioned "I'm sorry" might help. Says E. Gerald Dabbs, M.D., a New York City psychiatrist, "There's nothing wrong with a parent saying to a small child, 'I made a mistake, I lost control, let's start over.' "

"There are two ways to parent," Dr. Leventhal remarks. There's the *authoritarian*, who teaches for fear. Children follow because they're physically intimidated. And there's the *authoritative* parent, who teaches from a position of knowledge. Children follow because they want to learn.

Cultural and Societal Influences

- Social Issues (Articles 27–32)
- Special Challenges (Articles 33–36)

Social scientists and developmental psychologists have come to realize that children are influenced by a multitude of social forces that surround them. In this unit we present articles to illuminate how American children are influenced by broad factors such as economics, culture, politics, and media. These influences also affect the family, which is a major context of child development, and many children are now faced with more family challenges than ever. In addition, analysis of exceptional or atypical children gives the reader a more comprehensive account of child development. Thus, articles are presented on special challenges of development, such as poverty, violence, sexual abuse, autism, and attention deficit disorders.

Both "School and Family in the Postmodern World" and "Buried Alive" raise difficult and provocative issues about how American children today are faced with the challenge of unprecedented levels of change in the family, society, and larger popular culture. For example, the connection between broader societal values and the concomitant pressures exerted on educational practices have placed more demands on schools. At the same time, while we may espouse the need to hold onto certain core societal values, our popular culture often appears to directly contradict these core values. These two thoughtful essays help us to take stock of the complex ways in which our society sometimes sends conflicting messages to our unsuspecting children.

Having a home is no guarantee of optimal, safe development for children. In 1993 there were one million confirmed cases of child neglect and abuse in the United States (and likely many more that went unreported). "Why Leave Children with Bad Parents?" raises important issues about how America cares for its children at risk. For example, the child welfare system in many states tries to keep families intact rather than remove at-risk children and place them with foster parents.

Another influence on children is television, the "electronic family member." Nearly all American homes have a television set, and two-thirds of homes have at least two. In fact, more families in the United States have a television set than a telephone. Given that by the time children graduate from high school they will have spent more time watching television than attending school, their exposure to television is likely to affect many aspects of development. "Violence, Reel to Real" discusses many of the potentially negative and dangerous effects of television violence on children's development in our society today, while "Get 'em While They're Young" describes how advertisers now go to great lengths to market products to shape vulnerable young audiences in influencing their parents' buying behaviors.

Some children all around the world are faced with challenges such as attention deficit disorder, autism, sexual abuse, and other forms of exploitation. These children are often misunderstood and mistreated and pose special challenges to parents, teachers, and society. Are schools and families prepared to deal with such children? Teachers and parents need information to be better able to identify and deal with these children. These issues are discussed in "Victimization of Children," "Resilience in Development," "Child Labor in Pakistan," "Young Children with Attention Deficits," and "Life in a Parallel World."

Looking Ahead: Challenge Questions

Due to changes in family structure, child abuse, and so on, many American children are at risk. What should our nation do to help children? If family breakdown is related to numerous problems for children, should public policy be designed to help families stay intact? How can the enormous number of children living in poverty in our country be reduced? What do you believe should be done for children in high-risk families, such as those discussed in "Why Leave Children with Bad Parents?" In light of the fact that many states have a policy of striving to keep problematic families intact, what additional measures or safeguards would you recommend to improve the chances for children from these at-risk families?

What is the role of television in child development? How might television contribute to many of children's and society's problems? What advantages does television have for children's development? What can parents and schools do to help children become more "media literate" to protect them from influences on television and advertising? How do you balance our First Amendment rights

to free speech with the data showing a correlation between media violence and murder rates in this country? Is censorship warranted or necessary? Can you think of any ways in which advertisers may have affected your attitudes when you were growing up?

As a child, did you ever suffer from some form of victimization or exploitation? What were the responses of the adults and peers around you? What suggestions would you have to prevent what appears to be a very high incidence of childhood victimization?

School and Family in The Postmodern World

The schools have already undergone a major transformation—independent of any conscious reform agenda—simply in response to changes in the society and in the family, Mr. Elkind points out.

DAVID ELKIND

DAVID ELKIND is a professor in the Eliot-Pearson Department of Child Study, Tufts University, Medford, Mass. He is the author of Ties That Stress: The New Family Imbalance *(Harvard University Press, 1994).*

THE SCHOOL is the mirror of society and of the family. As society and the family change, so too must the school. Over the past half century there has been a major structural change in how we think about, perceive, and value ourselves and our world. This change has transformed our arts and our sciences, our industries and commerce, and our families. It has been labeled the shift from *modernity* to *postmodernity*.[1] Of necessity the school has reflected these changes and is a far different institution today than it was at midcentury. This transformation of the school has come about not by a conscious pursuit of education reform, but rather as an adaptive response to the changes in the family and in the larger society.

In what follows I describe how the modern school reflected modern society and the nuclear family and how the postmodern school mirrors postmodern society and the permeable family.[2] However, before I proceed with this discussion, we need to look first at the shift from modern to postmodern themes and then at how these themes are translated into modern and postmodern family ties. Only then can we appreciate how the modern school was a complement to the nuclear family and how the postmodern school is a mirror of the permeable family. I must say as well that, while the postmodern perspective has already been extended to education, I find most of these discussions quite abstract and removed from the practical issues of everyday pedagogy and child rearing. One of my aims in this article is to make concrete the postmodern as it applies to schools and families.

Fundamental Beliefs Of Modernity

It is not possible here to give anything like a complete account of the movement from modernism to postmodernism or of the debates that the use of these terms has engendered.[3] For our purposes, we can assume that the movement represents a fundamental paradigmatic shift in our abiding world view.

In the broadest sense, modernity arose as a revolt against the autocracy of the premodern world. It eventually overturned the medieval forms of government, religion, science, art, and education. Modernity was a continuing revolution in the sense that it did not occur all at once. Nor was it restricted to one particular country or to one specific domain of society. Rationalism, humanism, democracy, individualism, and romanticism were all modern ideas that took root and flourished at different times and in different places. Moreover, modernism was largely a Western phenomenon, and even today one can still find non-Western societies that are more feudal than modern.

Although modernity emerged at different times and in different places, it did have a single, unifying motif. It celebrated the individual as opposed to established authority. René Descartes is often credited with being among the first to express this faith in human thought with his assertion "I think, therefore I am." Descartes rooted authority not in objective agencies but in subjective thought and reasoning. The supremacy of reason, of the individual, and of individual freedom have been the abiding tenets of modernity. Protestantism in religion, self-expression in the arts, experimentation in science, and democracy in government all echo these modern themes.

As modernity spread in Western society, it established three basic beliefs that were the foundation for our modern perception and understanding of the world. The first of these was the belief in the concept of social *progress*: the idea that society and the lot of individuals within that society are gradually improving. The vision of social progress was closely tied up with the belief in the growth of scientific knowledge and in its necessary benefits for mankind. With the modern focus on progress, the medieval idea of a fixed body of knowledge, provided by an authoritative text, was abandoned. In the modern

From *Phi Delta Kappan*, September 1995, pp. 8-14. © 1995 by Phi Delta Kappa, Inc. Reprinted by permission.

world knowledge is viewed as cumulative, a product of scientific endeavor. Through the growth of knowledge and understanding, humankind can move toward a world in which all individuals can enjoy the rights to life and liberty.

A second fundamental truth of modernity was the belief in *universals*. The modern belief in universal "natural" laws was a repudiation of the medieval laws promulgated on the basis of the divine right of kings or of high church officials. It was this belief in universal natural laws that encouraged the grand theories in science, such as those of Newton, Darwin, Marx, Freud, and Einstein — all of whom believed that they had discovered universal principles of nature. The belief that the creative and rational thought of individuals could transcend social and historical boundaries was an assumption common to workers in the arts as well as in the sciences.

The third belief that was fundamental to modernity was that of *regularity*. The belief in the regularity and predictability of natural phenomena was a reaction against the often arbitrary and willful dictates of premodern authorities. Modern science was established as the search for the universal and regular natural laws that governed the physical and social worlds. Newtonian physics was perhaps the first great accomplishment of modernity and established the regularity of celestial phenomena according to the principles of universal gravitation. In like manner, Darwin established the regularity of biological phenomena with his concepts of variation and natural selection. In chemistry the construction of the periodic table of the elements was but another demonstration of the regularity inherent in the natural world.

Fundamental Beliefs Of Postmodernity

Postmodernism has been germinating for a long time. However, it is not a revolt against the beliefs of modernity. Rather, it is perhaps best regarded as a set of attitudes and efforts designed to modify and correct modern ideas that have been perverted and modern beliefs that have proved to be too broad or too narrow. For example, while modernism regarded reason as the engine of human progress, rational arguments have also been used to justify barriers to human progress, such as slavery, colonialism, imperialism, and fascism. Likewise, modernity stressed the freedom of

the individual, but this freedom was often restricted to male, Anglo-Saxon, Christian individuals. The modern belief in the unmitigated benefits of scientific and technological progress did not anticipate the use of advanced knowledge to create ever more powerful weapons of destruction, nor did it take into account the contribution of technological progress to the degradation of the environment. Modern beliefs were not entirely wrong, but they were often idealized and blind to the dark side of human nature, of scientific discovery, and of technological development.

Like modernism, postmodernism is largely a Western phenomenon. And, as happened with the rise of modernism, the rise of postmodernism is occurring not all at once but at different times, in different places, and in a variety of social institutions. Nonetheless, it has its own basic model and correlated themes. Modernity

> *The modern nuclear family has been regarded as the end of an evolutionary progression toward an ideal family form.*

celebrated reason and paid homage to the ideal of liberty and freedom for all individuals. Postmodernism venerates language, rather than thought, and honors human diversity as much as it does human individuality.

The ascendancy of language over reason as the true groundwork of human existence began in the last century. Nineteenth-century philosophers, such as Nietzsche and Kierkegaard — and later Wittgenstein — played "language games" to demonstrate that there is no such thing as "pure" reason and that our thinking can never be abstracted from our language.[4] Through their use of parody, irony, and satire, they demonstrated that language is inherently ambiguous and that the truths of reason, which must employ language, must thus be ambiguous as well.

When language, rather than reason, is taken as the fundamental model of how the world works, an alternative set of themes moves into prominence. First, languages do not "progress" — or at least not necessarily in a positive direction. For example, *Franglais* and TexMex are language developments that many would not regard as evidence of linguistic progress. Languages are characterized by their differences from one another and by their embeddedness within a social, cultural, and historical context. Even within the same country, language varies greatly, depending on the community in which it is employed. Postmodern writers are generally much more concerned with elucidating sociocultural *differences* than with demonstrating linear progress.

Second, although reason may be taken as universal to mankind, language surely is not. Language is always *particular* to a given culture at a given time. To be sure, the potential for language is a universal human characteristic, but in the real world there is not one language common to all. Likewise, even though languages can be translated, every language contains a great deal of surplus cultural meaning that cannot be conveyed by words. Thus postmodern writers are much more concerned with the particular, with domain-specific issues and discourses rather than with grand universals.

Finally, unlike reason, language is often as *irregular* as it is regular. To be sure, rules of grammar and orthography are generally regular, but many exceptions exist as well. Pluralization is a good example. While *boy* and *girl* are regularly pluralized as *boys* and *girls, man* and *woman* are irregularly pluralized as *men* and *women*. Indeed, too much regularity in language can have a negative impact. Trite and hackneyed phrases and dead metaphors are examples of the adverse impact that excessive regularity can have in the realm of language. Accordingly, many postmodern writers find the *irregular* to be as legitimate and as worthy of exploration as the regular.

These postmodern themes of difference, particularity, and irregularity are increasingly transforming science, the arts, and industry. They have also transformed the family and, increasingly, are transforming that mirror of the family, the school. We now need to look at the shift from the modern nuclear family to the postmodern permeable family to see how this shift is being echoed in our schools.

The Modern Family

The family can be defined as a social system characterized by a kinship system and by certain sentiments, values, and perceptions. These components of the modern nuclear family reflected the fundamental beliefs of modernity. The postmodern family reflects the basic assumptions of postmodernity and thus can be described as "permeable."

With regard to kinship, the modern nuclear family — two parents, with one working and one staying home to care for the children — has been regarded as the end of an evolutionary progression toward an ideal family form. The modern nuclear family has been seen as the configuration best suited to the rearing of caring, responsible, and productive citizens. Indeed, it came to be regarded as the regular or "normal" family form, the standard against which all other family structures had to be measured. It was also believed to be a family form that would eventually become universal, predominating in all societies the world over.

The sentiments that characterize the modern nuclear family are those associated with romantic love, maternal love, and domesticity. *Romantic love* is the idea that, for each one of us, there exists one and only one person in the whole world who would be the ideal mate. On meeting that person, we fall in love, marry, and live happily ever after. The sentiment of romantic love is one reason that couples "saved themselves" for their marital partners. It also implies a lifelong commitment to the relationship and regards divorce as an admission that a marriage was not made in heaven. Because of the dominance of the sentiment of romantic love, many couples stayed in unhappy and unloving relationships.

Maternal love is a sentiment based on the notion that mothers have an instinctive need to love and care for their children. Here we see the impact of Darwinian ideas on the family. After much controversy, Darwin's ideas finally became widely accepted, and our animal ancestry was used to explain much of our behavior. The maternal instinct could be observed in animals, and something similar was attributed to human mothers. But in human societies matters are much more complex, and the maternal instinct also served as a rationale for keeping women out of the work force when there was an excess of labor.

The third sentiment that characterizes the modern nuclear family is *domesticity*, the belief that each family member owes primary allegiance to the home. Within this context the mother was often seen as providing the nurturing and care for the emotional needs of all family members, while also providing a comfortable, livable nest. At one time there were some creative outlets for mothers in such activities as quilt-making, weaving, needlepoint, canning, and so on. At the turn of the century, however, the "Betty Crocker mentality" — that all things made in the home could be made more cheaply and more efficiently by machines — carried the day. Increasingly, mothers became consumers, rather than creators, of domestic products.

Although we often think of such virtues as honesty, thrift, fidelity, hard work, and responsibility as family values, they are in fact social, cultural, or religious values. While these values are transmitted by the family, they do not originate in the family. A value that does originate in the family is one that grows out of the family sentiments. In the case of the nuclear family, the value that is the amalgam of romantic love, maternal love, and domesticity is *togetherness*. The essence of the value of togetherness is that the family must be placed ahead of self and that doing things for and with the family must take precedence over doing things for oneself and with friends.

In the recent past, perceptions of the nuclear family have been in keeping with its sentiments and values. Parents were perceived as intuitively knowledgeable about child rearing. Modern writers for parents, such as Donald Winnicott and Benjamin Spock,[5] told parents they did not have to go to college or read heavy books to be good parents. They had only to use their clear-headed common sense and their natural inclinations, and they would easily be "good enough" parents. Much of the child-rearing literature was designed to inform parents about how children grow and develop; these were "how-do" books that left it up to parents to translate child development knowledge into the parenting practices most appropriate for their children.

Children in the modern age were seen as innocent and in need of parental guidance, limit-setting, and protection. Childhood itself was seen as a very precious time, to be cherished and protected. The literature for children of this era — *The Wind in the Willows*, *Peter Pan*, *Winnie the Pooh*, *The Secret Garden*, *The Adventures of Tom Sawyer*, and so on — reflected the perception of childhood as a magical time that children should be able to look back on with great pleasure and no regrets.

Adolescents were perceived as immature, as very much in need of adult limit-setting, guidance, and support. The many adult-led clubs for junior and senior high school students were evidence of this perception. There were debating teams, garden clubs, chess clubs, and stamp clubs. Many of these were led by school faculty members who saw directing such clubs as part of their teaching responsibilities. In addition, such programs as the Explorer Scouts and Seascouts were popular. Portrayals of adolescents in the media reflected this perception and often showed young people getting into typical adolescent scrapes from which they had to be extricated by annoyed, but wise and patient adults.

The Modern School

The kinship structure and the sentiments, values, and perceptions of the nuclear family were mirrored in the modern school. In the U.S., universal free public schooling was fairly well established by the middle of the 19th century. But it was John Dewey who, in the early 20th century, introduced an educational theory in keeping with the tenets of modernity and with the sentiments, values, and perceptions of the nuclear family.[6] Echoing the beliefs of modernism, Dewey offered a grand theory of progressive education that was built on the notions of progress, universality, and regularity. Historian Lawrence Cremin gave one of the best descriptions of this sweeping, idealistic view of the aims of the modern educational agenda:

First, it meant the broadening of the function of the school to include direct concern for health, vocation, and the quality of family and community life. Second, it meant applying in the classroom the pedagogical principles derived from new scientific research in psychology and in the social sciences. Third, it meant tailoring instruction more and more to the different kinds of classes of children who were being brought within the purview of the school. . . . Finally, progressivism implied the radical faith that culture could be democratized without being vulgarized, the faith that everyone could share not only in the benefits of the new sciences but in the pursuit of the arts as well.[7]

Progressive education became to varying degrees the template for late modern education in the United States. Because public schools took the nuclear family as a given, they reflected its sentiments and values as much by acts of omission as by acts of commission. The kindergarten as it functioned during the first half of this century is a case in point. In many states and in many communities, there were no publicly supported kindergartens. In those school districts that did provide kindergartens, attendance was not compulsory. Kindergarten itself was a half-day program. Children attending kindergarten played "dress-up," listened to stories, engaged in arts and crafts, and went on field trips to farms and firehouses. The noncompulsory, play-oriented modern kindergarten thus indirectly supported the sentiments of maternal love and domesticity. It reinforced the idea that young children should not be separated from their mothers or from their homes for long periods. Full-day kindergartens, so common today, would have been regarded (and in some circles still are) as a threat to the togetherness of the nuclear family.

Other modern educational practices also give evidence of how the sentiments of the nuclear family were reinforced by omission rather than commission. The personal information forms that children and adolescents were required to fill out presupposed the sentiment of enduring romantic love and made no provisions for young people from families of divorce or remarriage. Likewise, many elementary schools were built without cafeterias because it was taken for granted that children would go home for lunch or bring their lunches to school. This presumed the sentiment of domesticity (a mother at home to prepare lunch for her offspring).

The family value of togetherness was enshrined in the public schools' focus on *personal adjustment*. Progressive education was meant to facilitate children's adaptation to the larger society. In the process, however, many children met with frustration. Modern educational psychologists used the term *adjustment* to describe the child's response to frustration:

> Frustration can be conceptualized as a response to the disruption of ongoing behavior.... The responses elicited by the stimuli of frustration are adjustments. Adjustment as such is not valuative or conformative. Whatever response is made to the frustrating situation is termed adjustive. It may be socially desirable or undesirable from a valuative point of view and conformative or nonconformative or combine elements of both.[8]

The focus on adjustment and the use of the terms "well-adjusted" and "maladjusted" underscored the importance modern education placed on children's adaptation to the social world. Educators assumed that children would come to school already grounded in the basics of "social adjustment" — thanks to the family value of togetherness. Children's successful adjustment to the order of the school and the larger society was, therefore, premised on their prior adjustment within the family. If children did not adjust well to school, it was clearly the fault of their parents. This reflected the belief that parents knew about child rearing intuitively and that, if they did a bad job, it was because of bad character.

Progressive education also built on the perceptions of childhood innocence and adolescent immaturity. There was little in the curriculum that might be considered controversial, and both children and adolescents were presented with what today would be called overly sanitized views of American history and carefully censored literature. Little attention was paid to cultural diversity, for it was commonly believed that all families were "melting" toward the ideal model of the nuclear family. In these and in many other ways, the modern school reflected and reinforced the sentiments, values, and perceptions of the nuclear family.

The Postmodern Family

The postmodern assumptions of difference, particularity, and irregularity are the fundamental notions that underlie the postmodern conception of the permeable family. Today we recognize that the nuclear family is but one of many different family forms, each of which can provide high-quality child rearing. Single-parent, two-parent working, remarried, and adoptive families are just some of the permeable kinship structures that are evident in America today. While the nuclear family kinship structure may be the least stressful in present-day society, this is true only insofar as the family is emotionally healthy and financially secure. Many nuclear families are far from the ideal, while many non-nuclear families do an excellent job of child rearing.

In the permeable family, the sentiment of romantic love has given way to the sentiment of *consensual love*. With the sexual revolution of the 1960s and the social acceptance of premarital sex, the linchpin of romantic love — saving oneself for one's fated partner — disappeared. Young people began to have sexual relations with those whom they had no intention of marrying. Individuals now have sexual relations by mutual consent and without a lifelong commitment. The notion of consensual love has extended to marriage, and both men and women today marry with the awareness that divorce may well be in their future.

With the social acceptance of working mothers, the nuclear family sentiment of maternal love has also been transformed. What has replaced the sentiment of maternal love is the new sentiment of *shared parenting*. Today parenting is seen as shared not only between mother and father, but also with other caregivers. It is certainly true, of course, that despite this changed sentiment mothers still do the lion's share of child rearing and homemaking. Nonetheless, fathers do more today than was true in the past, and out-of-home care, while still not always easy to arrange, is more readily available than in earlier times.

With the advent of television, inexpensive cars, superhighways, and jet travel, families have become much more involved with the external world than they were during the modern era, when the family was looked on as a "haven in a heartless world." Accordingly, the third sentiment of the postmodern family is *urbanity*, in the sense that the boundaries between home and workplace, public and private life, and child and adult are much more open and flexible than they were during the modern era. Many people now work at home, and many workplaces have child-care facilities. Private lives are on public display every day on television shows such as "Oprah," "Donahue," and "Sally Jesse Raphael." In a world where children are exposed to anything and everything, the information barriers between children and adults are much more porous.

In keeping with the new sentiments of the permeable family, a new value has emerged that reflects the direction of these sentiments. This new value is *autonomy*, whereby each family member pursues his or her own interests and puts these interests before those of the family. In the modern family, where togetherness reigned, having meals together took precedence over individual pursuits. Today, soccer practice, music lessons, and business meetings take precedence over sharing mealtimes. If the nuclear home was a haven, the permeable home is more like a busy railway station with people coming in for rest and sustenance before moving out on another track.

The perception of parents in the permeable family reflects these new sentiments and values. Parenting is now seen as a matter of *learned technique* rather than unlearned intuition. Postmodern writers for parents emphasize the "how-to" and say very little about the "how-do." That is, these writers tell parents how to talk to children, but they say nothing about the important differences in how children of different ages use and comprehend language. These writers, such as Haim Ginott and Thomas Gordon,[9] place great emphasis on not evaluating children, but they do not hesitate to evaluate parents and teachers and to tell them what they are doing wrong and how to do it right.

Children, in turn, are now seen as *competent*: ready and able to deal with all of life's vicissitudes. This new perception of children, however, did not appear because of some new and revolutionary finding about children. It emerged because postmodern parents *need* competent children. We need children who can deal with out-of-home child care from an early age, who can cope with divorce, and who will be left unfazed by seeing people murdered in the streets or behaving wildly on drugs. The media reflect this new image of child competence. The title of the movie *Home Alone* is a nice metaphor for the postmodern competent child who not only is able to manage quite well on his own but can even outwit some stupid adult skullduggery.

The perception of adolescent immaturity is no longer a fitting sequel to the image of childhood competence. Accordingly, adolescents today are seen as *sophisticated*, as quite knowledgeable about drugs, sex, sexually transmitted diseases, AIDS, and modern technology. This new perception is again reflected in media portrayals of teenagers who are sexually active, who may be using drugs, and who consider themselves equal to their parents in decision-making competence.

The Postmodern School

Postmodern schools mirror the kinship structure, sentiments, values, and perceptions of the permeable family. Consider the sentiment of consensual love. Schools now recognize many different family kin-

ship systems, and the forms that children have to fill out provide for non-nuclear families. Many schools also have support groups for children whose parents are divorced. The schools' mirroring and support of the sentiment of consensual love is most apparent in the high schools. Sex education is often mandatory, and, while premarital sex is not condoned, the message to use protection is very clear. Some high schools now dispense condoms.

There is also direct acceptance and support for the sentiment of shared parenting. Full-day kindergartens are now common in school districts across the country. The full-day kindergarten speaks to the need of working parents to have high-quality, affordable, full-day care for their children. Extended-day programs for the children of working parents are also becoming more common in school districts across the country. Some school systems even subsidize child care for children as young as six weeks of age. Thus schools not only acknowledge *shared parenting* but also play an ever-increasing role in support of that sentiment.

Schools are also reflecting and bolstering the permeable family sentiment of urbanity. Multicultural and anti-bias curricula are being introduced at all grade levels, including early childhood.[10] At all age levels children are now taught about drug abuse, sexual abuse, and AIDS. Curriculum materials are also more sophisticated. Contemporary history books give more realistic portrayals of our past. For example, some texts now detail the violence, cruelty, and destruction that accompanied the conquest of the New World. The important contributions to science and culture made by women, by African Americans, and by other minorities are increasingly recognized. While this acknowledgment of diversity is welcome, some of its side effects, such as overzealous political correctness, are less so.

Autonomy, another of the values of the permeable family, is also reflected and reinforced in postmodern education. The current advocacy of a voucher system for parents is a good example. With vouchers, parents would have a choice about the schools their children would attend. While there is a good deal of controversy over whether a voucher system would work, the popularity of the concept itself reflects the new emphasis on giving parents more autonomy in the matter of school choice.

The value of autonomy is also reflected in the postmodern educational emphasis on *self-esteem*, in contrast to the mod-

ern focus on *personal adjustment*. This new orientation goes along with the shift from broad to specific educational goals. The new focus on self-esteem makes it clear that competition and individual achievement take precedence over social adjustment. While professionals continue to argue over what *self-esteem* means, the term is omnipresent in postmodern discussions of education:

> Self-esteem refers specifically to our self-evaluations — that is to our judgments about our own worth. . . . Self-esteem develops in part from our being able to perceive ourselves as competent. Perceived competence reflects our beliefs about our ability to succeed at particular tasks.[11]

Self-esteem has become important in education because it is believed to be critical to success in all domains, especially academic achievement. But it also reflects the permeable family value of autonomy and the need of each individual to be able to go it alone if necessary. Parents have been led to believe that, if children have self-esteem, they will not only do well academically but will be able to cope with any and all of life's vicissitudes. Yet self-esteem, unlike adjustment, is regarded as largely the child's problem, not the joint responsibility of parents and schools.

Schools also reflect the postmodern conception of child competence. In many school districts the curriculum is being pushed downward. Decimal fractions, once taught in the sixth grade, may now be taught in the fourth grade. In many school districts some 10% to 20% of children are retained or put in transition classes because they are "not ready" for first grade. (In a few communities the figure approaches 50%.) At the secondary level the acceptance of the perception of adolescent sophistication has meant that there are few adult-organized activities for young people — on the assumption that adolescents are entirely capable of arranging their own social and extracurricular activities.

I have tried to demonstrate how the schools have already undergone a major transformation — independent of any conscious reform agenda — simply in response to changes in the society and in the family. Space precludes discussing how the schools are beginning to reflect other postmodern societal changes, such as role "dedifferentiation," Total Quality Management,[12] downsizing in industry, and so on.

Nonetheless, I do hope that I have been able to show that there has already been a major transformation in our schools over the past half century, quite apart from the many different reform initiatives undertaken during that time.

Very simply, the schools in postmodern times have continued the historical trend of gradually assuming parental functions. In the modern era, when families moved from farm to city, schools took over vocational training and some health responsibilities, such as vaccinations and screening for hearing and visual defects. In addition, our schools today are providing much more in the way of child care, education for children with special needs, child support services, sex education, drug education, values education, and parent education than they did in the modern era.

These changes are already in place and need to be recognized. Unfortunately, the current education reform initiative toward national standards seems to presuppose a rather narrow, strictly pedagogical role for teachers and schools. Education reform geared toward improving academic performance simply ignores the many new functions the schools have assumed over the past half century. If our students are doing less well academically, perhaps it is at least partly because our schools are devoting more of their resources to meeting the nonacademic needs of students.

From this perspective, what we need most is not more reform, but rather more recognition and support for what the schools are already doing. In keeping with our families and our society, our schools are already postmodern. It is the reformers who need to be reformed.

1. Seymour Best and Donald Kellner, *Postmodern Theory: Critical Interrogations* (New York: Guilford, 1991).

2. David Elkind, *Ties That Stress: The New Family Imbalance* (Cambridge, Mass.: Harvard University Press, 1994).

3. Jean-François Lyotard, *The Postmodern Condition: A Report on Knowledge* (Minneapolis: University of Minnesota Press, 1984); and Jurgen Habermas, *The Philosophical Discourse of Modernity: Twelve Lectures* (Cambridge, Mass.: MIT Press, 1987).

4. Friedrich Nietzsche, *Human, All Too Human*, trans. R. J. Hollingdale (New York: Cambridge University Press, 1986); Søren Kierkegaard, *Stages on Life's Way* (Princeton, N.J.: Princeton University Press, 1945); and Ludwig Wittgenstein, *Letters from Wittgenstein*, ed. Peter Englemann, trans. Leon Furtmuller (New York: Oxford University Press, 1967).

5. Donald Winnicott, *The Child, the Family, and the Outside World* (Reading, Mass.: Addison-Wesley, 1957), p. 162; and Benjamin Spock, *Baby and Child Care* (New York: Hawthorne, 1968).

6. John Dewey, *Democracy in Education* (1916; reprint, New York: Free Press, 1944).

7. Lawrence Cremin, *The Transformation of the School: Progressivism in American Education: 1876-1957* (New York: Alfred A. Knopf, 1961), p. 349.

8. James M. Sawrey and Charles W. Teleford, *Educational Psychology* (Boston: Allyn and Bacon, 1965), p. 146.

9. Haim Ginott, *Between Parent and Teenager* (New York: Avon, 1969), pp. 79, 81; and Thomas Gordon, *Teaching Children Self-Discipline* (New York: Random House, 1989), pp. 53-54.

10. Bonnie Neugebauer, ed., *Alike and Different: Exploring Our Humanity with Young Children* (Washington, D.C.: National Association for the Education of Young Children, 1992).

11. Hermine M. Marshall, "The Development of Self-Concept," *Young Children*, vol. 44, 1989, p. 48.

12. Michael J. Schmoker and Richard B. Wilson, *Total Quality Education: Profiles of Schools That Demonstrate the Power of Deming's Management Principles* (Bloomington, Ind.: Phi Delta Kappa Educational Foundation, 1993).

BURIED ALIVE

Our children and the avalanche of crud.

DAVID DENBY

MAX, my older son, who just turned thirteen, once had a thick green carpet in his room, a tufted and matted shag that my wife and I inherited from the previous owners of our West End Avenue apartment, in New York. When Max was six or seven, we spent a good deal of time kneeling in the carpet, cleaning up his toys, and down there in the green we got to thinking about the moral nature of his education. Pennies, rubber bands, paper clips, marbles, peanut shells, dirty socks, toy soldiers, wooden blocks, G.I. Joes, crayons, dollops of synthetic slime—a sort of kiddies' bouillabaisse, a thickening brew of plastic and metallic stuff—gathered in the shag. It was the landscape of the American child.

One day, the carpet was covered with hundreds of pieces of plastic, and I sat among them, overwhelmed. A friend of Max's had just been over, and the boys had dumped boxes of toys on the floor. There were Legos, of course—the plugged and stamped modular pieces that fit together in innumerable combinations—but also the mobile olive-green figures of the Teenage Mutant Ninja Turtles, along with He-Man and Skeletor, and odd figures from "Sesame Street" and two or three toy groups I couldn't identify. On the floor was the plastic detritus of half a dozen . . . what? Not toys, exactly, but toy systems, many of which were also available as a television show or a movie, or both, with links to computer games, video-arcade games, comic books, regular children's books, clothes, and cereal boxes. Each part of the toy system sold another part, and so Max was encased in fantasy props—*stuff*—virtually to the limits of his horizon.

Idly, I extracted one of the superheroes from the carpet and broke off its arm.

To my surprise, I find myself welcoming, or at least not opposing, the advent of the V-chip—the little device that is to be installed in new television sets sold from 1998 on and that will allow parents to block out programs they don't want their children to see. Many parents I know have similar feelings, and quite a few are surprised by the depths of their ambivalence and in some cases misery on the subject of the plastic on the carpet—upset by the way pop culture in all its forms has invaded their homes, and the habits, manners, and souls of their children. My friends are drawn from a small circle of well-educated New Yorkers; we are a fairly compact and no doubt privileged group. Yet our anguish about bringing up children is, I believe, widely shared by parents of all kinds. Child-rearing is at once the most prosaic and the most mesmerizing subject in the world. The nagging, repetitive tasks it requires—and the wrenching obsessions—reach across regional, class, and political lines. "Married . . . with Children" and the computer game Doom are the same in Montana and in Manhattan.

No one I know expects that the V-chip will make much difference. The chip is no more than a finger in a dike that has already sprung a thousand leaks. In the past two decades or so, pop has triumphed, defeating all but a few pockets of resistance, absorbing or marginalizing the older, "high" arts, humbling the schools, setting the tone for an entire society. The children live in it, but, of course, their parents also live in it, and this is part of the confusion. How can you fight what you enjoy yourself? I am

a film critic and I see more than a hundred movies every year, which puts me in the worst possible position when I berate my children for watching too many movies. My wife, a novelist, loves the new crop of girl rockers. In our family, "The Simpsons" is a source of wonder and "The Empire Strikes Back" an endlessly repeated pleasure.

Even parents who enjoy their share of pop are feeling wary and sore, as if someone has made fools of them. And a few parents I know have given themselves over to bitter rage and are locked in an unwinnable struggle to shut out pop culture and the life of the streets—the two are now indistinguishable—from their children's experience. Acting out of fear and love, and perhaps out of spiritual ambition, too, they have turned themselves into authoritarians, banning television, banning many kinds of "unsuitable" movies. There is so much to forbid—perhaps a whole culture to forbid! And in so doing, these parents risk making the forbidden glamorous and dangerous; they risk cutting the children off from their friends and bringing them up as alienated strangers in the electronic world of the future.

I don't want to be like them, but I understand their absolutism. We are all in the same boat, afloat in the boundless sea. For both relaxed and authoritarian parents, the real issue is much larger than bad TV shows and movies. (There are always some good ones.) We all believe in "choice," but our children, to our chagrin, may no longer have the choice *not* to live in pop. For many of them, pop has become not just a piece of reality—a mass of diversions, either good or bad, brilliant or cruddy—but the very ground of reality. The danger is not mere exposure to occasional violent or prurient images but the acceptance of a degraded environment that devalues everything—a shadow world in which our kids are breathing an awful lot of poison without knowing that there's clean air and sunshine elsewhere. They are shaped by the media as consumers before they've had a chance to develop their souls.

The usual response to such complaints is a sigh or a shrug or, alternatively, exhortations like "Get tough with them. Take control of what they see, what they read and listen to." Parents who think of themselves as conservatives often say this, and their assumptions give them a tactical advantage: they don't have to make so many choices; they are more likely to establish inflexible general principles for what their children can see and do and to insist on parental authority regardless of any contrary evidence or argument. If sex is something children should not see in movies, that's the end of the discussion. Yet the issue is not so simple, especially for parents like me and my wife, who are not eager to stand over the children, guiding their progress all day long like missionaries leading the savages to light. To assume control over their habits and attitudes, we would have to become bullies.

In fact, our two boys are far from addicted to television, but like many American children they consider themselves entitled to a certain amount of TV and to video games and movies as well. As far as they are concerned, such pleasures come with the territory: consuming media, they think, is part of what children do. No doubt I should have been tougher with them; I should have made it clear when they were younger that watching TV was not an entitlement but a privilege. (The awful word makes me wince, but I'm sorry now that I didn't say it.) At this point, we are stuck with the usual compromise, which the children accept in principle: We establish limits—only so much TV, only certain movies, and so on. But there are always arguments, discussions, trades, and other negotiations, and we have come to realize that asserting control over the boys' tastes is no longer possible be-

yond a certain point. How can you control what they breathe?

MANDATED as part of the Telecommunications Act (signed earlier this year), the V-chip is an attempt to give parents more control (or, realists would say, the illusion of control). At this moment, the Motion Picture Association of America, which has administered the movie ratings since 1968, is hoping to get a workable system in place by next January, a year before the V-chipped sets come out. Just like movies, television shows will be rated according to their suitability for children. Parents at home, using a secret code and a remote control, will set their new TVs at whatever rating level they are comfortable with. Any show rated above that level will automatically be shut out.

But how do you rate an endless sea? There are broadcast network and broadcast local shows, network cable and local cable shows, and public television, too: perhaps a thousand hours or more a day of programming. It is less a series of discrete shows than a nation's shared environment—our communal glop, our feed, our ether, our *medium*. Movies are currently rated by a group of thirteen Los Angeles–area citizens with experience as parents, but no group of ten, twenty, or fifty citizens, not even one chained to the spot like the inhabitants of Plato's cave, can sit and rate all the shows. What to do? Jack Valenti, who is the head of the M.P.A.A., and an industry advisory board have decided that the distributors of programming—networks, stations, cable operators—perhaps in consultation with the writers and producers of the shows, will assign the ratings to themselves.

Can the producers and distributors rate themselves? It seems a dubious procedure. In any case, the sheer amount of stuff overwhelms any rational attempt to assess it. Such criteria as intelligence, dramatic interest, and style will not play much of a role in the ratings. A few shows that I might want my older son to see are likely to receive the equivalent of an R—for instance, the occasional PBS series "Prime Suspect," made by England's Granada Television, and starring Helen Mirren as the London police detective Jane Tennison. One recent episode, "The Scent

of Darkness," detailed with grim intensity and admirable British levelheadedness the pursuit and capture of a serial killer. Most of Tennison's colleagues doubt her judgment in the case, and the true subject of the episode—and of Mirren's performance—is the moral gallantry of a woman fighting the coldness of male contempt. Burrowing deep within its peculiar, mazelike world, the drama was so convincing and intelligent that when my older son drifted in, my wife and I let him watch. (We shooed away Thomas, who is nine.) Mirren's fierce, driving anger, her sense that she has an obligation not only to the job but to herself—an obligation not to betray herself—is the essence of modern heroism, and Max, who has seen his share of thoughtlessly violent movies and TV shows, was impressed. Afterward, we talked it over. He wanted to go deeper into the plot and the characters, to understand everyone's motives. With the V-chip in place, however, viewers unfamiliar with the special qualities of "Prime Suspect" will probably not let their thirteen-year-olds see it.

POP culture hardly takes up all of my sons' lives. Their school gives them plenty of work. They read, though not as much as we'd like. (We also read to them and tell them stories and bits of history constantly.) They play basketball, go snowboarding, collect things, make friends everywhere; Max blades and rides, and Thomas plays the piano. If we put on Toscanini's recording of Beethoven's Seventh, they twirl and jump around the living room and carom off the furniture. They seem busier and more active than I was at nine or thirteen. Nevertheless, their absorption in pop is very intense.

When Max is at home on a Saturday, or on vacation, he may hit the computer as soon as he gets up, ignoring repeated entreaties to eat breakfast, and finally ignoring bowls of cereal placed under his nose as he plays one of the war-strategy games that he currently loves—Caesar II, say, set in ancient Rome, or Warcraft II, in which the player, in charge of the Humans, builds forts, towns, farms, and mills, all for the purpose of defeating the unspeakable Orcs, ardent little creatures who attack from many sides and emit anguished groans as they are hacked, maced, and cannonaded into the world below. (Children with a taste for perversity can take the side of the Orcs, or two kids can play against each other.) Warcraft is a big advance in complexity over the point-and-shoot games like Wolfenstein 3-D or Doom, in which the player passes through three-dimensional corridors and mows down endless assailants. (In Wolfenstein, after killing all the S.S. guards, one finally kills Hitler; I have played the game myself with a certain amount of pleasure.) In Warcraft, having won a particular battle, the player graduates to a more difficult level, and is greeted there by the game's narrator, who speaks the medieval fustian that seems to have spread from the Emperor in the "Star Wars" trilogy to many areas of the kiddie culture. "A great host of Orcs have reconstructed the Dark Portal and now lay siege to the land of Nethergarde," the narrator says. The voice rings out in the house like some lugubrious fake who won't go home after a dinner party.

Max may then meet some friends and go for some lunch at the nearest Burger King, where he will eat a Double Whopper and drink a Coke and sternly ignore (I hope) the free dolls and other promotional appeals for "The Hunchback of Notre Dame." Afterward, the group of boys may drift to a violent special-effects debauch like "Mission: Impossible." Later, they may play some basketball in the park (baseball is not the game of choice for media kids), or just hand out at home and (if we let them) watch TV or a rented movie. As the kids sit watching, we shove plates of raw vegetables and roast chicken in their faces, which they sample, all the while demanding chips, Fritos, and Pop-Tarts. And so on, into the night. We intervene, pulling Max away from his friends, but on these occasions when we're at work and can't intervene, he's spent his whole day in media junk, including the food—a day of pleasure, companionship, and maybe heightened alertness, but little else.

Crashing into the kitchen, my sons talk in the private languages they've worked up from exposure to the shows, movies, computer games, rap music, and basketball players that matter to them. Children have always spoken in tongues, living inside their jokes and insults—my

friends and I did it forty years ago—but in recent years the talk has grown quicker, more jangled and allusive, shifting at near-electronic speeds from, say, imitations of Apu, the Kwik-E-Mart manager in "The Simpsons," to Darth Vader, then to Snoop Doggy Dogg and on to jaw-jutting taunts from "Ace Ventura" and other Jim Carrey movies. The children channel-surf their own minds. They can talk logically and soberly, but they seem at their happiest bopping through the apartment, like Robin Williams on a roll, the older one with his high, serious forehead and dark-brown hair parted in the middle, like a German scientist from 1912, and the younger one singing and crowing and then tumbling over his own lines.

"Whooha! Whooha! It is *you*, young Skywalker, who are mistaken. Alrightee then! Power and the money, money and the power. Minute after minute, hour after hour. Thank you, come again!"

Someone is bound to say, "It was ever thus," meaning that, as far as their elders are concerned, every generation of children is immersed in something that's no good for them. New York kids in the eighteen-sixties grew up in a rough city with gangs, street violence, and prostitutes, and most of them were no doubt familiar with such raucous and unenlightening entertainments as cockfighting and bare-knuckle boxing. It was ever thus. After all, many of us watched a good bit of TV as children, yet we wound up O.K., didn't we? What has changed? In a famous essay from 1954, "Paul, the Horror Comics, and Dr. Wertham," the cultural critic Robert Warshow deplored the violence and nihilistic goofiness of such pulp as "The Vault of Horror" and "Crime Suspen-Stories," but concluded that parents were worrying too much about horror comics. Children, like his son Paul, were resilient; most of them would outgrow comic books and would pass on to more complex narratives.

In the nineties, a great deal more than horror comics is jabbing at children, but we can agree with Warshow that the kids stay interested in nothing for very long. The computer games and TV shows, for instance, mark and cut the path of their own extinction, quickly

creating a restlessness that causes the child to turn against the games and the shows themselves. Children go from one craving to another, discarding—I don't know—"Looney Tunes" for "Superman," and "Superman" for "MacGyver," and "MacGyver" for "The Wonder Years," and "The Wonder Years" for Wolfenstein, and Wolfenstein for Sim City, and Sim City for Myst, and Myst for Doom, and Doom for Doom II. Nothing lasts. The restlessness produced by each station on this Via Dolorosa annihilates any chance for real devotion, and the child passes on. Finally the child passes *out:* he emerges at the other end of the media tunnel—though perhaps still ungratified.

My boys, after all, do not seem to be in dire trouble. They can be determinedly earnest on moral questions; they stand up for their friends and for powerless people. They are not, I think, likely to behave violently or commit crimes (the rewards for staying straight are too obvious), and if they screw up they will, like most white upper-middle-class children, be given a second chance, and a third, and they will probably do all right—they will probably come through.

But with what internal injuries along the way? It is a miserable question. Social scientists, looking for quantifiable results, have devised clinical experiments that measure the different effects of violence on children. These effects, which are apparently greater on boys, can be placed in three categories: direct imitation, which is rare, and the more frequent effects of desensitization (acceptance of violence as the way of the world) and a generalized fearfulness, a learned distrust and wariness. But as I write these words, I realize that the test results, however disturbing, are not the point. No social scientist need prove a direct effect on children's behavior for some of us to hate the bullying, conformist shabbiness of the worst pop and the way it consumes our children. If children are living in pop culture, and a good part of it is ugly and stupid, that is effect enough; the sheer cruddiness is an affront.

Individually, the games or shows may have little effect—or, at least, no effect that can't be overcome. But collectively, I'm not so sure. Even if the child's character is not formed by a single TV show, movie, video game, or computer game, the endless electronic assault obviously leaves its marks all over him. The children grow up, but they become ironists—ironists of waste. They know that everything in the media is disposable. Everything on television is just for the moment—it's just television—and the kids pick up this devaluing tone, the sense that nothing matters. Sold a bill of goods from the time they are infants, many of today's children, I suspect, will never develop the equipment to fight off the system of flattery and propitiation which soothes their insecurities and pumps their egos. By the time they are five or six, they've been pulled into the marketplace. They're on their way to becoming not citizens but consumers.

It was not ever thus. Our reality has changed. The media have become three-dimensional, inescapable, omnivorous, and self-referring—a closed system that seems, for many of the kids, to answer all their questions. The older children teach the younger ones the games and movie references, so they have something to talk about when they're alone. I've just run into a three-year-old girl who knew the names of the characters in "Hunchback" before the movie opened. Disney has already claimed her. Pop has also absorbed the oppositional energies that used to be associated with the avant-garde and with minority cultures, making once brave gestures empty gestures, commodifying discontent, inbreeding it with the edgy, in-your-face tone that teen-agers adopt as the sound of independence. That jeering tone has spread like a rash through the whole culture. It's awesome. It sucks.

When my older boy lets fly a stream of epithets in the rancorous tones of an inner-city black teen-ager, I know that the joke is on me—the white liberal. But the joke is not on me alone, of course: rap is very popular in the suburbs. One of the most remarkable social transactions of our time is the widespread assumption by white middle-class boys of the attitudes of a genuinely dispossessed class of young black men. Commodification of rage plays strange tricks. When the triumphal or despairing rant leaves its source, where it serves

as a passionate expression of survival and protest, and goes into the heads of middle-class white children, it serves very different needs, fuelling the emotional demands of pre-teens and teens who may be afraid of women and of the adult world in general. The kids know that the profane rap lyrics are a violation; they speak the words with an almost ecstatic sense of release. Their parents, however, experience those words as an angry assault, and they can either roll with the punches, in which case they feel they've become teen-agers themselves, or sternly disapprove, like the squares in a fifties teen-rebel movie. "Make a stand," I tell myself as I disapprove and forbid, but dignity is not much to fall back on.

Some sort of commercialized aggression is always putting parents on the defensive—Jim Carrey with ketchup coming out of his ears in movie after movie, or Sylvester Stallone machine-gunning the population of Cleveland, or video arcades with so many shooting games that the noise level exceeds that of the Battle of the Somme. "Beavis and Butt-head" is a clever show—it mocks the cruddy teen culture even as it sells it to teens. The show brilliantly sends itself up. Still, it's hard to take. You have to listen to that warthog snort-giggle-snort, so reminiscent of advanced lunacy, as well as the frequent butthole-buttwipe exchanges. Hip parents may appreciate the wryness of B. & B.'s self-extinction, but it's dismaying that everything on teen TV—even irony—is a commodity.

The kids in the dating-game programs treat each other as commodities, the girls swinging their shoulders and smiling as they show themselves off, the audience whooping as the boys pull off their shirts and reveal their pecs and tattoos. Hardly the end of Western civilization, I admit, but the way the shows force teens to stereotype one another is awful. Children don't understand vulgarity as a concept, and the makers of commercial culture would be happy if they never understood it. Parents have to teach them what vulgarity is somehow. When I have the energy, I argue, I satirize, I get the boys to agree that the shows are stupid. Yet I don't turn off the set, because doing that would only cause them to turn it back

on when I'm not there. I want *them* to turn it off.

Whether the sets are off or on, the cruddy tone is in the air and on the streets. The kids pick it up and repeat it, and every week there are moments when I feel a spasm of fury that surges back and forth between resentment and self-contempt. In those moments, I don't like the way my boys talk—I don't like the way they think. The crude, bottom-line attitudes they've picked up, the nutty obsessive profanity, the echo chamber of voices and attitudes, set my teeth on edge. The stuff fits, and they wear it. What American parent hasn't felt that spasm? Your kid is rude and surly and sees everything in terms of winning or losing or popularity and becomes insanely interested in clothes and seems far, far from courage and selfhood.

Aided by armies of psychologists and market researchers, the culture industries reach my children at every stage of their desires and their inevitable discontent. What's lost is the old dream that parents and teachers will nurture the organic development of the child's own interests, the child's own nature. That dream is largely dead. In this country, people possessed solely by the desire to sell have become far more powerful than parents tortuously working out the contradictions of authority, freedom, education, and soul-making.

In "The Republic" Plato declares that the young should hear nothing—not even a few discordant lines from Homer—that would form their characters improperly. Plato can mischievous, but he appears to be saying that young people will adopt only the behavior that they have heard about. Today, fundamentalists have taken up this concept of education like a cudgel. Salman Rushdie's impressionistic, dream-filled novel "The Satanic Verses," in which the narrator makes fun of Muhammad, is an attack on all Islam. Kill the novelist! An American commercial movie—say, "Sleeping with the Enemy"—that has a bad marriage in it is seen not as the dramatization of a single, fictional marriage but as an attack on the institution of marriage itself. Save the institution of marriage! Well-educated American conservatives who vilify popular culture for political ends appear to want entertainment that is didactic, improving, hygienic.

In a true liberal-arts education, however, children are exposed to many stories, from many sources. They hear about all sorts of behavior—wickedness and goodness and the many fascinating varieties in between—and are taught what a narrative is and what its moral relation to life might be. Narratives give many pleasures, one of which, surely, is the working out of the story's moral significance, either simple and redundant or complex, layered, and exploratory. Parents and teachers still hope that a complicated narrative will serve as a prelude, preparing children for the complexities of life. They will learn good by studying evil as well as good.

Thinking back to my own lazy days at thirteen, I remember noodling around the house and eating my way through boxes of chocolate-chip cookies and watching old movies on TV—thirties comedies and musicals, forties thrillers and war movies, the narrative achievements of a studio system that, whatever else it did wrong, invariably managed to tell stories that pulled the viewer in. I was more passive, and certainly more isolated, than Max, but I was luckier in my movies: the movies were still a narrative medium.

The computer games, I suppose, offer a kind of narrative, but one that yields without resistance to the child's desire for instant gratification. Affording a momentary—and spurious—feeling of power, the summer's new big-budget action movies like "Mission: Impossible" and "The Rock" (and last year's "Batman Forever") offer larger versions of the same thing—increasingly jangled and incoherent narratives that also yield instantly to pleasure. I believe in pleasure, but I hate the way my boys are jacked up by the new movies without ever being drawn into the more enveloping and transforming enchantments of a beautifully worked-out story. They get used to feeling nothing but excitement. ("I don't like *drama*," I once heard one of Max's friends say with considerable exasperation.) An American adventure movie is now simply a violent movie—and, increasingly, an impersonally violent movie whose thrills refer almost entirely to earlier movie images. The Hollywood studios need to top last

year's explosions, so they keep the children bucking on a roller-coaster ride to nowhere.

I wouldn't mind the boys' seeing a certain amount of violence in movies or on TV if the violence were dramatized as serious or tragic, or even playful—anything more than an electric prod to their already overstimulated nerves. Children need secrets and hidden places, they need to tempt the forbidden. And they can really learn from tasting temptation. The thrill of danger is good for them: many of the classic stories and movies for children are about danger. But in the big new action movies, no one humanly vulnerable—no one children could identify with—is placed in jeopardy, so there's actually little sense of danger.

Because they haven't been touched or shaken, children think that having seen one violent film justifies seeing another. A parent who vetoes a movie is likely to be told, "I've seen much more violent things than this," by which he means "and yet I've survived." The kid wants to test himself against the movie, as if it were a wild ride at an amusement park, and the parent who doesn't utter an immediate and final "no" either argues endlessly, or allows himself to be dragged along with a heavy heart.

Film critics who are parents have a particularly rough time of it. A friend of mine who is also a film critic was confronted by her older son holding the videotape of a horror movie.

"Can I look at this?"

"No, you cannot."

"Why not?"

"Because it's scary, I didn't like it, and I don't want you to see it."

At that point, the child turned over the box and read aloud a rave quote from his mother's review.

My own personal calvary: Without my permission, Max saw "Pulp Fiction" on tape at a friend's house a few months ago, and enjoyed it as a bizarre collection of wicked thrills. I told him I wished he hadn't seen it, but I suppose that in one way I should have been relieved. He wasn't yet far enough along in his education in media irony to see how funny the movie was. "Pulp Fiction" is play, a mocking commentary on old genres, a celebration of pulp flagrancy and violation as pleasure—the

sport of a declining movie culture in which sincerity is the only unforgivable sin. Habitual moviegoers savor the fizz in the drink, including the S & M scene, which is deliberately absurd. But I didn't explain this to Max. I saw no reason to expand a twelve-year-old's interest in "Pulp Fiction."

But then, having seen "Pulp Fiction," he wanted to leverage himself into seeing Quentin Tarantino's earlier and much nastier (and more pointless) "Reservoir Dogs." No, I said. But why not? he asked. After all, his friends had seen it. I told him I couldn't stop him from seeing it at someone else's house, but I would prefer that he not. In such exchanges, Max is saying to me (in effect), "If I'm not old enough to see the movie, how come I'm old enough to understand the reasons I'm not supposed to see it?" That is the ultimate question posed to the parents of a media child.

Sometimes we win, but often we give in, because there are moments when my wife and I want to talk to each other or to a friend on the telephone, or read, or work. A hundred dollars for a moment of peace! It's the eternal parental cry. And in those moments and hours I let the kids watch what's on TV or play some inane point-and-shoot computer game. I am grateful that the boys have something that bottles them up for a time. The media have suffused the children with pleasure and their parents with guilt.

CONSERVATIVE critics attack the media easily and comfortably. But do they acknowledge any culpability for allowing pop culture and consumerism to become such an overwhelming force in our country's habits of child-rearing? Conservatives would like to believe that capitalism and its extraordinary executive tool, the marketplace, are not only productive and efficient but *good*. Thus they may criticize the "excesses" of a company like Time Warner; they may even criticize "greed," as if greed were some bizarre aberration normally unknown to capitalism. But they can rarely bring themselves to admit that capitalism in its routine, healthy, rejuvenating rampage through our towns, cities, and farmlands forces parents to work at multiple jobs, substitutes malls for small-city commercial streets and neighborhoods, and dumps formerly employed groups (like blacks in the inner cities) onto the street or into dead-end jobs. Or that these developments loosen parental control, and help create the very nihilism and anomie—the rootlessness of nowhere men—that find release in junk movies, rap, pornography, and the rest.

When it comes to pop culture, conservatives are the last innocents. Surely there's something pathetic about Bob Dole's calling for restraint from Time Warner, when it's precisely the unrestrained nature of capitalism that conservatives have always celebrated. Conservatives would make a lot more sense on the subject of popular culture if they admitted that the unregulated marketplace, in its abundant energy, is amoral, that it inspires envy and greediness, that it shreds "values" and offers little space or encouragement for what William Bennett calls "virtues." Parents deserve better than such ideologically motivated hypocrisies.

Nearly every parent, consciously or not, cherishes a kind of idealized timetable that proposes a mood—a state of readiness—in which a child can best be introduced to a new experience. Children's first responses—to nature, to death, to sex, to violence, to the arts, to the news that this world is often a dark and dirty place—obsess parents almost as much as providing proper food and education. In hoping to maintain a reasonable schedule, parents do not necessarily want to protect children's innocence. The schedule, after all, is a way of regulating the *loss* of innocence—opening up the world to children in a way that makes sense.

Parents can still control some of the schedule, but a large part of it has been wrenched out of their hands by pop culture. Is this a calamity? Not really. Middle-class parents are often squeamish and overprotective. Some children may be better off if they escape their parents' grip, healthier if they grow up wild and free and sort things out on their own. Still, the schedule is a lovely idea—one of the enduring talismans of middle-class family life. And parents, however discouraged they may have become, will always try to impose it.

They consider imposing it their right. For parents, the early responses are central to the poetry and moral charm of childhood. And to have those intimate moments and pleasures preempted by someone's marketing scheme is like receiving a blow to the chest.

If conservatives are going to oppose any sort of government regulation of the marketplace, they can't be surprised that the market overwhelms parents, and that parents then complain that they have lost control. When toys, movies, books, and television shows are all devoted to the same product or performer and are marketed by different branches of the same company, can we rationally speak of free choice in the marketplace? The producers and the distributors may be free, but are the children?

LIBERALS, too, have an accounting to make. There is a strain of opinion regarding the arts which has reigned during the last few decades in most of the bourgeois democracies—in the United States, Australia, Great Britain, France, Germany, and the rest of Western Europe. Let us call it cultural libertarianism (its god is John Stuart Mill). Cultural libertarianism insists on the paramount importance of free expression. Therefore, cultural libertarianism, when it has to, defends, as a corollary, the right of artists to use violence and sex in their work. That exploiters will use violence and sex, too, is exasperating, but such is the price of freedom. There is no way *in law* of curtailing exploiters without also curtailing artists. The market is tawdry, corrupt, and corrupting; it is also exhilarating. In a free society, art and schlock come joined together like ship and barnacle. The way to separate the two is with education and criticism.

Any other approach, cultural libertarians will argue, leads to censorship or (just as bad) self-censorship. In any case, politicized criticism of the media, whether from the left or the right, is often a form of self-righteous hysteria that inflames people against imaginary or relatively harmless dangers while diverting them from genuine social problems. In the United States, we should be less obsessed with popular culture than with the unequal distribution of goods and opportunities in an increasingly stratified society. Anyone can bring pres-

sure on Time Warner, but how do you change an inner-city neighborhood?

So goes the orthodoxy of enlightenment practiced for decades by many people (including me). Many cultural libertarians would agree, of course, that a different set of rules should be brought into play when we are talking about children. The children should be protected; they don't have the right to see and hear everything. But *can* they be protected anymore? Has our social reality changed so much that the automatic celebration of freedom in itself puts children at risk? Cultural libertarians are now faced with a number of unnerving challenges to their self-esteem.

For one thing, the tone of our common culture has coarsened in the last couple of decades. Everyone has said so, and everyone is right. The boasting polygamists on trash TV, the rap lyrics, the rancorous and openly racist talk-radio shows—these are just the most obvious examples. We left-wing types popularized rudeness and slangy candor as a style of public discourse thirty years ago—our language, we thought, would discredit the official hypocrisies—and now everyone is going in for it. With depressing effect: even those who love profanity may be dismayed to hear a former mayor of New York calling someone a "schmuck" on the radio. It is not the words that matter so much as the ravaging lack of dignity. The rout of gentility, which cultural libertarians sparked, has now been followed by the rout of self-respect. On ragged and exhausted nights, the wised-up tone of everything wears one down. As I go to sleep in our second-floor bedroom, I can hear couples dully cursing one another on the street, the words landing like blows. (That women now give as much as they get makes the sound no less melancholy.) When the clock radio clicks on in the morning, giggles and hoots accompany anyone trying to talk about a subject more serious than the weather. In the nineties, sarcasm is no longer a resistance to the marketplace; it *is* the marketplace. The constant atmosphere of selling creates a common ironic consciousness, the derisiveness of people in the know. And what do they know? That everyone is out for himself, that greed is what drives life forward. Derision has become the spirit of the jammed, crazy, relentless talk, the needling spritz of radio, of late-night TV, of kids teasing and threatening on the street. In these worlds, in our common world, no other kind of talk takes hold. If you aren't derisive, you're out of it. You're not in the market.

Adults learn to screen a lot of this out, but children don't necessarily do so. They enjoy it. They imitate it—and who can blame them? The media and the streets are far more exciting than school, where virtue so often comes packaged as learning.

Then there's the problem of pop growth: the huge increases in the formidability and quantity of mass culture—the new Fox network, the local and national cable operators, the Sony PlayStation and Sega and Nintendo systems, the innumerable computer games, and the rest. The problem is not simply that the stuff comes flooding in on children from all sides. The problem is that easy entertainment and self-serving communication of one sort or another (political speech, commercial messages, infotainment, advertorials, ego rants, self-promoting "confessions") increasingly push everything else to the margins. If you click through the channels, including the zillion cable channels, at different times of day, you will discover that serious communication of any sort is a tiny portion of what's available. One of the comedies of intellectual life in recent years has been the spectacle of the cultural left in the universities complaining that the words of women or minorities have been suppressed, when the exponential growth of mass communication has swamped just about anything of real consequence.

Cultural libertarians have been too complacently self-regarding in their defense of free expression. It's a noble position, a necessary position, never to be relinquished, but at this point it isn't enough. How valuable is the latest constitutional victory for freedom of speech if the general level of speech continues to be degraded? Moreover, some of the cultural libertarians, including me, have a minor crime to answer for—the too-easy use of such loaded words as "subversive" and "transgressive" to praise movies and rock albums that offer a little

more sex and violence than other good movies and albums. A few years ago, liberal-minded cultural critics, terrified of standing with the squares, got bullied out of any sort of principled public resistance to pop. They took themselves out of the game, and left the field open for William Bennett's iron moralism.

THOMAS becomes annoyed when I question him about the Saturday morning kiddies' shows, in which, it seems, the world is always being saved by uniformed teens from some basso-voiced monster and his wicked female companion. Whatever I may think about the homogenized nature of these shows, however, Thomas sees important differences among them. What he loved six months ago, for instance, he now regards as beyond the pale. The market has moved him along and made him contemptuous of what he has discarded. He's a very easygoing child, but, as far as he's concerned, his entertainment choices are not our business. Shyly, like suitors with hat in hand, we question his tastes and try to introduce him to the older arts, to the things we love. It may be ridiculous, but parents suffer a narcissistic wound when their children don't care about their favorite pictures, their books and music. Five years ago, we heard, on the car radio, Chuck Berry singing "Johnny B. Goode," and Max, who was then in the depth of his Billy Joel phase, said he liked it. We were absurdly happy. He likes Chuck Berry! When Tommy popped out of bed at eleven o'clock recently and, half asleep, asked me if we could listen immediately to all nine of the Beethoven symphonies, I began playing the "Eroica," and he fell back to sleep on the couch, a warrior at rest, as the music swirled over him.

Choice! It has to mean more for parents than an endless opening to the market. An active and engaged liberalism, while rejecting censorship, would encourage the breaking up of such vertically integrated culture monoliths as Disney, Sony, and Time Warner. It would ask for more regulation. (The V-chip is only the beginning.) It would, for instance, support the attempt of Reed Hundt, the reform-minded F.C.C. chairman, to require broadcasters to put

on three hours of educational television a week. (Which might mean three fewer hours of trash.) And it would go far beyond the mere celebration of choice. It would insist on discrimination—not in the racial sense but in the cultural arena, where liberals, so eager to appreciate everyone's point of view, are often milky and weak. If parents are not to feel defeated by the media and pop culture, they must get over their reluctance to make choices that are based on clear assertions of moral values. They cannot leave to the "virtuecrats" the defense of religion, high culture, the meritocracy, the Western literary classics, or anything else that implies a hierarchy of taste. They have to join the discourse and make it aesthetically and morally alive.

ON vacation, away from Media City, without a television or a movie theatre in sight, I read to Max the novel that begins, "My father's family name being Pirrip, and my Christian name Philip, my infant tongue could make of both names nothing longer or more explicit than Pip. So I called myself Pip, and came to be called Pip." The same novel was read to me at the same age—not by my father but by an elderly teacher who entertained her students after lunch by reciting both "Oliver Twist" and "Great Expectations" in a Midwesterner's gentle version of a thick Cockney accent. On vacation, Max became completely absorbed in the book, his eyes turning dreamy and inward-looking, and we read a great deal, for ninety minutes at a time. I was happy, too, because I was not on the carpet anymore, down there in the plastic rubble.

But then we returned to the metropolis. TV sets and computers, as well as school and friends, pressed in on all sides, and the reading slowly petered out. We read less every night, and after a while Dickens, who only weeks earlier had enchanted so tenderly, now seemed slow, laborious, convoluted, even boring. We've picked the book up a few times since, and my son is slowly climbing back into it—that he enjoys it, I have no doubt—but I don't know if we'll ever finish it. I would like to, and so would he, but Dickens's long, rolling sentences require peace and time, and the air is just too charged around here.

Why Leave Children With Bad Parents?

Family: Last year, 1,300 abused kids died—though authorities knew that almost half were in danger. Is it time to stop patching up dead-end families?

MICHELE INGRASSIA AND JOHN MCCORMICK

THE REPORT OF DRUG PED-dling was already stale, but the four Chicago police officers decided to follow up anyway. As they knocked on the door at 219 North Keystone Avenue near midnight on Feb. 1, it was snowing, and they held out little hope of finding the pusher they were after. They didn't. What they discovered, instead, were 19 children living in horrifying squalor. Overnight, the Dickensian images of life inside the apartment filled front pages and clogged network airwaves.

For the cops that night, it seemed like a scavenger hunt gone mad, each discovery yielding a new, more stunning, find. In the dining room, police said, a half-dozen children lay asleep on a bed, their tiny bodies intertwined like kittens. On the floor beside them, two toddlers tussled with a mutt over a bone they had grabbed from the dog's dish. In the living room, four others huddled on a hardwood floor, crowded beneath a single blanket. "We've got eight or nine kids here," Officer John Labiak announced.

Officer Patricia Warner corrected him: "I count 12." The cops found the last of 19 asleep under a mound of dirty clothes; one 4-year-old, gnarled by cerebral palsy, bore welts and bruises.

As the police awaited reinforcements, they could take full measure of the filth that engulfed this brigade of 1- to 14-year-olds. Above, ceiling plaster crumbled. Beneath their feet, roaches scurried around clumps of rat droppings. But nothing was more emblematic than the kitchen. The stove was inoperable, its oven door yawning wide. The sink held fetid dishes that one cop said "were not from that day, not from that week, maybe not from this year." And though the six mothers living there collected a total of $4,500 a month in welfare and food stamps, there was barely any food in the house. Twice last year, a caseworker from the Illinois Department of Children and Family Services (DCFS) had come to the apartment to follow up reports of serious child neglect, but when no one would let her in, the worker left. Now, it took hours to sort through the mess. Finally, the

police scooped up the children and set out for a state-run shelter. As they left, one little girl looked up at Warner and pleaded, "Will you be my mommy?"

Don't bet on it. Next month the children's mothers—Diane Melton, 31; Maxine Melton, 27; May Fay Melton, 25; Denise Melton, 24; Casandra Melton, 21, and Denise Turner, 20—will appear in Cook County juvenile court for a hearing to determine if temporary custody of the children should remain with the state or be returned to the parents. Yet, for all the public furor, confidential files show that the DCFS is privately viewing the 19 children in the same way it does most others—"Goal: Return Home."

Why won't we take kids from bad parents? For more than a decade, the idea that parents should lose neglected or abused kids has been blindsided by a national policy to keep families together at almost any cost. As a result, even in the worst cases, states regularly opt for reunification. Even in last year's budget-cutting frenzy, Congress earmarked nearly $1 billion for family-preservation programs over the next five years. Yet there is mounting evidence that such efforts make little difference—and may make things worse. "We've oversold the fact that all families can be saved," says Marcia Robinson Lowry, head of the Children's Rights Project of the American Civil Liberties Union. "All families *can't* be saved."

Last year there were 1 million confirmed

cases of abuse and neglect. And, according to the American Public Welfare Association, an estimated 462,000 children were in substitute care, nearly twice as many as a decade ago. The majority of families can be repaired if parents clean up their acts, but experts are troubled by what happens when they don't: 42 percent of the 1,300 kids who died as a result of abuse last year had previously been reported to child-protection agencies. "The child-welfare system stands over the bodies, shows you pictures of the caskets and still does things to keep kids at risk," says Richard Gelles, director of the University of Rhode Island's Family Violence Research Program.

Nowhere has the debate over when to break up families been more sharply focused than in Illinois, which, in the last two years, has had some of the most horrific cases in the nation. Of course, it's not alone. But unlike many states, Illinois hasn't been able to hide its failures behind the cloak of confidentiality laws, largely because of Patrick Murphy, Cook County's outspoken public guardian, who regularly butts heads with the state over its aggressive reunification plans. The cases have turned Illinois into a sounding board for what to do about troubled families.

The Chicago 19 lived in what most people would consider a troubled home. But to veterans of the city's juvenile courts, it's just another "dirty house" case. In fact, Martin Shapiro, the court-appointed attorney for Diane Melton, plans to say that conditions could have been worse. He can argue that Melton's children weren't malnourished, weren't physically or sexually abused and weren't left without adult supervision. He's blunt: "Returning children to a parent who used cocaine—as horrific as that might seem—isn't all that unusual in this building." If only all the cases were so benign.

What Went Wrong?

ON THE LAST NIGHT OF JOSEPH Wallace's life, no one could calm his mother's demons. Police say that Amanda Wallace was visiting relatives on April 18, 1993, with 3-year-old Joseph and his 1-year-old brother, Joshua, when she began raving that Joseph was nothing but trouble. "I'm gonna kill this bitch with a knife tonight," Bonnie Wallace later told police her daughter threatened. Bonnie offered to keep the boy overnight, but Amanda refused, so Bonnie drove them to their apartment on Chicago's impoverished West Side. It's unclear what forced Amanda's hand, but authorities tell a harrowing tale: at about 1:30 a.m., she stuffed a sock into Joseph's mouth and secured it with medical tape. Then she went to the kitchen, retrieved a brown extension cord and wrapped it around Joseph's neck several times. She carried her

son to the living room, stood him on a chair, then looped the cord around the metal crank arm over the door. In the last act of his life, Joseph waved goodbye.

Amanda Wallace, 28, has pleaded not guilty to charges of first-degree murder. No one ever doubted that Amanda was deeply troubled. When Joseph was born, she was a resident at the Elgin Mental Health Center in suburban Chicago, and a psychiatrist there warned that Amanda "should never have custody of this or any other baby." Three times, the DCFS removed Joseph from his mother. Yet three times, judges returned him to Amanda's dark world. Six months after the murder—which led to the firing of three DCFS employees—a blue-ribbon report blasted the Illinois child-welfare system, concluding that it had "surely consigned Joseph to his death."

Even in the most egregious instances of abuse, children go back to their parents time and again. In Cook County, the public guardian now represents 31,000 children. Only 963 kids were freed for adoption last year. But William Maddux, the new supervising judge of the county's abuse and neglect section, believes the number should have been as high as 6,000. Nationwide, experts say, perhaps a quarter of the children in substitute care should be taken permanently from their parents.

But it's not simply social custom that keeps families together, it's the law. The Adoption Assistance and Child Welfare Act of 1980 is a federal law with a simple goal—to keep families intact. The leverage: parents who don't make a "reasonable effort" to get their lives on track within 18 months risk losing their kids forever. The law itself was a reaction to the excesses of the '60s and '70s, when children were often taken away simply because their parents were poor or black. But the act was also one of those rare measures that conservatives and liberals embraced with equal passion—conservatives because it was cheap, liberals because it took blame away from the poor.

By the mid-'80s, though, the system began to collapse. A system built for a simpler time couldn't handle an exploding underclass populated by crack addicts, the homeless and the chronically unemployed. At the same time, orphanages began shutting their doors and foster families began quitting in droves. The system begged to know where to put so many kids. It opted for what was then a radical solution: keeping them in their own homes while offering their parents intensive, short-term support—child rearing, housekeeping and budgeting. But as family-preservation programs took off, the threat of severing the rights of abusive parents all but disappeared. What emerged, Gelles argues, was the naive philosophy that a mother who'd hurt her child is not much different from one who can't keep house—and that with enough supervi-

sion, both can be turned into good parents.

In hindsight, everyone in Chicago agrees that Joseph Wallace's death was preventable, that he died because the system placed a parent's rights above a child's. Amanda could never have been a "normal" parent. She had been a ward of the state since the age of 8, the victim of physical and sexual abuse. Between 1976 and Joseph's birth in 1989, her psychiatrist told the DCFS, she swallowed broken glass and batteries; she disemboweled herself, and when she was pregnant with Joseph, she repeatedly stuck soda bottles into her vagina, denying the baby was hers. Yet 11 months after Joseph was born, a DCFS caseworker and an assistant public defender persuaded a Cook County juvenile-court judge to give him back to Amanda, returning him from the one of the six foster homes he would live in. The judge dispatched Amanda with a blessing: "Good luck to you, Mother."

Over the next two years, caseworkers twice removed Joseph after Amanda attempted suicide. But a DCFS report, dated Oct. 31, 1992, said she had gotten an apartment in Chicago, entered counseling and worked as a volunteer for a community organization. And though the report noted her turbulent history, it recommended she and Joseph be reunited. Joseph Wallace was sent home for the last time 62 days before his death, by a judge who had no measure of Amanda's past. "Would somebody simply summarize what this case is about for me and give me an idea why you're all agreeing?" the judge asked. Amanda's lawyer sidestepped her mental history. Nevertheless, the DCFS and the public guardian's office signed on. When Amanda thanked the judge, he said, "It sounds like you're doing OK. Good luck."

Murphy says that deciding when to sever parents' rights should be obvious: "You remove kids if they're in a dangerous situation. No one should be taken from a cold house. But it's another thing when there are drugs to the ceiling and someone's screwing the kids." Ambiguous cases? "There haven't been gray cases in years."

No one knows that better than Faye and Michael Callahan, one of the foster families who cared for Joseph. When Joseph first came to them he was a happy, husky baby. When he returned after his first stretch with Amanda, "he had bald spots because he was pulling his hair out," Faye says. By the third time, she says, Joseph was "a zombie. He rocked for hours, groaning, 'Uh, uh, uh, uh'." The fact that he was repeatedly sent home still infuriates them. Says Michael: "I'd scream at those caseworkers, 'You're making a martyr of this little boy!'"

See No Evil, Hear No Evil

EARLY LAST THANKSGIVING, ARETHA McKinney brought her young son to the emergency room. Clifford Triplett was semiconscious, and his body was pocked with burns, bruises and other signs of abuse, police say. The severely malnourished boy weighed 17 pounds—15 percent less than the average 1-year-old. Except Clifford was 5.

This wasn't a secret. In a confidential DCFS file obtained by NEWSWEEK, a state caseworker who visited the family last June gave a graphic account of Clifford's life: "Child's room (porch) clothing piled in corner, slanted floor. Child appears isolated from family—every one else has a well furnished room. Child very small for age appears to be 2 years old. Many old scars on back and buttocks have many recent scratches." In April, another caseworker had confronted McKinney's live-in boyfriend, Eddie Robinson Sr., who claimed that Cliff was a "dwarf" and was suicidal—neither of which doctors later found to be true. Robinson added that Cliff got "whipped" because he got into mischief. "I told him that he shouldn't be beat on his back," the caseworker wrote. "Robinson promised to go easy on the discipline."

It's one thing to blame an anonymous "system" for ignoring abuse and neglect. But the real question is a human one: how can caseworkers walk into homes like Clifford's, document physical injury or psychological harm and still walk away? A Cook County juvenile-court judge ruled last month that both McKinney and Robinson had tortured Clifford (all but erasing the possibility that he'll ever be returned to his mother). But caseworkers are rarely so bold. In Clifford's case, the April worker concluded that abuse apparently had occurred, but nine days later another found the home "satisfactory." Says Gelles: "Caseworkers are programmed by everything around them to be deaf, dumb and blind because the system tells them, 'Your job is to work to reunification'."

Murphy charges that for the past two

SAONNIA BOLDEN

"The amount of stress and frustration has been reduced. Sadie appears to have a lot more patience with her children and she continues to improve her disciplinary techniques." The same day the worker wrote this, Sadie's daughter Saonnia died after boiling water was poured on her. An autopsy uncovered 62 injuries, many recent.

FROM CASEWORKER REPORT
ON SAONNIA BOLDEN

years, Illinois has made it policy to keep new kids out of an already-clogged system. "The message went out that you don't aggressively investigate," he says. "Nobody said, 'Keep the ----ing cases out of the system'." But that, he says, is the net effect. "That's just not true," says Sterling Mac Ryder, who took over the DCFS late in 1992. But he doesn't dispute that the state and its caseworkers may have put too much emphasis on reunification—in part because of strong messages from Washington.

The problems may be even more basic. By all accounts, caseworkers and supervisors are less prepared today than they were 20 years ago, and only a fraction are actually social workers. Few on the front lines are willing, or able, to make tough calls or buck the party line. In the end, says Deborah Daro, research director of the National Committee to Prevent Child Abuse, "the worker may say, 'Yeah, it's bad, but what's the alternative? I'll let this one go and pray to God they don't kill him'."

In most cases, they don't. Nevertheless, children who grow up in violent homes beyond the age of 8 or 10 risk becoming so emotionally and psychologically damaged that they can never be repaired. "The danger," says Robert Halpern, a professor of child development at the Erikson Institute in Chicago, "is not just the enormous dam-

age to the kid himself, but producing the next generation of monsters."

Clifford Triplett is an all-too-pointed reminder of how severe the injuries can be. He has gained eight pounds, and his physical prognosis is good. But there are many other concerns. "When he came, he didn't know the difference between a car and a truck, the difference between pizza and a hot dog," says his hospital social worker, Kathleen Egan. "People were not introducing these things to him." Robinson and McKinney are awaiting trial on charges of aggravated battery and felony cruelty. McKinney's attorney blames Robinson for the alleged abuse; Robinson's attorney declined to comment. Clifford is waiting for a foster home. A few weeks ago he had his first conversation with his mother in months. His first words: "Are you sorry for whipping me?"

Band–Aids Don't Work

ACCORDING TO THE CASEWORKER'S report, 2½-year-old Saonnia Bolden's family was the model of success. Over 100 days, a homemaker from an Illinois family-preservation program called Family First worked with Sadie Williams and her boyfriend Clifford Baker. A second helper—a caseworker—shopped with Sadie for shoes and some furniture for her apartment; she evaluated Sadie's cooking, housekeeping and budgeting. She even took her to dinner to celebrate her progress. On March 17, 1992, the caseworker wrote a report recommending that Sadie's case be closed: "Due to the presence of homemaker, the amount of stress and frustration has been reduced. Sadie appears to have a lot more patience with her children and she continues to improve her disciplinary techniques."

What the Family First caseworker evidently didn't know was that, just hours before she filed her report, Saonnia had been beaten and scalded to death. Prosecutors claim that Williams, angered because her young daughter had wet herself, laid the child in the bathtub and poured scalding water over her genitals and her buttocks. Williams and Baker were charged with first-degree murder; lawyers for Baker and Williams blame each other's client. Regardless of who was responsible, this wasn't

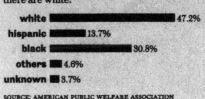

Race of Foster Children

Contrary to public opinion, foster care is not dominated by minorities. Nearly half the kids there are white.

white	47.2%
hispanic	13.7%
black	30.8%
others	4.6%
unknown	3.7%

SOURCE: AMERICAN PUBLIC WELFARE ASSOCIATION

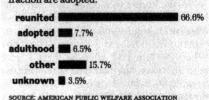

Where Do Children Go?

Two thirds of children who leave foster care are reunited with their parents; only a fraction are adopted.

reunited	66.6%
adopted	7.7%
adulthood	6.5%
other	15.7%
unknown	3.5%

SOURCE: AMERICAN PUBLIC WELFARE ASSOCIATION

A One-Man Children's Crusade

Twenty years ago, an angry young lawyer named Patrick Murphy wrote a book that exposed an injustice: state social workers too often seized children from parents whose worst crime was poverty. Today Murphy is the scourge of a child-welfare system that too often leaves kids with their abusive, drugged-out parents. He has not made the about-face quietly. In many cities, confidentiality laws protect caseworkers and judges from public outcries when their bad decisions lead to a parent's murder of a child. In Chicago, Murphy calls blistering press conferences to parcel out the blame. To those who say he picks on parents who are poor, black and victimized, he hotly retorts: "So are their kids."

Murphy is the Cook County (Ill.) public guardian, the court-appointed lawyer for 31,000 abused and neglected children. He's also a self-righteous crusader. last year, campaigning to rein in one "family preservation" program, Murphy sent every Illinois legislator color autopsy photos of a little girl scalded and beaten to death after caseworkers taught her family new disciplinary skills. It's a loner's life, poring over murder files and railing at fellow liberals who think the poor can do no wrong. "A lot of people hate my guts," Murphy shrugs. "I can't blame them."

His views on family reunification changed because child abuse changed. Drugs now suffuse 80 percent of the caseload; sexual and physical assaults that once taxed the imagination are now common. Murphy believes that most families should be reunited—but the child-welfare agencies waste years trying to patch up dead-end families when they should be hurrying to free children for early adoption. Murphy, 55, blames such folly on bleeding hearts like himself, who once lobbied for generous social programs without working to curb welfare dependency and other ills.

Now children of troubled families must pay the price—sometimes with their lives. "We inadvertently pushed a theory of irresponsibility," he says. "And we created a monster—kids having kids."

To Murphy's critics, that smacks of scorn for the less fortunate. "He's a classic bully," says Diane Redleaf of the Legal Assistance Foundation of Chicago, who represents parents trying to win back their kids. "Thousands of poor families are *not* torturing their children." Redleaf has drafted legislation that would force Murphy to get a judge's order each time he wants to speak about a case. That would protect children's privacy—and give the system a convenient hiding place. Murphy will fight to keep things as they are. His is the only job, he says, in which a lawyer knows that his clients are truly innocents.

J.M.

---

the first assault. The autopsy on Saonnia's visibly malnourished body found 62 cuts, bruises, burns, abrasions and wrist scars, among other injuries. Eleven were still healing—meaning they probably happened during the time the homemaker was working with the family.

Since Illinois's Family First program began in 1988, at least six children have died violently during or after their families received help. In many other instances, children were injured, or simply kept in questionable conditions. Such numbers may look small compared with the 17,000 children in Illinois who've been in the program. But to critics, the deaths and injuries underscore the danger of using reunification efforts for deeply troubled families. Gelles, once an ardent supporter of family preservation, is adamant about its failures. "We've learned in health psychology that you don't waste intervention on those with no intention of changing," he argues.

A University of Chicago report card issued last year gave the Illinois Family First program barely passing grades. Among the findings: Family First led to a slight *increase* in the overall number of children later placed outside their homes; it had no effect on subsequent reports of maltreatment; it had only mixed results in such areas as improving housing, economics and parenting, and it had no effect on getting families out of the DCFS system. John R. Schuerman, who helped write the report, says it's too simplistic to call Family First a

failure. Still, he concedes that the assumption that large numbers of households can be saved with intensive services "just may not be the case."

Nevertheless, in the last decade, family-preservation programs have become so entrenched there's little chance they'll be junked. Health and Human Services Secretary Donna Shalala carefully sidesteps the question of whether it's possible to carry the reunification philosophy too far. Asked where she would draw the line in defining families beyond repair, she diplomatically suggests that the answers be left to child-welfare experts. "Nobody wants to leave children in dangerous situations," says Shalala. "The goal is to shrewdly pick cases in which the right efforts might help keep a

family together." So far, not even the experts have come up with a sure way to do that.

Where Do We Go From Here?

POLICYMAKERS BELIEVE THAT IF THEY could just remove the stresses from a family, they wouldn't have to remove the child. But critics argue that the entire child-welfare network must approach the idea of severing parents' rights as aggressively as it now approaches family reunification. That means moving kids through the system and into permanent homes quickly—before they're so damaged that they won't fit in anywhere. In theory, the Adoption Assistance Act already requires that, but no state enforces that part of

CLIFFORD TRIPLETT

"I talked to him [Eddie Robinson, Cliff's mother's boyfriend] about Cliff and the old scars on his back. Robinson said . . . Cliff had a tendency to get into a lot of mischief," the caseworker noted. "This is why Cliff was whipped—however I told him that he shouldn't be beat on his back. Robinson promised to go easy on the discipline. (Said he wasn't doing the whipping.)"

FROM CASEWORKER REPORT ON CLIFFORD TRIPLETT

the law. Illinois is typical: even in the most straightforward cases, a petition to terminate parental rights is usually the start of a two-year judicial process—*after* the 18-month clean-up-your-act phase.

Why does it take so long? Once a child is in foster care, the system breathes a sigh of relief and effectively forgets about him. If the child is removed from an abusive home, the assumption is that he's safe. "There's always another reason to give the parent the benefit of the doubt," says Daro. "They lose their job, the house burns down, the aunt is murdered. Then they get another six-month extension, and it happens all over again. Meanwhile, you can't put a child in a Deepfreeze and suspend his life until the parent gets her life together."

In the most blatant abuse and neglect cases, parents' rights should be terminated immediately, reformers say. In less-severe cases, parents should be given no more than six to 12 months to shape up. "You have social workers saying, 'She doesn't visit her child because she has no money for carfare'," says Murphy. "But what parent wouldn't walk over mountains of glass to see their kids? You know it's a crock. You have to tell people we *demand* responsibility."

And if parents can't take care of them, where are all these children supposed to go? With just 100,000 foster parents in the system, finding even temporary homes is difficult. For starters, reformers suggest professionalizing foster care, paying parents decent salaries to stay home and care for several children at a time. Long range, many believe that society will have to confront its ambivalence toward interracial adoptions. Perhaps the most controversial alternative is the move to revive orphan-

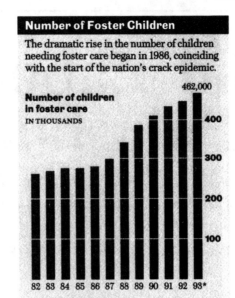

Number of Foster Children

The dramatic rise in the number of children needing foster care began in 1986, coinciding with the start of the nation's crack epidemic.

Number of children in foster care
IN THOUSANDS

462,000

*YEARS ARE FISCAL YEARS. 1993 IS AN ESTIMATE.
SOURCE: AMERICAN PUBLIC WELFARE ASSOCIATION

ages, at least for teenagers, who are the least likely to be adopted. One of the fiercest supporters is Maddux, the new supervising judge of Cook County's abuse section. Maddux, 59, says that his own family was so desperately poor they once lived in a shanty with two rooms—one of which was an old car. When the family broke up, he and his younger brother went to live at Boys Town, Neb. He believes that many foster children today could benefit from the nurturing-yet-demanding atmosphere of group living. "I wasn't raised in a family after the age of 12," Maddux says. "I didn't miss it. Thousands of kids at Boys Town knew that being in a destitute, nonfunctioning family was a lot worse than not

being in a family." In Illinois, some are taking the idea seriously—among the proposals is turning closed military bases into campuses for kids.

Ironically, Illinois could wind up with one of the best child-welfare systems in the nation. Pressed by public outrage over Joseph Wallace's death, state legislators last year passed a law that puts the best interest of children ahead of their parents'. Foster parents will be given a voice in abuse and neglect cases. And the DCFS is beefing up caseworker training, so that those in the field will learn how to spot dangerous situations more quickly.

Some of the toughest changes are already underway in Cook County. The much-criticized Family First program has been replaced with a smaller, more intensely scrutinized family-preservation project known as Homebuilders. And the county's juvenile-court system has been expanded so that there are now 14 judges, not eight, hearing abuse and neglect cases; that cuts each judge's caseload from about 3,500 to about 2,000 children per year. But reform doesn't come cheap. The DCFS budget has tripled since 1988, to $900 million, and it could top $1 billion in the next fiscal year.

Whether any of this can save lives, it's too soon to tell. In its report on Joseph Wallace's death, the blue-ribbon committee was pessimistic. "It would be comforting to believe that the facts of this case are so exceptional that such cases are not likely to happen again," the panel wrote with a dose of bitterness. "That hope is unfounded." The temptation, of course, is to blame some faceless system. But the fate of children really lies with everyone—caseworkers, supervisors, prosecutors, judges—doing their jobs.

Child Labor in Pakistan

Pakistan has recently passed laws greatly limiting child labor and indentured servitude—but those laws are universally ignored, and some 11 million children, aged four to fourteen, keep that country's factories operating, often working in brutal and squalid conditions.

JONATHAN SILVERS

Jonathan Silvers is a writer and an independent television producer specializing in international affairs and human-rights issues.

No two negotiations for the sale of a child are alike, but all are founded on the pretense that the parties involved have the best interests of the child at heart. On this sweltering morning in the Punjab village of Wasan Pura a carpet master, Sadique, is describing for a thirty-year-old brick worker named Mirza the advantages his son will enjoy as an apprentice weaver. "I've admired your boy for several months," Sadique says. "Nadeem is bright and ambitious. He will learn far more practical skills in six months at the loom than he would in six years of school. He will be taught by experienced craftsmen, and his pay will rise as his skills improve. Have no doubt, your son will be thankful for the opportunity you have given him, and the Lord will bless you for looking so well after your own."

Sadique has given this speech before. Like many manufacturers, he recruits children for his workshop almost constantly, and is particularly aggressive in courting boys aged seven to ten. "They make ideal employees," he says. "Boys at this stage of development are at the peak of their dexterity and endurance, and they're wonderfully obedient—they'd work around the clock if I asked them." But when pressed he admits, "I hire them first and foremost because they're economical. For what I'd pay one second-class adult weaver I can get three boys, sometimes four, who can produce first-class rugs in no time."

The low cost of child labor gives Sadique and his fellow manufacturers a significant advantage in the Western marketplace, where they undersell their competitors from countries prohibiting child labor, often by improbable amounts. Not surprisingly, American and European consumers are attracted to low-price, high-quality products, and imports of child-made carpets from Pakistan have trebled in the past two decades. Pakistan's carpet makers have satisfied this surging demand by expanding production at existing factories and opening new ones wherever they can. To maximize their returns, virtually all these factories employ children, and an increasing number do so exclusively. Somewhere between 500,000 and one million Pakistani children aged four to fourteen now work as full-time carpet weavers. UNICEF believes that they make up 90 percent of the carpet makers' work force.

Sadique delivers his speech at volume and accompanies it with an assortment of gestures—nods, waves, raised eyebrows—that are as theatrical as they are out of place in his shambles of a workshop. He concludes with a smile and, just in case Mirza does not appreciate his generosity, adds a wistful coda: "I wish my father had given me such an opportunity." Mirza seems doubtful, perhaps because his son is

EACH YEAR MILLIONS OF CHILDREN IN PAKISTAN ENTER THE LABOR FORCE, WHERE THEY COMPETE WITH ADULTS—OFTEN EVEN WITH THEIR PARENTS—FOR WHAT LITTLE WORK IS AVAILABLE. AT LEAST HALF THESE CHILDREN ARE UNDER THE AGE OF TEN.

seven years old, perhaps because he has seen too many of his neighbors' children suffer through similar opportunities. But he returns Sadique's smile and says in a faint voice that he hopes Nadeem will learn enough to work one day as a journeyman weaver or, better still, to open a workshop of his own.

Whatever misgivings Mirza has at the moment are overshadowed by his poverty, which is extreme and worsening. He supports a family of five by working at a nearby kiln, molding bricks by hand for up to eighty hours a week. The work pays poorly at the best of times, and on occasion it does not pay at all. Three weeks earlier a monsoon destroyed several thousand unfired bricks that had been left drying on factory grounds. The kiln owner held the workers accountable for the damage and refused to pay them for the two weeks they had spent making the bricks. The "fine," as the owner called it, proved ruinous. Already months behind on their rent and in debt to the village merchants, Mirza and his wife concluded that the only way to avoid eviction was to bond their eldest child to one of the district's manufacturers. Sadique was their first choice: he was prosperous, his workshop was near their home, and he was rumored to have an urgent need for child laborers, which they believed would translate into a high price for Nadeem.

They were half right. The workshop has a perpetual need for children, but Sadique is unwilling to pay a premium for them. For that matter, he is unwilling to pay market rates. Having dispensed with the niceties, he offers Mirza 5,000 rupees ($146) for five years of his son's labor. It's a paltry sum—roughly two months' earnings for an adult weaver. Mirza was expecting an offer at least three times as high. "Business is off this year," Sadique says, by way of preempting Mirza's objections. "When things improve, I may be able to give you another two or three hundred. Many fathers would be glad to get half this amount."

Mirza is distressed. He is a small man, stooped and wasted from his years at the kiln, his skin and tunic flecked with soot. Like most laborers, he is

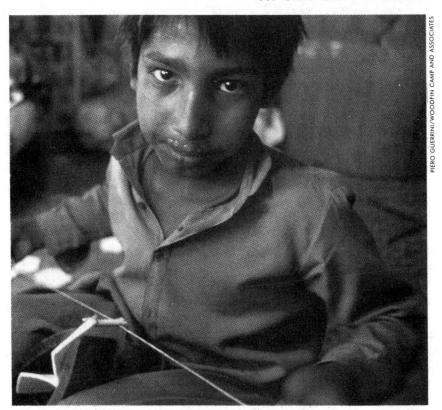

Stitching soccer balls in a factory in Sialkot

acutely aware of his caste, and in the presence of those whom he deems his betters is deferential to the point of abjectness. Bravely he asks Sadique for another thousand rupees, though he couches the request in the most self-deprecating terms he knows. "Sir, my family's survival depends on your charity. You will always be remembered in our prayers as our savior from beggary and destitution." To his relief, Sadique agrees at once, extending a manicured hand with a speed that suggests he was prepared to pay more and got a bargain. In any event, he can afford to be generous. The money he offers Mirza, called a *peshgi*, will be paid in installments, and he will deduct from it all costs associated with Nadeem's maintenance and training. Many of the deductions are contrived and inflated. Parents are charged for their children's food and tools, the raw materials they use, the errors they make, the amount of time the master spends "educating" them. Throughout Pakistan parents consider themselves fortunate if at the end of their child's service the master has paid them one third of the *peshgi*.

Mirza is unaware of these deductions and, eager to make his escape, does not ask questions that might complicate the proceedings. He consummates the deal by shaking Sadique's hand (after wiping his own on his tunic) and accepting from him a first installment of 200 rupees. The parties are bound only by their word: no contracts are signed; no witnesses are present. "Your boy now belongs to me," Sadique says as Mirza pockets the banknotes. "Please understand that so long as he works under my roof he is answerable only to me. Inform him that the needs of my shop take priority over those of his family, and he must do all he can to please me. If he does not, we will all be disappointed, him most of all." Mirza thanks the master for his kindness, bows low, and runs off to relay this information to his son.

An Inexhaustible Labor Pool

CHILD labor has assumed epidemic proportions in Pakistan. Statistics are unreliable, but the Human Rights Commission of Pakistan

(HRCP) last year estimated the number of Pakistani working children to be "realistically in the region of 11–12 million." At least half these children are under the age of ten. Despite a recent series of laws prohibiting child labor and indentured servitude, children make up a quarter of the unskilled work force, and can be found in virtually every factory, every workshop, every field. They earn on average a third of the adult wage. Certain industries, notably carpet making and brick making, cannot survive without them. One World Bank economist maintains that Pakistan's economic viability correlates with the number of children in its factories. The child labor pool is all but inexhaustible, owing in part to a birth rate that is among the world's highest and to an education system that can accommodate only about a third of the country's school-age children. Each year millions of children enter the labor force, where they compete with adults—often even with their parents—for what little work is available. In many regions the surplus of cheap child labor has depressed the already inadequate adult wage to the point where a parent and child together now earn less than the parent alone earned a year ago. As long as children are put to work, poverty will spread and standards of living will continue to decline.

To be sure, child labor is an institution throughout the Third World, and its incidence has been increasing in countries that are usually described as advanced. The worldwide population of children under fourteen who work full-time is thought to exceed 200 million. But few countries have done less to abolish or to contain the practice than Pakistan. And fewer still have a ruling class that opposes workplace reform and human-rights initiatives as vigorously. Given its relative prosperity, its constitutional prohibition against child labor, and its leaders' signatures on every UN human- and child-rights convention, Pakistan's de facto dependency on child labor is troubling and to its critics inexcusable.

"Inaction speaks louder than words," says I. A. Rehman, the director of the HRCP. "This government is in continuous violation of the Convention on the Rights of the Child, and has consistently refused to enforce those very laws it enacted to protect its most vulnerable citizens. We have far more in the way of resources and legal remedies than China, India, and Indonesia, and we do far less for our young than they. The problem is lack of political will. The problem is greed."

The median age of children now entering the Pakistani work force is seven. Two years ago it was eight. Two years from now it may be six. In the lowest castes, children become laborers almost as soon as they can walk. Much of the nation's farmland is worked by toddlers, yoked teams of three-, four-, and five-year-olds who plough, seed, and glean fields from dawn to dusk. On any given morning the canal banks and irrigation ditches in rural villages are lined with urchins who stand no taller than the piles of laundry they wash for their wealthier neighbors. Even the world-class industries of Islamabad, the modern capital, are staffed in large part by children and adolescents; politicians traveling to the National Assembly can't help noticing the ragged youths entering and exiting the brick factories, steel mills, and stone-crushing plants at all hours of the day and night. These children work with a minimum of adult supervision. An overseer comes by periodically to mark their progress and to give them instructions or a few encouraging blows, but for the better part of the workday they are left to themselves. "Children are cheaper to run than tractors and smarter than oxen," explains one Rawalpindi landowner. He prefers field hands between seven and ten years old, "because they have the most energy, although they lack discipline."

In rural areas children are raised without health care, sanitation, or education; many are as starved for affection as for food. As soon as they're old enough to have an elementary understanding of their circumstances, their parents teach them that they are expected to pay their

way, to make sacrifices, and, if necessary, to travel far from home and live with strangers. "When my children were three, I told them they must be prepared to work for the good of the family," says Asma, a Sheikhupura villager who bonded her five children to masters in distant villages. "I told them again and again that they would be bonded at five. And when the time came for them to go, they were prepared and went without complaint."

Bonding is common practice among the lower castes, and although the decision to part with their children is not made lightly, parents do not agonize over it. Neither, evidently, do the children, who regard bonding as a rite of passage, the event that transforms them into adults. Many look forward to it in the same way that American children look forward to a first communion or getting a driver's license. They are eager to cast off childhood, even if to do so means taking on adult burdens. Irfana, a twelve-year-old schoolgirl who spent four years as a brick worker before she was freed by an anti-slavery organization, remembers feeling relieved when her father handed her over at age six to a kiln owner. "My friends and I knew that sooner or later we'd be sent off to the factories or the fields. We were tired of doing chores and minding infants. We looked forward to the day when we'd be given responsibilities and the chance to earn money. At the time work seemed glamorous and children who worked seemed quite important."

She soon learned otherwise. "For the masters, bonded children are a commodity. My master bought, sold, and traded us like livestock, and sometimes he shipped us great distances. The boys were beaten frequently to make them work long hours. The girls were often violated. My best friend got ill after she was raped, and when she couldn't work, the master sold her to a friend of his in a village a thousand kilometers away. Her family was never told where she was sent, and they never saw her again."

Early in this decade the Pakistan National Assembly enacted two labor laws meant to curb such practices. The first, The Employment of Children Act of 1991, prohibited the use of child labor in hazardous occupations and environments. The second, The Bonded Labor Act of 1992, abolished indentured servitude and the *peshgi* system. As progressive as these laws were, the government failed to provide for their implementation and enforcement. It also neglected to inform the millions of working children and indentured servants that they were free and released from their debts. "We prefer to leave enforcement to the discretion of the police," says a Ministry of Labor official. "They understand best the needs of their community. Law is not an absolute. We must expect a certain flexibility on the part of those who enforce it. Could this sometimes mean looking the other way? Absolutely."

A Diminutive Entrepreneur

THE farther authorities are from a major city in Pakistan, the less likely are to pursue violators of the child-labor laws. To leave Lahore, the nation's intellectual and commercial center, is to enter a land populated and run by children. The change is as abrupt as it is extreme. The roads just beyond the city limits are congested with donkey carts, all of them driven by teamsters of eight or nine. Boys seem to have a monopoly on roadside attractions: gas stations, auto-repair centers, restaurants. When I pull into the Star Petroleum station on the Ferozpur Road, five miles from Lahore, three boys rush out of the garage to service my car. They are twelve, eight, and seven, and wear uniforms intended for men twice their size. The eldest has rolled up his pants and sleeves, but his colleagues helplessly trail theirs in the dirt. While the older boys fill my tank with a rusted hand pump, the youngest climbs into the hood and cleans the windshield with a dangling sleeve. When I pull away, the boys rush back to the garage and to a diesel engine they are attempting to rebuild between fill-ups. No adults are visible on the premises.

Adults are also in short supply at the crossroads markets that provide villagers with everything from prayer mats to surgical instruments. Twelve of the fifteen stands at the Tohkar Road market are managed by children under fourteen. The fruit stand is run by a tyrannical eight-year-old boy and his four- and five-year-old sisters. The boy spends his morning slicing melons with a knife half his size, while behind him the girls sort cartloads of fruit. At the next stall two eleven-year-old cousins fashion sandals out of discarded tires. They work from dawn to dusk six days a week, and make more than 1,200 pairs each week. Behind the last stall another boy is struggling to unload a stack of carpets from his donkey cart. He weighs seventy pounds. The twenty-odd carpets in his cart weigh sixty pounds apiece, and it takes him ten minutes of yanking, hefting, and cursing to get each one into the stall. The stall's proprietor watches him with interest, but his concern is strictly for the merchandise. He is a tall, heavyset forty-year-old who looks as if he could unload the entire cart in fifteen minutes without breaking a sweat. But he makes no move to help the boy, and seems to regard his exertions as routine. So do the passersby. And, for that matter, so does the boy.

His name is Faiz. A lively nine-year-old, he has been working as a hauler since he was six. He attended school for two years, but dropped out when an elderly neighbor offered him an advantageous lease on the cart and donkey. He runs the business alone, and spends his days scrounging for hauling jobs and shuttling produce, scrap metal, and crafts around six villages. He averages sixty miles a week—no easy feat with a donkey that trots at three miles an hour. "The work is painful and the days are long, but I earn enough to feed myself and tend the donkey," Faiz says with an entrepreneur's pride. The key to his success is underbidding the competition; his rates are a tenth of his pre-

decessor's. "It is reasonable that people should pay me less. My equipment is the same as an adult's, but I am small and have a fraction of an adult's strength. I take longer to make deliveries, so I must charge less. My hope is that the more goods I move, the stronger I will get and the more I can charge."

Soon after I arrived in Pakistan, I arranged a trip to a town whose major factories were rumored to enslave very young children. I found myself hoping during the journey there that the children I saw working in the fields, on the roads, at the marketplaces, would prepare me for the worst. They did not. No amount of preparation could have lessened the shock and revulsion I felt on entering a sporting-goods factory in the town of Sialkot, seventy miles from Lahore, where scores of children, most of them aged five to ten, produce soccer balls by hand for forty rupees, or about $1.20, a day. The children work eighty hours a week in near-total darkness and total silence. According to the foreman, the darkness is both an economy and a precautionary measure; child-rights activists have difficulty taking photographs and gathering evidence of wrongdoing if the lighting is poor. The silence is to ensure product quality: "If the children speak, they are not giving their complete attention to the product and are liable to make errors." The children are permitted one thirty-minute meal break each day; they are punished if they take longer. They are also punished if they fall asleep, if their workbenches are sloppy, if they waste material or miscut a pattern, if they complain of mistreatment to their parents or speak to strangers outside the factory. A partial list of "infractions" for which they may be punished is tacked to a wall near the entrance. It's a document of dubious utility: the children are illiterate. Punishments are doled out in a storage closet at the rear of the factory. There, amid bales of wadding and leather, children are hung upside down by their knees, starved, caned, or lashed. (In the interests of economy the foreman uses a lash made from scrap soccer-ball leather.) The punishment room is a standard feature of a Pakistani factory, as common as a lunchroom at a Detroit assembly plant.

The town's other factories are no better, and many are worse. Here are brick kilns where five-year-olds work hip-deep in slurry pits, where adolescent girls stoke furnaces in 160° heat. Here are tanneries where nursing mothers mix vats of chemical dye, textile mills where eight-year-olds tend looms and breathe air thick with cotton dust.

When confronted with questions from a foreigner about their use of child labor, industrialists respond in one of two ways: they attack the questioner or they deliver a lengthy lecture about the role of children in Pakistan's development. The attacks are not always verbal. Last June a Norwegian trade-union delegation was attacked at the Sialkot sporting-goods factory by three or four armed men who were believed to work for the factory's owner. The delegation's guide and cameraman were severly beaten and the latter required hospitalization. The police characterized the attackers as "civic-minded" and warned the delegation against inspecting other area factories and "unnecessarily antagonizing factory owners."

More common, though, is the industrialist who ushers the foreign investigator into his office, plies him with coffee and cake, and tells him in his friendliest manner that child labor is a tradition the West cannot understand and must not attempt to change. "Our country has historically suffered from a labor shortage, a deficit of able-bodied men," says Imran Malik, a prominent Lahore carpet exporter and the vice-chairman of the Pakistan Carpet Manufacturers and Exporters Association. "Children have compensated for this shortage. They have worked when adults could not. They have helped construct Pakistan's infrastructure and advanced its industry. For thousands of years children have worked alongside their parents in their villages. The work they now do in fac-

tories and workshops is an extension of this tradition, and in most ways an improvement on it. The children earn more than they would elsewhere. They contribute significantly to their family's security and raise their standard of living."

The industrialist's argument is accurate only in its assertion that Pakistani children have traditionally worked with their families. But children seldom worked *outside* the family until the 1960s, when the Islamic Republic made

At the carpet looms of Wasan Pura

a dramatic effort to expand its manufacturing base. This led to a spectacular and disproportionately large increase in the number of children working outside the home, outside the village, at factories and workshops whose owners sought to maximize profits by keeping down labor costs. The rise in child abuse was as meteoric as the rise in child labor. The children working in these

factories were beyond the reach or care of their families and were increasingly the victims of industrial accidents, kidnapping, and mistreatment.

A Mixed Curse

"IF employers would apply as much ingenuity to their manufacturing processes as they do to evading labor laws, we'd have no child-labor problem," says Najanuddin Najmi, the director general of the Workers Education Program, a government agency. "There's little doubt that inexpensive child labor has fueled Pakistan's economic growth. Entire industries have relocated to Pakistan because of the abundance of cheap child labor and our lax labor laws. At the same time, child labor has hindered our industrial development, especially in the use of advanced technologies.

Why should a manufacturer invest in labor-saving technology when labor-intensive mechanisms are so much cheaper? We are discovering more and more factories that have been redesigned and retooled so that only children can work there."

Child labor has been a mixed curse for all of southern Asia, expanding its industrial capacity while generating an unprecedented assortment of social problems. Not surprisingly, Pakistan's leaders are of two minds on the subject. Speaking officially, they deplore the practice and have nothing but pity for the roughly 11 million children working in factories, in fields, and on the streets. Speaking pragmatically, they regard the practice as a distasteful but unavoidable part of an emerging economy which time and prosperity will end. They are quick to take offense (and quicker to take the offensive) when human-rights activists suggest that they have ignored the problem.

"Westerners conveniently forget their own shameful histories when they come here," says Shabbir Jamal, an adviser to the Ministry of Labor. "Europeans addressed slavery and child labor only after they became prosperous. Pakistan has only now entered an era of economic stability that will allow us to expand our horizons and address social concerns. Just as we are catching up with the West in industrial development, so we are catching up in workplace and social reforms. We are accelerating the pace of reform and have resolved to create viable welfare and educational structures that will eradicate child labor in the foreseeable future."

Foreseeable may be a long way off. At the moment Prime Minister Benazir Bhutto seems more interested in outfitting her army than in reforming Pakistani society; her government has embarked on an ambitious military buildup that has already imperiled the region. Its first victims have been Pakistan's lower castes, the working poor who are accustomed to receiving little in the way of social services and must now make do with less. In 1994 military spending was 240 percent as high as spending on health and education combined; the disparity is expected to widen in years to come. Spending on education remains among the world's lowest. Only 37 percent of Pakistan's 25 million school-age children complete primary school—as compared with a world average of 79 percent and a South Asian average of approximately 50 percent. By the year 2000 less than a third of Pakistani children will attend school. The rest will enter the work force or become beggars.

Behind these statistics lurks an unpleasant truth: despite its modern views on warfare and industrialization, Pakistan remains a feudal society, committed to maintaining traditions that over the centuries have served its upper castes well. The lords—factory owners, exporters, financiers—reflexively oppose any reforms that might weaken their authority, lower their profit margins, or enfranchise the workers. "There is room for improvement in any society," the industrialist Imram Malik says. "But we feel that the present situation is acceptable the way it is. The National Assembly must not rush through reforms without first evaluating their impact on productivity and sales. Our position is that the government must avoid so-called humanitarian measures that harm our competitive advantages." On those rare occasions when a reform does squeak through, the backlash is fierce. For example, when the legislature last year approved a modest tax on bricks to fund an education program, brick-kiln owners staged a ten-day nationwide protest and threatened to suspend production, crippling construction, until the tax was repealed. Trade associations have used similar strong-arm tactics to fight minimum-wage legislation, occupational-safety regulations, and trade-union activity.

"The Charter of Freedom"

WITH a government that is at best ambivalent about social issues and an industrial sector resistant to workplace reform, the task of abolishing child labor has fallen to the human-rights community. But in a country where corruption is pervasive and education scarce, social activists are everyone's natural enemy. The ruling class despises them for assaulting its profitable traditions. The lower castes suspect them of ulterior motives. (Laborers are forever asking activists, "Why would an educated man trouble himself with the poor?") Consequently, activists are frequent targets of slander, police harassment, and lawsuits. They are beaten just as frequently, and on occasion they are killed.

Yet they persist, and sometimes they prevail. If human-rights organizations are judged by the number of people they have helped, the Bonded Labor Liberation Front is probably the most successful in Pakistan. Since its founding, in 1988, the BLLF has led the fight against bonded and child labor, liberating 30,000 adults and children—frequently entire families—from brick kilns, carpet factories, and farms, and placing 11,000 children in its own primary school system (its motto: "Struggle against slavery through education"). At the same time, it has won 25,000 high-court cases against abusive and unscrupulous employers, and helped to push the recent labor legislation through the National Assembly.

"Our victories amount to a hardship," says Ehsan Ulla Khan, the BLLF's founder and guiding force. "The state has done nothing to enforce the anti-slavery laws or even to inform the public that child and bonded labor have been outlawed. It's evident that if the enslaved workers are to be delivered from bondage, private citizens will have to do the delivering. That is, we will have to proclaim the end of slavery, educate workers, monitor employer compliance, and take legal action when necessary, because the state lacks the will and resources to do so."

With little funding, the BLLF wages a two-front war against enterprises that use child and bonded labor. While its legal advisers engage the courts and the legislature, its field staff shuttles around the country, informing workers of their recently acquired rights and distributing a pamphlet known as "The Charter of Freedom," which enumerates those rights in simple language. If a bonded laborer—child or adult—asks for its help, the BLLF takes whatever legal action is necessary to secure his or her release.

These days a surprising number of workers are refusing the pamphlet and turning their backs on BLLF staff members. This is an expression less of ingratitude than of fear. Employers throughout Pakistan are cautioning their workers against consorting with reformers who spread "false rumors" about the end of bonded labor. Many workers have been threatened with dismissal or violence if they speak with "the abolitionists" or are caught with "illegal communist propaganda."

So effective is the factory owners' disinformation campaign that workers literally flee when approached by BLLF staff members. This happened recently outside a Muridke brick factory to a BLLF leader I'll call Tariq. The fifty-odd kiln workers leaving the factory at the end of the workday scattered in all directions when they noticed Tariq lingering outside the factory gate, pamphlets in hand. One soot-covered girl of eight, left behind in the confusion, burst into tears when Tariq asked if she needed help. Between sobs the girl pleaded, "Please, sir, I have nothing to tell you. Please let me go."

Tariq did, albeit reluctantly. He has witnessed scenes like this countless times; they happen more and more often. If they discourage him (how could they not?), he takes care not to let anyone know. He describes his work as "an outgrowth of my patriotism." "What we do is meant not to shame Pakistan before the world but to create a Pakistan that respects the rights of all its peoples and encourages human potential." Tariq is a tall, pensive thirty-nine-year-old, an artist by training and by temperament. He traces his interest in child labor to an afternoon five years ago when an anti-slavery activist entered his graphic-design study in need of a brochure for his struggling organization. "Ehsan Ulla Khan had little money to spare, and he intimated that he'd rather not pay at all for the design work," Tariq told me. "I was just starting out in business and had no interest in politics or human rights. But I was moved by his photos of the children and agreed to do the work." Within six months Tariq was preparing all of the BLLF's documents; within a year he was overseeing its operations. Today he is its factotum: equal parts tactician, recruiter, instructor, fundraiser, morale booster.

IN THE LOWEST CASTES, CHILDREN BECOME LABORERS ALMOST AS SOON AS THEY CAN WALK. BY THE YEAR 2000 LESS THAN A THIRD OF PAKISTANI CHILDREN WILL ATTEND SCHOOL. THE REST WILL ENTER THE WORK FORCE OR BECOME BEGGARS.

Some days he is also part spy. In addition to their assigned duties, the BLLF's 600 staff members are encouraged to spend their free time scrounging for leads on factory owners who are especially abusive to children. All rumors are passed on to the BLLF's Lahore headquarters. Tariq does what he can to substantiate the worst of them, usually by touring the factories. It's a duty he dislikes. For one thing, it's exhausting: there are too many leads, too many rumors to verify. For another, it's dangerous: he's had numerous clashes with publicity-shy employers and their thugs. He prefers to travel alone, reasoning that one man is less conspicuous and less of a threat than is a group. And despite his reservations he is adept at subterfuge, at gaining entry to factories by masquerading as a laborer, a wholesaler, an exporter. "I do not misrepresent myself," he says. "But if a foreman mistakes me for a businessman or a wholesaler, I don't correct him."

His first stop one day last summer was a carpet workshop in a village twenty-four miles from Lahore. The village amounted to thirty brick huts, and the workshop was small in proportion—about the size of a subway car, and about as appealing. The long, narrow room contained a dozen upright looms. On each rough-hewn workbench between the looms squatted a carpet weaver. The room was dark and airless. Such light as there was came from a single ceiling fixture, two of its four bulbs burned out. A thermometer read 105°, and the mud walls were hot to the touch. A window promised some relief, but it was closed against fabric-eating insects.

Tariq entered quietly, in slacks, shirt, and patent-leather loafers. This outfit is uncommon in the provinces; he hoped it marked him as a person with Western tastes, and his vehicle, a Toyota Land Cruiser (donated to the BLLF by UNICEF), which he had parked conspicuously close to the entrance, marked him as a man of means—a buyer, a broker, an exporter. The weavers smiled at him, and a few bowed, but no one dared speak to him. Tariq took advantage of their reverence—and the master's absence—by circling the room, noting its conditions. After two circuits he began guessing the ages of the young weavers: "Are you twelve?" The boy nodded. Tariq pointed to the next.

"Fourteen?" Another nod and a smile. "Ten?" This time the nod was shy, and someone mentioned that the day before had been the boy's birthday. Tariq wished him health and happiness.

Of the twelve weavers, five were eleven to fourteen, and four were under ten. The two youngest were brothers named Akbar and Ashraf, aged eight and nine. They had been bonded to the carpet master at age five, and now worked six days a week at the shop. Their workday started at 6:00 A.M. and ended at 8:00 P.M., except, they said, when the master was behind on his quotas and forced them to work around the clock. They were small, thin, malnourished, their spines curved from lack of exercise and from squatting before the loom. Their hands were covered with calluses and scars, their fingers gnarled from repetitive work. Their breathing was labored, suggestive of tuberculosis. Collectively these ailments, which pathologists call captive-child syndrome, kill half of Pakistan's working children by age twelve.

Tariq and I watched Akbar in silence for some time. A hand-knotted carpet is made by tying short lengths of fine colored thread to a lattice of heavier white threads. The process is labor-intensive and tedious: a single four-by-six-foot carpet contains well over a million knots and takes an experienced weaver four to six months to complete. The finest, most intricate carpets have the highest density of knots. The smaller the knot, the more knots the weaver can cram into his lattice and the more valuable the finished carpet. Small knots are, of course, made most easily by small hands. Each carpet Akbar completed would retail in the United States for about $2,000—more than the boy would earn in ten years.

Observing a child carpet weaver at work generates in an American alternating currents of admiration and anger. At one moment the boy seems a prodigy, his carpet a lesson in geometry and colors. His patience is remarkable; his artistry seems effortless and of the highest order—comparable to, say, that of a great medieval tapestry

master. The next moment he fumbles with his scissors, and one notices a welt on his forearm. Suddenly the monotony of tying thousands of threads each hour seems like torture of the worst sort—like a death sentence, which in a way it is.

After ten minutes Tariq knelt by Akbar's side and said softly, "You're very good at this. The master must be quite pleased with you." The boy shook his head and grimaced. "The master says I am slow and clumsy."

Tariq placed a sympathetic hand on the boy's shoulder. "Have you been punished for poor work?" he asked. The boy shrugged and tied a red knot. Tariq repeated the question. This time the boy tied a dozen knots before answering him, in a conspiratorial whisper. "The master screams at us all the time, and sometimes he beats us," he said. "He is less severe with the younger boys. We're slapped often. Once or twice he lashed us with a cane. I was beaten ten days ago, after I made many errors of color in a carpet. He struck me with his fist quite hard on the face." By way of corroborating this, Akbar lifted a forelock, revealing a multicolored bruise on his right temple. Evidently the master did not consider the blow sufficient punishment: "I was fined one thousand rupees and made to correct the errors by working two days straight." The fine was added to Akbar's debt, and would extend his "apprenticeship" by several months.

"Do you like working here?"

"Oh, no, sir, staying here longer fills me with dread. I know I must learn a trade. But my parents are so far away, and all my friends are in school. My brother and I would like to be with our family. We'd like to play with our friends. This is not the way children should live."

Tariq listened to this outpouring without emotion. He has cultivated what he calls a surgeon's insensitivity to ravaged flesh, "because otherwise my heart would break ten times a day." Neither Akbar nor the others knew that child labor was illegal, that they were

free to leave the workshop whenever they wished.

Tariq left the factory and, on a whim, headed for the district police headquarters. As a rule BLLF members are closely observant of legal procedure, lest they be accused of subversive activity. The organization's legal advisers typically spend weeks drafting a formal complaint against a factory, based on members' espionage, before they register it with a high-court magistrate. Right now, however, Tariq was as interested in testing the responsiveness of the police as in penalizing the factory owner.

The nearest police station is a colonial relic on the Lahore road in Muridke. Tariq was caught up in the usual bureaucratic chaos on entering. The foyer was packed with police officers, soldiers, crime victims, and criminals, half of them shouting, the other half covering their ears against the noise. Every now and then the soldiers tried to impose order on the crowd, but with tattered uniforms and clipless rifles their authority went only so far. Familiar with such outposts, Tariq took his place in a line and forty minutes later was face-to-face with the district sergeant. It was ten in the morning. The sergeant had been at his post for two hours, but it could have been 200 for the way he looked. Tariq told him about the conditions in the workshop, about the children. The sergeant was perplexed. "Is this a crime?" he asked. "No one has ever complained before. What do you want us to do about it?" Tariq suggested sending officers to investigate, along with a medical-services crew for the children.

The sergeant left to consult his superior. Two minutes later he returned with the superintendent, a gracious, mustachioed man of fifty. "We are not unsympathetic to your complaint," the superintendent informed Tariq. "But the place you describe is registered as a home enterprise. It is run by a small landowner, and the workers are his immediate family. Family businesses are exempt from the labor laws. This enterprise is not illegal." The superintendent opened a binder and showed Tariq the workshop's registration certificate. Tariq attempted to correct him, but the superintendent said, "What you say may or may not be true. Unfortunately, our jurisdiction does not include child labor. I have no authority to investigate a private workplace. I have no evidence that the children are working there against their will or that their lives are in jeopardy. The mechanism for doing what you ask simply does not exist here."

Tariq was not disappointed, nor was he surprised. He expected no better, and was even pleased that he had rated an audience with the superintendent. Corruption is pervasive in the justice system: for a small consideration the police will look the other way when employers misuse their workers. In several districts the police are notorious for colluding with employers—supplying factories with children who have been abducted from itinerant poor families, orphanages, schools. Not long ago a boy of nine escaped from an abusive landowner and sought help from a police sergeant at this very station. The boy claimed that he had been held captive and tortured; he begged the police to return him to his parents. Instead the sergeant ordered the "fugitive" returned in shackles to the landowner. The sergeant later made the landowner a gift of the shackles, suggesting that they be used on other disruptive children.

The Death
of Iqbal Masih

IN 1992 Pakistani carpet exports fell for the first time in two decades. The fall was slight in absolute terms—no more than three or four percentage points—but it indicated that Western consumers were shying away from luxury goods made by Third World children. Carpet makers' fears were confirmed when in 1993 and 1994 sales fell sharply in several of the largest markets for Pakistani exports. Since carpets were an important source of foreign currency, the decline sent shock waves throughout the Pakistani economy. At a 1993 conference, officials of the Pakistan Carpet Manufacturers and Exporters Association blamed the decline on "subversive domestic organizations which are conducting misleading and false international media campaigns abroad about the use of child labor in our manufacturing processes." The conference concluded on an optimistic note: "The memory of Western consumers is brief and our enemies' meager resources cannot sustain their destructive campaign for much longer."

Whatever hopes the carpet makers had for a reversal of their misfortunes were dashed in 1994, when human-rights organizations around the world acclaimed a twelve-year-old former slave named Iqbal Masih for his crusade against child labor. A small, sickly boy, Iqbal had been bonded at age four to a village carpet maker. He spent much of the next six years chained to a loom, which he worked fourteen hours a day, six days a week. He was fed just enough to keep him functioning, and was beaten more often than the other children at the workshop, because, unlike them, he defied the master time and again, refusing to work and on occasion attempting to escape. At ten he slipped his chains and sought the help of the BLLF, which secured him his freedom and a place in a primary school.

Frail as he was, Iqbal was a child of rare gifts, possessed of an intellectual maturity beyond his years and a precocious sense of justice. He applied these gifts to the anti-slavery movement, and achieved results that would be impressive for a Nobel laureate, let alone a schoolboy. By his twelfth birthday he had helped to liberate 3,000 children from bondage at textile and brick factories, tanneries, steelworks—industries at the heart of the Pakistani economy. He was subsequently honored by the International Labor Organization, in Sweden; by Reebok, which presented him with its prestigious Human Rights Youth in Action Award (for "his courage and ingenuity in righting a centuries-old wrong") in Boston in December of 1994; and by ABC News, which featured him as its Person of the Week. He used his unlikely celebrity status to remind consumers that "the world's two hundred million enslaved children are your responsibility." Subsequent to his travels millions of people in the United States and Europe searched their souls and decided that they could do without products of doubtful origin from Pakistan, India, and Bangladesh.

Iqbal attained a corresponding notoriety in Pakistan, particularly among the politicians and industrialists whose feudal practices he opposed. They responded with smear campaigns and the occasional threat of violence. Iqbal dismissed these threats, telling his friends that they encouraged him to work harder. He reasoned that grown men would harm a child only as a last resort, when their own position proved vulnerable.

IQBAL ATTAINED NOTORIETY IN PAKISTAN, PARTICULARLY AMONG THE POLITICIANS AND INDUSTRIALISTS WHOSE FEUDAL PRACTICES HE OPPOSED. HE DISMISSED THREATS AGAINST HIM, TELLING HIS FRIENDS THAT THEY ENCOURAGED HIM TO WORK HARDER.

On the evening of April 16, 1995, Easter Sunday, Iqbal Masih was shot dead while visiting relatives in a rural village. Immediately afterward Ehsan Ulla Khan declared that the slain youth was the victim of "a mafia conspiracy." In the days that followed, Khan embellished his conspiracy theory for anyone willing to listen. "I emphatically say that the carpet mafia is responsible for this brutal killing . . . Iqbal has become a symbol of our struggle against slavery and was not afraid to expose the inhuman practices prevailing in the carpet industry. I have no doubt that the police are also a part of the conspiracy." However, Khan did not support his fulminations with evidence. "I do not rely on evidence," he told his critics. "I have my instinct. How else do you explain how, in a village where no murder has occurred for a decade, the one child who poses a threat to the carpet owners is gunned down? Coincidence is never so cruel." To the claim of the local police that Iqbal's murder was an isolated incident Khan retorts, "The evidence can be found if the police could be bothered to look." The killing remains unsolved.

Eight hundred mourners crowded into the Muridke cemetery for Iqbal's funeral. A week later 3,000 protesters, half of them under twelve, marched through the streets of Lahore demanding an end to child labor. A few days after the funeral Khan left Pakistan to consult with children's-rights activists in Europe. There he repeated his accusations to great effect at conferences, on television, before lawmakers. Iqbal was proclaimed a "martyr for the cause of bonded labor"; his murder became a cause célèbre among the intelligentsia. Khan called upon the Human Rights Commission of the United Nations to ban the import and sale of all products made by children, especially carpets. "I appeal to importers and consumers: say no and only no to child-made carpets," he said. "This is the last message of Iqbal. It would be an insult to his blood and memory if people continue to buy child-made products in any part of the world."

Western consumers have responded to Khan's plea. Sales of imported carpets have fallen precipitously in recent months. Bowing to public pressure, importers in the United States, Sweden, Italy, Britain, France, and Germany by last June had canceled carpet orders collectively valued at $10 million. At the same time, human-rights groups and individual sympathizers have donated large sums to support and expand BLLF operations. Ironically, Iqbal's death opened doors and purses that were previously closed to Khan.

Westerners, who have seen economic weapons used to achieve social reforms, might expect canceled orders to result in negotiation and, with luck, accommodation between industrialists and activists. Pakistan's industrialists, however, have chosen the questionable tactic of denying the existence of bonded labor in their factories. Shahid Rashid Butt, the president of the Islamabad Carpet Exporters Association, told his colleagues, "Our industry is the victim of enemy agents who spread lies and fictions around the world that bonded labor and child labor are utilized in the production of hand-knotted carpets. They are not and have never been." He condemned the BLLF and its allies as Jewish and Indian enemies who had launched a systematic campaign to damage the reputation of Pakistan's carpet industry for their own profit. His remarks were enthusiastically endorsed by the Pakistan Carpet Manufacturers and Exporters Association and echoed in the National Assembly.

"These charges flew in the face not just of reason but also of an extraordinary amount of evidence," says I. A. Rehman, the director of the Human Rights Commission of Pakistan. "Anywhere else they would have been laughed at and dismissed. Here they were accepted as fact and acted on." At the urging of politicians and industrialists, Javed Mahmood, the assistant director of Pakistan's Federal Investigation Agency (FIA), last May launched an inquiry into the BLLF on the strength of information he had received from highly placed sources suggesting that the organization was supported by "Pakistan's enemies." He later said, "I consider the information credible and will do all I can to protect our country's commercial interests from unscrupulous enemies." At the same time, Pakistan's leading newspapers began running "exposés" of abolitionist leaders, the nicest of which characterized Ehsan Ulla Khan as a philandering bigamist with "indisputable ties to Jewish and Indian agencies hostile to Pakistan." The publishers of these newspapers are suspected of having large financial interests in industries employing child labor.

The FIA is a secret police force, and one of its best-kept secrets is whom it works for. Nominally an organ of the state, it is not above accepting freelance assignments from prominent individuals and commercial groups. The extent of its extralegal activities is anyone's guess, but a highly respected human-rights investigator believes that "there is close cooperation between carpet interests, feudal lords, segments of the police force, and the administration—district commissioners, the courts, and government officials. Financially resourceful drug barons are also a part of the scene." Whoever the client, the FIA provides an assortment of services straight out of the KGB handbook; wiretaps, tails, searches, arrests, harassment, and varying degrees of corporal punishment.

These services were very much in evidence on a Thursday afternoon in late June, when the FIA raided the BLLF's Lahore headquarters. The detail consisted of ten men, all in plain clothes, who scrambled up four flights of stairs to the tiny office in no time flat. These were not ordinary policemen; this was not the usual surprise "inspection" (read "intimidation") to which all nongovernment organizations are periodically subjected. These were professional agents, lithe and expert, commanded by a severe officer in a freshly pressed safari suit. After lining the BLLF workers up against a wall, he ordered his troops to "confiscate anything that may incriminate them." The agents took a liberal view of "incriminate," and packed up computers, filing cabinets, fax machines, photocopiers, telephones, stationery, posters, bicycles—and the cashbox containing the monthly payroll. Their depredations were supervised by a small man who was distinctly not a policeman. He represented, it turned out, the Pakistan Carpet Manufacturers and Exporters Association. His purpose, he said, was "to protect the interests of legitimate businessmen." Every so often he consulted with the commander.

When one BLLF worker tried to protest, an agent threw her against a wall and held a rifle butt inches from her face. When another worker demanded to see a search warrant, the commander informed her that none was necessary, because "we are acting to prevent terrorism." The association representative nodded in agreement.

Fifteen minutes later the detail was gone, along with the office equipment and furnishings. All that remained was a heap of broken furniture, a workers'-rights poster, and a BLLF flag dangling out an open window. Several staff workers had been taken away as well, to an FIA holding center, where they were interrogated for three days.

Two days later another FIA detail raided the BLLF's "Freedom Campus" training facility in Lahore, along with several of its primary schools around the country. Once again the agents were undiscriminating. They seized everything movable ("items used to obstruct valid commercial interests") and mistreated the staff without respect for position or age. Teachers, drivers, secretaries, and peasant families seeking refuge from violent employers were interrogated along with administrators, advocates, attorneys, and fundraisers.

After an earlier raid on BLLF headquarters Fatima Ghulam, the director of the BLLF's women's-education program, was held for two days. "An officer promised to release me immediately if I agreed to inform against Ehsan Ulla Khan and some of the others," Ghulam says. "He wanted me to testify that Khan is a subversive, an enemy

agent, and that the BLLF receives money from foreign governments. He said he had tapped my telephone conversations and had recordings of me discussing treasonable acts. If I wanted to avoid prosecution, I would have to cooperate with the FIA. I refused, and he kept me without food or water. When I wouldn't speak to him the next day, he slapped me and dragged me around the room."

Not to be outdone, the Pakistani press stepped up its campaign against the BLLF. Last summer a number of newspapers whose editorial pages conceded that they were "troubled by the carpet export crisis" reported the following "facts": Khan himself had murdered Iqbal Masih to win sympathy for the BLLF; Khan had misappropriated BLLF funds to support his own decadent lifestyle; Khan routinely used BLLF schoolchildren as sex partners and house slaves; Iqbal Masih was a twenty-one-year-old midget whom Khan paid to masquerade as a carpet child; the BLLF was an outpost of India's intelligence agency; Khan was an Indian agent working to disgrace the Pakistani carpet trade. These same papers also "revealed" that carpet workers enjoy a higher standard of living than the average citizen, along with better working conditions. "The few children working on carpets," one editorial assured its readers, "do so after school, in their own homes, under the supervision of loving parents."

In the wake of these attacks BLLF operations—child-welfare programs, schools, training and education programs—nearly shut down for lack of funds and staff. Membership has suffered, and many of the legal advisers and support staff, fearing reprisals, have fallen away. Those who remain are subject to almost constant harassment: the fortunate ones have their telephones tapped; the less fortunate are shadowed around the clock. At the same time, the courts have ignored their complaints

about child labor and abusive treatment by employers.

Just in case the intention of the Federal Investigation Agency was unclear, Assistant Director Mahmood in early June charged Ehsan Ulla Khan, who was still abroad, and a BLLF strategist named Zafaryab Ahmad with sedition and economic treason, capital offenses punishable by death. According to Mahmood, "The accused men conspired with the Indian espionage agency to exploit the murder of Iqbal Masih . . . causing a recurring huge financial loss to Pakistan's business interests abroad and paving the way for India to wage economic warfare against Pakistan." Ahmad was arrested and taken to a Lahore jail, where, after repudiating the charges (he called them "foolish and absurd"), he was denied bail. The FIA has since refused to provide BLLF attorneys with evidence supporting the charges, although Mahmood assures them that it consists of "videotapes and recordings of telephone conversations that amount to firm proof." Mahmood has vowed to arrest Khan "the very moment he returns to Pakistan, the moment his aircraft touches down."

Ehsan Ulla Khan remains in Europe, an unhappy exile. "They will jail me if I return to Pakistan," he told me shortly after he left his country. "Our attorneys tell me I am of greater use to the BLLF here, speaking out against the authorities, than I would be inside a Lahore cell. I fear for my people. The police have harassed many of them, and so many more have left us out of fear. We are demoralized. We cannot pay our bills and our staff. Our schools may close and our thousands of students may end up in the very factories we saved them from. Our offices and homes are under surveillance. Our telephones are tapped. We are fighting for our survival. If the attacks do not stop soon, it is possible that the BLLF will perish. That would be tragic. What will become of the children of Pakistan?"

Violence, Reel to Real

'Copycat' crimes in New York's subways reignited the debate: Do TV and movies cause actual mayhem? The evidence isn't as clear as you might think.

John Leland

IN THE FILM "MONEY TRAIN," A MAN douses a New York subway token-booth clerk with a flammable liquid, lights a match and demands her money. When she pushes a bag of cash toward him, he tosses the match at her anyway, laughing sadistically that he isn't in it "for the money." For New York audiences, this was a horror revisited: in the 1980s, hoodlums terrorized subway clerks with firebombs and lighter fluid. The movie opened on Wednesday, Nov. 22, and grossed $15 million in its first five days.

But its impact seems to have extended beyond the box office. Late Saturday night, three days after the opening, two men in Brooklyn squirted flammable liquid into the token booth manned by Harry Kaufman and blew his small cubicle to pieces. Kaufman remains in critical condition, with burns over 75 percent of his body. By midweek two more token booths had been attacked or threatened by firebugs. The makers of "Money Train" ardently defended their film, claiming

they were only depicting a real crime method. But the incidents read like the latest case of life imitating art—or perhaps life imitating art *imitating life* (graphic). Bob Dole, who had reaped political mileage denouncing the entertainment industry in May, again lambasted Hollywood last week, calling for a boycott of the movie: "Those who continue to deny that cultural messages can and do bore deep into the hearts and minds of our young people are deceiving themselves and ignoring reality."

This was an easy shot, especially in the wake of such a reprehensible crime. Who could defend the values of "Money Train," a witless orgy of gratuitous mayhem? But as with most quick attempts to connect entertainments with real-world violence, the story under this was far more complicated. For starters, the hoods responsible haven't been arrested; no one knows whether they even saw the movie. More significant, the incident offers only the most facile look at how violence in

the media might affect us. Copycat crimes, even if they hold up under scrutiny, involve only a minuscule fraction of the millions of people who watch the same movie or show. Far more troubling is the question of how our daily immersion in violent media—in aggressive cartoons, brutal sporting events, graphic newscasts, shoot-'em-up movies and TV shows and harsh popular music—affect children and adults in the aggregate.

Beneath the huffy sound bites lie nearly 40 years of extremely murky scientific research on the subject. The evidence holds fascinating clues into how our entertainments act on our minds. But it is also far less certain than many of its adherents claim. Researchers routinely cite thousands of studies. Really, there are closer to 200; the rest are rehashes of data. The press in turn uncritically repeats numbers like annual figures for how many violent acts kids see each year, without noting that the figures include acts of nature, cartoon violence and slap-

Without TV a study says, we'd have 10,000 fewer murders per year

stick along with grisly fare. A closer look at the actual research literature reveals that what we don't know about media's effects is often as dramatic as what we do.

Nobody believes that media by themselves cause aggression. But Leonard Eron and Rowell Huesmann of the University of Michigan found in a 22-year study following kids from third grade through adulthood that the single best predictor of later aggression—more than poverty, grades, a single-parent home or exposure to real violence—was a heavy childhood diet of TV carnage. "Of course not every youngster is affected," says Eron. "Not everyone who gets lung cancer smoked cigarettes. And not everyone who smokes cigarettes gets lung cancer. But nobody outside the tobacco industry denies that smoking causes lung cancer. The size of the correlation is the same." Epidemiologist Brandon S. Centerwall goes so far as to assert that without TV there would be 10,000 fewer murders per year in the United States, 70,000 fewer rapes and 700,000 fewer assaults.

Much of the most effective research has been done on children, because they are considered most susceptible. As Centerwall puts it, "Later variations in exposure, in adolescence and adulthood, do not exert any additional effect." In the early '60s, Albert Bandura at Stanford was the first to show that kids learned behavior from TV, not just from their parents. Psychologists have used four theories of learning to describe how TV violence may influence kids: they learn to imitate what they see on TV, especially when it is rewarded; they learn from the frequency of violence on TV that it is normal; they become desensitized to real people's suffering, and they become aroused by images on television, triggering violent responses. Early researchers, following Aristotle, thought media violence

might be cathartic, purging violent urges, but experiments have not borne this out.

In a classic series of lab experiments in the early 1960s, researchers first frustrated a group of preschool kids, then showed them TV footage of a man hitting a "Bobo" or clown

Beware of Imitations

"Money Train" is just one of the movies and TV shows blamed for inspiring violence. But like that film's token-booth torchings, many of these "imitation" crimes happened first in real life.

Taxi Driver
This 1976 film in which a New York cabby (Robert DeNiro) attempts to assassinate a presidential candidate was reportedly the inspiration for John Hinckley Jr.'s shooting President Reagan in 1981.

The Burning Bed
A mere half hour after seeing this 1984 TV movie starring Farrah Fawcett, a Milwaukee man burned his estranged wife to death. Fawcett played a real battered wife who killed her husband that way in 1977.

The Program
Two teenagers were killed and another critically wounded (in separate incidents) when they copied a scene from this 1993 movie showing drunken college football players in a game of "chicken," lying in the middle of a highway at night. The scene was later cut.

Beavis and Butt-head
In 1993 they made a torch of an aerosol can, and three Ohio girls burned their room. In another Ohio incident, a mom blamed the cartoon duo for her son's starting a fatal fire.

Natural Born Killers
This 1994 Oliver Stone film, which depicts a 52-victim killing spree, was banned in Britain and Ireland because of "copycat" murders in the U.S. and France.

doll. Afterward, the kids who saw the violence were more likely to mimic it on a similar doll. Further studies showed that these kids would also spontaneously act out against a man dressed as a clown, indicating that TV violence might spill easily into the real world. In another twist, a group of kids saw a similar footage of a man hitting a doll, but then being spanked for his actions. These children were much less likely to attack the doll themselves.

These last results imply that what matters is the *type* or *treatment* of violence: that screen mayhem that's rewarded will encourage aggression, but when it's punished it will inhibit it. By this logic, a heroic John Wayne movie might be more damaging than a senseless slasher movie, especially if the villain is punished. The experiments also argue that simply tallying the number of violent acts is meaningless. In this case, seeing the most acts of violence (both a hit doll and a spanking) made kids the least likely to rumble themselves.

Working with adults, Brad Bushman at Iowa State has shown in lab situations that subjects not prone to aggression were not affected by what they saw, while those previously inclined toward violence were. "Highly aggressive people organize experiences in their memories differently," he says. Violent entertainment "activates their aggressive thoughts, angry feelings." Bushman came to his interest in TV violence the tough way. "My electronics teacher owned an audio store. Just before closing one day, two armed men came in and forced the owner and customers down into the basement, forced them to eat Drano and put duct tape over their mouths, just like in the movie 'Magnum Force.' At trial, one witness testified that these men watched 'Magnum Force' three times the day before."

The V-chip won't work, says one expert, it's 'a technocratic fantasy'

Other researchers have questioned whether it was the hyperkinetic *form* of TV, more than the content, that prompted aggression. Two studies published in the early '80s found that programs with heavy action but no violence were just as likely to provoke aggression as those that contained actual mayhem. Dorothy and Jerome Singer at Yale further found that even innocuous programs like the quick-cutting "Sesame Street" or variety and game shows were so stimulating that they prompted aggression. (The producers of "Sesame Street" have since slowed the show down.)

The problem with lab studies, though, is that their conditions are artificial and limited. They take material entirely out of context, and don't look at cumulative effects of our real viewing patterns. The responses measured—punching a doll or pushing a shock button—are not real violent responses, only approximations. Further, the responses all come with the sanction of the experimenter. They seem like acceptable behaviors, with no threat of retribution.

Two of the most compelling field studies have looked at the way television changed a culture when it was first introduced. In 1973, Tannis MacBeth Williams studied the kids in a Canadian town before and after the town got TV. She found that creativity dropped and that within two years after the arrival of the tube, rates of hitting, shoving and biting among first and second graders increased by 160 percent.

In a somewhat related experiment, Centerwall looked at murder rates in the United States, Canada and South Africa after the introduction of TV. In each country, 10 to 15 years after television came in, murder rates doubled. Centerwall explained the lag by reasoning that it took that long for the first young kids exposed to TV to come of age.

Even looking at other factors—the baby boom, urbanization, the rise of firearms—he claims that none was as viable an explanation as TV.

Neither of these studies dealt with the content of TV. Both suggest that it may be the *fact* of TV—the way it changes our social lives, decreases the time kids spend with parents, stimulates material desires—that makes our world aggressive, more than the body count in an episode of "NYPD Blue."

George Gerbner, professor and dean emeritus of The Annenberg School for Communication at the University of Pennsylvania, has been studying television and its effects since the 1950s. He argues that the question of whether violent media cause violence misses the point. "It's a shallow, superficial, law-enforcement approach." The violence on TV, he says, shapes a range of responses beyond aggression. So Gerbner devised what he calls a

---

Not So Quiet on the Set

Besides shoot-'em-up shows, researchers have found that a wide range of programs spark aggression, including game shows, ads, even "Sesame Street."

Sports
Children imitate violent behavior when they see it on the screen, especially when it is rewarded—as in the idolization of sports heroes.

Newscasts
Since the Vietnam War, TV news and documentaries have brought a new level of graphic bloodshed into the living room, often during family hours.

Children's Shows
Kids are most susceptible to TV violence. Yet kids' shows like the Power Rangers are five times more violent than prime-time fare.

Mean World Syndrome: a measure of how television cultivates "feelings of insecurity, vulnerability and mistrust, and—despite its supposedly 'entertaining' nature—alienation and gloom." He contends that violence is used to define social relations between characters. "The primary message of violence on TV," he says, "is who can get away with what against whom." In a study covering 1982 to 1992, for example, the researchers found that for every 10 prime-time male characters who commit violence, 11 were victims. But for every 10 female perps, there were 17 female victims. The numbers are even worse for minorities. For every 10 women of color given power, 22 are victimized. The elderly and the poor are also common victims on television. According to Gerbner, viewers then bend their views of the real world according to these ratios. People who watch a lot of television, he found, believed that women were more likely than men to be victims of violence (in fact, men are one and one-half times as likely to be victims of violent crimes). "Some kids see themselves as more likely to be victims than other kids, and they develop a greater sense of vulnerability. Or if they see themselves as more likely to perpetrate violence without consequences, they develop a greater sense of being able to prevail through aggression." He also found that heavy viewers were more likely to call for severe punishments for criminals, and to have bought new locks, watchdogs and guns "for protection."

Many researchers, though, question Gerbner's method of counting all acts of violence alike. He answers that no heavy viewer distinguishes between "Henry: Portrait of a Serial Killer" and "Arsenic and Old Lace" and that on TV, even natural phenomena like storms convey a message about power. His work also invites a counterexplanation: people who are predisposed to fear the world are also more likely to stay home and watch TV. Gerbner argues that because we watch TV all our lives, there is no such thing as predisposition, "no before and after. TV cultivates the predisposition."

Even if the evidence is inconclusive, it's hard to dismiss the likelihood of some connection between media and aggression. So what to do? Gerbner rejects the V-chip—a device that would allow parents to block out programs coded for violent content—as "a technocratic fantasy. It's a mindless mechanism. Who programs it? Do you let the fox guard the chicken coop? If government decides, it's unconstitutional."

Both the Singers and Huesmann have designed programs to try to inoculate children from the harmful effects of television. Huesmann asked a group of second graders to help make a videotape on the effects of TV violence, exploring how TV works: how it is not real life; how copying TV can hurt real people, and so on. Tested later, the kids showed a high skepticism toward media violence; they were also less aggressive in class. Parents can try similar techniques at home, or push schools to educate young kids about the biases and distortions of television. Unfortunately Huesmann does not think the effects of his program will be long-lasting. "I don't believe this kind of curriculum alone can solve the problem. It needs to be coupled with reduction in media violence."

For four decades the entertainment industry has resisted such pleas, no matter how great the pressures on it. The body of research against media violence, though spongy, grows larger each year. We may never understand fully just how our entertainments shape our behavior. For now, all we can say for sure is that the subway clerk Harry Kaufman lies in a hospital room, burned in a crime similar to one in a movie. It's cause for cautious examination, not sound bites. The research has a long way to go, further than its believers claim. But you still might think twice before letting your kids watch Power Rangers.

With ANDREW MURR *and*
ADAM ROGERS

Get 'em While They're Young

*With Kid Flavors, Bright Colors and Commercials That
Make Children Masters of Their Universe, Advertisers
Build Brand Loyalty That Will Last a Lifetime*

Karen Stabiner

Karen Stabiner is a contributing editor to the Los Angeles
Times Magazine. *Her book about the Chiat/Day advertising
agency,* Inventing Desire, *was published by Simon & Schuster
in 1993.*

I took my 3½-year-old daughter grocery shopping recently,
to a market we have walked through dozens of times. We
rolled past the yogurt case that we always pass on our
way from free-range chickens to lowfat milk—and like a child
possessed, she screeched to a halt, pointed to a package on
the uppermost shelf and announced, "I will like that. Let's get
some."

This from a child who willingly ate plain yogurt only until
she was able to hold the spoon herself who has never so much
as glanced at this display before. Why did she want a four-pack
of Dannon Sprinkl'ins, two strawberry-banana and two cherry-
vanilla four-ounce servings, each topped with a clear plastic
envelope of rainbow-hued candies?

"It has sprinkles," she explained, as though our house were
not a candy-free zone, as though she knew what a sprinkle
was.

"Have you seen them before?"

"Annie has them in her lunch box." She was fairly quivering
with desire. "Put them in the cart, mommy."

So I did. Just to see what would happen.

For The Dannon Co., that purchase represented a successful
step into the marketing equivalent of the Promised Land. Children are among the few consumers who still have time and
money on their hands. The recession gnaws away at adult discretionary income and at the exalted position that name brands
have always held over their discount competitors. The children's market continues to grow: American children between
the ages of 4 and 12 spent $8.6 billion in 1991, and their
spending power is on the rise. According to James U. McNeal,
Texas A&M University marketing professor and co-author of
a recent magazine article entitled "Born to Shop," children

with two working parents have become involved in an increasing number of purchase decisions. He estimates that the 12-
and-younger set has a vote on about $147 billion in spending
each year.

More to the point, children have decades of buying power
ahead of them—and unlike their parents, who carry awareness
of 1,500 brand names in their heads, they have no precon-
ceived preferences. They are a blank slate.

The combination—money to spend and an open mind—
makes children irresistible to American business, and places
them at the center of a heated controversy over whether, and
how much, to sell to an audience whose critical faculties are
still in the caterpillar stage. Critics like Peggy Charren, whose
Action for Children's Television advocacy group waged a 25-
year war for regulation of programming and commercials, believe that advertising takes advantage of impressionable
youngsters. "Children," says Charren, "are the only unpaid
sales force in the history of America. Advertisers don't expect
kids to buy the product. The kids are being used to sell the
product to the parent."

---

*'When a kid is 3, you can go after them
on television,' says one ad woman.*

"The point is not that advertising is wrong, but that often
it plays unfair," says Cynthia Scheibe, assistant professor of
psychology at Ithaca College and director of the Center for
Research on the Effects of Television, until recently a joint
project with Cornell University. "Some of the tricks are really
outrageous. Makeup artists, to make food look better? Kids
are taught it's wrong to lie, but they have to mature enough
cognitively to understand what's happening."

The opposing camp, the business community, believes that advertising sparks the commercial equivalent of patriotism—a pure faith in the value of certain brands, one that fosters the growth of a competitive economy. It is hardly ever too soon to start building allegiances. "Every kid is different," says Kid-vertisers Creative Director Deyna Vesey, who opened her eight-person New York agency in 1989 with the motto "The Agency that Majors in Minors." "But the general rule of thumb is that when a kid is 3, you can go after them on television."

What no one argues about is how important children are. Advertisers annually spend about $471 million on children's television advertising, according to recent trade estimates, and the investment grows while the rest of the advertising industry attempts to extricate itself from a three-year decline. Convenience-food manufacturers, toy companies and fast-food restaurants spend the most to reach kids.

"Children start asking for brand-name items at 2 years old," usually because they associate a brand name with an object.

"We have living proof" of the long-lasting quality of early brand loyalties "in the cradle-to-grave marketing at McDonald's, and how well it works," says McNeal. "We start taking children in for their first and second birthdays, and on and on, and eventually they have a great deal of preference for that brand. Children can carry that with them through a lifetime."

If Dannon Sprinkl'ins, which went into national distribution this past spring, succeeds, it guarantees both short-term sales increases and long-range customer loyalty. Liz Paley is an account supervisor at the Manhattan office of Grey Advertising, an international agency with $4.5 billion in billings that has established itself as an authority on children's advertising. Grey won the Dannon account in January, 1991, just as the company was beginning to develop a product for children. Paley knows what the mandate is. "The hope is that when kids get to the point where the sprinkles seem a little babyish to them, maybe they'll try Dannon blended, which is a bit more subtle. Then they can move on to Dannon's fruit on the bottom yogurt. When we say, 'a healthy habit for life,'" says Paley, quoting the Dannon tag line, "we mean it."

GETTING KIDS TO EAT YOGURT IS A TOUGHER MAR-keting proposition than getting them to buy a Barbie doll or a Nerf Master Blaster. As soon as they can wield their own cutlery and have enough words to object, most children abandon it—and they tend not to eat it again until teen-age weight concerns click in. "Kids don't like the tart taste, the runny texture, the pieces of fruit in it, the uneven texture," Paley says. "They like more intense flavors. They taste a real grape, it's not a grape to them. Grape is grape Kool-Aid."

But Dannon, a $400-million company owned by BSN, the largest food company in France, was determined to start the yogurt habit—and the customer's relationship with Dannon— early. The very future of the brand was at stake. This was a chance to form a lasting alliance with consumers just at the developmental point when they became receptive to commercial messages. According to McNeal, "Children start asking for brand-name items at 2 years old," usually because they associate a brand name with an object. "Mom says, 'Eat your Tony Tigers,' not 'Eat your Kellogg's Frosted Flakes,'" he says, "so when the child sees the picture on the box, they recognize it.

"By age 4, they are making evaluative judgments about brands, saying, 'I'll eat Cheerios and I won't eat anything but Cheerios,'" McNeal says. "Once they start school, they associate brands with people. It's, 'Billy eats Cheerios so I want to.'"

All of these factors—parents' habits, which amount to an endorsement; commercial messages and peer pressure—contribute to a child's preference for a specific brand, and make it difficult to dissuade him. Dannon, as well as competitors Light n' Lively and Yoplait, who have children's yogurts too, wanted to exploit what one Grey executive calls "the yogurt trough," a wasteland of 4-to-14-year-olds who would rather eat almost anything else. The White Plains, N.Y.-based company had been trying to figure out how to make yogurt fun, without abandoning Dannon's reputation for making healthful foods.

Grey Advertising provided the missing link. "Our typical process when we develop a new product is to create a team," says Bob Wallach, vice president of marketing for Dannon. "The company's marketing person is the hub of the wheel. We have supporting experts, and our communications experts are the people at the agency. We like to bring them in early. The interaction improves the concept. Maybe they'll say, 'Hey, if the Sprinkl'ins come in more than one color, we can do better ads.'"

"We wanted to integrate an element of fun right into the product, and not just do a smaller adult product," Paley says, but we were careful not to step over the line. There was no chocolate chip cookie yogurt."

What got out to the focus groups and taste-test sessions? During the year of testing, there were sweeter, thicker, more vividly colored yogurts with kid-friendly gimmicks. There were Dannosaurs, fruit-flavored yogurts enhanced by dinosaur-shaped gummy bears, with names like Bananasaurus Rex and Tricherrytops. There was yogurt that came with funny-shaped spoons attached to the cups, to be called either Crazy Spoons or Spoonatics. There were Cool Cups and rainbow layers of yogurt. None of them survived: Kids liked them, but they didn't like them enough.

Finally, Dannon came up with Sprinkl'ins—added sweeteners, added color, added flavors and a clear envelope of sprinkles attached to the top of each serving cup. "Sprinkl'ins seemed to break the bank," says Grey's Rob Mizrahi, a starched-shirted, perfectly coiffed art director. "It's not just yogurt—they didn't take blueberry blended yogurt and give you a sprinkle pack," says Mizrahi's partner, copywriter Andy Bohjalian, a young, slightly rumpled man who has worked on children's products for more than a decade. "It's a little sweeter, a little more fruity tasting. It's richer in color. A better kid flavor, and then these little sprinkle packs were the deal-breaker."

"Or," he says, breaking into an impish grin, "the deal-maker."

Dannon had done everything conceivable to please the pre-adolescent palate, but the fact remained that most kids hate yogurt. Advertising had to build the bridge between target consumers and a product they didn't want. "Can advertising create a want in children? I think it can, if it presents a product in such a manner that it creates a desirable attitude in the child," McNeal says.

"The most important need for children under 7 is play," he says. "If a product is presented in such a way that a child might say it's a lot of fun, then children might seek the product." All that Grey Advertising had to do was figure out the one thing that children wanted more than they didn't want yogurt.

GREY'S SENIOR VICE PRESIDENT, GROUP CREATIVE director Bob Skollar, tosses a navy double-breasted blazer over his shirt and jeans, a nod to his executive status, but everything about him shouts kid-at-heart, from his long auburn hair to a mischievous smile. Toys litter his corner office. Skollar has worked on the Kool-Aid account for six years, and he knows all about inventing fun. Kool-Aid's reputation as the best powdered fruit drink for kids is so strong that it has survived two devastating associations—with hallucinogenic drugs in the 1960s and with cyanide in the 1978 mass suicide in Jonestown.

About five years ago, it began to take heat from an unexpected adversary, the cheaper store brands that made sense in a tight economy. Suddenly there was a new advertising challenge—to explain to the consumer why to "take Kool-Aid rather than some[thing] else," according to Skollar.

"One really successful way to advertise to kids is to give them a sense of power, give them a place where they call the shots."

There were qualities that would appeal to parents: Kool-Aid was cheaper than carbonated beverages, and unsweetened Kool-Aid allowed parents to control the amount of sugar their children consumed. The drink was fortified with Vitamin C. And there was what Skollar called "the nostalgia factor" of

a drink parents had drunk when they were children. But it wasn't enough. There had to be something that appealed to kids and got them to ask for Kool-Aid instead of any other drink. What the product needed, Skollar says, was "a value added"—some benefit that derived from drinking that brand, and only that brand.

That is where brand advertising comes in. Essentially, it suggests to the consumer that there are advantages to a product that are not necessarily inherent in it; that drinking Kool-Aid will do much more for a child than merely quench his thirst. The image that Kool-Aid was trying to communicate, Skollar says, was "wacky and wild and fun and just for kids. The drink that's just for kids." So Grey developed a promotion called the Wacky Warehouse—an imaginary place, featured in the television campaign, that was full of gifts ranging from Kool-Aid hats to Nintendo games and Mattel troll dolls. All that children had to do was save up purchase coupons from their Kool-Aid packets, and they could send away for the prize of their choice. The promotion lured parents away from bargain brands by offering them a new way to save money: "After a couple of months, all of a sudden you turn around and give your kid a Nintendo gift," says Skollar. "That's pretty important for mom."

The agency also tweaked the Kool-Aid Man's personality, to make him seem a bit more modern. "When we started out, he was just a guy who brought Kool-Aid," says Skollar. "He's a cool kid now, he's in jeans. He has his jams. He has some sunglasses. So kids can identify, have something they can make part of their world." Today, Kool-Aid is the No. 1 powdered drink mix.

Andy Bohjalian worked on the Kool-Aid account 10 years ago, in what he calls "the dinosaur days of kid advertising." When he started working on Dannon 2½ years ago, he remembered the seminal lesson of his days on the fruit-drink account: Make a kid feel like he rules his universe, and he will likely desire the product that makes him feel that way.

"We discovered that if we had adults doing these slapstick reactions, falling on banana peels, wigs falling off, if we made adults look silly because they saw Kool-Aid Man and were shocked and frightened—the kids loved it because they were in control," says Bohjalian. "They called the Kool-Aid Man and he created chaos in the adult world.

"In the real world, kids are at the bottom of the food chain," he says, "and one really successful way to advertise to kids is to give them a sense of power, give them a place where they call the shots, instead of everyone telling them what to eat and when to go to bed and clean up their room."

"A key component of the advertising, which is probably true of anyone that works on kids' stuff, is 'kid mastery,' " adds Mizrahi.

The two men figured they were just the guys to make yogurt a mastery product. They share a uniquely appropriate dietary heritage: Bohjalian, whose family is Armenian, and Mizrahi, whose family is Turkish, grew up in homes where yogurt was a staple. They never knew about the yogurt trough until they became adults; they ate it as children, like to talk about its "probiotic" ability to nourish healthy bacteria in the body, and approach their task with almost messianic zeal. They felt they were in a position to improve the overall health of the youth of America, as soon as they figured out how to make Dannon Sprinkl'ins the food of choice for kids in charge.

So the team devised the Creation Station as a setting for Sprinkl'ins commercials, what Mizrahi calls "a Willy Wonka chocolate factory kind of thing," where children in lab coats and wild hairdos come up with the kinds of flavors they like to eat, where rainbow-colored sprinkles pour down from the heavens. It is a land where children who eat a particular brand of yogurt find themselves free of mundane constraints, where product and power are inextricably bound up together.

Do kids get the message? Dannon introduced Sprinkl'ins in test markets in one-third of the country last year, and expanded to 60% last September. A few months ago, Grey Advertising conducted focus groups to see what effect the Creation Station campaign had on its target audience. "The kids remembered the song, they remembered the name," Mizrahi says. "And they remembered the Creation Station."

"They could play back the copy, some of the kids," adds Bohjalian. "We like that."

Second-grade students at a Los Angeles-area school who were shown the commercials recognized them, and the product, immediately. Their consensus about the world of the Creation Station? "Impossible," about 40 children shouted in unison. They knew it wasn't real—but they thought it was a fabulous place.

"They're living out the fantasy of 'what would happen if Dannon came to me and I made a product for them?'" says Dannon's Wallach. The product, which cost $13 million to launch, is now available nationwide for a suggested $2.19. And Wallach, extrapolating from regional sales figures, expects sales of 2 million four-packs per month. It is "a small but growing part" of Dannon's sales, a company spokeswoman says.

"More than 10% of Sprinkl'ins volume came from new consumers, people who just didn't eat yogurt at all anymore," says Grey's Paley. "It's the, 'A spoonful of sugar makes the medicine go down' approach. The product is going like gangbusters."

IN THE PROCESS OF LAUNCHING SPRINKL'INS, DANnon and its advertising agency learned a happy lesson about brand loyalty. At the outset, Grey planned a two-pronged approach: the Creation Station campaign for children's television and a simultaneous print campaign in what Paley calls "mom magazines." Children are always nagging their parents for things they see advertised on television. There had to be a way to communicate to parents that this product was a worthy one; that Sprinkl'ins was the newest offspring in a brand family they already trust.

"Kids are still under the thumb of a gatekeeper," says Paley. "If you can convince parents that the name they trust has found a way to make yogurt palatable—that it tastes so good they won't know it's good for them—that was the big idea.

"With kids, you have to sell that it'll taste good, it'll make you the most popular kid in school," she says. "You have to sell it to the gatekeeper by saying, It's good for them.' The

---

Helping Children Beat the Blitz

Peggy Charren closed down her advocacy group, Action for Children Television, last year. But she continues to critique programming and commercials, and to find them wanting. So Charren, a grandmother of four, has devised ways to help parents and children navigate through the sea of advertising. Her suggestions:

1. Avoid commercials by watching public television.
2. Use home video.
3. Make a game of learning about commercials. For young children, Charren has made bingo boards that use products sold on children's television in place of letters. Each time there is a commercial for a particular product, the child puts a bean on that square. "It gives them a sense of how often they're sold something," says Charren, "so you can talk about what is advertised the most and does that make you want it the most? That helps undermine the message."

Ithaca College's Cynthia Scheibe also has a strategy. She recommends a game she calls "What are they selling?" "As soon as a commercial comes on, I say, 'OK. They're selling something. Who can be the first person in the room to say what it is?' My 2-year-old daughter could do it—and even if she was wrong, at least she understood that they were selling something."

—K.S.

---

mom says to herself, 'Oh, that's the new yogurt from Dannon, so it must be OK.'"

What the agency found, to its delight, was that Dannon had a foundation of brand loyalty that made the mom campaign unnecessary. They were preaching to the converted. The company decided to cancel the magazine campaign and use that money, instead, to increase the amount of children's television time it bought.

People tend to think that advertising is designed to increase sales, but that is only part of the bargain. Ronald Goodstein, UCLA assistant professor of marketing, believes that the best result of advertising is a lasting brand equity. "If you can't to boost sales, put a product on a promotion and you'll sell a lot more," he says. "Advertising talks about brand equity, about the value of a name. That equity can be used for premium pricing, the lifetime loyalty of the customer, and it helps with brand extensions. Brand advertising is equity building."

Once a brand has its hooks in the collective psyche, it is likely to hang on indefinitely, unless it becomes a casualty either of technology or of a misguided attempt to redefine the brand (Coca-Cola's market share has suffered ever since its decision, in 1985, to reformulate Coke). Martin Mayer, in his 1991 book, "Whatever Happened to Madison Avenue," lists companies that owned leading brands in several categories in 1923, and again in 1984. From Swift bacon to Wrigley chewing gum to Ivory soap, 16 of the 18 companies maintained their stranglehold. Only Hershey chocolates and Colgate toothpaste slipped, and only from first to second place.

This is not to say that the American public will buy anything that looks good in ads. Consumers might try a product once on the strength of an ad, but if the product doesn't meet their expectations, no amount of advertising will be able to persuade them to buy it again.

What brand advertising can do is enhance an acceptable product, wrap it up in what Goodstein calls "an image and a mystique." The consumer comes to believe that all athletic shoes, or cosmetics, or cars, are not created equal; that only a particular brand will successfully communicate who he is to the rest of the world.

Distinctions based on image have become ever more important to a product's success, because the consumer landscape is littered with parity products—goods that are essentially identical, whether they be batteries, midsize sedans or blue jeans, goods whose share of the market depends on created differences.

Image also persuades customers to pay the inflated price a particular brand demands, and is an important weapon in the war against anonymous discount brands. If the recession has proved a tenacious foe of brand equity—R.J. Reynolds recently rocked the business world by announcing a price reduction on its Marlboro cigarettes, in effect a capitulation to cheaper brands that were stealing customers, and leading diaper manufacturers are locked in a price war—the possible weakening of brand identities has made advertisers ever more concerned with shoring them up.

McNeal believes that successful advertising convinces the audience that a given product "potentially satisfies a need or set of needs." What distinguishes children from other viewers is not so much what advertisers show them, but how they interpret it. Children are literalists, which makes them more vulnerable to advertising's message. For them, seeing is believing.

Kidvertisers' Vesey has noticed that her year-old son loves the TV campaign for Michelin tires that features babies. "He's not buying a tire for a while," she says, laughing, "but can you imagine the brand loyalty?"

According to Ithaca's Scheibe, "Children can't distinguish the persuasive intent of commercials. There is enormous evidence that young children have various difficulties in understanding the nature of commercials. They give more credibility to the person speaking than they should, especially if it's someone they like, like Cap'n Crunch or Ronald McDonald, or someone who is a role model.

"Adults understand the purpose of advertising. They come with skepticism: These people may lie to you or distort the facts. Kids don't have that skepticism because they don't have what's called 'real world knowledge,'" she says.

But the notion that advertising somehow seduces youngsters into wanting things that they don't need irritates McNeal. He says that parents who complain about advertising, and the endless litany of product requests they get from their kids, ought to think about where they really learned to want what they want.

"What do you satisfy your appetites with?" asks McNeal. "With those things you've learned about, mainly from your parents. There is not a separate world that exists between marketers and kids, and the parents are omitted. I've never envisioned a helpless parent who couldn't say, 'No, you can't watch television,' or 'No, you can't have what you see in commercials.'"

"The wants children have, they've learned from somebody," he says. "They weren't born wanting Tony the Tiger."

PEGGY CHARREN, UNTIL LAST YEAR THE HEAD OF the Cambridge, Mass.-based advocacy group Action for Children's Television and the sharpest thorn in commercial television's side, emphatically agrees: No one was born wanting Tony the Tiger.

Her position, however, is that television, not parents, has taught kids to want that and other brands. Her criticisms of both programming and advertising aimed at children culminated in the 1990 Children's Television Act, which requires informational and educational programs from any station wishing to maintain its federal license—but she still despairs at how little is being done.

Charren doubts that even the most determined parent could withstand the onslaught of commercial messages a child encounters on TV. The Children's Television Act sets a limit of 10½ minutes of commercials per hour of programming, but even at that level, Charren worries that parents lack the skills to fight back. As far as she is concerned, television created a wild frontier for marketers, and products sprung up, not because anyone needed them, but because there was a new, improved way to sell them.

"With TV, suddenly the toy business started to do a year-round business, not just on holidays. The Barbie doll was an overnight success, and convinced the industry that television was the way to go. Television brought the picture with the message, and that's what kids respond to," Charren says.

She resents the "barrage" of commercials children see. "It's sort of incredible," she says, "to talk kids into spending money they don't have, on products that may not be good for them, when they can't yet cross the street alone."

If you don't want your kid to start saying, "Why can't I have it?" teach them very early on that that's not what it's about.

Marketers insist that the proliferation of brands is simply proof of a healthy economy. Agency people complain that it is up to parents to screen their children's requests and decide what is a worthwhile purchase. Parents critical of children's advertising point the finger at the marketers, who point right back at them.

"Parents have to take control," says Skollar, who has two young children. "If you don't want your kid to start saying, 'They have $100 sneakers, why can't I?' teach them very early on that that's not what it's about. I had the sneaker thing with my son. It wasn't kids' advertising that he saw, it was prime-time, adult advertising. But he sees who ever it is, Michael Jordan or Shaquille O'Neal, jumping up and doing the slam dunk, flying through the sky, and he says to me—this is when I think advertising's scary—he says to me, 'But, daddy, with those you could jump higher and run faster.'

"And I said, 'No, you can't. It's not the sneakers that do it."

Charren says that parents have to become more involved in their children's viewing habits—that the TV set is part of popular culture, not an electronic baby-sitter. But she chuckles at the idea that the people who make the advertising are innocent bystanders. "Then maybe the problem is with society as a whole," she says, "and not just the brand managers."

MY DAUGHTER DIDN'T CARE FOR SPRINKL'INS, ONCE she got past the brightly colored cardboard package, the thrill of spilling the candies in herself and the visual jolt of watching them leave pastel trails in the strawberry-banana yogurt. She decided that it was too sweet.

She loved the concept: Rather than abandon the yogurt on the first try, she insisted on sampling all four containers in the pack. But she didn't like the product; each cup went into the garbage three-quarters full. Now she prefers a recipe of her own devise, plain yogurt mixed with pesto sauce, a combination not likely to be mass-marketed at any time soon.

Still, it was hard for her to give up her romance with the brand. I kept the cardboard outer packaging, in the interest of research, and every now and then she pulls it out of the cabinet, studies it, and wonders when we might buy Sprinkl'ins again. Reminded that she didn't care for the yogurt on the first try, she suggests, "But I will like it next time," already loyal to her brand of choice.

Victimization of Children

David Finkelhor and Jennifer Dziuba-Leatherman

David Finkelhor and Jennifer Dziuba-Leatherman, Family Research Laboratory, University of New Hampshire.

Nadine M. Lambert served as action editor for this article.

We thank the Boy Scouts of America for financial support. We would also like to thank Kyle Ruonala for help in preparing the manuscript and Lucy Berliner, David Chadwick, Kathy Kaufer Christoffel, James Collins, Pat Crittenden, Howard Davidson, James Garbarino, Malcolm Gordon, Elizabeth Kandel, Kathy Kendall-Tackett, David Kerns, Ben Saunders, Murray Straus, James Tucker, members of the Family Violence Research Seminar, and several anonymous reviewers for helpful comments on the article.

Correspondence concerning this article should be addressed to David Finkelhor, Family Research Laboratory, University of New Hampshire, 126 Horton Social Science Center, Durham, NH 03824.

Children suffer more victimizations than do adults, including more conventional crimes, more family violence, and some forms virtually unique to children, such as family abduction. On the basis of national statistics, these victimizations can be grouped into three broad categories: the pandemic, *such as sibling assault, affecting most children; the* acute, *such as physical abuse, affecting a fractional but significant percentage; and the* extraordinary, *such as homicide, affecting a very small group. They can also be differentiated by the degree to which they result from the unique dependency status of children. A field called the victimology of childhood should be defined that adopts a developmental approach to understanding children's vulnerability to different types of victimizations and their different effects.*

Although the issue of child victimization has elicited considerable attention from professionals and the public, the interest has largely been fragmented. Writers and advocates have tended to confine themselves to certain specific topics, such as child abuse, child molestation, or stranger abduction, and few have considered the larger whole (for exceptions, see Best, 1990; Christoffel, 1990; McDermott, Stanley, & Zimmerman-McKinney, 1982; Morgan & Zedner, 1992). Unfortunately, this fragmentation has inhibited the recognition and development of what should be a very important field: the general victimology of childhood. Such a general victimology would highlight more clearly the true vulnerability of children to victimization, the overlap and co-occurrence of different types of victimization, and the common risk factors and effects. It is our goal to assemble disparate statistics and knowledge about the victimization and maltreatment of children in order to define such a field. We will review findings on the incidence, risk factors, and effects of child victimization and suggest integrative concepts.

Children Are More Victimized Than Adults

One reality, not widely recognized, is that children are more prone to victimization than adults are. For example, according to the 1990 National Crime Survey (NCS; Bureau of Justice Statistics, 1991), the rates of assault, rape, and robbery against those aged 12–19 years are two to three times higher than for the adult population as a whole (Table 1). Homicide is the only violent crime category for which teens are somewhat less vulnerable than adults.[1]

This disproportionate victimization of children is also confirmed in studies that gather information from adults on their lifetime experience with crime. For example, in the first national survey to ask adult women about their lifetime experiences of forcible rape, 61% of the rapes occurred before the age of 18 (Kilpatrick, 1992). This translates roughly into a fivefold higher rape risk for children.

The disproportionate victimization of children would be even more evident if the NCS and other studies were not so deficient in their counting of incidents of family violence (Garbarino, 1989), to which children are enormously more vulnerable than adults. For example, in the National Family Violence Survey (Straus, Gelles, & Steinmetz, 1980), adults reported that they inflicted almost twice as much severe violence (which includes beating up, kicking, hitting with a fist or object) against a child in their household than they did against their adult partner (Table 2). When to family violence we add the frequent occurrence of peer and sibling assaults against younger children—experiences that have virtually no equivalent among adults (Pagelow, 1989)—evidence strongly suggests that children are more victimized than adults are.

Statistics on Child Victimization

To illustrate the spectrum of child victimization, we have arrayed the national statistics gleaned from more than a dozen sources in Table 3 in rough order of magnitude. (See Appendix for list of sources.) We limited our notion

---

[1] Unfortunately, this contrast is muddied by the fact that the NCS does not have rates on children under 12 years of age, and, although they are usually classified as young adults, 18- and 19-year-olds—a very high-risk group—are treated as children. Even if one reclassifies 18- and 19-year-olds as adults and assumes no victimizations at all for children younger than 12, the overall rate for children, based on NCS data, would still be higher than the overall rate for adults.

of victimization to crimes, interpersonal violence (acts carried out with the intention or perceived intention of physically hurting another person, Gelles & Straus, 1979), child abuse, and certain related acts, such as abduction, that have been highlighted in the current wave of interest in child victimization. We included only forms of victimization for which there were scientifically defensible national estimates.

One of the interesting features of child victimology is that children suffer from certain types of violence that have been largely excluded from traditional criminologic concern. The first is assaults against young children by other children, including violent attacks by siblings. Prevailing ideology has tended to treat these as relatively inconsequential.[2] But from the point of view of the child, it is not clear, for example, why being beaten up by a peer would be any less traumatic or violative than it would be for an adult (Greenbaum, 1989).

An even more problematic type of noncriminalized violence toward children is spanking and and other forms of corporal punishment. There are signs that a normative transformation is in progress regarding corporal punishment (Greven, 1990). A majority of states have banned it in schools, and several Scandinavian countries have outlawed its use even by parents. Some social scientists have begun to study it as a form of victimization with short- and long-term negative consequences (Daro & Gelles, 1991; Hyman, 1990; Straus, in press).

This is far from an exhaustive inventory of all the victimizations children could be said to suffer. For example, bullying and emotional abuse by peers have received some deserved attention (Olweus, 1978). Moreover, children have been plausibly described as victims when crimes are committed against other members of their household (Morgan & Zedner, 1992). Finally, there are many types of criminal victimizations, such as involvement in child prostitution, for which we could identify no reliable national statistics.

Table 1

Crime Victimization Rate per 1,000:
Adolescents Versus Adults

Crime	Age in years	
	12–19	20+
Assault[a]	58.45	17.85
Robbery[a]	11.53	4.73
Rape[a]	1.60	0.50
Homicide[b]	0.09[c]	0.10

Note. Some figures shown in this table did not appear in original source but were derived from data presented therein.
[a] National Crime Survey, 1990 (Bureau of Justice Statistics, 1992).
[b] Uniform Crime Report, 1991 (Federal Bureau of Investigation, 1992).
[c] Rate is for ages 10–19.

Table 2

Family Violence Victimization Rate per 1,000:
Children Versus Adults, 1985

Perpetrator–victim relationship	Any violence	Severe violence[a]
Spouse to spouse	158	58
Parent to child	620	107

Note. Source: National Family Violence Resurvey, 1985 (Straus & Gelles, 1990).
[a] Includes kicking, biting, hitting with fist or object, beating up, using or threatening to use knife or gun.

Typology of Child Victimizations

Examining the figures in Table 3 and recognizing their methodological limitations, definitional imprecision, and variability, we nonetheless suggest that the types of child victimization reflected there should be broken into three broad categories according to their order of magnitude (Figure 1). First, there are the pandemic victimizations that occur to a majority of children in the course of growing up. At a minimum these include assault by siblings, physical punishment by parents, and theft, and probably also peer assault, vandalism, and robbery. Second, there are what might be called acute victimizations. These are less frequent—occurring to a minority, although perhaps a sizable minority, of children—but may be of generally greater severity. Among these we would include physical abuse, neglect, and family abduction. Finally, there are the extraordinary victimizations that occur to a very small number of children but that attract a great deal of attention. These include homicide, child abuse homicide, and nonfamily abduction.

Several observations follow from this typology. First, there has been much more public and professional attention paid to the extraordinary and acute victimizations than to the pandemic ones. For example, sibling violence, the most frequent victimization, is conspicuous for how little it has been studied in proportion to how often it occurs. This neglect of pandemic victimizations needs to be rectified. For one thing, it fails to reflect the concerns of children themselves. In a re-

---

[2] The following quote in a discussion of the meaning of the NCS statistics on adolescents is an example: "A student who is coerced into surrendering the Twinkies in his or her lunchbox to a school bully is, by strict definition, a victim of robbery. These events, although unpleasant and perhaps frightening, are not as alarming as suggested by the labels 'assault' and 'robbery'" (Garofalo, Siegel, & Laub, 1987, p. 331). This is common stereotypy of peer victimizations, even though the kind of chronic bullying, terrorizing, and intimidation that characterizes the lives of many children in school and in their neighborhood has almost no equivalent for adults, except perhaps in the case of battered wives (Greenbaum, 1989). There is also a tendency to see violence among children, particularly young children, as fighting and not as victimization. It is important to point out that this is not a distinction made in any of the statistics regarding adult victimization. That is, an adult who is assaulted in a fight he or she may have "started" (according to some observers) will nonetheless be counted as a victim in the NCS.

Table 3

Rate and Incidence of Various Childhood Victimization

Type of violence/age in years	Rate per 1,000	No. victimized	Year	Source	Report type[a]
Sibling assault					
3–17	800.0	50,400,000[b]	1975	NFVS-1	C
3–17	530.0	33,300,000[c]	1975	NFVS-1	C
Physical punishment					
0–17	498.6	31,401,329[d]	1985	NFVS-2	C
Theft					
11–17	497.0	—	1978	NYS	S
12–15	89.2	—	1990	NCS90	S
Assault					
11–17	310.6	—	1978	NYS	S
Grade 8	172.0	—	1988	NASHS	S
12–15	53.3	—	1990	NCS90	S
Vandalism					
11–17	257.6	—	1978	NYS	S
Robbery					
11–17	245.8	—	1978	NYS	S
Grade 8	160.9	—	1988	NASHS	S
12–15	13.6	—	1990	NCS90	S
Rape					
Grade 8	118.0	—	1988	NASHS	S
11–17	78.0	—[e]	1978	NYS78	S
12–15	1.8	—	1990	NCS90	S
Physical abuse					
0–17	23.5	1,480,007	1985	NFVS-2	C
0–17	10.5	673,500	1991	50-SS	A
0–17	4.9	311,500	1986	NIS-2	A
Neglect					
0–17	20.2	1,293,120	1991	50-SS	A
0–17	11.3	710,700[f]	1986	NIS-2	A
Sexual abuse					
0–17	6.3	404,100	1991	50-SS	A
0–17	2.1	133,600	1986	NIS-2	A
Family abduction					
0–17	5.6	354,100[g]	1988	NISMART	C
0–17	2.6	163,200[h]	1988	NISMART	C
Psychological maltreatment					
0–17	3.0	188,100	1986	NIS-2	A
0–17	2.5	161,640	1991	50-SS	A
Nonfamily abduction					
0–17	0.05–0.07	3200–4600[i]	1988	NISMART	A
0–17	0.003–0.005	200–300[i]	1988	NISMART	A
Homicide					
0–17	0.035	2,233	1991	UCR91	A
Abduction homicide					
0–17	0.001–0.002	43–147	1988	NISMART	A

Note. Some figures shown did not appear in original source but were derived from data presented therein. Dash = Unable to compute for entire population (0–17). NFVS-1 = National Family Violence Survey, 1975 (Straus & Gelles, 1990); NFVS-2 = National Family Violence Resurvey, 1985 (Straus & Gelles, 1990); NYS = National Youth Survey (Lauritsen, Sampson, and Laub, 1991); NCS90 = National Crime Survey, 1990 (Bureau of Justice Statistics, 1992); NASHS = National Adolescent Student Health Survey (American School Health Association, 1985); NYS78 = National Youth Survey, 1978 (Ageton, 1983); 50-SS = Annual Fifty State Survey, 1990 (Daro & McCurdy, 1991); NIS-2 = National Study of the Incidence and Severity of Child Abuse and Neglect, 1988 (Sedlak, 1991); NISMART = National Incidence Study of Missing, Abducted, Runaway and Thrownaway Children, 1990 (Finkelhor, Hotaling, & Sedlak, 1990); UCR91 = Uniform Crime Reports, 1991 (Federal Bureau of Investigation, 1992). Categories listed are not necessarily distinct and mutually exclusive. Under some victimization categories, estimates of several studies have been listed, sometimes showing widely divergent numbers. These differences stem from two factors in particular: the source of the report and the definition of the activity. Of the three main sources of reports—children themselves, caretakers knowledgeable about children's experiences, and agencies such as police and child protection services—children and caretakers are quite likely to provide many more accounts than are available from agencies alone. Estimates also diverge because some studies used more careful or restrictive definitions.

[a] Report type: A = agency; C = caretaker; S = self-report. [b] Any violence. [c] Severe violence. [d] Excludes corporal punishment in schools. [e] Girls only. [f] Physical and emotional neglect. [g] Broad scope. [h] Policy focal. [i] Legal definition. [j] Stereotypical kidnapping.

Figure 1
Typology of Child Victimization

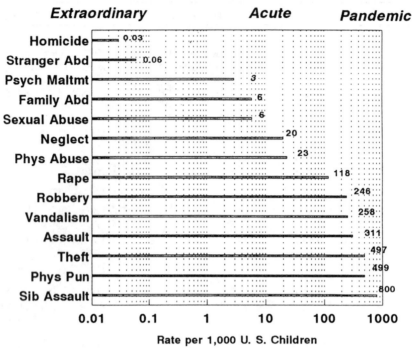

Note. Abd = abduction. Psych Maltmt = psychological maltreatment. Phys = physical. Pun = punishment. Sib = sibling.

cent survey of 2,000 children aged 10–16 years, three times as many were concerned about the likelihood of being beaten up by peers as were concerned about being sexually abused (Finkelhor & Dziuba-Leatherman, in press-b). The pandemic victimizations deserve greater attention, if only because of their alarming frequency and the influence they have on children's everyday existence.

Second, this typology can be useful in developing theory and methodology concerning child victimization. For example, different types of victimization may require different conceptual frameworks. Because they are nearly normative occurrences, the impact of pandemic victimizations may be very different from extraordinary ones, which children experience in relative isolation.

Finally, the typology helps illustrate the diversity and frequency of children's victimization. Although homicide and child abuse have been widely studied, they are notable for how inadequately they convey the variety and true extent of the other victimizations that children suffer. Almost all the figures in Table 3 have been promoted in isolation at one time or another. Viewed together, they are just part of a total environment of various victimization dangers with which children live.

Why Is the Victimization of Children So Common?

When the victimization of children is considered as a whole and its scope and variety more fully appreciated, it prompts a number of interesting and important theoretical questions. The first concerns why the victimization of children is so common. Obviously this is a complex question; a complete answer will undoubtedly require the explanation of elevated risks for different categories of children for different kinds of victimization. However, some generalizations may apply. Certainly the weakness and small physical stature of many children and their dependency status put them at greater risk. They cannot retaliate or deter victimization as effectively as can those with more strength and power. The social toleration of child victimization also plays a role. Society has an influential set of institutions, the police and criminal justice system, to enforce its relatively strong prohibitions against many kinds of crime, but much of the victimization of children is considered outside the purview of this system.

Another important generalization about why children are at high risk for victimization is that children have comparatively little choice over whom they associate with, less choice perhaps than any segment of the population besides prisoners. This can put them in more involuntary contact with high-risk offenders and thus at greater jeopardy for victimization. For example, when children live in families that mistreat them, they are not free or able to leave. When they live in dangerous neighborhoods, they cannot choose on their own to move. If they attend a school with many hostile and delinquent peers, they cannot simply change schools or quit. The absence of choice over people and environments affects children's vulnerability to both intimate victimization and street crime. Although some adults, like battered women and the poor, suffer similar limitations, many adults are able to seek divorce or change their residences in reaction to dangerous conditions. Adults also have more ready access to cars and sometimes have the option to live and work alone. Children are obliged to live with other people, to travel collectively, and to work in high density, heterogenous environments, which is what schools are. In short, children have difficulty gaining access to the structures and mechanisms in society that help segregate people from dangerous associates and environments.

Differential Character of Child Victimization

A second interesting theoretical question concerns how the victimization of children differs from the victimization of adults. Children, of course, suffer from all the victimizations that adults do (including economic crimes like extortion and fraud), but they also suffer from some that are particular to their status. The main status characteristic of childhood is its condition of dependency, which is a function, at least in part, of social and psychological immaturity. The violation of this dependency status results in forms of victimization, like physical neglect, that are not suffered by most adults (with the exception of those, like the elderly and sick, who also become dependent).

The dependency of children creates a spectrum of vulnerability for victimizations. Interestingly, the victimization categories that we have identified in Table 3 can be arrayed on a continuum, according to the degree to which they involve violations of children's dependency status (Figure 2). At one extreme is physical neglect, which has practically no meaning as a victimization except in the case of a person who is dependent and needs to be cared for by others. Similarly, family abduction is a dependency-specific victimization because it is the unlawful removal of a child from the person who is supposed to be caring for him or her. Psychological maltreatment happens to both adults and children, but the sensitive psychological vulnerability of children in their dependent relationship to their caretakers renders such parental behavior a major threat to normal child development (Claussen & Crittenden, 1991; Hart & Brassard, 1987). This is why society considers psychological maltreatment of children a form of victimization that warrants an institutional response.

At the other end of the continuum are forms of victimization that are defined without reference to dependency and which exist in similar forms for both children and adults. Stranger abduction is prototypical in this instance because both children and adults are taken against their will and imprisoned for ransom or sexual purposes. Homicide is similar; the dependency status of the victim does little to define the victimization. In some cases, to be sure, children's deaths result from extreme and willful cases of neglect, but there are parallel instances of adult deaths resulting from extreme and willful negligence.

Finally, there are forms of child victimization that should be located along the midsection of the dependency continuum. Sexual abuse falls here, for example, because it encompasses at least two different situations, one dependency related, one not. Some sexual abuse entails activities, ordinarily acceptable between adults, that are deemed victimizing in the case of children because of their immaturity and dependency. But other sexual abuse

Figure 2
Dependency Continuum for Child Victimization Types

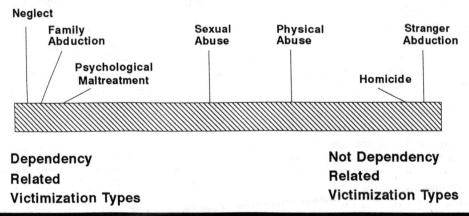

involves violence and coercion that would be victimizing even with a nondependent adult.

In the case of physical abuse, there is also some mixture. Although most of the violent acts in this category would be considered victimizing even between adults, some of them, like the shaken baby syndrome, develop almost exclusively in a caretaking relationship in which there is an enormous differential in size and physical control.

The dependency continuum is a useful concept in thinking about some of the unique features of children's victimizations. It is also helpful in generating hypotheses about the expected correlates of different types of victimization, such as variations according to age.

Developmental Victimology

Childhood is such an extremely heterogenous category—4-year-olds and 17-year-olds having little in common—that it is inherently misleading to discuss child victimization in general without reference to age. We would expect the nature, quantity, and impact of victimization to vary across childhood with the different capabilities, activities, and environments that are characteristic of different stages of development. A good term for this might be *developmental victimology*. Unfortunately, we do not have good studies of the different types of victimization across all the ages of childhood with which to examine such changes.

There are two plausible propositions about age and child victimization that could be a starting place for developmental victimology. One is that victimizations stemming from the dependent status of children should be most common among the most dependent, hence the youngest, children. A corollary is that as children grow older, their victimization profile should more and more resemble that of adults.

One can examine such propositions in a crude way with the data that are available. In fact, it is apparent (Table 4) that the types of victimization that are most concentrated in the under-12 age group are the dependency related ones (see the dependency continuum in Figure 2), particularly family abduction and physical neglect. Victimizations such as homicide and stranger abduction, which we grouped at the nondependency end of the continuum, involve a greater percentage of teenagers. However, not everything falls neatly into place; sexual abuse seems anomalously concentrated among teenagers, too. We believe this to be an artifact of the National Incidence Study (NIS) data on sexual abuse (National Center on Child Abuse and Neglect, 1981), which was based only on reported cases and thus undercounted sexual abuse of young children.[3] When the incidence of sexual abuse is based on data from retrospective self-reports, 64% of victimizations occur before age 12 (Finkelhor, Hotaling, Lewis, & Smith, 1990), a pattern more consistent with the hypothesis and the place of sexual abuse on the dependency continuum.

For additional insights about development and victimization, one can look also at child homicide, the type

Table 4

Victimization of Younger Children

Type of victimization	% of victims under 12 years of age	Source
Family abduction	81[a]	NISMART (R)
Physical neglect	70	NIS-2C
Psychological maltreatment	58[b]	NIS-2C, NSCANR
Physical abuse	56	NIS-2C
Sexual abuse	40	NIS-2C
Stranger abduction	27	NISMART (R)
Homicide	21[c]	UCR91

Note. Some figures shown in this table did not appear in original source but were derived from data presented therein. NISMART (R) = National Incidence Study of Missing, Abducted, Runaway and Thrownaway Children, 1990 (Authors' reanalysis of published data; Finkelhor, Hotaling, & Sedlak, 1990); NIS-2C = National Study of the Incidence and Severity of Child Abuse and Neglect, 1988 (Powers & Eckenrode, 1992); NSCANR = National Study on Child Abuse and Neglect Reporting, 1983 (American Association for Protecting Children, 1985); UCR91 = Uniform Crime Reports, 1991 (Federal Bureau of Investigation, 1992).
[a] Broad scope.   [b] Reflects midpoint of two divergent estimates.   [c] Age group for this category is under 10.

of victimization to which a developmental analysis has been most extensively applied (Christoffel, 1990; Crittenden & Craig, 1990; Jason, 1983). Child homicide has a conspicuous bimodal frequency, with high rates for the very youngest and oldest children (Figure 3). But the two peaks represent very different phenomena. The homicides of young children are primarily committed by parents, most often using their hands—so-called "personal weapons." In contrast, the homicides of older children are committed mostly by peers and acquaintances, most often with the use of firearms.

Although the analysts do not agree entirely on the number and age span of the specific developmental categories for child homicides, a number of propositions are clear. There is a distinct group of neonaticides, or children killed on the first day or within the first few weeks of life. Homicide at this age is generally considered to include many isolated mothers dealing with unwanted children. After the neonatal period, there follows a period in which homicides are still primarily committed by caretakers using personal weapons, but the motives and circumstances are thought to be somewhat different. These appear to be mostly cases of fatal child abuse that occur as a result of parents' attempts to control child behavior (Christoffel, 1990; Crittenden & Craig, 1990). As children become of school age and older, the nature of child homicide becomes incrementally more like adult homicide. Killings

---

[3] The undercount stems from two problems: (a) Most sexual abuse reports, unlike other forms of child maltreatment, start from children's own disclosures, which are more difficult for younger children to make. (b) Much sexual abuse goes on for extended periods of time before being disclosed, and the age data in the NIS are based on age at the time of report, not age at onset.

Figure 3
Relationship of Child Homicide Victims to Perpetrators

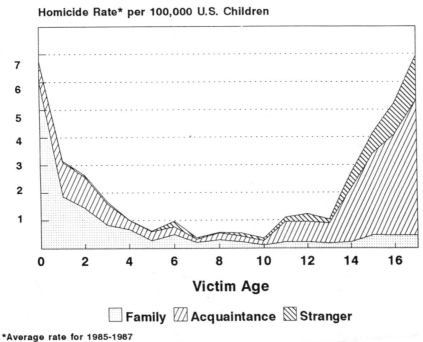

Homicide Rate* per 100,000 U.S. Children

Victim Age

☐ Family ▨ Acquaintance ▧ Stranger

*Average rate for 1985-1987

by parents and caretakers decline, and those by peers and acquaintances rise. Firearms become the predominant method.

These trends clearly suggest that the types of homicide suffered by children are related to the nature of their dependency and to the level of their integration into the adult world. These trends provide a good case for the importance and utility of a developmental perspective on child victimizations and a model of how such an approach could be applied to other types of victimization.

Intrafamily Victimization

Unlike many adults, children do not live alone; most live in families. Thus, another plausible principle of developmental victimology is that more of the victimization of children occurs at the hands of relatives. We illustrated this in Table 2 and also Table 3, showing the sheer quantity of victimization by relatives apparent in the elevated figures on sibling assault (Table 3), which outstrip any other kind of victimization.

The findings on homicide also suggest a developmental trend: Younger children have a greater proportion of their victimizations at the hands of intimates and correspondingly fewer at the hands of strangers. They live more sheltered lives, spend more time in the home and around family, and have less wealth and fewer valuable possessions that might make them attractive targets for strangers.

An additional possible principle is that the identity of perpetrators may vary according to the type of victimization and its place on the dependency continuum (Figure 2). Victimizations that are more dependency related should involve more perpetrators who are parents and family members. Accordingly, parents are 100% of the perpetrators of neglect and psychological maltreatment (Sedlak, 1991), the most dependency-related victimizations. However, they represent only 51% of the perpetrators of sexual abuse (Sedlak) and 28% of the perpetrators of homicide (Jason, Gilliand, & Taylor, 1983). This pattern occurs because the responsibilities created by children's dependency status fall primarily on parents and family members. They are the main individuals in a position to violate those responsibilities in a way that would create victimization. Thus, when a sick child fails to get available medical attention, it is the parents who are charged with neglecting the child, even if the neighbors also did nothing.

Gender and Victimization

Developmental victimology needs to take account of gender as well. On the basis of the conventional crime statistics available from the NCS and Uniform Crime Reports (UCR), boys would appear to suffer more homicide (2.3:1), more assault (1.7:1), and more robbery (2.0:1) than girls, whereas girls suffer vastly more rape (8.1:1). But this primarily pertains to the experience of adolescents and does not consider age and gender variations.

Figure 4
Gender Differences in Victimization Rates

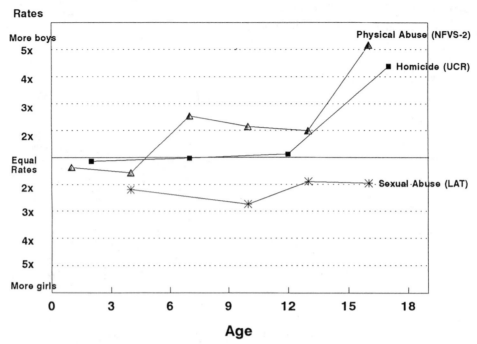

Note. NFVS-2 = National Family Violence Resurvey, 1985 (Straus & Gelles, 1990); UCR = UCR91, Uniform Crime Report (Federal Bureau of Investigation, 1992). LAT = *Los Angeles Times* Poll (Finkelhor, Hotaling, Lewis, & Smith, 1990).

Because gender differentiation increases as children grow older, a developmental hypothesis might predict that the pattern of victimization would be less gender-specific for younger children. That is, because younger boys and girls are more similar in their activities and physical characteristics, there might be less difference between sexes in the rate of victimization.

This pattern does indeed appear to be the case at least for homicide, the type of victimization for which we have the best data (Figure 4). Rates of homicide are quite similar for younger boys and girls, even up to age 14, after which point the vulnerability of boys increases dramatically.

However, this increased differentiation with age is less apparent for other types of victimization. In contrast to homicide, for example, for sexual abuse we might expect that it would be girls who would become increasingly vulnerable as they age. However, the national data do not

Table 5
Rate of Physical Injury Due to Childhood Victimization

Type of victimization	Rate of injury per 1,000 children	% of all victims sustaining injury	Source	Age in years
Assault	19.23	33	NCS90	12–19
Physical abuse	3.59	84	NIS-2	0–17
Robbery	2.71	24	NCS90	12–19
Physical neglect	1.39	52	NIS-2	0–17
Family abduction	0.22	04	NISMART	0–17
Sexual abuse	0.09	05	NIS-2	0–17
Stranger abduction	0.007–0.015	14–21	NISMART	0–17

Note. Some figures shown in this table did not appear in original source but were derived from data presented therein. NCS90 = National Crime Survey, 1990 (Bureau of Justice Statistics, 1992); NIS-2 = National Study of the Incidence and Severity of Child Abuse and Neglect, 1988 (Sedlak, 1991); NISMART = National Incidence Study of Missing, Abducted, Runaway and Thrownaway Children, 1990 (Finkelhor, Hotaling, & Sedlak, 1990).

show this. They show girls at roughly twice the risk of boys throughout childhood, with no increase during adolescence.

So it looks as though a developmental pattern in gender differentiation may apply to some forms of victimization but not others. This mixed picture in regard to gender and age merits more study. Some victimization types may have unique gender patterns reflecting their particular dynamics. However, we may also be suffering from inadequate data that are clouding the true situation.

Effects of Child Victimization

Homicide is currently one of the five leading causes of child mortality in the United States (Goetting, 1990). In addition to the more than 2,000 homicide deaths that occur each year (FBI, 1992), one needs to add a sizable proportion of 1,200 child abuse and neglect fatalities, an estimated two thirds of which are not often counted in the homicide statistics (Ewigman, Kivlahan, & Land, 1993). Victimization also results in a substantial toll of nonfatal injuries that are more difficult to count accurately. The NIS estimated that 317,700 children suffered serious or moderate physical injuries in one year (Table 5) as a result of physical abuse or neglect or sexual abuse, that is, injuries for which observable symptoms, such as bruises, lasted at least 48 hours. From the NCS, one can estimate that approximately 523,300 twelve- to 19-year-olds sustained physical injury due to an assault in 1990, and approximately 132,900 received hospital care as a result of any kind of violent crime. A Massachusetts study suggested that each year 1 in every 42 teenage boys receives hospital treatment for an assault-related injury (Guyer, Lescohier, Gallagher, Hausman, & Azzara, 1989).

Children's level of development undoubtedly influences the nature and severity of injuries resulting from victimization, although few analyses have taken such a developmental approach. An obvious example is the greater vulnerability of small children to death and serious harm as a result of inflicted blows. Another obvious example is the higher likelihood of older children to contract sexual-abuse-related HIV infection, because older children suffer more penetrative abuse (Kerns & Ritter, 1991).

In addition to physical injury, there is a growing literature documenting that victimization has grave short- and long-term effects on children's mental health. For example, sexually victimized children appear to be at a nearly fourfold increased lifetime risk for any psychiatric disorder and at a threefold risk for substance abuse (Saunders, Villeponteaux, Lipovsky, Kilpatrick, & Veronen, 1992; Scott, 1992). Scott estimated that approximately 8% of all psychiatric cases within the population at large can be attributed to childhood sexual assault.

Although they do not involve such specific epidemiological assessments, other studies have also demonstrated increased rates of mental health morbidity for other types of childhood victimization, including physical abuse (Kolko, 1992), psychological maltreatment (Briere

& Runtz, 1990), and physical punishment (Straus, in press).

In addition to general mental health impairments, a proposition that has been established across various types of victimization is that a history of such victimization increases the likelihood that someone will become a perpetrator of crime, violence, or abuse. Although this popular shibboleth has been criticized and qualified (Kaufman & Ziegler, 1987), evidence to support it comes from a wide variety of methodologies, such as longitudinal follow-ups (McCord, 1983; Widom, 1989a), studies of offender populations (Hanson & Slater, 1988), and surveys of the general population (Straus et al., 1980) and concerns a wide variety of perpetrations, including violent crime, property crime, child abuse, wife abuse, and sexual assaults (for review, see Widom, 1989b). An important qualification is that victims are not necessarily prone to repeat their own form of victimization. But the proposition that childhood victims are more likely to grow up to victimize others is firmly established.

Theory about posttraumatic stress disorder (PTSD) is being applied to, and may be a unifying concept for, understanding common psychological effects of a wide variety of child victimizations (Eth & Pynoos, 1985), including abuse in schools (Hyman, Zelikoff, & Clarke, 1988). Terr (1990) has made some effort to cast PTSD in a more developmental framework, but its application is mostly anecdotal.

Sexual abuse is the only area in which a developmental approach to the psychological impact of victimization has advanced on the basis of empirical studies (Kendall-Tackett, Williams, & Finkelhor, 1993). For example, in reaction to sexual abuse, symptoms of sexualization seem to appear more frequently among preschool than among school-age girls, who seem more aware of appropriate and inappropriate sexual conduct (Friedrich et al., 1992). This is the direction the whole area of child victimization needs to take.

Research Needs

The research needs in this field of child victimization are vast and urgent, given the size of the problem and the seriousness of its impact, and they range from studies of risk factors to studies of treatment efficacy. In the limited space of this review, we mention only three important points.

First, if we are to take child victimization seriously, we need much better statistics to document and analyze its scope, nature, and trends. We need comprehensive, yearly, national and state figures on all officially reported crimes against children and forms of child abuse. These need to be supplemented by regular national studies (one is currently in progress; Finkelhor & Dziuba-Leatherman, in press-a) to assess the vast quantity of unreported victimization, including family violence and child-to-child and indirect victimizations. Currently, the NCS records crime victimizations only down to age 12. The UCR in the past has made no age information available about crimes, with the exception of homicide. Because the national data collection system for child abuse fails to include all states and has severe methodological limitations, the information cannot be aggregated nationally or compared across states (National Center on Child Abuse and Neglect, 1992).

Second, we need theory and research that cuts across and integrates the various forms of child victimization. One example is the research illustrating how forms of victimization occur together (Claussen & Crittenden, 1991) or create vulnerability for one another (Russell, 1984). Another good example is the work on PTSD in children, which has been applied to the effects of various victimizations: sexual abuse, corporal punishment-related abuse in schools, stranger abduction, and the witnessing of homicide (Eth & Pynoos, 1985; Hyman et al., 1988; Terr, 1990). Similar cross-cutting research could be done on other subjects, such as what makes children vulnerable to victimization or how responses by family members buffer or exacerbate the impact of victimization. To be truly synthetic, this research needs to study the pandemic victimizations, not just the acute and the extraordinary, which have been the main foci in the past.

Finally, the field needs a more developmental perspective on child victimization. This would start with an understanding of the mix of victimization threats that face children of different ages. It would include the kinds of factors that place children at risk, including ecological factors, and the strategies for victimization avoidance that are appropriate at different stages of development. It would also differentiate how children, with all their individual differences, react and cope at different stages with the challenges posed by victimization. It is only through this more differentiated approach that we can understand how victimization leaves its mark on children's lives.

REFERENCES

Ageton, S. S. (1983). *Sexual assault among adolescents.* Lexington, MA: Lexington Books.

American Association for Protecting Children. (1985). *Highlights of official child neglect and abuse reporting, 1983.* Denver, CO: American Humane Association.

American School Health Association. (1985). *The national adolescent student health survey: A report on the health of America's youth.* Kent, OH: Author.

Best, J. (1990). *Threatened children: Rhetoric and concern about child-victims.* Chicago: University of Chicago Press.

Briere, J., & Runtz, M. (1990). Differential adult symptomatology associated with three types of child abuse histories. *Child Abuse and Neglect, 14,* 357–364.

Bureau of Justice Statistics. (1991). *Teenage victims: A national crime survey report* (NCJ-128129). Washington, DC: U.S. Department of Justice.

Bureau of Justice Statistics. (1992). *Criminal victimization in the United States, 1990: A national crime victimization survey report* (NCJ-134126). Washington, DC: U.S. Department of Justice.

Christoffel, K. K. (1990). Violent death and injury in U.S. children and adolescents. *American Journal of Diseases of Children, 144,* 697–706.

Claussen, A. I. E., & Crittenden, P. M. (1991). Physical and psychological maltreatment: Relations among types of maltreatment. *Child Abuse and Neglect, 15,* 5–18.

Crittenden, P. A., & Craig, S. E. (1990). Developmental trends in the nature of child homicide. *Journal of Interpersonal Violence, 5,* 202–216.

Daro, D., & Gelles, R. (1991). *Public attitudes and behaviors with respect to child abuse prevention 1987–1991* (Working paper No. 840). Chicago: National Center on Child Abuse Prevention Research, National Committee for Prevention of Child Abuse.

Daro, D., & McCurdy, K. (1991). *Current trends in child abuse reporting and fatalities: The results of the 1990 annual fifty state survey* (Working paper No. 808). Chicago: National Center on Child Abuse Prevention Research, National Committee for Prevention of Child Abuse.

Eth, S., & Pynoos, R. S. (1985). *Post-traumatic stress disorder in children.* Washington, DC: American Psychiatric Press.

Ewigman, B., Kivlahan, C., & Land, G. (1993). The Missouri Child Fatality Study: Underreporting of maltreatment fatalities among children younger than five years of age: 1983 through 1996. *Pediatrics, 91,* 330–337.

Federal Bureau of Investigation. (1992). *Crime in the United States, 1991: Uniform crime reports.* Washington, DC: U.S. Department of Justice.

Finkelhor, D., & Dziuba-Leatherman, J. (in press-a). Children as victims of violence: A national survey. *Pediatrics.*

Finkelhor, D., & Dziuba-Leatherman, J. (in press-b). Victimization prevention programs: A national survey of children's exposure and reactions. *Child Abuse and Neglect.*

Finkelhor, D., Hotaling, G. T., Lewis, I. A., & Smith, C. (1990). Sexual abuse in a national survey of adult men and women: Prevalence, characteristics, and risk factors. *Child Abuse and Neglect, 14,* 19–28.

Finkelhor, D., Hotaling, G. T., & Sedlak, A. (1990). *Missing, abducted, runaway, and thrownaway children in America: First report.* Washington, DC: Juvenile Justice Clearinghouse.

Friedrich, W. N., Grambsch, P., Damon, L., Hewitt, S. K., Koverola, C., Wolfe, V., Lang, R. A., & Broughton, D. (1992). Child Sexual Behavior Inventory: Normative and clinical comparisons. *Psychological Assessment, 4,* 303–311.

Garbarino, J. (1989). The incidence and prevalence of child maltreatment. In L. Ohlin & M. Tonry (Eds.), *Family violence* (pp. 219–261). Chicago: University of Chicago Press.

Garofalo, J., Siegel, L., & Laub, J. (1987). School-related victimizations among adolescents: An analysis of National Crime Survey narratives. *Journal of Quantitative Criminology, 3,* 321–338.

Gelles, R. J., & Straus, M. A. (1979). Determinants of violence in the family: Towards a theoretical integration. In W. R. Burr, R. Hill, F. I. Nye, & I. L. Reiss (Eds.), *Contemporary theories about the family* (Vol. 1). New York: Free Press.

Goetting, A. (1990). Child victims of homicide: A portrait of their killers and the circumstances of their deaths. *Violence and Victims, 5,* 287–296.

Greenbaum, S. (1989). *School bullying and victimization* (NSSC resource paper). Malibu, CA: National School Safety Center.

Greven, P. (1990). *Spare the child: The religious roots of punishment and the psychological impact of physical abuse.* New York: Knopf.

Guyer, B., Lescohier, I., Gallagher, S. S., Hausman, A., & Azzara, C. V. (1989). Intentional injuries among children and adolescents in Massachusetts. *The New England Journal of Medicine, 321,* 1584–1589.

Hanson, R. L., & Slater, S. (1988). Sexual victimization in the history of sexual abusers: A review. *Annals of Sex Research, 4,* 485–499.

Hart, S. N., & Brassard, M. R. (1987). A major threat to children's mental health: Psychological maltreatment. *American Psychologist, 42,* 160–165.

Hyman, I. A. (1990). *Reading, writing and the hickory stick: The appalling story of physical and psychological abuse in American schools.* Lexington, MA: Lexington Books.

Hyman, I. A., Zelikoff, W., & Clarke, J. (1988). Psychological and physical abuse in the schools: A paradigm for understanding post-traumatic stress disorder in children and youths. *Journal of Traumatic Stress, 1,* 243–267.

Jason, J. (1983). Child homicide spectrum. *American Journal of Diseases of Children, 137,* 578–581.

Jason, J., Gilliand, J. C., & Taylor, C. W. (1983). Homicide as a cause of pediatric mortality in the United States. *Pediatrics, 72,* 191–197.

Kaufman, J., & Ziegler, E. (1987). Do abused children become abusive parents? *American Journal of Orthopsychiatry, 57,* 186–192.

Kendall-Tackett, K. A., Williams, L. M., & Finkelhor, D. (1993). Impact of sexual abuse on children: A review and synthesis of recent empirical studies. *Psychological Bulletin, 113,* 164–180.

Kerns, D. L., & Ritter, M. L. (1991, September). *Data analysis of the medical evaluation of 1,800 suspected child sexual abuse victims.* Paper presented at the Ninth National Conference on Child Abuse and Neglect, Denver, CO.

Kilpatrick, D. (1992). *Rape in America: A report to the nation.* Charleston, SC: Crime Victims Research Center.

Kolko, D. J. (1992). Characteristics of child victims of physical violence: Research findings and clinical implications. *Journal of Interpersonal Violence, 7,* 244–276.

Lauritsen, J. L., Sampson, R. J., & Laub, J. H. (1991). The link between offending and victimization among adolescents. *Criminology, 29,* 265–292.

McCord, J. (1983). A forty year perspective on effects of child abuse and neglect. *Child Abuse and Neglect, 7,* 265–270.

McDermott, M. J., Stanley, J. E., & Zimmerman-McKinney, M. A. (1982). The victimization of children and youths. *Victimology, 7,* 162–177.

Morgan, J., & Zedner, L. (1992). *Child victims: Crime, impact, and criminal justice.* Oxford, England: Clarendon Press.

National Center on Child Abuse and Neglect. (1981). *Study findings, National Study of the Incidence and Severity of Child Abuse and Neglect* (OHDS Publication No. 81-30325). Washington, DC: Department of Health and Human Services.

National Center on Child Abuse and Neglect. (1992). *National child abuse and neglect data system* (Working paper No. 1): *1990 summary data component* (DHHS Publication No. ACF 92-30361). Washington, DC: Department of Health and Human Services.

Olweus, D. (1978). *Aggression in the schools: Bullies and whipping boys.* Washington, DC: Hemisphere.

Pagelow, M. D. (1989). The incidence and prevalence of criminal abuse of other family members. In L. Ohlin & M. Tonry (Eds.), *Family violence* (pp. 263–314). Chicago: University of Chicago Press.

Powers, J., & Eckenrode, J. (1992, March). *The epidemiology of adolescent maltreatment.* Paper presented at the Fourth Biennial Meeting of the Society for Research on Adolescence, Washington, DC.

Russell, D. (1984). *Sexual exploitation: Rape, child sexual abuse, and workplace harassment.* Beverly Hills, CA: Sage.

Saunders, B. E., Villeponteaux, L. A., Lipovsky, J. A., Kilpatrick, D. G., & Veronen, L. J. (1992). Child sexual assault as a risk factor for mental disorders among women: A community survey. *Journal of Interpersonal Violence, 7,* 189–204.

Scott, K. D. (1992). Childhood sexual abuse: Impact on a community's mental health status. *Child Abuse and Neglect, 16,* 285–295.

Sedlak, A. J. (1991). *Supplementary analyses of data on the national incidence of child abuse and neglect.* Rockville, MD: Westat.

Straus, M. A. (in press). Corporal punishment of children and depression and suicide in adulthood. In J. McCord (Ed.), *Coercion and punishment in long-term perspective.* Cambridge, England: Cambridge University Press.

Straus, M. A., & Gelles, R. J. (1990). *Physical violence in American families: Risk factors and adaptations to violence in 8,145 families.* New Brunswick, NJ: Transaction.

Straus, M., Gelles, R., & Steinmetz, S. K. (1980). *Behind closed doors: Violence in the American family.* Garden City, NY: Anchor Press.

Terr, L. (1990). *Too scared to cry.* New York: Harper/Collins.

Widom, C. S. (1989a). The cycle of violence. *Science, 244,* 160–166.

Widom, C. S. (1989b). Does violence beget violence? A critical examination of the literature. *Psychological Bulletin, 106,* 3–28.

APPENDIX

Sources of Data

Acronym	Survey
50-SS	Annual Fifty State Survey, 1990 (Daro & McCurdy, 1991).
LAECA	Los Angeles Epidemiologic Catchment Area data (Scott, 1992).
LAT	*Los Angeles Times* Poll (Finkelhor, Hotaling, Lewis, & Smith, 1990).
NASHS	National Adolescent Student Health Survey (American School Health Association, 1985).
NCS90	National Crime Survey, 1990 (Bureau of Justice Statistics, 1992).
NCSTEEN	National Crime Survey, 1979–1988 (as presented in Bureau of Justice Statistics, 1991).
NFVS-1	National Family Violence Survey, 1975 (Straus & Gelles, 1990).
NFVS-2	National Family Violence Resurvey, 1985 (Straus & Gelles, 1990).
NISMART	National Incidence Study of Missing, Abducted, Runaway and Thrownaway Children, 1990 (Finkelhor, Hotaling, & Sedlak, 1990).
NSCANR	National Study on Child Abuse and Neglect Reporting, 1983 (American Association for Protecting Children, 1985).
NIS-1	National Study of the Incidence and Severity of Child Abuse and Neglect, 1981 (National Center on Child Abuse and Neglect, 1981).
NIS-2	National Study of the Incidence and Severity of Child Abuse and Neglect, 1988 (Sedlak, 1991).
NIS-2C	National Study of the Incidence and Severity of Child Abuse and Neglect, 1988 (as presented in Powers & Eckenrode, 1992).
NYS	National Youth Survey (Lauritsen, Sampson, & Laub, 1991).
NYS78	National Youth Survey, 1978 (Ageton, 1983).
UCR91	Uniform Crime Reports, 1991 (Federal Bureau of Investigation, 1992).

Resilience in Development

Emmy E. Werner

Emmy E. Werner is Professor of Human Development at the University of California, Davis. Address correspondence to Emmy E. Werner, Department of Applied Behavioral Sciences, University of California, Davis, 2321 Hart Hall, Davis, CA 95616.

During the past decade, a number of investigators from different disciplines—child development, psychology, psychiatry, and sociology—have focused on the study of children and youths who overcame great odds. These researchers have used the term resilience to describe three kinds of phenomena: good developmental outcomes despite high-risk status, sustained competence under stress, and recovery from trauma. Under each of these conditions, behavioral scientists have focused their attention on protective factors, or mechanisms that moderate (ameliorate) a person's reaction to a stressful situation or chronic adversity so that his or her adaptation is more successful than would be the case if the protective factors were not present.[1]

So far, only a relatively small number of studies have focused on children who were exposed to biological insults. More numerous in the current research literature are studies of resilient children who grew up in chronic poverty, were exposed to parental psychopathology, or experienced the breakup of their family or serious caregiving deficits. There has also been a growing body of literature on resilience in children who have endured the horrors of contemporary wars.

Despite the heterogeneity of all these studies, one can begin to discern a common core of individual dispositions and sources of support that contribute to resilience in development. These protective buffers appear to transcend ethnic, social-class, and geographic boundaries. They also appear to make a more profound impact on the life course of individuals who grow up in adversity than do specific risk factors or stressful life events.

Most studies of individual resilience and protective factors in children have been short-term, focusing on middle childhood and adolescence. An exception is the Kauai Longitudinal Study, with which I have been associated during the past three decades.[2] This study has involved a team of pediatricians, psychologists, and public-health and social workers who have monitored the impact of a variety of biological and psychosocial risk factors, stressful life events, and protective factors on the development of a multiethnic cohort of 698 children born in 1955 on the "Garden Island" in the Hawaiian chain. These individuals were followed, with relatively little attrition, from the prenatal period through birth to ages 1, 2, 10, 18, and 32.

Some 30% of the survivors in this study population were considered high-risk children because they were born in chronic poverty, had experienced perinatal stress, and lived in family environments troubled by chronic discord, divorce, or parental psychopathology. Two thirds of the children who had experienced four or more such risk factors by age 2 developed serious learning or behavior problems by age 10 or had delinquency records, mental health problems, or pregnancies by age 18. But one third of the children who had experienced four or more such risk factors developed instead into competent, confident, and caring adults.

PROTECTIVE FACTORS WITHIN THE INDIVIDUAL

Infancy and Early Childhood

Our findings with these resilient children are consistent with the results of several other longitudinal studies which have reported that young children with good coping abilities under adverse conditions have temperamental characteristics that elicit positive responses from a wide range of caregivers. The resilient boys and girls in the Kauai study were consistently characterized by their mothers as active, affectionate, cuddly, good-natured, and easy to deal with. Egeland and his associates observed similar dispositions among securely attached infants of abusing mothers in the Minnesota Mother-Child Interaction Project,[3] and Moriarty found the same qualities among infants with congenital defects at the Menninger Foundation.[4] Such infants were alert, easy to soothe, and able to elicit support from a nurturant family member. An "easy" temperament and the ability to actively recruit competent adult caregivers were also observed by Elder and his associates[5] in the resourceful children of the Great Depression.

By the time they reach preschool

age, resilient children appear to have developed a coping pattern that combines autonomy with an ability to ask for help when needed. These characteristics are also predictive of resilience in later years.

Middle Childhood and Adolescence

When the resilient children in the Kauai Longitudinal Study were in elementary school, their teachers were favorably impressed by their communication and problem-solving skills. Although these children were not particularly gifted, they used whatever talents they had effectively. Usually they had a special interest or a hobby they could share with a friend, and that gave them a sense of pride. These interests and activities were not narrowly sex typed. Both the boys and the girls grew into adolescents who were outgoing and autonomous, but also nurturant and emotionally sensitive.

Similar findings have been reported by Anthony, who studied the resilient offspring of mentally ill parents in St. Louis;[6] by Felsman and Vaillant, who followed successful boys from a high-crime neighborhood in Boston into adulthood;[7] and by Rutter and Quinton, who studied the lives of British girls who had been institutionalized in childhood, but managed to become well-functioning adults and caring mothers.[8]

Most studies of resilient children and youths report that intelligence and scholastic competence are positively associated with the ability to overcome great odds. It stands to reason that youngsters who are better able to appraise stressful life events correctly are also better able to figure out strategies for coping with adversity, either through their own efforts or by actively reaching out to other people for help. This finding has been replicated in studies of Asian-American, Cauca-

sian, and African-American children.[2,9,10]

Other salient protective factors that operated in the lives of the resilient youths on Kauai were a belief in their own effectiveness (an internal locus of control) and a positive self-concept. Such characteristics were also found by Farrington among successful and law-abiding British youngsters who grew up in high-crime neighborhoods in London,[11] and by Wallerstein and her associates among American children who coped effectively with the breakup of their parents' marriages.[12]

PROTECTIVE FACTORS WITHIN THE FAMILY

Despite the burden of chronic poverty, family discord, or parental psychopathology, a child identified as resilient usually has had the opportunity to establish a close bond with at least one competent and emotionally stable person who is attuned to his or her needs. The stress-resistant children in the Kauai Longitudinal Study, the well-functioning offspring of child abusers in the Minnesota Mother-Child Interaction Project, the resilient children of psychotic parents studied by Anthony in St. Louis, and the youngsters who coped effectively with the breakup of their parents' marriages in Wallerstein's studies of divorce all had received enough good nurturing to establish a basic sense of trust.[2,3,6,12]

Much of this nurturing came from substitute caregivers within the extended family, such as grandparents and older siblings. Resilient children seem to be especially adept at recruiting such surrogate parents. In turn, they themselves are often called upon to take care of younger siblings and to practice acts of "required helpfulness" for members of their family who are ill or incapacitated.[2]

Both the Kauai Longitudinal

Study and Block and Gjerde's studies of ego-resilient children[9] found characteristic child-rearing orientations that appear to promote resiliency differentially in boys and girls. Resilient boys tend to come from households with structure and rules, where a male serves as a model of identification (father, grandfather, or older brother), and where there is some encouragement of emotional expressiveness. Resilient girls, in contrast, tend to come from households that combine an emphasis on risk taking and independence with reliable support from a female caregiver, whether mother, grandmother, or older sister. The example of a mother who is gainfully and steadily employed appears to be an especially powerful model of identification for resilient girls.[2] A number of studies of resilient children from a wide variety of socioeconomic and ethnic backgrounds have also noted that the families of these children held religious beliefs that provided stability and meaning in times of hardship and adversity.[2,6,10]

PROTECTIVE FACTORS IN THE COMMUNITY

The Kauai Longitudinal Study and a number of other prospective studies in the United States have shown that resilient youngsters tend to rely on peers and elders in the community as sources of emotional support and seek them out for counsel and comfort in times of crisis.[2,6]

Favorite teachers are often positive role models. All of the resilient high-risk children in the Kauai study could point to at least one teacher who was an important source of support. These teachers listened to the children, challenged them, and rooted for them—whether in grade school, high school, or community college. Similar findings have been reported by Wallerstein and her associates from their long-term observations of youngsters who coped effectively with their parents' divorces[12] and by Rutter and his associates from their studies of inner-city schools in London.[13]

Finally, in the Kauai study, we found that the opening of opportunities at major life transitions enabled the majority of the high-risk children who had a troubled adolescence to rebound in their 20s and early 30s. Among the most potent second chances for such youths were adult education programs in community colleges, voluntary military service, active participation in a church community, and a supportive friend or marital partner. These protective buffers were also observed by Elder in the adult lives of the children of the Great Depression,[14] by Furstenberg and his associates in the later lives of black teenage mothers,[15] and by Farrington[11] and Felsman and Vaillant[7] in the adult lives of young men who had grown up in high-crime neighborhoods in London and Boston.

PROTECTIVE FACTORS: A SUMMARY

Several clusters of protective factors have emerged as recurrent themes in the lives of children who overcome great odds. Some protective factors are characteristics of the individual: Resilient children are engaging to other people, adults and peers alike; they have good communication and problem-solving skills, including the ability to recruit substitute caregivers; they have a talent or hobby that is valued by their elders or peers; and they have faith that their own actions can make a positive difference in their lives.

Another factor that enhances resilience in development is having affectional ties that encourage trust, autonomy, and initiative. These ties are often provided by members of the extended family. There are also support systems in the community that reinforce and reward the competencies of resilient children and provide them with positive role models: caring neighbors, teachers, elder mentors, youth workers, and peers.

LINKS BETWEEN PROTECTIVE FACTORS AND SUCCESSFUL ADAPTATION IN HIGH-RISK CHILDREN AND YOUTHS

In the Kauai study, when we examined the links between protective factors within the individual and outside sources of support, we noted a certain continuity in the life course of the high-risk individuals who successfully overcame a variety of childhood adversities. Their individual dispositions led them to select or construct environments that, in turn, reinforced and sustained their active approach to life and rewarded their special competencies.

Although the sources of support available to the individuals in their childhood homes were modestly linked to the quality of the individuals' adaptation as adults, their competencies, temperament, and self-esteem had a greater impact. Many resilient high-risk youths on Kauai left the adverse conditions of their childhood homes after high school and sought environments they found more compatible. In short, they picked their own niches.

Our findings lend some empirical support to Scarr and McCartney's theory[16] about how people make their own environment. Scarr and McCartney proposed three types of effects of people's genes on their environment: passive, evocative, and active. Because parents provide both children's genes and their rearing environments, children's genes are necessarily correlated with their own environments. This is the passive type of genotype-environment effect. The evocative type refers to the fact that a person's partially heritable characteristics, such as intelligence, personality, and physical attractiveness, evoke certain responses from other people. Finally, called an active genotype-environment effect. In line with this theory, there was a shift from passive to active effects as the youths and young adults in the Kauai study left stressful home environments and sought extrafamilial environments (at school, at work, in the military) that they found more compatible and stimulating. Genotype-environment effects of the evocative sort tended to persist throughout the different life stages we studied, as individuals' physical characteristics, temperament, and intelligence elicited differential responses from other people (parents, teachers, peers).

IMPLICATIONS

So far, most studies of resilience have focused on children and youths who have "pulled themselves up by their bootstraps," with informal support by kith and kin, not on recipients of intervention services. Yet there are some lessons such children can teach society about effective intervention: If we want to help vulnerable youngsters become more resilient, we need to decrease their exposure to potent risk factors and increase their competencies and self-esteem, as well as the sources of support they can draw upon.

In *Within Our Reach*, Schorr has isolated a set of common characteristics of social programs that have successfully prevented poor outcomes for children who grew up in high-risk families.[17] Such programs typically offer a broad spectrum of health, education, and family support services, cross professional boundaries, and view the child in the context of the family, and the family in the context of the community. They provide children with sustained access to competent and caring adults, both professionals and volunteers, who teach them problem-solving skills, enhance their communication skills and self-esteem, and provide positive role models for them.

There is an urgent need for more systematic evaluations of such programs to illuminate the process by which we can forge a chain of protective factors that enables vulnerable children to become competent, confident, and caring individuals, despite the odds of chronic poverty or a medical or social disability. Future research on risk and resiliency needs to acquire a cross-cultural perspective as well. We need to know more about individual dispositions and sources of support that transcend cultural boundaries and operate effectively in a variety of high-risk contexts.

Notes

1. A.S. Masten, K.M. Best, and N. Garmezy, Resilience and development: Contributions from the study of children who overcame adversity, *Development and Psychopathology, 2,* 425–444 (1991).

2. All results from this study that are discussed in this review were reported in E.E. Werner, Risk resilience, and recovery: Perspectives from the Kauai Longitudinal Study, *Development and Psychopathology, 5,* 503–515 (1993).

3. B. Egeland, D. Jacobvitz, and L.A. Sroufe, Breaking the cycle of child abuse, *Child Development, 59,* 1080–1088 (1988).

4. A. Moriarty, John, a boy who acquired resilience, in *The Invulnerable Child*, E.J. Anthony and B.J. Cohler, Eds. (Guilford Press, New York, 1987).

5. G.H. Elder, K. Liker, and C.E. Cross, Parent-child behavior in the Great Depression, in *Life Span Development and Behavior,* Vol. 6, T.B. Baltes and O.G. Brim, Jr., Eds. (Academic Press, New York, 1984).

6. E.J. Anthony, Children at risk for psychosis growing up successfully, in *The Invulnerable Child*, E.J. Anthony and B.J. Cohler, Eds. (Guilford Press, New York, 1987).

7. J.K. Felsman and G.E. Vaillant, Resilient children as adults: A 40 year study, in *The Invulnerable Child*, E.J. Anthony and B.J. Cohler, Eds. (Guilford Press, New York, 1987).

8. M. Rutter and D. Quinton, Long term follow-up of women institutionalized in childhood: Factors promoting good functioning in adult life, *British Journal of Developmental Psychology, 18,* 225–234 (1984).

9. J. Block and P.F. Gjerde, *Early antecedents of ego resiliency in late adolescence,* paper presented at the annual meeting of the American Psychological Association, Washington, DC (August 1986).

10. R.M. Clark, *Family Life and School Achievement: Why Poor Black Children Succeed or Fail* (University of Chicago Press, Chicago, 1983).

11. D.P. Farrington, *Protective Factors in the Development of Juvenile Delinquency and Adult Crime* (Institute of Criminology, Cambridge University, Cambridge, England, 1993).

12. J.S. Wallerstein and S. Blakeslee, *Second Chances: Men, Women and Children a Decade After Divorce* (Ticknor and Fields, New York, 1989).

13. M. Rutter, B. Maughan, P. Mortimore, and J. Ousten, *Fifteen Thousand Hours: Secondary Schools and Their Effects on Children* (Harvard University Press, Cambridge, MA, 1979).

14. G.H. Elder, Military times and turning points in men's lives, *Developmental Psychology, 22,* 233–245 (1986).

15. F.F. Furstenberg, J. Brooks-Gunn, and S.P. Morgan, *Adolescent Mothers in Later Life* (Cambridge University Press, New York, 1987).

16. S. Scarr and K. McCartney, How people make their own environments: A theory of genotype → environment effects, *Child Development, 54,* 424–435 (1983).

17. L. Schorr, *Within Our Reach: Breaking the Cycle of Disadvantage* (Anchor Press, New York, 1988).

Recommended Reading

Haggerty, R., Garmezy, N., Rutter, M., and Sherrod. L., Eds. (1994). *Stress, Risk, and Resilience in Childhood and Adolescence* (Cambridge University Press, New York).

Luthar, S., and Zigler, E. (1991). Vulnerability and competence: A review of research on resilience in childhood. *American Journal of Orthopsychiatry, 61,* 6–22.

Werner, E.E., and Smith, R.S. (1992). *Overcoming the Odds: High Risk Children From Birth to Adulthood* (Cornell University Press, Ithaca, NY).

Editor's Note: *Most children who are diagnosed by competent mental health professionals as having attention-deficit hyperactivity disorder do; but as early childhood educators, we must always ensure that our classrooms are developmentally appropriate and that children are not being inappropriately labeled because our classroom is inappropriate.*

Young Children With Attention Deficits

Steven Landau and Cecile McAninch

Steven Landau, Ph.D., is a professor of psychology at Illinois State University. Previously a school psychologist, his research interests include ADHD and problems associated with peer rejection.

Cecile McAninch, M.A., is completing her doctorate in clinical psychology at the University of Kentucky. Her areas of interest include children's self-concept and social cognition.

Three-year-old Jamie was expelled from preschool after frequent fights with other children. If Jamie and the other boys were playing with trucks, Jamie was the first one to start crashes, which escalated into wild behavior. In the sandbox it was always Jamie who threw sand in someone's face or grabbed the shovel from another child. After a month of preschool, Jamie's teacher became worried that Jamie might seriously hurt another child, and she asked Jamie's mother to keep him home.

Jamie's parents were dismayed by this request. They knew that he was a difficult child. They found Jamie hard to manage because he seemed to have an excessive activity level and a short attention span and was prone to numerous temper outbursts. Indeed, he had been "difficult" since infancy; however, they wanted to believe that this was simply a phase he was going through—a difficult period of development—and that he would outgrow these problems sometime soon. They even considered the possibility that Jamie's preschool teacher didn't understand him—that she could intervene more before he became too excited and wound up. These problems were thus simply developmental (i.e., he is just "all boy"), or they were best understood as a function of an intolerant preschool teacher. Maybe a better preschool would be the answer.

Jamie, who was first described by Campbell (1988), is representative of many young children referred for atten-tion-deficit hyperactivity disorder (ADHD). What is ADHD, and how does it differ from hyperactivity? ADHD is the current psychiatric term used to describe a set of symptoms reflecting excessive inattention, overactivity, and impulsive responding. It is important to note that the presence of these symptoms must be established in the context of what is developmentally appropriate for the child's age and gender group. ADHD is found in 3 to 5% of the childhood population (American Psychiatric Association, 1987) and is clearly a disorder that is far more prevalent in males; sex differences among children referred for treatment average about six males to one female. Because ADHD is the formal diagnostic label from the psychiatric classification scheme (i.e., the *Diagnostic and Statistical Manual of Mental Disorders* [DSM–III–R]; American Psychiatric Association, 1987), this is the term used by family physicians, pediatricians, psychiatrists, and other mental health clinicians. Indeed, all professionals who deal with children, *except* professionals in the public school system, employ the psychiatric classification scheme and, thus, the term ADHD.

The fact that children considered "in need of special services" by their school according to Public Law 94–142 are not required to have a formal DSM–III–R psychiatric diagnosis for placement creates confused communication among parents, school personnel, and community professionals. Confusion is further increased by the fact that the nomenclature pertaining to this disorder has changed several times over the years. The disorder has previously been known as "brain damage syndrome"; "minimal brain dysfunction"; "hyperkinetic reaction to childhood"; "attention deficit disorder (with and without hyperactivity)"; and, most recently, "attention-deficit hyperactivity disorder." Although frustrating for some, this trend of changing terminology clearly represents improved understanding of the disorder (Schaughency & Rothlind, 1991).

Primary symptoms

The preceding overview of evolving terminology makes it apparent that there has been a shift in emphasis regarding what is considered most central to the disor-

The column in this issue was edited by Laura E. Berk, Ph.D., professor of psychology at Illinois State University.

der. Many researchers agree that a deficit in *sustained attention,* the inability to remain vigilant, represents the area of greatest difficulty for the child with ADHD (Douglas, 1983); thus, children with ADHD show significantly less persistence than their classmates. Even though many teachers use the term *distractible* to characterize their observations of school performance, distractibility implies that the child with ADHD seems unable to select relevant from irrelevant stimuli that compete for their attention (i.e., a *selective attention* deficit). The bulk of current research, however, suggests that their greatest difficulties stem from an inability to *sustain a response* long enough to accomplish assigned tasks, that is, they lack perseverance in their efforts. As a consequence, parents and teachers attribute to them characterizations such as "doesn't seem to listen," "fails to finish assigned tasks," "can't concentrate," "can't work independently of supervision," "requires more redirection," and "confused or seems to be in a fog"—all apparently the result of this inability to sustain attention (Barkley, 1990).

It is important to stress, however, that even though inattention may be the source of some difficulty in a less structured, free-play setting, highly structured academic settings create the greatest problem for these children (Milich, Loney, & Landau, 1982). The specific expectations within a setting and the degree of structure in that setting thus play important roles in determining the presence of the disorder. This may explain, in part, why parents and teachers do not tend to agree when rating the symptoms of these children (Achenbach, McConaughy, & Howell, 1987). Expectations in the home environment are simply different from those at school. This point was recently reinforced in a study by Landau, Lorch, and Milich (1992). These investigators were intrigued by the surprising but frequent parent report that their child with ADHD is able to attend to television (e.g., "What do you mean he can't pay attention in school? He sits glued to the TV for hours!"). In fact, a recent advice column in *Parents* magazine suggested that parents could rule out thoughts of ADHD if their child was able to pay attention to television. Results of the study by Landau and his colleagues indicated that boys diagnosed with ADHD who were extremely inattentive in the classroom were able to attend to educational television programming to a high degree, and their attention was indistinguishable from that of normal agemates under some circumstances. It seems evident that television may hold greater intrinsic appeal than schoolwork for the child with ADHD, plus TV does not represent the historical source of frustration and failure associated with classroom performance. Apparently the nature of the task seems crucial when determining if the child has significant difficulty paying attention.

Related to problems with inattention, children with ADHD are *impulsive;* they experience difficulty *inhibiting* their response in certain situations (Barkley, 1990). As with inattention, impulsivity is a multidimensional construct; it can be defined in several ways (Olson, 1989). Children with ADHD, for example, are impulsive when confronted with academic tasks. They are extremely quick to respond without considering all alternatives; thus they are known as fast but careless and inaccurate problem solvers. This type of response style can have a profound influence on the child's ability to perform in an academic setting. Besides affecting cognitive performance, impulsivity can also manifest itself as an inability to suppress inappropriate behavior. As such, children with ADHD are also known to be high-risk takers, as evidenced by their running out in traffic. In addition, they seem unable to delay gratification (Campbell, Szumowski, Ewing, Gluck, & Breaux, 1982). In school they experience difficulty waiting their turn in line, blurt out answers in class, constantly touch other children, and tend to be undesirable playmates because of their difficulty with turn taking, sharing, and cooperation, and their low tolerance for frustration while playing games (Landau & Moore, 1991).

The third primary symptom involves motor excess, or *overactivity.* Historically overactivity was considered the hallmark characteristic of the disorder and served as the source for the enduring "hyperactivity" label applied to these children. This is probably because overactivity remains the most salient symptom and possibly the symptom most annoying to others. In fact, parents of children with ADHD retrospectively report overactivity to be an early marker of the disorder (Campbell, 1988), even though it is also a common complaint from parents of normal children (Lapouse & Monk, 1958; Richman, Stevenson, & Graham, 1982). As with the other symptoms, overactivity can take many forms but is especially apparent as excessive body movements (both major and minor motor) and vocalizations; for example, these children are described as "always on the go" or "squirmy and fidgety," or as a child who "can't sit still," "hums and makes other odd noises," "talks incessantly," and "climbs excessively" (Barkley, 1990).

When children with ADHD engage in table activities or academic seatwork, they constantly get up and down from the desk (or do all seatwork while standing). Many show minor motor fidgeting, such as pencil tapping or leg shaking, and they seem unable to keep their hands off objects unrelated to the task at hand. During individual psychological testing, children with ADHD can be extremely challenging subjects because they attempt to manipulate the examiner's test materials throughout the evaluation. Finally, they are often overactive and incessantly talkative in the context of social play—behaviors that seem to have a negative effect on peer relations (Landau & Moore, 1991). Again, it is important to remember that setting demands—in particular, the degree of structure in the environment—affect the extent to which these children are problems to their teachers. The child with ADHD may be considered quite troublesome, for example, in a highly structured academic setting, with desks placed in rows and all work to be accomplished in one's seat. In contrast, in the open-classroom setting where cooperative learning is encouraged and children are expected to move about and collaborate with others, the child with ADHD may be less distinctive and disturbing to others (Jacob, O'Leary, & Rosenblad, 1978).

Secondary symptoms or associated characteristics

Children with ADHD experience numerous difficulties that go beyond inattention, impulsive responding, and overactivity. Although these problems are not related to the diagnosis of ADHD, the fact that children with ADHD present these added difficulties accounts for the extreme heterogeneity among ADHD cases.

First, children with ADHD are at elevated risk for problems related to conduct disorder. Although the rates of overlap vary with each study, most investigators agree that at least one half of all children with ADHD also meet diagnostic criteria for conduct disorder. In these children one finds extreme stubbornness, noncompliance, hostility, rule violations, stealing, lying, and aggressive acts (Hinshaw, 1987). Studies of children with ADHD indicate that those who show conduct disorder not only are more difficult to manage as children but also will have more serious adolescent and adult adjustment problems (Weiss & Hechtman, 1986).

Second, many children with ADHD are rejected by their peers (Landau & Moore, 1991). In fact, many boys with ADHD who are not aggressive seem to be more "disliked" than their classmates who are highly aggressive but do not have ADHD (Milich & Landau, 1989), and this negative reputation may be established after only brief contact with unfamiliar children (Pelham & Bender, 1982). This effect on others is not surprising, as children with ADHD tend to be bossy, intrusive, disruptive, and easily frustrated while in the play group. They have few, if any, friends. Peer rejection is a serious outcome of ADHD because children who are rejected early in life tend to be at high risk for many adult adjustment difficulties, including job terminations, bad-conduct discharge from the military, negative contact with police, and psychiatric hospitalization (Parker & Asher, 1987).

Third, children with ADHD are at high risk for achievement difficulties, and many meet special-education placement criteria as learning disabled (McGee & Share, 1988). Because children with ADHD in the academic setting are typically off task, noisy, disruptive, out-of-seat, and do not finish schoolwork or homework, parents and teachers complain of underachievement. These children's work tends to be highly inefficient and disorganized, and their performance often shows great fluctuations.

Finally, these children seem to experience problems dealing with the numerous transitions in school (such as going from recess back to class). They have difficulty adapting their behaviors as situational expectations change (Landau & Milich, 1988). Consequently, there may be a grave discrepancy between actual achievement in school and the child's estimated potential for learning. As children with ADHD accumulate a history of negative feedback from parents, teachers, and peers, it is little wonder that they are also at risk for low self-esteem and depression as they mature.

Effects on the classroom

Children with ADHD can be an extremely negative force in the classroom setting. They tend to evoke numerous negative interactions with their teachers and take teacher time away from other children. They are disruptive to learning activities; try to dominate social situations; and, to make matters worse, do not perform well academically. Indeed, the presence of a child with ADHD in the preschool setting serves as a catalyst for significantly more negative teacher feedback to all children in the classroom (Campbell, Endman, & Bernfeld, 1977).

Causal hypotheses

Many causal explanations for ADHD have been proposed over the years. First, research indicates that the role of genetic transmission must be taken seriously. Parents and siblings of children diagnosed with ADHD are more likely to have the disorder, and studies of twins indicate that identical twins are much more likely to share the disorder than are fraternal twins. Second, researchers are currently working on identifying a neurobiological cause, such as a deficit in the neurotransmitters that control attention, although none has yet been isolated (Hynd, Hern, Voeller, & Marshall, 1991). Third, there is intriguing correlational evidence that maternal smoking and/or alcohol use during pregnancy may be linked to increased risk for ADHD. Fourth, in spite of widespread belief among lay persons and the popularity of the "Feingold Diet" (1975), sugar consumption does *not* seem to be related to the symptoms of ADHD (Wolraich, Milich, Stumbo, & Schultz, 1985). Finally, there is no evidence to suggest that parenting or childrearing is in any way related to the primary symptoms of the disorder; however, some of the secondary problems associated with ADHD (such as conduct disorder and self-esteem problems) may be the consequence of factors in the child's social environment.

Assessment of ADHD

Because symptoms of impulsivity, poor attention, and excessive activity may differ among children with ADHD and across various situations, a multidimensional approach to assessment is necessary. Parent, teacher, and possibly even peer reports, plus observation in the naturalistic setting, are considered in the evaluation of ADHD. This assessment is designed to go beyond offering an actual diagnosis. A comprehensive school-based evaluation should provide data to develop a thorough intervention plan for the child.

Parents

Parents are, of course, an important source of information about children's behavior because they observe the children daily and in a variety of settings. In addition, parents are in a position to notice fluctuations in behavior in response to different situations and varying responses to treatment. Parent reports are not sufficient in the evaluation of ADHD, however, for two reasons. First, parents do not have exposure to the full range of child behavior. They may be unaware of developmental norms and what constitutes age-appropriate behavior. Second, as stated earlier, the symptoms of ADHD may not be as troublesome in the home, a setting that typically is less structured than school. Although parent reports are necessary, information from other sources must be considered as well.

Teachers

Teachers serve as an essential source in the assessment of ADHD, and there are several rating scales by which teachers may easily communicate their knowledge and concerns regarding the child. These scales provide a normative comparison; teachers are asked to rate the degree to which the child's behavior differs from the behavior of other children in the class. Like parents, teachers have almost daily contact with these children. Unlike parents, teachers are also exposed to many other children of the same age and are able to use their *normative perspective* to determine if the referred child is behaving in age-inappropriate ways. In addition, teachers observe these children in unstructured play settings as well as highly structured academic settings, where symptoms of ADHD are more likely to emerge. Teacher input is thus integral in the assessment of ADHD (see Barkley, 1990, for a review of these rating scales).

Naturalistic observation data

An important source of information regarding the child with ADHD—one that has direct implications for treatment planning—involves systematic observation of the child in classroom and play settings. By using previously defined code categories that quantify the amount of time the child with ADHD spends engaged in on-task behavior and in various inappropriate off-task behaviors, it is possible to get *direct* information about how the child is functioning. In addition, it is helpful to collect these data on the same-sex classmates of the child. In this way it is possible to determine that Billy, who presents symptoms suggestive of ADHD, attends to math or storytime 22% of the time, while the other boys in his class attend an average of 84% during that same observation session. Because parent and teacher reports are based on previous contact with the child (i.e., numerous *retrospective* observations) and may be biased by the disruptive nature of the child's behavior, direct observation of the child with ADHD is the only way to provide data on *current* behavior, and these data will facilitate interpretation of the reports from parents and teachers.

Peers

One final area to be considered in the assessment process involves the child's peer interactions. Classroom sociometric assessment, which can provide information about peer popularity and rejection, in combination with measures of social loneliness and social anxiety offers valuable information about the child's social functioning and may highlight areas for intervention (see Landau & Milich, 1990, for a discussion of appropriate measures).

Preschool issues

Special issues arise in the assessment of preschool-age children. Most measures used to diagnose ADHD, for example, are not normed for preschoolers and may be developmentally inappropriate for this age group (Barkley, 1990). Furthermore, high activity level and noncompliance in very young children may either signify

Many children with ADHD are rejected by their peers. Children with ADHD tend to be bossy, intrusive, disruptive, and easily frustrated while in the play group. They have few, if any, friends. Peer rejection is a serious outcome of ADHD because children who are rejected early in life tend to be at high risk for many adult adjustment difficulties, including job terminations, bad-conduct discharge from the military, negative contact with police, and psychiatric hospitalization.

problems or simply represent normal development. In assessing preschoolers, therefore, special emphasis must be placed on the severity and frequency of a disruptive behavior rather than on its presence or absence (Campbell, 1990). Parents who are unaware of developmental norms tend to overreport problems with their children due to unrealistic expectations, thereby engendering additional conflict. On the other hand, some parents may be overly lenient and thus fail to notice potential problems.

Finally, teacher reports of behavior are obviously unavailable for those young children who do not attend preschool. Problems exist, however, even when teacher reports are obtainable (Barkley, 1990). As mentioned earlier, the public school classroom is an important arena in which to assess ADHD due to its structure; preschool settings are generally less structured and can therefore accommodate children with attentional deficits more easily. Preschool-based assessments thus may yield much less informative information than assessments conducted in grade school. Activities of daily living (e.g., eating, dressing) are more likely to be the source of conflict at this age. Even in this area, however, it is important to not confuse the child's normal attempts at autonomy with ADHD-related management difficulties.

Treatment of ADHD

Once assessment has indicated a possibility of ADHD, what can teachers and caregivers do? It is important to remember that children with ADHD benefit from the same environments that all children do; thus, designing classrooms appropriately for the child's development is an important step toward managing the behavior of a child with ADHD. For young children this means a loosely structured environment in which active involvement is an integral part of the learning process. In addition, tailoring work to fit the child's individual needs and encouraging collaboration and cooperation are practices recommended for children with ADHD, as they are for all children.

The two primary methods of intervention are stimulant medication and behavioral management; however, the most effective treatment involves a combination of the two (Pelham, in press).

5. CULTURAL AND SOCIETAL INFLUENCES: Special Challenges

Medication therapy

The most common treatment for ADHD is medications that stimulate the central nervous system (Barkley, 1990). Research suggests that children with ADHD may not be as sensitive to feedback from the social and physical environment as other children; stimulant medication appears to render these children more sensitive by lowering response thresholds in the nervous system (Barkley, 1989). Ritalin, or methylphenidate (the generic drug name), is the most common stimulant used. Approximately 70 to 75% of children responded positively to this medication, while about one fourth are unaffected (Pelham, 1987); thus, these medications will help many but not all children with ADHD.

Effects of medication. For those children who do respond positively, the effects are immediate and typically quite strong. Attention, impulse control, and short-term memory may all be improved (Barkley, 1990). Children talk less, are less disturbing, follow rules better, and exhibit less aggression (Pelham, 1987). These changes often lead to improved relations with parents, teachers, and peers. As these children become more cooperative, the need for close adult supervision should diminish; however, in spite of substantial reduction in disruptive behavior, the majority of children with ADHD will still show problem behaviors. Medication is thus often helpful, but not sufficient, in managing the disorder.

In addition to reducing disruptive behavior, stimulant medication has been found to help children attend better when involved in organized athletic play with other children (Pelham et al., 1990). Because these activities, such as soccer or T-ball, involve peer interactions, medication may indirectly improve the peer relations and self-esteem of children with ADHD. Even while on medication, however, it is difficult for most children with ADHD to gain peer acceptance (Pelham & Milich, 1984).

Children with ADHD who are on medication are also better able to concentrate on schoolwork. They complete more assignments and are more careful and accurate; thus, they show improved academic *performance* (Barkley, 1990). Medication is much less effective in improving children's scores on academic *achievement* tests, however. In other words, medication does not necessarily help children with ADHD master more difficult tasks and may not directly relate to enhanced learning; thus, academic achievement *per se* appears to be only minimally improved by medication, if at all.

Recently there has been growing interest in the effects of medication on the attitudes and motivation of children with ADHD. Some experts have suggested, for example, that medication may cause children to believe that they are responsible for their own misbehavior—that they must rely on some external agent (the drug) for control of their difficulties. Consequently, when children behave inappropriately or do not succeed at schoolwork, they might conclude that the medication must not be working that day—in other words, these problems are not their fault. In contrast, other researchers suggest that because medication leads to improved performance, children with ADHD may be able to personalize this newly discovered success and thus feel greater responsibility for their own behavior than

if they had not been medicated—they have greater control than before. Although more study is necessary, current results support the second hypothesis: Medicated children with ADHD seem to credit themselves for good performances (i.e., they *internalize* and personalize their successes) while *externalizing* or blaming poor performance on factors beyond their control (Milich, 1993). The fact that these children attribute successes to their personal responsibility, and not to the medication, may contribute to their self-esteem. In summary, medication seems to improve behavior in a variety of ways and may also help children to feel better about themselves.

Despite the important effects of medication, several cautions should be kept in mind. First, as mentioned earlier, not all children with ADHD benefit from stimulant medication. Second, four- to five-year-old children do not experience improvement to the same extent as do older children (Barkley, 1989). In a review of medication studies with preschoolers, Campbell (1985) noted that few benefits were obtained and that side effects, such as increased solitary play and clinging, appeared serious enough to potentially disrupt social development. Third, all of the medication-induced benefits represent short-term effects only; that is, improvements are noticeable only while the child is taking the medication. In the evenings, weekends, and summers, when children are typically not medicated, their symptoms generally return to pretreatment levels; thus medication brings no lasting benefits.

Side effects. Many parents express concern about potential negative side effects of stimulant medication; for example, there is evidence that mild insomnia and lessened appetite, especially at lunchtime, can occur (Barkley, 1990). This latter effect has been thought to lead to suppressed weight and height gains. Research indicates, however, that effects on growth can be corrected by altering dosage and tend to occur only during the first year of medication therapy (Barkley, 1990). Height and weight tend to catch up to age norms in subsequent years even if medication is continued (Mattes & Gittleman, 1983). There is little research on this side effect in pre-school children, however, even though medication is sometimes given to children as young as age three (Campbell, 1990). As a consequence, medication is not recommended for children in this age group. Because medication effects tend to wear off within a four-hour period, most children with ADHD receive a noontime dose to cover their afternoon activities at school. One simple way to avoid the lunchtime appetite loss is to have the child eat lunch prior to taking the afternoon medication dose.

Mild headaches and stomachaches may also occur, but they tend to disappear within a few weeks (Barkley, 1990). These problems, along with mood changes, such as irritability, and individual reactions (e.g., lip licking, rashes) may be alleviated by a simple dosage adjustment. Research indicates that there are no known long-term side effects; for example, these children do not appear to be at increased risk for drug abuse later in life. Any side effects, therefore, tend to be mild, short term, and easily relieved.

One unfortunate consequence of drug treatment is that many parents and teachers tend to rely on medication exclusively and not invest in other, more lasting interventions. Within the past few years, the lay press has expressed alarm about overmedication of children. If parents seek medication for their child to manage home-based behavior problems, this concern may be valid; however, if medication is used to help the child attend to important classroom instruction and adjust well to school, this concern seems to be exaggerated. It is important to remember that medicated children with ADHD, although improved, are not made symptom free. For these reasons, medication is not adequate by itself as a treatment for children with ADHD. The "best practice," based on research, is to combine medication and behavioral treatments in the management of ADHD. This is done not only because medication is insufficient in the treatment of most cases but also because it permits the use of a lower dose of medication. There is strong evidence that a low dose of Ritalin, in combination with behavioral intervention, results in at least the same improvement—and sometimes greater improvement—in the child as does a high dose of Ritalin alone (Pelham, in press). In addition, when the low dose is used, most undesirable side effects can be avoided. In fact, it has been suggested that behavioral interventions be attempted in school *before* thought is given to the use of medication (National Association of School Psychologists, 1992).

Behavioral treatment

Because many children with ADHD demonstrate an inability to follow rules and govern their own behavior (Barkley, 1989), behavioral treatment is necessary for these self-regulatory difficulties. Aspects of successful behavioral intervention include rewarding appropriate behavior, giving effective directions and requests, and using consistent methods of discipline. If teachers can receive assistance from consultants (such as school psychologists) to implement these procedures, most children with ADHD can have their educational and social needs met in the regular education setting. In addition, collaboration with parents is essential because home-based support for school behavior and performance will enhance the success of programs at school.

Appropriate behavior. Many parents and teachers do not think that children should be rewarded simply for "doing what they ought to do," and most children do not need a heavy overlay of rewards to promote acceptable behavior; however, if a child with ADHD seldom engages in an important behavior (such as playing cooperatively), then rewards may be necessary to promote the behavior. As the child learns the behavior, rewards should be gradually removed. Research shows that the use of rewards is particularly helpful when dealing with children who have ADHD (Pelham, 1992). Their inappropriate behavior tends to be extremely compelling; adults cannot ignore it. As a consequence, much of the feedback these children receive from parents, teachers, and peers is expressed as a complaint or reprimand. It is little wonder that many children with ADHD develop self-concept difficulties and depression. Rewarding positive behaviors thus not only encourages the child to continue behaving well but also provides the child with desperately needed success, thereby building self-esteem.

Verbal praise is crucial for a child with ADHD and is especially powerful when the positive behavior is also clarified (e.g., "I like the way you are playing so nicely with the other boys"). Praise may not, however, provide adequate incentive initially due to the child's lower sensitivity to feedback from the social environment; thus, children with ADHD often require more frequent and powerful rewards for a time (Barkley, 1990). At first, parents and teachers may need to give material rewards, along with praise, to teach appropriate behavior; subsequently they may use praise alone to maintain the behavior—for example, smiley faces or gold stars may be given to the child every half hour for engaging in appropriate classroom behavior. A star chart on which different classroom activities (e.g., storytime) are separated as intervals can make implementation of such a reward system easier. To avoid a problem with classroom equity (other children wondering why they do not earn these rewards), the smiley faces could be granted discreetly, perhaps on a special card to be taken home at the end of each day. Even though some teachers may find these procedures intrusive and distracting, the fact remains that the use of behavioral intervention disrupts classroom routine less than does an untreated child with ADHD.

Directions. Unfortunately, the disruptive behavior of children with ADHD causes parents and teachers to often find themselves issuing numerous directives and commands to these youngsters throughout the day. To increase the likelihood that the child will cooperate with adult requests, directions should be specific and brief (Pelham, 1992). Those that are vague or issued in question format (e.g., "Let's get back to work, shall we?") or that involve several directives strung together are not likely to be obeyed. Instead, adults should obtain the child's attention, issue the direction (e.g., "Joey, finish picking up those blocks now"), and wait a few seconds. The child should then be praised for cooperating. Research shows that these techniques are effective. They prevent adult interactions from escalating into impatience and reduce the tendency of children with ADHD to ignore or resist adult direction.

In instances in which a child with ADHD does not respond to adult guidance, school psychologists can work with teachers to implement a variety of other behavioral interventions. Ignoring mildly negative behaviors may prove effective, but often increased adult monitoring and immediate consequences to reduce disruptive acts (e.g., asking the child to sit out an activity) are necessary. If the child engages in aggressive outbursts or is extremely uncooperative, a time-out procedure may also have to be implemented (Barkley, 1990). Consistency is essential for all of these methods to work well.

Daily report card. Parents can serve as an effective back-up to school-based interventions. An important behavior-management strategy involves sending home a brief daily report card reflecting the child's performance for each day (Barkley, 1990). Parents may thus praise the child for success in school, thereby supporting teachers'

> *Acknowledging teachers' need for effective consultation and collaboration in this area, the National Association of School Psychologists (NASP) recently issued the following position statement describing a "best-practice" approach for dealing with children with attention deficits.*
>
> NASP believes that effective intervention should be tailored to the unique learning strengths and needs of every student. For children with attention deficits, such interventions will include the following:
>
> 1) Classroom modifications to enhance attending, work production, and social adjustment;
>
> 2) Behavioral management systems to reduce problems in arenas most likely to be affected by attention deficits (e.g., large group instruction, transitions, etc.);
>
> 3) Direct instruction in study strategies and social skills, within the classroom setting whenever possible to increase generalization;
>
> 4) Consultation with families to assist in behavior management in the home setting and to facilitate home-school cooperation and collaboration;
>
> 5) Monitoring by a case manager to ensure effective implementation of interventions, to provide adequate support for those interventions, and to assess progress in meeting behavioral and academic goals;
>
> 6) Education of school staff in characteristics and management of attention deficits to enhance appropriate instructional modifications and behavior management;
>
> 7) Access to special education services when attention deficits significantly impact school performance;
>
> 8) Working collaboratively with community agencies providing medical and related services to students and their families.
>
> NASP believes appropriate treatment may or may not include medical intervention. When medication *is* considered, NASP *strongly* recommends:
>
> 1) That instructional and behavioral interventions be implemented before medication trials are begun;
>
> 2) That behavioral data be collected before and during medication trials to assess baseline conditions and the efficacy of medication; and
>
> 3) That communication between school, home, and medical personnel emphasize mutual problem solving and cooperation. (National Association of School Psychologists, 1992)

efforts. In addition, parents should consider using small toys and special activities (e.g., going to a movie) as back-up rewards for positive school performance because these children need rewards of high salience. Parents should target small successes first (e.g., remaining seated throughout storytime) then gradually increase expectations as the child demonstrates mastery.

Preschool issues. Unfortunately, dealing with ADHD symptoms among preschool-age children can be quite a challenge because some of these problems simply represent individual differences in developmental rates. Excessive activity, impulsive responding, and an inability to pay attention—all symptoms of ADHD among school-age children—may not be particularly unusual behaviors for many preschool-age children. Even so, some preschool children receive a diagnosis of ADHD. In these cases—such as Jamie, who was described earlier in this article—parents may feel overwhelmed with the child's discipline problems at home and with aggressive conduct with playmates. The primary symptoms of ADHD *per se* thus do not represent the major source of difficulty, and a diagnosis of ADHD would be premature. Parent training, however, may be an appropriate intervention, in which Jamie's parents are given systematic guidance on how to manage his behavior at home. If Jamie continues to experience difficulties once he reaches school age, when classroom demands require a greater restraint on activity and more persistent attention, a diagnosis of ADHD may be given serious consideration.

Conclusion

ADHD is a problem that has many facets and affects the child in many areas of functioning, including academic performance, interpersonal relations, and emotional well-being. Because of ADHD's complexity, successful treatment requires a multidisciplinary approach reflecting the collaboration of many professionals. Teachers must have assistance in dealing with children with ADHD.

References

Achenbach, T.M., McConaughy, S.H., & Howell, C.T. (1987). Child/adolescent behavioral and emotional problems: Implications of cross-informant correlations for situational specificity. *Psychological Bulletin, 101,* 213–232.

American Psychiatric Association. (1987). *Diagnostic and statistical manual of mental disorders* (3rd ed., revised). Washington, DC: Author.

Barkley, R.A. (1989). Attention deficit-hyperactivity disorder. In E.J. Mash & R.A. Barkley (Eds.), *Treatment of childhood disorders* (pp. 39–72). New York: Guilford.

Barkley, R.A. (1990). *Attention-deficit hyperactivity disorder: A handbook for diagnosis and treatment.* New York: Guilford.

Life in a Parallel World

A bold new approach to the mystery of autism

SHARON BEGLEY AND
KAREN SPRINGEN

ADAM ELDER, 8, SPENDS AN HOUR A day tearing paper and cereal boxes into confetti. Words must be wrested from him like an impacted molar; it is a small miracle when his mother gets him to say "cheetos." His sister, Lily, 6, lives in a parallel universe, too, whose impassable borders are defined by autism. She flaps her hands and covers her ears obsessively. She is so afraid of open eyes that she doesn't look at people. She even blacks out the eyes of the figures in her coloring books.

The cause of autism remains largely unknown, and a cure isn't even on the horizon. But a few scientists are taking a wholly new approach to the syndrome. They are defining autism as a "spectrum" disease. At one end is the child crouched in a corner; at the other is, for example, Mark Romoser, 81, a research assistant at Yale University who has also managed to hold corporate jobs—as long as they don't require interacting with customers. If autism can present such a range

of symptoms and severity, suggests the new model, then it strikes not 2 to 5 people per 10,000, but 15 per 10,000, says Dr. Eric Hollander of Mount Sinai Medical Center in New York, who is presenting a sort of unified field theory of autism this week at the annual meeting of the American Psychiatric Association.

The new approach doesn't just redefine the incidence of autism. It also suggests that there are three core components of the syndrome, each with its own cause in the brain and, possibly, its own cure. Autistic children—four times more boys than girls—have huge difficulty communicating and cannot read emotions on faces. They shrink from people. They often behave compulsively; if it is not Adam's paper-tearing, then it is Dustin Hoffman's meticulous arranging of pens in the movie "Rain Man." Although about 80 percent of children with autism are mentally retarded, about 5 percent are "autistic savants," with unusual abilities that involve rote memory or visual skills. Child psy-

chiatrist Fred Volkmar of Yale knows one autistic boy who has an IQ of about 60 but can recite the daily lottery numbers for the past several years. Think of the components of autism—social phobia, compulsive behavior, trouble communicating and, rarely, savantism—as the colors on a child's paint palette. Different mixes of red, blue and yellow produce a rainbow of hues. Similarly, different combinations of autism's components produce the array of conditions known by the umbrella term autism.

Obsessive-compulsive disorder, for instance, is linked to low levels of the brain chemical serotonin. Prozac, which increases the amount of serotonin sloshing around brain circuits, seems to reduce the compulsivity of autism. The social phobia of autism may be linked to the brain chemical oxytocin. This molecule, best known for inducing labor and lactation, also promotes maternal and other bonds and so has come to be known as the sociability molecule. when Hollander administered oxytocin to five autistic patients, it made them four times more talkative and, according to the patients, twice as "happy."

What causes the abnormalities in brain chemistry? Scientists suspect a subtle interplay of the DNA we inherit and the experiences we have. The case for "autism genes" is circumstantial, says Dr. Edwin Cook of the University of Chicago: if one identical twin is autistic, there is a 90 percent chance that the other twin will be, too. But there must be more to autism than genetics. Almost no autistics have children—most can't even manage a date—so any genes that directly caused autism would disappear from the population. Unless, that

is, they remained quiescent, not causing any disease until triggered by some event such as brain damage. "Without the brain damage," Hollander suggests, "you get a disorder marked by great social phobias, or else these 'odd' family members who have special skills such as being human calculators." But with brain damage, "you get autism."

Finding the cause of that brain damage represents the next frontier for autism research. One suspect is a virus that disturbs the migration of neurons in the fetal brain. Ellen Feifarek of Towson, Md., whose 10-year-old son is autistic, has long wondered whether the viral infection she got in her 10th week of

pregnancy could have anything to do with Scott's condition. "One searches one's heart of hearts all the time," she says. A more controversial theory focuses on pitocin, a hormone given to women to speed up their labor. Pitocin is the manmade analogue of oxytocin. "Most of the mothers of patients we see have had pitocin-induced labor," says Hollander. He suspects that pitocin somehow messes up the newborn's oxytocin system, producing the social phobias of autism. This idea is very preliminary, but it's an improvement on the theory hatched when autism was first identified 53 years ago. Then, scientists blamed it on unloving mothers.

Index

Credits/Acknowledgments

Cover design by Charles Vitelli

1. Conception to Birth
Facing overview—UNICEF illustration of "Mother and Child" by Oskar Kokoschka. 7—© 1994 by Bob Sacha. 9—Photo by Nick Kelsh. 11—Photos courtesy of Drs. E. Fuller Torrey and Daniel R. Weinberger, National Institute of Mental Health Neuroscience Center, Washington, DC. 12—American Philosophical Society photo. 17—Century City Hospital photo.

2. Cognition, Language, and Learning
Facing overview—United Nations photo by Shelley Rotner.

3. Social and Emotional Development
Facing overview—United Nations photo by Marcia Weistein.

4. Parenting and Family Issues
Facing overview—*Children Today* photo by Jacquine Roland.

5. Cultural and Societal Influences
Facing overview—United Nations photo by Y. Nagata. 200—Photo by Jonathan Silvers.

PHOTOCOPY THIS PAGE!!!

ANNUAL EDITIONS ARTICLE REVIEW FORM

■ NAME: _____ DATE: _____

■ TITLE AND NUMBER OF ARTICLE: _____

■ BRIEFLY STATE THE MAIN IDEA OF THIS ARTICLE: _____

_____

■ LIST THREE IMPORTANT FACTS THAT THE AUTHOR USES TO SUPPORT THE MAIN IDEA:

_____

_____

_____

_____

■ WHAT INFORMATION OR IDEAS DISCUSSED IN THIS ARTICLE ARE ALSO DISCUSSED IN YOUR TEXTBOOK OR OTHER READINGS THAT YOU HAVE DONE? LIST THE TEXTBOOK CHAPTERS AND PAGE NUMBERS:

_____

_____

_____

_____

_____

■ LIST ANY EXAMPLES OF BIAS OR FAULTY REASONING THAT YOU FOUND IN THE ARTICLE:

_____

_____

_____

_____

■ LIST ANY NEW TERMS/CONCEPTS THAT WERE DISCUSSED IN THE ARTICLE, AND WRITE A SHORT DEFINITION:

_____

_____

_____

_____

_____

*Your instructor may require you to use this ANNUAL EDITIONS Article Review Form in any number of ways: for articles that are assigned, for extra credit, as a tool to assist in developing assigned papers, or simply for your own reference. Even if it is not required, we encourage you to photocopy and use this page; you will find that reflecting on the articles will greatly enhance the information from your text.

We Want Your Advice

ANNUAL EDITIONS revisions depend on two major opinion sources: one is our Advisory Board, listed in the front of this volume, which works with us in scanning the thousands of articles published in the public press each year; the other is you—the person actually using the book. Please help us and the users of the next edition by completing the prepaid article rating form on this page and returning it to us. Thank you for your help!

ANNUAL EDITIONS: CHILD GROWTH AND DEVELOPMENT 97/98
Article Rating Form

Here is an opportunity for you to have direct input into the next revision of this volume. We would like you to rate each of the 36 articles listed below, using the following scale:

1. **Excellent: should definitely be retained**
2. **Above average: should probably be retained**
3. **Below average: should probably be deleted**
4. **Poor: should definitely be deleted**

Your ratings will play a vital part in the next revision. So please mail this prepaid form to us just as soon as you complete it.
Thanks for your help!

Rating	Article	Rating	Article
	1. Eugenics Revisited		19. The EQ Factor
	2. Making Babies		20. Children without Friends
	3. Waiting Game		21. Girls and Boys Together . . . but Mostly Apart
	4. In the Name of the Children		22. Little Big People
	5. The Fantastic Voyage of Tanner Roberts		23. Fathers' Time
	6. Putting a New Spin on the Birth of Human Birth		24. Life-Span Adjustment of Children to Their Parents' Divorce
	7. The Most Intimate Bond		25. How Children Learn to Resolve Conflicts in Families
	8. The Amazing Minds of Infants		26. Why Spanking Takes the Spunk Out of Kids
	9. Ten Myths about Child Development		27. School and Family in the Postmodern World
	10. Your Child's Brain		28. Buried Alive
	11. Vygotsky's Theory: The Importance of Make-Believe Play		29. Why Leave Children with Bad Parents?
	12. How Do Infants Learn about the Physical World?		30. Child Labor in Pakistan
	13. Malnutrition, Poverty, and Intellectual Development		31. Violence, Reel to Real
	14. What Should Children Learn?		32. Get 'em While They're Young
	15. How Kids Learn		33. Victimization of Children
	16. The IQ Puzzle		34. Resilience in Development
	17. Early Experience and Emotional Development: The Emergence of Wariness of Heights		35. Young Children with Attention Deficits
	18. The Moral Power of Good Stories		36. Life in a Parallel World

(Continued on next page)

ABOUT YOU

Name _____ Date _____

Are you a teacher? ❑ Or a student? ❑

Your school name _____

Department _____

Address _____

City _____ State _____ Zip _____

School telephone # _____

YOUR COMMENTS ARE IMPORTANT TO US!

Please fill in the following information:

For which course did you use this book? _____

Did you use a text with this *ANNUAL EDITION*? ❑ yes ❑ no

What was the title of the text? _____

What are your general reactions to the *Annual Editions* concept?

Have you read any particular articles recently that you think should be included in the next edition?

Are there any articles you feel should be replaced in the next edition? Why?

Are there other areas of study that you feel would utilize an *ANNUAL EDITION?*

May we contact you for editorial input?

May we quote your comments?

No Postage
Necessary
if Mailed
in the
United States

ANNUAL EDITIONS: CHILD GROWTH AND DEVELOPMENT 97/98

BUSINESS REPLY MAIL

First Class   Permit No. 84   Guilford, CT

Postage will be paid by addressee

Dushkin/McGraw·Hill
Sluice Dock
Guilford, Connecticut 06437